Who's Who
IN THE
BIBLE

CONTRIBUTING EDITOR:
Dietrich Gruen

CONTRIBUTING WRITERS:
Dietrich Gruen, Julia Pferdehirt, Anna Trimiew,
Carol Troyer-Shank, Sue Vander Hook

CONSULTANT:
David M. Howard, Jr., Ph.D.

PUBLICATIONS INTERNATIONAL, LTD.

Dietrich Gruen is an ordained minister, with an M.Div. from Bethel Theological Seminary. He is executive editor of The Gruen Group, which develops small group curricula and Bible-related products. He has collaborated on more than 20 books and Bible projects, including his first solo book, *Fathers Who Made a Difference.*

Julia Pferdehirt studied theology at Fuller Seminary and works as a freelance writer. Her writing projects include multicultural unit studies on ethnic America and a children's fairy tale, *Nothing at All.*

Anna Trimiew is a freelance writer and a former school teacher who holds a master's degree from Gordon-Conwell Theological Seminary. Her work includes *Bringing the New Testament to Life* and numerous Christian education materials, including ready-made Bible studies.

Carol Troyer-Shank works as a Quaker First Day School teacher and as an editor in the elementary publishing center she helped to establish. She holds a B.A. from Goshen College and an M.Ed. from Tufts University.

Sue Vander Hook is an English, journalism, and Bible teacher at Faith Christian School. She has contributed to a variety of published works, including the *Serendipity Family Bible.*

David M. Howard, Jr. is associate professor of Old Testament and Semitic Languages at Trinity Evangelical Divinity School and holds a Ph.D. in Near Eastern Studies from the University of Michigan. He is a member of the Society of Biblical Literature and the Institute for Biblical Research.

Front Cover: *Clockwise from top right:* Adam and Eve expelled from Paradise; Noah releases the raven from the ark; Mary and the infant Jesus; Peter the apostle; God, the eternal father; Daniel in the lions' den; Moses and the Ten Commandments. **Back Cover:** *Top:* Abraham attempts to sacrifice his son Isaac; *Bottom:* Jesus at Emmaus after the resurrection. **Title Page:** Joseph, Mary, and Jesus flee to Egypt. **Contents Page:** *Top:* Jesus raises Lazarus from the dead; *Bottom:* Moses parts the Red Sea; *Background:* Abraham takes his family to find the Promised Land.

Contents

STUDYING THE BIBLE
THROUGH ITS CHARACTERS

Learning about the lives of the Bible's characters can be a fascinating endeavor, for several reasons. First, many of the Bible's famous characters have found permanent places in the popular Western imagination. Who has not heard of Samson and his great strength, or of his lover Delilah and her betrayal? Who does not understand the apple as a symbol of Eve's temptation of her husband Adam and of their joint temptation by the serpent? Who does not know Moses and the Ten Commandments, King David and Bathsheba, Daniel in the lion's den, Jonah and the great fish? Who does not know of Jesus, whom the Bible presents as a sinless human being, a great teacher, and the Son of God?

The Bible's characters also exhibit many positive virtues that can be emulated. Abraham's great faith enabled him to establish a unique religious heritage for his descendants. Deborah's strength of character helped her to deliver her people from oppression. Ruth showed great loyalty and selflessness in staying with her widowed and destitute mother-in-law Naomi. Elijah and Elisha, the Israelite prophets, spoke the truth in the face of great danger and overwhelming opposition. Mary, Martha, and Lazarus were siblings who offered staunch and reliable friendship to Jesus.

Yet, the Bible does not gloss over evil, either. Many villainous characters play a role in biblical stories: the Egyptian Pharaoh in Moses's day; David's sons Amnon, who raped his sister Tamar,

and Absalom, who killed Amnon and rebelled against his father's throne; innumerable kings in Israel and Judah who promoted the worship of pagan deities; Herod, who beheaded John the Baptist; and Judas Iscariot, who betrayed Jesus.

Interestingly enough, even the Bible's heroes are shown to have flaws. Despite Abraham's faith, he showed a lack of trust in God when he tried to pass his wife off as his sister on two different occasions. Moses, Israel's great leader and lawgiver, sinned against God and forfeited his right to enter the Promised Land. The great King David was guilty of adultery and premeditated murder. Peter, one of Jesus's closest apostles, vigorously insisted he would never deny Jesus and then did precisely that in Jesus's time of crisis. This realism with which the Bible presents its heroes and villains can provide an inspiring example to readers. The Bible shows God accomplishing many great things using people whose lives were not models of virtue, but were rather ordinary and everyday. In today's complex and challenging world, that lesson can be comforting and encouraging.

The Bible also contains a wealth of minor, rather obscure characters who are nonetheless intriguing. Characters such as Enoch, Miriam, Caleb, Abigail, Micaiah, Naaman, Elizabeth, Onesimus, and a host of others have inspiring stories, yet most are relatively unknown.

Who's Who in the Bible will serve as a useful tool for exploring the lives and deeds of the

Bible's prominent and obscure players. A combination of several features makes it unique and especially useful. First, every character named in the Bible is included, for a total of nearly 4000 entries that cover the Old and New Testaments plus the Apocrypha, which is used in Roman Catholic and Eastern Orthodox traditions. Entries have been assigned different lengths, reflecting the characters' relative importance. Some 400 entries, ranging in length from 50 words to 1500 words, offer detailed information about the individuals' lives and religious significance. The remaining entries briefly identify the individuals; in many instances, little or nothing is known about these people except their names and perhaps their ancestors or descendants.

Each entry—long or short—gives the first biblical reference for a character, and many entries include additional references at the end for further study. A date is also given for each character when the historical record allows. In the cases of kings, the dates indicate when they actually ruled. Otherwise, most dates are given only by century. Readers should understand that dating schemes for Old Testament times vary somewhat, and that dates prior to 1000 B.C. are accurate only to within a century or two. After 1000 B.C., our modern-day knowledge of ancient dates is much more precise, thanks to accurate dating records kept by the Assyrians, Babylonians, Persians, and Egyptians, based mainly on astronomical observations.

Pronunciations are given for each character's name. These are how the biblical names should sound in English, not necessarily how they were pronounced in Hebrew, Greek, or the other ancient languages reflected in the Bible. Meanings also are given for most names. However, readers should again know that in many cases, the meanings given are merely educated guesses by scholars. Sometimes the Bible makes a point of a wordplay about a character's name; for example,

Moses's Hebrew name was Mosheh, because he had been "drawn up" (Hebrew *mashah*) out of the waters by Pharaoh's daughter. However, in the vast majority of cases, the meaning of names had no particular significance to the biblical writers.

Several features make this book unique, distinguishing it from others about Bible characters. First is the beautiful artwork, which has been chosen from a wide range of famous paintings, stained glass windows, and other sources. Second, the book is all-inclusive, encompassing even the apocryphal characters, which is something seldom found elsewhere. It also includes discussions of people groups (Philistines, Assyrians, Hittites, etc.), pagan gods (Baal, Asherah, Milcom, Artemis, etc.), and even angels (Gabriel, Michael, etc.). The combination of dates, pronunciations, and meanings in this book is seldom found together in other such books. Finally, although the Bible is the primary source of information, extra-biblical material about individual Bible characters is introduced where it is especially relevant.

This book is written for a general adult audience, with no sectarian or confessional slant intended. The attempt has been made to keep the book strictly text-based, that is, to make only claims that are supported by the text of the Bible itself (or in the extra-biblical works, as noted). Individual readers may have differing interpretations of the Bible on any given point, but the characters in this work are shown as they are portrayed in the Bible.

Many readers will enjoy the information in these pages on a purely secular level, as a resource of interesting characters, many of whom are important in Western culture. Others will enjoy it for more personal, spiritual reasons, as a study of characters to be learned from and of examples to be emulated or avoided. For all readers, however, it should prove to be a worthwhile endeavor.

AARON (AIR uhn) meaning unknown; 15 century B.C.; Ex 4:14

Aaron—brother of Moses and oldest son of Amram and Jochebed—came from the tribe of Levi. He married Elisheba and they had four sons: Nadab, Abihu, Eleazar, and Ithamar. Aaron's place in the biblical story began when God commissioned Moses to release the people of Israel from slavery in Egypt. Since Moses feared that he would be an ineffective speaker for the mission, God assigned Aaron to assist his brother in freeing and leading the Hebrews.

Moses and Aaron went before the Israelites and told them of God's plan to free them; then they approached Pharaoh. The brothers worked tirelessly to bring an end to the oppression of God's covenant people. In all their efforts, God directed Moses, then Moses in turn told Aaron what to say to the people. Instructed by Moses, Aaron performed miracles to help bring about the release of the Hebrews by demonstrating God's power. On one occasion, his miraculous rod turned into a living snake that swallowed the rods of the Egyptian magicians. Another time, Aaron used his rod to strike the waters of Egypt and turn them to blood. He even caused a plague of frogs to cover the land by simply stretching his rod over the streams and lakes of Egypt. Through these and other demonstrations, Aaron and Moses convinced Pharaoh to respect God's power and heed his directive to free the Israelites.

Along with Moses, Aaron received special instructions from God for observing the festivals of Passover and unleavened bread. Old traditions were given new meaning as God's people celebrated their deliverance from Pharaoh's enslaving hand during the Exodus from Egypt. As the Israelites wandered in the wilderness after their release, Aaron helped Moses keep order and govern the people. This was no easy task. Both men were singled out when the people complained about tough wilderness conditions. They challenged the leadership of Moses and Aaron, and even threatened to find another leader to take them back to Egypt. Yet, the rebellion was quelled, and the group pressed on in spite of struggles over food and water, hot days and cold nights, and the danger of fierce desert tribes.

On the way to Sinai, the Israelites were challenged by the Amalekites, a nomadic clan that controlled the wilderness in the region of Kadesh. As Joshua commanded the Israelite troops against Amalek and his warriors, the real battle took place

The rod of Aaron turns into a living snake, swallowing the rods of Egyptian magicians.

on a hilltop nearby. There, Moses held the rod of God aloft to the heavens; as long as he did so, the Israelites would keep the upper hand in the battle. As the conflict raged on, Aaron and his brother-in-law Hur helped Moses by supporting his weary arms, thereby securing victory for Israel.

Clearly, Aaron's most distinctive role in the Exodus events was that of high priest. When the tabernacle (the main sanctuary of worship) was established for the Israelites, Aaron became head of the priesthood and was in charge of national worship. When Aaron's authority was questioned by some, his staff budded, blossomed, and bore ripe almonds, a dramatic and colorful gesture that indicated God's choice of Aaron and his descendants as priests. In his position as religious leader, Aaron wore special robes and was instructed by God on how to be a priest and run the tabernacle. Only Aaron, serving as the high priest, could enter the Holy of Holies (the most sacred part of the tabernacle) once a year to represent the people on the Day of Atonement.

Even though he was one of the spiritual leaders of the nation, Aaron occasionally disobeyed God and demonstrated poor leadership. During the time that Moses was on Mt. Sinai receiving God's commandments, Aaron allowed the Israelites to build an idol to worship, and he even gave them instructions on how to make the statue. When Moses learned of what had happened in his absence, Aaron was saved from God's anger only because Moses intervened on his brother's behalf.

Later, Aaron and his sister Miriam sided together against Moses. They questioned his authority and criticized him for marrying a Cushite woman. In their discontent, Aaron and Miriam challenged Moses's status as the leader of the Hebrew people. In a swift and dramatic move, God put an end to their insubordination. Miriam was struck by leprosy and banished from the encampment. Once again, Moses begged God to show mercy, and God relented.

At the end of the wilderness journey, Aaron and Moses were kept out of the Promised Land because of the times that they had shown a lack of trust in God. Aaron died at the age of 123 on Mt. Hor, and his priestly garments were handed to his oldest living son, Eleazar. The house of Israel mourned Aaron for 30 days.

For further study, see Ex 4; 6–7; 17; 28–29; 32; Nu 4; 12; 14–15; 18; 20.

ABADDON (uh BAD uhn) *destruction;* Rev 9:11; angel of the Abyss; Hebrew form of Apollyon

ABAGTHA (uh BAG thuh) *happy* or *prosperous;* 5 century B.C.; Est 1:10; steward of Ahasuerus

ABDA (AB duh) *servant* or *worshiper*
1. 10 century B.C.; 1Ki 4:6; father of Adoniram the overseer of forced labor
2. 5 century B.C.; Ne 11:17; chief Levite in Jerusalem following the Exile; also called Obadiah 11

ABDEEL (AB dee el) *servant of God;* 7 century B.C.; Jer 36:26; father of Shelemiah; servant of Jehoiakim

ABDI (AB dee) *servant of the Lord*
1. 11 century B.C.; 1Ch 6:44; grandfather of Ethan; a music minister
2. 8 century B.C.; 2Ch 29:12; father of Kish the Levite in Hezekiah's time
3. 5 century B.C.; Ezr 10:26; one who married and divorced foreigner after Exile

ABDIEL (AB dee el) *servant of God;* 1Ch 5:15; ancestral family head in Gad's genealogy

ABDON (AB dahn) *service*
1. 1Ch 8:23; Benjaminite living in Jerusalem
2. 11 century B.C.; Jdg 12:13; wealthy minor judge who led Israel for eight years
3. 11 century B.C.; 1Ch 8:30; firstborn of Jeiel and Maacah; uncle of Saul
4. 7 century B.C.; 2Ch 34:20; one of Josiah's officials; also called Achbor 3

ABEDNEGO (uh BED neh goh) *servant of Nego;* 7 century B.C.; Da 1:7; companion of Daniel; also called Azariah 20; see Shadrach

ABEL (AY buhl) *breath* or *vapor* or *son;* possibly *meadow;* Gen 4:2
The story of Adam and Eve's sons, Cain and Abel, introduces the Old Testament system of sacrifices and the universal standard of faith. Though nothing was inherently wrong with Cain's farming or his offering of some of the fruits of his labors, God "had regard" for (saw and approved of) the faith evident in Abel's animal offering because, unlike Cain, he had presented the first products of his labor, mak-

ing it a "more acceptable" (Heb 11:4) sacrifice. Ironically, the blood of Abel, killed by his angry and jealous brother Cain, became the prototype for future blood sacrifices, even that of Christ on the cross. For further study, see Gen 4:1-25; Mt 23:34-35; Lk 11:49-52; Heb 11:1-4; 12:24; 4Mac 18:11.

ABI (AY bye) *my father;* 8 century B.C.; 2Ki 18:2; mother of Hezekiah; a form of Abijah 7

ABI-ALBON (AY bye AL buhn) *father of strength;* 11 century B.C.; 2Sa 23:31; military leader; mighty man of David; also called Abiel 2

ABIASAPH (uh BYE uh saf) *my father has gathered;* Ex 6:24; son of Korah; ancestor of Levite gatekeepers; also called Asaph 1, Ebiasaph

ABIATHAR (uh BYE uh thahr) *father of abundance* or *the father is preeminent;* 11 century B.C.; 1Sa 22:20

Abiathar was the son of Ahimelech, the high priest. Father and son lived in the town of Nob, just outside Jerusalem. When King Saul heard that Ahimelech and the priests of Nob had helped the outlaw David, the king was enraged and gave orders for all the priests of the Lord to be killed. Doeg the Edomite attacked the priests, killed 85 of them, including Abiathar's father, and destroyed the town of Nob.

Abiathar fled the massacre. He brought the ephod (a ceremonial garment, like a heavy apron) with him and sought out David for protection. David comforted the young priest and pledged to

Abiathar accompanying the ark of the covenant to Jerusalem.

protect him. Abiathar stayed with David throughout his days as a fugitive and then went with David to Jerusalem.

Abiathar and Zadok were both high priests when David, now king, ordered the ark of the covenant brought to Jerusalem. David was establishing temple worship, and he wanted a proper place to put God's written covenant with Israel. When David's son Absalom tried to take the throne, David was forced to flee Jerusalem, but he would not let Abiathar or Zadok remove the ark from the city. He told the high priests to turn back with their sons and act in the king's interests in Jerusalem. After Absalom was defeated, Zadok and Abiathar implored the leaders of Judah to call for David's return.

At the close of David's reign, Abiathar supported David's son Adonijah in his bid for the throne. But Solomon, the younger brother, was crowned instead. Because Abiathar continued to favor Adonijah, Solomon expelled Abiathar from office and banished him from Jerusalem to his estate in Anathoth, sparing his life for his lengthy and devoted service to David.

For further study, see 1Sa 22:20-23; 2Sa 15:24; 1Ki 1–2; 1Ch 15:11; 18:16; 27:34.

ABIDA (uh BYE duh) *father of knowledge* or *my father knows;* 20 century B.C.; Gen 25:4; grandson of Abraham; son of Midian

ABIDAN (uh BYE duhn) *my father is judge;* 15 century B.C.; Nu 1:11; leader of Benjamin's tribe under Moses

ABIEL (AY bee el) *my father is God*
1. 12 century B.C.; 1Sa 9:1; grandfather of Saul; also called Jeiel 2
2. 1Ch 11:32; see Abi-albon

ABIEZER (AY bih EE zuhr) *my father is help*
1. Jos 17:2; descendant of Manasseh; clan leader; a form of Iezer
2. 11 century B.C.; 2Sa 23:27; Benjaminite; mighty man of David

ABIEZRITES (AY bih EEZ ryts) Jdg 6:11; descendants of Abiezer 1 who settled in Manasseh

ABIGAIL (AB uh gayl) *my father rejoices*
1. 11 century B.C.; 1Sa 25:3

Abigail begs David's forgiveness and offers provisions for his troops.

Abigail displayed the wisdom and kindness that were absent in her foolish and mean-spirited husband Nabal. When approached by David's warriors for food rations, Nabal refused their request despite the fact that David's men had been protecting Nabal's property from warring factions in the land. Knowing this insult could mean retaliation and death for Nabal's entire household, Abigail intervened with David, begging forgiveness and offering the provisions he needed. David blessed her and accepted her offering. That night, a drunken Nabal suffered a heart attack; he died ten days later. David then married the widow Abigail and later had a child Chileab (Daniel) by her. She also uttered remarkable prophecies about David's future. For further study, see 1Sa 25; 30; 2Sa 2:2; 3:3; 1Ch 3:1.
2. 11 century B.C.; 1Ch 2:16; stepsister of David; mother of Amasa; a form of Abigal

ABIGAL 2Sa 17:25; see Abigail 2

ABIHAIL (AB uh hayl) *my father is strength*
1. 15 century B.C.; Nu 3:35; father of Zueriel; a Levite
2. 1Ch 2:29; wife of Abishur; in genealogy of Jerahmeel

3. 10 century B.C.; 2Ch 11:18; daughter-in-law of David; mother-in-law of Rehoboam
4. 1Ch 5:14; descendant of Gad
5. 6 century B.C.; Est 2:15; father of Esther; uncle of Mordecai

ABIHU (uh BYE hoo) *my father is he;* 15 century B.C.; Ex 6:23; son of Aaron; died profaning God's sacrifice

ABIHUD (uh BYE huhd) *my father is majesty;* 19 century B.C.; 1Ch 8:3; third son of Bela; grandson of Benjamin

ABIJAH (uh BYE jah) *my father is the Lord*
1. 19 century B.C.; 1Ch 7:8; grandson of Benjamin; son of Becher
2. 1Ch 2:24; wife of Judah's descendant Hezron
3. 11 century B.C.; 1Sa 8:2; son of Samuel; corrupt judge of Israel
4. 11 century B.C.; 1Ch 24:10; head of one of David's priestly divisions
5. 10 century B.C.; 1Ki 14:1; son of Jeroboam I
6. ruled 913–910 B.C.; 2Ch 13:1; second king of Judah; son of Rehoboam; form of Abijam
7. 2Ch 29:1; see Abi

8. 6 century B.C.; Ne 12:1; head of priestly family after Exile
9. 5 century B.C.; Ne 10:7; priest who signed covenant

ABIJAM 1Ki 14:31; see Abijah 6

ABIMAEL (uh BIM ay el) *my father is God;* Gen 10:28; ninth son of Joktan; descendant of Shem

ABIMELECH (uh BIM uh lek) *my father is king*
1. and **2.** 21–20 century B.C.; Gen 20:2

According to the Genesis account, Abraham and Isaac both signed separate treaties with a king of Gerar named Abimelech. Also, both Hebrew patriarchs tricked a king named Abimelech in like manner—by passing off their wives as their sisters to assure safe passage for their family through enemy territory.

Perhaps Abraham and Isaac hoodwinked the same king twice, one century apart. More likely, the first King Abimelech had a successor by the same name. That coincidence has also led some scholars to believe Abimelech was not a name but

By dropping a millstone on his head, a Shechem woman kills Abimelech and fulfills Jotham's prophecy.

actually a common title for Philistine kings, in the same way that Pharaoh was a common title for Egyptian rulers.

The first Abimelech made a treaty with Abraham regarding the well at Beersheba, and the second Abimelech made a similar treaty with Isaac regarding water and grazing rights.

For further study, see Gen 20:1-18; 21:22-32; 26:1-30.
3. ruled 1129–1126 B.C.; Jdg 8:31

Abimelech was born to Gideon by a concubine from Shechem. The pagan lords of his mother's clan raised him and financially backed his effort to establish a monarchy over Israel. In his bid for the throne, Abimelech hired mercenaries to slaughter his 70 half-brothers, all sons of Gideon by various wives. This bloody massacre had but one survivor—Jotham, the youngest son. He went into hiding and later emerged to prophesy destruction for Abimelech. Abimelech worked against God's mandate for the Israelite judges, who were supposed to eliminate idolatrous Baal worship. True to Jotham's prophesy, Abimelech was done in by his own followers when the people of Shechem rebelled. He was fatally injured when a woman dropped a millstone on his head. For further study, see Jdg 8:31–9:57.
4. Ps 34; see Achish 1

ABINADAB (uh BIN uh dab) *my father is generous*
1. 11 century B.C.; 1Sa 7:1; man who stored the ark of the covenant for 20 years
2. 11 century B.C.; 1Sa 16:8; second son of Jesse; brother of David
3. 11 century B.C.; 1Sa 31:2; son of Saul; slain by Philistines

ABINOAM (uh BIN oh am) *my father is delight;* 13 century B.C.; Jdg 4:6; father of military general Barak

ABIRAM (uh BYE ruhm) *my father is exalted*
1. 15 century B.C.; Nu 16:1; rebel who defied Moses's authority
2. 9 century B.C.; 1Ki 16:34; son of Hiel; died when Jericho fell

ABISHAG (AB uh shag) possibly *my father was a wanderer;* 10 century B.C.; 1Ki 1:3

When King David was old and weak, a beautiful young woman was found to take care of him.

David restrains Abishai from murdering the sleeping King Saul.

Her name was Abishag, and she was from the town of Shunem, near Nazareth. Although she served David as a nurse, Abishag was considered part of the royal harem. After David's death, his ambitious son Adonijah asked permission to marry Abishag. David's successor, King Solomon, was indignant when he heard this request. Since Abishag was a member of King David's harem, she was royal property. Adonijah's attempt to marry Abishag would be seen as a bold claim to the throne. King Solomon made arrangements to have Adonijah killed immediately. As for Abishag, it is possible that she remained in the royal harem, passed on from David to Solomon. For further study, see 1Ki 1:1-15; 2:13-22.

ABISHAI (AB ih shy) meaning unknown; 11 century B.C.; 1Sa 26:6

Abishai, a loyal yet violent companion, would battle anyone for David, whom he revered as the national hope of Israel. He helped hunt down Amasa and Sheba, two of David's enemies; and, in one battle, Abishai is credited with single-handedly killing 300 of David's enemies. On another occasion, he saved David's life by killing a giant.

His distinguished military career as the chief enforcer in David's select band of 30 warriors is somewhat tainted by his violent impulses. He was good at taking orders but tended to act without thinking. In two separate instances, Abishai would have killed both the sleeping King Saul and the spiteful Shimei if not for David's restraining hand. Abishai was told to "deal gently" in corralling David's rebellious son Absalom and did so. After defeating Absalom's rebel force, Abishai also effectively dealt with the Ammonites who had insulted David's goodwill ambassadors.

Abishai's fierce loyalty to King David likely stemmed from strategic family ties and royal ambitions. His mother was David's sister, and his brother, Joab, was David's commander-in-chief, under whom Abishai served as second in command.

For further study, see 1Sa 26; 2Sa 2:18-32; 3:22-39; 10:9-14; 16:5-14; 18:9-15; 19:18-24; 20:4-13; 21:15-17; 23:18-19.

ABISHALOM (uh BISH uh lohm) *father of peace;* 10 century B.C.; 1Ki 15:2; grandfather of King Abijah of Judah; possibly Absalom 1

ABISHUA (uh BISH oo uh) *my father is deliverance*
1. 19 century B.C.; 1Ch 8:3; fourth son of Bela
2. 1Ch 6:4; descendant of Aaron; ancestor of Ezra

ABISHUR (uh BYE shur) possibly *my father is a wall;* 1Ch 2:28; Judahite; in genealogy of Jerahmeel

ABITAL (uh BYE tuhl) *my father is the dew;* 11 century B.C.; 2Sa 3:4; wife of David; mother of Shephatiah

ABITUB (uh BYE tub) *my father is good;* 1Ch 8:11; listed in genealogy of Benjamin

ABIUD (uh BYE ud) *my father is majesty;* 6 century B.C.; Mt 1:13; son of Zerubbabel; ancestor of Christ

ABNER (AB nuhr) *father is a lamp;* 11 century B.C.; 1Sa 14:50

Abner, the son of Ner, was King Saul's cousin and the powerful commander of the king's army.

After Saul died, Abner gathered his army at Mahanaim and chose Saul's youngest and least capable son, Ishbaal, to take over the throne. All the tribes of Israel gave allegiance to the new king, except for Judah, which allied itself with David.

Abner and his troops advanced to Gibeon, where they were met by Joab in command of David's forces. Abner and Joab agreed upon a fighting tournament between 12 strong men picked from either side. When all of these men were killed and victory remained undecided, the trial of strength degenerated into a real military brawl in which Abner's army was defeated. As David's men pursued the retreating army, Abner killed Joab's brother Asahel and so started a blood feud between Joab and himself.

Sometime later, Abner and Ishbaal quarreled over one of Saul's mistresses. Disappointed with Ishbaal's character, Abner resolved to side with David and to bring all of Israel with him. The proposed union was sealed with a feast hosted by David.

When Joab learned of the new alliance, he tried unsuccessfully to turn David against Abner. Taking matters into his own hands, Joab sent for Abner and murdered the commander, avenging Asahel's death and eliminating a possible rival for his position as leader of David's army.

David was devastated when he heard the news. He lamented that "a prince and a great man has fallen..." (2Sa 3:38), and he gave Abner an honorable burial at Hebron.

For further study, see 1Sa 17:55-58; 26:5,13-16; 2Sa 2–4.

ABRAHAM (AY bruh ham) *father of a multitude;* 22 century B.C.; Gen 11:26

Abram, as he was first called, was a descendant of Noah's son Shem. He was a man of profound faith, and he was highly regarded wherever he went. He made his mark across the Near Eastern world nearly 4000 years ago, from Haran in Mesopotamia to Egypt. His story takes place primarily in the central hill country of Canaan, the land promised to him and his descendants, who were to be the chosen people of God.

Abram was born in Ur of the Chaldees and lived there with his wife Sarai (later called Sarah), his father, Terah, and his brothers. Abram and his nephew Lot moved their family group to Haran, a trading center in the Euphrates valley. They made Haran their home, and it was there that Terah died.

When Abram was 75 years old, God made a dramatic call on his life. God told Abram to leave Haran for a new land that God would show him. He promised that he would make of Abram "a great nation" (Gen 12:2) and vowed to bless Abram and give him a great name. In answering God's bidding, Abram gave up his pagan beliefs, ties to his people, and his status as a wealthy landowner. He and his family traveled through Shechem and Bethel into Canaan. Along the way, Abram honored the Lord, and the Lord reminded Abram that he would keep his promise to Abram and his descendants.

Walking by faith, however, was no easy task and not always the choice Abram made. During this

Abraham departs Haran with his family for the new land promised to him by God.

time, there was a famine in the region, and Abram and his company went to Egypt because food was available there. While in Egypt, Abram lied about Sarai, claiming that she was his sister. She was indeed his half-sister, but he didn't want the Egyptians to know that she was also his wife. No doubt the motive for his deception was based on the social laws of that time: In enemy territory, a husband could be killed if someone wanted his wife. Clearly Abram wanted to protect himself, but it almost cost him dearly.

Pharaoh brought Sarai into his household to add her to his harem. Abram was lavishly compensated for her with servants and livestock, but losing her would have meant that his promised blessings from God could not be realized. Fortunately for Abram, God intervened by sending plagues on the palace. Indignant when he discovered the truth about Abram and Sarai, Pharaoh returned Abram's wife to him and gave orders for the Hebrew family to take their belongings and go.

They left Egypt and returned to the hills north of Jerusalem. Soon, however, it became clear that there was not enough room or grazing ground for the large encampments of Abram and his nephew Lot. Abram resolved the problem by agreeing to let Lot move to the fruitful Jordan valley—part of Abram's Promised Land. Abram and his camp settled in the plain of Mamre near Hebron. Once there, Abram renewed his worship and faith by setting up an altar to the Lord.

Lot pitched his tents near the corrupt cities of Sodom and Gomorrah. In an attack orchestrated by four northern kings, Lot and his family were taken captive. Abram mustered an effective army and defeated the invaders in a night assault. Abram chased the enemy all the way beyond Damascus, then returned with Lot, his family, and other captives. This military victory was a remarkable achievement for Abram. He not only vanquished four notorious kings and established his military

might, but his triumph was also symbolic of his spiritual strength and faith.

Later, God told Abram that he intended to destroy the cities of Sodom and Gomorrah, where Lot lived, for the wicked practices of their inhabitants. Alarmed, Abram earnestly bargained with God to spare the cities if they contained as few as ten righteous people, but not even that number was found, so Sodom and Gomorrah were destroyed.

When Abram was 99 and Sarai was 90, God spoke to him again, giving him the name Abraham and reminding him that he would be the father of many nations. God instructed Abraham that he and all his male descendants should adopt circumcision as a sign to mark this covenant. Also at this time, God changed Sarai's name to Sarah and told Abraham that she would finally give birth to a son. Abraham laughed at this news but was later reminded of this promise by three strangers (angels in disguise) who visited him. Sarah, well past child-bearing age, also laughed when she overheard this announcement, but in time Isaac was born to them, as had been promised. This was a memorable event, and Abraham gave a grand feast when the baby was weaned.

Still, there was trouble in Abraham's clan: Some years earlier, the childless Sarah had given her maid to her husband so that their household would have an heir. Hagar, the slave-girl, bore Abraham a son called Ishmael. As a result of Ishmael's birth, Hagar threatened to replace Sarah as the mother of Israel. Bitterness and jealousy grew between Sarah and Hagar over Ishmael and Isaac, and finally on the day of the feast, Sarah told Abraham to get rid of Hagar and Ishmael. Sarah did not want Ishmael to share Isaac's inheritance. Abraham was troubled by Sarah's request, but the Lord instructed him to do as Sarah asked and also told him that his descendants through Ishmael would be a great nation. Abraham gave Hagar and Ishmael supplies and sent them off.

> ➤ ⬅
>
> *"I will make your offspring as numerous as the stars of heaven and as the sand that is on the seashore…by your offspring shall all the nations of the earth gain blessing for themselves."*
>
> Gen 22:17-19

Three angels remind Abraham of God's promise that Sarah would give birth to a son.

At this time, Abraham journeyed south, into the territory of the Philistine king Abimelech. There was trouble over use of a well, and resolving the issue brought the two men together. Through the solemn covenant they established, Abraham was able to secure land rights in Beersheba. He planted a tamarisk tree at the place where their oath of friendship and peace had been established.

Abraham's faith was most severely tested when God told him to kill his son as a sacrificial offering. Obediently, Abraham started toward the land of Moriah on his donkey, taking with him two servants, his son Isaac, and some firewood. On the third day of the journey, they were near the mountain where the sacrifice would take place. Abraham and Isaac walked the rest of the way alone. Isaac questioned his father about the sacrificial lamb. Resolutely, Abraham assured Isaac that God would provide the animal.

When they reached the place, Abraham built an altar, bound Isaac, laid him on the firewood, and took up the knife to kill his son. At the last moment, God intervened by providing a substitute offering: Abraham saw a ram trapped in a nearby thicket, and the animal was sacrificed instead of the boy. In this one act, Abraham performed an extreme demonstration of his faith, and God indicated that the common pagan practice of child sacrifice would not be tolerated in the Hebrew faith. God then renewed the promise of blessing to Abraham and his numerous descendants. After this, Abraham and Isaac returned to Beersheba.

Sarah was 127 years old when she died. Abraham purchased the Cave of Machpelah in Hebron as a family burying place, and here Sarah was laid to rest. Abraham, now elderly, sent his servant to Haran to look for a wife for Isaac from among Abraham's relatives there. Rebekah was found (the granddaughter of one of Abraham's brothers), and Isaac married the young girl.

Abraham then married Keturah, and their sons became the ancestors of the tribes of Dedan and Midian. After giving his possessions to Isaac and making provisions for his other sons, Abraham died at the age of 175. He, like Sarah, was buried in the Cave of Machpelah.

The story of Abraham marks the founding of Israel as a people, their move toward a land of their own, and most importantly, their commitment to monotheism. In the New Testament, Abraham is honored as a righteous man and the father of the Levitical priesthood. His consistent obedience to his call is described as the Bible's most outstanding example of faith. Abraham held many titles— landowner, entrepreneur, family man, grand patriarch of the Hebrews, and even friend of God.

For further study, see Gen 11:27–25:11; Ac 13:26; Ro 4; Heb 7:5; 11:8; 19.

ABSALOM (AB suh luhm) *father of peach*

1. 10 century B.C.; 2Sa 3:3

When King David failed to punish his oldest son, Amnon, for the rape of his half-sister Tamar, Absalom took matters into his own hands. He

A fleeing Absalom is killed by David's men when his hair becomes entangled in tree branches.

lured his older half-brother Amnon to his death two years later on a pretense of tending sheep in the country and banqueting with family. With Amnon dead, Absalom became the crown prince and heir to David's throne, but he had to lie low for a few more years. David was furious and inconsolable in grief over the sordid acts of his children, and he refused to allow Absalom to be in his presence for some time.

Once back from exile and reinstated into David's good graces, Absalom conspired to attain his father's throne by posing as a populist figure, promising justice, and charming the people. Absalom intercepted people coming to David for justice and persuaded them to join his rebel following instead. This attempt to steal the hearts of the people continued for four years and became so successful that David finally had to flee Jerusalem for his life.

Absalom sealed his takeover bid by sleeping with David's concubines. However, his carefully timed rebellion soon came to a violent end. A group of David's men caught and killed the fleeing Absalom when his hair became entangled in the branches of a tree. Ironically, Absalom had always flaunted his full and luxuriant hair as a symbol of his strength and vigor.

For further study, see 2Sa 13-19.

2. 10 century B.C.; 2Ch 11:20; (grand)father of Maacah 9; a form of Abishalom; possibly Absalom 1; also called Uriel 2

3. 2 century B.C.; 1Mac 11:70; father of two Maccabean army captains

4. 2 century B.C.; 2Mac 11:17; King Antiochus's courier to Judas Maccabeus

ABUBUS (uh BOO buhs) meaning unknown; 2 century B.C.; 1Mac 16:11; father of Ptolemy; related to Simon the priest

ACCOS (AK kus) *thorn;* 3 century B.C.; 1Mac 8:17; grandfather of Eupolemus the courier to Rome

ACHAICUS (uh KAY uh kuhs) *belonging to Achaia;* 1 century A.D.; 1Co 16:17; Corinthian who visited Paul

ACHAN (AY kuhn) *troubler* or *troubled;* 15 century B.C.; Jos 7:1

Despite being a wealthy man from Judah, Achan wrongly sought to increase his material possessions.

Achan and his family are stoned to death for defying Joshua's command.

During the Israelites' campaign in Canaan, he disobeyed Joshua's command by taking silver and gold from the spoils of Jericho that were to be "devoted" (destroyed in worship) to God. Achan's singular disobedience immediately brought God's punishment on all of Israel with an unexpected defeat at Ai, sending Israel's leadership into disarray.

Not until Achan was exposed, indicted, and stoned to death for this far-reaching individual sin did God return his hand of blessing on Israel and grant victory in the second battle with little Ai. Achan, the troublemaker, was buried in the Valley of Achor, which means *trouble.*

For further study, see Jos 6:17–8:2. Also called Achar.

ACHAR 1Ch 2:7; see Achan

ACHBOR (AK bohr) *mouse*
1. Gen 36:38; father of Edomite King Baal-hanan
2. 7 century B.C.; Jer 26:22; father of Elnathan

3. 7 century B.C.; 2Ki 22:12; queried Huldah about Law of Moses; see Abdon 4; possibly Achbor 2

ACHIM (AY kuhm) meaning unknown; Mt 1:14; ancestor of Jesus through Joseph

ACHIOR (AK ee or) *brother of light;* 5 century B.C.; Jdt 5:5; Ammonite chief; converted to Judaism

ACHISH (AY kish) meaning unknown
1. 11 century B.C.; 1Sa 21:10; ruler of Gath; protected David; also called Abimelech 4
2. 10 century B.C.; 1Ki 2:39; ruler of Gath; possibly Achish 1

ACHSAH (AK suh) *anklet* or *ornament;* 15 century B.C.; Jos 15:16; daughter of Caleb; won by Othniel as his wife

ADAH (AY duh) *adorned*
1. Gen 4:19; wife of Lamech; mother of Jabal and Jubal
2. 20 century B.C.; Gen 36:2; wife of Esau; daughter of Elon the Hittite

ADAIAH (uh DAY uh) *the Lord has adorned*
1. 7 century B.C.; 2Ki 22:1; father of Jedidah; grandfather of Josiah

2. 1Ch 6:41; Levite music minister under David; possibly Iddo 2
3. 1Ch 8:21; in genealogy of Benjamin
4. 9 century B.C.; 2Ch 23:1; his son Maaseiah helped overthrow Queen Athaliah
5. 6 century B.C.; Ne 11:5; descendant of Maaseiah; lived in Jerusalem after Exile
6. 5 century B.C.; 1Ch 9:12; priest who lived in Jerusalem after Exile
7. 5 century B.C.; Ezr 10:29; married foreign wife in Ezra's time
8. 5 century B.C.; Ezr 10:39; married foreign wife in Ezra's time

ADALIA (uh DAYL yah) meaning unknown; 5 century B.C.; Est 9:8; fifth of Haman's ten sons killed by Jews

ADAM (AD uhm) *human being* or *humanity;* Ge 1:26-27

On the sixth day of creation, God made humanity. He carefully shaped Adam from earthy clay, breathed life into his body, and made him a living person. He made a garden for Adam in Eden and instructed him to take care of it. God brought the animals and birds to Adam so that Adam could name them. Adam's world was pleasant and harmonious, but he was alone. God then created a woman, Eve, from Adam's rib, and Adam and Eve lived and worked together in the garden.

Earlier, God had warned Adam not to eat the fruit from the tree of knowledge of good and evil. But the serpent pursuaded Eve to try the fruit; she, in turn, gave some to Adam. Immediately, they felt ashamed of themselves and their nakedness and covered themselves with leaves.

At the time of the evening breeze, God was walking in the garden. Feeling guilty and anxious because of what they had done, Adam and Eve hid from their creator. God confronted them and dealt with their disobedience: He cursed the serpent to crawl forever on its belly in the dust; he confined the woman to painful childbearing and to potential domination by Adam; and he handed Adam over to a life of unending hardship as a farmer. Then God banished

God creating Adam. Michelangelo (1475–1564), Sistine Chapel, Rome.

the pair from Eden forever. With their actions, Adam and his family brought sin and death into the world.

After their expulsion, Adam and Eve had three sons—Cain, Abel, and Seth. Their descendants formed a line of redemption and blessing, down to Noah and his sons—particularly Shem—and on through Jesus Christ. The apostle Paul emphasized the spiritual relationship between Adam and Jesus, saying that the first man was an example of disobedience and death, while Christ—the second Adam—was the ultimate example of obedience and eternal life.

For further study, see Gen 1–4; Ro 5:12-21; 1Co 15:20-49.

ADBEEL (AD bee el) *languishing for God;* 21 century B.C.; Gen 25:13; third son of Ishmael

ADDAR (AD dahr) *noble;* 19 century B.C.; 1Ch 8:3; grandson of Benjamin through Bela; possibly Ard

ADDI (AD ee) *my witness;* Lk 3:28; ancestor of Jesus through Joseph

ADIEL (AY dee el) *God is my ornament*
1. 11 century B.C.; 1Ch 27:25; father of Azmaveth; David's treasurer
2. 8 century B.C.; 1Ch 4:36; Simeonite leader in Hezekiah's time
3. 5 century B.C.; 1Ch 9:12; priest; father of Maasai

ADIN (AY din) *ornament*
1. Ezr 2:15; ancestor of Jews who returned to Judah after Exile
2. 5 century B.C.; Ne 10:16; leader; sealed covenant in Nehemiah's time; possibly Adin 1

ADINA (AD uh nuh) *delicate* or *ornament;* 10 century B.C.; 1Ch 11:42; Reubenite chief; mighty man of David

ADLAI (AD lay) meaning unknown; 11 century B.C.; 1Ch 27:29; father of Shaphat the overseer of David's herds

ADMATHA (ad MAY thuh) meaning unknown; 5 century B.C.; Est 1:14; noble who advised King Ahasuerus to banish Vashti

ADNA (AD nuh) *pleasure*
1. 6 century B.C.; Ne 12:15; head of priestly family; returnee from Exile
2. 5 century B.C.; Ezr 10:30; one who married and divorced foreign wife after Exile

ADNAH (AD nuh) *pleasure*
1. 11 century B.C.; 1Ch 12:20; man of Manasseh; joined David's army at Ziklag
2. 9 century B.C.; 2Ch 17:14; commander under Jehoshaphat

ADONI-BEZEK (uh DOH nye BEH zek) *lord of Bezek;* 15 century B.C.; Jdg 1:5; king of Bezek; captured by Israel

ADONIJAH (AD oh NI juh) *the Lord is my Lord*
1. 10 century B.C.; 2Sa 3:4
Adonijah, born in Hebron to David and Haggith, was David's fourth son. After the death of his three older brothers (Amnon, Absalom, and Chileab), the handsome Adonijah aspired to the throne. When David was old, Adonijah decided to set about taking his father's place. He consulted with Joab and Abiathar, who agreed that Adonijah should naturally succeed David. Adonijah prepared a grand feast for his supporters at En-rogel, a spring in the Kidron valley outside the city walls. However, Adonijah did not invite his younger brother Solomon, the prophet Nathan, the military leader Benaiah, or the high priest Zadok. Alarmed by what Adonijah was doing, these men took action.

The prophet Nathan spoke to Bathsheba, Solomon's mother, and she approached David. She reminded the aging king that he had promised the throne to Solomon. David immediately decided to resign in favor of Solomon. He told Zadok, Nathan, and Benaiah to go with Solomon to the spring of Gihon (also in the Kidron valley) and anoint Solomon king in public. When Adonijah and his supporters heard the merrymaking from Solomon's coronation, they panicked. Adonijah's supporters hurried home, and Adonijah, fearing for his life, grabbed the altar for protection. Solomon spared Adonijah's life.

After David died, Adonijah once again made an unwise move: He asked to marry Abishag, the young Shunammite girl who had looked after David in his old age. His request to take a wife from the royal harem was viewed as yet another bid for the throne. King Solomon immediately sent for

Benaiah and had his ambitious older brother Adonijah killed.

For further study, see 1Ki 1–2.

2. 9 century B.C.; 2Ch 17:8; Jehoshaphat's teacher of the Law in Judah

3. 5 century B.C.; Ne 10:16; sealed covenant in Nehemiah's time; possibly Adonikam

ADONIKAM (ad uh NYE kuhm) *my lord is exalted;* Ezr 2:13; ancestor of family living in Judah after Exile; possibly Adonijah 3

ADONIRAM (ad uh NYE ruhm) *my lord has risen;* 1Ki 4:6; supervisor of forced labor under three Israelite kings; also called Adoram and Hadoram 3

ADONI-ZEDEK (uh DOH ni ZEH dek) *my lord is righteousness;* 15 century B.C.; Jos 10:1

King Adoni-zedek of Jerusalem was afraid. He had heard that Joshua and the Israelites had destroyed the cities of Ai and Jericho on their march into Canaan, and that the Gibeonites had made peace with Israel. Unhappy with this alliance, Adoni-zedek invited four other Amorite kings to join him in attacking the Gibeonites. To stave off this threat, Gibeon implored Joshua and the Israelites for help. Assured of victory by God, Joshua and his forces attacked the enemy in a battle marked by hailstones and a call for the sun and moon to "stand still" until victory was complete. After their defeat, Adoni-zedek and the four kings hid in a cave at Makkedah. Pursued by Joshua, they were executed and buried in the same cave. For further study, see Jos 10:1-27.

ADORAM 2Sa 20:24; see Adoniram

ADRAMMELECH (uh DRAM muh lek) *Ader is king*

1. 2Ki 17:31; Babylonian deity who received human sacrifice

2. 7 century B.C.; 2Ki 19:37; son who murdered his father Sennacherib

ADRIEL (AY dree el) *my help is God;* 11 century B.C.; 1Sa 18:19; husband of Saul's daughter Merab

ADUEL (AD oo el) *God is an ornament;* Tob 1:1; ancestor of Tobit

ADULAMITES (uh DULL uh myts) Gen 38:1; inhabitants of Adullam, a Canaanite town

AENEAS (eh NEE uhs) *praise;* 1 century A.D.; Ac 9:33; paralytic in Lydda; healed by Peter

AGABUS (AG uh buhs) *he loved* or *locust;* 1 century A.D.; Ac 11:28; Christian prophet who predicted Paul's arrest

AGAG (AY gag) *warlike or violent*

1. Nu 24:7; powerful king mentioned in Balaam's oracle

2. 11 century B.C.; 1Sa 15:8; Amalekite king; spared by a disobedient Saul

AGAGITES (AY guh gyts) Est 3:1; descendants of King Agag of the Amalekites; Haman of Persia was one

AGEE (AG ee) *fugitive;* 11 century B.C.; 2Sa 23:11; father of Shammah

AGRIPPA Ac 25:13; see Herod Agrippa II (Herod 7)

AGUR (AY guhr) *gatherer;* Pr 30:1; son of Jakeh; author of many proverbs

AHAB (AY hab) *father is brother*

1. ruled 874–853 B.C; 1Ki 16:28

Ahab was a compelling figure—politically astute, clever at foreign policy, and an economic genius. During his rule as the seventh king of Israel's northern kingdom, he fortified Israelite cities, maintained peace with the southern kingdom of Judah, and strengthened economic ties with Phoenician seaports. Ahab undertook a major renovation of his own capital, Samaria, even adorning the palace with ivory. He was known for his love of wealth and showy extravagance. Ahab began his reign in a strong position, thanks to his father and predecessor King Omri who had set the pattern for the kingship to be dynastic, with absolute authority passed on through inheritance.

Despite his successes in political and military affairs, Ahab went against the mandated religious practices of Israel by allowing and even practicing paganism. In fact, the biblical record states that Ahab did more to displease the Lord than any of the previous kings of Israel.

King Ahab dies in battle as foretold by the prophet Micaiah.

the prophet fled for his life across the Jordan River. In the last year of the drought, at God's urging, Elijah returned to challenge King Ahab to a showdown with 450 prophets of Baal on Mt. Carmel. Ahab agreed to the competition. In the ensuing drama, the Baal worshipers tested their god from morning until evening, but there was "no voice, no answer, and no response" (1Ki 18:29). Elijah mocked the worshipers and claimed that their god was preoccupied and useless.

When it was his turn, the Hebrew prophet prepared an offering before all the people and prayed to the God of Israel. Elijah's offering was suddenly consumed by "the fire of the Lord" (1Ki 18:31). The people were awed and acknowledged the God of Israel as the true Lord. Elijah then had the false prophets put to death, and a great storm, sweeping in from the Mediterranean Sea, brought the drought to an end.

After this victory for monotheism, Ahab drove back in his chariot through the downpour. An ecstatic Elijah ran down the mountain, outracing king Ahab in his chariot. When Jezebel heard the news, she was furious and swore to have Elijah killed, but once again, the prophet escaped.

Another significant incident in Ahab's life involved a neighbor's vineyard. Adjacent to Ahab's winter quarters at Jezreel was a fruitful vineyard that the king wanted for himself. But Naboth, the owner, refused to sell his family inheritance. When the king couldn't have his way, Jezebel took charge and had Naboth stoned to death on false charges of blasphemy. The vineyard then became Ahab's by default, as the property of a convicted criminal reverted to the king. Furious at this treachery and murder, Elijah pronounced destruction on Ahab and his household. Frightened at the prophet's curse, Ahab repented. According to the biblical record, God accepted his penitence and postponed judgment on him.

Israel's most oppressive foe during Ahab's reign was Ben-hadad II of Syria. On one occasion, Ben-hadad marched his army to the gates of Samaria and besieged the city. However, Ahab surprised the enemy by launching a daytime attack. The Syrians fled, and their king narrowly escaped on horseback. Later, in a battle near Aphek, Ahab defeated Ben-

Ahab's marriage to Jezebel and his relationship with her father Ethbaal influenced his rule over Israel's religious life. Jezebel used her position as queen to champion her native Phoenician religion. Ahab agreed to build a temple with all of its pagan trappings dedicated to the god Baal. He actively served Baal and introduced pagan rituals that were anathema to the Hebrews. Cultic practices sprang up everywhere, including promiscuous ceremonial rites dedicated to the fertility goddess, Asherah (Astarte).

The king's palace also supported false prophets who promoted the creeds of the pagan gods. Jezebel persecuted and killed off many prophets of the Lord. However, some of God's prophets were saved thanks to Ahab's minister Obadiah, who hid them in caves.

Elijah, the prophet of Israel at the time, was aghast at what was taking place. He warned the king that Israel's paganism would be punished with a prolonged drought. After delivering his message,

hadad but agreed to spare his life in return for political and commercial concessions. For his lenient actions toward Ben-hadad, Ahab was warned by an unknown prophet that he would lose his own life.

After this, Israel and Syria enjoyed peace for three years, probably because both nations were threatened by the imperial power of Assyria. Assyrian records indicate that Ahab supported Ben-hadad with chariots and men against the northern invader, and their common front succeeded in halting the Assyrian advance. Their alliance was short-lived, however. Once more, Ahab fought against Syria, this time with the help of Jehoshaphat, king of Judah. Even though Ahab's death in this battle was predicted by the prophet Micaiah, the king disguised himself and brazenly went into the fray. A stray arrow pierced Ahab, and by day's end he died in a pool of his own blood. Ahab was buried in Samaria, and his son Ahaziah became king.

For further study, see 1Ki 16:28–22:40; 2Ch 18:1-34; Hos 1:4; Mic 6:16.
2. 6 century B.C.; Jer 29:21; false prophet during Exile

AHARAH (uh HAR uh) *brother's follower;* 19 century B.C.; 1Ch 8:1; son of Benjamin; form of Ahiram; possibly Aher; also called Ehi

AHARHEL (uh HAR hel) *brother of Rachel;* 1Ch 4:8; clan leader; descendant of Judah

AHASBAI (uh HAS bye) *blooming;* 11 century B.C.; 2Sa 23:34; father of Eliphelet the army commander

AHASUERUS (uh HAZ yoo AYR uhs) meaning unknown
1. 6 century B.C.; Da 9:1; father of Darius the Mede
2. ruled 486–465 B.C.; Ezr 4:6

In extra-biblical history, he is known as Xerxes I (Greek name) or Khshayarsha (Persian name). As

King Ahasuerus with Esther, whom he married after divorcing the virtuous Queen Vashti. Rembrandt (1606–1669).

the son of Darius I the Great and grandson of Cyrus the Great, he succeeded them to rule over a vast Persian empire, embracing some 50 nations from India to Ethiopia. His many military and cultural accomplishments were largely overshadowed by a devastating defeat by Greek allies in 480–79 B.C. But in Scripture, Ahasuerus is best known for marrying Esther after divorcing the beautiful Queen Vashti.

Vashti was his virtuous wife and the beautiful cohost of Ahasuerus's lavish and prolonged palace feasts. But she was deemed insubordinate on one such occasion for refusing to show off her beauty for ogling guests. Her defiance embarrassed the king, and some guests worried that her example would inspire other women in the kingdom to assert themselves against their husbands. Ahasuerus's advisors persuaded the indecisive king to reject the noble Vashti and conduct a kingdomwide search for someone "better than she" (Est 1:19).

After a long search, the king married Esther, the Jewish adopted daughter of Mordecai. As the king's wife and father-in-law, they would later use their influence to thwart a conspiracy hatched by Ahasuerus's prime minister Haman to persecute the Jews. An enlightened Ahasuerus later executed Haman and granted political freedom for the Jews, an event still celebrated as the feast of Purim.

For further study, see Est 1–3; 6–10.

AHAZ (AY haz) *he grasped* or *he possessed*
1. 10 century B.C.; 1Ch 8:35; son of Micah; father of Jehoaddah
2. ruled 735–715 B.C.; 2Ki 15:38

Ahaz had a promising start and heritage. He was raised a son of the godly King Jotham and Queen Jerusha and the grandson of Azariah (also called Uzziah), under whom Judah had reached new heights, spiritually and geopolitically. Yet Ahaz departed radically from the righteous ways of these two kings and revived the cultic practices of child sacrifice, pagan idolatry, and witchcraft.

Ahaz invited the wrath of Syria and Israel when he declined to join their alliance against Assyria. The prophet Isaiah offered Ahaz the prophesy of Immanuel ("God is with us") that foretold the coming of Christ, and he counseled that by renewing their faith in God, Ahaz and his people would not fall before Israel and Syria. Ahaz refused to listen to Isaiah, and Judah was overrun. Ravaged and desperate, he turned to Assyria for protection and at the same time embraced the pagan gods of Damascus. Rather than putting his faith in the power of the Lord God, Ahaz relinquished his nation to the armies and gods of

King Ahaz. Stained glass. Durham Cathedral, Durham, England.

foreign lands, going so far as to surrender his political autonomy and to sacrifice his own son in a pagan ritual.

The legacy of the evil Ahaz lingered for generations. His pagan practices and institutions, including the new altar modeled after the one in Damascus and adopted for sun worship of the Assyrian gods, survived even the purges of reformist King Josiah almost 100 years later.

Despite his brutally idolatrous ways, Ahaz did produce one godly son, Hezekiah. Though to succeed Ahaz as king, of course, Hezekiah had to survive Ahaz's practice of burning sons at pagan altars—no small feat.

For further study, see 2Ki 16; 2Ch 28; Isa 7–12.

AHAZIAH (AY huh ZI uh) *the Lord sustains*
1. 853–852 B.C.; 1Ki 22:40

This son of King Ahab and Queen Jezebel adopted the practices of his mother's pagan religion. When he was injured in a fall from a window, Ahaziah consulted with the oracles of the fertility god Baal to treat his condition. The prophet Elijah foretold that Ahaziah would die in bed of his injuries for entrusting his recovery to a pagan deity rather than to God. The king tried to nullify Elijah's curse of death by taking him captive, but his actions made no difference; Elijah was shown to be a true prophet when Ahaziah soon died. For further study, see 1Ki 22:40–2Ki 1:18; 2Ch 20:35,37.
2. ruled 841 B.C.; 2Ki 8:24

This youngest son of the wicked King Joram and Queen Athaliah succeeded his father at age 22 as the sixth king of Judah. Ahaziah died after only one year in office, yet he lived long enough to produce an heir—Joash—and to establish a path of idolatry. Following the lead of his maternal grandparents Ahab and Jezebel, Ahaziah promoted the sexually indulgent rituals associated with the worship of the fertility god Baal. This association with Ahab and Baal worship proved to be his undoing. When Jehu was anointed a righteous king of Israel, he immediately hunted down and killed any rivals related to Ahab, including King Ahaziah of Judah. For further study, see 2Ki 8:24-29; 9:16-29; 1Ch 3:11; 2Ch 22. Also called Jehoahaz.

AHBAN (AH bahn) *brother of intelligence;* 1Ch 2:29; Judahite; descendant of Jerahmeel

AHER (AY huhr) *one who is behind* or *another;* 1Ch 7:12; descendant of Benjamin

AHI (AY high) *my brother*
1. 1Ch 7:34; son of Shomer; in genealogy of Asher
2. 1Ch 5:15; head of family; descendant of Gad

AHIAH (uh HIGH uh) *the Lord is my brother;* 5 century B.C.; Ne 10:26; Jewish leader; sealed covenant in Nehemiah's day

AHIAM (uh HIGH uhm) *a mother's brother;*
11 century B.C.; 2Sa 23:33; mighty warrior under
David

AHIAN (uh HIGH uhn) *brotherly;* 1Ch 7:19;
listed in genealogy of Manasseh

AHIEZER (AY high EE zuhr) *brother is help*
1. 15 century B.C.; Nu 1:12; leader of tribe of
Dan in Moses's time
2. 11 century B.C.; 1Ch 12:3; Benjaminite
military leader; defected from Saul to David

AHIHUD (uh HIGH hud) *brother of majesty*
1. 1Ch 8:7; son of Gera; descendant of Benjamin
2. 15 century B.C.; Nu 34:27; leader appointed
by Moses to help divide Canaan

AHIJAH (uh HIGH juh) *the Lord is brother*
1. 1Ch 2:25; son of Jerahmeel; descendant of
Judah
2. 11 century B.C.; 1Sa 14:3; son of Ahitub; army
priest; possibly Ahimelech 2
3. 11 century B.C.; 1Ch 11:36; mighty man of
David; also called Eliam 2
4. 11 century B.C.; 1Ch 26:20; Levite in charge
of temple treasuries under David
5. 10 century B.C.; 1Ki 4:3; a secretary for
Solomon
6. 10 century B.C.; 1Ki 11:29; prophet who
foretold the division of Israel and the death of
Jeroboam's son
7. 10 century B.C.;1Ki 15:27; father of evil king
Baasha
8. 1Ch 8:7; see Ahoah
9. 2Esd 1:1; father of Ahitub and supposed
ancestor of Ezra

AHIKAM (uh HIGH kuhm) *my brother has risen;*
7 century B.C.; 2Ki 22:12; Josiah's official; spared
Jeremiah

AHIKAR (uh HIGH kuhr) possibly *precious
brother;* 8 century B.C.; Tob 1:21; nephew of
Tobit; Assyrian royal treasurer

AHILUD (uh HIGH luhd) *a brother born*
1. 11 century B.C.; 2Sa 8:16; father of
Jehoshaphat 1
2. 11 century B.C.; 1Ki 4:3; father of Baana;
possibly Ahilud 1

AHIMAAZ (uh HIM ay az) *brother of wrath*
1. 11 century B.C.; 1Sa 14:50; father of Saul's
wife Ahinoam
2. 10 century B.C.; 2Sa 15:27; son of Zadok;
loyal to David during revolt
3. 10 century B.C.; 1Ki 4:15; district governor;
married Solomon's daughter Basemath

AHIMAN (uh HIGH muhn) *brother of fortune*
1. 15 century B.C.; Nu 13:22; descendant
of Anak
2. 5 century B.C.; 1Ch 9:17; temple gatekeeper in
Jerusalem after Exile

AHIMELECH (uh HIM eh lek) *my brother is king*
1. 11 century B.C.; 1Sa 26:6; Hittite; fled from
Saul with David
2. 11 century B.C.; 1Sa 21:1
   When David and his fugitive band came begging for provisions at Nob, a priestly sanctuary outside of Jerusalem, Ahimelech showed mercy. He offered the only food on hand—the "bread of the
Presence" (bread consecrated for use at the sacred
sanctuary). Ahimelech also gave David the sword
of Goliath. Little did Ahimelech know that for aiding and abetting Saul's enemy, he and 85 other
priests at Nob would be executed by Saul's agent,
Doeg the Edomite.
   Jesus later used the story of Ahimelech to show
that the ceremonial laws, such as those restricting
holy bread to priests and excluding laity (Lev 24:9),
are subordinate to God's laws, such as those that
tell us to do good by helping those in need.
   For further study, see 1Sa 21–22; Mt 12:1-8; Lk
6:1-5.
3. 10 century B.C.; 2Sa 8:17; son of Abiathar;
grandson of Ahimelech 2

AHIMOTH (uh HIGH moth) *brother is death;*
1Ch 6:25; Levite; ancestor of Samuel

AHINADAB (un HIN uh dab) *brother is noble;*
10 century B.C.; 1Ki 4:14; district governor under
Solomon

AHINOAM (uh HIN oh am) *brother is delight*
1. 11 century B.C.; 1Sa 14:50; wife of Saul;
daughter of Ahimaaz
2. 11 century B.C.; 1Sa 25:43; wife of David;
mother of Amnon

AHIO (uh HIGH oh) *his brother*
1. 1Ch 8:14; listed in genealogy of Benjamin
2. 11 century B.C.; 1Ch 8:31; eighth son of Jeiel; uncle of Saul
3. 11 century B.C.; 2Sa 6:3; son of Abinadab 1; moved ark to Jerusalem

AHIRA (uh HIGH ruh) *brother of evil;* 15 century B.C.; Nu 1:15; leader of the Naphtali tribe

AHIRAM Nu 26:38; see Aharah

AHISAMACH (uh HIS uh mahk) *my brother supports;* 15 century B.C.; Ex 31:6; father of Oholiab

AHISHAHAR (uh HISH uh hahr) *brother of dawn;* 1Ch 7:10; in genealogy of Benjamin

AHISHAR (uh HIGH shahr) *my brother has sung;* 10 century B.C.; 1Ki 4:6; overseer of Solomon's palace

AHITHOPHEL (uh HITH oh fel) *brother of foolishness;* 10 century B.C.; 2Sa 15:12
    Ahithophel's family ties reveal a possible reason for his changing allegiance from David to Absalom. His son Eliam, a mighty man among David's Thirty, is likely the same Eliam who fathered Bathsheba (2Sa 11:3). If so, he may have chosen to side against David when he learned that David and Bathsheba had had an affair and that David had arranged the death of Bathsheba's husband, Uriah.
    This sage member of David's cabinet gave unusually poor advice to Absalom: to lie with David's harem. That sin was tantamount to Absalom assuming the throne and doomed his rebellion to a fatal end. When his military advice to Absalom went unheeded and he saw that the flawed rebellion was doomed, Ahithophel committed suicide rather than facing charges as a coconspirator in treason.
    For further study, see 2Sa 11:3; 12:8-12; 15–17; 23:34.

AHITUB (uh HIGH tuhb) *brother is good*
1. 11 century B.C.; 1Sa 14:3; father of Ahimelech the priest of Nob
2. 11 century B.C.; 2Sa 8:17; father of Zadok the priest; possibly Ahitub 1

3. 1Ch 6:11; descendant of Ahitub 2

AHLAI (AH lah eye) meaning unknown
1. 1Ch 2:31; child of Sheshan; descendant of Judah
2. 11 century B.C.; 1Ch 11:41; his son Zabad was a mighty man of David

AHOAH (uh HO uh) *brotherly;* 1Ch 8:4; a son of Bela the Benjaminite; also called Ahijah 8

AHUMAI (uh HOO may ee) *brother of water;* 1Ch 4:2; clan leader; descendant of Judah

AHUZZAM (uh HUZ uhm) *possessor;* 1Ch 4:6; descendant of Judah

AHUZZATH (uh HUZ ath) *held fast;* 21 century B.C.; Gen 26:26; advisor to Abimelech during Isaac's time

AHZAI (UH zih) *the Lord sustains;* Ne 11:13; ancestor of Amashsai the priest; possibly Jahzerah

AIAH (AY yuh) *vulture*
1. 20 century B.C.; Gen 36:24; son of Zibeon; brother of Anah; contemporary of Esau
2. 11 century B.C.; 2Sa 3:7; father of Saul's concubine Rizpah

AKAN (AY kan) *intelligent* or *twisted;* 20 century B.C.; Gen 36:27; son of Ezer; Horite chief; also called Jaakan

AKKUB (AK ub) *cunning* or *one who lies in wait*
1. Ezr 2:42; ancestral head of family of gatekeepers
2. Ezr 2:45; ancestral head of family of temple servants
3. 5 century B.C.; 1Ch 9:17; gatekeeper of temple in Jerusalem
4. 5 century B.C.; Ne 8:7; Levite in Jerusalem; taught the Law with Ezra
5. 1Ch 3:24; descendant of Zerubbabel; in line of David
6. 1Esd 5:28; ancestor of gatekeepers after Exile

ALCIMUS (AL si muhs) *valiant;* 2 century B.C.; 1Mac 7:5
    Alcimus's appointment to the priesthood was full of pretense and controversy, inciting riots,

death, and all-out war. Without any inherited (legitimate) claim to the priesthood, Alcimus appealed to the new Seleucid king, Demetrius I Soter, who granted his unusual request and enforced it with a Syrian army escort to Jerusalem. Judas Maccabeus contested the appointment with an armed rebellion that was squashed by an even larger military contingent. Though Alcimus was eventually restored to his powerful priestly office, he died from a paralyzing stroke shortly thereafter. According to Jewish legend, Alcimus's death was God's retribution for breaking down the inner wall of the temple separating Gentiles from the inner courts reserved only for legitimate Jewish priests. For further study, see 1Mac 7:5-25; 9:1-4, 54-57; 2Mac 14:3-13,26.

ALEMETH (AL uh meth) *hidden* or *youthful vigor*
1. 19 century B.C.; 1Ch 7:8; last son of Becher; grandson of Benjamin
2. 1Ch 8:36; descendant of Saul through Jonathan

Alexander the Great, 356–323 B.C., whose empire spread Hellenism across the known world.

ALEXANDER (al ig ZAN duhr) *defender of men*
1. Alexander the Great; ruled 336–323 B.C.; 1Mac 1:1

Alexander of Macedonia, son of King Philip II, was educated by the Greek philosopher Aristotle to have a passion for learning and an unshakable belief in the superiority of Greek (Hellenistic) culture. At age 16, Alexander administered Macedonia in his father's absence, during which time he distinguished himself as a commander. When Philip was assassinated, Alexander became king of Greece.

That same year, Alexander attacked the Medo-Persian rulers to free Greeks living under their thumb in Asia Minor. One victory led to another and by 324 B.C., the conquest of Asia Minor was complete; Hellenism was now the international norm for civilization. Alexander's shrewd genius, visionary leadership, and outstanding military command helped him accomplish his ambitions. He was also driven by personal grandeur of epic and biblical proportions. From exile in Babylon centuries before, the prophet Daniel anticipated in a vision that "the first king of Greece" would defeat Medo-Persia.

In establishing his sprawling empire, Alexander went beyond Hellenism and embraced racial and cultural cooperation. He took Persians into his army, encouraged his soldiers to marry Asians, and began to establish Greek cities in the East, many named Alexandria. His forces marched eastward as far as India, but after a great victory there, weary soldiers refused to go farther and Alexander was forced to return home.

Alexander died in Babylon at the young age of 32. His vast empire, divided among his successor-generals, became three dynasties: the Antigonids of Macedonia, the Ptolemies of Egypt, and the Seleucids of Syria. Alexander's legacy eventually contributed to the rise of the Roman empire and to the spread of Christianity.

For further study, see Da 8:1-22; 11:3; 1Mac 1:1-9.
2. Alexander Balas (al ig ZAN duhr BAH luhs); ruled 150–145 B.C.; 1Mac 10:1

The pretender Alexander Balas did not descend from the Seleucid dynasty, which began with one of the generals under Alexander the Great and ruled Syria from 281 to 64 B.C. Nonetheless, this virtually unknown and lowborn Greek successfully wrested away the throne from the incumbent Seleucid ruler, Demetrius I Soter, by posing as the son of the legendary Antiochus Epiphanes. In his campaign to usurp the throne, Alexander Balas (Epiphanes) bought the allegiance of the controversial Jewish priest Jonathan. Jonathan then came to his aid when Alexander Balas was challenged militarily by Demetrius II Nicator, son of the deposed Demetrius I Soter. Although Jonathan won the war, Alexander Balas lost his five-year hold on power through gross ineptitude and was beheaded. For further study, see 1Mac 10:1–11:17.

3. 1 century A.D.; Ac 4:6; member of Sanhedrin; kinsman of Annas the priest

4. 1 century A.D.; Mk 15:21; son of Simon of Cyrene identified with Jesus's cross

5. 1 century A.D.; Ac 19:33

Thrust forward by fellow Jews, Alexander tried calming the mob of silversmiths who were protesting the work of Paul and other early evangelists. The Ephesian metalworkers made great profits filling the demand for silver idols of the goddess Artemis, and the monotheism spread by Paul and other leaders of the new church was taking away their business. He never got to speak over the tumult, and it is not known whether Alexander would have supported the local trade unions or the Gospel. While appearing to be on the side of Paul and his companions, he may have later turned on Paul. See Alexander 6 and 7.

6. 1 century A.D.; 1Ti 1:20

This Alexander may have suffered economically under the impact of the Gospel on the silversmiths at Ephesus. Although Alexander had converted to Christianity, his economic motives may have caused him to speak against Paul. Paul felt compelled to give up on this believer-turned-blasphemer, as he mentions in his letter to Timothy. See Alexander 5 and 7.

7. 1 century A.D.; 2Ti 4:14

Progressive hostility and antagonism could have turned this Alexander, a coppersmith from Asia, from public dismay to open heresy to bitter opposition of Paul and his message. Paul mentions some "harm" that this Alexander inflicted on him; it may have been some false charges that sent Paul first to jail and then to Rome. All this gave Paul another reason to warn Timothy about this dangerous, vengeful heretic. In either event, Alexander seems to be one that Paul had frequent and unfortunate run-ins with. Alexander 5, 6, and 7 may well be the same person. For further study, see Ac 19:23-41; 1Ti 1:19-20; 2Ti 4:14-18.

ALEXANDRIANS (al ig ZAN dree uhns) Ac 6:9; inhabitants of Macedonia (modern Greece), founded by Alexander the Great in 330 B.C.

ALIAH 1Ch 1:51; see Alvah

ALIAN 1Ch 1:40; see Alvan

ALLON (AL luhn) *oak tree;* 1Ch 4:37; in genealogy of Simeon

ALMODAD (al MOH dad) *agitator* or *the beloved;* Gen 10:26; eldest son of Joktan

ALPHAEUS (al FEE uhs) *leader of a thousand*
1. 1 century A.D.; Mk 2:14; his son Levi became the apostle Matthew
2. 1 century A.D.; Mt 10:3; father of apostle James 3; possibly Alphaeus 1

ALVAH (AL vuh) *high* or *sublimity;* Gen 36:40; descendant of Esau; chief of Edom; form of Aliah

ALVAN (AL vun) *tall* or *sublime;* 20 century B.C.; Gen 36:23; firstborn son of Shobal of Seir; form of Alian

AMAL (AY mahl) *laborer;* 1Ch 7:35; listed in genealogy of Asher

AMALEK (AM uh lek) *warlike;* 20 century B.C.; Gen 36:12; son of Eliphaz and concubine Timna; grandson of Esau

AMALEKITES (AM uh leh kites) Gen 14:7

From Amalek, grandson of Esau, came this tribe that first attacked Israel as they entered Canaan. Amalekites fought Moses, Joshua, the judges, Saul, and David. For further study, see Gen 36:12-16; Dt 1; Ex 17:8-16; Nu 14:25-45; 24:20; Jdg 6:3,33; 1Sa 15; 2Sa 1; 8:12.

AMARIAH (am uh RI uh) *the Lord has said*
1. 12 century B.C.; 1Ch 6:7; grandfather or great-grandfather of Zadok
2. 1Ch 6:11; descendent of Amariah 1
3. 1Ch 23:19; descendant of Kohath the son of Levi
4. 9 century B.C.; 2Ch 19:11; high priest during Jehoshaphat's time

5. Zep 1:1; ancestor of prophet Zephaniah
6. 8 century B.C.; 2Ch 31:15; Levite; distributed tithes in Hezekiah's time
7. 6 century B.C.; Ne 10:3; ancestral head of priestly family
8. 5 century B.C.; Ezr 10:42; one who married and divorced foreign wife after Exile
9. Ne 11:4; ancestor of Ahaiah; stayed in Jerusalem

AMASA (uh MAS uh) *burden-bearer*
1. 10 century B.C.; 2Sa 17:25
   Though a nephew to David (born to David's sister Abigail), Amasa joined and led the opposition forces under his rebel cousin Absalom. When Amasa's army was defeated and Absalom and Abner were killed in battle by Joab, David appealed to his blood relative to switch sides. Amasa accepted this offer of a second chance, reaffirmed his loyalty to the king, and became the commander of David's army. This reconciling move on David's part was both political and personal, as he wanted to reunite the various warring factions and replace the bloodthirsty Joab. However, Joab was not as forgiving as David and would soon exact his revenge. Through an act of treachery, he killed Amasa. For further study, see 2Sa 19:13–20:13.
2. 8 century B.C.; 2Ch 28:12; Israelite leader; opposed enslaving Judah's captives

AMASAI (AM uh sigh) *burden-bearer*
1. 1Ch 6:25; Levite; ancestor of David's temple minister
2. 11 century B.C.; 1Ch 12:18; chief of David's mighty men; possibly Abishai; possibly Amasa 1
3. 11 century B.C.; 1Ch 15:24; priest; blew trumpet in bringing ark to Jerusalem

AMASHSAI (uh MASH sigh) *burdensome;* 5 century B.C.; Ne 11:13; priest in Jerusalem in Nehemiah's time; also called Maasai

AMASIAH (AM ah SIGH uh) *the Lord bears;* 9 century B.C.; 2Ch 17:16; army commander under Jehoshaphat

AMAZIAH (AM uh ZYE uh) *the Lord is mighty* or *strength of the Lord*
1. 11 century B.C.; 1Ch 6:45; Levite; temple musician under David
2. ruled 796–767 B.C.; 2Ki 12:21

Like his father, King Joash of Judah, Amaziah "did right" early in his political career but later lapsed into foolishness and was judged for it. Amaziah's big mistake was boastfully taking on the mightier Israelite army under King Jehoash. His defeat resulted in years of captivity as a king in exile, the sacking of the Jerusalem temple, and the subjugation of Judah to Israel. When released from prison, he was killed by political conspirators. Altogether, he ruled as Judah's ninth king for 29 years, the last 24 in a co-regency with son Azariah. For further study, see 2Ki 13:12; 14:1–15:3; 1Ch 3:12; 2Ch 24:27–26:4.
3. 8 century B.C.; Am 7:10; priest at Bethel; Amos cursed him
4. 8 century B.C.; 1Ch 4:34; Simeonite leader in Hezekiah's day

AMI (AY mih) *faithful;* 10 century B.C.; Ezr 2:57; servant of Solomon; also called Amon 2

AMITTAI (uh MIT eye) *truthful;* 8 century B.C.; 2Ki 14:25; father of prophet Jonah

AMMIEL (AM ee el) *God is my kinsman*
1. 15 century B.C.; Nu 13:12; Danite chosen to explore Canaan
2. 11 century B.C.; 2Sa 9:4; father of David's ally Machir
3. 11 century B.C.; 1Ch 3:5; father of Bath-shua; grandfather of Solomon; also called Eliam 1
4. 11 century B.C.; 1Ch 26:5; son of Obed-edom; gatekeeper in David's day

AMMIHUD (uh MI hud) *my kinsman is glorious*
1. 15 century B.C.; Nu 1:10; Ephraimite leader under Moses
2. 15 century B.C.; Nu 34:20; Simeonite; appointed by Moses to divide Canaan
3. 15 century B.C.; Nu 34:28; Naphtali tribe leader; authorized to divide Canaan
4. 11 century B.C.; 2Sa 13:37; father of Absalom's ally King Talmai
5. 5 century B.C.; 1Ch 9:4; descendant of Judah through Perez

AMMINADAB (uh MIN uh dab) *my kinsman is noble*
1. 1Ch 6:22; descendant of Kohath the son of Levi

2. 15 century B.C.; Ex 6:23; father of Nahshon; father-in-law of Aaron; tribal leader
3. 11 century B.C.; 1Ch 15:10; head of Levite family who carried ark to Jerusalem

AMMISHADDAI (am mi SHAD eye) *Almighty is kinsman;* 16 century B.C.; Nu 1:12; father of Ahiezer the leader of tribe of Dan

AMMIZABAD (uh MIZ uh bad) *my kinsman has given;* 10 century B.C.; 1Ch 27:6; commander of David's bodyguards

AMMONITES (AM oh nights) Gen 19:28

Descended from Ben-ammi, the son of Lot, this tribe of the Trans-Jordan area was first accepted as near relatives by Israel on their return to Canaan. However, the two groups became adversaries for much of the remaining Old Testament record. For further study, see Dt 2:19-37; Jdg 10:6–12:3; 1Sa 11; 14; 2Sa 10–12; 1Ki 11; 2Ki 23–24; Ne 2; 4; 13; Jer 9; 27; 40–41; 49; Eze 21; 25.

AMNON (AM nahn) *faithful*
1. 1Ch 4:20; descendant of Judah
2. 10 century B.C.; 2Sa 3:2

This son of King David by Ahinoam was a half-brother of the beautiful Tamar, who was his sole consuming interest. Amnon raped his half-sister,

which ultimately brought hatred and strife to the whole family. The eldest son and crown prince, he was in line to inherit the throne of David. But before he could assume any royal office, his half-brother Absalom avenged Tamar's rape and abuse by murdering Amnon. For further study, see 2Sa 13:1-31; 1Ch 3:1.

AMOK (AY muhk) *deep;* 6 century B.C.; Ne 12:7; priest who returned to Judah after Exile

AMON (AM muhn) *trustworthy*
1. Jer 46:25; Egyptian god of Thebes
2. Ne 7:59; see Ami
3. 9 century B.C.; 1Ki 22:26; governor of city of Samaria under Ahab
4. ruled 642–640 B.C.; 2Ki 21:18; idolatrous king of Judah

AMORITES (AM uh rights) Gen 10:16

This group from western Saudi Arabia and southern Syria was conquered by Joshua. Survivors became subservient to Israel, fulfilling Noah's curse of Canaan. For further study, see Gen 9:25-27; 15:16; Jos 10–13; Dt 1:4-44; Jdg 1:34-36; 10–11; 1Ki 9:20-23.

AMOS (AY muhs) *burden-bearer*
1. 8 century B.C.; Am 1:1

Amos, a sheep farmer and a dresser of fig trees, was a pioneer among prophets. A plainspoken rustic from the small Judean village of Tekoa, he was not brought up in the class from which prophets usually came, nor was he trained in the prophetic schools or guilds for the difficult task that God called him to do: that of speaking harsh words to the northern kingdom of Israel during the prosperous and peaceful reign of Jeroboam II.

This prophet denounced the nation for numerous crimes against humanity, including war and violence. He warned that the people would be punished for breaking and rejecting God's law. Amos thundered against Israel for luxurious self-indulgence and showing callous treatment to others, particularly the poor. He spoke against the hypocrisy of keeping up a religious front while turning "justice into poison and the fruit of righteousness into

David mourns the death of his son Amnon at the hands of Amnon's half-brother Absalom.

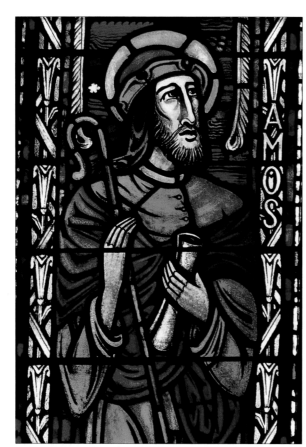

The prophet Amos. Stained glass. Hamline United Methodist Church, St. Paul, Minnesota.

wormwood" (Am 6:12). According to Amos, Israel had become profane, immoral, and inhuman. They had trampled their covenant with God.

The prophet warned that if the people did not repent, none would escape God's punishment. Amos spoke of judgment using analogies of devouring grasshoppers, a consuming fire, the builder's plumbline, summer fruit, and the smitten sanctuary. He warned of famine and drought, blight and disease, invasion and destruction. Yet his uncompromising lament was followed by an appeal to return to God, moral purity, and social justice. Amos assured the people that repentance would bring the promise of a brighter day.

Israel turned a deaf ear to the prophet, just as they did to his contemporary, Hosea. The priest Amaziah told Amos to leave Bethel, go to Judah, and preach his message there.

For further study, see the Book of Amos.
2. Lk 3:25; ancestor of Christ

AMOZ (AY mahz) *strong;* 8 century B.C.; 2Ki 19:2; father of prophet Isaiah

AMPLIATUS (AM plee AY tuhs) *large;* 1 century A.D.; Ro 16:8; Roman Christian; Paul sent him greetings

AMRAM (AM ram) *the kinsman is exalted*
1. 15 century B.C.; Ex 6:18; father of Moses, Aaron, and Miriam
2. 5 century B.C.; Ezr 10:34; one who married and divorced foreign wife after Exile

AMRAPHEL (AM rah fel) *powerful people;* 22 century B.C.; Gen 14:1; king who helped defeat the kings of Sodom and Gomorrah

AMZI (AM zih) *my strength*
1. 1Ch 6:46; ancestor of Ethan the music minister under David
2. Ne 11:12; ancestor of Adaiah

ANAH (AY nuh) *answered*
1. 20 century B.C.; Gen 36:2; son of Zibeon; father-in-law of Esau; possibly Beeri 1
2. 20 century B.C.; Gen 36:20; uncle of Anah 1; Horite chief in Esau's time

ANAIAH (uh NYE uh) *the Lord has answered*
1. 5 century B.C.; Ne 8:4; stood with Ezra while he read the Law
2. 5 century B.C.; Ne 10:22; leader; sealed Nehemiah's covenant; possibly Anaiah 1

ANAK (AY nak) *long-necked;* Nu 13:28; ancestral source of Anakites

ANAKIM, ANAKITES (AY nuhk im, AY nuh kyts) Nu 13:22; people of giant stature; descendants of Anak the founder of Hebron

ANAMIM (AN uh mim) Gen 10:13; tribe or nation related to the Egyptians

ANAMMELECH (uh NAM uh lek) *the king answers;* 2Ki 17:31; Babylonian deity; received child sacrifices

ANAN (AY nuhn) *cloud;* 5 century B.C.; Ne 10:26; leader; sealed Nehemiah's covenant renewal

ANANI (uh NAH nih) *my cloud;* 1Ch 3:24; descendant of Zerubbabel; in David's lineage

ANANIAH (an uh NYE uh) possibly *the Lord has covered;* 6 century B.C.; Ne 3:23; grandfather of Azariah 23

ANANIAS (an uh NYE us) *protected by the Lord* or *the Lord is gracious*
1. Jdt 8:1; ancestor of Judith
2. 9 century B.C.; Tob 5:13; descendant of prophet Shemaiah
3. 9 century B.C.; Tob 5:12; relative of Tobit; claimed by angel Raphael as father
4. 1 century A.D.; Ac 5:1

Ananias and his wife Sapphira, a land-owning couple in Jerusalem, wanted to appear generous, so they said they had donated all proceeds from a real estate sale to the early church. In truth, they kept back something for themselves. For having deceived the Holy Spirit, they fell dead. Death for hypocrisy and deceit may seem overly harsh, perhaps even cruel. However, God may have made the couple pay with their lives to establish the discipline necessary to grow the church in its foundational years. For further study, see Ac 5:1-11.
5. 1 century A.D.; Ac 9:10

God used Ananias as an instrument to help change Saul of Tarsus—a notorious persecuter of Christians—into Paul, champion of the Christian faith. Although Ananias knew of Saul's hatred of the church, he followed God's directive to seek Saul out and welcome him by laying hands upon him. When he did so, Saul was cured of the blindness God had inflicted on him. This incident prompted Saul's conversion and began his career as the church's premier missionary. For further study, see Acts 9:10-19; 22:12-16.
6. 1 century A.D.; Ac 23:2

Pharisees loved to debate various political, religious, and judicial issues, especially before the Sanhedrin, the Jewish council in Palestine and puppet government under Roman rule. To this council Paul was taken to defend his qualifications and controversial views about "the hope of the resurrection" (Ac 23:6). Ananias, the council chairman, in-

Following God's instructions, Ananias cures Saul of his blindness.

sulted Paul in a most unpriestlike manner, so Paul branded him, in effect, "The Great White-Washed Tomb." In his latter years, Ananias became more open to bribes and extortion, and was more of a collaborator with Rome. He was killed by Jewish Zealots in A.D. 66 for his pro-Roman activities. For further study, see Ac 22–24.

ANATH (AY nath) 13 century B.C.; Jdg 3:31; father of Shamgar the minor judge

ANATHOTH (AN uh thath) *answers*
1. 19 century B.C.; 1Ch 7:8; eighth son of Becher; grandson of Benjamin
2. 5 century B.C.; Ne 10:19; leader; sealed Nehemiah's covenant

ANDREW (AN droo) *manly;* 1 century A.D.; Mt 4:18
Born in the fishing village of Bethsaida and raised a fisherman with his brother Simon Peter, Andrew joined a fishing partnership with two sons of Zebedee, James and John. He was among the first called by Jesus to become a "fisher of men."

Andrew, a fisherman who followed John the Baptist before becoming a disciple of Jesus.

From John's Gospel, it is apparent that Andrew and another unnamed disciple, perhaps Philip, were followers of John the Baptist before becoming followers of Jesus. Andrew thus was steeped in the Jewish expectations of the coming Messiah, whom John the Baptist identified as Jesus. Upon coming to this realization, Andrew told his brothers and business partners, "We have found the Messiah" (Jn 1:41). For further study, see Mt 10:2; Mk 1:16–18,29; 3:18; 13:3; Lk 6:14; Jn 1:35– 44; 6:8–12; 12:20–22; Ac 1:13.

ANDRONICUS (an DRON uh kuhs) *conqueror*
1. 2 century B.C.; 2Mac 4:31; minister of Antiochus IV Epiphanes
2. 2 century B.C.; 2Mac 5:23; governor at Gerizim under Antiochus IV Epiphanes
3. 1 century A.D.; Ro 16:7; highly regarded apostle; partner of Junia(s); see Junia(s)

ANER (AY nuhr) *sprout* or *affliction* or *waterfall;* 21 century B.C.; Gen 14:13; Amorite ally of Abraham; helped rescue Lot

ANIAM (uh NI uhm) *lamentation of the people;* 1Ch 7:19; descendant of Manasseh

ANNA (AN uh) *grace*
1. 9 century B.C.; Tob 1:20; wife of Tobit
2. 1 century A.D.; Lk 2:36-38
Anna was the daughter of Phanuel of the tribe of Asher. She was a godly woman who followed the prophetic tradition of Miriam, Deborah, and Huldah. Like them, she cared passionately about Israel and their dealings with the Lord. After seven years of marriage, Anna's husband died, and she devoted herself to serving God. The elderly prophet lived in the temple at Jerusalem and spent her days and nights fasting, praying, and worshiping God. When Joseph and Mary brought the child Jesus to the temple, an elderly devout man named Simeon blessed the family, honored God, and declared that he had now seen the Lord's Messiah. Then Anna approached and also announced that the child was the long-awaited Messiah, and she praised God for fulfilling his promises.

ANNAS (AN uhs) *grace;* 1 century A.D.; Lk 3:2
The priesthood was a family affair for Annas, his five sons, one son-in-law (Caiaphas), and one grandson (Matthias). As head of this prominent

Anna and Simeon recognize the infant Jesus as the Messiah at his presentation in the temple.

priestly clan, Annas's ministry spanned the lives of John the Baptist, Jesus, and Peter. Although his official term of office was cut short (A.D. 6–15), he and his family remained influential over the political and religious life of Jerusalem until A.D. 65. A man of aristocratic wealth, Annas had a spacious house and courtyard to which Jesus was taken the night of his arrest in Gethsemene. There Peter denied knowing his Lord three times. Peter himself was later tried by Annas's supreme court for bold preaching but was acquitted. For further study, see Jn 18:13-24; Ac 4:5-6.

ANTHOTHIJAH (AN thoh THIGH jah) *answers of the Lord;* 1Ch 8:24; in genealogy of Benjamin

ANTIOCHIS (an TYE uh kis) meaning unknown; 2 century B.C.; 2Mac 4:30; concubine of Antiochus IV Epiphanes

ANTIOCHUS (an TIE uh kuhs) *opposer* or *withstander*
1. Antiochus III (the Great); 3 century B.C.; 1Mac 1:10

The Seleucid dynasty, founded by one of the generals under Alexander the Great, ruled Syria from 281–64 B.C. Antiochus III, surnamed Megas (the Great), succeeded his older brother, Seleucus III Soter, to the throne. The Seleucid kings of Syria had warred with the Ptolemaic kings of Egypt ever since the death of Alexander the Great. This period of empires at war was anticipated by the prophet Daniel. Many see Antiochus III as Daniel's "king of the north" who would prevail over the "king of the south." If so, then Daniel foresaw the victory of Antiochus III over the Egyptian general Scopas that gave the Seleucids complete control over Palestine. Without an enemy to preoccupy them, the Seleucids began a systematic persecution of Jews. For further study, see Dan 11:10-19; 1Mac 8:6–8.
2. Antiochus IV Epiphanes (an TIE uh kuhs uh PIF uh neez); 2 century B.C.; 1Mac 1:10

Antiochus IV Epiphanes, the eighth ruler in the Seleucid dynasty that began with one of the generals under Alexander the Great, was the most cruel and vain of the Seleucid kings. The empire he inherited from his father included Palestine, and he plundered the temple treasury, butchered many Jerusalem Jews, and began to systematically dismantle the Jewish religion. He declared that every citizen had to give up their particular customs and adopt the king's Greek religion. Sabbath worship was banned and worship of Zeus installed. Antiochus IV is likely the king regarded in Daniel's prophecy as the one who establishes the "abomination that makes desolate" (Da 11:31). Religious repression under Antiochus IV resulted in a popular

The second son of King Demetrius I Soter, Antiochus VII assumed the Seleucid throne after his older brother Demetrius II Nicator was captured by Parthians. But first he had to deal with the treacherous army commander Trypho. The usurper Trypho installed a puppet king (the son of Alexander Balas), with himself as regent. That puppet king was shortly ousted when Trypho himself took the reigns. Antiochus VII Sidetes regained the throne with help from Simon the Maccabean Jew. They pursued and besieged Trypho until he eventually took his own life. But Antiochus VII Sidetes then turned on Simon and John Hyrcanus, Simon's son and the new Jerusalem high priest. Antiochus VII Sidetes himself met death when the Parthians attacked again in 129 B.C. For further study, see 1Mac 15:1-38.

ANTIPATER (AN tih PAY tuhr) *against father;* 2 century B.C.; 1Mac 12:16; son of Jason; Jewish envoy to Rome

ANTIPAS (AN tih puhs) *against all*
1. 1 century A.D.; Rev 2:13; Christian martyr from Pergamum
2. see Herod Antipas (Herod 3)

ANUB (AY nub) *ripe* or *strong;* 1Ch 4:8; descendant of Judah

APELLES (uh PEL eez) *separate* or *exclude;* 1 century A.D; Ro 16:10; greeted by Paul as "approved in Christ"

APHERRA (uh FEER ruh) meaning unknown; 1Esd 5:34; servant of Solomon

APHIAH (uh FYE uh) possibly *striving;* 1Sa 9:1; Benjaminite; ancestor of Saul

APOLLONIUS (AP uh LOH nee uhs) *of Apollo*
1. 2 century B.C.; 2Mac 12:2; son of Gennaeus; district governor
2. 2 century B.C.; 1Mac 3:10; military governor in Samaria during Maccabean revolt
3. 2 century B.C.; 2Mac 3:5; from Tarsus; envoy to Ptolemy VI's coronation
4. 2 century B.C.; 2Mac 5:24; Mysian captain; massacred Jerusalem Jews on the Sabbath
5. 2 century B.C.; 1Mac 10:69; military general under Seleucid ruler Demetrius II

The Seleucid kings, Antiochus IV (top) *and Antiochus VII* (bottom) *imprinted on Tyrean coins.*

revolt led by Judas Maccabeus, who restored temple worship. Antiochus IV then retreated to Persia, went insane, and died. For further study, see 1Mac 1:1–6:16; 2Mac 9:5-28.
3. 2 century B.C.; 1Mac 12:16; father of Nemuenius the envoy to Rome from Judas Maccabeus
4. Antiochus V Eupator (an TIE uh kuhs yoo PAY tor); ruled 163–162 B.C.; 1Mac 6:15; Seleucid king
5. Antiochus VI; ruled 145–139 B.C.; 1Mac 11:40; king of Seleucid Empire
6. Antiochus VII Sidetes (an TIE uh kuhs si DEET ez) 2 century B.C.; 1Mac 15:1

APOLLOPHANES (uh pahl OFF uh neez) meaning unknown; 2 century B.C.; 2Mac 10:37; Syrian leader captured by Judas Maccabeus

APOLLOS (uh PAH lohs) possibly *a destroyer;* 1 century A.D.; Ac 18:24

Apollos (an Alexandrian Jew) was an enthusiastic and gifted speaker. He had a profound understanding of the Old Testament, and he loved sharing his knowledge with others. He arrived in Ephesus when Paul the apostle was away in Palestine. Apollos was familiar with the story of Jesus, but he knew little of the purpose and development of the early Christian movement. Yet he eagerly spoke about all that he knew, and his listeners were impressed by his knowledge and eloquence.

Aquila and Priscilla (partners with Paul in Christian evangelism) heard Apollos and recognized that the capable speaker had an incomplete picture of the "Way of God" (Ac 18:26). So they took Apollos aside to round out his Christian education.

From Ephesus, Apollos went to Corinth to the fledgling Christian community there. He proved to be a very effective Christian teacher to the Jews, and his persuasive preaching attracted many. Soon, the Christian community at Corinth became divided—some following Paul, others forming an Apollos party. Apollos did not promote the split, and Paul did not hold him accountable for it. However, Paul confronted the congregation about their divisiveness, admonishing them for their spiritual immaturity. Paul pointed out that he and Apollos were both working together under the hand of God. They were simply God's tools and God alone produced the results. Later, Paul encouraged Apollos to revisit Corinth, and it appears that this gifted leader did make another journey for the sake of the church.

For further study, see Ac 18:24–19:7; 1Co 1:12; 3:4-6; 16:12; Tit 3:13.

APOLLYON (uh PAHL ee ahn) *destroyer* or *destruction;* Rev 9:11; angel of the Abyss; Greek form of Abaddon

APPAIM (AP ay im) *faces* or *nostrils;* 1Ch 2:30; in genealogy of Jerahmeel

APPHIA (AF ee uh) 1 century A.D.; Phm 1:2 Christian woman addressed in Paul's letter

APPHUS 1Mac 2:5; see Jonathan 16 the Maccabean

AQUILA (uh KWIL luh) *eagle;* 1 century A.D.; Ac 18:2; tentmaker with Paul and Priscilla; see Priscilla

ARA (AR uh) *strong;* 1Ch 7:38; descendant of Asher

ARABS (AYR uhbz) 2Ch 17:11

Descendants of the Ishmaelites, Midianites, and others, the Arabs of the Sinai Peninsula interacted with a variety of biblical figures as trading partners and military adversaries. For further study, see 2Ch 21:16; 22:1; 26:7; Ne 4:7; Isa 13:20; Ac 2:11.

ARAD (AIR ad) *fugitive;* 1Ch 8:15; a Benjaminite

ARAH (AIR uh) *wanderer* or *traveler*
1. 1Ch 7:39; descendant of Asher
2. Ezr 2:5; ancestor of family that returned to Judah after Exile

ARAM (AIR uhm) *high* or *exalted*
1. Gen 10:22; last son of Shem; ancestor of Arameans
2. 21 century B.C.; Gen 22:21; son of Kemuel; grandnephew of Abraham
3. 1Ch 7:34; descendant of Asher
4. Mt 1:3; ancestor of Christ

ARAMEANS (AIR uh mee uhnz) Gen 25:20

Nomadic descendants of Aram, the Arameans lived in Syria; Rebekah, Leah, Rachel (wives of the patriarchs), and the Ben-hadad dynasty came from this group. Sometimes allies and sometimes enemies of Israel, they were conquered by kings Ahab and David. For further study, see 2Sa 8; 10; 1Ki 20; 2Ki 6–7; 1Ch 19. Also called Syrians.

ARAN (AIR ahn) *wild goat;* 20 century B.C.; Gen 36:28; son of Dishan the Horite chief

ARAUNAH (uh RAH nuh) *the Lord is firm;* 2Sa 24:15; Jebusite whose threshing floor David purchased; also called Ornan

ARBA (AR buh) *four* or *croucher;* Jos 14:15; father of Anakim; founder of Kiriath-arba (Hebron)

ARBATHITES, ARBITES (AR ba thyts, AR bytes) 2Sa 23:31,35; natives of Arba (Hebron), two of whom were among David's mighty men

ARCHELAUS see Herod Archelaus (Herod 2)

ARCHIPPUS (ahr KIP uhs) *chief groom;* 1 century A.D.; Col 4:17; Christian minister at Colossae

ARCHITES (AHR kyts) 2Sa 15:32; residents of Archi (border city of Ephraim), one of whom was David's friend

ARD (AHRD) meaning uncertain; Gen 46:21; son of Benjamin; possibly Addar

ARDON (AHR dahn) *descendant;* 1Ch 2:18; descendant of Judah

ARELI (uh REE li) *valiant;* 19 century B.C.; Gen 46:16; last son of Gad; head of his own clan

ARETAS (AHR uh tuhs) *goodness* or *excellence*
1. 1 century A.D.; 2Co 11:32
The reign of Aretas crossed the path of Saul when the future apostle had just been converted. If the governor of Damascus appointed by Aretas had done his job correctly, Saul may never have become the apostle Paul; he would have been arrested before his Christian career even got going. Instead, Saul escaped when his followers lowered him in a basket through an opening in the wall of that blockaded city. Aretas, the fourth Nabatean king by that name, was also a force to be reckoned with in Roman political circles, as Herod Antipas found out. The daughter of Aretas was married to Herod Antipas, who then divorced her in favor of Herodias. For this insult, Aretas invaded Antipas's territory to kill him, but Antipas managed to escape with his life.
2. Aretas 2; 2 century B.C.; 2Mac 5:8; Arabian prince; captured high priest Jason

ARGOB (AHR gahb) *a mound;* 8 century B.C.; 2Ki 15:25; Israelite official assassinated by Pekah

ARIARATHES (ah ree uh RAY theez) meaning unknown; 2 century B.C.; 1Mac 15:22; king of Cappadocia; ally of Rome

ARIDAI (AIR uh dye) *gift of Ari* [a tribe]; 5 century B.C.; Est 9:9 one of Haman's ten sons killed by Jews in Persia

ARIDATHA (AHR uh DAY thuh) *gift of Ari* [a tribe]; 5 century B.C.; Est 9:8; one of Haman's ten sons killed by Jews in Persia

ARIEH (AIR yah) *lion of the Lord;* 8 century B.C.; 2Ki 15:25; official slain by Pekah

ARIEL (AIR ee el) *lion of God;* 5 century B.C.; Ezr 8:16; Ezra's envoy sent to get servants from Casiphia

ARIOCH (AHR ee ahk) *lionlike*
1. 22 century B.C.; Gen 14:1; king in coalition that captured Lot
2. 7 century B.C.; Da 2:14; commander ordered to kill Babylonian wise men
3. 7 century B.C.; Jdt 1:6; king of Elymeans; lived between Tigris and Euphrates

ARISAI (AHR uh sigh) *lives among the Ari* [a tribe]; 5 century B.C.; Est 9:9; one of Haman's ten sons killed by Jews in Persia

ARISTARCHUS (AIR uhs TAHR kuhs) *best ruler;* 1 century A.D.; Ac 19:29
For at least seven pivotal years, as recorded in the Acts of the Apostles and the Letters of Paul, Aristarchus was Paul's staunch companion. He had many of the same experiences as the apostle Paul—brutal beatings, false imprisonment, travel weariness, and even a shipwreck. At Ephesus in particular, Aristarchus and his companion Gaius seem to have borne the brunt of the mob brutality intended for Paul. Despite the hardships and brutal mistreatment, Aristarchus remained at Paul's side to the end. Judging from Paul's letter to the church at Colossae, Aristarchus was among those "fellow prisoners" who took turns staying with Paul in his Roman jail cell. For further study, see Ac 19:29–20:5; 27:1-2; Col 4:10; Phm 1:24.

ARISTOBULUS (air is TOB yuh luhs) *best advisor*
1. 2 century B.C.; 2Mac 1:10; tutored Egyptian ruler Ptolemy VII
2. 1 century A.D.; Ro 16:10; Roman greeted by Paul

ARIUS (AYR ee us) meaning unknown; 3 century B.C.; 1Mac 12:7; king of Sparta who was friendly to Jews

ARKITES (AR kights) Gen 10:17; descendants of Canaan who settled in Arka, a city of Phoenicia (modern Lebanon)

ARMONI (ahr MOH nee) *belonging to the palace;* 11 century B.C.; 2Sa 21:8; son of Saul and concubine Rizpah

ARNA (AHR nuh) meaning unknown; 2Esd 1:2; ancestor of Ezra

ARNAN (AHR nuhn) *joyous* or *strong;* 1Ch 3:21; descendant of Zerubbabel; in David's lineage

ARNI (AHR nye) *rejoicing;* Lk 3:33; ancestor of Jesus through Joseph; also called Ram 2

AROD Nu 26:17; see Arodi

ARODI (AIR oh dee) *posterity;* 20 century B.C.; Gen 46:16; sixth son of Gad; a form of Arod

AROERITES (uh ROH uhr yts) 1Ch 11:44; inhabitants of Aroer, a Moabite city condemned by Isaiah and Jeremiah

AROM (AIR uhm) meaning unknown; 1Esd 5:16; ancestor of returnees to Jerusalem

ARPACHSHAD (ahr PAKS ad) *one that releases;* Gen 10:22; son of Shem; ancestor of Jesus through Joseph; form of Arphaxad 2

ARPHAXAD (AHR fuhk zad) *one who releases*
1. 7 century B.C.; Jdt 1:1; king of Media
2. Lk 3:36; form of Arpachshad

ARSACES (uhr SAY kus) *title* or *hero;* 2 century B.C.; 1Mac 14:2; Parthian king; ally of Rome

Artaxerxes I of Persia giving Ezra a letter authorizing government money for the reestablishment of Jerusalem.

ARTAXERXES (AHR tuh ZERK sees) *Arta's kingdom;* ruled 464–423 B.C.; Ezr 4:7

Artaxerxes I Longimanus of Persia, the son and successor of King Xerxes I (also called Ahasuerus), was noted for his generosity to the Jews in general and to Ezra and Nehemiah specifically for aiding them in their effort to reestablish the city of Jerusalem. He wrote letters of authorization, opened up the government treasuries for Ezra, and called for freewill offerings from the Babylonians. Likewise, Artaxerxes granted Nehemiah a leave of absence from his cupbearer's job, a military escort, letters of authorization, and a government grant of timber and financial aid. God moved the king's heart in response to Nehemiah's prayer and faith and in accord with his grand redemptive plan for restoring Jerusalem. For further study, see Ezr 4:6-24; 6:14; 7:1–8:1; Ne 1:11–2:9; 5:14; 13:6.

ARTEMAS (AHR teh muhs) *gift of Artemis;* 1 century A.D.; Tit 3:12; Christian companion of Paul

ARTEMIS (AR tih muhs) Ac 19:28

This Greek huntress and moon deity was identified with the Roman goddess Diana. Widely wor-

Marble statue of the Greek huntress and moon deity, Artemis, from the second or third century A.D.

shiped, her temple at Ephesus was deemed one of the seven wonders of the ancient world. For further study, see Ac 19:28-34.

ARVADITES (AHR vuh dyts) Gen 10:18; descendants of Canaan and inhabitants of Ruad (an island off the Syrian coast)

ARZA (AHR zuh) *firm* or *delight;* 10 century B.C.; 1Ki 16:9; steward of Eliah; Eliah was killed in his house

ASA (AY suh) *created or healer*
1. ruled 910–869 B.C.; 1Ki 15:8

Facing the threat of a million Ethiopian soldiers led by Zerah the Cushite, Judah seemed certain to be overwhelmed. The nation could offer no military match to Zerah's forces, but King Asa recognized that their faith in God was a more powerful weapon than any available to Zerah. In response to Asa's faith, the Lord defeated the Ethiopians by making "the fear of the Lord" come upon them.

Moved by this same faith, Asa reversed the religious policies of his apostate fathers and "did what was right in the eyes of the Lord," as had King David. Early in his reign as Judah's third king, Asa acknowledged total dependence on God, not on military might. He rebuilt the religion and the po-

litical security of the people in ways that Solomon, his grandfather, never did. Later kings would be measured against the reformist legacy of Asa. During a reign noted for peace and prosperity, he also refortified the walled cities.

Yet Asa did not persevere in faith. He came to rely on foreign alliances to win even more fortified cities and spoils in periodic forays to the north. For this, Asa was rebuked by the prophet Hanani. When he later fell sick, Asa again failed to rely on the Lord by not turning to him for healing. After his death, he was succeeded in office by his son Jehoshaphat.

For further study, see 1Ki 15–16; 22:41-46; 1Ch 3:10; 14–16; 20:32-33; 21:11-15; Jer 41:9.
2. 1Ch 9:16; ancestor of Berechiah the returnee to Jerusalem

ASAHEL (AS uh hel) *God has made*
1. 11 century B.C.; 2Sa 2:18; brother of Joab; nephew of David; killed by Abner
2. 9 century B.C.; 2Ch 17:8; Levite sent by Jehoshaphat to teach in Judah
3. 8 century B.C.; 2Ch 31:13; temple treasurer under Hezekiah

King Asa of Judah. Stained glass. Lincoln Cathedral, Lincoln, England.

4. 5 century B.C.; Ezr 10:15; opponent of Ezra's plan to cast out foreign wives

ASAIAH (AY suh EYE uh) *the Lord has made*
1. 11 century B.C.; 1Ch 6:30; Levite; son of Haggiah
2. 8 century B.C.; 1Ch 4:36; Simeonite clan leader in Hezekiah's time
3. 7 century B.C.; 2Ki 22:12; Josiah's attendant; spoke with Huldah about the Law
4. 5 century B.C.; 1Ch 9:5; Shionite; returned after Exile; also called Maaseiah 17

ASAIAS (uh SAY ee uhs) *the Lord has made;* 5 century B.C.; 1Esd 9:32; one who had a foreign wife

ASAPH (AY saf) *collector* or *gatherer*
1. 1Ch 26:1; see Abiasaph
2. 10 century B.C.; 1Ch 6:39
   Asaph was composer and chief musician for David and Solomon, an office that may have been hereditary. Both his father and four named sons were chief musicians; even their descendants were singers—all 148 of them. Upon their return from exile in Babylon, they established a school or guild of musicians to help revive the nation's faith with their music. Asaph loved to sound the bronze cymbals on special occasions, such as the return of the ark of the covenant. He wrote and collected psalms, 12 of which bear his name (Ps 50; 73–83). His psalms are forceful, spiritual, and prophetic. For further study, see 1Ch 6:39; 9:15; 15:17–16:37; Ne 7:5,44; 11:17,22; Ps 50; 73–83.
3. 1Ch 9:15; descendant of Shemaiah the returnee to Jerusalem
4. 8 century B.C.; 2Ki 18:18; father of Hezekiah's recorder Joah
5. 5 century B.C.; Ne 2:8; king's forester; provided timber for Jerusalem

ASAREL (AS uh rel) *meaning uncertain;* 1Ch 4:16; descendant of Judah

ASARELAH (AS uh REH luh) *upright toward God;* 11 century B.C.; 1Ch 25:2; son of Asaph; music minister; also called Jesarelah

ASENATH (AS en ath) *belonging to Neit;* 19 century B.C.; Gen 41:45; Egyptian wife of Joseph

ASHBEL (ASH bel) *man of Baal;* 19 century B.C.; Gen 46:21; third son of Benjamin

ASHDODITES (ASH dah dyts) Ne 4:7; inhabitants of Ashdod, a Philistine city

ASHER (ASH uhr) *happy;* 20 century B.C.; Gen 30:13
   Jacob's eighth son Asher was his second son by Zilpah, the maidservant provided by Leah for the purpose of adding to Jacob's large blended family. Motivated by jealousy, Asher and his brothers sold their youngest brother Joseph into slavery and then went through a series of travels and travails that led to reconciling with Joseph and migrating to Egypt. By the time of their big move, Asher had four sons and a daughter. On his deathbed, Jacob blessed Asher with "rich food." That promise came true when Asher was alloted the fertile highlands of western Galilee near Mt. Carmel. For further study, see Gen 30:13; 35:26; Nu 1:13,40-41; 26:44-47; Dt 33:24; Jos 17; 19; Jdg 1:31; 5:17; Eze 48:2-3,34; Lk 2:36; Rev 7:6.

ASHERAH (uh SHEER uh) meaning unknown; 1Ki 15:13
   Throughout the Old Testament, Israelites were frequently drawn from their religious traditions to-

Pottery figurines of the fertilty goddess Asherah from approximately 1200 B.C.

ward the worship of this Canaanite fertility goddess along with her consort Baal. King Ahab and Queen Jezebel encouraged the worship of Asherah and Baal among Israelites, which led to a dramatic confrontation with Elijah. For further study, see Jdg 3:7; 1Ki 15:13; 18:19; 2Ki 21:7; 23:4-7.

ASHERITES (ASH uh ryts) Nu 2:27; descendants of Jacob's son Asher

ASHHUR (ASH uhr) *happy* or *freeman;* 1Ch 2:24; descendant of Judah; leader of Tekoa

ASHIMA (ah SHIH muh) *heaven;* 2Ki 17:30; Hittite deity worshiped by people of Hamath in Samaria; also called Ashimah

ASHIMAH Am 8:14; form of Ashima

ASHKENAZ (ASH keh nahz) *a fire that spreads;* Gen 10:3; son(s) of Gomer; the latter-day Cimmerians (Ukraine and eastern Turkey)

ASHPENAZ (ASH peh naz) meaning unknown; 7 century B.C; Da 1:3; Nebuchadnezzar's supervisor of Daniel and friends

ASHURITES (ASH uh ryts); 2Sa 2:9; inhabitants of northern Israel; possibly the same as the Asherites

ASHVATH (ASH vath) *fashioned;* 1Ch 7:33; in genealogy of Asher

ASIEL (AYZ ee el) *made by God*
1. Tob 1:1; ancestor of Tobit; member of Naphtali tribe
2. 1Ch 4:35; ancestor of Jehu

ASMODEUS (az moh DEE uhs) meaning unknown; Tob 3:8; wicked demon

ASNAH (AS nah) *thorn-bush;* Ezr 2:50; ancestral head of temple servants who returned to Judah

ASPATHA (as PAY thuh) *horse-given;* 5 century B.C.; Est 9:7; one of Haman's ten sons killed by Jews in Persia

ASPHARASUS (as FAIR uh sus) meaning unknown; 5 century B.C.; 1Esd 5:8; leader of returning Exiles

ASRIEL (AS ree el) meaning unknown; 15 century B.C.; Nu 26:31; descendant of Manasseh; clan leader

ASSAPHIOTH (as SAF ee oth) meaning unknown; 1Esd 5:33; a servant of Solomon

ASSHUR (ASH uhr) *level plain;* Gen 10:22; son(s) of Shem who became the Assyrians in northern Mesopotamia

ASSHURIM (ASH uhr eh eem) Gen 25:3; Arabian desert tribe descended from Abraham and Keturah through Dedan

ASSIR (AS uhr) *captive*
1. Ex 6:24 Levite; son or descendant of Korah
2. 1Ch 6:23; son of Ebiasaph; great-grandson of Assir 1

ASSYRIANS (uh SIHR ee uhnz) 2Ki 19:35
Originating in Mesopotamia, the warlike Assyrians became the dominant power in the Middle East from late in the 9th century through the 7th century B.C. Their prominent rulers include Tiglath-pileser and Sargon II the Great, who car-

Assyrian warriors with spoils from their conquest of the Jewish city of Lachish. Relief sculpture from the palace of King Sennacherib in Niniveh.

ried Israel into captivity. For further study, see 2Ki 15–19; Isa 10–11; 19–20; 36–37; Eze 23.

ASTARTE (uh STAR tee) Jdg 2:3
The mother goddess of the deities in ancient Canaanite religion, Astarte is identified with violence and promiscuous sexuality. For further study, see Jdg 10:6; 1Sa 7:3-4; 12:10; 31:10; 1Ki 11:5,33; 2Ki 23:13; Jer 7:18.

ASTYAGES (ass TYE uh jeez) meaning unknown; 6 century B.C.; Bel 1:1; Babylonian king after Cyrus the Persian

ASYNCRITUS (uh SING krih tuhs) *incomparable;* 1 century A.D.; Ro 16:14; slave or freedman at Rome

ATARAH (AT uh ruh) *crown;* 1Ch 2:26; wife of Jerahmeel; mother of Onam

ATER (AY tuhr) *bound*
1. Ezr 2:16; ancestral head of family that returned to Judah
2. Ezr 2:42; ancestor of gatekeepers who returned to Judah
3. 5 century B.C.; Ne 10:17; leader who sealed covenant renewal under Nehemiah

ATHAIAH (uh THAY uh) *the Lord is helper;* 5 century B.C.; Ne 11:4; Judahite; lived in Jerusalem after Exile

ATHALIAH (ATH uh LYE uh) *the Lord is strong* or *the Lord is exalted*
1. 1Ch 8:26; third son of Jeroham the Benjaminite who lived in Jerusalem
2. ruled 841–835 B.C.; 2Ki 8:26
Athaliah was not the only female ruler or regent with a record for doing evil (Jezebel set the standard). Nor was she the only murderous ruler to sit on the throne of Judah or Israel. However, she stands alone as the only woman to sit on the throne of either Hebrew kingdom. Upon learning of her son Ahaziah's death in office, Athaliah set about to kill off all claimants to the throne in the royal family. She succeeded with all but one-year-old Joash, who was taken into protective custody and pre-

Athaliah murdering claimants to the throne of Judah so she could claim it for herself.

sented six years later as the rightful king of Judah. When Athaliah challenged this "treason," she was executed. For further study, see 2Ki 8:26; 11:1-20; 2Ch 22; 23; 24:7.
3. 5 century B.C.; Ezr 8:7; father of Jeshaiah the head of Elamites who returned to Judah

ATHENIANS (ATH uh NEE unz) Ac 17:21; people of Athens, Greece; did not accept Paul's teachings

ATHENOBIUS (ath uh NO bee us) meaning unknown; 2 century B.C.; 1Mac 15:28; diplomat under Antiochus VII

ATHLAI (ATH lay eye) *the Lord is great;* 5 century B.C.; Ezr 10:28; descendant of Bebai; married and divorced foreigner

ATTAI (AT ay eye) *timely*
1. 1Ch 2:35; in genealogy of Jerahmeel; descendant of Judah

2. 11 century B.C.; 1Ch 12:11; Gadite warrior; joined David at Ziklag
3. 10 century B.C.; 2Ch 11:20; second son of Rehoboam by Maacah

ATTALUS II (AT uh luhs) meaning unknown; ruled 159–138 B.C.; 1Mac 15:22; king of Pergamum; ally of Rome

ATTHARATES (at thuh RAY teez) meaning unknown; 5 century B.C.; 1Esd 9:49; inspiring speaker when Ezra read the Law

ATTHARIAS (at thuh RYE uhs) meaning unknown; 1Esd 5:40; helped Nehemiah with decisions about priests after Exile

AURANUS (ah RAY nuhs) meaning unknown; 2 century B.C.; 2Mac 4:40; old man used by Lysimachus to calm mob

AVVIM (AY vim) Dt 2:23; pre-Philistine inhabitants of Avim (a city near Bethel); also called Avvites

AVVITES 2Ki 17:31; see Avvim

AZAEL (AYE zuh ehl) meaning unknown; 5 century B.C.; 1Esd 9:34; one who left his foreign wife

AZALIAH (AZ uh LY uh) *the Lord has set aside;* 7 century B.C.; 2Ki 22:3; father of Shaphan the secretary of Josiah

AZANIAH (AZ uh NYE uh) *the Lord has heard;* 5 century B.C.; Ne 10:9; his descendant Jeshua sealed covenant renewal

AZAREL (AZ uh rel) *God has helped*
1. 11 century B.C.; 1Ch 12:6; Korahite; joined David's army at Zilag
2. 11 century B.C.; 1Ch 25:18; son of Heman; temple musician under David; also called Uzziel 3
3. 11 century B.C.; 1Ch 27:22; son of Jeroham; officer under David
4. 5 century B.C.; Ne 11:13; father of Amashsai the returnee to Jerusalem
5. 5 century B.C.; Ezr 10:41; descendant of Binnui; married and divorced foreigner
6. 5 century B.C.; Ne 12:36; priest; musician at dedication of walls of Jerusalem

AZARIAH (AZ uh RYE uh) *the Lord has helped*
1. 1Ch 2:8; in genealogy of Judah
2. 1Ch 6:36; descendant of Heman the musician; ancestor of Samuel
3. 1Ch 2:38; in genealogy of Jerahmeel the descendant of Judah
4. Ezr 7:3; ancestor of high priest Zadok
5. 10 century B.C.; 1Ch 6:9; son of Ahimaaz; grandson of Zadok; grandfather of Azariah 6
6. 10 century B.C.; 1Ki 4:2; descendant of Zadok; chief priest under Solomon
7. 10 century B.C.; 1Ki 4:5; son of Nathan; official over 12 governors under Solomon
8. 10 century B.C.; 2Ch 15:1; son of Oded; prophet during reign of Asa
9. 9 century B.C.; 2Ch 21:2; son of Jehoshaphat; killed by his brother Jehoram
10. 9 century B.C.; 2Ch 23:1; son of Jeroham; army commander who helped put Joash on throne
11. 9 century B.C.; 2Ch 23:1; son of Obed; army commander who helped put Joash on throne
12. see Uzziah 3
13. 8 century B.C.; 2Ch 26:17; priest who opposed King Uzziah
14. 8 century B.C.; 2Ch 28:12; Israelite who opposed enslaving captives of Judah
15. 8 century B.C.; 2Ch 29:12; father of Joel the temple reformer
16. 8 century B.C.; 2Ch 29:12; Levite; son of Jehallelel; temple reformer
17. Tob 5:13

According to an apocryphal Jewish tale, the angel Raphael assumes the human form of Azariah to cure Tobias's father Tobit, the righteous Israelite taken captive in Nineveh who was suffering from blindness and near death. In the story, Azariah befriends Tobias as he travels to Media on an errand for his father. He tells Tobias how to use the entrails of a fish to drive a demon from a Median woman named Sarah, whom Tobias then marries. Again using the fish, Tobias is able to cure his father's illness. After Tobit is healed, Azariah reveals himself as the angel Raphael. For further study, see the Book of Tobit.
18. 8 century B.C.; 2Ch 31:10; descendant of Zadok 1; a high priest under Hezekiah; possibly Azariah 15
19. 1Ch 6:13; son of Hilkiah the high priest in Josiah's time
20. Da 1:7; Hebrew name of Daniel's friend Abednego

21. 6 century B.C.; Jer 43:2; son of Hoshaiah; ignored advice of Jeremiah
22. 6 century B.C.; Ne 7:7; returnee after Exile; possibly Azariah 21; also called Seraiah 8
23. 5 century B.C.; Ne 3:23; son of Maaseiah who rebuilt walls of Jerusalem
24. 5 century B.C.; Ne 8:7; Levite; taught people the Law with Ezra
25. 5 century B.C.; Ne 10:2; priest; sealed covenant renewal under Nehemiah
26. 5 century B.C.; Ne 12:33; leader of Judah when Jerusalem walls dedicated
27. 5 century B.C.; 1Ch 9:11; head of priestly family; son of Azariah 19; also called Seraiah 11
28. 2 century B.C.; 1Mac 5:18; commander in Jerusalem who disobeyed Judas Maccabeus

AZAZ (AY zaz) *powerful;* 1Ch 5:8; in genealogy of Reuben

AZAZIAH (AZ uh ZYE uh) *the Lord is strong*
1. 11 century B.C.; 1Ch 27:20; father of Hoshea
2. 11 century B.C.; 1Ch 15:21; Levite; played harp upon return of ark to Jerusalem
3. 8 century B.C.; 2Ch 31:13; temple treasurer in Hezekiah's day

AZBUK (AZ buk) meaning unknown; 5 century B.C.; Ne 3:16; father of Nehemiah 3

AZEL (AY zel) *noble;* 1Ch 8:37; descendant of Saul's son Jonathan

AZETAS (uh ZEE tuhs) meaning unknown; 1Esd 5:15; ancestor of family that returned from Exile

AZGAD (AZ gad) *Gad is strong*
1. Ezr 2:12; ancestor of family that returned from Exile
2. 5 century B.C.; Ne 10:15; Jewish leader who sealed covenant renewal

AZIEL (AY zee el) *God is power;* 11 century B.C.; 1Ch 15:20; Levite; played lyre for ark's return; form of Jaaziel

AZIZA (ah ZYE zuh) *strong;* 5 century B.C.; Ezr 10:27; one who married and divorced foreigner after Exile

AZMAVETH (AZ muh veth) *strength of death*
1. 11 century B.C.; 2Sa 23:31; one of David's military leaders
2. 11 century B.C.; 1Ch 12:3; father of Jeziel and Pelet who were David's allies at Ziklag; possibly Azmaveth 1
3. 11 century B.C.; 1Ch 27:25; chief storehouse official under David
4. 1Ch 9:42; descendant of Saul's son Jonathan

AZOR (AY zor) *helper;* Mt 1:13; ancestor of Jesus

AZRIEL (AZ ree el) *God is my helper*
1. 11 century B.C.; 1Ch 27:19; father of Jerimoth; of Naphtali tribe
2. 8 century B.C.; 1Ch 5:24; family head of Manasseh tribe
3. 7 century B.C.; Jer 36:26; father of Seraiah the officer who arrested Jeremiah

AZRIKAM (AZ rih kam) *my help has risen*
1. 1Ch 8:38; Benjaminite; descendant of Jonathan and Saul
2. 8 century B.C.; 2Ch 28:7; chief official of palace under Ahaz
3. 1Ch 9:14; ancestor of Shemaiah the Levite who resettled in Jerusalem
4. 1Ch 3:23; descendant of Zerubbabel

AZUBAH (uh ZOO buh) *forsaken*
1. 1Ch 2:18; first wife of Caleb; in genealogy of Judah
2. 10 century B.C.; 1Ki 22:42; mother of King Jehoshaphat of Judah

AZZAN (AZ zuhn) *strong* or *sharp;* 15 century B.C.; Nu 34:26; his son Paltiel helped divide Canaan under Moses

AZZUR (AZ uhr) *helper*
1. 7 century B.C.; Jer 28:1; his son Hananiah was a false prophet who opposed Jeremiah
2. 6 century B.C.; Eze 11:1; father of Jaazaniah from Ezekiel's vision
3. 5 century B.C.; Ne 10:17; leader; sealed covenant renewal

BAAL (BAY ul) *master or lord*
1. Nu 22:41

Worship of Baal, the fertility and nature god of the Canaanites, continually led the Israelites away from their religious tradition. Reformist kings (Josiah) and prophets (Elijah) made efforts to defeat those practices, while other rulers (Ahab) allowed or even encouraged them. For further study, see Jdg 6; 1Ki 18; 2Ki 10–11; 23; Jer 32:29-35; Ro 11:4.
2. 1Ch 5:5; in genealogy of Reuben
3. 1Ch 8:30; fourth son of Jeiel; brother of Saul's ancestor Kish

BAAL OF PEOR (BAY uhl, PEE or) *lord of the opening;* Ps 106:28; local deity or idol worshiped in Moab

BAAL-BERITH (BAY uhl buh RITH) *lord of the covenant;* Jdg 8:33; god worshiped by Canaanite cities in covenant

BAAL-HANAN (BAY uhl HAY nuhn) *Baal is gracious*
1. Gen 36:38; pre-Israelite king of Edom
2. 11 century B.C.; 1Ch 27:28; Gederite; regional overseer of David's groves

BAALIS (BAY uhl is) *lord of joy;* 6 century B.C.; Jer 40:14; king of Ammonites after fall of Jerusalem

BAALS Jdg 2:11; see Baal 1

BAAL-ZEBUB (BAY uhl ZEE bub) *lord of the flies;* 2Ki 1:2; Philistine god that Ahaziah wished to consult; see Beelzebul

BAANA (BAY an nuh) *son of oppression*
1. 10 century B.C.; 1Ki 4:12; son of Ahilud; Solomon's governor
2. 10 century B.C.; 1Ki 4:16; son of Hushai the governor under Solomon
3. 5 century B.C.; Ne 3:4; father of Zadok 4

BAANAH (BAY ah nuh) *son of oppression*
1. 11 century B.C.; 2Sa 23:29; father of Heleb the military man of David
2. 11 century B.C.; 2Sa 4:2; military leader; murdered Saul's son Ishbaal
3. 6 century B.C.; Ezr 2:2; one who returned from Exile with Zerubbabel
4. 5 century B.C.; Ne 10:27; leader who sealed covenant renewal

BAARA (BAY ah ruh) meaning unknown; 1Ch 8:8; divorced wife of Shaharaim; in line of Benjamin

Bronze figurine of Baal, the fertility and nature god of the Canaanites, from the late Bronze Age.

BAASEIAH (BAY uh SEE yuh) *the Lord is bold;* 1Ch 6:40; ancestor of Asaph the music minister at temple

BAASHA (BAY uh shuh) meaning unknown; ruled 908–886 B.C.; 1Ki 15:16

After deposing the last ruler in the Jeroboam-Nadab dynasty, the usurper Baasha became the first self-appointed king of Israel and founded the second brief dynasty of the northern kingdom of Israel. By killing Nadab and taking the throne in a bloody coup, Baasha was executing God's judgment on Jeroboam's idolatrous reign. However, in his 22-year reign, Baasha went beyond God's purposes in trying to attack Judah and Jerusalem under King Asa. God judged the militaristic King Baasha in the same way he had Jeroboam and Nadab, using Zimri to kill Baasha's son and successor, Elah, and all his family after only two years on the throne. Thus the Baasha dynasty ended much as it began—violently. For further study, see 1Ki 15:16–16:8; 21:22; 2Ki 9:9; 2Ch 16:1-6; Jer 41:9.

BABYLONIANS (BAB ih LO nee uhnz) Ezr 4:9

A powerful nation centered between the Tigris and Euphrates rivers in modern Iraq, this group succeeded the Assyrians in dominating the Middle East under kings Merodach-baladan, Nabopolassar, and Nebuchadnezzar. For further study, see 2Ki 17; 20; 24–25; 2Ch 36; Ezr 5–7; Isa 13–14; 39; Jer 20–29; 32–52; Eze 17; 23; 29–30; Da 1–7. Also called Chaldeans.

BACCHIDES (BAK uh deez) meaning unknown; 2 century B.C.; 1Mac 7:8; general who fought Maccabeans

BACENOR (buh SEH nohr) meaning unknown; 2 century B.C.; 2Mac 12:35; Maccabean officer who fought Gorgias

BAGOAS (buh GO az) *eunuch;* 5 century B.C.; Jdt 12:11; chief servant of Holofernes

BAKBAKKAR (bak BAK uhr) *searcher;* 5 century B.C.; 1Ch 9:15; Levite; resettler after Exile; form of Bakbukiah 3

BAKBUK (BAK buk) *bottle* or *flask;* Ezr 2:51; ancestor of temple servants who returned to Judah

An angel appears to Balaam on his journey to King Balak of Moab.

BAKBUKIAH (BAK buh KI uh) *wasted by the Lord*
1. 6 century B.C.; Ne 12:9; Levite; returned to Jerusalem after Exile
2. 5 century B.C.; Ne 12:25; Levite gatekeeper of temple storehouse
3. Ne 11:17; see Bakbakkar; possibly Bakbukiah 2

BALAAM (BAY luhm) possibly *devourer;* 15 century B.C.; Nu 22:5

Balaam, son of Beor, was a famous priest-diviner from Mesopotamia. It was believed that Balaam could not only foresee coming events but could shape their outcome by his predictions. King Balak of Moab feared the power of the Israelites as they marched toward the Promised Land and offered to reward Balaam if he would put a curse on them while they were encamped in the plains of Moab.

Balaam declined, explaining that God would not allow him to curse a people who were "blessed" (Nu 22:12). Balak persisted and finally persuaded the magician to visit him. On the way, Balaam's donkey balked several times because she saw an angel and was afraid. Angered by her behavior, Balaam struck the donkey three times. The animal spoke and admonished Balaam for his actions. Balaam then saw the angel and was confronted by the Lord. It became clear to Balaam that he could only continue on this mission if he were directed by the Lord.

Although Balaam's methods were not part of Israel's law, he cooperated with God as he prepared and delivered a number of oracles to the people of Israel. Instead of cursing them, he blessed the Israelites. Disappointed, the king sent Balaam home without paying him but without daring to harm the powerful soothsayer either.

Sometime later, Balaam embraced paganism, becoming involved with the Midianite nomads. Israel was enticed into their idolatry and immorality, and God pronounced judgment in a holy war against the Midianites. Thousands were killed in the ensuing battle, including Balaam. In the New Testament, Balaam is roundly denounced as a turncoat, a treacherous teacher, and a bad influence.

For further study see Nu 22–24; 31; 2Pe 2:15; Jude 11.

BALADAN (BAL uh duhn) *he has given a son;* 8 century B.C.; 2Ki 20:12; father of King Merodach-baladan of Babylon

Barabbas, the prisoner chosen by the crowd over Jesus for release from the sentence of crucifixion.

BALAK (BAY lak) *devastator;* 15 century B.C.; Nu 22:2

When King Balak of Moab (son of Zippor) saw the Israelite army encamped on his doorstep, he sent for Balaam, the diviner, to come and curse his enemies. Balak believed that Balaam's curse could shape future events between his own nation, Moab, and the adversary, Israel. After an encounter with an angel of the Israelite God, Balaam arrived and delivered four oracles, all of which portrayed Israel as a nation that would thrive. Balak was furious. Neither bribe, nor threat, nor three altars erected to pagan gods would budge Balaam from the message that God had revealed to him. Balak refused to pay Balaam and sent him home. Throughout Jewish lore, Balak remained an example of the futility of man trying to thwart the sovereign will of the Lord. For further study, see Nu 22–24; Jos 24:9-10; Jdg 11:25; Mic 6:5; Rev 2:14.

BANI (BAY ni) *posterity* or *built*
1. 1Ch 6:46; ancestor of chief music minister under David
2. 11 century B.C.; 2Sa 23:36; one of David's mighty men
3. 1Ch 9:4; Judahite; ancestor of Uthai who settled in Jerusalem
4. Ezr 2:10; ancestor of family that returned to Jerusalem after Exile; also called Binnui 2
5. Ezr 10:34; ancestor of some who married and divorced foreigners after Exile; possibly Bani 4
6. 5 century B.C.; Ne 3:17; father of Rehum 4
7. 5 century B.C.; Ne 11:22; father of Uzzi the chief Levite in Jerusalem
8. 5 century B.C.; Ne 8:7; Levite; taught the Law with Ezra
9. 5 century B.C.; Ne 9:4; Levite; led worship
10. 5 century B.C.; Ne 10:13; Levite; sealed covenant renewal with God; possibly Bani 7 or 8
11. 5 century B.C.; Ne 10:14; leader; sealed covenant renewal after Exile

BARABBAS (buh RAB uhs) *father's son* or *son of Abba;* 1 century A.D.; Mt 27:16

Barabbas, a Jewish prisoner, was a political terrorist and a murderer. He might even have been a Zealot, a freedom fighter dedicated to getting rid of the despised Roman occupation forces in Judea. At the Passover festival, it was customary to release a prisoner to the crowd. When Pilate, the Roman governor, offered to release either Barabbas or

The apostles Paul and Barnabas on a missionary journey to Lystra.

BARKOS (BAHR kuhs) *son of Kos* [a god]; Ezr 2:53; ancestor of temple servants in Judah after Exile

BARNABAS (BAHR nuh buhs) *son of encouragement;* 1 century A.D.; Ac 4:36

Barnabas (also called Joseph) came from a Jewish-Cypriot priestly family and was an early Christian convert. Known as a good man, full of faith and the Holy Spirit, Barnabas personified a ministry of encouragement. His characteristic warm-heartedness and spiritual insight consistently won converts and bore fruit in the Christian community.

When the early Christians emphasized sharing and stewardship, Barnabas sold his land and gave the proceeds for distribution to needy church members. He showed the same responsive spirit when Saul (renamed Paul), the newly converted persecuter of Christians, arrived in Jerusalem. The former archenemy of the church was given a chilly reception, but Barnabas cared for him and convinced church leaders of Paul's conversion and integrity.

Barnabas chose Paul to assist him in a fruitful ministry at Antioch. They worked together for a year, encouraging disciples and evangelizing the Gentiles. When the pair visited Jerusalem with contributions for famine relief, their call to Gentile missionary work was recognized.

The first missionary journey (covering 1400 miles) resulted in the formation of many Gentile churches. On the journey, the men experienced formidable opposition, miraculous events, and even hero worship—some mistook Barnabas for the Roman god Zeus.

When the pair returned to Jerusalem, they participated in the debate over the admission of Gentiles into the church. On the next proposed journey, Paul took the lead but parted company with Barnabas in a dispute over Mark (cousin of Barnabas). Barnabas took the young Mark under his wing and returned to his Gospel ministry in Cyprus.

For further study, see Ac 11:22-30; 12:25–15:41; Gal 2; Col 4:10.

Jesus, the people chose Barabbas. Pilate challenged their choice: Jesus was blameless and should go free. But the crowd, influenced by the chief priests and the elders, clamored for Barabbas's release and Jesus's crucifixion. Reluctantly, Pilate granted their request. For further study, see Mt 27; Mk 15; Lk 23; Jn 18.

BARACHEL (BAHR uh kel) *God blesses;* Job 32:2; father of Job's advisor Elihu

BARACHIAH Mt 23:35; see Berechiah 4

BARAK (BAYR ak) *lightning;* 12 century B.C.; Jdg 4:6; military leader under the judge Deborah who freed Israelites from foreign oppression

BARBARIANS (bahr BAIR ee uhnz) Ro 1:14; any non-Greek, non-Jewish, or non-native groups of people

BARIAH (buh RYE uh) *fugitive;* 1Ch 3:22; descendant of Zerubbabel and David

BAR-JESUS (BAHR JEE suhs) *son of Jesus;* 1 century A.D.; Ac 13:6; Jewish sorcerer who became blind after Paul denounced him

The apostle Bartholomew being flayed alive in Armenia.

BARODIS (buh ROH dis) meaning unknown; 1Esd 5:34; Solomon's servant; ancestor of returnees from Exile

BARSABBAS (bahr SAHB uhs) *son of Saba* or *son of the Sabbath*
1. Ac 1:23; nickname of Joseph 13
2. Ac 15:22; nickname of Judas 7

BARTACUS (BAR tuh kuhs) meaning unknown; 1Esd 4:29; father of King Darius's concubine

BARTHOLOMEW (bahr THAHL uh myoo) *son of Talmai;* 1 century A.D.; Mt 10:3
Together with the other 11 disciples of Jesus, Bartholomew participated in the events that led to the crucifixion of their Master. He participated in the early church movement, too, as he was present in the decisive Upper Room meeting, but he is not named elsewhere in the Acts of the Apostles. Tradi-

tion holds that he brought the Gospel to India and was flayed alive in Armenia (eastern Asia Minor). The Synoptic Gospels (of Matthew, Mark, and Luke) always link Bartholomew with the apostle Philip; but John's Gospel (1:45-51) links Nathanael with Philip, while Bartholomew is conspicuously missing. Hence, many scholars identify Nathanael with Bartholomew. Bartholomew is simply a patronym (a name that tells who his father was), so Nathanael could have been his personal name. For further study, see Mk 3:18; Lk 6:14; Jn 21:2; Ac 1:13.

BARTIMAEUS (BAHR tuh MAY uhs) *son of Timaeus;* 1 century A.D.; Mk 10:46
Bartimaeus is the first person in Mark's Gospel to openly acknowledge that Jesus was the Messiah. Jesus and his followers passed by Bartimaeus as the blind man sat by the road to Jericho. Bartimaeus called out not "Jesus of Nazareth" but "Jesus, Son of David, have mercy on me." That title was fraught with Jewish expectations of a Messiah or Deliverer. Attempts to quiet him did not work, as Bartimaeus persisted in his urgent and insightful appeal to the Messiah. In response to such faith, Jesus healed him of his blindness. For further study, see Mt 20:29-34; Mk 10:46-52; Lk 18:35-43.

BARUCH (BAIR uhk) *blessed*
1. 7 century B.C.; Jer 32:12
Baruch, son of Neriah and companion to Jeremiah, took copious notes of Jeremiah's teachings and prophecies. Shortly after the Book of Jeremiah

Jesus cures Bartimaeus of blindness. Stained glass. Westminster Presbyterian, Minneapolis, Minnesota.

The prophet Baruch. Giotto (1266–1337). Arena Chapel, Padua, Italy.

was dictated to Baruch, the manuscript fell into the hands of King Jehoiakim of Judah. Upon hearing prophecies that were fairly damning to Jehoiakim, the king shredded Jeremiah's scrolls, piece by piece, and burned them.

Baruch got in the last word, however. He took dictation a second time from Jeremiah, and the transcript survives largely intact to this day. A surviving apocryphal work, written in the second century B.C., is also attributed to Baruch.

For further study, see Jer 32:12-16; 36; 43:1-7; 45:1-5; the Book of Baruch.
2. 5 century B.C.; Ne 11:5; father of Maaseiah the returnee to Jerusalem
3. 5 century B.C.; Ne 3:20; helped rebuild wall of Jerusalem
4. 5 century B.C.; Ne 10:6; priest; signed covenant renewal; possibly Baruch 3

BARZILLAI (bahr ZIL ay eye) *of iron* or *iron-maker*
1. 11 century B.C.; 2Sa 21:8; father of Adriel; son-in-law of Saul
2. 11 century A.D.; 2Sa 17:27

When King David was fleeing from Absalom's rebellion, he was given refuge and fresh supplies by Barzillai, a wealthy Gileadite. Among the supplies given were beds, wash basins, cookware, wheat, barley, honey, cheese, and sheep (for clothing or meat). Barzillai's political contribution did not go unrewarded; David later summoned Barzillai to come to the nation's capital to patronize and provide for him. The 80-year-old Barzillai declined, preferring instead to die among his own people. Never one to take no for an answer, David took in Barzillai's sons and told his successor, Solomon, to care for Barzillai's family in his absence. For further study, see 2Sa 17:27-29; 19:31-39; 1Ki 2:7.
3. 10 century B.C.; Ezr 2:61; ancestor of priests who could not prove priestly heritage

BASEMATH (BAHS uh math) *fragrant*
1. 20 century B.C.; Gen 26:34; wife of Esau; daughter of Elon the Hittite
2. 20 century B.C.; Gen 36:3; another wife of Esau; daughter of Ishmael; also called Mahalath
3. 10 century B.C.; 1Ki 4:15; daughter of Solomon; wife of Ahimaaz 3

BATHSHEBA (bath SHE bah) *daughter of an oath* or *daughter of abundance;* 10 century B.C.; 2Sa 11:2

The story of Bathsheba begins with a tranquil and intimate portrait of a beautiful woman: While bathing outdoors one afternoon, she was spotted by King David as he was walking nearby. Attracted to her, he wanted to know who she was. David discovered that her father was Eliam (or Ammiel), that her grandfather was Ahithophel (one of David's advisors), and that she was the wife of Uriah the Hittite, a soldier in David's army. Aroused by passion for her, David sent for this lovely, married woman, and they had an affair. When Bathsheba told King David that she was pregnant with his child, David carried out a series of deceptions against Uriah to cover up his own sin. These efforts finally led to Uriah's untimely death. After mourning her dead husband, Bathsheba married her royal lover and gave birth to their child.

Nathan the prophet confronted David about his wrongdoing, and the king expressed remorse for his actions. Yet Bathsheba's tiny newborn became ill and died, and the royal household mourned. In time, David and Bathsheba produced four more children—Shimea, Shobab, Nathan, and Solomon.

In David's later years, Bathsheba became a strong political force in the life of the court: With the prophet Nathan's help, she convinced David to make Solomon the next king of Israel and blocked the attempt of Adonijah, another of David's sons, to get the throne for himself. After David's death, she continued to exert power and influence as the mother of King Solomon.

This strong, colorful woman—whose life was marked by passion, tragic circumstances, and grand events—is also mentioned in the genealogy of Jesus.

For further study, see 2Sa 11–12; 1Ki 1–2; 1Ch 3:5; Mt 1:6. Also called Bath-shua.

BATH-SHUA (bath SHOO uh) *daughter of abundance*
1. 1Ch 2:3; wife of Judah; also called Shua
2. 1Ch 3:5; see Bathsheba

BAZAN (BAY zan) meaning unknown; 5 century B.C.; AddEst 1:10; eunuch servant of King Artaxerxes

BAZLITH (BAZ luth) meaning unknown; Ezr 2:52; ancestor of temple servants who returned to Judah

Bathsheba, bathing outdoors, attracts the attention of King David.

BEALIAH (BEE uh LYE uh) *the Lord is lord;* 11 century B.C.; 1Ch 12:5; kinsman of Saul; defected to David's army

BEBAI (BEE buh eye) *fatherly*
1. Ezr 2:11; ancestor of family that returned to Judah after Exile
2. 5 century B.C.; Ne 10:15; leader who sealed covenant renewal

BECHER (BEE kuhr) *young camel*
1. 19 century B.C.; Gen 46:21; second son of Benjamin
2. Nu 26:35; descendant of Ephraim; also called Bered

BECORATH (beh KOHR ath) *firstborn;* 1Sa 9:1; Benjaminite; ancestor of Saul

BEDAD (BEE dad) *alone;* Gen 36:35; father of Hadad the pre-Israelite king of Edom

BEDAN (BEE dan) meaning unknown; 1Ch 7:17; in genealogy of Manasseh

BEDEIAH (beh DYE yuh) *servant of the Lord;* 5 century B.C.; Ezr 10:35; descendant of Bani; married and divorced foreigner

BEELIADA (bee uh LYE ah duh) *the lord knows* or *Baal knows;* 11 century B.C.; 1Ch 14:7; son of David; also called Eliada 1

BEELZEBUL (bee El zee buhl) *exalted Baal* or *lord of the exalted abode* or *lord of the manure pile;* Mt 10:25

This ancient pagan god consulted by the Philistines was known to Israelites by the more derisive name of Baal-zebub ("lord of the flies"). The deity was given new life in Jesus's day when the early church mockingly adopted Beelzebul as a name for the devil. Jewish opponents tried to stick this degrading name on Jesus, accusing him of being a demon; that was their way of explaining the irrefutable spiritual authority he exhibited. Jesus used this moniker to show his spiritual power could not be from Satan. On the contrary, why would the devil em-

Belshazzar of Babylon is unable to decipher the handwriting on the wall warning of his sudden death.

power Jesus to cast out Satan's subjects? That would, in effect, be Satan attacking himself. Furthermore, Jesus claimed to be Lord of the house, not lord of the pagan temple or manure pile, as was his adversary. For further study, see 2Ki 1:2-16; Mt 12:24-27; Mk 3:22-26; Lk 11:15-26.

BEERA (BEER uh) *well;* 1Ch 7:37; in genealogy of Asher

BEERAH (BEER uh) *well;* 8 century B.C.; 1Ch 5:6; Reubenite leader; captive of king of Assyria

BEERI (BEER ee) *man of the springs*
1. 20 century B.C.; Gen 26:34; father-in-law of Esau; possibly Anah 1
2. 8 century B.C; Hos 1:1; father of Hosea the prophet

BEEROTHITES (BEE uh rah thyts) 2Sa 4:5; inhabitants of Beeroth, a Gibeonite city assigned to Benjamin

BEL (BEL) *lord;* Isa 46:1
This chief god of the Babylonians was also known as Merodach or Marduk. Daniel's Babylonian name, Belteshazzar, means *may Bel protect his life.* For further study, see Jer 50:2; 51:44; Bel 1:1-42.

BELA (BEE luh) *consumer*
1. 19 century B.C.; Gen 46:21; firstborn son of Benjamin
2. Gen 36:32; pre-Israelite king of Edom
3. 1Ch 5:8; clan leader in genealogy of Reuben

BELIAL (BEE lee uhl) *worthlessness;* 2Co 6:15; name for Satan

BELNUUS (BEL noo uhs) meaning unknown; 5 century B.C.; 1Esd 9:31; returnee from Exile who married and divorced a foreign wife

BELSHAZZAR (bel SHAZ uhr) *may Bel protect the king;* ruled 550–539 B.C.; Da 5:1
Belshazzar ruled over Babylon for some 11 years while the true king, his father Nabonidus, cam-

Benaiah, the head of David's and Solomon's royal guard, descends into a pit to kill a lion.

paigned in Arabia to strengthen his weakening empire. Belshazzar, generally considered a weak and self–indulgent monarch, is immortalized in the Bible as the man who could not make out the "handwriting on the wall." During the course of an extravagant and drunken festival held at the royal palace, he ordered that sacred vessels taken from the Jewish temple be brought forth so that he and his guests could drink from them. The instant that he performed this act of profanity, a disembodied hand appeared and wrote a cryptic message on the wall. Terrified, Belshazzar demanded an interpretation of the strange words from his astrologers, sorcerers, and magicians. However, only Daniel the prophet could interpret God's message. The prophet explained that the words *mene, mene, tekel,* and *parsin* indicated that the king's days were numbered (*mene*), that he had been weighed (*tekel*) and found wanting, and that his kingdom would be divided (*parsin*). Belshazzar was killed that same night, and the Babylonian Empire soon fell to the Medes and Persians under Darius the Mede. For further study, see Da 5:1-30; 7:1; 8:1.

BELTESHAZZAR (BEL tuh SHAZ uhr) *may Bel protect his life;* Da 1:7; see Daniel 3

BELTETHMUS (bel TEHTH mus) meaning unknown; 5 century B.C.; 1Esd 2:16; protested rebuilding of Jerusalem

BEN-ABINADAB (BEN ah BIN uh dab) *son of Abinadab;* 10 century B.C.; 1Ki 4:11; governor; Solomon's son-in-law

BENAIAH (beh NAY yuh) *the Lord has built* or *the Lord builds*
1. 11 century B.C.; 1Ch 27:34; father of Jehoiada 3
2. 10 century B.C.; 2Sa 8:18
This son of Jehoiada the priest became a distinguished warrior and cabinet-level military commander, heading up David's and Solomon's royal guard. Benaiah is best known for three heroic warrior feats: descending into a pit on a snowy day and killing a lion, killing two lionlike warriors from Moab, and killing an Egyptian giant with the giant's own weapon. He is also known for performing three political executions for Solomon: Adonijah, Joab, and Shimei. In Solomon's day, political murders helped solidify one's hold on public office. After three killings on command, not only was Solomon's kingdom established but so was Benaiah's reputation as a political assassin. For further study, see 2Sa 8:18; 20:23; 23:20-23; 1Ki 1–2; 4:4; 1Ch 11:22-24; 18:17; 27:5-6.
3. 11 century B.C.; 2Sa 23:30; the Pirathonite; one of David's mighty men
4. 11 century B.C.; 1Ch 15:18; musician; played lyre in temple
5. 11 century B.C.; 1Ch 15:24; priest; blew trumpet before ark; possibly Benaiah 4
6. 10 century B.C.; 2Ch 20:14; grandfather of Jahaziel the priest under Jehoshaphat
7. 8 century B.C.; 1Ch 4:36; Simeonite clan leader in Hezekiah's day
8. 8 century B.C.; 2Ch 31:13; supervised money collection in temple in Hezekiah's day
9. 7 century B.C; Eze 11:1; father of Pelatiah from Ezekiel's vision
10. 5 century B.C.; Ezr 10:25; one of four who married and divorced foreign wife after Exile
11. 5 century B.C.; Ezr 10:30; one of four who married and divorced foreign wife after Exile
12. 5 century B.C.; Ezr 10:35; one of four who married and divorced foreign wife after Exile

13. 5 century B.C.; Ezr 10:43; one of four who married and divorced foreign wife after Exile

BEN-AMMI (ben AHM ee) *son of my people;* 21 century B.C.; Gen 19:38; son of Lot; father of the Ammonites

BEN-DEKER (ben DEE kuhr) *son of Dekar;* 10 century B.C.; 1Ki 4:9; a district governor under Solomon

BEN-GEBER (ben GEE buhr) *son of Geber;* 10 century B.C.; 1Ki 4:13; a district governor under Solomon

BEN-HADAD (ben HAY dad) *son of Hadad* [a god]
1. Ben-hadad I; 9 century B.C.; 1Ki 15:18
  Ben-hadad was the son of Tabrimmon and grandson of Hezion, kings of Aram (Syria). Ben-hadad I ruled Aram during the reigns of Judah's King Asa (910–869 B.C.) and Israel's King Baasha (908–886 B.C.). He is best known as the greedy, unprincipled king who broke a nonaggression pact with Baasha of Israel and joined forces with Asa of Judah. As a result of this merger and collusion, Ben-hadad I captured several key cities and trade routes of northern Israel. Scripture does not say how he died; evidently he was succeeded by a son, Ben-hadad II. For further study, see 1Ki 15:18-20; 2Ch 16:2-6.

2. Ben-hadad II; 9 century B.C.; 1Ki 20:1
  Apparently the son of Ben-hadad I, this Syrian ruler besieged Samaria but was turned back and routed by a surprise attack from the city. Ben-hadad II begged for his life from Israel's King Ahab. Ahab extended mercy in exchange for the cities the Syrian King's father had taken a generation earlier. The two opposing kings later formed an alliance against the Assyrians under Shalmaneser III. As predicted by the prophet Elijah, King Ben-hadad II died some years later after a prolonged illness when he was smothered in bed by his military general and opportunistic successor, Hazael. For further study, see 1Ki 19:15; 20:1-34; 22:1-36; 2Ki 6:8-24; 8:7-15.
3. Ben-hadad III; 8 century B.C.; 2Ki 13:3
  Though he adopted the dynastic name of his predecessors, this particular Ben-hadad was no son of theirs but a son of Hazael, the murderer and usurper of Ben-hadad II. Ben-hadad III continued the conflict with Israel that typified his predecessors. Because Israel's King Jehoahaz (814–798 B.C.) continued to do evil in the sight of the Lord, Israel was permitted to fall prey to Syrian domination under Ben-hadad III. Not until King Joash succeeded to the throne (798–782 B.C.) and three times defeated Ben-hadad III did Israel fully regain its independance from Syria. For further study, see 2Ki 13:1-25; Jer 49:27; Am 1:4.

BEN-HAIL (ben HAYL) *son of strength;* 9 century B.C.; 2Ch 17:7; taught the Law in Judah under Jehoshaphat

BEN-HANAN (ben HAY nuhn) *son of grace;* 1Ch 4:20; descendant of Judah

BEN-HESED (ben HEH sed) *son of loving-kindness;* 10 century B.C.; 1Ki 4:10; district governor under Solomon

BEN-HUR (ben HUHR) *son of Hur;* 10 century B.C.; 1Ki 4:8; district governor under Solomon

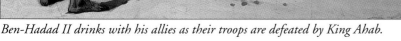
Ben-Hadad II drinks with his allies as their troops are defeated by King Ahab.

A silver cup planted by Joseph in his brother Benjamin's sack leads to Benjamin's arrest.

BENINU (buh NYE noo) *our son;* 5 century B.C.; Ne 10:13; Levite; sealed covenant renewal

BENJAMIN (BEN juh min) *son of the right hand*
1. 20 century B.C.; Ge 35:18

The birth order in Jacob's clan foretells the significance of Benjamin: He was the youngest and most beloved of Jacob's 12 sons, the second by Rachel (Jacob's favorite wife, who died giving birth to Benjamin), and the only full brother to Joseph. Benjamin was the object of universal family affection and loyalty—a sharp contrast to the hatred and jealousy shown for Joseph that drove the other brothers to sell him into slavery.

Later, when the brothers traveled to Egypt to purchase grain because of a famine in their homeland, they met Joseph, but failed to recognize him. Joseph planted a silver cup in Benjamin's sack and then had him arrested. The brothers felt that the loss of the beloved Benjamin would precipitate their father's death, and they begged Joseph to keep any one of them as bondsman in Benjamin's place.

In due time, Joseph revealed himself to the brothers, who then pledged to bring their father Jacob back to Egypt, so the reunited family could survive the coming famine.

In Jacob's last will and testament, he blessed Benjamin by picturing fruitfulness for his tribe and praising his martial qualities. Those qualities would come into play for the tribe of Benjamin, whose allotment in the Promised Land included Jerusalem, the most prized and fought-over city in Canaan. Benjamin fathered ten sons who became a large tribe; the Benjaminites, in turn, produced the likes of King Saul and Saul of Tarsus, who became the apostle Paul.

For further study, see Ge 35; 42–46; 49:27; Ex 1:3; Dt 33:12; 1Ch 2:2; 7:6. Also called Ben-oni.
2. 1Ch 7:10; in genealogy of Benjamin
3. 5 century B.C.; Ezr 10:32; descendant of Harim; married and divorced foreigner after Exile
4. 5 century B.C.; Ne 3:23; helped rebuild Jerusalem wall

5. 5 century B.C.; Ne 12:34; helped dedicate Jerusalem wall; possibly Benjamin 4

BENJAMINITES (BEN juh min ights) Nu 1:36
   The descendants of Jacob's son Benjamin and the heirs to the Promised Land, this tribe settled Jerusalem, Jericho, and Bethel. King Saul and the apostle Paul came from the Benjaminite tribe. For further study, see Nu 1:36-37; 7:60; Jos 18:11-28; Jdg 1:21; 20–21; 1Sa 9:1,21; Ne 11:1-9; Php 3:5.

BENO (BEE noh) *his son;* 1Ch 24:26; Levite; descendant of Merari

BEN-ONI Gen 35:18; see Benjamin 1

BEN-ZOHETH (ben ZOH heth) *son of Zoheth;* 1Ch 4:20; descendant of Judah

BEOR (BEE ohr) *shepherd*
1. Gen 36:32; father of Bela the pre-Israelite king of Edom
2. 15 century B.C.; Nu 22:5; father of Baalam the seer who refused to curse the Israelites

BERA (BEER uh) meaning unknown; 22 century B.C.; Gen 14:2; king of Sodom whom Abram assisted

BERACAH (BAIR uh kah) *blessing;* 11 century B.C.; 1Ch 12:3; Benjaminite; joined David's army at Ziklag

BERAIAH (buh RAY yuh) *the Lord has created;* 1Ch 8:21; in genealogy of Benjamin

BERECHIAH (BAIR uh KI uh) *the Lord has blessed*
1. 11 century B.C.; 1Ch 6:39; father of Asaph the music minister under David
2. 11 century B.C.; 1Ch 15:23; doorkeeper for ark under David
3. 8 century B.C.; 2Ch 28:12; leader who opposed enslaving Jews during the time of Ahaz
4. 6 century B.C.; Zec 1:1; father of prophet Zechariah; also called Barachiah
5. 6 century B.C.; 1Ch 3:20; son of Zerubbabel in David's royal lineage
6. 5 century B.C.; Ne 3:4; father of Meshullam 16
7. 5 century B.C.; 1Ch 9:16; Levite; resettled near Jerusalem

BERED 1Ch 7:20; see Becher 2

BERI (BEER ee) *wisdom;* 1Ch 7:36; descendant of Asher

BERIAH (buh RYE uh) *misfortune*
1. 19 century B.C.; Gen 46:17; youngest son of Asher
2. 19 century B.C.; 1Ch 7:23; son of Ephraim
3. 1Ch 8:13; head of Benjaminites that lived in Aijalon
4. 1Ch 23:10; in genealogy of Levites descended from Gershon

BERNICE (buhr NIH see) *victorious;* 1 century A.D.; Ac 25:13; daughter of Herod Agrippa I

BESAI (BEE sigh) *downtrodden;* Ezr 2:49; ancestor of temple servants that returned to Judah

BESODEIAH (BEZ uh DEE yuh) *in the confidence of the Lord;* 5 century B.C.; Ne 3:6; father of Meshullam 17

BETHLOMON (beth LOH muhn) *house of bread;* 1Esd 5:17; ancestor of returning exiles; some scholars consider this a place rather than a person

BETHUEL (be THOO uhl) *dweller in God;* 21 century B.C.; Gen 22:22; son of Nahor; father of Rebekah and Laban

BETH-ZUR (BETH zoor) *house of rock;* 1Ch 2:45; son of Maon; descendant of Caleb

BEZAI (BEE zay eye) *shining*
1. Ezr 2:17; ancestor of family that returned to Judah after Exile
2. 5 century B.C.; Ne 10:18; leader; sealed covenant renewal

BEZALEL (BEZ uh lel) *protected by God* or *in the shadow/protection of God*
1. 15 century B.C.; Ex 31:2
   Bezalel the craftsman was gifted with wisdom by the Spirit of God to construct the tabernacle in the wilderness—much as Solomon was gifted with God's wisdom to construct the temple in Jerusalem. Bezalel worked closely with an assistant,

Oholiab, son of Ahisamach, from the tribe of Dan. Both Bezalel and Oholiab were technically adept at casting and carving designs in metal, jewelry, and wood, and at weaving and embroidering designs in cloth. They also stood out for being spiritually endowed with the ability to teach others. Bezalel was the son of Judah through Perez, Hezron, Caleb, Hur, and Uri. For further study, see Ex 31:1-11; 35:30–36:2; 1Ch 2:18-20; 2Ch 1:5-10.
2. 15 century B.C.; Ezr 10:30; married and divorced foreigner after Exile

BEZER (BEE zuhr) *strong;* 1Ch 7:37; in genealogy of Asher

BICHRI (BIK rih) *youth* or *firstborn;* 2Sa 20:1; Benjaminite; father or ancestor of Sheba; possibly Becher 1

BIDKAR (BID kahr) *stabber;* 9 century B.C.; 2Ki 9:25; chariot officer of King Jehu of Judah

BIGTHA (BIG thuh) *gift of fortune;* 5 century B.C.; Est 1:10; steward under Ahasueras; possibly Bigthan

BIGTHAN (BIG thun) *gift of fortune;* 5 century B.C.; Est 2:21; plotted death of Ahasueras; also called Bigthana

BIGTHANA Est 6:2; see Bigthan

BIGVAI (BIG vah eye) *happy*
1. Ezr 2:2; ancestor of family who returned to Judah after Exile
2. 5 century B.C.; Ne 10:16; leader of family who sealed covenant renewal

BILDAD (BIL dad) *Bel* [a god] *has loved;* Job 2:11; one of three comforters of Job; see Eliphaz 1

BILGAH (BIL guh) *brightness*
1. 11 century B.C.; 1Ch 24:14; head of a priestly division under David
2. 6 century B.C.; Ne 12:5; head of priestly family that returned to Judah

BILGAI (BIL gay eye) *cheerfulness;* 5 century B.C.; Ne 10:8; head of family that sealed covenant renewal

BILHAH (BIL hah) *foolish* or *simple;* 20 century B.C.; Gen 29:29; Rachel's maidservant; mother of Dan and Naphtali

BILHAN (BIL han) *foolish* or *simple*
1. 20 century B.C.; Gen 36:27; son of Ezer the Horite chief in the land of Seir
2. 1Ch 7:10; son of Jediael

BILSHAN (BIL shan) *inquirer;* 6 century B.C.; Ezr 2:2; head of family that returned to Judah

BIMHAL (BIM hal) *circumcised;* 1Ch 7:33; in genealogy of Asher

BINEA (BIN ee uh) *wanderer* or *structure;* 1Ch 8:37; descendant of Saul's son Jonathan

BINNUI (BIN noo i) *built* or *building*
1. Ezr 10:38; ancestor of some who married and divorced foreigners
2. Ne 7:15; ancestor of family that returned to Jerusalem after Exile; also called Bani 4
3. 6 century B.C.; Ne 12:8; Levite; returned to Judah after Exile
4. 5 century B.C.; Ezr 8:33; father of Noadiah the Levite
5. 5 century B.C.; Ezr 10:30; married and divorced foreign wife after Exile
6. 5 century B.C.; Ne 3:18; Levite; repaired Jerusalem walls; sealed covenant renewal

BIRSHA (BUHR shuh) *thick* or *strong;* 22 century B.C.; Gen 14:2; king of Gomorrah; rebelled against king of Elam

BIRZAITH (buhr ZAY uhth) *well of olives;* 1Ch 7:31; son of Malchiel; great-grandson of Asher

BISHLAM (BISH luhm) *peaceful;* 5 century B.C.; Ezr 4:7; one who wrote letter against Jews

BITHIAH (bih THI uh) *daughter of the Lord;* 1Ch 4:18; daughter of Pharaoh; married Mered the Judahite

BIZTHA (BIZ thuh) *eunuch;* 5 century B.C.; Est 1:10; steward under Ahasueras

BLASTUS (BLAST uhs) *bud* or *sprout;* 1 century A.D.; Ac 12:20; personal servant of Herod Agrippa I

BOANERGES (boh uh NUHR jeez) *sons of thunder;* 1 century A.D.; Mk 3:17; nickname of James 2 and John 3

BOAZ (BOH az) *quickness* or *strength;* 12 century B.C.; Ru 2:1

Boaz was a wealthy landowner in Bethlehem. He was a man of faith who was capable, wise, and kind. When Boaz discovered Ruth (the widow of his relative Mahlon) in his fields picking up after the reapers, he welcomed her and praised Ruth for her devotion to her mother-in-law, Naomi. Boaz instructed his servants to take care of Ruth. Sometime later, Naomi urged Ruth to find a husband, and she helped Ruth present herself to Boaz. Flattered by her humble trust, Boaz followed local Israelite cus-

The widow Ruth meets her future husband, Boaz, while gleaning his fields.

tom and discussed Ruth's marital status with her closest male relative. Ruth's relative declined to marry her, so Boaz married Ruth and claimed responsibility for the property of Elimelech, the deceased husband of Naomi and father-in-law of Ruth. Boaz and Ruth had a son, Obed, and were the great-grandparents of King David. For further study, see Ru 1–4; 1Ch 2:11-12; Mt 1:5-6.

BOCHERU (BO kuh roo) *firstborn;* 1Ch 8:38; son of Azel the Benjaminite

BOHAN (BO han) *thumb;* Jos 15:6; son of Reuben

BUGATHAN (boo GAY thuhn) meaning unknown; 5 century B.C.; AddEst 7:9; eunuch under Artaxerxes

BUKKI (BUHK eye) *proven*
1. 15 century B.C.; Nu 34:22; a Danite whom Moses appointed to divide Canaan
2. 1Ch 6:5; descendant of Aaron; ancestor of scribe Ezra

BUKKIAH (buh KYE uh) *the Lord has proven;* 11 century B.C.; 1Ch 25:4; son of Heman; temple musician

BUNAH (BOO nuh) *intelligence;* 1Ch 2:25; son of Jerahmeel; in genealogy of Judah

BUNNI (BUHN eye) *to build*
1. Ne 11:15; his descendant Shemaiah 17 resettled in Jerusalem after Exile
2. 5 century B.C.; Ne 9:4; Levite who helped with worship in Ezra's time
3. 5 century B.C.; Ne 10:15; Jewish leader; sealed covenant renewal

BUZ (BUHZ) *contempt*
1. 21 century B.C.; Gen 22:21; second son of Abraham's brother Nahor
2. 1Ch 5:14; in genealogy of Gad

BUZI (BOO zye) *contempt;* 7 century B.C.; Eze 1:3; father of prophet Ezekiel

BUZITES (BOO zights) Job 32:2; citizens of a kingdom near Tema and Dedan (northwest Arabia)

CAESAR (SEE zuhr) title of Roman emperors; see Claudius, Nero, Tiberius

CAIAPHAS (KAY uh fuhs) meaning unknown; 1 century A.D.; Mt 26:3

Joseph, called Caiaphas, ruled as Jewish high priest (A.D. 18–36) when Christianity was founded. His father-in-law, Annas, had been appointed high priest by Pilate the Roman governor. Annas and his family—including five sons, a grandson, and Caiaphas—became the political and religious power behind the throne.

While Caiaphas was in office, Jewish religious leaders became restless with Jesus's growing influence, messianic claims, and alleged miracles. They tried to offset his impact by expressing official disapproval and by contradicting his claims. But this

Jesus declares he is Christ to the high priest Caiaphas, who then condemns Jesus to death.

popular hero, believed by some to be the Messiah, became a growing threat to the religious status quo.

When Jesus raised Lazarus from the dead, the chief priests and the Pharisees were so alarmed they decided to call an emergency session of the Sanhedrin (the supreme court at Jerusalem). Caiaphas presided at the meeting and concluded that Jesus must die if the Jewish nation was to remain in Rome's favor. The council then devised a plan to destroy Jesus. After Passover, they arrested Jesus at Gethsemene, rushed him through a preliminary trial at Annas's house, and then brought him before Caiaphas. Caiaphas tore his mantle in disbelief when Jesus admitted he was the Christ. The Sanhedrin condemned Jesus to death and delivered him to Pilate for execution.

Caiaphas continued to exert ecclesiastical influence in the early church movement. He threatened its leaders not to preach or teach, brought some apostles before his court, and presided over the trial of Stephen. Following Stephen's death, Caiaphas gave Saul authority to severely persecute all Christians under his jurisdiction.

For further study, see Mt 26:3-5,57-68; 27:1-2; Lk 3:2; Jn 11:43-57; 18; Ac 4:1-21; 6:8-14; 7:54–8:1.

CAIN (KAYN) *to acquire;* Ge 4:1

The story of Cain is one of obedience and disobedience, hope and faithlessness, life and death. The first son of Adam and Eve, Cain was a farmer by occupation. His younger brother Abel was a herder. They both brought offerings to the Lord; Cain gave some of his produce, but Abel offered the best of what he had: the fat portions of the firstlings of his flock. God accepted Abel's offering, but rejected Cain's. Disappointed and angry, Cain was unwilling to listen to the Lord's explanations or advice about the matter. Instead, Cain took his brother out into a field and murdered him.

Later, when Cain denied killing his brother, God punished him by sending him away to become an unproductive wanderer. Cain complained

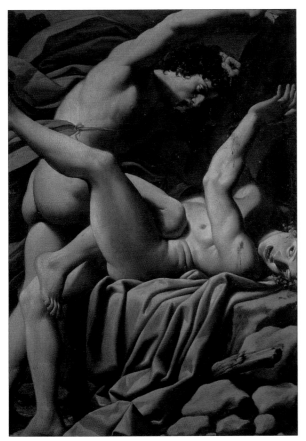

Cain slays his brother Abel after God accepts Abel's offering but rejects Cain's.

that the punishment was too harsh, and that his life was in danger. God then put a mark on Cain so that no one would kill him.

Cain settled in Nod, east of Eden, where he started a family and had a son called Enoch. He built a city and named it after his son. Among Cain's descendants were Jabal, the forerunner of tent-dwelling cattle-keepers; Jubal, the creator of music by harp and pipe; Tubal-cain, the chief of the metalsmiths; and Lamech, a man known for violence and arrogance. This early urban society started by Cain developed in a land away from God. It was a prosperous culture that produced music, weapons, and agricultural devices. Yet, unmistakably, it also bore the mark of Cain and produced lawlessness and destruction.

For further study, see Ge 4:1-24; He 11:4.

CAINAN (KAY nuhn) *acquisition*
1. Lk 3:37; ancestor of Christ; also called Kenan
2. Lk 3:36; son of Arphaxad; ancestor of Christ

CALAMOLALUS (cahl uh MAHL uh lus)
meaning unknown; 1Esd 5:22; ancestor of returnees from Exile

CALCOL (KAL kahl) meaning unknown; 1Ki 4:31; wise son of Mahol; descendant of Judah; see 1Ch 2:6

CALEB (KAY leb) *dog* or *rabid*
1. 1Ch 2:18; son of Hezron; in lineage of Judah; also called Chelubai
2. 15 century B.C.; Nu 13:6

Caleb served as one of the 12 tribal leaders commissioned as spies by Moses to survey the Promised Land at the end of the Exodus from Egypt. His minority report, filed along with Joshua's, advocated proceeding into Canaan, but the other spies felt dwarfed by the challenge and died in the wilderness for their lack of faith in God's promises. At age 85, after 40 years of wandering in the wilderness, faithful Caleb received his long-awaited reward—Hebron became his territory in the Promised Land. Caleb proved magnanimous in victory: He gave his daughter Achsah in marriage to Othniel for capturing the neighboring city of Debir. For further study, see Nu 13–14; 32:12; 34:19; Jos 14:6-15; 15:13-20; 21:12; Jdg 1:12-15; 1Ch 4:15; 6:56.

CALLISTHENES (kuh LIS thuh neez) meaning unknown; 2 century B.C.; 2Mac 8:33; Syrian; burned temple gates

CANAAN (KAY nuhn) meaning unknown; Gen 9:18

The story of Canaan begins with an episode of shame between two of his family members: Canaan's grandfather, Noah, became drunk one day and lay naked inside his tent. Canaan's father, Ham, saw Noah like this and told his brothers Shem and Japheth. They, in turn, covered their father without looking at him. In their culture, seeing one's father naked was a breach of family values of the worst sort. Ham's transgression was made even worse when he talked about what he had seen. Noah's dignity, power, and even his authority became a mockery. When Noah became sober and found out what had happened, he was humiliated by Ham's actions. In order to exact justice, he cursed Ham's son Canaan and his offspring. What seemed to be a small, unfortunate incident became a major tragedy. Noah's oracle predicted that

Noah cursing his grandson Canaan and his offspring for the actions of Canaan's father, Ham.

Canaan's offspring would be in servitude to the Shemites and the Japhethites, who, by contrast, would be blessed. In the Old Testament, where the blessing-cursing motif is central, the Canaanites were often dispossessed and dominated in order for Israel (descendants of Shem) to thrive. For further study, see Gen 9:20-27; 10:6,15; 1Ch 1:8,13.

CANAANITES (KAY nuh nyts) Gen 10:18
In a broad sense, Canaanites were any residents of Canaan (Syria and Palestine) regardless of ethnic identity. In a tribal sense, Canaanites were the descendants of Noah's grandson Canaan and were culturally akin to the Amorites and Phoenicians. Canaanites worshiped a pantheon of gods, chief of which was Baal, and were a corrupting pagan influence on Israel, whose task it was to drive the Canaanites from the Promised Land. For further study, see Gen 10:15-19; 12:5-7; 13:7-12; 15:19-21; 28:1-8; Ex 13:5,11; 23:23-33; 34:11-16; Nu 13:17-29; 14:25-45; 21:1-3; 34:2-29; Jos 3:10; 9:1; 11:3; 12:8; 24:11; Jdg 1; 4–5; Mt 15:21-28; Ac 13:19.

CANDACE (KAN duh see) *pure;* 1 century A.D.; Ac 8:27; title of ancient Ethiopian queens

CAPHTORIM (KAF tor eem) Gen 10:14; descendants of Egypt; possibly ancestors of the Philistines

CARKAS (KAHR kuhs) *vulture;* 5 century B.C.; Est 1:10; steward of Ahasuerus

CARMI (KAHR mi) *fruitful* or possibly *vineyard*
1. 19 century B.C.; Gen 46:92; son of Reuben; went to Egypt
2. 15 century B.C.; Jos 7:1; father of Achan the thief who brought judgment on Israel

CARPUS (KAHR puhs) *fruit* or *harvest;* 1 century A.D.; 2Ti 4:13; Troas resident; Paul left his cloak with him

CARSHENA (kahr SHEE nuh) meaning unknown; 5 century B.C.; Est 1:14; prince who advised Ahasuerus

CASLUHIM (KAS loo eem) meaning unknown; Gen 10:14; descendants of Egypt; ancestors of Philistines

CATHUA (kath YOO uh) meaning unknown; 1Esd 5:30; ancestor of temple servants returning from Exile

CENDEBEUS (sen DAY bee us) meaning unknown; 2 century B.C.; 1Mac 15:38; general defeated by Simon's sons Judas and John

CEPHAS Jn 1:42; see Peter

CHABRIS (CHAB ris) meaning unknown; 5 century B.C.; Jdt 6:15; Bethulian magistrate who aided Judith

CHAEREAS (kah AYR ee us) meaning unknown; 2 century B.C.; 2Mac 10:32; Gazarian commander killed by Maccabean forces

CHALDEANS (kal DEE uhnz) Gen 11:28
The Chaldean dynasty (627–539 B.C.) of Nabopolassar, Nebuchadnezzar, and Belshazzar controlled all of Babylon (modern Iraq), so that Chaldean came to mean Babylonian. Abraham was a Chaldean but was unrelated to the later ruling dynasty. For further study, see Isa 13:19; 23:13;

43:14; 47:1,5; 48:14-20; Jer 32; 37–40; 50–52; Eze 23:14-23; Da 1–5.

CHALPHI (KAL fih) *child replacing one who has been lost;* 2 century B.C.; 1Mac 11:70; father of Judas Maccabeus

CHARMIS (KAHR mis) meaning unknown; 5 century B.C.; Jdt 6:15; Bethulian magistrate who aided Judith

CHEDORLAOMER (KEHD or lay OH muhr) 22 century B.C.; Gen 14:1; King of Elam defeated in battle by Abraham

CHELAL (KEE lahl) *perfection;* 5 century B.C.; Ezr 10:30; descendant of Pahath-moab; married and divorced foreigner after Exile

CHELUB (KEE lub) *basket*
1. 1Ch 4:11; descendant of Judah
2. 11 century B.C.; 1Ch 27:26; father of Ezri; supervised David's field workers

CHELUBAI 1Ch 2:9; see Caleb 1

CHELUHI (KEL uh high) meaning unknown; 5 century B.C.; Ezr 10:35; one who married and divorced foreigner

CHEMOSH (KEE mosh) Nu 21:29
  Solomon built a shrine to Chemosh, god of the Moabites and Ammonites, which Josiah and Jeremiah destroyed 300 years later through their reformist actions and prophecies. For further study, see Jdg 11:24; 1Ki 11:7,33; 2Ki 23:13; Jer 48.

CHENAANAH (kuh NAY uh nuh) *merchant*
1. 1Ch 7:10; warrior; son of Bilhan
2. 9 century B.C.; 1Ki 22:11; father of King Ahab's false prophet Zedekiah

CHENANI (kuh NAY ni) *firm;* 5 century B.C.; Ne 9:4; Levite; led confession at covenant renewal

CHENANIAH (KEN uh NIGH uh) *the Lord is firm*
1. 11 century B.C.; 1Ch 15:22; Levite choir leader in procession returning the ark
2. 10 century B.C.; 1Ch 26:29; Levite; official of David

CHERAN (KEER uhn) meaning unknown; 20 century B.C.; Gen 36:26; son of Esau's brother-in-law Dishon

CHERETHITES (KAIR uh thyts) 1Sa 30:14; Philistine tribe; bodyguards for David

CHESED (KEH sed) meaning unknown; Gen 22:22; son of Abraham's brother Nahor

CHIDON (KYE duhn) *a javelin;* 1Ch 13:9; owner of threshing floor where Uzzah died; also called Nacon

CHILEAB (KIL ee ab) meaning unknown; 10 century B.C.; 2Sa 3:3; son of David and Abigail; also called Daniel 2

CHILION (KIL ee uhn) *sickly;* Ru 1:2; son of Elimelech and Naomi; brother-in-law of Ruth

CHIMHAM (KIM ham) *longing;* 11 century B.C.; 2Sa 19:37; one who accompanied David after Absalom's death

CHISLON (KIZ lahn) *hope* or *trust* or *strong;* 15 century B.C.; Nu 34:21; his son Elidad helped divide Canaan

CHLOE (KLOH ee) *tender shoot;* 1 century A.D.; 1Co 1:11; her people reported Corinthians' problems to Paul

CHRIST (KRYST) *anointed one;* Mt 1:18; title of the promised savior assumed by Jesus; see Jesus

CHRISTIANS (KRIS chuhnz) Ac 11:26
  The followers of Jesus Christ were known by a variety of names early on, and many of these appear in the Bible—the Church, Nazarenes, followers of the Way, disciples, believers, servants of Christ, and several others. They are called Christians three times in Scripture, and the name became commonly used by both Christians and non-Christians beginning in the second century. For further study, see Ac 26:28; 1Pe 4:16.

CHUZA (KOO zuh) meaning unknown; 1 century A.D.; Lk 8:3; Herod's household manager; wife healed by Jesus

Cleopas and his companion finally recognize the risen Jesus as they dine together at Emmaus.

CLAUDIA (KLAW dee uh) meaning unknown; 1 century A.D.; 2Ti 4:21; Roman Christian who sent Timothy greetings

CLAUDIUS (KLAW dee uhs) meaning unknown; ruled A.D. 41–54; Ac 11:28

Being a sickly, rather ugly, and ill-mannered child, Claudius was considered unfit for public life. Nonetheless, Tiberius Claudius Nero Germanicus assumed leadership of the Roman Empire following the murder of Octavian. He married and divorced three wives in succession, by whom he had five children. His fourth wife, Agrippina, poisoned him, but not before she forced Claudius to adopt her son and make him (the emperor Nero) heir over Claudius's own son.

Symptomatic of Claudius's unpopular reign, the worldwide famine recorded in the Acts of the Apostles happened while he was in power. Claudius was plagued by religious groups who couldn't get along with each other and caused trouble. For the sake of peace, he banned Jews and some Christians from Rome. Such persecution actually aided the spread of the early Christian church.

For further study, see Ac 11:28; 18:1-2.

CLAUDIUS LYSIAS (KLAW dee uhs LIS ee us) meaning unknown; 1 century A.D.; Ac 23:26

Claudius Lysias, the Roman tribune overseeing troops at Fort Antonia in Jerusalem, played a leading role in the highly charged events surrounding the apostle Paul when he was at the temple. After he was nearly lynched, Paul was taken to Fort Antonia for protection. Claudius Lysias let Paul speak to the mob and then prepared him for interrogation. When the tribune realized that Paul was a Roman citizen by birth (something Claudius himself had purchased for a large sum), he released Paul to appear before the entire Sanhedrin (Jewish high council). Since Paul's life was still in danger, Claudius Lysias provided him with a letter of explanation and a cavalry escort to take him to the Roman governor, Felix. For further study, see Ac 21–23.

CLEMENT (KLEM uhnt) *mild* or *merciful;* 1 century A.D.; Php 4:3; Philippian Christian and Paul's fellow worker

CLEOPAS (KLEE uh puhs) *renowned father;* 1 century A.D.; Lk 24:18-35

On the first Easter Day, two disciples were walking from Jerusalem to Emmaus discussing recent events. Jesus joined them, but they did not recognize him. He questioned the two about their discussion and their sad demeanor. Incredulous at the stranger's lack of knowledge, Cleopas related the story of Jesus of Nazareth—his life, death, and reported resurrection. Jesus chided them for not understanding and believing, and he explained from the Scriptures what had been said about the Messiah. Later that day, as they shared the evening meal together, the two finally recognized Jesus, and he vanished. Cleopas and his companion hurried back to Jerusalem to affirm the resurrection to the other disciples.

CLEOPATRA (KLEE oh PAT rah) *sprung from a famous father;* 2 century B.C.; AddEst 11:1; daughter of Ptolemy VI Philometer; wife of Alexander Balas

CLOPAS (KLOH puhs) meaning unknown; 1 century A.D.; Jn 19:25; witnessed death of Jesus on the cross

COL-HOZEH (kahl HOH zuh) *all seeing*
1. Ne 11:52; Judahite; ancestor of Maaseiah 17
2. 5 century B.C.; Ne 3:15; his son Shallun helped rebuild the wall of Jerusalem

CONANIAH (KOH nuh NIGH uh) *made by the Lord*
1. 8 century B.C.; 2Ch 31:12; in charge of temple collections under Hezekiah
2. 7 century B.C.; 2Ch 35:9; chief Levite under Josiah

CONIAH Jer 22:24; see Jehoiachin

CORINTHIANS (coh RIN thee uhnz) Ac 18:8; residents of Corinth (in Greece), where Paul the tentmaker ministered

CORNELIUS (kohr NEEL ee uhs) meaning unknown; 1 century A.D.; Ac 10:1

This army captain was caught between two loyalties: one to Rome for the Italian Regiment under his command, and another to his neighboring Jews in his hometown of Caesarea, in hostile Palestine, where he and his men were stationed to keep the peace. Somehow Cornelius was drawn to Jewish monotheism as opposed to the pagan idolatry of his peers. This God-fearing, alms-giving man had the respect of both camps, Roman and Jewish, but was still divided in his soul. To resolve his inner turmoil, Cornelius sent a delegation of three men to Joppa to fetch Simon Peter, whom he was told could teach him the Gospel.

A stubborn, dumb-founded Peter choked at the prospect of preaching Christianity to a barbaric, unclean Gentile. So God had to repeat his confirming instructions to Peter three times: "What God has made clean, you must not call profane" (Ac 10:15). Finally Peter was convinced that God wanted him to cross this major cultural barrier and have dinner with Cornelius and his household. Upon hearing the Gospel for the first time, Cornelius and his household converted to Christ and were baptized by the Holy Spirit. The incident

Peter preaching the Gospel to Cornelius. Stained glass. All Saints Cathedral, Albany, New York.

helped establish the idea that Christianity is open to all believers.

For further study, see Ac 10:1–11:18.

COSAM (KOH suhm) *diviner;* Lk 3:28; ancestor of Christ

COZBI (KAHZ bee) meaning unknown; 5 century B.C.; Nu 25:15; Midianite woman killed by Aaron's grandson

CRATES (KRAY teez) meaning unknown; 2 century B.C.; 2Mac 4:29; Syrian commander in Jerusalem under Antiochus IV Epiphanes

CRESCENS (KRES uhnz) *increasing;* 1 century A.D.; 2Ti 4:10; companion of Paul; left Rome for Galatia

CRETANS (CRE tans) Ac 2:11; inhabitants of Crete, a southern Greek island

CRISPUS (KRIS puhs) *curled;* 1 century A.D.; Ac 18:8; ruler of Corinthian synagogue; Christian convert

CUSH (KOOSH) *black*
1. Gen 10:62; firstborn of Ham; ancester of Cushites
2. 11 century B.C.; Ps 7; Benjaminite enemy of David

CUSHAN-RISHATHAIM (KOOSH an RISH uh THAY uhm) meaning unknown; 14 century B.C.; Jdg 3:8; Mesopotamian king; ruled Israel for eight years

CUSHI (KOOSH eye) *an Ethiopian*
1. 7 century B.C.; Jer 36:14; his descendant Jehudi brought Jeremiah's scroll to Jehoiakim
2. 7 century B.C.; Zep 1:1; father of prophet Zephaniah

CUSHITES (KUSH ights) Nu 12:1; people from the territory south of Egypt; Moses's wife Zipporah was a Cushite

CUTHA (KOO thuh) meaning unknown; 1Esd 5:32; ancestor of returning temple servants; also called Cuthah

CUTHAH 2Ki 27:24; see Cutha

CYAXARES (sy AHKZ uh reez) meaning unknown; Tob 14:15; king of Media who imprisoned people of Ninevah

CYRENIANS (sy REE neh uhnz) Ac 6:9; inhabitants of Cyrene (a Lybian city)

CYRUS THE GREAT (SY ruhs) *son;* ruled 559–530 B.C.; 2Ch 36:22

Cyrus's father was King Cambyses I of Anshan in eastern Elam, and his mother was Mandane, daughter of King Astyages of Media. As Cyrus II, or Cyrus the Great, he unified and ruled over the Medes and Persians for 30 years, establishing the largest empire the world had yet seen. In doing so, he also fulfilled certain prophecies of Jeremiah and Isaiah regarding the liberation of the Hebrews from Babylonian captivity and the rebuilding of the temple in Jerusalem.

In one of the many military conquests that built the vast Persian Empire, Cyrus overran the crumbling empire of the Babylonians. His forces met little resistance, and he marched into the city of Babylon to assume the throne unchallenged in 539 B.C. As he had done in other newly acquired regions, Cyrus freed captive peoples and encouraged religious tolerance. In this case, his policies were extended to the Jews, who had been enslaved and had suffered religious repression by the Babylonians throughout that century.

For further study, see 2Ch 26:22-23; Ezr 1:1-4; 7:11-26; Neh 2:1-8; Isa 44:28–45:5,13; 46:11; 48:15; Jer 25:11-12; Da 9:1–10:1. See Darius the Mede.

The Cylinder of Cyrus depicts the decree permitting the Jews to return to Judah and rebuild the temple.

DAGON (DAY gahn) *cloudy and rainy* or *grain;* Jdg 16:23

Worship of the Philistine weather and vegetation god Dagon was akin to worship of the Canaanite god Baal. When Israel's ark of the covenant was captured and placed in the temple at Ashdod, the idol of Dagon fell down and lost his hands and head. For further study, see 1Sa 5; 1Ch 10:10.

DAISAN (DAY ee suhn) meaning unknown; 1Esd 5:31; ancestor of temple servants who returned from Exile

DALPHON (DAL fahn) *crafty;* 5 century B.C.; Est 9:7; one of ten sons of Haman killed by the Jews

DAMARIS (DAM uh ris) *gentle;* 1 century A.D.; Ac 17:34; Athenian woman who became a Christian convert

DAN (DAN) *judge* or *he has vindicated;* 20 century B.C.; Gen 30:6

Dan was Jacob's fifth son and his first with Rachel. His name is the sign of God's favorable "judgment" or vindication of Rachel, and Dan was blessed with the ability to judge or govern his tribe with the help of others. According to Jacob's blessing, Dan was like a "snake" in his subtle and venomous attacks on the enemy. Moses referred to the tribe as a "lion's whelp," that is, fierce and vigorous fighters. Indeed, many fine fighters grew up from the ranks of the Danites, including the warrior-judge Samson. Descendants of Dan marched north to conquer Laish during the period of the Judges, which established the northernmost extremity of Israel: "from Dan to Beersheba." For further study, see Gen 30:1-6; 49:16-17; Nu 1:12,39; 10:25-26; 26:43; Dt 27:13; 33:22; Jdg 18.

DANIEL (DAN yuhl) *God is my judge*
1. Eze 14:14; righteous man referred to by Ezekiel; possibly Daniel 3

2. 1Ch 3:1; see Chileab
3. 6 century B.C.; Da 1:6

As a bright and gifted youth from a distinguished family, Daniel was the type of child most parents and teachers would happily brag about. It's no wonder King Nebuchadnezzar of Babylon desired him for his royal court during the time that the Hebrews lived in exile in Babylon.

While in exile in Babylon, Daniel and his companions Hananiah, Mishael, and Azariah were enrolled in a three-year program for courtiers. Their training was directed by Ashpenaz, the king's chief eunuch, who gave them each a Babylonian name: Daniel became Belteshazzar and the others became Shadrach, Meshach, and Abednego, respectively. Their palace education included Aramaic, science,

Daniel interprets a message on Belshazzar's palace walls, which tells of God's anger with the king.

diplomacy, and perhaps astrology and magic. Their food was the best in the land—wine and rich fare from the royal table. Daniel immediately showed discipline and leadership when he persuaded the palace to give them a simple vegetarian diet instead of the king's fancy rations. After a trial period, the boys demonstrated how healthy they were, and they were allowed to keep their strict regimen.

At the end of their training, the young men were brought before the king, who found Daniel and his friends not only superior to the other members of the school, but also wiser than all the royal magicians and enchanters. From that point on, Daniel lived and worked at the royal court until the overthrow of the Babylonian Empire in 539 B.C.—a span of almost 70 years.

While Daniel was there, King Nebuchadnezzar had a very disturbing dream. When his wise men could neither tell him the dream nor interpret the meaning, the king became enraged and ordered them all killed. Once Daniel and his three friends—part of the targeted group—became aware of the dangerous situation, they turned to God and asked for mercy. That night, in a vision, the king's dream was revealed to Daniel.

The next morning, Daniel told the king about the vision and explained its meaning. In his vision, Daniel saw an immense, frightening statue. The golden head of the image represented Nebuchadnezzar himself, and the other parts stood for lesser kingdoms that would eventually succeed the Babylonian kingdom. Finally, all of them would be swept aside by God, who would carve out his own universal, everlasting kingdom. The king was so surprised at the revelation that he credited Daniel's God and made Daniel prefect over all the wise men of the region and governor of the province of Babylon.

As time passed, Nebuchadnezzar forgot that he once recognized the God of the Jews as supreme. He set up a gigantic idol and demanded that every-

> ➵ ➴
>
> *"Soon Daniel distinguished himself above all the other presidents and satraps because an excellent spirit was in him, and the king planned to appoint him over the whole kingdom."*
>
> Daniel 6:3

one worship it. Unwilling to trade their faith for idolatry, Daniel's three friends would not comply. The angry king ordered the three young Hebrews to be bound and thrown into a blazing furnace. It was so hot that the servants who shoved them in burned to death. However, God sent an angel into the furnace to protect Daniel's friends, and they emerged from the flames without even the smell of smoke on them. Once again Nebuchadnezzar was amazed by this show of power, and he issued a decree that instructed his subjects to recognize and honor the Most High— the mighty God of Shadrach, Meshach, and Abednego.

Another time during Nebuchadnezzar's reign, the King had a dream that he told to his enchanters and wise men: In it he saw a tall, fruitful tree at the center of the earth. It provided food, shade, and shelter for all living creatures. A celestial being came along and had the tree cut down, leaving only the stump in the ground. Daniel interpreted the dream, telling the king that the tree represented Nebuchadnezzar in all his power and majesty. However, in order to humble him and teach him that the Lord ruled over everything, God would make him like an animal, driven away from people, with grass for food and dew for a covering. Daniel was dismayed by this revelation and advised the king to atone for his sins and show compassion to the needy so that he would continue to be prosperous.

A year later, while Nebuchadnezzar was strutting about and recounting his many accomplishments, he was attacked with a form of insanity in which he started behaving like an animal. And just as Daniel had predicted, the king ate grass and lived in the fields until his hair grew as long as feathers and his nails turned to claws. When the monarch eventually recovered his sanity, he worshiped God and was restored to his former greatness.

A number of years after Nebuchadnezzar's death, his successor King Belshazzar gave a great feast in the palace, and all his household and a thousand of his nobles attended. During the merriment, members of Belshazzar's household drank wine from holy temple vessels, and libations were poured out to pagan gods. Suddenly, a mysterious hand wrote a message on the palace walls. Belshazzar was dumbfounded by this and offered royal robes, gold, and prestige to anyone who could understand and interpret the strange words. Daniel, now elderly, was summoned to explain the meaning. The wise old man reminded the king how Nebuchadnezzar was punished for his pride and warned Belshazzar that by desecrating the temple vessels he had set himself against God. Daniel went on to decipher the Aramaic terms on the wall. They denoted numbers, weights, and divisions, and advised Belshazzar that his days were numbered, and that his kingdom would fall and be divided. That very night, Belshazzar was killed and his kingdom was overtaken by Darius the Mede.

Darius made Daniel one of the most powerful men in the kingdom. But there were those who were jealous of Daniel and sought ways to discredit him, particularly by attacking his religion. They convinced Darius to pass an edict ordering everyone to worship the king alone for a month, on penalty of being tossed to the lions. Daniel ignored the order. He continued his practice of openly praying to the God of the Hebrews three times each day. When the king was told about Daniel, he had no choice but to obey his own edict and cast Daniel into the pit with the lions. Daniel was as safe there as his friends had been in the furnace, for "God sent his angel and shut the lions' mouths" (Da 6:22). The king was greatly relieved when he discovered that Daniel was unscathed. After Daniel was released, the king promptly had Daniel's accusers and their families thrown to the lions. After this, Darius the Mede issued a proclamation calling for his people to honor the God of Daniel.

Daniel stands unscathed in the lion's den.

These stories from the Book of Daniel are set in Babylon around the time of the Persian conquest in the sixth century B.C. Although many are not told in extra-biblical sources, they do show how God placed Daniel in a position of influence at the center of the Babylonian Empire, and they also show how faithful Jews trusted God to take care of them among enemies.

The last portion of the Book of Daniel records a series of visions of current and future events. Writing in Aramaic and in a somewhat obscure style, Daniel endeavors to describe his own personal revelations from God.

In the first vision, four beasts come out of the sea. They represent the passing of kingdoms to make way for the kingdom of God. Some say the beasts depict the Babylonian, Medo-Persian, Seleucid Greek, and Roman empires. The ten-horned monster symbolizes the Seleucid kings, and the horn with the boastful mouth is Antiochus IV Epiphanes.

The second vision includes a ram and a male goat that depict Medo-Persia dominated by Alexander's Greek empire. The four horns show his empire divided into four kingdoms. The little horn indicates the campaigns of Antiochus IV Epiphanes.

In the prophecy of the 70 weeks, Judah's 70-year captivity spoken of by Jeremiah is almost over. Daniel asks God to let his people return to their homeland. God reveals that Israel's troubles are not over but that salvation will come.

In the fourth and final vision, Daniel is given insight into the continual battle raging in the spiritual world between those protecting God's people and those bent on their destruction. In this revelation, an angel (probably Gabriel) outlines the historical events from Alexander the Great to Antiochus Epiphanes. The report is continued into the future, when the existing political order will end in great turmoil. In the coming troubles, a God-fearing remnant will be saved. There will be a resurrection, and a time when all evil will be over.

The Book of Daniel is both prophetic and apocalyptic. Its stories and visions focus on meanings, symbols, and signs of past and present events, with a look toward a future where trouble and pain will give way to God's triumph and peace.

For further study, see the Book of Daniel; Jer 25:11-12; 29:10; 1Mac 1–6; Rev 1:12-16.
4. 5 century B.C.; Ezr 8:2; head of priestly family who lived in Judah after Exile

DANITES (DAN ights) Nu 2:25; northern tribe of Israel; fighters descended from Dan; Samson was one

DARA (DAHR uh) meaning unknown; 1Ch 2:6; son of Zerah in genealogy of Judah; possibly Darda

DARDA (DAHR duh) meaning unknown; 1Ki 4:31; son of Mahol; praised by Solomon

DARIUS (duh RI uhs) *he who upholds the good*
1. Darius the Mede; 6 century B.C.; Da 5:31
Darius the Mede acquired the kingdom of Babylon in 539 B.C. when King Belshazzar was slain

Darius I seated on his throne. Limestone relief sculpture from the fifth century B.C.

and that empire fell to the Medes and Persians. Darius set the prophet Daniel in a position of authority over the nation. The 120 satraps and administrators, jealous of Daniel's growing popularity, charged Daniel with treason for praying to Yahweh (God) rather than worshiping King Darius. By an "unalterable decree" that conspirators had tricked Darius into signing, Daniel had to be thrown to the lions despite his loyal character and an impeccable service record. After hoping all night for divine intervention, the king awoke to learn of Daniel's miraculous rescue and praised the God of Daniel. There is no extra-biblical record of Darius the Mede; this character is likely the Persian leader Cyrus II, who sat on the throne in Babylon at this time. For further study, see Da 5:30–6:28; 9:1.

2. Darius I; ruled 522–486 B.C.; Ezr 4:5

King Darius of Persia was surnamed "the Great" for good reason: His decisive military actions, efficient postal system, and brilliant architectural feats preserved the Achaemenid dynasty and Persian way of life. By killing the usurper Gautama and all other pretenders or potential threats to his throne, Darius I secured his empire for another century. When King Darius "made a decree" (Ezr 6), the people listened and acted with due diligence. Indeed, he was God's instrument in decreeing that construction on the second temple in Jerusalem would go forward as scheduled in 520 B.C. For further study, see Ezr 4:24–6:15; Da 11:2; Hag 1:1,15; 2:10; Zec 1:1,7; 7:1.

3. Darius II; ruled 424–404 B.C.; Ne 12:22; ruler of Persia; son of Artaxerxes

DARKON (DAHR kahn) meaning unknown; 10 century B.C.; Ezr 2:56; servant of Solomon; ancestor of family that lived in Judah

DATHAN (DAY thuhn) *strong;* 15 century B.C.; Nu 16:1; Reubenite son of Eliab; rebelled against Moses

DAVID (DAY vid) *beloved;* ruled 1003–970 B.C.; Ru 4:17

David was the son of Jesse of Bethlehem and the great-grandson of Ruth and Boaz. The youngest of eight brothers, he was brought up to be a shepherd, and this occupation taught him compassion and courage, traits he found especially useful later in life.

David, bolstered by his faith in God, was able to slay the giant Philistine soldier Goliath.

When David was young, Samuel, the prophet and priest, visited Bethlehem ostensibly to make a sacrifice to the Lord. Jesse, the prosperous sheep farmer, was summoned to the ceremony along with seven of his eight sons. David was out caring for the sheep. Samuel reviewed the boys and then requested that the youngest son be brought in. The handsome youngster was presented to Samuel, and with little fanfare or ceremony, David was anointed with oil, infused with the Spirit of the Lord, and secretly marked as Israel's next king. The job finished, Samuel returned to his home in Ramah, and Bethlehem returned to the quiet of pastoral life.

Previously, Samuel had crowned Saul as Israel's first king, but the relationship between the prophet and the monarch was often strained. The situation soured completely when Saul assumed Samuel's priestly duties. Samuel denounced him for this, and told Saul that God had looked for "a man after his own heart" to replace Saul as king (1Sa 13:14). After his falling out with Samuel, Saul became very depressed. Ironically David the shepherd—also a talented musician—was sent to the palace to lift the king's spirits. David did such a good job that the king made him his armor-bearer. Whenever one of Saul's bad moods appeared, David would play to him on the lyre, and Saul would feel renewed.

During this time, the Philistines and the Israelites were preparing to do battle. The Israelite forces were stationed at Elah, and Jesse sent David to the encampment with food for his warrior brothers. When he arrived, David saw a giant soldier, Goliath of Gath, parading about between enemy lines and taunting the Israelites to send out a champion to fight him. Though courageous, the soldiers were fearful of accepting his challenge. Bolstered by his faith in God, the lowly shepherd boy David agreed to meet the giant in battle. David knew he was no match for the mighty warrior, but he believed that the Lord, who had helped him protect his sheep from a lion and a bear, would also protect him from Goliath. Saul agreed to let him fight, and the stripling went out with only a staff, a sling, and five stones to face the intimidator. David stunned Goliath with a stone and then used Goliath's own sword to decapitate him. With their champion dead, the Philistines fled in terror, hotly pursued by the jubilant Israelites. David became the new champion of Israel, and Saul began to keep a wary eye on him.

After this, David remained in the king's service, and a warm friendship developed between David and Saul's son Jonathan. As David's fame and popularity grew, the king became increasingly jealous of his young rival and twice tried to kill him while he was playing music to soothe the troubled monarch. He also sent David on precarious, almost impossible military missions, hoping David would somehow be killed. However, David always returned victorious causing his dealings with Saul to

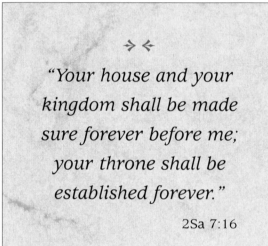

> ➤ ⭠
>
> *"Your house and your kingdom shall be made sure forever before me; your throne shall be established forever."*
>
> 2Sa 7:16

become progressively worse. Not only had the king tried to kill him several times, but he had reduced David's military honor, cheated David of his promised bride (the king's first daughter), and gave him Princess Michal instead.

Matters finally came to a head when King Saul sent men to David's house to kill him. With Michal's help, David fled to Samuel in Ramah. Unsafe there, it became clear to David—and his friend Jonathan—that the young national hero had become a fugitive. David's life was then marked by constant flight from Saul's unending pursuit. While on the run, David used his wits, courage, and military strategy to protect himself. His guerilla force, known as the Adullam band, moved through the countryside to escape the rage-obsessed king. Twice during this period David had opportunity to kill Saul yet spared his life out of respect for the divinely appointed office that Saul held. During this period, David took Abigail and Ahinoam to be his wives.

In a battle with the Philistines at Gilboa, Saul was killed along with his son Jonathan. David mourned greatly for the passing of the king, for his dear friend, and for the whole house of Israel. He expressed his sorrow in a moving dirge entitled "The Song of the Bow" and taught it to the people of Judah.

David was finally anointed king by the men of Judah, and he established his throne in Hebron. The first two years of his reign were marked by civil war between David's supporters and the old courtiers of Saul who supported Saul's son Ishbosheth. After the tragic murder of Ishbosheth and Abner (Saul's former commander), all Israel acclaimed David king. The 30-year-old monarch added more wives to his royal household, and each wife bore him a son.

David then turned his attention toward Jerusalem. He wrested it from the Jebusites and repulsed the Philistines along the way. With a strong military and political hold on Jerusalem, King David chose to turn it into the capital and religious center of the nation. When the ark of the covenant was finally safely installed there, a relieved and thankful David danced before it dressed in the short apron worn by priests. His wife Michal was displeased when she saw him behaving like this and confronted him. They argued, and the quarrel soured their relationship.

David wanted to build a temple in Jerusalem, but he had to be satisfied with preparing all the religious ritual and organization that would later enrich temple worship in his son Solomon's reign. According to the prophet Nathan, God wanted David to establish a vast, safe, and unified kingdom. For this, God promised David an unending dynasty on the throne of Jerusalem, a promise realized generations later by David's descendant Jesus. In response to Nathan's words, David developed the capital, built a palace, restored trade routes, and returned prosperity to the city. While in Jerusalem, David led the Israelites in decisive victories against their enemies, from the Philistines to the Moabites, from

King David. Stained glass. Ripon Cathedral, Ripon, England.

the Amalekites to the Ammonites. Taxes were reduced at home, and all of Israel benefited.

At the height of his success, however, David stumbled. During a siege against the Ammonites, David had an affair with Bathsheba, the wife of Uriah (a soldier in his army). Bathsheba became pregnant, and David had Uriah killed. Nathan condemned the king for his sin, and David repented deeply. After the baby was born, it became ill and died just as Nathan had warned would happen. David shook off his grief, took personal command of the siege against Ammon, and succeeded in making it a vassal state.

More strife came upon David's household. There was rape, murder, deception, and revenge among the king's children, and Absalom (popular and attractive like the young David) became estranged from his father. His resentment eventually took the form of open rebellion, and Absalom marched on Jerusalem in a surprise assault. David abandoned Jerusalem and fled for his life. He quickly assembled an army under the command of Joab and others. At Ephraim, a battle between the forces of father and son ensued, and Absalom was killed. David was heartbroken and even wished that he had died instead of his son. Absalom's rebellion was soon followed by a revolt from the northern kingdom, led by Sheba, a Benjaminite. This, too, was crushed by Joab, and David was once again firmly restored as monarch.

During his last days, the ailing king was cared for by Abishag the Shunammite. David withdrew from active involvement in state affairs, and the question of succession to the throne became pressing. The heir-apparent, Adonijah, prematurely asserted his claim. At the same time, David abdicated his throne (ending a reign of 40 years) in favor of his young son Solomon, and the coronation took place in the Kidron valley. On his deathbed, David told Solomon to be strong, courageous, and godly, and he instructed him in other matters. Then the old monarch died and was laid to rest in the city of David.

David's reign was marked by his great military and political strength. Under his rule, the Hebrew nation reached the peak of its unity and power. David himself stood out as a brilliant king, known for his diverse talents and extraordinary strengths. He was ambitious, tough, and politically astute. He was also tender, poetic, a writer of psalms, and a player of music. He had a deep and passionate love for family, friends, and most of all, for God. David was unswervingly loyal and also capable of great humility. His life was also marked by unworthy actions and profound failures. Even though the story of David is one of flawed greatness, he is a model of faith, a man close to the heart of God from whose line the promised Messiah was to come.

For further study, see 1Sa 16–31; the Second Book of Samuel; 1Ki 1–2.

DEBIR (DEE buhr) meaning unknown; 15 century B.C.; Jos 10:3; king of Eglon; one of the coalition defeated by Joshua

DEBORAH (DEB uhr uh) *bee*
1. 21 century B.C.; Gen 35:8; nurse of Isaac's wife Rebekah
2. 12 century B.C.; Jdg 4:4

The prophet Deborah lived near the border of Benjamin and Ephraim. She was one of Israel's great judges, and the only woman on record to hold this position of leadership over Israel. Her

Deborah speaks to her people of Sisera's defeat.

moral authority was regarded as appointed by the Lord, and her judgment was greatly sought and highly trusted. Deborah was often found sitting under a palm tree between Bethel and Ramah, north of Jerusalem, and Israelites from various tribes would consult her there to settle their disputes.

At that time, Israelites had lapsed into apostasy and were oppressed in the north by Jabin the Canaanite, king of Hazor. Conveying God's instructions, Deborah told Barak of Naphtali to gather an army on Mount Tabor against general Sisera and the army of Jabin. Even though Deborah prophesied that Sisera would die, Barak would only agree to go if Deborah went with the army: Her inspiring moral leadership was considered essential.

Barak assembled his men on Mount Tabor, and Sisera advanced his intimidating array of forces along the open plain. Suddenly a violent rainstorm flooded the Kishon river, turning the valley floor into mud. Sisera's army, including hundreds of horses and chariots, became completely bogged down. The Israelites descended upon the helpless Canaanites and overpowered them. Sisera fled and was killed, and on that day King Jabin's domination over the Israelites in the north was broken.

The story of Deborah's victory is recounted twice in the Book of Judges: first in prose and then in the Song of Deborah. The latter not only celebrates the Lord's triumph over Sisera in poignant imagery, but it provides details of Sisera's defeat not found in the prose narrative.

For further study, see Jdg 4–5.

DEDAN (DEE duhn) *low*
1. Gen 10:7; great-grandson of Noah through Raamah; ancestor of Dedanites
2. 21 century B.C.; Gen 25:3; son of Jokshan; grandson of Abraham

DEDANITES (DEE duhn ights) Isa 21:13; Arabian people from Dedan, near Sheba

DELAIAH (duh LAY uh) *the Lord has raised up*
1. 11 century B.C.; 1Ch 24:18; head of division of priests in David's day
2. Ezr 2:60; ancestor of family with no proof of Israelite ancestry
3. 7 century B.C.; Jer 36:12; official who advised against burning Jeremiah's prophecy scroll

Delilah learns that the secret of Sampson's strength is his uncut hair and betrays him to the Philistines.

4. 1Ch 3:24; descendant of David
5. 5 century B.C.; Ne 6:10; ancestor of Shemaiah the prophet who deceived Nehemiah

DELILAH (duh LY luh) *small* or *dainty;* 12 century B.C.; Jdg 16:4

In the midst of turmoil between the Israelites and the Philistines, Israel's judge and mighty warrior, Samson, fell in love with Delilah, a Philistine. The Philistine rulers lured Delilah with a large reward of silver to find out the secret of Samson's strength and then betray him. In her attempts to trick Samson, Delilah was outwitted three times. First Samson told her to bind him with seven bowstrings, then with new ropes, and finally to weave his hair with a spinning wheel. When none of these worked, Delilah pestered Samson until "he was tired to death" (Jdg 16:16) and revealed that his uncut hair was the secret of his strength. Delilah had Samson's hair cut as he slept on her lap and gave him to the Philistines, who gouged out his eyes and brought him in triumph to Gaza. For further study, see Jdg 16.

DELPHON (DEHL fohn) meaning unknown; AddEst 9:7; son of Mordecai's enemy Haman

DEMAS (DEE muhs) *popular;* 1 century A.D.; Col 4:14

During Paul's first Roman imprisonment (A.D. 60–62), the apostle was living under house arrest, which meant he could freely entertain visitors and close associates. Demas was among several Greek-speaking Asian associates (including Tychicus, Epaphras, Epaphroditus, Aristarchus, Luke, and Marcus) who apparently took turns with Paul in prison. While in Rome, Demas and the other brothers also conducted a street ministry that brought new believers to Paul for discipleship. However, by the time of Paul's second imprisonment (A.D. 67–68), Demas had deserted Paul, returned to his worldly ways, and taken up another line of work in Thessalonica. This is an inference from Paul's disparaging remark that Demas "loved this [present] world" (2Ti 4:10). For further study, see Ac 28:14-31; Phm 1:24; 2Ti 4:10.

DEMETRIUS (duh MEE tree uhs) *belonging to Demeter*
1. Demetrius I Soter (duh MEE tree uhs SOH tuhr); ruled 162–150 B.C.; 1Mac 7:1

The Seleucid dynasty had been ruling Judea and Syria since the death of Alexander the Great in 323 B.C., but their hold was slipping away when 10-year-old Demetrius seized the reins. Several factors prompted Demetrius to action: the assassination of his father Seleucus IV Philopator; the insanity of his uncle Antiochus IV Epiphanes; the premature ascent to the throne by his 9-year-old cousin Antiochus V Eupator; and the Maccabean revolt in Judea led by Judas. To secure the Seleucid dynasty, Demetrius seized the army and killed off his rivals. He then installed the reform-minded Alcimus as high priest and dispatched military generals Nicanor and Bacchides to crush the Maccabean revolt. In the waning years of his rule, Demetrius I Soter faced a rival claimant, Alexander Balas, and lost his life on the battlefield. For further study, see 1Mac 7–10; 15.

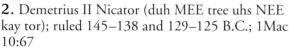

2. Demetrius II Nicator (duh MEE tree uhs NEE kay tor); ruled 145–138 and 129–125 B.C.; 1Mac 10:67

Demetrius II, son of Demetrius I, restored the Seleucid dynasty when he was 14 years old. He did so by allying himself with an Egyptian army and with mercenaries from Crete; the combined forces marched on Syria and defeated Alexander Balas.

Holding onto power proved more difficult than grasping it, however. Still a teenager, Demetrius II made too many mistakes and concessions, especially to Jonathan, the rebel Maccabean high priest. General Trypho mobilized disaffected troops, turned on Demetrius, and forced him to flee to Media, where he was captured and imprisoned. In the absence of Demetrius II, Alexander Balas's son (Antiochus VI Epiphanes Dionysus) was installed as puppet king but was quickly replaced by Trypho himself. Demetrius II later regained the throne upon his release from prison but was murdered in 125 B.C.

For further study, see 1Mac 10–15.

3. 1 century A.D.; Ac 19:24

This leader of the local craftsmen's guild at Ephesus had a vested interest in making silver statues of Diana, the Roman version of the Greek goddess Artemis. He profited from tourists the world over who visited the Seventh Wonder of the Ancient World, the temple to Diana. Naturally, he resented any evangelist who turned his market away from idol worship and therefore lessened the demand for idol making. Convincing the townspeople that "Great is Artemis of the Ephesians!" (Ac 19:34), he instigated a riot against the apostle Paul and his companions. The town clerk was able to quell the crowd, telling them to take their charges to the court. No charges were brought against Paul, however, and he left Ephesus unhindered.

4. 1 century A.D.; 3Jn 1:12; bearer of John's third letter

DEMOPHON (DEM uh fahn) meaning unknown; 2 century B.C.; 2Mac 12:2; Syrian military governor in Palestine under Antiochus V

DEUEL (DOO uhl) *knowledge of God;* 15 century B.C.; Nu 1:14; his son Eliasaph was a tribal leader under Moses

DIBLAIM (DIB lay uhm) *two cakes;* 8 century B.C.; Hos 1:3; father of Hosea's adulterous wife Gomer

DIBRI (DIB rye) *orator;* 15 century B.C.; Lev 24:11; Danite whose grandson was stoned to death

DIKLAH (DIK luh) *place of palms;* Gen 10:27; son of Joktan; descendant of Noah

DINAH (DY nuh) *justice;* 20 century B.C.; Gen 30:21

Dinah, on her way to visit the women of the neighboring country, was raped by Shechem, the son of Hamor, ruler of the Hivites. Through his father, Shechem asked Dinah's father Jacob for her hand in marriage, offering to do anything the Israelites asked in return. Concealing their anger that Shechem had defiled their sister, Dinah's brothers Simeon and Levi agreed to the marriage if all Hivite males would be circumcised like the Israelites. The Hivites agreed, but before the pain had subsided from the circumcisions, the brothers attacked the city, killing Hamor and Shechem as well as all the men in the city. Simeon and Levi were later cursed by their father for their violence. For further study, see Gen 34.

DIONYSIUS (DI uh NI see uhs) meaning unknown; 1 century A.D.; Ac 17:34

The Areopagus was the Athenian High Court that convened on Mars Hill to debate legal cases or philosophical issues. This central marketplace of ideas—located in full view of the Acropolis and the Parthenon—was where Paul the Jew debated about "Jesus" and "the Resurrection," which the Greek audience mistook for two deities. The debate was cohosted by Epicurean and Stoic philosophers of the day. Paul surveyed their religious monuments, affirmed how deeply religious his audience was, quoted from their Greek poets, then introduced Christianity as the revelation of "an unknown God," to whom the Greeks had erected an altar. Paul won few converts in Athens, but Dionysius was among them. Tradition holds that Dionysius became the first bishop of Athens and was later martyred under Emperor Domitian (A.D. 81–96). For further study, see Ac 17:17-34.

DIONYSUS (DI uh NI suhs) meaning unknown; 2Mac 6:7

The Greek god of wine, Dionysus was associated with wild excess and debauchery. He appears in the Apocrypha as a part of the Syrian oppressors' attempts to impose foreign religious practices on the people of Judea, which prompted the Maccabean revolt.

DIOTREPHES (dye AHT ruh feez) *nourished by Zeus;* 1 century A.D.; 3Jn 9; church leader; refused to receive disciples

DIPHATH (DIF ath) meaning unknown; 1Ch 1:6; descendant of Japhath; also called Riphath

DISHAN (DYE shan) meaning unknown; 20 century B.C.; Gen 36:21; son of Seir; Horite chief in Esau's day

DISHON (DYE shan) meaning unknown
1. 20 century B.C.; Gen 36:21; son of Seir; Horite chief
2. 20 century B.C.; Gen 36:25; son of Anah; Horite chief; brother-in-law of Esau

DODAI (DOH dye) *beloved;* 11 century B.C.; 1Ch 27:4; father of Eleazar the mighty man of David; also called Dodo 2

DODAVAHU (doh duh VAY hoo) *beloved of the Lord;* 9 century B.C.; 2Ch 20:37; father of Eliezer the prophet against Jehoshaphat

DODO (DOH doh) *beloved*
1. 12 century B.C.; Jdg 10:1; grandfather of Tola, Israelite judge
2. 2Sa 23:9; see Dodai
3. 2Sa 23:24; father of Elhanan the mighty man of David

DOEG (DOH eg) *anxious;* 11 century B.C.; 1Sa 21:7; the Edomite mercenary hired by King Saul to execute the priests of Nob who had assisted David and his troops

DORCAS Ac 9:36; see Tabitha

DORYMENES (dor YUM eh neez) meaning unknown; 2 century B.C.; 1Mac 3:38; son of Ptolemy; warrior

DOSITHEUS (do SITH ee us) meaning unknown
1. 2 century B.C.; 2Mac 12:19; Maccabean commander; released Timothy
2. 2 century B.C.; 2Mac 12:35; strong Jewish horseman; possibly Dositheus 1 the Maccabean commander
3. 2 century B.C.; AddEst 11:1; Jewish priest; brought Greek translation of Esther to Egypt
4. 3 century B.C.; 3Mac 1:3; Jew who saved Ptolemy IV

DRIMYLUS (drih MYE luhs) meaning unknown; 3Mac 1:3; father of Dositheus 4

DRUSILLA (droo SIL uh) meaning unknown; 1 century A.D.; Ac 24:24; Jewish wife of Judean governor Felix

DUMAH (DOO muh) *silence;* 21 century B.C.; Gen 25:14; son of Ishmael; grandson of Abraham

Dionysius and Damaris convert to Christianity after hearing Paul preach.

EBAL (EE bahl) *bare* or *stony*
1. 20 century B.C.; Gen 36:23; son of Shobal the Horite chief
2. 1Ch 1:22; son of Joktan; also called Obal

EBED (EE bed) *servant*
1. 12 century B.C.; Jdg 9:26; father of Gaal; conspired against Abimelech
2. 5 century B.C.; Ezr 8:6; descendant of Adin; returned to Judah after Exile

EBED-MELECH (EE bed MEL ehk) *king's servant;* 7 century B.C.; Jer 38:7; Ethiopian who freed Jeremiah from cistern

EBER (EE buhr) *cross over* or *other side*
1. Gen 10:21; descendent of Shem and ancestor of Abraham after whom the Hebrews are named
2. 1Ch 5:13; ancestor of Gad
3. 1Ch 8:12; Benjaminite family head
4. 1Ch 8:22; another Benjaminite family head
5. 6 century B.C.; Ne 12:20; head of priestly family after Exile

EBIASAPH 1Ch 6:23; see Abiasaph

EDDINUS (EHD dihn us) meaning unknown; 1Esd 1:15; temple singer

EDEN (EE duhn) *delight*
1. 8 century B.C.; 2Ch 29:12; Levite; purified temple in Hezekiah's day
2. 8 century B.C.; 2Ch 31:15; Levite; distributed offerings in Hezekiah's day; possibly Eden 1

EDER (EE duhr) *helper* or *flock*
1. 1Ch 8:15; descendant of Benjamin
2. 1Ch 23:23; Levite; descendant of Merari

EDNA (ED nuh) *delight;* Tob 7:2; wife of Raguel; mother-in-law of Tobit's son Tobias

EDOM Gen 25:30; see Esau

EDOMITES (EE duh myts) Gen 36:9
Descendants of Isaac's son Esau, the Edomites lived between the Dead Sea and the Gulf of Aqabah and were traditional enemies of Judah and Israel. The Nabothian dynasty ruled them for four centuries, well into New Testament times; the Herod family who ruled Palestine were Edomites. For further study, see Gen 32:3; 36; Nu 20; 24:18; 1Sa 22; 1Ki 11; 2Ki 3; Isa 34; Jer 49.

EGLAH (EG luh) *calf;* 1 century B.C.; 2Sa 3:5; wife of David; mother of Ithream

EGLON (EG lahn) *circle* or *calflike;* 14 century B.C.; Jdg 3:12; king of Moab; ruled over Israel 18 years

EGYPTIANS (EE jip shuhnz) Gen 10:6
One of the most sophisticated civilizations of the ancient world, Egypt is known for its achievements in architecture, art, literature, and social development as well as for its intriguing religious beliefs. The biblical account states that the Egyptian nation descended from Noah's son Ham. During its 3000-year history, this kingdom in northeast Africa played a major role in the Judeo-Christian saga.

While the polytheistic Egyptians readily borrowed beliefs and practices from nearly all cultures they knew, their society appears to have been almost unaffected by the Hebrew religion. Conversely, Egypt strongly influenced the many Israelites who spent significant time there. Abraham took his family to Egypt to avoid famine; Joseph rose to power and ruled Egypt; Moses freed his people from Egyptian slavery and revealed God's power in doing so; Jeremiah was exiled to Egypt; and Joseph, Mary, and Jesus sought refuge there. Egypt also influenced the history of Israel and Judah by waging numerous wars throughout the Middle East.

For further study, see Gen 12; 39–50; Ex 1–14; 18; Nu 33; Isa 19; Eze 20; 23; 29–32; Mt 2; Ac 7.

EHI Gen 46:21; see Aharah

EHUD (EE hud) *united* or *strong*
1. 13 century B.C.; Jdg 3:15
King Eglon of Moab, in alliance with neighboring Ammonites and Amalakites, held the Israelites subservient for 18 years. Israel cried out for deliverance, and Ehud, the left-hander, came to their rescue. Left-handedness was considered a rare handicap or weakness; the word, in Hebrew, means *hindered in the right hand.* Ironically, Ehud was a Benjaminite or "son of the right hand." For Ehud, being left-handed allowed him to sheathe his dagger on the right thigh and pull it out unexpectedly to stab king Eglon. With Eglon assassinated, Ehud then worked to help Israel subjugate Moab, giving Israel peace for 80 years. For further study, see Jdg 3:12–4:1.
2. 1Ch 7:10; descendant of Benjamin; possibly Ehud 1

Ehud flees after slaying King Eglon of Moab.

EKER (EE kuhr) *root;* 1Ch 2:27; descendant of Judah

ELA (EE luh) *oak;* 10 century B.C.; 1Ki 4:18; father of Solomon's governor Shimea

ELAH (EE luh) *oak*
1. Gen 36:41; chief of Edom; descendant of Esau
2. 14 century B.C.; 1Ch 4:15; son of Caleb; grandson of Jephunnen; spy in Canaan
3. ruled 886–885 B.C.; 1Ki 16:8; fourth king of northern Israel; son of Baasha
4. 8 century B.C.; 2Ki 15:30; father of Hoshea the last king of Israel
5. 1Ch 9:8; Benjaminite; lived in Jerusalem after Exile

ELAM (EE luhm) *highland*
1. Gen 10:22; firstborn son of Shem; founder of Elamites
2. 1Ch 8:24; descendant of Benjamin
3. 11 century B.C.; 1Ch 26:3; son of Meshelemiah the gatekeeper under David
4. Ezr 2:7; ancestor of family that returned to Judah after Exile
5. Ezr 2:31; ancestor of another family that returned to Judah after Exile
6. Ezr 10:26; his descendants married and divorced foreigners after Exile; possibly Elam 4 or 5
7. 5 century B.C.; Ne 10:14; sealed covenant renewal in Nehemiah's day; see Elam 4 and 5
8. 5 century B.C.; Ne 12:42; Levite singer at Jerusalem wall dedication

ELAMITES (EE luhm ights) Ezr 4:9; descendants of Elam 1; from Persia (modern Iran); military mercenaries

ELASAH (EL uh suh) *whom God made*
1. 7 century B.C.; Jer 29:3; son of Shaphan; took letter to exiles in Babylon
2. 5 century B.C.; Ezr 10:22; descendant of Pashhur; married and divorced foreigner after Exile

ELDAAH (el DAY uh) *called of God;* 19 century B.C.; Gen 25:4; son of Midian; grandson of Abraham

ELDAD (EL dad) *God has loved* or *called of God;* 15 century B.C.; Nu 11:26; elder with power to prophesy

ELEAD (EL ee ad) *God has testified;* 19 century B.C.; 1Ch 7:21; son of Ephraim; slain by men of Gath

ELEADAH (EL ee AY duh) *God has adorned;* 1Ch 7:20; descendant of Ephraim

ELEASAH (EL ee AY suh) *God has made*
1. 1Ch 2:40; descendant of Judah
2. 1Ch 8:37; Benjaminite; descendant of Saul

ELEAZAR (EL ee AY zuhr) *God has helped*
1. 1Ch 23:21; great-grandson of Levi
2. 15 century B.C.; Ex 6:23

As the third son born to Aaron and Elisheba, Eleazar stood to succeed to the high priesthood when his brothers, Nadab and Abihu, were killed by fire for dereliction of duty. Evidently, Eleazar learned from his family's painful lesson. He not only survived in office for decades without further scandal, but he proved to be a loyal lieutenant first to Aaron and Moses and later to Joshua. Eleazar and his younger brother Ithamar assisted Aaron in all priestly duties, especially in supervising the temple furniture and services. Eleazar rose to prominence after the rebellion of Korah and the death of Aaron. Thereafter, this chief of the Levites took charge of receiving worship offerings and participated in taking the census and distributing the allotted portions of the Promised Land. Through his son Phinehas, Eleazar established a line of 16 priestly families that included the house of Zadok. For further study, see Ex 6:23-25; 28:1; Lev 10:6-16; Nu 3:2-4; 16:31-50; 19:1-10; 20:23-29; 26:1-4,60-63; 27:19-23; 31; Jos 14:1; 17:4; 19:51; 21:1; 22:32; Jdg 20:28; 1Ch 24:4; Ezr 7:1-5.
3. 11 century B.C.; 1Sa 7:1; son of Abinadab the keeper of the ark
4. 11 century B.C.; 2Sa 23:9; one of David's mighty men
5. 5 century B.C.; Ezr 8:33; descendant of Phinehas the temple official in Ezra's day
6. 5 century B.C.; Ezr 10:25; descendant of Parosh; married and divorced foreigner
7. 5 century B.C.; Ne 12:42; priest/singer at Jerusalem wall dedication
8. Mt 1:15; ancestor of Christ through Joseph
9. 3 century B.C.; Sir 50:27; grandfather of Jesus Ben Sira the sage
10. 2 century B.C.; 1Mac 8:17; father of Jason the envoy to Rome

11. 2 century B.C.; 2Mac 6:18; Jerusalem Law teacher flogged to death by Antiochus IV Epiphanes
12. 2 century B.C.; 1Mac 2:5; son of Mattathias; priest who killed the war elephant, starting the Maccabean revolt

ELHANAN (el HAY nuhn) *God is gracious*
1. 11 century B.C.; 2Sa 21:19; warrior; killed Goliath's brother Lahmi
2. 11 century B.C.; 2Sa 23:24; mighty man of David

ELI (EE li) *uplifted;* 11 century B.C.; 1Sa 1:3

Eli was the temple priest at Shiloh who overheard the infertile Hannah praying for a son, although he did not recognize the true meaning of her prayers. When the Lord granted her prayers, Hannah dedicated her new son Samuel to the Lord's service and placed him in the custodial care of Eli. Ironically, Eli seemed to have greater success raising Samuel than his own two sons, Hophni and Phinehas.

When the corrupt Hophni and Phinehas violated Jewish custom and law regarding ritual sacrifices, they received only mild rebuke from the permissive Eli, who should have removed them from their priestly office. God responded by calling to

Eli and Samuel. Stained glass. St. Ita's Church, Chicago, Illinois.

Samuel at night and revealing his displeasure. The boy prophesied to Eli that God would end Eli's household. With the death of his sons in battle, the 98-year-old Eli recognized the fulfillment of this prophecy and fell dead himself.

The death of Eli marked the end of Israel's redemptive history. Before Eli, Israel was led by judges; after Eli, kings ruled. The boy Samuel became the last judge; he appointed Israel's first two kings—Saul and David.

For further study, see 1Sa 1–4; 14:3; 1Ki 2:26-27.

ELIAB (ee LYE uhb) *God is father*
1. 15 century B.C.; Nu 16:1; Reubenite whose sons rebelled against Moses
2. 15 century B.C.; Nu 1:9; leader of tribe of Zebulun during Exodus
3. 1Ch 6:27; ancestor of Samuel; also called Eliel 2 and Elihu 2
4. 11 century B.C.; 1Sa 16:6; son of Jesse; David's brother; father-in-law of Rehoboam; also called Elihu 5
5. 11 century B.C.; 1Ch 12:9; Gadite who joined David's army at Ziklag
6. 11 century B.C.; 1Ch 15:18; Levite musician under David
7. Jdt 8:1; ancestor of Judith

ELIADA (ee LYE ah duh) *God knows*
1. 2Sa 5:16; see Beeliada
2. 10 century B.C.; 1Ki 11:23; father of Rezon the Syrian enemy of Solomon
3. 9 century B.C.; 2Ch 17:17; Benjaminite commander under Jehoshaphat

ELIADAS (ee LYE ah duhs) meaning unknown; 5 century B.C.; 1Esd 9:28; one who married and divorced foreigner after Exile

ELIAHBA (ee LYE ah buh) *hidden by God;* 11 century B.C.; 2Sa 23:32; mighty man of David

ELIAKIM (ee LYE uh kim) *may God raise*
1. Lk 3:30; ancestor of Christ
2. 8 century B.C.; 2Ki 18:18; palace aide when Assyrians besieged Jerusalem
3. 2Ki 23:34; see Jehoiakim
4. 5 century B.C.; Ne 12:41; priest/singer at Jerusalem wall dedication
5. Mt 1:13; ancestor of Christ through Joseph

ELIAM (ee LYE um) *God's people*
1. 2Sa 11:3; see Ammiel 3
2. 2Sa 23:34; see Ahijah 3

ELIASAPH (ee LYE uh saf) *God will increase*
1. 15 century B.C.; Nu 1:14; tribal leader of Gad during Exodus
2. 15 century B.C.; Nu 3:24; Levite; led Gershonites in Moses's day

ELIASHIB (ee LYE uh shib) *restored of God*
1. 10 century B.C.; 1Ch 24:12; head of priestly division in David's day
2. 5 century B.C.; Ezr 10:6; high priest; angered Nehemiah by housing Tobiah in temple
3. 5 century B.C.; Ezr 10:24; Levite singer; married and divorced foreigner after Exile
4. 5 century B.C.; Ezr 10:27; descendant of Zattu; married and divorced foreigner after Exile
5. 5 century B.C.; Ezr 10:36; descendant of Bani; married and divorced foreigner after Exile
6. 1Ch 3:24; descendant of Zerubbabel

ELIATHAH (ee LYE ah thuh) *God has come;* 11 century B.C.; 1Ch 25:4; son of Heman; music minister

ELIDAD (ee LYE dad) *God has loved;* 15 century B.C.; Nu 34:21; Benjaminite leader Moses appointed to divide Canaan

ELIEHOENAI (el ih ee hoh EE nye) *toward the Lord are my eyes*
1. 10 century B.C.; 1Ch 26:3; son of Meshelemiah the gatekeeper under David
2. 5 century B.C.; Ezr 8:4; descendant of Pahath-moab

ELIEL (ee LYE uhl) *my God is God*
1. 1Ch 5:24; family head of half-tribe of Manasseh
2. 1Ch 6:34; see Eliab 3
3. 1Ch 8:20; descendant of Benjamin
4. 1Ch 8:22; descendant of Benjamin
5. 11 century B.C.; 1Ch 11:46; Mahavite; mighty man of David
6. 11 century B.C.; 1Ch 11:47; another mighty man of David
7. 11 century B.C.; 1Ch 12:11; Gadite commander; joined David at Ziklag; possibly Eliel 5 or 6

8. 11 century B.C.; 1Ch 15:9; chief Levite; helped return ark to Jerusalem
9. 8 century B.C.; 2Ch 31:13; supervised storage of temple offerings

ELIENAI (el eh EE nye) *God is my eyes;* 1Ch 8:20; descendant of Benjamin

ELIEZER (el eh EE zuhr) *God is help*
1. 18 century B.C.; Gen 15:2; chief servant of Abraham
2. 19 century B.C.; 1Ch 7:8; son of Becher; grandson of Benjamin
3. 15 century B.C.; Ex 18:4; son of Moses and Zipporah
4. 11 century B.C.; 1Ch 15:24; priest/trumpeter when ark returned to Jerusalem
5. 11 century B.C.; 1Ch 27:16; officer over Reubenites in David's time
6. 9 century B.C.; 2Ch 20:37; prophesied against Jehoshaphat
7. Lk 3:29; ancestor of Christ
8. 5 century B.C.; Ezr 8:16; leader Ezra sent to bring Levites to temple in Jerusalem
9. 5 century B.C.; Ezr 10:18; priest; married and divorced foreigner after Exile
10. 5 century B.C.; Ezr 10:23; Levite; married and divorced foreigner after Exile
11. 5 century B.C.; Ezr 10:31; descendant of Harim

ELIHOREPH (el uh HOHR uhf) *God of autumn;* 10 century B.C.; 1Ki 4:3; secretary for Solomon

ELIHU (el LYE hoo) *he is my God*
1. Job 32:2
Elihu, descendant of Abraham's brother Nahor, offered his opinion on the long-suffering Job to the three friends who were discussing his plight. God had taken Job's health, family, and estate as a test of his faith. Despite Job's claims of innocence, the first three counselors assumed that God was acting to punish Job for some sin. Elihu took a somewhat softer stand, suggesting that God was not punishing Job but rather building his spiritual character through adversity. He went on to chastise Job for his self-rightousness. When God later rebuked Job's friends for their comments (Job 42:7-9), Elihu was not mentioned, perhaps suggesting that his speculations were on the right track. For further study, see Job 32–37.

2. 1Sa 1:1; see Eliab 3
3. 11 century B.C.; 1Ch 12:20; Manasseh warrior; joined David at Ziklag
4. 11 century B.C.; 1Ch 26:7; descendant of Obed-edom; gatekeeper
5. 11 century B.C.; 1Ch 27:18; see Eliab 4

ELIJAH (ee LYE juh) *the Lord is my God*
1. 9 century B.C.; 1Ki 17:1
Elijah the Tishbite emerged, as if from nowhere, to become Israel's greatest miracle-worker since Moses. This great prophet from the northern kingdom of Israel was empowered by God to battle the forces of Baal, the Canaanite god of storm, rain, and fertility. Baal was acquiring a huge following among the Israelites who had forsaken their God or were attempting to worship both God and Baal.

The Israel of Elijah's day was in political as well as spiritual disarray. After the triumphant, solidifying reigns of King David and King Solomon, a political upheaval broke the nation into two kingdoms, Israel and Judah. As Israel suffered through the reigns of kings who did not follow the God of their fathers, Elijah emerged as a prophet to steer Israel from the brink of disaster.

Elijah lived in Israel during the reign of King Ahab, whose father, King Omri, had formed an alliance with Phoenicia. Their coalition was sealed by the marriage of Ahab to Jezebel, daughter of the king of Sidon. Ahab allowed her to establish the worship of the Phoenician god Baal and his consort Asherah throughout Israel. Ahab began to support this idolatrous Baal worship so enthusiastically that

The prophet Elijah awakened by an angel.

the Book of Kings denounced Ahab as the most wicked king of Israel.

Against this royal pagan backdrop, Elijah, dressed only in a leather loin cloth and a cloak made of hair, appeared before King Ahab to make a dramatic and harsh decree: Israel would suffer an extended drought. Before the king could order any retribution on this upstart prophet, Elijah vanished. During the drought and resulting famine, Elijah followed God's instructions and hid in a ravine next to a brook; ravens brought him meat and bread, and he drank from the brook until it dried up.

According to the Lord's instructions, Elijah was to seek help from a widow and her son in Phoenicia who were suffering the devastating consequences of the famine. When he asked her to bring him water and bread, the widow explained that she had only a handful of flour and a little oil. But Elijah told her to bring him her last piece of bread and God would make the flour and oil last until the end of the drought. The prophet helped the widow again a year later, when her son died and she blamed Elijah for his death. Elijah then stretched himself out on the boy's body and prayed three times, crying out to God for his life; the child came back to life, affirming to the widow that Elijah was truly a prophet of the Lord.

After three dry years, God instructed Elijah to present himself before Ahab and end the drought. Elijah challenged Ahab to a battle of the prophets—a contest between one prophet of God and the 450 prophets of Baal on Mt. Carmel. Ahab accepted the challenge. It was decided that each side would cut up a bull, lay it on wood with no fire, and then call on their god to take the offering by fire.

> ➤ ⬅
>
> *"... the prophet Elijah came near and said, 'O Lord, God of Abraham, Isaac, and Israel, let it be known this day that you are God in Israel, that I am your servant ... answer me, so that this people may know that you, O Lord, are God, and that you have turned their hearts back.'"*
>
> 1Ki 18:36-37

Before the contest, Elijah urged the assembled Israelites to abandon their dual theocracy by proclaiming, "How long will you go limping with two different opinions? If the Lord is God, follow him; but if Baal, then follow him" (1Ki 18:21). The ceremony began in the morning with the appeal to Baal. By noon, after Ahab's prophets had repeatedly cried out, "O Baal, answer us!" there was still no fire. Elijah taunted them with jeers that perhaps Baal was meditating, on a journey, or sleeping. Baal's prophets became agitated, and to get the attention of their god, they slashed themselves with their swords until they were covered with blood.

When there was still no response and the time came for the afternoon sacrifice, the spectators turned their attention to Elijah. He built an altar with 12 stones (to represent the 12 tribes of Israel), laid wood and the sacrificial bull on the altar, and dug a deep trench around it. He had 12 jars of water poured over the sacrifice and the wood until the altar was saturated and the trench was overflowing. Then Elijah stood by the altar and said, "O Lord, God of Abraham, Isaac, and Israel, let it be known this day that you are God in Israel" (1Ki 18:36). The fire of God consumed not only the pieces of the bull but the wood, the stones, the dust, even the water in the trench. The people were astounded and acknowledged Elijah's God as Lord. They seized the false prophets, who were then executed by Elijah in accordance with Jewish Law.

Elijah then announced that God would end the drought. He prayed seven times for rain with his face humbly between his knees. When a little storm cloud appeared on the horizon, Elijah ran down the mountain to the city, arriving ahead of the king's chariot to announce the coming of the rains.

Elisha watches Elijah's ascent into heaven.

spirit, was then separated from his beloved teacher by a fiery chariot and horses of fire, which took Elijah to heaven in a whirlwind. Elisha tore his clothes and picked up Elijah's mantle, which had fallen from the chariot—an act symbolic of Elisha taking up the great prophet's ministry.

Elijah set the standard against which all future prophets and messianic figures would be measured. The prophet Malachi ended the Old Testament with the promise that Elijah would reunite his people before "that great and dreadful day of the Lord comes" (Mal 4:5). Between the Testaments, Jesus Ben Sira reported that Elijah stands ready to "restore the tribes of Jacob" (Sir 48:10).

Several times in the Gospel, John the Baptist and even Jesus are compared to Elijah as a way to validate their status. Elisha's significance is further established when he appears alongside Moses at the Transfiguration, an event that affirms Jesus as the Son of God. For all his greatness, Elijah was simply a human being like us who raised the expectation that the persistent prayer of a "righteous" person will be "powerful and effective" (Jas 5:16-17).

For further study, see 1Ki 17–19, 21; 2Ki 1–2; Mal 4:5; Mt 11:14; 17:1-13; 27:47-49; Mk 6:15; 8:28; 9:1-13; Lk 1:16-17; 4:25-26; 9:7-9, 18-19, 28-36; Jn 1:21-25; Jas 5:16-18.

2. 1Ch 8:27; descendant of Benjamin

3. 5 century B.C.; Ezr 10:21; priest; married and divorced foreigner after Exile

4. 5 century B.C.; Ezr 10:26; descendant of Elam; married and divorced foreigner after Exile

5. Jdt 8:1; ancestor of Judith

ELIKA (el LYE kuh) meaning unknown; 11 century B.C.; 2Sa 23:25; mighty man of David

ELIMELECH (el LIM uh lek) *my God is king;* 12 century B.C.; Ru 1:2; husband of Naomi; father-in-law of Ruth

Upon hearing that her prophets had been killed, Queen Jezebel sought to execute Elijah. Instead of celebrating the victory of his God, Elijah now had to flee for his life. He went into the wilderness, where the despairing prophet was fed by an angel of God and instructed to keep traveling south. Then he went to Mt. Sinai, the place where God had revealed himself to Moses and had given his Law to Israel. On this holy mountain, God again exhibited a wonderful display of nature, starting with a mighty wind that split mountains and broke rocks into pieces. Then came an earthquake and a fire, followed by total silence broken only by God speaking in a quiet voice. Elijah was instructed to select Elisha as his successor and to anoint two kings (for Aram and Israel). Upon returning to Samaria, Elijah accused Ahab of murder and predicted the deaths of Ahab and Jezebel. When Ahab repented, the Lord delayed judgment on him but, as predicted, Jezebel was thrown out a window and trampled by horses.

When God was ready to take Elijah to heaven, an insistent, devoted Elisha aggressively stayed with his mentor. In a miracle reminiscent of God parting the Red Sea for the Israelites exiting from Egypt, Elijah saw God stop the waters of the Jordan River so he could walk across on dry ground. Elisha, after receiving a double portion of Elijah's

ELIOENAI (EL ee oh EE ni) *toward the Lord are my eyes*
1. 19 century B.C.; 1Ch 7:8; son of Becher; grandson of Benjamin
2. 1Ch 4:36; clan leader; descendant of Simeon
3. 5 century B.C.; Ezr 10:22; priest; married and divorced foreigner after Exile
4. 5 century B.C.; Ezr 10:27; descendant of Pashhur; married and divorced foreigner after Exile
5. 5 century B.C.; Ne 12:41; priest/singer at Jerusalem wall dedication
6. 1Ch 3:23; descendant of David

ELIPHAL (el LYE fuhl) *judged of God;* 11 century B.C.; 1Ch 11:35; military man of David; same as Eliphelet 1

ELIPHAZ (EL uh faz) *my God is fine gold* or *God is victorious*
1. Job 2:11
When the God-fearing, law-abiding Job was made to suffer by God as a test of his faith, he turned to three counselors to find an explanation for his plight. The leader and eldest of these was Eliphaz from Teman, south of the Dead Sea. He was a ruler of men and was considered both wise and rich. In keeping with orthodox religious thought of the time, he reasoned that Job must have sinned at some point, as there seemed to be no other way to account for such treatment from God. In three addresses to Job (Job 4–5; 15; 22), he became more and more put out with Job; even so, Eliphaz did hold out the prospect of God's mercy.

Bildad, the second of Job's friends, was a Shuhite from the nomadic tribe in southeast Palestine. As with Eliphaz, his counsel was very orthodox. When Job denied any sin, Bildad blustered at the notion that God's justice could be in any way impugned by Job. Bildad surmised that Job's children must have sinned, since they were suddenly killed, but he offered no consolation to Job.

Zophar, the third of Job's friends, was from Na-maah in northern Arabia. His philosophy was very rigid, even by standards of biblical orthodoxy. Zophar was the most harsh in his treatment of Job, presuming that Job deserved even more suffering than he had experienced thus far—judging from the wickedness and hypocrisy alleged by Eliphaz and Bildad.

In the end, Job was vindicated by God, and his health and household were returned. All three counselors were rebuked for their presumptuousness.

For further study, see the Book of Job.
2. 20 century B.C.; Gen 36:4; son of Esau by Adah

ELIPHELEHU (uh LIF uh LEE hoo) *may God distinguish;* 1 century B.C.; 1Ch 15:18; Levite; harp player when ark was brought into Jerusalem

ELIPHELET (uh LIF uh let) *God is deliverance*
1. 2Sa 23:34; see Eliphal
2. 10 century B.C.; 1Ch 3:6; son of David born in Jerusalem; also called Elpelet
3. 10 century B.C.; 2Sa 5:16; another son of David born in Jerusalem
4. 1Ch 8:39; descendant of King Saul
5. 5 century B.C.; Ezr 8:13; descendant of Adonikam; returned to Judah after Exile
6. 5 century B.C.; Ezr 10:33; descendant of Hashum; married and divorced foreigner after Exile

ELISHA (ee LYE shuh) *God is salvation;* 9 century B.C.; 1Ki 19:16
Elisha was the protégé of the great prophet Elijah, who prepared his disciple to assume the role of the leading prophet of Israel. Elijah treated his successor the way a loving father would treat his son. When they parted company, Elisha asked for a double portion of Elijah's spirit, a blessing very similar to the typical inheritance of a firstborn son.

Elijah's ministry was to bring the Israelites back to a monotheistic worship of the God of their fathers. By miracles equal only to the phenomenal feats of Moses, Elijah proved that the God of Israel

The prophet Elijah casts his mantle on Elisha.

The youths who taunted Elisha are mauled by bears.

riages, and crop failure in Jericho. After throwing a new bowl of salt into the spring, Elisha announced to the residents of Jericho that God had made the water healthful. The spring of Ain es-Sultan, which still provides lushness to the Jericho oasis, is traditionally known as the "Spring of Elisha."

Elisha's third miracle had a vengeful aspect. As he was leaving Jericho, a large group of small boys followed him, jeering and taunting him with their insulting chant, "Go away, baldhead! Go away, baldhead!" Elisha looked at them and cursed them in the name of the Lord, whereupon two female bears came out of the woods and mauled 42 of the boys. Although harsh, this incident pointed to the extreme holiness of the prophet and the reverence he embodied; this man of God could not be mocked without severe repercussions.

Many of Elisha's miracles took place in the company of a large group of prophets who often lived and ministered together. A widow of one of those prophets came to Elisha about an angry creditor who was going to take her children away as slaves. Using her only possession (a jar of oil) as a resource for a miracle, Elisha instructed her to borrow as many empty containers as she could find and fill them from her single jar of oil. She did as Elisha said, filling so many jars that she was able to pay her husband's debt and live on the income from the excess oil.

As these prophets were suffering the effects of famine, Elisha fed them soup made from just a handful of meal and a poisonous yellow gourd, but his miraculous power prevented any deaths. Elisha also fed 100 of the prophets by multiplying some loaves of bread and ears of wheat. Another time, he helped his comrades rescue a borrowed axe-head which had fallen into the river by making it float to the surface.

When Elisha was not living with the group of prophets, he stayed in a room built especially for him at the home of a couple from Shunem. Out of gratitude, Elisha predicted the childless couple would have a son. But when this child later became ill and died, his mother sent for Elisha. When his servant Gehazi was unable to raise the boy, Elisha came himself. After he prayed and stretched himself upon the body of the child, the boy was restored to life.

Elisha's healing ministry at times extended to Israel's enemies. When Naaman, a leprous Syrian army commander, came to him for a cure, Elisha

was greater than the Canaanite god Baal. At the end of his ministry, he was taken to heaven in a whirlwind, accompanied by a fiery chariot. As he was whisked away, Elisha caught Elijah's cloak as it fell from the chariot, an act symbolic of the great prophet's ministry passing on to his beloved disciple and spiritual son.

Elisha's first miracle was identical to Elijah's last miracle. Beginning his ministry where Elijah left off, he struck the water of the Jordan River with his inherited mantle, parting the waters to provide a dry path. Other observing prophets recognized that Elisha had the spirit of Elijah and bowed down before him in reverence, accepting him as their leader even though they still searched for the "missing" Elijah.

Elijah's ministry was intense and aggressive; Elisha's was more gentle. Elijah's life was solitary; Elisha was people oriented, often living with groups of other prophets. Elisha showed the social aspect of his ministry when, as his second miracle, he purified the water that had been causing death, miscar-

instructed him to go dip himself seven times in the Jordan River. At first questioning why Israel's rivers would be any better than Syria's, Naaman finally obeyed and was healed.

Elisha's entire ministry was interspersed with government affairs, advising and anointing kings, and warning his country of imminent danger. He not only predicted future kings, but also anointed new sovereigns and foresaw military defeats and victories.

Even in his death, Elisha's body evidently retained some of his power to heal and restore life. Shortly after Elisha's death, a corpse was inadvertently thrown into his grave and it came to life just by touching the bones of this powerful prophet.

For further study, see 1Ki 19:15-21; 2Ki 2–9.

ELISHAH (el LYE shuh) *my God is salvation;* Gen 10:4; ancestor of coastland people who settled either Cyprus or Sicily

ELISHAMA (ee LISH ah muh) *my God hears*
1. 15 century B.C.; Nu 1:10; led tribe of Ephraim during Exodus; grandfather of Joshua
2. 1Ch 2:41; descendant of Judah
3. 10 century B.C.; 2Sa 5:16; son of David born in Jerusalem
4. 9 century B.C.; 2Ch 17:8; priest; taught Law under Jehoshaphat
5. 7 century B.C.; 2Ki 25:25; grandfather of Ishmael the assassin of Gedaliah
6. 7 century B.C.; Jer 36:12; Jehoiakim's secretary

ELISHAPHAT (ee LISH uh fat) *my God has judged;* 9 century B.C.; 2Ch 23:1; military commander; planned overthrow of Athaliah

ELISHEBA (ee LISH uh buh) *my God is [my] oath;* 15 century B.C.; Ex 6:23; wife of Aaron

ELISHUA (el uh SHOO uh) *my God is salvation;* 10 century B.C.; 2Sa 5:15; son of David born in Jerusalem

ELIUD (ee LYE uhd) *God is my praise;* Mt 1:14; ancestor of Christ

ELIZABETH (ee LIZ uh beth) *God is my oath;* 1 century A.D.; Lk 1:5

Elizabeth, a descendant of Aaron, was the wife of Zechariah the priest and the mother of John the

Mary visits Elizabeth. Stained glass. Notre-Dame Cathedral, Ottawa.

Baptist. Her husband was visited by the angel Gabriel, who said that the elderly, childless couple would soon be blessed with a son that they should name John. Elizabeth stayed in seclusion the first five months of her pregnancy. In her sixth month, she was visited by her cousin Mary, who was pregnant with Jesus. Elizabeth's baby jumped inside her womb when Mary entered their house. Recognizing the importance of her cousin's pregnancy, Elizabeth called Mary "the mother of my Lord" (Lk 1:43) and pronounced her blessed. When her baby was born, Elizabeth named him John, against the advice of her friends and neighbors. For further study, see Lk 1.

ELIZAPHAN (ee LIZ uh fan) *God has protected*
1. 15 century B.C.; Nu 3:30; Kohathite leader of Levites during Exodus; also called Elzaphan
2. 15 century B.C.; Nu 34:25; Zebulunite leader Moses appointed to divide Canaan

ELIZUR (el LYE zuhr) *God is a rock;* 15 century B.C.; Nu 1:5; Reubenite leader during Exodus

ELKANAH (el KAY nuh) *God has possessed* or *God has taken possession*
1. Ex 6:24; Levite; grandson of Korah
2. 1Ch 6:26; ancestor of Samuel
3. 11 century B.C.; 1Sa 1:1
   Elkanah claimed an impressive family history, with his lineage tied to the Levites, the Zuphites, and the Ephraimites. He fathered several sons and daughters by one wife, Peninnah, but was unable to produce any offspring with his other wife, Hannah. Only after persistent prayer by Hannah and her promise that she would give up her child to God's service did she conceive a son, Samuel, the last of the judges and the anointer of kings Saul and David. After Samuel's birth, Elkanah and Hannah produced five more children.
4. 11 century B.C.; 1Ch 12:6; Korahite; joined David at Ziklag
5. 11 century B.C.; 1Ch 15:23; Levite; doorkeeper for ark; possibly Elkanah 4
6. 8 century B.C.; 2Ch 28:7; second in command to Ahaz; killed by Israelites
7. 1Ch 9:16; his descendant Berekiah settled in Jerusalem

ELKIAH (el KYE uh) meaning unknown; Jdt 8:1; ancestor of Judith

ELMADAM (el MAY duhm) meaning unknown; Lk 3:28; ancestor of Christ

ELNAAM (el NAY uhm) *God is pleasant* or *delightful;* 11 century B.C.; 1Ch 11:46; father of Jeribai and Joshaviah, David's mighty men

ELNATHAN (el NAY thuhn) *God has given*
1. 7 century B.C.; 2Ki 24:8; servant of Jehoiakim; grandfather of Jehoiachin
2. 5 century B.C.; Ezr 8:16; leader sent to bring Levites back from Casiphia
3. 5 century B.C.; Ezr 8:16; another leader sent to bring Levites back from Casiphia
4. 5 century B.C.; Ezr 8:16; scholar sent by Ezra for Levites in Casiphia

ELON (EE lahn) *oak* or *terebinth*
1. 20 century B.C.; Gen 26:34; Hittite; father-in-law of Esau

2. 19 century B.C.; Gen 46:14; son of Zebulun; source of clan
3. 12 century B.C.; Jdg 12:11; Israelite judge for ten years

ELPAAL (el PAY uhl) *God has wrought;* 1Ch 8:11; descendant of Benjamin

ELPELET (el PAY let) *God is deliverance;* 10 century B.C.; 1Ch 14:5; son of David born in Jerusalem; see Eliphelet 2

ELUZAI (ee LOO zye) *God is my strength;* 11 century B.C.; 1Ch 12:5; relative of Saul; joined David's army

ELYMAS Ac 13:6; see Bar-Jesus

ELZABAD (el ZAY bad) *God has given*
1. 11 century B.C.; 1Ch 12:8; Gadite in David's army at Ziklag
2. 10 century B.C.; 1Ch 26:7; Levite; temple gatekeeper

ELZAPHAN (el ZAY fan) *God has protected;* 15 century B.C.; Ex 6:22; son of Uzziel; kinsman of Moses; see Elizaphan 1

Enoch is taken by God. Enamel on gilded copper, from the Verdun Altar in Klosterneuburg, Austria.

EMIM (EE mim) *terrors;* Gen 14:5; giant race of Anakim living near Dead Sea and Moab; attacked in Abraham's day

ENAN (EE nuhn) *two springs;* 15 century B.C.; Nu 1:15; father of Ahira the tribal head during Exodus

ENOCH (EE nuhk) *dedicated* or *initiated*
1. Gen 4:17; son of Cain
2. Gen 5:18
What set Enoch apart from his contemporaries was not his relatively short life span—365 years as compared to Methuselah's 969—but his distinctive spirituality. Enoch "walked with God" for 300 years. That suggests a conversion experience at age 65, following the birth of Methuselah, the first of his many sons and daughters. Though Enoch did not die, "God took him" (Gen 5:24) directly into his presence; he represents immortality in the same way as Elijah, who was also taken by God, or transported to heaven, in a sudden and mystifying way. For further study, see 2Ki 2:10-11; Heb 11:5.

ENOS (EE nahs) *mortal;* Lk 3:38; ancestor of Christ; also called Enosh

ENOSH Gen 4:26; see Enos

EPAENETUS (eh PEE nuh tuhs) *praised;* 1 century A.D.; Ro 16:5; first Christian convert in Asia

EPAPHRAS (EP uh fras) *handsome* or *charming;* 1 century A.D.; Col 1:7
Epaphras likely converted to Christianity during Paul's extended visit to Ephesus (A.D. 53–56). He then evangelized in the Lycus valley 100 miles inland from Ephesus until churches at Colossae, Laodicea, and Hierapolis were established. Epaphras was among several Greek-speaking Asian associates who took turns staying with Paul in prison in Rome. Epaphras was Paul's "fellow-prisoner" when Paul corresponded with Philemon in A.D. 60. Epaphras may also have been visiting Rome during this time to bring disaster relief to the churches in the Lycus valley, which, according to one historical source, had been rocked recently by an earthquake. For further study, see Ac 28:14-31; Col 1:3-8; 4:12; Phm 1:23.

EPAPHRODITUS (eh PAF roh DY tuhs) *handsome* or *charming;* 1 century A.D.; Php 2:25
Epaphroditus traveled from Philippi to Rome to bring gifts from the church to the imprisoned Paul. The mission nearly cost him his life, as he became ill in Rome and almost died. After Epaphroditus's recovery, Paul sent him back to Philippi with a letter in which Paul described him as his "brother, co-worker, and fellow soldier, your messenger and minister to my need." For further study, see Php 4:14-19.

EPHAH (EE fah) *dark one*
1. Gen 25:4; son of Midian; grandson of Abraham
2. 1Ch 2:46; concubine of Caleb and mother of three sons
3. 1Ch 2:47; son of Jahdai

EPHAI (EE fye) meaning unknown; 7 century B.C.; Jer 40:8; ancestor of some who remained in Judah during Exile

EPHER (EE fuhr) *young deer*
1. 20 century B.C.; Gen 25:4; son of Midian; grandson of Abraham
2. 1Ch 4:17; descendant of Judah
3. 1Ch 5:24; head of Manasseh family exiled by king of Assyria

EPHESIANS (ee FEE zyuhnz) Ac 19:28; inhabitants of Epheseus, the heart of Greco-Roman society and of paganism in western Turkey; see Artemis

EPHLAL (EF lal) *judgment;* 1Ch 2:37; descendant of Judah

EPHOD (EE fahd) *a vest;* Nu 34:23; his son Hanniel helped Moses divide Canaan

EPHRAIM (EE free uhm) *fruitful;* 19 century B.C.; Gen 41:52
When Jacob's health and sight were failing, Joseph brought his sons Ephraim and Manasseh to their grandfather to be blessed regarding their future. When Jacob first put his hand on the younger Ephraim, Joseph corrected him. However, Jacob insisted that he intended to bless Ephraim and thereby make him a greater nation. Indeed, after Jacob's blessing, Ephraim's descendants became

Jacob blesses his grandsons Ephraim and Manasseh.

more fruitful, eventually becoming the prominent tribe of the northern kingdom. Later known as the tribe of Israel, the Ephraimites inherited the hill country between the Jordan and the Mediterranean. In later times, they would become embroiled in civil strife with their rival tribe, Judah. For further study, see Gen 46:20; 48:1-20; Nu 26:28; Dt 33:17; 1Ch 7:20-22.

EPHRAIMITES (EE fruh im ights) Nu 7:48

The descendants of Joseph's son Ephraim, the Ephraimites inherited the hill country between the Jordan River and the Mediterranean Sea. They were leading figures in the northern kingdom of Israel after the monarchy was divided. For further study, see Gen 48; Nu 1–2; Jos 16–17; Jdg 12; Eze 37; Hos 4–12.

EPHRATH (EF rath) *fruitfulness;* 1Ch 2:19; second wife of Caleb; a form of Ephrathah

EPHRATHAH 1Ch 2:50; see Ephrath

EPHRATHITES (EF ruh thights) Ru 1:2; inhabitants of Bethlehem (Judah), the home of Naomi's sons Mahlon and Kilion

EPHRON (EE frahn) *fawnlike;* 21 century B.C.; Gen 23:8; Hittite who sold Abraham a burial cave for Sarah

EPICUREANS (epp uh kyoo REE anz) Ac 17:18; followers of Epicurus the Greek philosopher

ER (UHR) *watcher*
1. 19 century B.C.; Gen 38:3; son of Judah; first husband of Tamar
2. 1Ch 4:21; descendant of Shelah and Judah
3. Lk 3:28; ancestor of Christ

ERAN (EE ran) *watchful;* Nu 26:36; descendant of Ephraim; ancestral origin of Eranites

ERASTUS (uh RAS tuhs) *beloved*
1. 1 century A.D.; Ac 19:22; Christian whom Paul sent to Macedonia with Timothy
2. 1 century A.D.; Ro 16:23; Corinthian director of public works
3. 1 century A.D.; 1Ti 4:20; Christian whom Paul left in Corinth; possibly Erastus 1 or 2

ERI (EE rye) *my watcher;* 19 century B.C.; Gen 46:16; son of Gad; grandson of Jacob

ESAR-HADDON (EE suhr HAD uhn) *Assur* [a god] *has given a brother;* ruled 680–669 B.C.; 2Ki 19:37

This son of King Sennacherib and grandson of King Sargon II (the Great) became ruler of Assyria when two other sons, Adrammelech and Sharezer, murdered their father in 681 B.C. During his reign, Esar-haddon proved to be a very capable expansionist monarch for the powerful Assyrian Empire. He gained ground by raiding and occupying Lower Egypt and by exacting tribute from 13 vassal kings and their city-states along the eastern Mediterranean seacoast. King Manasseh of Judah was listed in Assyrian archives as among those paying tribute to Esar-haddon. Esar-haddon also had a hand in repopulating Israel during the Babylonian Exile with people who ended up frustrating the efforts of returning Jews to rebuild Jerusalem. For further study see Ezr 4:1-5; Is 37:38.

ESAU (EE saw) *hairy* or *shaggy;* 20 century B.C.; Gen 25:25

Before the twins Jacob and Esau were born to Rebekah and Isaac, it was predicted that the elder would serve the younger. Red-haired Esau was born first, followed by Jacob, clutching his brother's heel.

Esau grew up to become a skillful hunter, while Jacob chose to work as a cultivator. On his return from a hunting trip one day, a ravenous Esau impulsively sold his birthright—the firstborn's double-share of the inheritance—to Jacob in return for bread and lentil stew. When a blind and aging Isaac was preparing to give his blessing to Esau, Jacob sought to claim what his brother had sold him. With the help of Rebekah, he disguised himself as Esau, went before his father, and took his blessing.

Esau was devastated. He begged for another blessing and hated Jacob for cheating him. Esau threatened to kill Jacob, but the younger brother fled to safety. After this, Esau took his wives and settled in the land of Seir south of the Dead Sea, while Jacob and his family inhabited Canaan. Many years passed before the brothers met again. They reconciled, thanks to Esau's forgiving spirit and his willingness to accept Jacob's gift of restitution and appeasement to him. Esau was the ancestral father of the Edomites, a nation in repeated conflict with Jacob's descendants, that is, Israel.

In the story of these twins, Jacob was not censured for his duplicity, although he paid a heavy price for the blessing. Esau, however, was chastised for his worldliness—that is, for abandoning spiritual values for something immediate and temporal.

For further study, see Gen 25–28; 32–33; 36; Nu 20:18-21; Heb 12:16. Also called Edom.

Jacob offers Esau food in exchange for his birthright.

ESDRIS (EZ drihs) meaning unknown; 2 century B.C.; 2Mac 12:36; Maccabean commander in battle in Idumea

ESH-BAAL 1Ch 8:33; see Ishbaal

ESHBAN (ESH ban) *man of understanding;* 20 century B.C.; Gen 36:26; son of Dishon the Horite chief in Seir

ESHCOL (ESH kahl) *cluster of grapes;* 22 century B.C.; Gen 14:13; Amorite; helped Abraham rescue Lot

ESHEK (EE shek) *oppressor;* 1Ch 8:39; descendant of Saul through Jonathan

ESHTEMOA (ESH tuh MOH uh) *listening post* **1.** 1Ch 4:17; son of Ishbah; descendant of Judah **2.** 1Ch 4:19; son of Hodiah 1; descendant of Judah

ESHTON (ESH tuhn) *restful;* 1Ch 4:11; descendant of Judah

ESLI (ES lye) *reserved;* Lk 3:25; ancestor of Christ

ESTHER (ES tuhr) *star;* 5 century B.C.; Est 2:7

The book of Esther is primarily about the Jewish queen of King Ahasuerus (Xerxes) of Persia, and how she defeated Haman, the chief minister of the king, in order to save her people. To climax a six-month display of wealth and power, King Ahasuerus gave a banquet on the palace grounds at Susa for all his officials and ministers. After several days of merrymaking, the king sent for his wife, Queen Vashti, to show her off. She refused to make a command appearance, which embarrassed and angered Ahasuerus. On the advice of his astrologers, he deposed Vashti and ordered a search for a new queen to replace her.

Among the beautiful young women brought to the king was a Jewish girl named Hadassah (the Hebrew word for *myrtle*), whose Persian name was Esther. Orphaned when she was very young, she had been adopted by her cousin, Mordecai, a devout Jew from Jerusalem who lived in exile in Susa. Esther delighted Ahasuerus, as well as all the royal court, and she was crowned queen. The king then declared a public holiday, gave a great wedding feast, and generously distributed gifts to his subjects in honor of his marriage to the lovely Esther.

Even after her move to the palace, Mordecai continued to keep a custodial eye on Esther and advised her to keep her Jewish identity hidden. One day he overheard two of the king's chamberlains plotting to kill their master. He told Esther to warn the king, who then had the men executed. Mordecai's service was recorded by the scribes in the official court annals.

Shortly after this, Ahasuerus appointed Haman, the Agagite, as his chief minister and ordered all palace officials to show deference by bowing down to the grand vizier. Mordecai alone refused. As a Benjaminite, he would not pay such an honor, as it would be tantamount to idolatry. Angered by Mordecai's refusal to prostrate himself, Haman plotted the destruction not just of Mordecai but of the entire Jewish population. Haman had the magicians cast lots to pick the day for his evil design, then he went to the king to malign the Jews. In order to get his way, he offered Ahasuerus a fabulous bribe. The king rejected the bribe but gave Haman his signet ring and the freedom to do as he pleased with the Jews.

Haman gave orders, had them published, then dispersed the royal decrees throughout the provinces. In the spring, on the 13th day of Adar, all Jews were to be killed and their possessions seized. Mordecai implored Esther to go to the king and plead for the lives of her people. It was against the law, and dangerous, for her to approach the king unbidden, but because of the urgent circumstances, she courageously agreed, declaring "... if I perish, I perish" (Est 4:16).

The queen fasted for three days, dressed herself in regal robes, and then approached Ahasuerus. He received her, and Esther cleverly invited the king and Haman to dinner. After the meal, she invited them to a second banquet the following day. Haman was pleased at this newfound royal attention, but his high spirits gave way to anger when he came across his nemesis, Mordecai, at the palace gate.

> ⇥ ⇤
>
> *"...these days of Purim should be observed at their appointed season, as the Jew Mordecai and Queen Esther enjoined on the Jews..."*
>
> Est 6:31

Ignoring his own edict concerning the Jews, Haman decided to go after Mordecai. He ordered gallows built on the spot, intending to ask the king the next day to have Mordecai hanged. Fortunately, though, a sleepless night gave the king an opportunity to have the court records read to him, and from them he was reminded how Mordecai had earlier saved his life and had gone unrewarded.

The next morning when Haman appeared before the king, Ahasuerus immediately wanted to know "What shall be done for the man whom the king wishes to honor?" (Est 6:6). Believing that the king meant him, Haman smugly suggested that such a man should have a grand royal procession with many accompanying honors. Then in a dramatic twist of events, the king ordered Haman to do just that for Mordecai.

When Haman and the king were brought to Esther for the second dinner, Esther revealed her Jewish identity and told the king about Haman's plot to exterminate her people. Overcome with rage toward Haman, the king rushed out of the room. Haman, desperate for his life, violated harem law when he threw himself down on the couch beside the queen. Worse, the king found the frightened grand vizier like this when he returned from the garden and ordered Haman to be hanged that very day on the gallows he had built for Mordecai.

Then Ahasuerus gave the queen Haman's estate and appointed Mordecai chief minister in Haman's place. Esther once again approached the king, this time concerning Haman's edict against the Jews. She begged the king to cancel it. The king refused since Persian law made a formal edict irrevocable, even by the king himself. Instead, Ahasuerus gave Mordecai authority to send out another decree neutralizing the first one by providing new instructions: Jews were given the right to bear arms in self-defense. And on the day Haman had appointed for their annihilation, Esther's people turned on their enemies and wiped them out, including the ten sons of Haman. On the 14th day of Adar—after the killing and mayhem—the Jews celebrated not only their survival but their amazing and complete victory. Later, Mordecai and Esther sent letters to all the Jews, establishing that the Feast of Purim should be commemorated each year to mark their deliverance from Haman and their enemies. On a concluding note, the writer of Esther observed that Ahasuerus continued to enjoy great political strength, and that Mordecai had significant influence and popularity among the people.

Because of Esther's story, Purim has become an important part of the Jewish calendar and is celebrated in a jubilant atmosphere. At Purim, the Book of Esther—last of the five scrolls (the Megillah)—is read in the synagogue, and some of the observed traditions include fancy dress parades, masquerades, and the making and eating of special cakes.

In addition to providing the basis for an important festival among Jews, Esther is also a significant religious work that shows God influencing the affairs of humanity unannounced. As many scholars have noted, God is never mentioned in Esther, and the story does not include the typical Jewish conventions, such as the Law, the covenant, prayer, and so on, that are found in other Old Testament literature. Some scholars have also questioned the canonicity of the book because of its ethical tone. The basic Judaic values of mercy, kindness, and forgiveness are missing from Esther and have been replaced by malice, cruelty, and vengeance. For example, Haman's consuming hatred is matched by the bloodthirsty revenge of Mordecai and Esther. On the other hand, some godly concepts are both presupposed and suggested in the text. In one instance, Mordecai infers that God will deliver his people (Est 4:14); and Esther mandates fasting (and by implication, prayer) as a religious exercise (Est 4:16).

The book was written some time after the death of Ahasuerus. But the writer's nationalism and fa-

Queen Esther, King Ahasuerus, and the chief minister Haman. Rembrandt (1606–1669).

Illuminated scroll of Esther read during the feast of Purim. Germany, seventeenth century.

miliarity with Persian history, customs, and vocabulary make it likely that the unknown author was a Jew who lived in Persia. In the Greek version, Esther is placed among the historical books and has been lengthened by six additional passages containing 107 verses not found in the Hebrew text. The additional material found in the Apocrypha mentions God and prayer, the covenant with Israel, and several other Hebraic motifs.

In spite of the book's unusual traits, Esther is an intriguing story that speaks clearly of wisdom, courage, deliverance, and God's providential care for a covenant people.

For further study, see the Book of Esther and Additions to Esther.

ETAM (EE tuhm) *lair of wild beasts;* 1Ch 4:3; descendant of Judah

ETHAN (EE thuhn) *enduring*
1. 1Ki 4:31; wise man; author of Psalm 89
2. 1Ch 6:42; Levite musician; descendant of Asaph
3. 11 century B.C.; 1Ch 6:44; chief minister of music in David's time; also called Jeduthun 1

ETHANUS (eh THAY nuhs) meaning unknown; 5 century B.C.; 2Esd 14:23; scribe who worked with Ezra

ETHBAAL (ETH bay uhl) *with Baal* or *man of Baal;* 9 century B.C.; 1Ki 16:31; king of Sidon; father-in-law of Ahab

ETHIOPIANS (ee thih OH pih uhnz) 2Ki 19:9
Also called Nubia and Cush, Ethiopia ventured into many wars of the Middle East during Old Testament times. An Ethiopian eunuch to Queen Candace brought Christianity to Africa in the first century A.D. after being baptized by Philip 8. For further study, see 2Sa 18:21-23; Isa 20:3-5; Eze 29–30; Jer 38:7-12; 2Ch 14; Ac 8:26-40.

ETHNAN (ETH nuhn) *hire* or *gift;* 1Ch 4:7; descendant of Judah

ETHNI (ETH ni) *gift;* 1Ch 6:41; Levite ancestor of music minister in David's time

EUBULUS (yoo BYOO luhs) *well advised* or *good counsel;* 1 century A.D.; 2Ti 4:21; Christian who sent greetings to Timothy

EUMENES (YOO me neez) *well disposed;* 2 century B.C.; 1Mac 8:8; king of Pergamum; fought Antiochus III

EUNICE (YOO nis) *good victory;* 1 century A.D.; 2Ti 1:5; mother of Timothy

EUODIA (yoo OH dee uh) *prosperous journey* or *success;* 1 century A.D.; Php 4:2; key Christian woman at Philippi

EUOPATOR (YOO pah tor) *good father;* 2 century B.C.; 1Mac 6:17; son of Antiochus IV Epiphanes

EUPOLEMUS (yoo PO leh mus) *skillful in war;* 2 century B.C.; 1Mac 8:17; son of John; grandson of Accos; Maccabean envoy to Rome

EUTYCHUS (YOO tuh kuhs) *fortunate;* 1 century A.D.; Ac 20:9; youth revived by Paul after dying from a fall

EVE (EEV) *life-giver;* Gen 3:20

When God made Adam, he put him in the garden of Eden. Although surrounded by a pleasant environment of birds, animals, and plants, Adam was alone. So, God set out to create a new being, a helper and partner, to provide the companionship that Adam needed. God caused Adam to sleep, removed one of his ribs, and made it into a woman.

When Adam saw the woman, he recognized that she shared part of his being, and he named her Woman (Gen 2:23). Thus, Adam and the woman came together in an interdependent relationship, guiltless before each other and before God.

While in the idyllic garden, the clever serpent talked the woman into tasting the fruit from the tree of the knowledge of good and evil, the one thing that God had instructed them to avoid. She gave some to Adam as well. Feeling guilty and anxious because of their disobedience, Adam and the woman covered their nakedness and hid from God. When he confronted them about what they had done, the woman told God that the serpent had tricked her. The Lord dealt with the serpent, and he also punished Adam and the woman for their sin. Her curse was to experience suffering in childbirth, the most fundamental human process, and to have her mutual partnership with Adam give way to a relationship of conflict and inequity.

Then Adam named his wife Eve "because she was the mother of all living" (Gen 3:20). God gave them protective clothing and sent them out of the

Adam and Eve in Paradise. Peter Paul Rubens (1577–1640).

garden forever. After this, Eve bore Adam many children: Cain, Abel, Seth, and other sons and daughters.

For further study, see Gen 1:26-31; 2:18-25; 3; 4:1-2, 25; 2Co 11:3; 1Ti 2:13.

EVI (EE vye) *desire;* 15 century B.C.; Nu 31:8; Midianite king defeated and killed by Israelites

EVIL-MERODACH (EE vuhl MAIR uh dahk) *man of* [the god] *Marduk;* ruled 562–560 B.C.; 2Ki 25:27; king of Babylon

EZBAI (EZ bah eye) *shining* or *beautiful;* 1 century B.C.; 1Ch 11:37; father of mighty man of David

EZBON (EZ bahn) meaning unknown
1. 19 century B.C.; Gen 46:16; son of Gad; also called Ozni
2. 19 century B.C.; 1Ch 7:7; son of Bela; grandson of Benjamin

EZEKIEL (ee ZEE kee uhl) *God strengthens;* 6 century B.C.; Eze 1:3

Ezekiel was both a prophet and a priest to the Hebrew people in exile, and he ranks among the major prophets of the Old Testament, along with Isaiah, Jeremiah, and Daniel. Ezekiel lived during the greatest crisis in Israel's history—when their homeland and the temple, the center of their theocracy, were destroyed and the people were held in captivity in Babylon for 70 years. Ezekiel was among the Hebrews taken to Babylon by King Nebuchadnezzar in his second invasion of Judah in 597 B.C. His contemporary, Daniel, was taken captive in the first invasion in 605 B.C. Nebuchadnezzar invaded Judah yet a third time (586 B.C.), destroying the temple and the entire city.

Ezekiel's prophecy, which began "In the thirtieth year...as I was among the exiles" (Eze 1:1), may be dated to 593 B.C. The "thirtieth year" probably refers to Ezekiel himself, meaning he was 30 years old when taken to a Babylonian refugee camp at Tel-Abib on the River Chebar. The only other personal notes in the Book of Ezekiel refer to his living and marital status. He had his own house and was married; evidently, Ezekiel's wife died on the eve of Jerusalem's destruction. The remainder of the book deals with his warnings and prophecies to the exiled Jews.

To a nation that had abandoned their God and given themselves to the idols of foreign nations, Ezekiel had one central message, which he repeated 70 times: "You [or they] shall know that I am the Lord." The Book of Ezekiel consists of several verbal messages, enhanced by and intertwined with intricate visions, some of which are acted out.

Ezekiel's opening chapter focused on his call and commission from God, which came in the form of a vision—a whirlwind and a fire, followed by four cherubim with the faces of a lion, an ox, a man, and an eagle. Next, Ezekiel directed his message to the Jews in Babylon, warning them of God's judgment for their sin and rebellion. Under the leadership of several evil kings in the past, Judah had deserted the Lord, and the people had worshiped the

Vision of the prophet Ezekiel. Raphael (1483–1520).

gods of foreign countries, defiling the temple with foreign idols and altars.

Ezekiel employed elaborate, sometimes confusing allegories; he depicted the nation as a vine and as an adulterous woman, for instance. He also relied on dramatic, somewhat strange demonstrations to speak to his people. In one instance, he laid on his side for over a year in front of a picture of Jerusalem to represent the siege of the city. Through such devices, he showed that the Exile in Babylon was the result of the Israelites' losing God's favor through their wicked ways; he also emphasized that each individual was responsible for choosing to return to God in order to regain his blessing and bring an end to the suffering of the nation.

The Israelites were not the sole focus of his prophecies, however. Ezekiel also addressed the surrounding nations that ravaged and plundered Israel. He specifically foretold the judgment on Ammon, Moab, Edom, Philistia, Tyre, Sidon, and Egypt. He then spoke to the Jewish exiles with a message of comfort and a promise that they would someday return to Jerusalem. This prophecy of Israel's restoration in their own land was supported by his vision of the valley of dry bones. In this unusual vision, Ezekiel spoke to the lifeless bones, telling them God would cause breath to enter them, making them come alive. God attached tendons to these bones and gave them flesh and skin. The vision symbolized the nation of Israel's restoration from exile as if it were a resurrection of the dead. In another vision, God instructed Ezekiel to join two sticks, one representing Judah and the other Israel, together into one, hinting that the two kingdoms would one day be reunited.

Ezekiel detailed the final assault of the kingdom of God upon the nations of the world and their destruction through the might of Jehovah. The final vision described the ideal kingdom of God with its restored land and temple, detailing the new tem-

> *"Mortal, I have made you a sentinel for the house of Israel; whenever you hear a word from my mouth, you shall give them warning from me."*
>
> Ese 3:17

ple's measurements and interior decorations. Ezekiel also envisioned the glory of the Lord returning to the temple.

Because the prophet Ezekiel could foresee the destruction of Jerusalem and its temple, he first preached repentance to the exiled Jews, demanding a change in their old practices of pagan idol worship. He followed this harsh message with the hope of deliverance and restoration to their homeland, emphasizing a future time of bounteous blessing.

For partial fulfillment of these prophecies, historians point to the times that Nebuchadnezzar laid siege to Jerusalem, completely destroying it by fire, confiscating all the temple treasures for his own temple god, and bringing captive Jews back to Babylon.

Even though the Bible tells little about Ezekiel's personal life, we know that he played a major public role in restoring the Jewish people. Not only did Ezekiel call them to repentance in their period of unfaithfulness to God, but he gave them hope of a future restoration—one that was national and eternal, as well as personal and temporal.

For further study, see the Book of Ezekiel.

EZER (EE zuhr) *help*
1. 20 century B.C.; Gen 36:21; Horite chief; lived in Seir during Esau's time
2. 19 century B.C.; 1Ch 7:21; son of Ephraim; killed when caught stealing cattle
3. 1Ch 4:4; descendant of Judah
4. 11 century B.C.; 1Ch 12:9; Gadite chief who joined David at Ziklag
5. 5 century B.C.; Ne 3:19; Levite; son of Jeshua 7; helped fix Jerusalem walls
6. 5 century B.C.; Ne 12:42; musician/priest at Jerusalem wall dedication

EZORA (eh ZOR uh) meaning unknown; 1Esd 9:34; ancestor of some who married foreigners

Ezra reads the Law. Wall painting from Dura Europos, one of the earliest known synagogues, approximately 245

EZRA (EZ ruh) *help* or *helper*
1. Ne 12:1; priest; refugee from Exile; also called Azariah 24
2. 5 century B.C.; Ezr 7:1

Ezra's lineage can be traced back to the priestly Hebrew tribe, the Levites, with the high priest Aaron as one of his forefathers. He was a dedicated teacher who devoted himself to the study and observance of the Law. But the Bible first places him in Babylon under the reign of a foreign king. He was part of the exiled Jews who remained captive in Babylon for 70 years after their sacred city of Jerusalem was destroyed and the temple was burned down. In 539 B.C., King Cyrus of Persia conquered Babylon and then allowed the Jews to return to Jerusalem, where they restored the city and the temple under the leadership of Nehemiah.

A small group of exiles remained in Babylon, however, either because they knew no other homeland or because they had influential positions that they were unwilling to give up. Ezra was part of this remnant and probably one of those holding an official position. He not only kept the remnant on track spiritually, but he organized a financial support group to help their comrades in Jerusalem with their rebuilding efforts. He was even able to procure support from the king himself.

After helping his homeland by proxy for many years, Ezra himself returned to Jerusalem with approximately 5000 other Jews. They took with them gold, silver, and sacred articles for the temple. Ezra was hesitant to ask the king for the protection of soldiers and horsemen on their journey because he had once told him of God's ability to protect and care for those who followed him. So in humility, Ezra proclaimed a fast prior to setting off on his 900-mile trip "so that we might humble ourselves before our God and ask him for a safe journey" (Ezr 8:21).

Three days after Ezra's group arrived in Jerusalem, the treasures were delivered to the temple and burnt offerings were sacrificed to God. Ezra then began his central purpose for coming to Jerusalem—to restore temple worship and observance of the Law. But Ezra soon faced the greatest moral and religious crisis of this restoration period. He met with a group of concerned leaders who told how the Israelites had married people from the neighboring countries and adopted foreign "detestable practices" in direct violation of God's commands. Upon hearing this news of Israel's unfaithfulness, Ezra was so appalled that he tore his clothes and pulled hair from his head and beard. What followed was an anguished prayer for his people in penitence for their corporate sins. As he demonstrated his concern for his sinful nation, a group of repentant people joined him, ultimately deciding that all mixed marriages should be abandoned, thus restoring the exclusiveness of the Israelites.

In the cold and rain, the Hebrew people assembled at the square in front of the temple to hear Ezra speak. In a sermon that was short and to the point, he cited the people's sins, instructing them to confess and separate from their foreign spouses. The people were saddened by this edict but were undoubtedly prepared for the message since all but four immediately affirmed their agreement with Ezra. Judges were appointed to handle the divorce proceedings, which took about three months. A total of 113 Jews had become involved in mixed marriages with unbelieving Gentiles. While this is only a small portion of the many returned exiles, roughly a fourth of the offenders were religious leaders who were obligated to set an example for their community.

As marriages were dissolved, guilt offerings were presented in keeping with the Law. Though painful in its administration, Ezra's purge of foreigners was considered successful by the Israelites since it preserved their national identity and religious adherence to the Law for one more generation.

No record exists of Ezra's activities for the next 13 years, but during the time of the Jewish governor Nehemiah, Ezra began to fulfill his original purpose in coming to Jerusalem. He began to establish the Law among the people as the basis for their daily lives. At an assembly at the square in front of the Water Gate, Ezra took out the Scriptures he had brought with him from Babylon. Standing above the people in clear sight of everyone, he began to read aloud. So attentive were the people that he read continually from sunrise until noon. His audience was so moved by what he read that they wept openly, lifting their hands and shouting, "Amen! Amen!" The crowd became so emotional that Governor Nehemiah encouraged them to go home and get something to eat and drink, for it was not a day to grieve but to rejoice in the strength of the Lord. The people did eat and drink and turn their sadness to joy, returning the next day for more of Ezra's instruction.

Through Ezra's teaching, the Hebrew people were motivated to repent of their national sins and renew their obedience to God. Along with Ezra's reform concerning mixed marriages, the people also returned to a strict observance of the Sabbath, a reinstitution of the Sabbatical Year, and a reinstitution of temple tithes and offerings. The people also renewed their religious festivals and enthusiastically built booths to live in during the seven-day Feast of the Tabernacle.

Ezra played a major role in reestablishing Israel after the Exile in Babylon. On returning to Jerusalem, the nation was united—physically due to the efforts of Nehemiah, and spiritually due to Ezra's efforts.

For further study, see the books of Ezra and Nehemiah.

EZRAH (EZ ruh) *help;* 1Ch 4:17; descendant of Judah

EZRI (EZ rye) *my help;* 10 century B.C.; 1Ch 27:26; farm overseer for David's royal lands

FELIX (FEE liks) *happy;* 1 century A.D.; Ac 23:24

As the Roman governor of Judea, Felix had influence with the Roman courts and was tyrannical in suppressing Zealots and Sicarri (assassins), but he was also corrupt and easily bribed. Living in Caesarea, the administrative center of Roman rule in Palestine, Felix was insulated from heavy Roman influence in his governorship.

When the apostle Paul was falsely accused by the Jews of violating temple laws, he appeared before Felix to be judged. Felix made no decision on the trumped up charges but held Paul in custody for the remaining two years of his rule, hoping to be offered a bribe for the apostle's release. When Felix was recalled to Rome, his successor Festus inherited custody of Paul. For further study, see Ac 23–24.

FESTUS (FES tuhs) *joyful;* 1 century A.D.; Ac 24:47

Porcius Festus was a competent Roman governor of Judea. With this position, he inherited the case of the apostle Paul, who was accused of misconduct by the Jews and held in custody for two years. Hearing the case along with King Herod Agrippa II and Herod's sister Bernice, Festus clearly saw Paul's innocence. However, when Paul spoke of Christ and the resurrection, Festus responded "Paul, you are mad; your great learning is turning you mad" (Ac 26:23-24). Although Festus would have released him, Paul invoked his right as a Roman citizen to have Caesar hear his charges. So, Festus had no choice but to send him to Rome for trial. For further study, see Ac 24:27–26:32.

FORTUNE (FOHR choon) Isa 65:11; heathen god worshiped by Israelites, along with Destiny

FORTUNATUS (FOHR choo NAH tuhs) *fortunate;* 1 century A.D.; 1Co 16:17; Corinthian Christian; visited Paul in Rome

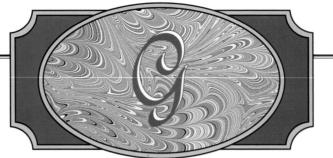

GAAL (GAY uhl) *scarab* or *loathing;* 12 century B.C.; Jdg 9:26; man of Shechem; rebelled against Abimelech

GABAEL (GAH bah el) meaning unknown
1. Tob 1:1; ancestor of Tobit
2. Tob 4:1; relative of Tobit who stored 10 silver talents

GABBAI (GAB eye) *collector;* 5 century B.C.; Ne 11:8; Benjaminite; returned to Jerusalem after Exile

GABRI (GAY brye) meaning unknown; Tob 1:14; brother of Gabael 2

GABRIAS (GA bree uhs) meaning unknown; Tob 4:20; father of Gabael 2

GABRIEL (GAB rih el) *God is a warrior;* Da 8:16

The angel Gabriel makes three dramatic appearances in the Bible: to Daniel, to interpret visions of the future for the distraught prophet in Babylon; to Zechariah, the aged priest on duty in the temple, to announce that his wife would give birth to John the Baptist; and to the young virgin Mary, to announce that she would carry the Christ child. All three appearances are linked to the coming Messiah. Gabriel is also traditionally considered the angel who will trumpet Christ's return and who holds the key to the bottomless pit at the Last Judgment. In apocryphal and Jewish folklore, Gabriel is linked with many Old Testament events (the finding of Joseph's brothers, the burial of Moses, the slaughter of Assyrians) and is linked with the angels Michael, Raphael, and Uriel. For further study, see Da 8:16-27; 9:20-27; Lk 1:11-38; 1Th 4:16; Rev 9:1; 20:1.

GAD (GAD) *good fortune*
1. 20 century B.C.; Gen 30:11

The angel Gabriel. Gerard David (1460–1523).

Gad was the seventh son of the Jewish patriarch Jacob by Zilpah, the maidservant of Jacob's wife Leah. Gad's younger full brother was Asher, but he had ten other half brothers. The events of Gad's life are intertwined with the story of his whole family. He was involved with selling his brother Joseph, and later he accompanied his family to Egypt. On his deathbed, Jacob blessed all his sons, bestowing on Gad a future as an excellent raider. Gad's descendants, one of the 12 tribes of Israel, were successful at raiding and acquiring extensive territories. For further study, see Gen 35:26; 46:16; 49:19; Ex 1:4; Dt 33: 20, 21.
2. 11 century B.C.; 1Sa 22:5; prophet and advisor to David

GADARENES (gad uh REENZ) Mt 8:28; residents of Gadara, a Greek city and capital of Perea

GADDI (GAD dih) *my fortune*
1. 15 century B.C.; Nu 13:11; leader of tribe of Manasseh; explored Canaan
2. 1Mac 2:2; see John 3

GADDIEL (GAD ee uhl) *fortune of God;* 15 century B.C.; Nu 13:10; Zebulun tribal leader who explored Canaan

GADI (GAH dih) *my fortune;* 8 century B.C.; 2Ki 15:14; Manassite leader who explored Canaan

GADITES (GAD ights) Nu 2:14
The Gadites were members of the Israelite tribe founded by Jacob's son Gad. They settled east of Jordan in the region known as Gilead, between the Sea of Galilee and the Dead Sea.

GAHAM (GAY ham) *burning;* 21 century B.C.; Gen 22:24; son of Nahor; nephew of Abraham

GAHAR (GAY hahr) *hiding place;* Ezr 2:47; ancestor of temple servants who returned to Judah

GAI (GAY ee) meaning unknown; 5 century B.C.; AddEst 2:8; eunuch in charge of Esther

GAIUS (GAY yuhs) *commended*
1. 1 century A.D.; Ac 19:29; Paul's companion; seized in riot in Ephesus
2. 1 century A.D.; Ac 20:4; Christian from Derbe; traveled with Paul
3. 1 century A.D.; Ro 16:23; Corinthian Christian who housed Paul
4. 1 century A.D.; 1Co 1:14; Corinthian baptized by Paul; possibly Gaius 3
5. 1 century A.D.; 3Jn 1:1; addressee of John's third letter

GALAL (GAY lal) *rolling*
1. 5 century B.C.; 1Ch 9:15; Levite; returned to Jerusalem after Exile

2. 1Ch 9:16; ancestor of Obadiah 11 the returnee to Jerusalem after Exile

GALATIANS (guh LAY shih uhns) Ac 16:6; Gallic, Celtic, and Roman inhabitants of Galatia (in modern Turkey)

GALILEANS (gal uh LEE uhns) Jos 12:23; inhabitants (mostly Gentile) of Galilee in northern Palestine, who were despised by Jews

GALLIO (GAL ee oh) *who lives on milk;* 1 century A.D.; Ac 18:12; proconsul of Achaia; refused to try Paul in Corinth

GAMAEL (GAHM ah uhl) meaning unknown; 1Esd 8:29; ancestor of leaders returning from Exile

GAMALIEL (guh MAY lee uhl) *God is my reward*
1. 15 century B.C.; Nu 1:10; Manassite leader during the Exodus
2. 1 century A.D.; Ac 5:34
Studying under his grandfather, the great Rabbi Hillel, Gamaliel became one of the most respected scholars of religious teachings in his day. His interpretations and applications of the Law tended to be merciful and tolerant, putting him at the head of the liberal movement within the Pharisees. Another great legal mind of the time was Shammai, who led

Entrance to the tomb of Rabbi Gamaliel in Beth Shearim.

Gamaliel and Paul. Stained glass. Hugenot Memorial Church, Pelham, New York.

the Sadducees in a stricter, more literal view of Hebrew Law.

When the apostles Peter and John were brought to the court of the Sanhedrin for preaching Christian doctrine in the temple, Gamaliel convinced his fellow priests to release them. He argued that if Jesus were a false prophet, the Christian movement would self-destruct, as had all the other movements that sprang up around pseudo-messiahs, but if Jesus and his teachings truly came from God, the Sanhedrin would never be able to stop the spread of the Gospel.

Gamaliel is also known as a one-time teacher of Saul, the Pharisee who relentlessly persecuted Christians until God intervened to make him one of the church's leading evangelists. Gamaliel's religious and legal thinking is still respected today by Jewish scholars. The Talmud (a collection of Jewish commentary from A.D. 200–600) says, "Since the Rabban Gamaliel died, the glory of the Law has ceased." For further study, see Ac 5:33-42; 22:3.

GAMUL (GAY mul) *rewarded;* 11 century B.C.; 1Ch 24:17; appointed head of the priests in David's day

GAREB (GAIR eb) *scabrous;* 11 century B.C.; 2Sa 23:38; one of David's mighty men

GAS (GAS) meaning unknown; 1Esd 5:34; ancestor of family returning from Exile with Zerubbabel

GATAM (GAY tuhm) *puny;* 19 century B.C.; Gen 36:11; son of Eliphaz 2; grandson of Esau

GAZERA (gah ZEE rah) meaning unknown; 1Esd 5:31; ancestor of temple servants returning from Exile

GAZEZ (GAY ziz) *shearer*
1. 1Ch 2:46; son of Caleb; descendant of Judah
2. 1Ch 2:46; grandson of Caleb

GAZITES (GAY zights) Jdg 16:2; inhabitants of Gaza, a Canaanite city that later became a part of Philistia

GAZZAM (GAZ uhm) *consuming;* Ezr 2:48; ancestor of temple servants who returned to Judah after Exile

GEBALITES (GHEE buhl ights) Jos 13:5; people from Gebal, a seaport in north Phoenicia famous for trade and books

GEBER (GEE buhr) *man* or *strong one;* 10 century B.C.; 1Ki 4:19; a district governor Solomon appointed over Gilead

GEDALIAH (gad uh LYE uh) *the Lord is great*
1. 11 century B.C.; 1Ch 25:3; music minister at temple in David's time
2. Zep 1:1; ancestor of prophet Zephaniah
3. 7 century B.C.; Jer 38:1; an official who threw Jeremiah into cistern
4. 6 century B.C.; 2Ki 25:22

Gedaliah was a peace advocate who supported the prophet Jeremiah instead of deporting him. After the fall of Jerusalem to Babylon, this governor of Judah made Mizpah his headquarters. Gedaliah urged his fellow Jews to accommodate themselves to life under Babylonian rule; his moderate policies attracted throngs of peaceful settlers to the land of Judah. However, his term was cut short after only two months in office when the radical Ishmael and his thugs assassinated the politically moderate Gedaliah and his supporters. With the death of Gedaliah, the Jews who had remained in Judah fled Babylonian rule and settled in Egypt. Gedaliah's death is now commemorated on October 7 as a Jewish day of fasting. For further study, see 2Ki 25:22-26; Jer 40–41.

5. 5 century B.C.; Ezr 10:18; priest; married and divorced foreigner after Exile

GEDDUR (GEH dur) meaning unknown; 1Esd 5:30; ancestor of returning temple servants

GEDERITES (GHED uh rights) 1Ch 27:28; inhabitants of Geder, a Canaanite city near Debir

GEDOR (GHEE dohr) *wall*
1. 1Ch 4:4; son of Penuel; descendant of Judah
2. 1Ch 4:18; descendant of Judah
3. 11 century B.C.; 1Ch 8:31; Benjaminite; son of Jeiel 2; uncle of King Saul

GEHAZI (guh HAY zee) *valley of vision;* 9 century B.C.; 2Ki 4:12

To repay a Shunammite woman for hospitality shown toward his master Elisha, Gehazi told Elisha that the woman wished for a child. With Elisha's blessing, the woman and her elderly husband were able to conceive. She gave birth to a son the next year, only to see that child fall sick and die. Gehazi was commissioned to revive the son, but when his efforts failed, Elisha intervened and restored the boy to life.

Later, Gehazi exhibited deceit and dishonesty in dealing with Naaman, the Syrian army commander healed of leprosy by Elisha. Although Elisha had refused any payment for healing the soldier, the enterprising Gehazi implied otherwise and accepted Naaman's generous gift for himself. When Elisha found out, Gehazi lost his chance to succeed Elisha, and he and his descendants were cursed with leprosy.

For further study, see 2Ki 4–5.

GEMALLI (guh MAL ih) *camel driver;* 15 century B.C.; Nu 13:12; father of Ammiel 1 the explorer of Canaan

GEMARIAH (gem uh RYE uh) *the Lord has accomplished*
1. 7 century B.C.; Jer 36:10; official who urged Jehoiakim to preserve Jeremiah's scroll
2. 7 century B.C.; Jer 29:3; emissary who took Jeremiah's message to exiles in Babylon

GENNAEUS (jen NAY ee uhs) meaning unknown; 2 century B.C.; 2Mac 12:2; father of Apollonius the Syrian governor and general

GENTILES (JEN tyelz) Mt 4:15

Greeks, barbarians, and all other foreigners were called Gentiles by the Jews to distinguish them as outside the Jewish covenant with God. For further study, see Mt 15:21-28: Mk 7:24-30; Lk 7:1-10; Ac 10; 15; Ro 1:13-16; Eph 2:14; Col 3:11

GENUBATH (guh NOO bath) meaning unknown; 10 century B.C.; 1Ki 11:20; son of Hadad the Edomite; nephew of Pharaoh of Egypt

GERA (GEER uh) meaning unknown
1. 19 century B.C.; Gen 46:21; son of Benjamin
2. 19 century B.C.; 1Ch 8:3; son of Bela; grandson of Benjamin
3. 19 century B.C.; 1Ch 8:5; son of Bela; grandson of Benjamin
4. 14 century B.C.; Jdg 3:15; Benjaminite father of Ehud the judge
5. 11 century B.C.; 2Sa 16:5; ancestor of David's opponent Shimei

GERASENES (GAIR uh seens) Mk 5:1; inhabitants of an area near the Sea of Galilee, whose chief city was Gerasa

GERSHOM (GUHR shuhm) possibly *an alien there*
1. 1Ch 6:1; see Gershon
2. 15 century B.C.; Ex 2:22; son of Moses by Zipporah
3. Jdg 18:30; the head of a family of fraudulent Danite priests; possibly Gershom 2
4. 5 century B.C.; Ezr 8:2; descendant of Phinehas; returned to Judah after Exile

GERSHOMITES (GUHR shuhm ights) 1Ch 6:62; descendants of Gershom the son of Moses; akin to sons of Eliezer

GERSHON (GUHR shuhn) meaning unknown; 19 century B.C.; Gen 46:11; son of Levi; also called Gershom 1

GERSHONITES (GUHR shuhn ights) Nu 3:21; descendants of Gershon the son of Levi; lived at north end of Jordan River

GESHAN (GESH uhn) *firm;* 1Ch 2:47; descendant of Judah

GESHEM (GESH uhm) *rainstorm;* 5 century B.C.; Ne 2:19; Arabian enemy of Nehemiah; opposed building Jerusalem wall

GESHURITES (GESH yoo rights)
1. Dt 3:14; inhabitants of Geshur, an Aramean kingdom east of the Jordan River
2. 1Sa 27:8; a people living south of Philistia near Sinai; raided by King David

GETHER (GEE thuhr) *fear;* Gen 10:23; son of Aram; great-grandson of Noah

GEUEL (GOO uhl) *majesty of God;* 15 century B.C.; Nu 13:15; leader of tribe of Gad; explored land of Canaan

GIBBAR (GIB ahr) *mighty;* Ezr 2:20; ancestral head of family that returned to Judah

GIBEA (GIB ee uh) *hill* or *highlander;* 1Ch 2:49; grandson of Caleb

GIBEONITES (GIB ee uhn ights) Jos 10:6; inhabitants of Gibeon, a Hivite (Canaanite) city; tricked Joshua into a peace treaty

GIDDALTI (guh DAL tih) *I have magnified* [God]; 11 century B.C.; 1Ch 25:4; son of Heman; temple musician under David

Gideon's triumphant battle against the superior forces of the Midianites.

GIDDEL (GID uhl) *very great*
1. Ezr 2:47; temple servant whose descendants returned to Judah after the Exile
2. 10 century B.C.; Ezr 2:56; Solomon's servant whose descendants returned to Judah after the Exile

GIDEON (GID ee uhn) *cutter* or *hewer*
1. 12 century B.C.; Jdg 6:11
Although Gideon was one of the 12 judges, he did not lead or rule Israel in the same way that some of the other judges did. A meek farmer from a lesser tribe, he led an unusual military campaign to rid the Hebrews of the Midianites, a nomadic tribe that raided and plundered at will throughout Canaan.

Gideon was selected by an angel of God to show his people that their plight stemmed from their turning away from God in favor of idol worship. The angel instructed Gideon to destroy the temples erected to the pagan god Baal and his consort in the city of Ophrah. Fearful of reprisals from his countrymen, Gideon carried out the destruction at night in secret. Although he was found out and threatened with death, his father intervened and convinced the crowd to spare him.

After that incident, Gideon raised an army to combat the Midianites. Lacking confidence, he asked for a sign of victory from God—that a fleece left on the threshing room floor overnight would gather dew on it while the floor remained dry. After receiving this sign, he was still doubtful and so asked for another confirmation—this time that the fleece would remain dry while the floor gathered dew. This done, God imposed a test on Gideon's faith, ordering him to reduce the size of his army to a mere 300 men so that all would know their victory came from God rather than from their military might. Facing a force of thousands, Gideon's men surrounded the Midianite camp at night and sowed confusion by simultaneously blaring trumpets and breaking pottery jars. Frightened and misled by the tumult, the Midianites fled from what they thought was a superior force, and Israel was freed from their plundering.

After the victory, Gideon was offered kingship but declined, taking instead a hoard of gold. Ironically, he fashioned the booty into an ephod, a pagan image that the people began to worship. He had been commissioned to lead his people away from idolatry and back to God; while he did so

briefly, his success was short-lived. Still, Gideon is celebrated as a hero of faith from early on (Ps 83:11; Isa 9:4; 10:26; Heb 11:32). His story is traditionally viewed as one of the prime examples of relying on the power of God even when circumstances and common sense might dictate another course of action.

For further study, see Jdg 6–8.
2. Jdt 8:4; ancestor of Judith

GIDEONI (gid ee OH nee) *hewer;* 15 century B.C.; Nu 1:11; father of Abidan the leader of the Benjaminites during the Exodus

GILALAI (guh LAY lih) *weighty;* 5 century B.C.; Ne 12:36; priest/musician at Jerusalem wall dedication

GILEAD (GIL ee ad) *rocky*
1. 19 century B.C.; Nu 26:29; grandson of Manasseh; source of Gileadite clan
2. 12 century B.C.; Jdg 11:1; father of judge Jephthah
3. 1Ch 5:14; descendant of Gad

GILEADITES (GIL ee ad ights) Nu 26:29; descendants of Jacob's son Gilead; settled mountainous Trans-Jordan area

GINATH (GIH nath) *garden;* 10 century B.C.; 1Ki 16:21; father of Tibni the challenger for the Israelite throne

GINETHOI (GIN uh thoy) *gardener;* 5 century B.C.; Ne 12:4; chief priest who returned to Jerusalem after Exile; possibly Ginnethon

GINNETHON (GIN uh thahn) *gardener;* 5 century B.C.; Ne 10:6; priest; sealed covenant renewal with God; possibly Ginethoi

GIRGASHITES (GUR guh shights) Gen 10:16; a Canaanite tribe; locale unknown

GIRZITES (GUHR zights) 1Sa 27:8; Canaanites of Gezer (central Palestine); conquered by Joshua

GISHPA (GISH puh) meaning unknown; 5 century B.C.; Ne 11:21; Levite in charge of temple servants under Nehemiah

God the eternal father. Giovanni Guercino (1591–1666).

GITTITES (GIT tights) 2Sa 15:18; giants of Gath, a Philistine city; befriended and conquered by David

GOD (GAHD) Gen 1:1

The biblical narrative is the story of God and his dealings with humanity. From Genesis ("In the beginning when God created...") to Revelation ("I am the Alpha and the Omega"), God is pictured as the beginning and the end of history—its Creator, Sustainer, and Redeemer. No formal definition of God exists in the Bible. Nor do any of its authors argue specifically for his existence, which is assumed throughout Scripture. Yet the central personality and driving force in biblical literature is unmistakably God himself.

The biblical picture of God unfolds in his dealings with people. We see him as a compassionate creator concerned about Adam's loneliness and as a shaper of history who called Abraham to faith. God revealed himself both as a moral authority, thundering from Mt. Sinai, and as a glad father, proudly watching the baptism of Jesus his son. Although something of God's character can be known through his many recorded interactions with people, Scripture tells us that no one can fully know him in essence. That is because God is limitless—higher than the heavens, deeper than the earth, and too glorious to comprehend.

The Bible speaks not only of his great love and mercy but also of his terrible anger and flattening judgments that resound through history. God calls some people to himself, yet turns his back on others. He blesses, he curses, and he even changes his mind in response to human behavior. God is described as perfect, unchangeable, holy, and good.

Even so, we are left with many questions: Is this God capricious, or is he consistent and trustworthy? What do those in Scripture say about him? And what does God say about himself?

In conversation with a Samaritan woman, Jesus affirmed "God is spirit" (Jn 4:24) meaning infinite spirit—without the limitations of his created beings. The Psalmist testifies that in relation to time, God is eternal; in relation to space, he is everywhere; in relation to the universe, he is both within it and outside it (Ps 139). Isaiah says that although God is present and powerful within the world, he is beyond and above it all as its Creator and Judge (Isa 40:12-17).

God is also described as a personal being with moral character traits we can relate to. Some attributes of the divine personality parallel attributes that humans (made in God's image) possess—such as wisdom, truth, goodness, righteousness, justice, anger, and love. The Bible testifies repeatedly to such divine characteristics. For example, David cannot say enough about God's goodness (Ps 31:19), and the Hebrew prophets decry oppression and warn of a just God who will punish wrongs.

However, God also has divine perfections that are not like anything in human form. For example: self-existence, complete and absolute knowledge, unchangeableness, the ability to be wholly present everywhere all the time—there is no human counterpart to these divine attributes. God's creative power, another of his attributes, is unlike limited human power. God can—and did—make a world out of nothing, just by the creative energy of his spoken word.

Perhaps the one attribute of God that most sets him apart from his creation is that of perfect holiness. Because he alone is holy and pure, he delights in goodness and hates evil. This holy God has a design for all of life. God acts both sovereignly to bring about his purposes and passively to allow circumstances to take their course; either way, his actions are consistent with his holy, loving character.

However, when God created human beings, he gave them free will to make real choices with natural consequences. God respects the human will and interacts with it. Since Adam and Eve, humans have sometimes chosen evil over good in exercising this free will. The endless stuggle within every human being creates a struggle between humanity and God that defines their relationship. Nevertheless, all choices in this life come under the authority and will of God—as does the ultimate fate of humanity.

God proved himself sovereign over the chaos of sin, deception, and death as recorded in Genesis. He disciplined his wayward people and restored Israel from Exile as prophesied by Isaiah and Jeremiah. God was the power behind the phenomenal spread of Christianity throughout the known world of the first century as seen in the Acts of the Apostles. He is also the victor in the consummation of history as recorded in Revelation.

God's covenant with Israel, especially his promises to David, nurtured fervent expectations for a messiah or redeemer-king to be born from the line of David. The New Testament sees Jesus of Nazareth as that long-anticipated Messiah and universal Savior. The biblical accounts of Jesus's life, death, and resurrection show God's hand entering human history in the most direct way possible. The death of his Son was the deepest expression of God's love for sinful humanity; in effect, he sacrificed himself to allow humanity the chance to redeem itself.

Prophets of Old and New Testaments confirm that God gives his people "a future with hope" (Jer 29:11). The apocalyptic imagery of John in Revelation reveals that God will even bring "a new heaven and a new earth" (Rev 21:1). Such imagery calls to mind the loveliness of creation before that picture was destroyed by sin. By coupling what is yet to be with what has already been, the Bible makes it evident that the whole of history lies within the purview and purpose of God.

God is known in Scripture by many titles or descriptions. The following list borrows insight from the actual words in Hebrew and Greek that the Bible uses to describe him. This list is merely suggestive; a further look at each title will provide more insight into the nature of God:

(1) GOD. In both Hebrew (*elohim*) and Greek (*theos*), the words for God are broad terms that can refer to pagan deities as well as to the God of Israel. Although the Hebrew term is plural, implying fullness or richness, it is used with singular verbs. The singular Hebrew term *el* is less commonly used, possibly because El was also the name of a Canaanite god. However, it is sometimes used in poetry to describe the God of Israel. On occasion, it is coupled with a second word or phrase to form a

> ➤ ᛕ
>
> *"'I am the Alpha and the Omega,' says the Lord God, who is and who was and who is to come, the Almighty. "*
>
> Rev 1:8

special title, such as "God Most High" (El elyon, Gen 14:18-20) or "God Almighty" (El shaddai, Gen 17:1).

(2) YAHWEH. Usually translated "the Lord" and sometimes "Jehovah," this is by far the most distinctive and popular term for God in the Hebrew Scriptures. Yahweh is the personal name of God. When the name originated, it consisted of four consonants (*YHWH* or *JHVH*). By the third century B.C., it was thought too holy to be spoken aloud, so the Hebrew word for Lord (*Adonai*) was substituted. The name Jehovah was created by combining the consonants *JHVH* with the Hebrew vowel sounds of *Adonai*.

Appearing more than 6800 times in the Bible, the name Yahweh was first revealed to Moses from the burning bush (Ex 3:11-15). That incident of special self-revelation ("I am who I am") provides insight into God's holy nature, his independent existence, and his active presence throughout history.

Memorable places and altars were named after Jehovah, commemorating his role in biblical events. Abraham named the place where his faith was most severely tested Jehovah-jireh, meaning "the Lord provides" (Gen 22:14). After defeating the Amalekites, Moses built an altar and called it Jehovah-nissi, meaning "the Lord is my banner" (Ex 17:15).

(3) THE LORD OF HOSTS. Aware of the power of this title, the Hebrew prophets, particularly Jeremiah, used it often. This psalmist also speaks of Yahweh in this regard as the great Savior and Protector of his people (Ps 24:10).

(4) LORD GOD OF ISRAEL. Deborah the judge used this title in her song of victory (Jdg 5:3) and it was frequently used by other prophets to emphasize Israel's unique relationship with God.

(5) THE HOLY ONE OF ISRAEL. This favorite of Isaiah's titles for God is also found in the Book of Jeremiah and the Psalms; similarly, Samuel speaks of "the Mighty One of Israel" and "the Glory of Israel" (1Sa 15:29).

(6) ANCIENT ONE. The prophet Daniel used this phrase to picture God on his throne, judging the great empires of the world (Da 7:9,13,22).

GOG (GAHG) *mountain*
1. 1Ch 5:4; descendant of Reuben
2. Eze 38:3; prince of Magog; leader of army in Ezekiel's prophecies; see Magog

GOLIATH (goh LY uth) *exile* or *soothsayer*
1. 11 century B.C.; 1Sa 17:4

Goliath was likely one of those legendary "descendants of Anak" (Nu 13:28) or Nephilim ("giants of the earth") that loomed large and persistently haunted the advance of Israel into Canaan. This professional warrior hailed from Gath, an old Canaanite city in Judah, whose residents were called Gittites. Among the Gittites were the Anakim, warriors known for their extraordinary height. At more than nine feet tall ("six cubits and a span," 1Sa 17:4), Goliath stood out from the rest.

Tall and bold, Goliath paraded along the valley stream that separated the Philistine army from King Saul and his army. Neither side dared attack each other wholesale, and no Israelite dared accept Goliath's challenge of one-on-one combat to settle the conflict. After 40 days, the shepherd boy David arrived with provisions

Creation of the Sun and Moon. Michelangelo (1475–1564), Sistine Chapel, Rome.

David slays the Philistine warrior Goliath.

for his brothers in Saul's army and accepted Goliath's challenge. Relying on his faith in God, he marched into battle unprotected by armor and slew the giant with a stone from a sling. As David took the fallen Goliath's head with his own sword, the Philistines fled in panic.

For further study, see Gen 6:4; 1Sa 21:9; 22:10.
2. 11 century B.C.; 2Sa 21:19; possibly son of Goliath 1

GOMER (GOH muhr) *ember* or *completion*
1. Gen 10:2; son of Japheth
2. 8 century B.C.; Hos 1:3

When the Hebrew prophet Hosea was told by God to marry a prostitute, he chose Gomer, and she repeatedly and openly cuckolded him. She gave birth to three children, to whom the Lord gave names that symbolized his displeasure with Israel. Gomer left her family, prostituting herself with any man who had money to spend. Finally, she sold herself into slavery as a mistress. God told Hosea to bring Gomer home. When he discovered her, weak and ill, Hosea purchased Gomer from her owner and accepted her back as his wife. Gomer's adultery symbolized Israel's abandonment of God for idols of stone and metal, and her children's names symbolized God's anger toward the Hebrew people. As an illustration of God's promise to love Israel back to faithfulness, Hosea and Gomer's reconciliation was marked not by judgment but by love. For further study, see Hos 1–3.

GORGIAS (GOR gee us) meaning unknown; 2 century B.C.; 1Mac 3:38

In the middle of the second century B.C., the Seleucid king Antiochus IV conquered Israel and outlawed Jewish religious practices. In a rebellion known as the Maccabean revolt, pious Jews fought for their faith. Three "friends of the king" were each given command of 40,000 Seleucid troops and assigned to wipe the Jews from the land of Israel. Afterward, Antiochus intended to enslave the Israelites and settle Judea with more cooperative subjects. One of these commanders, Gorgias, tried to attack the Jews' camp at night. However, they had been forewarned and fled. Although the Jews were outnumbered, their leader, Judas Maccabeus, spurred them on, saying, "Then [the Seleucids] will know . . . there is one who redeems and saves Israel." The Jews attacked their former pursuers at dawn, routing Gorgias's troops and chasing them for miles. For further study, see 1Mac 3:38–4:18.

GOTHOLIAH (goth uh LYE ah) meaning unknown; 1Esd 8:33; father of one who returned after the Exile

GOTHONIEL (go THON ih el) meaning unknown; Jdt 6:15; father of magistrate at trial of Achior

GREEKS (GREEKS) Da 8:21

The Greeks were an Indo-European people of the southeast Mediterranean. Their pagon religion, sophisticated culture, and powerful military force dominated the Middle East between the fourth and second centuries B.C. For further study, see Jn 7:35; Ro 1:13-16; Ac 17–21; 1Co 1; 1Mac 1; 8–10; 2Mac 4–6; 11.

GUNI (GOO nih) *colored*
1. 19 century B.C.; Gen 46:24; son of Naphtali; descendant of Jacob
2. 1Ch 5:15; descendant of Gad

HAAHASHTARI (HAY uh HASH tuh rye) *courier;* 1Ch 4:6; son of Ashhur and descendant of Judah

HABAIAH (hah BYE ah) *the Lord has hidden;* Ezr 2:61; father of excommunicated priests; form of Hobaiah

HABAKKUK (huh BAK uhk) *embracer* or *wrestler;* 7 century B.C.; Hab 1:1

The author of the Book of Habakkuk wrestled with a problem commonly raised in the Bible—why does God allow evil in the world? Habakkuk's ultimate answer to this age-old question was that God brings judgment and punishment on all evildoers in the end. This prophet saw Israel practicing corruption and injustice and predicted its defeat and enslavement by the Babylonians in 597 B.C. as God's judgment of them. Further, he saw that God's justice would eventually cause the Babylonians to fall due to their wickedness and idolatry. Habakkuk saw God as the judge of all humans and saw history as a testimony to God's final, if not immediate, judgments. Habakkuk also composed a psalm extolling the virtues of his own encounter with God. For further study, see the Book of Habakkuk.

HABAZZINIAH (HAB uh zuh NIGH uh) meaning unknown; 7 century B.C.; Jer 35:3; grandfather of Jaazaniah 4

HACALIAH (HAK uh LYE uh) *darkness of the Lord;* 5 century B.C.; Ne 1:1; father of Nehemiah

HACHMONI (HAK moh nih) *wise;* 1Ch 11:11; family of Jehiel and caretakers for David's sons

HACHRATHEUS (hak RAY thee uhs) meaning unknown; 5 century B.C.; AddEst 4:5; eunuch attending Esther

HADAD (HAY dad) *thunderer*
1. Gen 25:15; son of Ishmael; grandson of Abraham
2. Gen 36:35; pre-Israelite king who succeeded Husham
3. 10 century B.C.; 1Ki 11:14; Edomite; enemy of Solomon

HADAD-RIMMON (HAY dad RIM muhn) Zec 12:11; Assyrian god of vegetation and stormy weather

HADADEZER (HAY dad EE zuhr) *Hadad is help;* 11 century B.C.; 2Sa 8:3; King of Zobah whom David defeated

HADAR (HAY dahr) meaning unknown; Gen 36:39; ruler of Edom; succeeded Baal-hanan

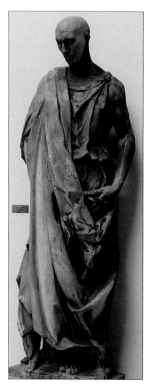

The prophet Habakkuk. Donatello (1386–1466), Cathedral of Florence.

HADASSAH (huh DAS uh) *myrtle;* 5 century B.C.; Est 2:7; either Esther's Hebrew name or a title given her, meaning *bride*

HADLAI (HAD lye) meaning unknown; 8 century B.C.; 2Ch 28:12; father of Amasa the Ephraimite leader

HADORAM (huh DOHR uhm) *Hadad* [a god] *is exalted*
1. Gen 10:27; son of Joktan; ancestor of unidentified Arabian tribe
2. 10 century B.C.; 1Ch 18:10; son of Tou; brought father's congratulatory gift to David; also called Joram 2
3. 2Ch 10:18; see Adoniram

HAGAB (HAY gab) *locust;* Ezr 2:46; ancestor of temple servants who returned to Judah

HAGABA (HAG uh buh) *locust;* Ne 7:48; ancestor of exiles who returned to Judah; form of Hagabah

HAGABAH Ezr 2:45; see Hagaba

HAGAR (HAY gahr) *one who flees* or *flight;* 22 century B.C.; Gen 16:1

Hagar served the Old Testament patriarch Abraham and his wife, Sarah. Her life was grim, like that of any slave. Subject to her owners' every whim, Hagar's only value lay in providing labor or children. As Hagar's story unfolded, her ability to bear children placed her in the very center of Israel's history.

God had promised Abraham he would father a great nation, yet Sarah was barren. In desperation, Sarah chose a culturally acceptable solution to infertility; she offered her servant as a surrogate mother, and Hagar conceived.

This outwardly acceptable arrangement was inwardly disastrous. Hagar's scant value rose because of the child she carried, and she began to look at Sarah with contempt. Sarah's pain came out in harshness. Finally, Hagar ran away into the desert.

During Hagar's flight, she had an encounter with an angel of Abraham's God near the springs of

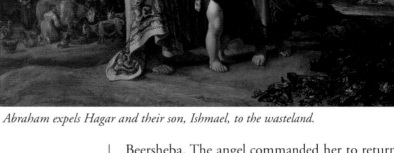

Abraham expels Hagar and their son, Ishmael, to the wasteland.

Beersheba. The angel commanded her to return to her mistress. In prophecy and promise, the angel said her child would be a son, named Ishmael (meaning *God hears*), a "wild ass of a man," fighting neighbors and kin alike.

When Hagar returned, Sarah was still bitter. After Sarah also had a son, Isaac, she begged Abraham to send Hagar and Ishmael away. Hagar was sent away to preserve Isaac's undisputed place as heir, but God promised that Ishmael would also father a great nation. Even Hagar, the slave, had a heritage in that promise. Ishmael's family line became the great Arab nations, so Hagar's descendants continue, even today, as powerful forces in the history of the world.

For further study, see Gen 15–18.

HAGGAI (HAG eye) *festive;* 6 century B.C.; Ezr 5:1

Judging from his name, Haggai the prophet was born during a major Jewish festival in Babylon. Living among those who would return to Jerusalem in 538 B.C., Haggai was a contemporary of Zechariah the prophet, Joshua the high priest, Zerubbabel the governor, and Cyrus and Darius the Persian kings. He is best known for his impassioned concern for rebuilding the temple at a time when most Israelites were overwhelmed with apa-

Ham looks upon the nakedness of his drunken father, Noah.

HAKKATAN (HAK uh tan) *the little one;* 5 century B.C.; Ezr 8:12; descendant of Azgad; father of one who returned to Judah

HAKKOZ (HAK ahz) *thorn*
1. 11 century B.C.; 1Ch 24:10; head of division of priests under David
2. Ezr 2:61; ancestor of priests unable to prove Israelite descent; possibly Hakkoz 1
3. Ne 3:4; ancestor of Meremoth the rebuilder of the Jerusalem wall; possibly Hakkoz 1 and 2

thy. Returning to the bleak city of Jerusalem after years in Babylon, the Jews undoubtedly focused on their own material and survival needs. Through his four oracles or messages, Haggai directed them to reconsider their priorities and focus on God and their spiritual responsibilities. For further study, see Ezr 5:1; 6:14; the Book of Haggai.

HAGGEDOLIM (hag uh DOH lim) *the great* [men]; 5 century B.C.; Ne 11:14; father of Zabdiel the priest in Jerusalem after Exile

HAGGI (HAG eye) [born on] *a feast day;* 19 century B.C.; Gen 46:16; son of Gad

HAGGIAH (hah GYE uh) *feast of the Lord;* 1Ch 6:30; descendant of Merari

HAGGITH (HAG ith) [born on] *a feast day;* 11 century B.C.; 2Sa 3:4; wife of David; mother of Adonijah

HAGRI (HAG rye) *wanderer;* 11 century B.C.; 1Ch 11:38; father of Mibhar the mighty man of David

HAGRITES (HAG rights) 1Ch 5:10; family of David's herdsmen; possibly descendants of Hagar

HAKUPHA (huh KOO fuh) *crooked;* Ezr 2:51; ancestor of temple servants who returned to Judah

HALLOHESH (hah LOH hesh) *the whisperer;* 5 century B.C.; Ne 3:12; leader whose son rebuilt Jerusalem wall

HAM (HAM) meaning unknown; Gen 5:32
As part of the eight surviving humans aboard the ark, Noah's second son, Ham, and his wife shared in the responsibility of repopulating the earth after the flood. Ham's family did quite well in that regard. He fathered four sons—Cush and Put, whose tribes settled parts of Africa; Egypt, forefather of the Egyptians; and Canaan, whose descendants settled Phoenicia and Palestine. Canaan was accursed because Ham had looked upon the nakedness of a drunken Noah. The curse on Canaan meant that his immediate descendants would be dispossessed from the Promised Land and become subservient to Israel, the descendants of Shem who would possess the land instead. For further study, see Gen 5:32; 7:13; 9:18-27; 10:1-20; 1Ch 1:4,8; 4:40; Ps 78:51; 105:23,27; 106:22.

HAMAN (HAY muhn) 5 century B.C.; Est 3:1
As the prime minister of Persia under King Ahasuerus, Haman was in a position to express his per-

sonal animosities toward Jews as a racial public policy. When Haman commanded that all the king's staff bow down before him, Mordecai the Jew refused because he viewed such an act as idolatry. Haman's anger toward Mordecai turned to hatred of all Jews, whom he then targeted for extermination by royal decree.

Haman's hatred for Jews went beyond one man's snub, but had its roots in history. Haman's people, the Agagites, and Mordecai's people, the Hebrews, had battled each other since the days of Joshua and Saul—always to the death. This age-old war was now being played out 500 years later through Haman the Agagite and Mordecai the Jew.

Haman plotted to frame and hang Mordecai and then annihilate all Jews. That plan was foiled by Mordecai and his niece, Queen Esther. In the end, Mordecai was vindicated and then honored in Haman's stead. After his evil intentions were brought out in the open, Haman was executed by the king on the very gallows he intended for Mordecai, while Mordecai was promoted to Haman's position as prime minister.

For further study, see Ex 17:8-16; 1Sa 14:47-48; 15; the Book of Esther.

Haman, prime minister of Persia, is accused by Queen Esther of plotting to destroy her people.

HAMATHITES (HAY meh thights) Gen 10:18; Aramean-Hittite people of Hamath, capital of Syria

HAMMEDATHA (HAM uh DAY thuh) *given by Ham;* 6 century B.C.; Est 3:1; father of Haman the official under Ahasuerus

HAMMOLECHETH (hah MOHL uh keth) *the queen;* 1Ch 7:18; female descendant of Manasseh

HAMMUEL (HAM yoo uhl) *God's warmth;* 1Ch 4:26; descendant of Simeon

HAMOR (HAY mohr) *ass;* 20 century B.C.; Gen 33:19; Hivite ruler; father of Shechem; killed by Simeon and Levi

HAMRAN (HAM ran) meaning unknown; 1Ch 1:41; son of Dishon the Horite chief; also called Hemdan

HAMUL (HAY muhl) *spared;* 19 century B.C.; Gen 46:12; son of Perez; grandson of Judah

HAMUTAL (huh MOO tuhl) meaning unknown; 7 century B.C.; 2Ki 23:31; wife of Josiah; mother of King Jehoahaz and King Zedekiah

HANA (HAN uh) meaning unknown; 1Esd 5:30; ancestor of family returning from Exile

HANAEL (HAN uh ehl) meaning unknown; Tob 1:21; brother of Tobit

HANAMEL (HAN uh mehl) *grace of God;* 7 century B.C.; Jer 32:7; cousin of Jeremiah the prophet; sold a field to Jeremiah

HANAN (HAY nuhn) *grace*
1. 1Ch 8:23; descendant of Benjamin
2. 11 century B.C.; 1Ch 11:43; mighty man of David
3. 1Ch 8:38; descendant of King Saul through Jonathan
4. Ezr 2:46; ancestor of temple servants who returned to Judah
5. 7 century B.C.; Jer 35:4; son of Igdaliah; his sons lived near the temple
6. 5 century B.C.; Ne 8:7; Levite who helped Ezra teach people the Law

7. 5 century B.C.; Neh 10:10; Levite who sealed covenant renewal; possibly Hanan 6
8. 5 century B.C.; Ne 10:22; Jewish leader who sealed covenant renewal after Exile
9. 5 century B.C.; Ne 10:22; another Jewish leader who sealed covenant renewal
10. 5 century B.C.; Ne 13:13; son of Zaccur; Nehemiah's assistant temple treasurer

HANANI (huh NAY nee) *gracious*
1. 10 century B.C.; 1Ch 25:4; son of Heman the music minister for David
2. 10 century B.C.; 1Ki 16:1; prophet imprisoned by King Asa; father of prophet Jehu
3. 5 century B.C.; Ezr 10:20; priest who married and divorced foreigner after Exile
4. 5 century B.C.; Ne 1:2; brother of Nehemiah; interim governor of Jerusalem
5. 5 century B.C.; Ne 12:36; priest/musician at Jerusalem wall dedication

HANANIAH (HAN uh NYE uh) *the Lord is gracious*
1. 1Ch 8:24; descendant of Benjamin
2. 10 century B.C.; 1Ch 25:4; son of Heman; musician under David
3. 8 century B.C.; 2Ch 26:11; royal official; military commander under Uzziah
4. 7 century B.C.; Jer 37:13; grandfather of Irijah the soldier who imprisoned the prophet Jeremiah
5. 7 century B.C.; Jer 36:12; father of Zedekiah the official under King Jehoiakim
6. 7 century B.C.; Jer 28:1; false prophet who opposed the prophet Jeremiah
7. 7 century B.C.; Da 1:6; see Shadrach
8. 6 century B.C.; 1Ch 3:19; descendant of Judah
9. 6 century B.C.; Ne 12:12; head of family of priests under Joiakim
10. 5 century B.C.; Ezr 10:28; one who married and divorced foreigner after Exile
11. 5 century B.C.; Ne 3:8; perfume maker; helped repair Jerusalem wall
12. 5 century B.C.; Ne 3:30; helped repair Jerusalem wall
13. 5 century B.C.; Ne 7:2; officer placed in charge of Jerusalem by Nehemiah; possibly Hanani 4
14. 5 century B.C.; Ne 10:23; Jewish leader; sealed covenant renewal
15. 5 century B.C.; Ne 12:41; priest/trumpeter at Jerusalem wall dedication

HANANIEL (huh NAN ih ehl) *favor of God;* Tob 1:1; grandfather of Tobit

HANNAH (HAN nuh) *grace;* 12 century B.C.; 1Sa 1:2

Imagine a woman longing for a child, taunted by her husband's second wife, and living in a culture where barrenness is considered punishment for some dark, hidden sin. This was Hannah.

During her family's annual trip to worship in the sanctuary at Shiloh, she pleaded with God for a child and vowed that she would dedicate him to the Lord. Hannah was praying with such emotion that Eli, the priest, accused her of drunkenness, not understanding that she was, as she put it, "pouring out my soul before the Lord."

God heard her prayer, and when the family returned home, Hannah conceived and gave birth to a son, Samuel, who later became Israel's first prophet. Hannah and her husband, Elkanah, chose a name that sounds like the Hebrew word "God has heard." This child was Hannah's sign that God had heard and cared.

Hannah kept her vow, and when the boy was weaned, she took him to the sanctuary to live with Eli and learn from him. Hannah brought both her child and her gratitude to God. "For this child I prayed," she said. "Therefore I have lent (him) to

Hannah and Samuel. Stained glass. Ripon Cathedral, Ripon, England.

the Lord; as long as he lives, he is given to the Lord."

Hannah's prayer of thanksgiving is recorded in First Samuel 2:1-10. She praised God's care for weak and hurting people, saying, "There is no Holy One like the Lord, no one beside you." Many years later, Hannah's words were used by one of the authors of Psalms and by Mary, Jesus's mother, in their own songs of praise. Throughout history, Hannah has been honored both as Samuel's mother and as a woman of faith.

For further study, see 1Sa 1–3; Ps 113; Lk 1:46-56.

HANNIEL (HAN ee uhl) *God is gracious*
1. 15 century B.C.; Nu 34:23; Manassite tribal leader who helped divide Canaan
2. 1Ch 7:39; descendant of Asher

HANOCH (HAY nahk) meaning unknown
1. 20 century B.C.; Gen 25:4; son of Midian; grandson of Abraham
2. 20 century B.C.; Gen 46:9; son of Reuben; grandson of Jacob

HANUN (HAY nuhn) *gracious*
1. 11 century B.C.; 2Sa 10:1; Ammonite; successor of Nahash; defeated in war by David
2. 5 century B.C.; Ne 3:13; helped repair Jerusalem wall
3. 5 century B.C.; Ne 3:30; son of Zalaph; helped repair Jerusalem wall

HAPPIZZEZ (HAP uh zehz) *hasty;* 11 century B.C.; 1Ch 24:15; head of division of priests under David

HARAN (HAIR uhn) *mountainous*
1. 22 century B.C.; Gen 11:26; brother of Abraham; father of Lot
2. 1Ch 2:46; son of Caleb and Ephah
3. 10 century B.C.; 1Ch 23:9; Levite descendant of Gershon

HARARITES (HAIR uh rights) 2Sa 23:11; natives of Judah hill country; an epithet hurled at David's mighty men

HARBONA (hahr BOH nuh) *donkey driver;* 5 century B.C.; Est 1:10; eunuch servant of King Ahasuerus

HAREPH (HAHR ef) *scornful;* 1Ch 2:51; founder of town of Beth-gader; descendant of Judah

HARHAIAH (hahr HAY uh) *the Lord protects;* 5 century B.C.; Ne 3:8; his son Uzziel helped rebuild the Jerusalem wall

HARHAS (HAHR hahs) *splendor;* 7 century B.C.; 2Ki 22:14; his grandson Shallum married the prophet Huldah; also called Hasrah

HARHUR (HAHR huhr) *fever;* Ezr 2:51; ancestor of temple servants who returned to Judah

HARIM (HAIR uhm) *consecrated*
1. 11 century B.C.; 1Ch 24:8; head of division of priests under David
2. Ezr 2:32; ancestor of family that returned to Judah after Exile
3. Ezr 2:39; ancestor of priests that returned from Exile; possibly Harim 1
4. Ezr 10:31; ancestor of some who married and divorced foreigners after Exile; possibly Harim 2
5. 5 century B.C.; Ne 10:27; Jewish leader; sealed covenant renewal

HARIPH (HAIR if) meaning unknown
1. Ne 7:24; see Jorah
2. 5 century B.C.; Ne 10:19; Jewish leader; sealed covenant renewal

HARNEPHER (HAHR nuh fuhr) meaning unknown; 1Ch 7:36; descendant of Asher

HAROEH (huh ROH uh) *the seer;* 1Ch 2:52; descendant of Caleb

HARSHA (HAHR shuh) *enchanter;* Ezr 2:52; ancestor of temple servants who returned to Judah after Exile

HARUM (HAIR uhm) *high;* 1Ch 4:8; descendant of Judah

HARUMAPH (huh ROO mahf) *slit-nosed;* 5 century B.C.; Ne 3:10; his son Jedaiah helped rebuild the Jerusalem wall

HARUPHITES (huh ROO fights) 1Ch 12:5; Benjaminite soldiers; Shephatiah was one

HARUZ (HAIR uhz) meaning unknown; 8 century B.C.; 2Ki 21:19; father of Meshullemeth

HASADIAH (HAS uh DI uh) *the Lord is kind*
1. 5 century B.C.; 1Ch 3:20; son of Zerubbabel
2. Bar 1:1; ancestor of Baruch the scribe of Jeremiah

HASHABIAH (HASH uh BYE uh) *the Lord has taken account*
1. 1Ch 6:45; descendant of Ethan 3
2. 10 century B.C.; 1Ch 25:3; son of Jeduthun; division head of musicians under David
3. 10 century B.C.; 1Ch 26:30; Hebronite; official of David
4. 10 century B.C.; 1Ch 27:17; son of Kemuel; officer over Levites in David's day
5. 7 century B.C.; 2Ch 35:9; chief Levite under Josiah
6. 1Ch 9:14; ancestor of Shemaiah 17
7. Ne 11:22; ancestor of Uzzi the chief of returning Jerusalem Levites
8. 6 century B.C.; Ne 12:21; head of priestly family during Joiakim's priesthood
9. 5 century B.C.; Ezr 8:19; Levite; returned to Judah after Exile
10. 5 century B.C.; Ne 3:17; ruler over half of Keilah during rebuilding of Jerusalem wall

HASHABNAH (huh SHAB nuh) *regarded;* 5 century B.C.; Ne 10:25; leader; sealed covenant renewal

HASHABNEIAH (HASH uhb NEE uh) *the Lord has considered*
1. 5 century B.C.; Ne 3:10; helped repair Jerusalem wall
2. 5 century B.C.; Ne 9:5; Levite; led prayer before covenant renewal

HASH-BADDANAH (hash BAD duh nuh) *thoughtful judge;* 5 century B.C.; Ne 8:4; helped Ezra read the Law

HASHEM (HAY shehm) meaning unknown; 11 century B.C.; 1Ch 11:34; mighty man of David; also called Jashen

HASHUBAH (huh SHOO buh) *esteemed;* 5 century B.C.; 1Ch 3:20; son of Zerubbabel

HASHUM (HAY shuhm) *opulent*
1. Ezr 2:19; ancestor of family that returned to Jerusalem after Exile
2. Ezr 10:33; ancestor of some who married and divorced foreigners after Exile; possibly Hashum 1
3. 5 century B.C.; Ne 8:4; stood with Ezra when Law was read to people
4. 5 century B.C.; Ne 10:18; leader; sealed covenant renewal
5. Gen 46:23; see Hushim 1

HASIDEANS (hass uh DEE uhnz) 1Mac 2:42; very orthodox Jews from whom the Pharisees and Essenes came

HASRAH 2Ch 34:22; see Harhas

HASSENAAH (has uh NAY uh) *thorny;* Ne 3:3; ancestor of rebuilders of Fish Gate; also called Senaah

HASSENUAH (has uh NOO uh) meaning unknown; 1Ch 9:7; his descendant Sallu returned to Jerusalem after Exile

HASSHUB (HASH uhb) *thoughtful*
1. 5 century B.C.; 1Ch 9:14; father of Shemaiah the returnee to Jerusalem after Exile
2. 5 century B.C.; Ne 3:11; rebuilder of Jerusalem wall
3. 5 century B.C.; Ne 3:23; rebuilder of Jerusalem wall
4. 5 century B.C.; Ne 10:23; sealed covenant renewal; possibly Hasshub 2 or 3

HASSOPHERETH (hah SAHF uh reth) *the scribe;* 10 century B.C.; Ezr 2:55; servant of Solomon; also called Sophereth

HASUPHA (huh SOO fuh) *stripped;* 10 century B.C.; Ezr 2:43; servant of Solomon

HATHACH (HAY thak) meaning unknown; 5 century B.C.; Est 4:5; eunuch of King Ahasuerus; attendant of Esther

HATHATH (HAY thath) *fear;* 14 century B.C.; 1Ch 4:13; son of judge Othniel

HATIPHA (HAT i fuh) *seized* or *captive;* Ezr 2:54; ancestor of returnees to Judah

HATITA (HAT i tuh) *dug up;* Ezr 2:42; ancestor of temple gatekeepers who returned to Judah

HATTIL (HAT uhl) meaning unknown; 10 century B.C.; Ezr 2:57; servant of Solomon; ancestor of returnees to Judah

HATTUSH (HAT uhsh) *assembled*
1. 6 century B.C.; Ne 12:2; chief priest; returned to Judah
2. 5 century B.C.; 1Ch 3:22; descendant of Shecaniah the son of Zerubbabel; returned to Judah
3. 5 century B.C.; Ne 3:10; son of Hashabneiah the rebuilder of Jerusalem wall; possibly Hattush 1
4. 5 century B.C.; Ne 10:4; priest/sealer of covenant renewal

HAVILAH (HAV uh luh) *sandy*
1. Gen 10:7; son of Cush whose descendants became an Arab nation
2. Gen 10:29; descendant of Shem

HAZAEL (HAY zee uhl) *God sees;* 9 century B.C.; 1Ki 19:15
When Hazael was serving as a high official in the court of King Ben-hadad II God told Elijah that Hazael would be the next king of Syria. Later, the very sick Ben-hadad sent Hazael to ask the prophet Elisha whether or not the King would recover from his illness. Elisha's response was puzzling to Hazael, for he told him the king's illness was not fatal, but he would still die. Through his tears, Elisha also told him that Hazael himself would become the next king, committing appalling atrocities upon the people of Israel. The day after, Hazael smothered Ben-hadad with a wet cloth and assumed the throne. Israel soon became a powerless vassal to Syria, and all its territory east of the Jordan River was occupied by Hazael. For further study, see 1Ki 19:15-17; 2Ki 8:8-15; 13:3, 22-25.

HAZAIAH (huh ZAY yuh) *the Lord sees;* Ne 11:5; ancestor of Maaseiah 17

HAZARMAVETH (hay zuhr MAY veth) *court of death;* Gen 10:26; Semitic ancestor of settlers in southern Arabia

HAZIEL (HAY zee uhl) *God sees;* 1Ch 23:9; family head; descendant of Gershon

HAZO (HAY zoh) *seer;* 21 century B.C.; Gen 22:22; son of Nahor; nephew of Abraham

HAZZELELPONI (HAZ uh lehl POH nye) *coming shadows;* 1Ch 4:3; daughter of Etam; descendant of Judah

HEBER (HEE buhr) *companion*
1. 19 century B.C.; Gen 46:17; grandson of Asher
2. 13 century B.C.; Jdg 4:11; Kenite whose wife Jael killed Canaanite commander
3. 1Ch 4:18; descendant of Judah
4. 1Ch 8:17; descendant of Benjamin

HEBREWS (HEE brooz) Gen 14:13
The Semitic descendants of Abraham, Isaac, and Jacob (Israel) were Hebrews who derived their names from Shem's grandson Eber. Former slaves, they wandered across the Sinai Peninsula after the Exodus from Egypt and crossed the Jordan River to settle the land of Canaan. For further study, see Ex 1–10; 2Co 11:22; Php 3:5. See Israelites, Jews.

HEBRON (HEB ruhn) *league* or *association*
1. 19 century B.C.; Ex 6:18; grandson of Levi
2. 1Ch 2:42; descendant of Judah

HEBRONITES (HEE bruhn ights) Nu 3:27; descendants of Hebron the third son of Kohath the priest

HEGAI (HEHG eye) meaning unknown; 5 century B.C.; Est 2:3; eunuch in charge of King Ahasuerus's harem

HEGEMONIDES (HEHJ uh MOH ni deez) possibly *guide;* 2 century B.C.; 2Mac 13:24; trustworthy Syrian officer

HELAH (HEE luh) meaning unknown; 1Ch 4:5; wife of Ashhur; descendant of Judah

HELDAI (HEL dye) meaning unknown
1. 11 century B.C.; 1Ch 27:15; commander in David's army; possibly Heleb
2. 6 century B.C.; Zec 6:10; bringer of gold and silver to returning exiled Jews

HELEB (HEE lehb) meaning unknown; 11 century B.C.; 2Sa 23:29; mighty man of David; also called Heled; possibly Heldai 1

HELED 1Ch 11:30; see Heleb

HELEK (HEE lehk) *portion* or *lot;* Nu 26:30; ancestor of clan in tribe of Manasseh

HELEM (HEE luhm) *strength;* 1Ch 7:35; descendant of Asher

HELEZ (HEE lehz) *strong*
1. 11 century B.C.; 2Sa 23:26; mighty man of David
2. 1Ch 2:39; descendant of Jerahmeel

HELI (HEE lye) *climbing;* 1 century B.C.; Lk 3:23; father of Joseph; ancestor of Christ

HELIODORUS (heh lih uh DOHR uhs) *gift of Helios* [sun god]; 2 century B.C.; 2Mac 3:7; Seleucid official

HELKAI (HEL kye) *the Lord is my portion;* 6 century B.C.; Ne 12:15; head of priestly family under Joiakim

HELON (HEE lahn) *strength* or *valor;* 15 century B.C.; Nu 1:9; father of Eliab the leader of Zebulunites

HEMAN (HEE muhn) *faithful*
1. 20 century B.C.; Gen 36:22; son of Lotan the Horite chief in Esau's day; also called Horam
2. 1Ch 2:6; son of Zerah; the Ezrahite author of Ps 88
3. 1Ki 4:31; son of Mahol; wise man comparable to Solomon
4. 11 century B.C.; 1Ch 6:33; Levite seer and chief temple musician in David's day

HEMDAN Gen 36:26; see Hamran

HENADAD (HEN uh dad) *favor of Hadad* [weather god]; Ne 3:18; ancestor of temple rebuilders; also called Hodaviah 1

HEPHER (HEE fuhr) *pit*
1. Nu 26:32; descendant of Gilead; source of a clan in tribe of Manasseh
2. 1Ch 4:6; descendant of Judah
3. 11 century B.C.; 1Ch 11:36; mighty man of David

The massacre of the innocents, as ordered by King Herod the Great.

HEPHZIBAH (HEF zib uh) *my delight is in her;* 8 century B.C.; 2Ki 21:1; wife of Hezekiah 1; mother of Manasseh 2

HERESH (HEER esh) meaning unknown; 5 century B.C.; 1Ch 9:15; Levite resettler in Jerusalem

HERMAS (HUHR muhs) meaning unknown; 1 century A.D.; Ro 16:14; slave in the church at Rome

HERMES (HUHR meez) *messenger*
1. Ac 14:12; messenger of Greek gods in the pantheon; also called Mercury by the Romans
2. 1 century A.D.; Ro 16:14; slave or freedman in the church at Rome

HERMOGENES (huhr MAHJ uh neez) *born of Hermes* [Greek god]; 1 century A.D.; 2Ti 1:15; Christian who deserted Paul

HEROD (HAIR uhd) *sprung from a hero*

1. Herod the Great; ruled 37–4 B.C.; Mt 2:1

Twenty-five years after Jerusalem was destroyed by the Roman army in 63 B.C., Herod the Great reconstructed its various pieces into a kingdom under his domain. He skillfully served Rome while appeasing his Jewish subjects. But his main legacy was architectural, not political, outdoing even Solomon at his peak. Herod the Great reconstructed many public buildings, including the Jerusalem temple that Jesus visited and that the Romans later destroyed. Despite his greatness, Herod was insanely jealous of another "king of the Jews" born in Bethlehem. In an act of cruel barbarism, this Herod ordered the murder of all male babies born around the same time as Christ. For further study, see Mt 2:1-23; Lk 1:5.

2. Herod Archelaus (HAIR uhd ahr kuh LAY uhs); ruled 4 B.C.–A.D. 6; Mt 2:22; eldest son and successor of Herod the Great; a cruel local ruler over all Judea excluding Galilee

3. Herod Antipas (HAIR uhd AN ti puhs); ruled 4 B.C.–A.D. 39; Mt 14:1

The ruler of Galilee and Perea during the ministries of Jesus and John the Baptist, Herod Antipas is best remembered for the role he played in their arrests and deaths. John the Baptist lost his life after condemning Herod Antipas for violating the Law by adulterously marrying his brother's wife, Herodias. Herodias had John imprisoned for this affront, but she wanted further punishment for him. When an impulsive Antipas promised Herodias's daughter Salome anything she wanted in appreciation for pleasing the king with her dancing, Salome (prompted by her mother) demanded, "Give me the head of John the Baptist here on a platter" (Mt 14:8). And so it was done.

Herod Antipas also played a role in the arrest, mockery, and eventual execution of Jesus. At first a secret admirer of Jesus, Antipas was eager to see the Galilean perform miracles. But Antipas turned against him when Jesus refused to perform on command. Neither defending nor condemning him, Antipas left the decision of Jesus's fate up to Pontius Pilate.

Antipas's contribution to these major events comes through his weakness; he let others take charge instead of controlling the outcomes of these situations himself. This weakness is also evident in his political life. He was unable to extend his control beyond Galilee, and in A.D. 39, he lost what power he had to Herod Agrippa I and spent his remaining years in exile.

For further study, see Mt 14:1-12; Mk 6:14-29; Lk 3:19-20; 8:3; 9:7-9; 13:31-35; 23:6-12; Ac 4:26-27; 13:1.

4. Herod Philip I; 1 century A.D.; Mt 14:3; son of Herod the Great; father of Salome and first husband of Herodias

5. Herod Philip II; ruled 4 B.C.–A.D. 34; Lk 3:1; son of Herod the Great and Cleopatra; husband of Salome; ruler over Iturea and Traconitus

6. Herod Agrippa I (HAIR uhd uh GRIP uh); ruled A.D. 37–44; Ac 12:1

This King Herod was Agrippa I, the son of Aristobulus and grandson of Herod the Great. He was politically linked with the Roman emperors Caligula and Claudius. In the diplomatic tradition of his grandfather, this Jewish monarch eventually ruled over and united Judea, Samaria, and Idumea. He staunchly defended Jewish policies and persecuted the early church. He arraigned the apostle Peter on false charges and executed James the son

The executioner presents the head of John the Baptist to Salome, stepdaughter of King Herod Antipas.

of Zebedee. Luke records his sudden and unpleasant demise, saying "an angel of the Lord struck him down, and he was eaten by worms and died." His kingdom was then divided among his son and three others. For further study, see Ac 12:1-23.

7. Herod Agrippa II (HAYR uhd uh GRIP uh); ruled A.D. 50–93; Ac 25:13

Six years after his father and namesake died suddenly in office (Ac 12:20-23), 23-year-old Herod Agrippa II became the tetrarch (ruler of a fourth part), serving Rome as he ruled over Judea. He attempted to mediate between the Jewish Zealots and his Roman overseers, but even his great diplomatic skill could not avert the Jewish War (A.D. 66–70). He presided over the affairs of Palestinian Jews the longest of any Herodian, but he died childless, ending the Herodian dynasty. A witness to the start-up of the early church, Agrippa II consulted with Governor Festus regarding the apostle Paul's trial for heretical teaching. He tried to help Paul but was powerless to intervene on Paul's behalf once the apostle appealed to Rome for a ruling. For further study, see Ac 25:13–26:32.

HERODIANS (heh ROH dee uhns) Mt 22:16; partisans of Herod who opposed Jesus

HERODIAS (huh ROH dee uhs) meaning unknown; 1 century A.D.; Mt 14:3

Herodias used her beauty to marry her powerful brother-in-law. When Herod Antipas, Israel's Roman ruler, left his wife for Herodias, their adultery horrified his Jewish subjects. John the Baptist, a radical preacher, publicly reproached them, and for this reason, Herodias hated John the Baptist and wanted him dead.

Herod arrested John but was fearful of executing him because of his popularity and his authority as a prophet. Herodias, however, had no such qualms. She found her opportunity for vengeance on Herod's birthday—a drunken celebration where her daughter, Salome, danced. Salome so enticed Herod that he offered her anything, even half his wealth, as gratitude for her performance. At her mother's urging, Salome asked for and received the head of John the Baptist. For further study, see Mk 6:17-29; Mt 14:1-12; Lk 3:19-20; 9:7-9

HERODION (huh ROH dee uhn) *heroic;* 1 century A.D.; Ro 16:11; Paul's kinsman at Rome, whom he greets

HEZEKIAH (HEZ uh KYE uh) *the Lord is my strength*

1. ruled 729–686 B.C.; 2Ki 16:20

When Hezekiah took the throne of Judah, he was only 25, Assyrian invaders were threatening the borders, and the nation was in spiritual and economic ruin. Yet, Hezekiah's reign is a spot of light in a mostly dark period of Jewish history.

When Israel split into separate Hebrew nations, Israel and Judah, neither country followed God.

The water reservoir constructed by King Hezekiah to lessen Jerusalem's vulnerability to siege.

People and rulers alike worshiped idols, made war against their brothers, and became like the surrounding pagan nations. From the day Jeroboam worshiped a golden calf in Israel until Hezekiah's own father, Ahaz, practiced child sacrifice in Judah, nearly every generation ignored the ways of God. Hezekiah and the prophet Isaiah stood virtually alone, symbols of the few faithful Jews God had promised would always remain.

Hezekiah wanted to be a king like David. He understood how God abhorred the worship of idols, so he struck down altars and destroyed sites of idol worship. He pulled down the sacred pole of the Canaanite goddess Asherah and ground it to dust. Then Hezekiah rebuilt the temple, which had been neglected for generations. He fortified Jerusalem, rebuilding walls, towers, and battlements. In a feat of ambitious engineering, he commissioned the digging of a tunnel to connect the spring outside the city walls with a reservoir inside. The 600-yard tunnel gave the city a direct water supply and lessened its vulnerability to siege. Only Hezekiah's own commitment and spirited leadership made these tremendous projects possible.

During the first years of Hezekiah's reign, Israel was conquered by Assyria. A few years later, the Assyrians tried to add Judah to their kingdom as well. Faced with such a threat, Hezekiah aligned himself with other nations to fight the Assyrian onslaught. However, just as they had taken Israel, the Assyrians claimed city after city in Judah. They forced people from their homes to make room for troops and arms. Their military might overcame Judah's armies, and finally, Hezekiah himself was placed under house arrest.

Hezekiah's submission and defeat was not enough for the Assyrian king. The final trophy for King Sennacherib was the heart of Judah—its capital, Jerusalem. He sent envoys and nearly 200,000 soldiers to the city gates with a demand of surrender, knowing Judah could not fight such an army. Sennacherib sent a message mocking the God of the Jews. His envoys called out to the people on Jerusalem's walls, saying they were fools to follow Hezekiah, and greater fools to think their God would save them.

God spoke to the prophet Isaiah, saying Sennacherib would never enter Jerusalem but would return to die by the sword in his own land. The next morning, 185,000 Assyrian soldiers were dead, killed by an angel of the Lord. By the time

Hezekiah turns his face to the wall and prays when Isaiah tells him he will die.

the terrified survivors reached home, King Sennacherib was battling invading armies on all fronts. The king finally fled to Nineveh, where he was murdered with a sword. As God said, Jerusalem stood unconquered, while Sennacherib fell.

Some years later, when Hezekiah was near death, the prophet Isaiah told him to set his house in order and prepare to die. At this, Hezekiah turned his face to the wall and wept. He prayed, asking God to remember how he had walked before God in faithfulness "with a whole heart" and tried to do right all his life. God heard Hezekiah's prayer. He stopped Isaiah in the middle of the courtyard and said, "Go and say to Hezekiah . . . I have heard your prayer" (Isa 38:5).

God promised Judah's king 15 more years of life and protection from the Assyrians for Jerusalem. When Isaiah told him these things, Hezekiah asked for a sign that the promises would happen. Isaiah cried out to the Lord, and when God made the shadow on the sundial move backward "ten intervals," there was no doubt. Hezekiah recovered and went to the temple on the third day. He lived those

15 years, and during that time, invaders did not take the city of Jerusalem.

Hezekiah is known more for his faith in God than his wisdom as a ruler. In the end, political ambition and military mistakes were his undoing. While he believed in the God of Israel, he did not always follow the counsel of God's prophet, Isaiah. Perhaps seeking peaceful coexistence, he made alliances with Babylon and opened the secrets of his kingdom to their ambassadors. The king continued offers of friendship even after Isaiah received a prophetic vision warning that an alliance with Babylon would be the beginning of Judah's destruction. In the vision, Isaiah saw palace treasures carried off to Babylon and young Hebrew men taken to be made eunuchs for Babylon's courts. Hezekiah ignored the warning, trading peace and prosperity in his own time for the lives of his descendants. Still, when Hezekiah died, all Judah honored him.

For further study, see 2Ki 18–20; 2Ch 29–32; Isa 1:1; 36–39; Jer 26:18-19; Hos 1:1; Mic 1:1.
2. Zep 1:1; ancestor of prophet Zephaniah
3. 6 century B.C.; Ezr 2:16; head of family that resettled in Judah after Exile
4. 5 century B.C.; Ne 10:17; sealer of covenant renewal with God; possibly Hezekiah 3

HEZION (HEZ ee uhn) *vision;* 10 century B.C.; 1Ki 15:18; grandfather of Ben-hadad 1; possibly Rezon

HEZIR (HEZ uhr) *boar*
1. 11 century B.C.; 1Ch 24:15; head of division of priests in David's time
2. 5 century B.C.; Ne 10:20; sealer of covenant renewal in Nehemiah's time

HEZRO (HEZ roh) meaning unknown; 11 century B.C.; 2Sa 23:35; mighty man of David

HEZRON (HEZ ruhn) *enclosure*
1. 19 century B.C.; Gen 46:9; son of Reuben; grandson of Jacob
2. 19 century B.C.; Gen 46:12; son of Perez; grandson of Judah; ancestor of Jesus

HIDDAI (HID eye) meaning unknown; 11 century B.C.; 2Sa 23:30; mighty man of David; also called Hurai

HIEL (HIGH uhl) *God lives;* 9 century B.C.; 1Ki 16:34; rebuilt Jericho; Joshua foresaw death of Hiel's sons

HIERONYMUS (high RUHN ee muhs) meaning unknown; 2 century B.C.; 2Mac 12:2; Syrian military governor in Palestine

HILKIAH (hil KYE uh) *the Lord is my portion*
1. 1Ch 6:45; ancestor of David's music minister Ethan
2. 10 century B.C.; 1Ch 26:11; Levite; son of Hosah the temple gatekeeper under David
3. 8 century B.C.; 2Ki 18:18; father of Eliakim the palace administrator under Hezekiah
4. 7 century B.C.; 2Ki 22:4

When Josiah was king in Judah, Hilkiah was chief priest. Most citizens of Israel and Judah had long ago abandoned their faith in God to worship idols, such as the Canaanite god Baal. Josiah, however, wanted to be a king like his ancestor David. To bring his people back toward the God of Israel, he ordered Hilkiah to repair the neglected temple. During the repairs, an ancient Book of the Law was found hidden in the temple treasury. Hilkiah brought the book to Josiah. When it was read aloud, Josiah saw how far his people had strayed from God's ways and tore his clothes in distress, realizing that the nation deserved God's punishment. He sent Hilkiah to a respected prophet, Huldah, who confirmed that God would punish Judah, but not until the penitent Josiah's reign had ended. Then, at Josiah's command, Hilkiah cleared the temple of all traces of Baal worship. For further study, see 2Ki 22; 23:4.
5. 7 century B.C.; Jer 1:1; priest of Anathoth; the father of the prophet Jeremiah
6. 7 century B.C.; Jer 29:3; father of Gemariah the ambassador to Babylon
7. Jdt 8:1; ancestor of Judith
8. Bar 1:1; ancestor of Baruch the scribe of Jeremiah
9. 6 century B.C.; Sus 1:2; his daughter Susanna was falsely accused of adultery
10. 6 century B.C.; Ne 12:7; chief priest; returned to Judah after Exile
11. 5 century B.C.; 1Ch 9:11; father of a priest who resettled in Jerusalem
12. 5 century B.C.; Ne 8:4; stood with Ezra as the Law was read

HILLEL (HIL ehl) *he has praised;* 12 century B.C.; Jdg 12:13; father of minor judge Abdon

HIRAH (HIGH ruh) *nobility;* 20 century B.C.; Gen 38:1; Adullamite with whom Judah stayed

HIRAM (HIGH ruhm) *my brother is exalted*
1. ruled 978–944 B.C.; 2Sa 5:11

Tyre of Phoenicia (present-day Lebanon) was a mighty sea power and a commercial rival to Israel. Though frequently denounced by Hebrew prophets as a pagan influence, Tyre was courted by David and Solomon as a trading partner. King Hiram of Tyre supplied rich timber, gold, expert carpenters and stonecutters, plus on-site supervision in Lebanon to help with the temple and other building projects. Hiram also sent Solomon experienced

Hiram the craftsman and the bronze pillars he created for Solomon's temple.

seamen and ships to help launch Solomon's fledgling shipping industry. Over a 20-year period, Solomon incurred a trade imbalance, for which 20 cities along the Galilee-Phoenicia border were held as collateral (and later returned) by Hiram. For further study, see 1Ki 5:1-18; 9:10-27; 10:11-22; 1Ch 14:1; 2Ch 8:2-18; 9:10,21. Also called Huram 2.
2. 10 century B.C.; 1Ki 7:13

Before Hiram's father died, he passed down his great skill as a craftsman in bronze to his son. When it came time for Solomon to put the finishing touches on the temple of Jerusalem, he naturally sent to Tyre for Hiram, who was "full of skill, intelligence, and knowledge in working bronze" (1Ki 7:14). Hiram was responsible for the two great bronze pillars called Jachin and Boaz, which stood approximately 27 feet high and 18 feet around. He also crafted the elaborate bronze capitals and the intricate pomegranates and lily work on top of the pillars. He made the molten sea and the 12 oxen on which it rested. His smaller works included ten bronze bases, ten bronze basins, and the pots, shovels, and bowls used in the temple. For further study, see 1Ki 7; 2Ch 2:7-16. Also called Huram 3 and Huram-abi.

HITTITES (HIT tights)
1. Gen 15:20; descendants of Heth the son of Canaan; natives living in Judean hills near Hebron who were dispossessed by Israelites
2. 2Sa 11:3; citizens of or mercenaries from the Anatolian or neo-Hittite Empire of Syria, or possibly an unrelated group living in Canaan

HIVITES (HIGH vights) Gen 10:17; Canaanites in Lebanon; Solomon used some as slave laborers; akin to Horites

HIZKI (HIZ kye) *strong;* 1Ch 8:17; descendant of Benjamin

HIZKIAH (hiz KYE uh) *the Lord is my strength;* 1Ch 3:23; descendant of Zerubbabel

HOBAB (HOH bahb) *beloved;* 15 century B.C.; Nu 10:29; son of Reuel the Midianite

HOBAIAH Ne 7:63; see Habaiah

HOD (HAHD) *majesty;* 1Ch 7:37; descendant of Asher

Judith and her servant flee Holofernes's camp with his head.

HODAVIAH (hahd uh VYE uh) *honorer of the Lord*
1. Ezr 2:40; see Henadad
2. 8 century B.C.; 1Ch 5:24; family head in tribe of Manasseh
3. 1Ch 9:7; ancestor of Sallu the Benjaminite resettler in Jerusalem
4. 1Ch 3:24; descendant of Zerubbabel

HODESH (HOH desh) *new moon;* 1Ch 8:9; third wife of Shaharaim; descendant of Benjamin

HODEVAH (HOH deh vuh) meaning unknown; 6 century B.C.; Ne 7:43; ancestor of Levites returning from Babylon

HODIAH (hoh DYE uh) *splendor of the Lord*
1. 1Ch 4:19; descendant of Judah
2. 5 century B.C.; Ne 8:7; Levite interpreter of Law as read by Ezra
3. 5 century B.C.; Ne 10:10; Levite sealer of covenant renewal; possibly Hodiah 2
4. 5 century B.C.; Ne 10:13; Levite sealer of covenant renewal; possibly Hodiah 2
5. 5 century B.C.; Ne 10:18; sealer of covenant renewal

HOGLAH (HAHG luh) *partridge;* 15 century B.C.; Nu 26:33; daughter of Zelophehad; petitioned with her sisters to receive her father's inheritance

HOHAM (HOH ham) meaning unknown; 15 century B.C.; Jos 10:3; king of Hebron defeated by Joshua

HOLOFERNES (hol uh FUR neez) meaning unknown; 5 century B.C.; Jdt 2:4

King Nebuchadnezzar's commanding officer, Holofernes, paid with his life for ignoring the God of Israel. Holofernes invaded Israel in spite of a warning that no one could defeat the Jews if they had been obedient to their God. Holofernes discounted the warning, saying, "Who is God except Nebuchadnezzar?" At Bethulia, he captured the water supply and laid siege to the city. A pious Jewess named Judith believed God would rescue the city. She dressed elegantly and went to Holofernes, claiming she would betray her people to him. Holofernes believed her story and held a banquet, hoping to seduce her, but Judith waited until he was helplessly drunk and then cut off his head with his own sword. Without Holofernes's leadership, his troops scattered before the Israelite offensive. For further study, see the Book of Judith.

HOLY SPIRIT (HOH lee SPEER it) Gen 1:2

The Holy Spirit was present throughout biblical history. He was there at Creation: "Let us make humankind in our image" (Gen 1:26). He was there to inspire God's law-givers, judges, and prophets in speaking God's message, living it out, and writing it down. He was there to baptize and anoint Jesus for a healing ministry. He was there at the birth of the church—regenerating, sanctifying, and equipping believers. He will be there also at the end of history to reveal and enable special activities and manifestations of God's power.

In most biblical narratives, the Holy Spirit is unnamed; this person of the Godhead is self-effacing and does not call attention to himself but brings glory to God the Father or to Christ the Son (Jn 16:13-15). However, in some accounts of God's work, the behind-the-scenes agent is specifically named as the "eternal Spirit," the "spirit of God," the "spirit of the Lord," the "Spirit of truth," the "Spirit of Jesus," or the "Spirit of holiness." Images of God's Spirit at work are also conjured up by rich symbols used to describe him: "the Advocate,"

"Helper," "Comforter," "Counselor." Elsewhere, the Spirit is associated with "streams of living water," "tongues of fire," and "mighty wind."

In the Pentecost narrative of Acts 2, observers sensed "the rush of a violent wind," and in the Creation account of Genesis 1, "a wind from God swept over the waters." In these instances, wind is a play on words that indicates the invisible power of the Holy Spirit; the biblical words for spirit (in Hebrew, *ruah*; in Greek, *pneuma*) also mean *wind*.

The historical and prophetic books of the Old Testament record interactions between the Holy Spirit and a variety of people—from childless women to babes in the womb, from soldiers in battle to fugitives in hiding, from kings to peasants, and from priests to beggars. Most Old Testament narratives of the Spirit's work tell about individuals upon whom God placed his Spirit intermittently. Of the mighty Samson, for example, it is said "the

The Holy Spirit descends upon Jesus at his baptism by John the Baptist.

Spirit of the Lord rushed on him" (Jdg 14:5,19; 15:14), then left just as quickly "but he did not know the Lord had left him" (16:20).

By comparison, the New Testament image of the Spirit's work is more often corporate and ongoing. Not only is the Holy Spirit said to "dwell" in the "inner person" (Ro 8:9-11) and "seal" one's salvation (Eph 1:14), but he also gives spiritual gifts "for the common good" (1Co 12:7) and "to equip the saints for the work of ministry" (Eph 4:12).

This idea, that God's Spirit resides in people to bring about life-changing results, is found scattered throughout the Old Testament; but in the New Testament, this direct, ongoing relationship with the Spirit becomes the norm. Yet that New Testament norm has always been hard to define and to accept, especially at first. God unexpectedly exceeded all norms when the Holy Spirit empowered Gentiles to believe the Gospel. The apostles were shocked to see the Spirit working cross-culturally outside their inner circle of Jewish believers.

At other times, believers praying and obedient to God were said to be "filled with the Holy Spirit." Many were blessed with such a connection to the Spirit: John the Baptist in his mother's womb and during his radical ministry; the apostles Peter, John, and Paul in their bold preaching; Philip and the other deacons in their table service and witness; Stephen in his martyrdom. As for Jesus, his entire life and healing ministry was marked by unparalleled demonstrations of the Spirit's power.

The Gospels describe the Holy Spirit as a personal being and divine power with specific abilities and tasks, especially in relation to Jesus. At Jesus's baptism, "the Holy Spirit descended upon him in bodily form like a dove," accompanied by a voice proclaiming the Father's good pleasure and inaugurating Jesus's public ministry. When Jesus preached his first sermon, he read from Isaiah and identified himself as the fulfillment of this prophecy: "The Spirit of the Lord is upon me, because he has anointed me to bring good news to the poor" (Lk 4:18; see Isa 61:1). Jesus credited the Holy Spirit for his ability to heal broken lives, bind Satan, and inaugurate the Kingdom. At the Last Supper, Jesus told his disciples "the Advocate," meaning the Holy Spirit, would convict the world of all sin, righteousness, and judgment (Jn 16:8). However, this would not happen until 50 days after Jesus's death, resurrection, and ascension—that is, beginning at Pentecost.

The followers of Christ are filled with the Holy Spirit at Pentecost.

Pentecost was the annual occasion of thousands of Jews gathering in Jerusalem for a feast day. So, too, the loyal disciples of Jesus gathered in Jerusalem—in a secret room, waiting and praying for the Holy Spirit, as instructed by Jesus. What happened on that day far exceeded what the disciples could have expected or prayed for: They were "filled with the Holy Spirit" (Ac 2:4) to preach the news of Jesus's death and resurrection to the ends of the earth.

The outpouring of the Spirit on each believer sounded like a rush of mighty wind and appeared like tongues of fire; it filled their hearts and prompted each of them to preach in a nonnative language. Jews from all over—Mesopotamia, Judea, Asia, Egypt, Libya, Rome, and beyond— heard the Word of God in their own languages.

After this amazing demonstration of the Spirit's power, Peter preached his first sermon. He explained that the Spirit-filled believers were not drunk, as some observers supposed, but were empowered just as Joel prophesied: "In the last days...I will pour out my Spirit upon all flesh, and your sons and your daughters shall prophesy, and your young men shall see visions and your old men shall dream dreams" (Ac 2:17; see Joel 2:28-29).

Peter continued, telling how Jesus had been crucified and rose from the dead. Many in the audience were "cut to the heart" by the Spirit. When Peter urged them to repent and be baptized in Jesus's name to receive forgiveness of sins and the "gift of the Holy Spirit," 3000 converts were made.

Paul's letters and the Acts of the Apostles include a great many accounts of people being infused with the Holy Spirit. Paul often lists "gifts" of the Holy Spirit that bear fruit in the individual and corporate lives of Christians. Practical gifts of service—teaching, preaching, evangelism, and leadership—work alongside gifts of the heart—wisdom, love, prophecy, mercy, faith, and healing. Still other spiritual gifts were more sensational—speaking in tongues, interpreting tongues, or discerning spirits. The Book of Revelation, which foretells the second coming of Christ, also speaks of the Holy Spirit's work at the end of time. Indeed, John's entire vision is received "in the Spirit."

These gifts of the Holy Spirit were evident in the early church and were valued as tools by which Christians understood the mysteries of life and met the needs of people. Even so, the church has struggled for centuries to understand the nature and role of the Holy Spirit. Many still wonder today: How does the New Testament concept of God the Father, God the Son, and God the Holy Spirit fit in with the Old Testament teaching that one and only one God exists? Did the Holy Spirit give gifts for all Christians, in every age, or only for the first century church? What are "tongues" and the "interpretation of tongues"?

The quest for answers continues. Since God, Jesus, and the Holy Spirit are equally and indivisibly attributed with divine power by the New Testament authors, the church has coined a term to convey this mystery. They call the one God, who reveals himself in three forms, the *Trinity*.

As for the nature, extent, and expression of spiritual gifts, this has been variously understood within the historic Christian church. Some Christians believe these gifts expired in the first century, as if they were needed just to establish the early church. Others today report speaking in tongues, receiving prophecies, and receiving miraculous healing through the Holy Spirit, and they look to Scripture to confirm their experiences.

Unlike other Bible characters whose earthly lives begin and end, the Holy Spirit is eternal. Although Christians have long struggled to understand him, that difficulty does not limit their faith in the ongoing work of the Spirit in human hearts.

> → ←
>
> *"But the Advocate, the Holy Spirit, whom the Father will send in my name, will teach you everything and remind you of all that I have said to you."*
>
> John 14:26

For further study, see Gen 1:26; Ex 31:3; Nu 24:2; Jdg 14:6,19; 15:14,19; 16:20; 1Sa 16:13; Ps 51:1-11; Isa 61:1; Eze 11:5; Joel 2:28-32; Mt 12:28; Lk 3:21-22; 4:1,14-21; Jn 3:5-8; 7:37-39; 14:17,26; 16:7-16; Ac 1–2; 6:3-6; 7:51-56; 8:9-40; 10:44-48; 19:1-7; Ro 5:5; 8:2-27; 1Co 2; 12; 14; 2Co 3; Gal 5:16-26; 6:1,8; Eph 1:13-14; 4:1-16; Rev 1:10; 2–3; 4:2.

HOMAM 1Ch 1:39; see Heman 1

HOPHNI (HAHF ni) meaning unknown; 12 century B.C.; 1Sa 1:3

Sons of the temple priest Eli, Hophni and his brother, Phinehas, violated the Law regarding ritual sacrifices at Shiloh. They greedily kept the best parts of the meat sacrifices for themselves rather than giving them to God. Furthermore, they profaned a holy place by sleeping with women in the sanctuary. Hophni and Phinehas were also guilty of profaning the ark of the covenant, not only because it ended up captured by the Philistines but because the two sons shared a pagan superstition. They identified the divine presence with the material object and incorrectly thought they could curry God's favor by manipulating the symbol as a good luck charm. For their impious behavior, God ordained

Eli's sons Hophni and Phinehas violate laws regarding the ritual sacrifice at Shiloh.

that they would be killed in battle and that Eli's house would end with them. Hophni's and Phinehas's foster brother, Samuel, prophesied their fate and rose up as the last of Israel's judges after their fall. For further study, see 1Sa 2:12-36; 4:1-22.

HOPHRA (HAHF ruh) meaning unknown; ruled 589–570 B.C.; Jer 44:30; Pharaoh who aided Zedekiah; see Pharaoh

HORAM (HOH ram) *elevated;* 15 century B.C.; Jos 10:33; king of Gezer defeated by Joshua

HORI (HOHR eye) *noble*
1. 20 century B.C.; Gen 36:22; son of Lotan; grandson of Seir; Horite chief
2. 15 century B.C.; Nu 13:5; his son Shaphat the Simeonite was sent by Moses to explore Canaan

HORITES (HOHR ights) Gen 14:6

The Eastern Horites, inhabitants and "cave-dwellers" of Seir (Edom), were akin to Edomites and Hivites. The Western Horites were non-Semites, unrelated to the Eastern Horites but akin to the Hurrians of central Asia Minor, a people who are not mentioned in the Bible. For further study, see Gen 36.

HORONITES (HOHR uh nights) Ne 2:10; possibly natives of Beth-horon; an epithet hurled at Sanballat

HOSAH (HOH zuh) *refuge;* 11 century B.C.; 1Ch 16:38; chief temple gatekeeper under David

HOSEA (ho ZAY uh) *the Lord has saved;* 8 century B.C.; Hos 1:1

The Bible is filled with images of marriage; God is called a husband to widows, Jesus the bridegroom, and the church his bride. In the first three chapters of the Old Testament Book of Hosea, however, one marriage symbolizes the history of God's love and Israel's betrayal.

Hosea was an Israelite prophet who was told by God to marry a prostitute named Gomer. He offered her his love, but she continued to sell herself to any man with money.

Gomer repeatedly betrayed Hosea with many lovers. In the same way, the Jews betrayed their covenant with God, worshiping at festivals, pagan temples, and roadside altars. As Gomer ran after her lovers, Israel ran after the idols and gods of every surrounding nation.

Children were born and given names that embodied God's own pain at Israel's betrayal. The oldest son, Jezreel, was named to recall an unwarranted slaughter by an earlier king of Israel in the valley of Jezreel. The next child was a daughter named Lo-ruhama (meaning *not pitied*). At the birth of Gomer's second son, God said, "Name him Lo-ammi [meaning *not my people*], for you are not my people and I am not your God."

Gomer finally left her children and husband for her lovers. When God told Hosea to bring Gomer home, he found her ill, broken, and a slave. Hosea bought her from her lover and took her back home. In the same way, God said he would bring Israel back to himself. "I will take you for my wife forever," God said. Hosea loved Gomer again as his wife. The younger children's names were changed to mean *pitied* and *you are my people*.

This story of Hosea's life in the first three chapters of his Book is followed by 11 chapters of prophecy from Hosea concerning the apostasy of Israel, its imminent punishment from God, and its eventual redemption through the love of God. Hosea, the only writing prophet to live in the northern kingdom, criticized his nation for displacing God from their hearts in favor of foreign idols, political and social accomplishments, and personal affluence. He placed blame on the civil and religious leaders for taking their people astray, and he warned of a time of submission and exile at the hands of Assyrian invaders. He also prophesied a time in the future when, through God's grace, Israel would be restored to righteousness.

For further study, see the Book of Hosea.

HOSHAIAH (hoh SHAY yuh) *the Lord has saved*
1. 7 century B.C.; Jer 42:1; father of Azariah 21 and Jezaniah
2. 5 century B.C.; Ne 12:32; leader at dedication of rebuilt Jerusalem wall

HOSHAMA (HOSH uh muh) *the Lord has heard;* 6 century B.C.; 1Ch 3:18; son or grandson of Jehoiachin

HOSHEA (hoh SHEE uh) *may the Lord save*
1. Nu 13:8; see Joshua 1
2. 11 century B.C.; 1Ch 27:20; Ephraimite tribal officer under David

3. ruled 732–722 B.C.; 2Ki 15:30

Hoshea, the son of Elah and successor to Pekah (whom he murdered), was the last king of Israel before the northern kingdom was engulfed and dispersed by the Assyrian invasion. By the time Hoshea took the throne, the Assyrians were already annexing parts of Israel and installing their own governors. Hoshea served the Assyrians as their leader over Israel; he was a puppet king who ruled in name only and paid Assyria for the privilege.

When Assyrian King Tiglath-pileser III died, Hoshea naively tried to form a military alliance with Egypt and together throw off the burdensome Assyrian yoke. But Assyria's new monarch, Shalmaneser V, crushed the independence movement, besieged Samaria, and took its inhabitants captive in 722 B.C.

For further study, see 2Ki 17:1-6; 18:9-13.
4. 5 century B.C.; Ne 10:23; sealer of covenant renewal in Nehemiah's day

HOTHAM (HOH thuhm) *seal*
1. 1Ch 7:32; descendant of Asher
2. 11 century B.C.; 1Ch 11:44; father of Shama and Jeiel, two of David's mighty men

HOTHIR (HOH thuhr) *abundance;* 10 century B.C.; 1Ch 25:4; son of Heman; temple musician under David

HUBBAH (HUB buh) meaning unknown; 1Ch 7:34; descendant of Asher

HUL (HUHL) *circle;* Gen 10:23; son of Aram; grandson of Shem

HULDAH (HUHL duh) *weasel;* 7 century B.C.; 2Ki 22:14

When Huldah was a respected prophet in Judah, so many generations had abandoned the God of Israel that not even the priests knew much about God's Law. When a Book of the Law was found hidden in the treasury, the king panicked. The book (perhaps some or all of Deuteronomy) showed in glaring terms how absolutely the nation had broken God's Law. Josiah sent priests to Huldah, a prophet who could still hear God. She spoke harshly, predicting disaster because the Jews' abandonment of God and worship of idols had earned God's wrath. She also said that because King Josiah loved and wanted to obey God, the nation would not be punished in his lifetime. For further study, see 2Ki 3–20; 2Ch 34:8-33.

HUPHAM (HOO fuhm) *coast-inhabitant;* Nu 26:39; ancestor of Benjaminite clan; also called Huppim

HUPPAH (HUP uh) *protection;* 11 century B.C.; 1Ch 24:13; head of division of priests under David

HUPPIM Gen 46:21; see Hupham

HUR (HUHR) meaning unknown
1. 16 century B.C.; Ex 31:2; Calebite descendant of chief craftsman of tabernacle
2. 15 century B.C.; Ex 17:10; helped Aaron hold up Moses's hands for Amalekite defeat
3. 15 century B.C.; Nu 31:8; Midianite king defeated by Moses and Israelites
4. 5 century B.C.; Ne 3:9; father of Rephaiah the rebuilder of the Jerusalem wall

HURAI 1Ch 11:32; see Hiddai

HURAM (HYOOR uhm) [my] *brother is exalted;*
1. 19 century B.C.; 1Ch 8:5; son of Bela; grandson of Benjamin
2. 2Ch 2:3; see Hiram 1
3. 2Ch 4:11; see Hiram 2

HURAM-ABI 2Ch 2:13; see Hiram 2

HURI (HUHR eye) meaning unknown; 1Ch 5:14; descendant of Gad

HUSHAH (HOO shuh) *haste* or *passion;* 1Ch 4:4; descendant of Judah

HUSHAI (HOO shye) *my brother's gift*
1. 10 century B.C.; 2Sa 15:32

Living up to his position as the trusted friend of King David, Hushai followed David as he fled Jerusalem during the rebellion of David's son Absalom. Arriving at the top of the Mount of Olives with "his coat torn and earth on his head" (2Sa 15:32), Hushai accepted David's assignment to return to Jerusalem as a spy, pretending to support Absalom. When Absalom questioned Hushai's defection, Hushai deceived him, saying he was bound to serve the man chosen by God and the Israelites.

Ahithophel, Absalom's chief advisor, counseled that they should pursue David immediately and destroy him. Hushai advised that Absalom should wait to attack. Absalom accepted Hushai's errant advice, and so David was allowed enough time to regroup and ultimately defeat his usurper. For further study, see 2Sa 15–17; 1Ch 27:33.
2. 10 century B.C.; 1Ki 4:16; father of Solomon's district governor Baana; possibly Hushai 1

HUSHATHITES (HYOO shuh thights) 2Sa 21:18; native of Hushah; Sibbecai the warrior was one

HUSHAM (HOO shuhm) *haste* or *passion;* Gen 36:34; pre-Israelite king of Edom; descendant of Esau

HUSHIM (HOO shim) *haste* or *passion*
1. 19 century B.C.; Gen 46:23; son of Dan; a form of Hashum; also called Shuham
2. 1Ch 8:8; wife divorced by Shaharaim; in Benjamin's genealogy

HYMENAEUS (HY muh NEE uhs) *pertaining to Hymen* (god of marriage); 1 century A.D.; 1Ti 1:20

The early church faced a great many struggles, not the least of which was conflicting interpretations of dogma by teachers such as Hymenaeus. The specifics of Hymenaeus's teachings are not known, but one way he clearly departed from the church's stand related to the final resurrection. Hymenaeus, it seems, did not accept the concept of an ultimate bodily resurrection but said rather that resurrection was strictly a spiritual experience, perhaps occurring at the time of baptism. In any event, Paul mentioned Hymenaeus with disdain in his letters to Timothy as one who had "suffered shipwreck in the faith" (1Ti 1:19). Paul excommunicated Hymenaeus from the church and turned him, along with Alexander and Philetus, over to Satan because of their blasphemy. Paul warned Timothy that they were guilty of profane chatter that spread like gangrene, upsetting the faith of some Christians with their false teaching. For further study, see 1Ti 1:19-20; 2Ti 2:14-19.

HYRCANUS (huhr CAY nuhs) *from Hercania;* 2 century B.C.; 2Mac 3:11; wealthy son of Tobias with funds deposited in temple

IBHAR (IB hahr) *he chooses;* 10 century B.C.; 2Sa 5:15; son of David born in Jerusalem

IBNEIAH (ib NEE yuh) *the Lord builds up;* 5 century B.C.; 1Ch 9:8; Benjaminite resettler in Jerusalem

IBNIJAH (ib NIGH juh) *the Lord builds up;* 1Ch 9:8; ancestor of Benjaminite resettler in Jerusalem

IBRI (ib REE) *a Hebrew;* 11 century B.C.; 1Ch 24:27; descendant of Merari

IBSAM (IB sam) *fragrant;* 1Ch 7:2; descendant of Issachar

IBZAN (IB zan) *active;* 11 century B.C.; Jdg 12:8; minor Israelite judge from Bethlehem

ICHABOD (IK uh bahd) *there is no glory;* 11 century B.C.; 1Sa 4:21; son of Phinehas; grandson of Eli

IDBASH (ID bash) *honey-sweet;* 1Ch 4:3; descendant of Judah

IDDO (ID oh) *beloved* or *adorned* or *timely*
1. 1Ch 6:21; Levite; descendant of Gershon; possibly Adaiah 2
2. 11 century B.C.; 1Ch 27:21; officer over Manassite tribe within Gilead
3. 10 century B.C.; 1Ki 4:14; father of Ahinadab; father-in-law of Solomon's daughter
4. 10 century B.C.; 2Ch 9:29; seer who knew much about the reigns of Solomon, Rehoboam, and Abijah
5. 6 century B.C.; Ezr 5:1; grandfather of prophet Zechariah
6. 6 century B.C.; Ne 12:4; chief priest; returned to Judah after Exile
7. 5 century B.C.; Ezr 8:17; leader of Levites from whom Ezra chose temple servants

IDUEL (id YOO ehl) meaning unknown; 5 century B.C.; 1Esd 8:43; courier sent by Ezra

IEZER Nu 26:30; see Abiezer 1

IGAL (EYE gal) *may he redeem*
1. 15 century B.C.; Nu 13:7; leader from Issachar tribe who explored Canaan
2. 11 century B.C.; 2Sa 23:36; son of Nathan; mighty man of David; also called Joel 7
3. 1Ch 3:22; descendant of Zerubbabel

IGDALIAH (IG duh LYE uh) *the Lord is great;* Jer 35:4; possibly a prophet; ancestor of Hanan

IKKESH (IK esh) *crooked* or *subtle;* 11 century B.C.; 1Ch 11:29; father of Ira the mighty man of David

ILAI (IHL eye) *supreme;* 11 century B.C.; 1Ch 11:29; mighty man of David; also called Zalmon

IMLAH (IM luh) *fullness;* 10 century B.C.; 1Ki 22:8; father of Micaiah the prophet

IMMANUEL (ih MAN yoo el) *God with us;* Isa 7:14; name given in Isaiah's prophecy to child of the virgin

IMMER (IM uhr) *lamb*
1. 11 century B.C.; 1Ch 24:14; head of division of priests under David
2. Ezr 2:37; ancestor of priestly family that resettled in Judah
3. 1Ch 9:12; ancestor of Amashsai the priest who resettled in Jerusalem
4. 7 century B.C.; Jer 20:1; temple priest whose son Pashhur had Jeremiah beaten

IMNA (IM nuh) *he keeps back;* 1Ch 7:35; descendant of Asher

IMNAH (IM nuh) *meaning unknown*
1. 19 century B.C.; Gen 46:17; firstborn son of Asher
2. 8 century B.C.; 2Ch 31:14; Levite; keeper of East Gate of Jerusalem wall during Hezekiah's day

IMRAH (IM ruh) *stubborn;* 1Ch 7:36; descendant of Asher

IMRI (IM rye) *my lamb*
1. 1Ch 9:4; ancestor of Uthai the resettler in Jerusalem
2. 5 century B.C.; Ne 3:2; father of Zaccur the rebuilder of Jerusalem wall

IPHDEIAH (if DEE yuh) *the Lord redeems;* 1Ch 8:25; descendant of Benjamin

IR (EER) *city;* 1Ch 7:12; descendant of Benjamin; ancestral source of Huppites and Shuppites

An angel intervenes as Abraham is about to sacrifice his son Isaac. Rembrandt (1606–1669).

IRA (EYE ruh) *meaning unknown*
1. 11 century B.C.; 2Sa 20:26; Jairite; not a Levite but still served as David's priest
2. 11 century B.C.; 2Sa 23:26; mighty man of David; son of Ikkesh
3. 11 century B.C.; 2Sa 23:38; Ithrite; mighty man of David

IRAD (EYE rad) *meaning unknown;* Gen 4:18; son of Enoch; grandson of Cain

IRAM (EYE ram) *meaning unknown;* Gen 36:43; chief of Edom; descendant of Esau

IRI (IH rye) *meaning unknown;* 1Ch 7:7; descendant of Benjamin; possibly Ir

IRIJAH (ih RYE juh) *the Lord sees;* 7 century B.C.; Jer 37:13; captain of guards; arrested Jeremiah

IR-NAHASH (ur NAY hash) *serpent city;* 1Ch 4:12; son (or city) of Tehinnah

IRU (EYE roo) *meaning unknown;* 15 century B.C.; 1Ch 4:15; son of Caleb; spy Moses sent to explore Canaan

ISAAC (I zak) *laughing* or *he laughed;* 21 century B.C.; Ge 17:19

Isaac was the "child of promise." God promised a 99-year-old man and his 90-year-old wife a child. Although at first the couple laughed at the prospect, Isaac was born as Abraham's heir and the father of the next generation of God's chosen people.

Isaac's story is one of faithfulness and favoritism. He learned faithfulness from his father in an unsettling event that has become one of the strongest examples of dedication to God in the Judeo-Christian heritage. Isaac was young when God told Abraham to sacrifice his only son on a mountain altar. Abraham obeyed, binding Isaac and raising a knife against him. At the last moment God sent an angel to intervene, and a ram was sacrificed in Isaac's place.

Isaac learned favoritism from his father as well. In his youth, Isaac saw his half-brother, Ishmael, sent away to ensure an undisputed inheritance. As Isaac approached manhood, other brothers were exiled also to secure his place as heir.

Isaac brought these childhood lessons into his own home. In faithfulness, he married Rebekah, his father's relative, instead of one of the idol-worshiping Canaanite women nearby. He put his faith in God when he and his wife were unable to conceive a child, and in the end was given twin sons. He also followed God's directives in settling his family.

Favoritism also affected Isaac's family. Isaac favored his son Esau, while Rebekah favored Jacob. This division of love produced competition such that Jacob managed to take his brother's birthright. Later, an elderly, blind Isaac was tricked when Jacob dressed as his brother so that Isaac would give him the blessing that was intended for Esau.

For further study, see Ge 15:1-6; 16–18; 21–29; Gal 4:28; Ro 9:6-13.

ISAIAH (I ZAY uh) *the Lord is salvation;* 8 century B.C.; 2Ki 19:2

Hebrew prophets were men and women, rich and poor, eccentric and scholarly. Some used poetry to communicate and others used drama. Amidst these differences was their consistent, unchanging dedication to revealing the will of their God to their people. By almost any measure, Isaiah is among the greatest of ancient Israel's prophets. He was a scholar, statesman, and poet, and during 50 years of prophetic ministry in Israel, he confronted evil, foretold future events, communicated God's will to rulers and citizens, and trumpeted an ongoing call to return to the ways of God.

At age 25, Isaiah had a vision in which God asked for a prophet willing to speak God's word. When Isaiah answered, "Here am I. Send me!" (Isa 6:8), his life's direction was set in motion. His ministry spanned 50 years and the reigns of four kings, beginning at the death of King Uzziah and lasting through the reigns of Jotham, Ahaz, and Hezekiah.

Isaiah lived in a time of political and spiritual upheaval. Israel had split into the separate monarchies of northern Israel and southern Judah; Assyrian and Egyptian military assaults kept every small nation in fear; and few God-fearing kings had sat on Judah's throne. Amid this confusion, Isaiah was called to speak for God.

Isaiah often addressed political and military issues. Because of the threat of invasion, particularly from Assyria, both Judah and Israel tried to find safety through ever-shifting alliances with various powerful neighbors. As a statesman and prophet, Isaiah repeatedly warned against looking for safety in armies and nations. His faith and vision taught

Vision of Isaiah, from the twelfth-century Bible of Saint-Suplice of Bourges.

him that God, and only God, had established and would protect the nation. During the reigns of Ahaz and Hezekiah, Judah was in such imminent danger that invading troops stood at the gates of Jerusalem. The kings were desperate for help, but Isaiah warned each of them that alliances with Assyria or Babylon might bring temporary aid but would not bring peace. Both kings, father and son, ignored Isaiah and made alliances that ended in Judah being swallowed up by the nations they put their trust in. "Woe to the rebellious children," the Lord said, "who carry out a plan, but not mine…" (Isa 30:1).

Isaiah lived all his recorded life in Jerusalem. His love for the city and his unveiled understanding of its failings are apparent in his writings. He called Jerusalem both a "faithful city" and a "harlot." The Book of Isaiah records God warning Jerusalem to turn from idol worship or he would "turn from [the city] in disgust and make [it] a desolation…," yet in Isaiah's lifetime, God miraculously saved Jerusalem from invaders twice, when King Ahaz and King Hezekiah were each on the throne. Both times, the city was hopelessly surrounded by superior forces, and the kings had ignored Isaiah's counsel, yet, God spoke through Isaiah that he would not permit the city to be taken.

Isaiah was more than a prophetic advisor to Judah's kings. He spoke publicly about idol worship and God's Law. He also criticized the outwardly religious who did not inwardly follow God, and he reiterated the traditional view of a righteous lifestyle.

Until King Hezekiah, Judah's citizens and rulers alike worshiped idols of the surrounding nations' gods. Much of the Book of Isaiah records his attempts to warn, reason with, and even shock those who committed idolatry. The prophet reasoned, "Who would fashion a god or cast an image that can do no good? Look, all its devotees shall be put to shame" (Isa 44:10-11). Later, when his people worshiped idols, he called them whores and said, "When you cry out, let your collection of idols deliver you" (Isa 57:13).

Isaiah also had harsh words for rich, comfortable Hebrews who ignored the poor and gained wealth at their expense. Prophets Micah and Amos spoke about these social justice issues, but they were rural farmers and may have been poor themselves. Isaiah spoke to the wealthy as a peer, and his words of condemnation were perhaps harsher because of it.

Isaiah had a vision for righteous living. When he saw God's people "adding house to house and field to field," and women adorning themselves with jewelry and costly clothing like Egyptian court maidens, he spoke in judgment and grave disappointment. He spoke of God's grief at the disobedience and hard hearts of Judah's kings and people. He commanded the rich and comfortable to share with the hungry and bring the homeless poor into their homes. "Is this not the fast that I choose: to loose the bonds of injustice, to undo the thongs of the yoke, to let the oppressed go free and to break every yoke?" (Isa 58:6). His words are similar to

> ➤ ⬅
>
> *"For a child has been born for us, a son given us; authority rests upon his shoulders; and he is named Wonderful Counselor, Mighty God, Everlasting Father, Prince of Peace."*
>
> Isa 9:6-7

Jesus's teachings about social justice in the Sermon on the Mount.

Isaiah may be best known for his prophecies about the messiah. Jews in every era have waited and hoped for God's promised savior, and Christians consider many chapters of the Book of Isaiah to be direct prophecies pointing to Jesus. Isaiah wrote passionately about the messiah. Chapter 53 of his book portrays the messiah in powerful terms as a servant who suffers for the redemption of sin. "He was wounded for our transgressions, crushed for our iniquities; upon him was the punishment that made us whole, and by his bruises we are healed" (Isa 53:5) is seen by Christians as a prediction of Jesus's death.

Jesus identified himself with Isaiah's messianic prophecies. This is apparent in Luke's narrative about the beginning of Jesus's ministry in the synagogue in Nazareth. He stood to read the scroll of the Book of Isaiah, choosing Chapter 61, verses 1 and 2. Jesus read, "The Spirit of the Lord is upon me, because he has anointed me to bring good news to the poor…" He then closed the scroll, turned to the congregation, and said that he was the fulfillment of this prophecy.

Traditional Jewish teaching on these writings is varied. Many theologians believe Isaiah's prophecies were about only the Assyrian oppression of Judah and Israel. Still others hold that the messianic chapters refer either to the reestablishment of Israel or to the hope of a messiah still to come. To this day, religious Jews wait and hope for the messiah whom Isaiah called "Yahweh's anointed one."

Ancient copies of Isaiah's writings have been discovered as part of the Dead Sea Scrolls; these manuscripts were found by Bedouin children in 1946. Although most of the discovery consisted of scroll fragments, some sealed jars contained complete scrolls. One, a 24-foot-long scroll made of sewn leather sheets, contained all 66 chapters of the

A portion of the Book of Isaiah found among the Dead Sea Scrolls at Qumran.

Book of Isaiah. This unprecedented discovery excited the theological and archaeological communities. Before the Dead Sea Scrolls were found, the earliest known version of the Hebrew Bible was the Masoretic Text, dated to the 10th century A.D. Remarkably, the writings of Isaiah from the Dead Sea Scrolls, dated some 1000 years earlier, are nearly identical with the Masoretic Texts.

Isaiah's life and writings are examples of faithfulness under pressure. During an era when Hebrew kings and commoners alike turned away from the traditions of God, Isaiah stood alone and harshly called for a return to the Law.

For further study, see 2Ki 19:1-7; the Book of Isaiah.

ISCAH (IZ kuh) meaning unknown; 21 century B.C.; Gen 11:29; daughter of Haran; sister of Milcah

ISCARIOT (is KAIR ee uht) *man of Kerioth;* see Judas Iscariot, Simon Iscariot

ISDAEL (IHZ dah ehl) meaning unknown; 10 century B.C.; 1Esd 5:33; servant of Solomon; ancestor of returnees

ISHBAAL (ISH bay uhl) *man of Baal* [a Canaanite god]; 11 century B.C.; 2Sa 2:8

This youngest son of King Saul is known by two names. Called Ish-Bosheth (meaning *man of shame*) by Hebrews in retrospect, he was first known by followers of Baal as Esh-baal or Ishbaal. In the power vacuum created by Saul's death in battle, the 40-year-old Ishbaal was made puppet king of Israel for two years in a vain attempt by Saul's cousin Abner to repudiate David's claim to the kingdom. The question of royal succession by heredity—favoring Ishbaal and Abner—or by charisma—favoring David—was eventually settled in favor of David, who ruled for 33 years over all of Israel and Judah following the assassination of Ishbaal. For further study, see 2Sa 2:8–5:5; 1Ch 8:33; 9:39. Also called Ishvi 2.

ISHBAH (ISH buh) *praising;* 1Ch 4:17; descendant of Judah

ISHBAK (ISH bak) meaning unknown; 21 century B.C.; Gen 25:2; son of Abraham by Keturah

ISHBI-BENOB (ISH bih BEE nahb) *dweller at Nob;* 11 century B.C.; 2Sa 21:16; Philistine warrior slain by Abishai

ISHHOD (ISH hahd) *vitality;* 1Ch 7:18; descendant of Manasseh

ISHI (ISH eye) *my husband*
1. 1Ch 2:31; descendant of Jerahmeel
2. 1Ch 4:20; descendant of Judah
3. 1Ch 4:42; ancestor of Simeonites who ran Amalekites out of Seir
4. 8 century B.C.; 1Ch 5:24; head of Manassite family exiled by king of Assyria

ISHMA (ISH muh) meaning unknown; 1Ch 4:3; descendant of Judah

ISHMAEL (ISH may uhl) *God heard*
1. 22 century B.C.; Gen 16:11
Ishmael's story began when his father, Abraham, received a promise from God that he would father

Ishmael and his mother are aided by an angel in the wilderness.

and established a clan of desert dwellers considered to be the ancestors of today's Arab nations.

For further study, see Gen 16–17.

2. 1Ch 8:38; Benjaminite descendant of Jonathan 4

3. 10 century B.C.; 2 Ch 9:11; father of Zebadiah the judge appointed by Jehoshaphat

4. 9 century B.C.; 2Ch 23:1; military commander; helped install Joash as king of Judah

5. 6 century B.C.; 2Ki 25:23; assassin of Gedaliah 4

6. 6 century B.C.; Ezr 10:22; priest; married and divorced foreigner after Exile

ISHMAELITES (ISH may el ights) Gen 37:25; Arab descendants of Abraham through Ishmael; from Paran wilderness

ISHMAIAH (ish MAY uh) *the Lord hears*
1. 11 century B.C.; 1Ch 12:4; Gibeonite; leader of David's mighty men
2. 11 century B.C.; 1Ch 27:19; officer over tribe of Zebulun under David

ISHMERAI (ISH muh rye) *guard* or *protector;* 1Ch 8:18; descendant of Benjamin

ISHPAH (ISH puh) meaning unknown; 1Ch 8:16; descendant of Benjamin

ISHPAN (ISH pan) *he will hide;* 1Ch 8:22; descendant of Benjamin

ISHTAR see Queen of Heaven

ISHVAH (ISH vuh) meaning unknown; 19 century B.C.; Gen 46:17; son of Asher

ISHVI (ISH vye) *equal*
1. 19 century B.C.; Gen 46:17; son of Asher
2. 1Sa 14:49; see Ishbaal

a great nation. Because Abraham and his wife, Sarah, were childless and elderly, they thought the promise could never be fulfilled. In their day, barren women sometimes used a substitute childbearer to produce a family; thus, Sarah offered her slave Hagar to Abraham as a concubine, hoping for the "child of promise" through her.

When Hagar became pregnant, she used her new status to look down upon her mistress. Sarah became so angry that Hagar fled into the desert in fear. There, an angel promised her that she would have a son, Ishmael, and ordered her to return.

Ishmael grew up as Abraham's son and heir. At 13, he was circumcised, marking him as a participant in Abraham's covenant with God. But then, Abraham was told by angels that the promise of his great nation was to be fulfilled not through Ishmael but through a child conceived by Sarah. When this son, Isaac, was born, Ishmael became dispossessed. Sarah asked that Ishmael be sent away, as he posed a threat to Isaac's inheritance. Abraham was reluctant to banish his son, but God instructed him to do so, telling Abraham that from Ishmael would come another great nation.

Wandering in the wilderness, Hagar and Ishmael almost died of thirst. An angel directed them to a well, and there they settled. Ishmael married

ISMACHIAH (IZ muh KIGH uh) *the Lord sustains;* 9 century B.C.; 2Ch 31:13; supervised tithes and offerings

ISRAEL (IZ ree uhl) *who strives with God*
1. Gen 32:28; see Jacob
2. Jdt 8:1; ancestor of Judith

ISRAELITES (IZ rih uhl ights) Gen 32:32
   Israelites are the descendants of Abraham through the 12 sons of Jacob. Also called Hebrews, they were chosen by God to receive the Law; to be guided by deliverer-judges, kings, and prophets; to endure God's judgment in the form of the Babylonian Exile; to be granted restoration into God's favor; and to receive the promise of a messiah. The nation was divided in 930 B.C.: Two of its tribes formed the southern nation of Judah, and the other ten tribes formed the northern nation of Israel. Israel was also known as Ephraim, after its principle tribe, and Samaria, after its capital city. See Hebrews, Jews.

ISSACHAR (IHZ uh kahr) *rewarded*
1. 20 century B.C.; Gen 30:18
   Issachar was the ninth son of Jacob and the fifth son of Leah. He and his 11 brothers became heads of the 12 tribes of Israel. Together with nine of his brothers, Issachar sold his brother Joseph as a slave to the Midianites, who in turn sold him to the Egyptians. Years later when the brothers traveled to Egypt to buy food during a famine, they encountered Joseph, who then held a prominent position in Pharaoh's court. With Jacob, they took their families and moved to Egypt. Issachar died in Egypt, but his descendants increased to over 64,000 by the time the Israelites returned to Canaan. For further study, see Gen 35:23; 46:13; 49:14-15; Nu 26:23; Dt 33:18-19; 1Ch 2:1; 7:1.
2. 10 century B.C.; 1Ch 26:5; temple gatekeeper under David

ISSHIAH (ish EYE uh) *there is the Lord*
1. 1Ch 7:3; descendants of Issachar
2. 1Ch 24:21; descendant of Levi
3. 1Ch 23:20; descendant of Levi
4. 11 century B.C.; 1Ch 12:6; mighty man of David

ISSHIJAH (ish EYE juh) *there is the Lord;* Ezr 10:31; 5 century B.C.; married and divorced foreigner after Exile

ISTALCURUS (iss tahl KYOO ruhs) meaning unknown; 5 century B.C.; 1Esd 8:40; father of returnee from Exile

ITHAI 1Ch 11:31; see Ittai 2

ITHAMAR (ITH uh mahr) *island of the palm tree;* 15 century B.C.; Ex 6:23; son of Aaron

ITHIEL (ITH ee uhl) *God is with me;* Ne 11:7; ancestor of Benjaminite resettler in Jerusalem

ITHMAH (ITH muh) *bereavement* or *purity;* 11 century B.C.; 1Ch 11:46; mighty man of David

ITHRA (ITH ruh) *excellence;* 10 century B.C.; 2Sa 17:25; brother-in-law of David; father of Amasa; also called Jether 5

ITHRAN (ITH ran) *excellent*
1. 20 century B.C.; Gen 36:26; son of Dishon the Horite chief in Esau's day
2. 1Ch 7:37; descendant of Asher; possibly Jether 3

ITHREAM (ITH ree uhm) *populous* or *remnant;* 10 century B.C.; 2Sa 3:5; son of David by Eglah

ITTAI (IT eye) meaning unknown
1. 10 century B.C.; 2Sa 15:19; Philistine military leader; with David against Absalom
2. 10 century B.C.; 2Sa 23:29; one of David's mighty men; also called Ithai

IZHAR (IZ hahr) *shining forth;* Ex 6:18; descendant of Levi through Kohath

IZLIAH (iz LYE uh) meaning unknown; 1Ch 8:18; descendant of Benjamin

IZRAHIAH (IZ ruh HIGH uh) *the Lord shines forth;* 1Ch 7:3; descendant of Issachar

IZRI (IZ rye) *one who forms;* 10 century B.C.; 1Ch 25:11; head of division of priests under David

IZZIAH (iz EYE uh) *the Lord purifies;* 5 century B.C.; Ezr 10:25; married and divorced foreigner after Exile

JAAKAN 1Ch 1:42; see Akan

JAAKOBAH (JAY uh KOH buh) *heel catcher;* 8 century B.C.; 1Ch 4:36; Simeonite; fought Hamites and Amalekites

JAALA (JAY ah luh) *mountain goat;* 10 century B.C.; Ne 7:58; servant of Solomon; ancestor of returnees to Judah; also called Jaalah

JAALAH Ezr 2:56; see Jaala

JAARE-OREGIM (JAY uh ree OHR uh jim) *woodsmen;* 10 century B.C.; 2Sa 21:19; father of Elhanan 1; also called Jair 3

JAARESHIAH (JAIR uh SHY uh) *the Lord plants;* 1Ch 8:27; descendant of Benjamin

JAASIEL (jay AY zee uhl) *God does* or *God makes*
1. 11 century B.C.; 1Ch 11:47; mighty man of David
2. 11 century B.C.; 1Ch 27:21; son of Abner; Benjaminite officer; possibly Jaasiel 1

JAASU (JAY uh soo) *maker* or *doer;* 5 century B.C.; Ezr 10:37; married and divorced foreigner

JAAZANIAH (jay az uh NYE uh) *the Lord hears*
1. 7 century B.C.; Eze 8:11; son of Shaphan; idol-worshiper
2. 7 century B.C.; Eze 11:1; son of Azzur; gave false advice in Ezekiel's vision
3. 6 century B.C.; 2Ki 25:23; aide to Gedaliah 4; also called Jezaniah; possibly Azariah 21
4. 6 century B.C.; Jer 35:3; Rechabite who refused wine

JAAZIAH (JAY uh ZYE uh) *the Lord strengthens;* 1Ch 24:26; ancestor of some Levites in time of David

JAAZIEL 1Ch 15:18; see Aziel

JABAL (JAY buhl) *stream;* Gen 4:20; son of Lamech; ancestral father of the first herdsmen

JABESH (JAY besh) *dry;* 8 century B.C.; 2Ki 15:10; father of King Shallum

JABEZ (JAY bez) *sorrow;* 1Ch 4:9; descendant of Judah; more pious than his brothers

JABIN (JAY bin) *intelligent* or *discerning*
1. 15 century B.C.; Jos 11:1; king of Hazor; defeated by Joshua
2. 13 century B.C.; Jdg 4:2; king of Hazor; oppressed Israel 20 years; defeated by Deborah

JACAN (JAY kuhn) *affliction;* 1Ch 5:13; ancestor of Gadite family

JACHIN (JAY kin) *he will establish*
1. 20 century B.C.; Gen 46:10; son of Simeon 1; also called Jarib 1
2. 10 century B.C.; 1Ch 24:17; head of division of priests under David
3. 5 century B.C.; 1Ch 9:10; priest; resettler in Jerusalem after Exile

JACOB (JAY kuhb) *supplanter*
1. 20 century B.C.; Gen 25:26

Jacob's birth was a metaphor for his life. In the womb, he struggled with his twin brother, Esau, and was born clutching the elder Esau's heel. While his name means *supplanter,* a more literal, albeit less polite, meaning is *grabber;* and grab he did.

When Rebekah was pregnant, the Lord said she carried "two nations" in her womb. He prophesied that the two nations would be divided, and the firstborn would serve the younger. "Jacob I loved, Esau I hated," creates an image of harshness not quite in keeping with God's treatment of Esau. However, God's blessing went to Jacob, not Esau.

Jacob was favored by his mother, while his father, Isaac, favored Esau. Jacob and Esau's struggle for primacy in the womb continued throughout their lives, aggravated by their parents' favoritism. In this struggle, Jacob became manipulative and deceitful; he literally grabbed everything Esau had. Because Esau was firstborn, he received the birthright. In ancient cultures this traditionally meant twice the inheritance of money and property, headship of the family, and a social and spiritual position of leadership. Jacob, clearly, was not content with one third of the inheritance and a subservient position, so he schemed to take his brother's birthright.

Jacob found his opportunity one day when Esau, an avid outdoorsman, was returning from a hunting trip exhausted and starving. In a move that has symbolized sibling rivalry for centuries, the wily farmer Jacob offered his brother food in exchange for his birthright, and Esau accepted. Whether Esau did not value his birthright or was desperate and truly starving is not clear. Later, Jacob added to this deception by stealing the blessing that Isaac intended for Esau. The paternal blessing of children was a common Middle Eastern custom and conveyed more than good wishes; it

Jacob meets his uncle Laban's daughter Rachel at a well.

was a stamp of approval and transfer of authority. Isaac reserved this blessing for his favorite son, Esau, but because Isaac was old and nearly blind, Jacob and his mother, Rebekah, were able to trick him. At Rebekah's suggestion, Jacob covered his arms and neck with lamb's wool to appear like his hairy older brother. Isaac was deceived and gave his blessing to Jacob instead of Esau.

When Esau discovered that Jacob had again grabbed something intended for him, he was enraged and vowed to kill his brother. Rebekah was afraid, and under the guise of sending him to seek a wife from her extended family, she sent Jacob north, to her homeland. About 60 miles from home, Jacob had a dream in which God stretched a ladder between heaven and earth. God stood at the top, assuring Jacob that the promise Abraham received would be made good for him, as Abraham's descendant. When Jacob woke, he poured oil over the stone under his head to mark the place of God's presence.

In Paddanaram, Rebekah's home, Jacob the grabber met his match. His trip became a 20-year exile, and he experienced deception in a new way—from the receiving end. Seeking his uncle Laban, he stopped at a well to ask directions of the local men. They not only knew Laban but pointed out his daughter Rachel, who was approaching with a herd of sheep. In a show of hospitality common to the times, Laban hosted Jacob for a month. Then, he asked what wages Jacob might take to stay and work with Laban's herds. Jacob had come to love

Shortly after Jacob leaves home to seek a wife, God appears to him in a dream.

Rachel, and said, "I will serve you seven years for your younger daughter, Rachel." Laban agreed.

After seven years, Jacob and Rachel's marriage was celebrated and Laban's true nature was revealed. Jacob took his veiled bride into a dark tent to consummate the marriage. The morning sun showed that Laban had veiled Leah, Rachel's older sister, and Jacob had married her instead. It is not known whether Laban forced his daughters to comply with this plan or whether Leah agreed in order to marry Jacob, but the results of this deception lasted more than one lifetime. Laban did eventually agree that Jacob could marry Rachel also after the feast for Leah was ended; however, he required seven more years of labor as a price for her.

The 14 years in Haran greatly changed Jacob and his family. Leah gave birth to four sons, while Rachel did not conceive. Following the example of her ancestor Sarah, Rachel gave her maid, Bilhah, to Jacob, and he fathered two more sons by her. After these births, Jacob fathered children by Zilpah, Leah's maid, and Leah gave birth to two more sons and a daughter. Jacob never loved Leah; only Rachel had his heart. Leah hoped that the six sons and one daughter she bore might win her husband's love. This did not happen. When, at last, Rachel conceived and gave birth to Joseph, Jacob favored him over his ten other sons. By repeating his own father's favoritism, he continued his family's pattern of hurt and rivalry into another generation.

When Jacob had worked 14 years for Leah and Rachel, he asked to return home. Jacob was an able shepherd, and since Laban did not want to lose such a skilled worker, he planned yet another trick. Laban asked what wages Jacob wanted for his work. Jacob asked no pay but the speckled, spotted, and black sheep and goats in the flock; those were considered blemished and were worth less. Laban agreed to this, but when Jacob was off with part of the flock, Laban's sons culled all these animals and drove them three days' journey away.

> ➤ ⬅
>
> *"You shall no longer be called Jacob, but Israel, for you have striven with God and with humans, and have prevailed."*
>
> Gen 32:28

Jacob was left with a hard choice: He could take the few multicolored or black animals in the small flock he was herding, or bide his time in hope of justice. He chose to stay, and devised a clever plan to turn Laban's deception against him. Jacob stripped fresh branches and set them in front of the troughs where the flocks drank. Because the animals bred near the trough, Jacob set apart only the strongest ewes to mate with speckled, spotted, or black sheep. He continued this practice, setting apart only the strongest for himself and returning the rest to Laban. In this way he became wealthy and Laban's flocks were poor.

As Jacob's success became increasingly obvious, Laban's sons were angry. God spoke to Jacob, telling him to return home, a proposal to which his wives agreed. When Laban was gone, Jacob left with his wives and children, servants and concubines. Although Laban pursued and tried to stop them, Jacob and his family never returned to Haran again.

As they approached his home, Jacob sent gifts ahead, hoping to soften Esau's anger. That night, Jacob sent everyone to the far side of the river and stayed alone, in case Esau should come. During the night, an angel in human form wrestled with him. At daybreak the angel pulled away, but Jacob clung to him, saying he would not let go without the angel's blessing. The angel asked Jacob's name and said, "You shall no longer be called Jacob, but Israel" (Gen 32:28). Jacob's hip was dislocated, but he persevered to receive the blessing, a name meaning *One who strives with God*. Esau then met his brother in welcome and forgiveness. Jacob settled in Canaan while Esau remained across the Jordan River in Seir.

In the years that followed, God spoke directly to Jacob, confirming the angel's word that Jacob would now be named Israel. God assured Jacob once again that, as Abraham's descendants, his family would produce nations and kings. In this period, Jacob and his family moved repeatedly. On

Jacob wrestles with an angel and then receives a blessing.

2. 1 century B.C.; Mt 1:15; father of Joseph; grandfather of Jesus

JADA (JAY duh) *caring* or *wise;* 1Ch 2:28; descendant of Judah

JADDAI (JAD eye) *beloved;* 5 century B.C.; Ezr 10:43; married and divorced foreigner after Exile

JADDUA (JAD oo uh) *known*
1. 5 century B.C.; Ne 10:21; sealer of covenant renewal in Nehemiah's day
2. 5 century B.C.; Ne 12:22; great-grandson of Eliashib; priest during reign of Darius

JADON (JAY dahn) *he will judge;* 5 century B.C.; Ne 3:7; man from Meronoth; rebuilder of Jerusalem wall

JAEL (JAY el) *mountain goat;* 13 century B.C.; Jdg 4:17

Jael was a capable woman—quick, clever, and fearless. She is honored for killing Sisera, a Canaanite military leader who had oppressed Israel for 20 years. When the people finally turned to God for help, they realized a total victory over the Canaanites. Sisera fled to the Kenites, a neighboring tribe at peace with Canaan. In the Kenite camp, Jael took Sisera into her tent to hide him from the Israelites, but her promise of safety was only a pretense. Jael waited until the commander fell asleep and then drove a tent peg into his temple, killing him instantly. Although history does not record the motivation for her act, Jael was honored in the Israelites' song of victory as the "most blessed of women." For further study, see Jdg 5:24-27.

one journey to Ephrath, Rachel went into labor. She received her longed-for second son but died in childbirth. Joseph named the boy Benjamin and grieved deeply for his wife.

The remainder of Jacob's life is strongly linked to his son Joseph. Joseph's brothers sold him into slavery in Egypt, where, through his own skill and God's protection, he became a powerful man. During a famine, Jacob, his sons, and their families were brought to Egypt by Joseph. When Jacob died, Joseph and his brothers took their father's body, as he requested, and buried it in Canaan. Then, they returned to Egypt where their descendants would remain for centuries, become enslaved, and finally be led to freedom during the Exodus under the leadership of Moses.

Jacob's grandfather, Abraham, was called the father of the Hebrew people. In a symbolic sense, Abraham conceived the nation, his son Isaac carried the seed, and Jacob gave birth to the child. The 12 tribes of Israel came from Jacob's 12 sons, in fulfillment of God's promise to Abraham.

For further study, see Gen 26–35; 37:18-28; 38–47; Ro 9:13.

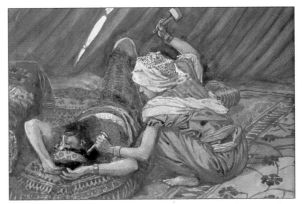

Jael kills the Canaanite military leader Sisera, who had oppressed Israel for 20 years.

JAHATH (JAY hath) *he will snatch up*
1. 1Ch 4:2; descendant of Judah
2. 1Ch 6:20; Levite clan leader; ancestor of Asaph; musician
3. 1Ch 23:10; descendant of Levi through Gershon; possibly Jahath 2
4. 10 century B.C.; 1Ch 24:22; Levite during David's day
5. 7 century B.C.; 2Ch 34:12; Levite supervisor of temple reconstruction

JAHAZIEL (juh HAY zee uhl) *God sees*
1. 11 century B.C.; 1Ch 12:4; Benjaminite in David's army
2. 11 century B.C.; 1Ch 16:6; priest/trumpeter when David brought ark to Jerusalem
3. 10 century B.C.; 1Ch 23:19; Levite during David's day
4. 9 century B.C.; 2Ch 20:14; priest who prophesied before King Jehoshaphat
5. 5 century B.C.; Ezr 8:5; father of Shecaniah 7

JAHDAI (JAH dye) *leader* or *the Lord leads;* 1Ch 2:47; descendant of Caleb and Judah

JAHDIEL (JAH dee uhl) *God gives joy;* 8 century B.C.; 1Ch 5:24; head of Manassites exiled by Tiglath-pileser III

JAHDO (JAH doh) *joyful;* 1Ch 5:14; descendant of Gad

JAHLEEL (JAH lee uhl) *God waits;* 19 century B.C.; Gen 46:14; last son of Zebulun; grandson of Jacob

JAHMAI (JAH mye) *the Lord protects;* 1Ch 7:2; descendant of Issachar

JAHZEEL (JAH zee uhl) *God apportions;* Gen 46:24; head of one clan of Naphtali; also called Jahziel

JAHZEIAH (JAH zee yuh) *the Lord sees;* 5 century B.C.; Ezr 10:15; opposed Ezra's decree to divorce foreign wives

JAHZERAH 1Ch 9:12; see Ahzai

JAHZIEL 1Ch 7:13; see Jahzeel

JAIR (JAIR) *may he shine forth* or *he enlightens*
1. 15 century B.C.; Nu 32:41; descendant of Manasseh
2. 12 century B.C.; Jdg 10:3; Gileadite; leader of Israel; possibly descendant of Jair 1
3. 1Ch 20:5; see Jaare-oregim
4. 6 century B.C.; Est 2:5; Benjaminite; father of Esther's cousin Mordecai

JAIRUS (JAYR uhs) *the Lord enlightens;* 1 century A.D.; Mk 5:22

Jairus, president of the local synagogue in the Gerasene region, ordered worship services and saw that religious tradition was upheld in the community. When tragedy threatened his family, this distinguished ruler turned to Jesus for help. In front of a crowd, Jairus knelt, begging Jesus to heal his dying 12-year-old daughter. Before they reached her, she was pronounced dead, but Jesus told Jairus to keep his faith and continued on. On reaching Jairus's house, Jesus said that the girl was merely sleeping and went over and revived her. He told the girl's amazed parents to feed her and not to speak to anyone of what had happened. For further study, see Mt 9:18-26; Mk 5:21-43; Lk 8:40-56.

JAKEH (JAY kuh) *pious* or *discerning;* Pr 30:1; father of Agur the author of a proverb

Jesus restores Jairus's daughter to life.

JAKIM (JAY kim) *he will establish*
1. 1Ch 8:19; descendant of Benjamin
2. 10 century B.C.; 1Ch 24:12; head of division of priests

JALAM (JAY luhm) meaning unknown; 20 century B.C.; Gen 36:5; son of Esau by Oholibamah

JALON (JAY lahn) meaning unknown; 1Ch 4:17; descendant of Judah

JAMBRES (JAM breez) meaning unknown; 15 century B.C.; 2Ti 3:8; Egyptian sorcerer; opposed Moses; see Jannes

JAMBRI (JAM brye) meaning unknown; 2 century B.C.; 1Mac 9:36; head of family that attacked wedding party

JAMES (JAYMZ) *supplanter*
1. 1 century A.D.; Lk 6:16; father of the apostle Judas
2. 1 century A.D.; Mt 4:21

James left his father Zebedee and the family fishing business to follow Jesus with the other chosen apostles. Along with his brother John and their partner Peter, James became one of Jesus's favored followers. These three men personally witnessed the life, ministry, death, and resurrection of Jesus. James was at Jesus's side for the glory of the Transfiguration and the agony in the garden of Gethsemane. James and John were described in the Gospel accounts as the "Sons of Thunder." They earned that nickname for their tendency to rush to judgment, as when they called for God to rain thunder and lightning on a village full of Samaritan unbelievers. The brothers showed their ambitious natures when they asked Jesus for positions of honor in the kingdom he came to establish. Jesus warned the two that they did not know what they were asking for and that they were unprepared to drink from the same cup as he, a reference to his impending death. Yet James would be the first to taste death for his master. The ambitious, short-tempered James was the church's first martyr; he was executed at the hands of Herod Agrippa I, 15 years after Jesus died. For further study, see Mt 10:2; 17:1-13; Mk 1:16-20; 3:17; 10:35-41; 13:3; 14:32-42; Lk 5:1-10; 6:14; 8:51; 9:28,54; Ac 1:13; 12:2.

James and his brother John leave the family fishing business to follow Jesus.

3. 1 century A.D.; Mt 10:3; son of Alphaeus; an apostle; possibly brother of Matthew
4. 1 century A.D.; Mt 27:56; son of Clopas and Mary; possibly James 2
5. 1 century A.D.; Mt 13:55

James, considered by most scholars to be the brother of Jesus, found his faith in Christ late. During the ministry of Jesus, James was known as his brother, not his follower. In fact, church tradition is that James's conversion occurred only when Jesus appeared to him after the resurrection, but his life from that point was unwavering.

James was probably the primary leader of the Jerusalem Christians. He was known for wisdom and integrity, amply illustrated in the Book of James, where he wrote about righteous behavior and good works as evidence of faith. The apostle Paul respected and consulted him.

During James's tenure as church leader, the movement changed drastically. As Gentiles joined the church, their non-Jewish attitudes and practices

James, son of Clopas and Mary. El Greco (1541–1614).

JAMIN (JAY min) *lucky* or *the right hand*
1. 20 century B.C.; Gen 46:10; son of Simeon and grandson of Jacob
2. 1Ch 2:27; grandson of Jerahmeel
3. 5 century B.C.; Ne 8:7; Levite; helped Ezra teach the Law to people

JAMLECH (JAM lek) *may he give dominion;* 1Ch 4:34; clan leader; descendant of Simeon

JANAI (JAY nye) *may he answer;* 1Ch 5:12; Gadite chief; descendant of Gad

JANNAI (JAH nye) *answered;* Lk 3:24; descendant of Zerubbabel; ancestor of Jesus

JANNES (JAN ez) possibly *he who seduces;* 15 century B.C.; 2Ti 3:8

Though unnamed in Exodus, Jannes and Jambres are identified in Jewish tradition as the two Egyptian sorcerers who countered Moses's efforts to convince Pharaoh to free Israel. Using magic, they duplicated the miracles that Moses and Aaron had performed with the assistance of God, and so for a time kept Pharaoh unimpressed with the Hebrew God. Jannes and Jambres appear in many traditional Jewish stories, and they also show up in pagan and Christian literature from the first century. In Paul's last letter to Timothy, he cites Jannes and Jambres as traditional examples of the deception and opposition young Timothy might face while pastoring at Ephesus. For further study, see Ex 7–8; 2Ti 3:1-9.

JAPHETH (JAY feth) *may God enlarge;* Gen 5:32

This third son of Noah was one of eight human survivors of the Flood. Along with his brother Shem, he was particularly blessed by Noah for having discreetly covered their father's drunkenness and nakedness. They did so by walking toward him backward and covering him with a blanket without looking at him, thus saving him from embarassment. Noah's blessing on Japheth conveyed a sense of multiple, far-ranging descendants. The descendants of Japheth may be identified as the 14 Indo-European (Caucasian) nations mentioned in Genesis 10: From Gomer came the ancient Cimmerians; from Magog, the Scythians; from Madai, the Medes; from Javan, the Ionians or Greeks; from Tubal and Meshech, peoples of eastern Turkey; from Tiras, certain Aegean islanders, including per-

forced a confrontation between them and the Jewish believers who thought Gentiles should become Jews and be circumsized before they could be baptized as Christians. James headed the council faced with this conflict. Under James's leadership, the council refused to bind Gentile Christians to Jewish Law, requiring them only to avoid practicing pagan sexual rituals and offering meat in sacrifice to idols.

James was called "the Just," perhaps to honor his leadership of the early church. In his epistle, he humbly called himself only "a servant of God and of the Lord Jesus Christ," placing his brother above himself. The Jewish historian Josephus recorded James's death by stoning in A.D. 62.

Some Roman Catholic scholars see the description "brother of Jesus" as symbolic rather than literal, assigning a brotherhood within the family of God, or distant kinship, rather than shared parentage; such an interpretation is consistent with the Catholic doctrine of the perpetual virginity of Mary.

For further study, see the Letter of James; 1Cor 15:7; Ac 21:17-26.

haps the Etruscans. For further study, see Gen 6:10; 7:13; 9:18-27; 10:1-5; 1Ch 1:4-5.

JAPHIA (juh FYE uh) *splendor*
1. 15 century B.C.; Jos 10:3; Amorite king of Lachish; defeated by Joshua
2. 10 century B.C.; 2Sa 5:15; son of David

JAPHLET (JAF luht) *delivered;* 1Ch 7:32; descendant of Asher

JARAH (JAY ruh) *honeycomb;* 1Ch 9:42; descendant of Jonathan and Saul; also called Jehoaddah

JARED (JAIR uhd) *descent;* Gen 5:15; father of Enoch; ancestor of Noah

JARHA (JAR hah) meaning unknown; 1Ch 2:34; Egyptian servant; married a female descendant of Judah

JARIB (JAIR uhb) *he contends*
1. 1Ch 4:24; see Jachin
2. 5 century B.C.; Ezr 8:16; envoy sent by Ezra to retrieve Levites for temple service

3. 5 century B.C.; Ezr 10:18; descendant of Jeshua the high priest who married and divorced foreigner after Exile

JAROAH (juh ROH uh) *new moon* or *mouth;* 1Ch 5:14; descendant of Gad

JASHAR (JAY shahr) *upright;* Jos 10:13; author of the Book of Jashar, which is quoted twice in the Old Testament

JASHEN 2Sa 23:32; see Hashem

JASHOBEAM (juh SHOH bee uhm) *to whom the people turn*
1. 11 century B.C.; 1Ch 11:11; leader of David's mighty men; also called Josheb-basshebeth
2. 11 century B.C.; 1Ch 12:6; Korahite; joined David at Ziklag
3. 10 century B.C.; 1Ch 27:2; son of Zabdiel; in charge of division of David's army; possibly Jashobeam 1

JASHUB (JAY shuhb) *may he return*
1. 19 century B.C.; Gen 46:13; son of Issachar; grandson of Jacob
2. 5 century B.C.; Ezr 10:29; married and divorced foreigner after Exile

JASON (JAY suhn) *healing* or *salvation*
1. 2 century B.C.; 1Mac 8:17; son of Eleazar; Maccabean envoy to Rome
2. 2 century B.C.; 2Mac 2:23

The Maccabean revolt occurred in the years between the Old and New Testaments. A family of pious Jews rebelled when Judea's political masters, the Seleucid Empire, forbade traditional religious practices and tried to control the Jews through appointed chief priests. Jason the Cyrene, a writer and historian, recorded this history in a five-volume work that

Japhet and Shem cover the nakedness of their father, Noah. Michelangelo (1475–1564), Sistine Chapel, Rome.

has since disappeared. The Book of Second Maccabees, written between 104 and 63 B.C., credits Jason with compiling a "mass of material" from which the apocryphal history was condensed. Second Maccabees contains rich literary images that may have come from Jason. The historian may have been recognized as a scholar outside of Israel as well, since his name was inscribed on the temple of Pharaoh Thutmose III in Egypt. For further study, see 2Mac 1–15.
3. 1 century A.D.; Ac 17:5; Thessalonian Christian arrested for housing Paul and Silas
4. 1 century A.D.; Ro 16:21; relative of Paul; sent greetings to Roman church; possibly Jason 3

JATHNIEL (JATH nee el) *God-given;* 10 century B.C.; 1Ch 26:2; son of Meshelemiah; chief temple gatekeeper

JAVAN (JAY vuhn) meaning unknown; Gen 10:2; son of Japheth; a maritime people of Ionia (southern Greece)

JAZIZ (JAY ziz) meaning unknown; 11 century B.C.; 1Ch 27:30; Hagrite shepherd for King David

JEATHERAI (jee ATH uh rye) meaning unknown; 1Ch 6:21; descendant of Levi

JEBERECHIAH (juh BAIR uh KYE uh) *the Lord blesses;* 8 century B.C.; Isa 8:2; father of Zechariah the witness to a prophecy by Isaiah

JEBUSITES (JEB yoo sights) Gen 10:16; Canaanite tribe; inhabitants of Jebus (Jerusalem) captured by David

JECHONIAH (JEK oh NIGH uh) *the Lord establishes;* Mt 1:11; ancestor of Jesus; a form of Jeconiah

JECOLIAH (JEK uh LYE uh) *the Lord is able;* 9 century B.C.; 2Ki 15:2; mother of Azariah the tenth Judean king

JECONIAH (JEK uh NIGH uh) *the Lord establishes*
1. 1Sa 6:19; see Jechoniah and Jehoiachin
2. 6 century B.C.; Bar 1:7; son of Jehoiakim 2

JEDAIAH (jeh DAY yuh) *the Lord knows*
1. 11 century B.C.; 1Ch 24:7; priest in charge of a divsion under David
2. Ezr 2:36; ancestor of family of priests who returned to Judah
3. 1Ch 4:37; ancestor of Ziza the Simeonite chief
4. 6 century B.C.; Ne 12:6; one of two priests who returned to Judah
5. 6 century B.C.; Ne 12:7; one of two priests who returned to Judah
6. 6 century B.C.; Zec 6:10; brought gold and silver to Jerusalem; possibly Jedaiah 4 or 5
7. 5 century B.C.; Ne 3:10; son of Harumaph; repairer of Jerusalem wall
8. 5 century B.C.; 1Ch 9:10; priest; resettled in Jerusalem after Exile

JEDIAEL (jeh DYE uhl) *God knows*
1. 1Ch 7:6; descendant of Benjamin
2. 11 century B.C.; 1Ch 11:45; mighty man of David
3. 11 century B.C.; 1Ch 12:20; Manassite who joined David at Ziklag; possibly Jediael 2
4. 10 century B.C.; 1Ch 26:2; son of Meshelemiah; temple gatekeeper

JEDIDAH (jeh DYE duh) *beloved;* 7 century B.C.; 2Ki 22:1; mother of Josiah the sixteenth king of Judah

JEDIDIAH (JED uh DYE uh) *beloved of the Lord;* 10 century B.C.; 2Sa 12:25; Solomon's birth name; see Solomon

JEDUTHUN (jeh DOO thuhn) *praiseworthy*
1. 1Ch 9:16; see Ethan 3
2. 11 century B.C.; 1Ch 16:38; father of David's gatekeeper Obed-edom

JEHALLELEL (jeh HAL uh lel) *may God shine forth*
1. 1Ch 4:16; descendant of Judah
2. 8 century B.C.; 2Ch 29:12; father of Azariah the Levite who helped purify the temple

JEHDEIAH (jeh DEE yuh) *may the Lord rejoice*
1. 10 century B.C.; 1Ch 24:20; Levite who served under David
2. 10 century B.C.; 1Ch 27:30; official responsible for David's donkeys

JEHEZKEL (jeh HEZ kel) *God strengthens;* 10 century B.C.; 1Ch 24:16; leader of priests under David

JEHIAH (jeh HIGH uh) *the Lord lives;* 11 century B.C.; 1Ch 15:24; gatekeeper for ark upon its return

JEHIEL (jeh HIGH uhl) *God lives*
1. 11 century B.C.; 1Ch 15:18; Levite; played lyre upon ark's return
2. 11 century B.C.; 1Ch 23:8; Levite; temple treasurer; also called Jehieli
3. 10 century B.C.; 1Ch 27:32; caretaker of sons of King David
4. 9 century B.C.; 2Ch 21:2; killed when his brother Jehoram became king of Judah
5. 2Ch 31:13; see Jehuel
6. 7 century B.C.; 1Ch 35:8; chief temple administrator under Josiah
7. 5 century B.C.; Ezr 8:9; father of Obadiah 12
8. 5 century B.C.; Ezr 10:2; father of Shecaniah 8
9. 5 century B.C.; Ezr 10:21; priest who married and divorced foreigner after Exile
10. 5 century B.C.; Ezr 10:26; married and divorced foreigner; possibly Jehiel 8

JEHIELI 1Ch 26:21; see Jehiel 2

JEHIZKIAH (JEE hiz KYE uh) *the Lord strengthens;* 8 century B.C.; 2Ch 28:12; opposed enslaving prisoners

JEHOADDAH 1Ch 8:36; see Jarah

JEHOADDAN (juh HOH uh dan) possibly *the Lord delights;* 9 century B.C.; 2Ch 25:1; mother of King Amaziah; a form of Jehoaddin

JEHOADDIN 2Ki 14:2; see Jehoaddan

JEHOAHAZ (juh HOH uh haz) *the Lord has grasped*
1. 2Ch 21:17; see Ahaziah 2
2. ruled 814–798 B.C.; 2Ki 10:35
At the time Jehoahaz succeeded to the throne, Israel was in decline under the dominance of Aram (Syria). Israel's spiral accelerated downward under Jehoahaz, whose army was badly defeated by Syrian King Hazael and his successor Ben-hadad III. Late in his reign, however, Jehoahaz appealed to the Lord, who granted Israel a "savior." That savior took the form not of some deliverer-judge, as in years past, but of a diversion; the Israelites experienced temporary relief when the oppressive Syrian military moved north to head off a threat from Assyria. Despite this reprieve from God, the people under Jehoahaz continued to practice idolatry as they had for the previous 11 administrations. For further study, see 2Ki 13:1-9.
3. ruled 609 B.C.; 2Ki 23:30
Jehoahaz succeeded to the throne of Judah at age 23, following his father Josiah's death in battle against Pharaoh Neco. Jehoahaz, the fourth and youngest son of Josiah, may have been chosen over his older brothers because his policies were anti-Egyptian, as were the policies of Josiah. However, like his father, Jehoahaz was no match for Pharaoh Neco. Summoned to a meeting with Neco, Jehoahaz was arrested, placed in chains, deposed, and deported from Judah to Egypt, where he died. Pharaoh Neco installed Jehoiakim, the older half-brother of Jehoahaz as a puppet king in his place; thus Judah became a vassal state, paying tribute to Egypt. For further study, see 2Ki 23:31-35. Also called Shallum 10.

JEHOASH (juh HOH ash) *the Lord has given*
1. 2Ki 11:21; see Joash 7
2. ruled 798–782 B.C.; 2Ki 13:10
The obituary for Jehoash, the twelfth king of Israel, reads like an indictment: "He did what was evil in the sight of the Lord," abandoning God, worshiping idols, and causing all Israel to follow

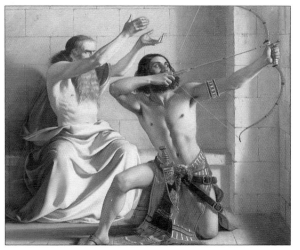

Elisha orders King Jehoash to shoot the arrow of victory for Israel.

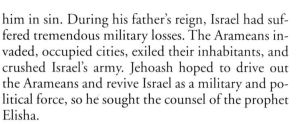

him in sin. During his father's reign, Israel had suffered tremendous military losses. The Arameans invaded, occupied cities, exiled their inhabitants, and crushed Israel's army. Jehoash hoped to drive out the Arameans and revive Israel as a military and political force, so he sought the counsel of the prophet Elisha.

Jehoash went to Elisha's deathbed, weeping about Israel's position and his own despair. Elisha told him to shoot an arrow from the east window; he called it "the Lord's arrow of victory." Elisha then instructed Jehoash to strike the ground with a fistful of arrows; he struck three times. As Elisha predicted, Jehoash's army defeated the Arameans and reclaimed their cities, but, because Jehoash lacked faith and struck only three times, Israel took only three victories, defeating but not crushing the Arameans.

Jehoash is best known for utterly defeating Israel's southern neighbor, Judah. King Amaziah of Judah, heady after defeating the Edomites, issued a challenge to Israel as well. Jehoash of Israel did not want to fight fellow Hebrews and told Amaziah to "be content with [his] glory, and stay at home," but Amaziah refused to withdraw. The two armies met at Bethshemesh in Judah, and Amaziah's forces were badly beaten. Jehoash showed his contempt for Judah and the Lord by destroying a 600-foot stretch of the wall surrounding Jerusalem and by looting both the temple and palace.

For further study, see 2Ki 13:10-19; 2Ki 14:1-14. Also called Joash 8.

JEHOHANAN (jeh hoh HAY nuhn) *the Lord is gracious*
1. 10 century B.C.; 1Ch 26:3; gatekeeper; son of Meshelemiah
2. 9 century B.C.; 2Ch 17:15; chief commander under King Jehoshaphat
3. 9 century B.C.; 2Ch 23:1; father of Ishmael 4; possibly Jehohanan 2
4. 6 century B.C.; Ne 12:13; head of priestly family of Amariah 7
5. 5 century B.C.; Ezr 10:6; high priest; also called Johanan 8
6. 5 century B.C.; Ezr 10:28; descendant of Bebai; married and divorced foreigner after Exile
7. 5 century B.C.; Ne 6:18; his father Tobiah opposed Jerusalem wall construction
8. 5 century B.C.; Ne 12:42; priest who helped dedicate Jerusalem wall

JEHOIACHIN (je HOY uh chin) *the Lord will uphold;* ruled 598–597 B.C.; 2Ki 24:6
When Judah's King Jehoiakim died, his 18-year-old son Jehoiachin began his short reign of only three months and ten days. In spite of the brevity of his regime, Jehoiachin established a reputation as a godless king, consistent with his father's previous administration. His reign was cut short by the invasion of the Babylonians, led by King Nebuchadnezzar, who took all but the very poor captive to Babylon. According to the prophet Jeremiah, the people of Judah looked to Jehoiachin as their ruler even in exile, while the Babylonians treated him with contempt. After 37 years of captivity, Jehoiachin was released from prison by the new Babylonian king, Amel-Marduk, who gave him an honored place in his court. For further study, see 2Ki 24–25; 1Ch 3:16-17; 2Ch 36:8-9; Est 2:6; Jer 22:24-30; 24:1; 37:1; 52:31-34; Eze 1:2-3. Also called Coniah and Jeconiah 1.

JEHOIADA (jeh HOY ah duh) *the Lord knows*
1. 11 century B.C.; 2Sa 8:18; father of David's bodyguard Benaiah
2. 11 century B.C.; 1Ch 12:27; descendant of Aaron; joined David at Hebron
3. 10 century B.C.; 1Ch 27:34; advisor of David
4. 9 century B.C.; 2Ki 11:4
The elderly Jehoiada was a sage priest whose timely, well-organized support allowed Joash to rightfully take the throne of Judah from the murderous Queen Athaliah. Under Jehoiada's guidance, King Joash led the people to a covenant of restoration and returned them to the God of Israel. As long as young Joash (also called Jehoash) listened to the advice of the elder Jehoiada, the king and the nation fared well. "Jehoash did what was right in the sight of the Lord all his days, because the priest Jehoiada instructed him" (2Ki 12:2). But as soon as the king strayed from the strict religious tradition of Jehoiada, he paid the ultimate price—his life. For further study, see 2Ki 11–12; 2Ch 23–24.
5. 7 century B.C.; Jer 29:26; replaced Zephaniah as priest at temple
6. Ne 13:28; see Joiada 2

JEHOIAKIM (jeh HOY ah chim) *God established* or *the Lord will establish*
1. ruled 609–598 B.C.; 2Ki 23:34
Eliakim was renamed Jehoiakim when Pharaoh Neco made him a puppet king of Judah. Jehoiakim

ruled Judah for 11 years. He was subservient to Egypt's Neco for the first four years and to Babylon's Nebuchadnezzar for three more, until he was temporarily able to oust the Babylonians. Jehoiakim's regime was violent, greedy, dishonest, and oppressive. He murdered the prophet Uriah and would have killed the prophet Jeremiah and his companion Baruch if it weren't for the protection of friends within Jehoiakim's regime. Jeremiah denounced the ways of Jehoiakim and Judah and predicted their downfall in the prophetic scrolls he dictated to Baruch. Jehoiakim shredded and burned the scrolls of Jeremiah, but to no avail. Jeremiah's words were borne out when the Babylonians recaptured Judah. Jehoiakim died violently and was given "the burial of a donkey—dragged off and thrown out beyond the gates of Jerusalem" (Jer 22:19). For further study, see 2Ki 23:34–24:8; 2Ch 36:4-8; Jer 22:13-30; 26:20-24; 36:1-32. Also called Eliakim.
2. 6 century B.C.; Bar 1:7; high priest in Jerusalem

JEHOIARIB (jeh HOY ah rib) *the Lord contends*
1. 10 century B.C.; 1Ch 24:7; leader of priests under David

2. 5 century B.C.; 1Ch 9:10; priest who resettled in Jerusalem

JEHONADAB 2Ki 10:15; see Jonadab 2

JEHONATHAN (juh HAHN uh thuhn) *the Lord has given*
1. 9 century B.C.; 2Ch 17:8; Levite; taught Law in Judah
2. 6 century B.C.; Ne 12:18; head of priestly family in time of Joiakim

JEHORAM (juh HOHR uhm) *the Lord is exalted*
1. ruled 852–841 B.C.; 2Ki 1:17
   The Jehoram of Israel (also called Joram) is not to be confused with the Jehoram/Joram who ruled Judah during the same decade. Israel's king, the son of Ahab and his Phoenician, Baal-worshiping wife Jezebel, inherited the throne from his brother Ahaziah. After a 12-year reign, Jehoram was killed by the usurper Jehu, who was anointed to wipe out the house of Ahab for their practice of the cultic Baal religion. Under Jehoram's rule, Israel lost control of neighboring Moab when King Mesha's revolt could not be suppressed. When Jehoram resumed Israel's perpetual war with its northern

Jehoram is treacherously killed with an arrow by the usurper Jehu.

neighbor Aram (Syria), he brought on a siege and food shortage that he then tried to blame on the prophet Elijah and his God. For further study, see 2Ki 3:1-27; 8:16-29; 9:14-29; 2Ch 22:1-7.

2. ruled 852–841 B.C.; 2Ki 8:16

As the son of King Jehoshaphat, Jehoram (also called Joram) was the rightful ruler of Judah, but it was his wife Athaliah, daughter of the wicked Ahab and Jezebel, who wielded the true power. Under her influence, Jehoram and the nation abandoned the God of Israel and practiced the cultic religion of the god Baal. After Jehoram's death, Athaliah attempted to wrest power from Jehoram's ancestral line of Judah by assassinating all of his offspring. One grandson, Joash, survived the queen's plan and later regained the throne from her. For further study, see 2Ki 8:16-24; 2Ch 21.

3. 9 century B.C.; 2Ch 17:8; priest; taught Law to people of Judah

JEHOSHABEATH (juh HAHSH uh buth) *the Lord is abundance;* 9 century B.C.; 2Ch 22:11; aunt who hid boy-king Joash; a form of Jehosheba

JEHOSHAPHAT (juh HAHSH uh fat) *the Lord has judged*
1. 10 century B.C.; 2Sa 8:16; recorder or historian for King David and King Solomon
2. 10 century B.C.; 1Ki 4:17; son of Paruah; governor under Solomon
3. ruled 872–848 B.C.; 1Ki 15:24

Jehoshaphat, the fourth king of Judah, learned a difficult lesson from his father and predecessor, King Asa. Although Asa followed God early in his reign, his pride later prompted him to reject God's judgment. Following the flattering words of false prophets rather than the will of God, Asa fell ill and died.

King Jehoshaphat of Judah. Stained glass. Lincoln Cathedral, Lincoln, England.

When Jehoshaphat assumed the throne, he became one of the few God-fearing kings of Judah or Israel. In addition to destroying many sites of idol worship and restoring the temple, he personally appointed judges and set the Law of Moses as their standard. He placed the chief priest over them to command judgment "in fear of the Lord, in faithfulness" (2Ch 19:9).

After this, three nations combined to invade Judah. When messengers reported approaching armies, Jehoshaphat's response was unlike that of any of Judah's kings either before or after him. He assembled the entire nation to pray. Jehoshaphat himself prayed, "O our God...we are powerless against this great multitude....We do not know what to do, but our eyes are on you" (2Ch 20:12).

Jehoshaphat's army went out to meet the invaders and found their corpses strewn across a valley; the invading armies had turned on each other and destroyed themselves. Jehoshaphat's army returned to Jerusalem singing praise to God for his protection. Jehoshaphat reigned for 25 years in Jerusalem and was succeeded by his son Jehoram, who began his rule by killing all six of his brothers and turning from his father's faith.

For further study, see 1Ki 22:1-50; 2Ch 17–20.

4. 9 century B.C.; 2Ki 9:2; father of King Jehu

JEHOSHEBA 2Ki 11:2; see Jehoshabeath

JEHOZABAD (juh HOH zuh bad) *the Lord gives*
1. 10 century B.C.; 1Ch 26:4; son of Obed-edom; a temple gatekeeper for David
2. 9 century B.C.; 2Ch 17:18; Benjaminite commander under Jehoshaphat
3. 9 century B.C.; 2Ki 12:21; official who plotted murder of King Joash

JEHOZADAK 1Ch 6:14; see Jozadak

JEHU (JEE hoo) *he is the Lord*
1. 1Ch 2:38; descendant of Judah 1
2. 11 century B.C.; 1Ch 12:3; Benjaminite defector to David's army
3. 10 century B.C.; 1Ki 16:1; son of Hanani; prophesied against King Baasha
4. ruled 841–814 B.C.; 1Ki 19:16

Jehu, son of Jehoshaphat, rose from the rank of a military commander to be selected and anointed by Elisha as the tenth king of Israel. He became Israel's head of state for one purpose: to destroy the

Jehu destroys an image of the god Baal. Michelangelo (1475–1564), Sistene Chapel, Rome.

house of Ahab. True to his calling, Jehu killed Jehoram, Jezebel, and all of Ahab's family, leaving no survivors of that wicked dynasty.

Queen Jezebel hung on him the derisive moniker of evil Zimri, who 45 years earlier had taken office after murdering the incumbent and his whole clan. Though murderous and self-centered, Jehu's bloody coup and purge was viewed as having divine sanction. However, Jehu was later condemned for going too far in his political coup and for not going far enough in his religious purge. The prophet Hosea condemns his excess as "bloodshed at Jezreel." Although he ruled Israel for 28 years, his purge of pagan worship was incomplete.

Jehu himself died a natural death, but his dynasty was killed off after four generations. Even so, his was the longest-lived dynasty of the northern kingdom, in fulfillment of a promise from God for eliminating the wicked house of Ahab. The downfall of Jehu's dynasty ushered in a period of political instability and decline, which precipitated the fall of the northern kingdom in 722 B.C.

For further study, see 1Ki 16:8-20; 21:18-24; 2Ki 9–10; 12:1; 13:1; 14:8; 15:12; 2Ch 22:7-9; 25:17; Hos 1:4-5.
5. 8 century B.C.; 1Ch 4:35; head of Simeonite family under Hezekiah

JEHUCAL (juh HOO kuhl) *the Lord is able;* Jer 37:3; official who put Jeremiah in cistern; a form of Jucal

JEHUDI (juh HOO dye) *Judean;* 7 century B.C.; Jer 36:14; official of Jehoiakim; read scroll of Jeremiah

JEHUEL (jee HYOO ehl) meaning unknown; 8 century B.C.; 2Ch 29:14; temple aide under Hezekiah; also called Jehiel 5

JEIEL (juh EYE uhl) meaning unknown
1. 1Ch 5:7; head of clan of Reubenites
2. 12 century B.C.; 1Ch 8:29; father of Ner; great-grandfather of King Saul
3. 11 century B.C.; 1Ch 11:44; mighty man of David; brother of Shama
4. 11 century B.C.; 1Ch 15:18; Levite gatekeeper and musician for ark upon its return
5. 11 century B.C.; 1Ch 16:5; another Levite musician who played when ark returned
6. 2Ch 20:14; descendant of Asaph and ancestor of Jahaziel 4
7. 8 century B.C.; 2Ch 26:11; secretary of King Uzziah
8. 7 century B.C.; 2Ch 35:9; chief Levite in Josiah's day
9. 5 century B.C.; Ezr 10:43; one who married and divorced foreigner

JEKAMEAM (JEK uh MEE uhm) possibly *may kinsman establish;* 10 century B.C.; 1Ch 23:19; Levite of Kohathite clan

JEKAMIAH (JEK uh MIGH uh) *may the Lord establish*
1. 1Ch 2:41; descendant of Judah 1
2. 6 century B.C.; 1Ch 3:18; son of Jehoiachin

JEKUTHIEL (juh KOO thee uhl) *may God sustain;* 1Ch 4:18; descendant of Judah 1

JEMIMAH (juh MYE muh) *little dove;* Job 42:14; daughter born to Job in his old age

JEMUEL (JEM yoo uhl) meaning unknown; 20 century B.C.; Gen 46:10; son of Simeon; also called Nemuel 1

JEPHTHAH (JEF thuh) *he opens;* 11 century B.C.; Jdg 11:1

The son of Gilead and a prostitute, Jephthah was rejected unjustly by his half-brothers and grew up a social outcast but later became a judge of Is-

Jephthah sacrifices his only child to keep his vow to God.

rael. He was offered leadership of his people if he could provide a victory over the invading Ammonite army. Jephthah vowed to God that he would sacrifice whoever first greeted him out of his house upon his return if he were victorious in battle. The vow secured him victory, but he was heartbroken when his daughter, a young virgin and his only child, was the first to welcome him home. Jephthah's daughter asked for and received two months to mourn her plight with her friends and then was burned to death. Although such barbarous human sacrifice was prohibited by Israelite Law, Jephthah went on to lead Israel for six more years. Through his actions as a leader, he emerged as a man of faith who is revered by Jews and Christians alike. For further study, see Jdg 10:6–12:7; 1Sa 12:11; Heb 11:32.

JEPHUNNEH (juh FUN uh) meaning unknown
1. 15 century B.C.; Nu 13:6; father of spy Caleb
2. 1Ch 7:38; descendant of Asher

JERAH (JEER uh) *moon;* Gen 10:26; descendant of Shem; ancestor of an Arabian tribe

JERAHMEEL (juh RAH mee uhl) *may God have mercy*
1. 1Ch 2:9; son of Hezron
2. 10 century B.C.; 1Ch 24:29; Levite in days of David
3. 7 century B.C.; Jer 36:26; officer who arrested Baruch and Jeremiah

JERECHUS (JAIR eh kuhs) meaning unknown; 6 century B.C.; 1Esd 5:22; ancestor of exiles returning with Zerubbabel

JERED (JEER ed) *descent;* 1Ch 4:18; father of Gedor

JEREMAI (JAIR uh mye) *exalted;* 5 century B.C.; Ezr 10:33; married and divorced foreigner after Exile

JEREMIAH (JAIR uh MYE uh) *the Lord establishes* or *the Lord is exalted*
1. 11 century B.C.; 1Ch 12:4; Benjaminite warrior who joined David at Ziklag
2. 11 century B.C.; 1Ch 12:10; Gadite warrior in David's force at Ziklag
3. 11 century B.C.; 1Ch 12:13; another Gadite warrior in David's force at Ziklag
4. 9 century B.C.; 2Ki 23:31; grandfather of King Jehoahaz of Israel
5. 8 century B.C.; 1Ch 5:24; Manassite head of family exiled by Tiglath-pileser
6. 7–6 century B.C.; 2Ch 35:25

Jeremiah was a man consumed by his commitment to God. He was scarcely out of childhood, age 12 or 13, when God called him to be a prophet. Jeremiah heard the words, "Before I formed you in the womb I knew you, and before you were born I consecrated you." When Jeremiah protested that he was only a boy, God replied, "Now I have put my words in your mouth" (Jer 1:5,9).

Josiah was king in Judah at this time. In previous generations, Judah and its rulers abandoned God and his Law. In Josiah's time, a Book of the Law (thought by many scholars to be part or all of Deuteronomy) was found in the temple treasury.

Josiah had the book read to him and was overcome with repentance. His reforms rocked Judah's society; he tore down altars for idols and restored the worship of the Lord in the temple. In Jerusalem, he commanded a celebration of Passover; this remembrance of God's faithfulness had not been observed for nearly 500 years. Jeremiah watched as his king "did what was right in the sight of the Lord." When Josiah died in battle with the Egyptians, Jeremiah wept.

For the next 40 years, Jeremiah watched king after king take Judah's throne. Jehoahaz, Josiah's son, was deposed by Pharaoh Neco of Egypt after only three months on the throne. Neco evidently preferred the older son, Jehoiakim, who is described as one who "did what was evil in the sight of the Lord" despite Jeremiah's protestations.

Jehoiakim was the first of many kings to threaten Jeremiah's life. These were not idle threats, since Jehoiakim dragged the prophet Uriah from Egypt, where he had fled, and killed him with his own hands.

Jehoiakim was a puppet of the Egyptians. When he opened Judah's door to Egyptian gods and began to worship their idols, Jeremiah spoke of God's warning. "If you do not...walk in my law...[and] heed the words of my prophets...then I will make this city a curse for all the nations of the earth" (Jer 26:6). His life was spared only because the priests and officials were afraid his words might be true. They remembered the prophet Micah, who had spoken similar warnings years ago. The few officials who acknowledged Judah's sin were enough to protect Jeremiah from Uriah's fate.

Though banned by Jehoiakim from speaking in the temple, the prophet was undeterred. He dictated his warnings of danger to his scribe and disciple, Baruch, who read Jeremiah's dictates on the temple grounds. Advisors to the king heard Baruch and demanded the scrolls, ostensibly so that the king could hear as well. In rage and disgust, he listened to each section, then cut off that portion of the scroll with a knife and tossed it into the fire. Unmoved and unchanged, Jehoiakim sent members of his guard to arrest Jeremiah and Baruch, but they could not be found.

After the first scroll was burned, Jeremiah wrote another, this time including special warnings for Jehoiakim. This second scroll recorded the earlier words of warning and added the prophecy that Jehoiakim would leave no one to sit upon the throne. This prophecy was fulfilled in an unexpected way. At Jehoiakim's death, his son Jehoiachin ruled, but for less than three months. King Nebuchadnezzar of Babylon conquered Jerusalem, carried away treasure from both temple and palace, and exiled the king. This left Judah's throne empty. One year later, Jeremiah's words were confirmed when Jehoiakim's brother, Zedekiah, ascended to the throne instead of Jehoiakim's son.

During Zedekiah's first years, Jeremiah spoke wherever he could, as fear of arrest fired him with urgency. The nation was in both spiritual demise and political danger: God's punishment hung over king and citizen alike, and the Babylonian army besieged Jerusalem. Although Zedekiah ignored Jeremiah's words, he was sufficiently concerned about

Jeremiah laments the destruction of Jerusalem. Rembrandt (1606–1669).

the Babylonians to send advisors to Jeremiah to ask him to pray. Meanwhile, Zedekiah heard that their Egyptian allies had sent troops to their aid. Jeremiah prayed, but the prophet's words were not what Zedekiah expected. "Even if you defeated the whole army of [Babylonians]...and there remained of them only wounded men in their tents, they would rise up and burn this city with fire" (Jer 37:10).

Zedekiah tried to make peace with the Babylonians, sending an envoy to communicate this desire. Jeremiah took this opportunity to draft a letter to the Hebrews still exiled in Babylon since Jehoiachin's brief reign. He prophecied that their Exile would last 70 years, after which they would return to their own land. Until that time, he told them to settle in Babylon, raise their families, and "seek the welfare of the city where [God has] sent you into exile...for in its welfare you will find your welfare" (Jer 29:7).

Jeremiah was arrested, falsely accused of treason, and imprisoned. When he boldly said the Babylonians would take Jerusalem, sparing only those who surrendered, Zedekiah handed Jeremiah over to men who hated him; they threw him into an empty cistern and left him to die of starvation.

An Ethiopian slave named Ebed-melech heard of Jeremiah's plight and pleaded with the king for his life. Zedekiah allowed Ebed-melech to pull Jeremiah from the cistern. However, this did not free Jeremiah; he remained under arrest in the guard's courtyard.

King Zedekiah was fast losing hope that Jerusalem could withstand the seige. He met with Jeremiah secretly to ask whether his life might be spared. Jeremiah knew he spoke to Judah's last king as he said that Zedekiah's only hope was in surrender. Zedekiah did not surrender, and after his capture, his sons were killed before his eyes. Then he was blinded and taken in chains to Babylon. As for Jerusalem, it was burned as Jeremiah foretold.

Jeremiah was not taken to Babylon. Evidently his fame had spread, because the Babylonian king commanded that he be treated well. He was allowed to stay in Judah with Gedaliah, the newly appointed interim governor. Gedaliah was assassinated shortly thereafter, and Jeremiah had to flee to Egypt. He remained there, and continued to prophesy. Little is recorded of those years, except that Jeremiah issued a warning to exiled Hebrews about idol worship.

Jeremiah was known for his dramatic prophecies and unusual life. For example, God told him not to marry, as a symbol of Judah's hopeless future. His harsh, prophetic warnings contrasted with his sensitive spirit. When rejected and hounded by the very kings he hoped would turn to God, he cried out in hurt and anguish, although God chided him, saying he should stop praying for people who would never change. Often he asked God why his life was so difficult, yet God's word burned in him, like a fire in his bones.

> ➤ ⬍
>
> *"O that my head were a spring of water, and my eyes a fountain of tears, so that I might weep day and night for the slain of my poor people!"*
>
> Jer 9:1

Jeremiah did not have Isaiah's brilliance or gift for poetic words, nor did he speak to the common man's pain with the sensitivity of Amos or Micah, but he was an example of amazing perseverance in spite of danger and rejection. Jeremiah was direct and confrontive; he once cut off his hair to illustrate mourning and smashed a clay pot to show how Judah would be shattered. He coldly described Judah and Israel as whores, who "refuse to be ashamed" (Jer 3:3). However, all of Jeremiah's prophetic words were not condemning; he also spoke of God's forgiveness with words like, "Return, O faithless children, I will heal your faithlessness" (Jer 3:22).

Jeremiah was often quoted by Jesus. Among the great Hebrew prophets, he stands as a model of perseverance and insight, and though he is not noted for messianic prophecies, his words often pointed to the relational, heart-to-heart, God-to-human faith described in the New Testament. Although the Book of Lamentations is sometimes credited to Jeremiah, his authorship is doubtful.

For further study, see 2Ch 35–36; the Book of Jeremiah; Mt 2:17-18; 27:3-10.

7. 7 century B.C.; Jer 35:3; Recabite; father of Jaazaniah 4

8. 6 century B.C.; 2Mac 15:14; prophet in Judas Maccabeus's dream

9. 6 century B.C.; Ne 12:1; priest who resettled in Judah

10. 5 century B.C.; Ne 10:2; priest; sealed covenant renewal; possibly Jeremiah 9

11. 5 century B.C.; Ne 12:34; leader who rededicated Jerusalem wall

JEREMIEL (jeh REHM ih el) possibly *may God have compassion;* 2Esd 4:36; archangel who spoke to Ezra about the coming age

JEREMOTH (JAIR uh mahht) *swollen*
1. 1Ch 7:8; descendant of Becher 1
2. 1Ch 8:14; descendant of Benjamin
3. 10 century B.C.; 1Ch 23:23; Levite descendant of Mushi; also called Jerimoth 3
4. 10 century B.C.; 1Ch 25:22; temple musician under David; also called Jerimoth 4
5. 5 century B.C.; Ezr 10:26; one who married and divorced foreigner after Exile
6. 5 century B.C.; Ezr 10:27; another who married and divorced foreigner after Exile
7. 5 century B.C.; Ezr 10:29; another who married and divorced foreigner after Exile

JERIAH (juh RYE uh) *the Lord sees;* 10 century B.C.; 1Ch 23:19; descendant of Hebron; also called Jerijah

JERIBAI (JAIR uh bye) *my adversary;* 11 century B.C.; 1Ch 11:46; son of Elnaam; mighty man of David

JERIEL (JEER ee uhl) *God sees;* 1Ch 7:2; descendant of Issachar 1

JERIJAH 1Ch 26:31; see Jeriah

JERIMOTH (JAIR uh mahht) *swollen*
1. 19 century B.C.; 1Ch 7:7; fourth son of Bela and Benjamin
2. 11 century B.C.; 1Ch 12:5; Benjaminite allied with David at Ziklag
3. 1Ch 24:30; see Jeremoth 3
4. 10 century B.C.; 1Ch 25:4; see Jeremoth 4
5. 10 century B.C.; 1Ch 27:19; officer over Naphtalites in David's day
6. 10 century B.C.; 2Ch 11:18; son of David; father-in-law of King Rehoboam
7. 8 century B.C.; 2Ch 31:13; Levite; temple treasurer under Hezekiah

JERIOTH (JAIR ee ahth) *tents;* 1Ch 2:18; wife of Caleb 1

JEROBOAM (JAIR uh BOH uhm) *may the people increase*
1. ruled 930–909 B.C.; 1Ki 11:26

Jeroboam was a man caught between God's plans and his own sin. Solomon, king of Israel, had broken faith with God by worshiping idols, so God told Solomon the kingdom would be taken from his family and given to a servant. Jeroboam was that servant—a laborer on Solomon's payroll.

The prophet Ahijah met Jeroboam on the road. Ahijah tore his garment into 12 pieces to show Jer-

King Jeroboam I breaks his pact with God by worshiping a golden calf.

oboam how the 12 tribes of Israel would split—two following Solomon's son Rehoboam and ten following Jeroboam. Ahijah said God promised to bless Jeroboam if he kept the commandments and lived obediently.

When Solomon heard this, he decided to kill Jeroboam, so Jeroboam fled to Egypt for safety. After Solomon's death, Rehoboam tried to rule by force and intimidation. Thus, when Jeroboam returned, ten tribes seceded, calling themselves Israel and crowning Jeroboam king. Only the tribes of Judah and Benjamin remained with Rehoboam.

Once in power, Jeroboam disregarded God's promise and built two golden calves to worship. If Israel had its own gods, Jeroboam reasoned, the people would not worship in Jerusalem nor return to Rehoboam. This began a pattern of idolatry that would lead to Israel's downfall. Jeroboam held a festival for his idols. As he stood by the altar, a prophet from Judah rose and prophesied that a future king, Josiah, would sacrifice idol-worshiping priests on that very altar. Sixteen generations later, King Josiah did just that.

The same prophet, Ahijah, who said God would give Jeroboam the kingdom, later prophesied his downfall. Jeroboam died leaving a legacy of idolatry that eventually destroyed Israel.

For further study, see 1Ki 12–14:20; 2Ki 23:15-20; 2Ch 10–11:16.

2. ruled 793–753 B.C.; 2Ki 13:13

Being the object of prophecy was a mixed blessing for King Jeroboam of Israel. He was criticized by two prophets, Hosea and Amos, and presented in a favorable light by a third, Jonah. Hosea saw Israel under Jeroboam in religious terms, as suffering from a spiritual vacuum that impoverished the people. Amos regarded the same national evils in more political terms, as a moral injustice where the rich oppressed the poor. Jeroboam's public actions, indeed, showed no true spirituality. However, Jonah noted that Jeroboam II was an expansionist king who extended Israel's borders to the north and east, recalling the glory years of David and Solomon. Israel under Jeroboam's peacetime economy experienced some prosperity, with new capital construction and ivory palaces in Samaria. After a 41-year reign, he died and was succeeded by his son Zechariah. For further study, see 2Ki 14:16-29; Hos 1:1; Am 1:1; 7:9-11.

JEROHAM (juh ROH ham) *God will have mercy*
1. 12 century B.C.; 1Sa 1:1; father of Elkanah; father-in-law of Hannah
2. 1Ch 8:27; descendant of Benjamin
3. 1Ch 9:8; ancestor of Benjaminite resettler in Jerusalem
4. 11 century B.C.; 1Ch 12:7; father of Benjaminite warriors who joined David at Ziklag
5. 10 century B.C.; 1Ch 27:22; father of Azarel the Danite officer under David
6. 9 century B.C.; 2Ch 23:1; father of Azariah the ouster of Athaliah
7. 5 century B.C.; 1Ch 9:12; father of Adaiah the priest in Jerusalem after Exile

JERUBBAAL Jdg 6:32; see Gideon

JERUSHA (juh ROO shuh) *possession;* 8 century B.C.; 2Ki 15:33; wife of King Uzziah; a form of Jerushah

JERUSHAH 2Ch 27:1; see Jerusha

JESARELAH 1Ch 25:14; see Asarelah

JESHAIAH (jeh SHAY yuh) *the Lord has saved*
1. 1Ch 26:25; ancestor of David's treasurer Shelomoth
2. 10 century B.C.; 1Ch 25:3; temple musician under David
3. Ne 11:7; ancestor of Benjaminite who returned to Jerusalem
4. 5 century B.C.; Ezr 8:7; descendant of Elam 1; returned to Judah after Exile
5. 5 century B.C.; Ezr 8:19; Levite; returned to Judah with Ezra
6. 1Ch 3:21; descendant of Zerubbabel

JESHEBEAB (juh SHEB ee ab) *father's place;* 10 century B.C.; 1Ch 24:13; leader of priests under David

JESHER (JEH shuhr) *uprightness;* 1Ch 2:18; son of Caleb 1

JESHISHAI (jeh SHISH eye) *aged;* 1Ch 5:14; descendant of Gad

JESHOHAIAH (JESH uh HAY yuh) *humble;* 8 century B.C.; 1Ch 4:36; Simeonite leader under Hezekiah

JESHUA (JESH oo uh) *salvation*
1. 10 century B.C.; 1Ch 24:11; leader of priests under David
2. 8 century B.C.; 2Ch 31:15; priest; distributed contributions among priests
3. Ezr 2:6; descendant of Pahath-moab
4. 6 century B.C.; Ezr 2:2; high priest; returned to Judah with Zerubbabel; also called Joshua 4
5. Ezr 2:40; Levite whose descendants returned to Judah with Zerubbabel
6. 5 century B.C.; Ezr 8:33; father of Jozabad the Levite in Ezra's day
7. 5 century B.C.; Ne 3:19; ruler of Mizpah
8. 5 century B.C.; Ne 10:9; Levite who sealed covenant renewal

JESHURUN (JESH uh ruhn) *upright;* Dt 32:15; name that personified Israel's history with God

JESIMIEL (jeh SIM ee uhl) *may God establish;* 8 century B.C.; 1Ch 4:36; head of Simeonite family

JESSE (JES ee) meaning unknown; 11 century B.C.; Ru 4:17

When judge Samuel came looking for a "son of Jesse" to assume the throne of Israel, the God-fearing Jesse proudly paraded seven sons, in sequence, before Samuel, who surprised everyone by selecting Jesse's eighth and youngest son, David, and anointing him Israel's king to replace Saul. Jesse sent young David to King Saul to serve as Saul's music therapist, armor-bearer, special courier, and later, giant-killer. David never forgot his roots. When fleeing Saul's wrath, David provided safety and protection for his aging parents in Moab. Centuries later, God raised up another "root of Jesse," Jesus Christ. For further study, see Ru 4:22; 1Sa 16; 17:12-58; 22:1-13; 1Ch 2:12-16; Isa 11:1-10; Mt 1:3-6; Lk 3:31-33; Ac 13:22; Ro 15:12.

JESUS (JEE zuhs) *salvation*
1. 2 century B.C.; Sir 50:27

Jesus, son of Sirach, also known as Jesus Ben Sira, was a philosopher, teacher, and scribe who composed a book of "wisdom literature" similar to the Old Testament books of Proverbs and Ecclesiastes. This apocryphal Book of Sirach is expressed in collections of maxims, moral tales, songs, prayers, and poetic reflections on life.

Ben Sira wrote after the reign of Alexander the Great when the Ptolemies of Egypt and the Seleucids of Syria rose to power from among many warring national and ethnic groups in the Middle East. Judea was under spiritual and cultural siege, as the Seleucids attempted to wipe all traces of non-Greek religion and culture from conquered nations. Hence, Ben Sira's wisdom was more than popular philosophy; he intended to present a model of righteous living and faith in God for people suffering under religious persecution. Ben Sira wrote sometime between 198 and 175 B.C., and 30 to 50 years later, the manuscripts were taken to Egypt by his grandson and translated into the Greek form known as Ecclesiasticus.

Ben Sira's wisdom cut across class and economic lines. He counseled merchants and tradesmen to be honest, while admitting that "buying and selling" made wrongdoing hard to avoid. He offered advice about topics like marriage, charity, forgiveness, overeating, and how to tell friends from enemies. Ben Sira is quoted 82 times in the Talmud, a collection of oral and written law and commentary dating from A.D. 200–500. In addition, the early Christians may have used it as a guidebook for life within the church.

For further study, see the Book of Sirach.
2. 1 century A.D.; Mt 1:1

Jesus was a common name among Jews during the period of Greco-Roman occupation, much as Joshua (the Hebrew equivalent) was in the Old Testament era. But Jesus of Nazareth was no common man. He is the historical figure whom Christians believe to be the Son of God incarnate, that is, God-in-the-flesh.

Shepherds visit the newborn Jesus in the manger.

Jesus had other titles ascribed to him—including Lord, Savior, Son of Man, the Word, Son of David, Lamb of God, Bread of Life, King of Kings, and Prince of Peace. The most common title ascribed to him was Christ, which is Greek for messiah, meaning *anointed one*. The messiah of long-held Jewish expectations was to be an anointed king in the line of David who would fulfill Old Testament prophecy concerning a savior-deliverer.

To Christians, Jesus was God's promised Savior, the one who would save all of humanity from sin and death through his own life, death, and resurrection. Scriptures say the birth of this Savior was remarkably humble in its circumstances yet divinely orchestrated in its conception. According to the apostolic creeds and based on the testimony of Scripture, Jesus was "conceived by the Holy Ghost, born of the Virgin Mary...the only-begotten Son of God,...Very God of Very God [who]...was made man."

Apart from the circumstances of his birth and circumcision, the biblical story of Jesus's first 12 years is silent. Luke records that at age 12, Jesus attended his first Passover feast in Jerusalem with his family. Afterward, Jesus stayed behind in the temple, listening to the rabbis and amazing everyone with his own unique wisdom and understanding.

The political climate of the times was extremely volatile, especially since Judea had come under direct Roman rule, but Jesus and his family did not get involved in the politics of his day. According to the biblical record, it was another 18 years before Jesus went public with his teachings. Jesus's public ministry began in earnest when his cousin, John the Baptist, saw him and announced: "Here is the Lamb of God who takes away the sins of the world!" (Jn 1:29). Jesus submitted to John's baptism of repentance on behalf of all Israel. As Jesus came up out of the Jordan River, "the Holy Spirit descended on him in bodily form like a dove" (Lk 3:22). Jesus then retreated to the desert where, according to the biblical record, he was tempted by Satan for 40 days but did not succumb.

> ⇢ ⇠
>
> *"And a voice from heaven said, 'This is my Son, the Beloved, with whom I am well pleased.'"*
>
> Mt 3:17

Two pivotal events that helped Jesus prepare for his ministry: the baptism by John and the temptation by Satan.

As reported in four Gospel accounts, Jesus's earthly ministry was characterized by many personal and powerful encounters as he traveled throughout cities of Galilee, proclaiming the kingdom of God. Of the many people he met in the course of his travels around Galilee, Jesus chose 12 men in particular to be his closest disciples. All he expected of them was their companionship, their obedience to his teachings, and their commitment to follow his example.

Jesus frequently used human and earthly analogies to express spiritual or eternal concepts. He often taught moral issues and spoke of humanity's relationship to God by using parables—brief narratives and analogies that illustrate a spiritual truth. The Gospels record Jesus's use of seeds, weeds, yeast, vineyards, fishnets, farmers, sheep, servants, widows, and bridesmaids to explain what the kingdom of God is like.

However, the Bible portrays Jesus as more than just a good teacher or great ethicist. In addition to Jesus's memorable sayings, Scripture has preserved numerous accounts of miracles performed by Jesus, supporting the idea that he is indeed the Son of God. Stories of Jesus making the blind see and the mute speak; causing the deaf to hear and the paralyzed to walk; feeding the masses with a few loaves of bread; curing diseases and even raising the dead—all these are meant to verify Jesus's claims of divinity.

While Jesus demonstrated power over the material world, it was his power over the unseen world of the demonic and his presumptive authority to forgive sins that aroused the most controversy and consequences with his critics. The Jewish Talmud records that Jesus was just a rabbi who was condemned for "practicing sorcery and leading Israel astray." Such thinking by the Sanhedrin, the Jewish high council, during Jesus's ministry led to charges of blasphemy against him for claiming to be the Son of God. Whenever Jesus taught or healed, the Jewish leaders sought a way to stop him. Led by Caiaphas the high priest, they finally met to plan his demise.

Their plan culminated before the Passover feast in Jerusalem a few days after Jesus had entered the city on a donkey thronged by people shouting "Hosanna!" During that week of Passover, Jesus ate with his disciples one last supper and prayed in the Garden of Gethsemane, where he was betrayed by Judas Iscariot (one of Jesus's original 12 disciples).

Jesus makes his triumphant entrance into Jerusalem.

The Sanhedrin convened hastily in special session and convicted Jesus of blasphemy. But since the Jews were not allowed to sentence anyone to death, they took him to Pontius Pilate, the Roman governor of Judea.

Pilate questioned Jesus in the Praetorium, not about blasphemy but about possible treason stemming from the itinerant preacher's claim of being King of the Jews. When Jesus explained that his kingdom was not of this world, Pilate announced to the crowd that he could find no fault in him. Thinking he could rid himself of any lingering liability, Pilate passed off Jesus to King Herod, who only mocked him and sent the would-be king back to Pilate.

To pacify the Jewish people, a prisoner of the people's choice was customarily released each year during Passover. Thinking he could calm the crowd with this proposal, Pilate offered to release Jesus as their annual appeasement. But the angry crowd insisted that he instead release Barabbas, a notorious assassin. When Pilate asked what he should do then

Jesus crowned with thorns during his trial.

with Jesus, the crowd shouted, "Crucify him! Crucify him!" With Jesus refusing to defend himself before Pilate and the crowd growing angrier and more insistent, Pilate finally washed his hands of the matter. He handed Jesus over to die a criminal's death on a Roman cross, between two common thieves.

Jesus's ministry of peace and hope and eternal life seemingly ended then and there, as Joseph of Arimathea and Nicodemus took his body from the cross, prepared it for burial, and placed it in Joseph's own unused tomb. However, the events that occurred three days later, as told in the Gospel accounts, restored the hopes of the disciples as well as Christian believers ever since. Coming to the tomb to anoint the body of Jesus, three women followers found the tomb empty. They were confronted by an angel at the entrance to the tomb and then they talked with someone who turned out to be Jesus himself, risen from the dead.

Jesus was then seen by his disciples and more than 500 others over the span of the next 40 days, at which point his disciples saw him ascend into heaven and there were no more reported citings of

Christ. This final experience with their teacher—seeing him come back from the dead as he said he would—left the disciples with an unshakable faith in their testimony that Jesus was the Son of God who had returned to his former glory and who would come again in glory.

For further study, see the books of Matthew, Mark, Luke, and John (on Jesus's life, death, and resurrection); other New Testament Books offer reflections on his significance to humanity.
3. 1 century A.D.; Col 4:11; Colossian Christian greeted by Paul; also called Justus 3

JETHER (JEE thuhr) *abundance*
1. 1Ch 2:32; descendant of Jerahmeel
2. 1Ch 4:17; descendant of Judah 1
3. 1Ch 7:38; descendant of Asher; possibly Ithran 2
4. 12 century B.C.; Jdg 8:20; oldest son of Gideon the judge
5. 11 century B.C.; 1Ki 2:5; see Ithra

JETHETH (JEE thehth) *subjection;* Gen 36:40; descendant of Esau

JETHRO (JETH roh) *excellence;* 15 century B.C.; Ex 3:1

As a young man, Moses killed an Egyptian and fled to the land of Midian on the Sinai Peninsula. There he met a tribe, the Kenites, who were shepherds in that region. Moses married Zipporah, the daughter of a wise Midianite priest named Jethro, and tended Jethro's sheep until God ordered him to return to Egypt. When Moses led the Israelites out of Egypt, Jethro brought Zipporah and her sons to their camp. Upon hearing the amazing way God had saved Israel from Pharaoh, Jethro said, "Now I know that the Lord is greater than all gods" (Ex 18:11). While he stayed with the Israelites, Jethro helped Moses by showing him how to delegate responsibility by appointing judges instead of governing alone. For further study, see Ex 2:11–3:12; Ex 18.

JETUR (JEE tuhr) meaning unknown; 20 century B.C.; Gen 25:15; grandson of Abraham; son of Ishmael

JEUEL (JOO uhl) *treasured* or *God has saved*
1. 8 century B.C.; 2Ch 29:13; Levite; helped cleanse temple for Hezekiah

2. 5 century B.C.; 1Ch 9:6; Judahite resettler in Jerusalem
3. 5 century B.C.; Ezr 8:13; descendant of Adonikam

JEUSH (JEE uhsh) meaning unknown
1. 20 century B.C.; Gen 36:5; son of Esau by Oholibamah
2. 1Ch 7:10; descendant of Benjamin
3. 10 century B.C.; 1Ch 23:10; head of Levite family; descendant of Gershon
4. 10 century B.C.; 2Ch 11:19; son of Rehoboam; grandson of Solomon
5. 1Ch 8:39; descendant of Saul through Jonathan

JEUZ (JEE uhz) meaning unknown; 1Ch 8:10; descendant of Benjamin

JEWS (JOOZ) Ezr 4:12
Toward the end of the Old Testament period, all descendants of the tribe of Judah or inhabitants of the land of Judah came to be called Jews. In the New Testament period, the emphasis shifted from geography and ethnicity to religion: The Jews were not everyone from Judea or everyone of Jewish descent, but only the leadership opposed to Christ—particularly the Pharisees, Sadducees, Zealots, and other partisan parties. The shift from ethnicity to religion as the defining criterion was made complete by the apostle Paul, who pressed for opening the church to all nations and people. Anyone who believed in Christ, though non-Jew by ethnic origin, became a part of Abraham's great nation. For further study, see Dt 10:16; Jer 4:4; the Book of Ezra; the Book of Nehemiah; the Book of Esther; 1Mac 8:23-29; Ro 2:28-29; 9–11; Php 3:3-5; Gal 1:13-14; 3:28-29; Col 3:11. Also see Judeans, Israelites.

JEZANIAH Jer 40:8; see Jaazaniah 3

JEZEBEL (JEZ uh bel) meaning unknown
1. 9th century B.C.; 1Ki 16:31
Jezebel is a name that has become synonymous with treachery and evil and is often used to label shamelessly deceitful women. The original Jezebel, the Phoenician wife of King Ahab of Israel, earned her reputation. After her marriage of political convenience to Ahab, she continued to worship Baal, the fertility god of her people. Ahab not only joined

Jezebel is cast from a window to her death during a rebellion.

her, but he built a temple for Baal and erected a pole for worship of the goddess Asherah, Baal's consort. Jezebel actively promoted Baal worship throughout the realm, using money from the treasury to pay 950 prophets of Baal and Asherah. She may even have been a priestess of Baal herself. Finally, to secure the stamp of her god upon Israel, Jezebel ordered the Hebrew prophets killed.

Some Hebrew prophets escaped by fleeing or hiding; Elijah, a patriarch among the prophets of Israel, was one of the few survivors. He challenged Jezebel's prophets, asking if Baal could send fire to burn a sacrifice. For an entire day, they cried to Baal, without response. Then, Elijah built an altar to the Lord, laid a bull upon it, and prayed. Fire flashed, consuming the sacrifice, wood, stone, and even the dust. Elijah then put the prophets of Baal to death, and Jezebel vowed to kill him.

Jezebel was noted for her cruelty. She even arranged the execution of an innocent man, Naboth, to acquire his land for Ahab's garden. In prophesy, Elijah said she would die and be eaten by dogs. She died during a rebellion; when her body was found, only the skull, feet, and the palms of her hands remained.

For further study, see 1Ki 16:31-33; 18:20-40; 19:1-10; 21:1-28; 2Ki 9:30-37.
2. 1 century A.D.; Rev 2:20; false prophetess in Thyatira

JEZER (JEE zuhr) *creature* or *formation;* 19 century B.C.; Gen 46:24; son of Naphtali; clan leader

JEZIEL (JEE zee uhl) *God gathers;* 11 century B.C.; 1Ch 12:3; warrior; joined with David at Ziklag

JEZRAHIAH (JEZ ruh HIGH uh) meaning unknown; 5 century B.C.; Ne 12:42; choir leader for dedication of Jerusalem wall

JEZREEL (JEZ ree uhl) *God sows*
1. 1Ch 4:3; descendant of Judah 1
2. 8 century B.C.; Hos 1:4; son of Hosea; name symbolized judgment of King Jehu

JEZREELITES (JEZ reel ights) 1Ki 21:1; inhabitants of Jezreel, a city near Mt. Gilboa

JEZRIELUS (jez rih EHL us) meaning unknown; 5 century B.C.; 1Esd 9:27; returnee from Exile; married and divorced a foreigner

JIDLAPH (JID laf) *weeping;* 21 century B.C.; Gen 22:22; son of Nahor; nephew of Abraham

JOAB (JOH ab) *the Lord is father*
1. 10 century B.C.; 2Sa 2:13

As King David's commander-in-chief, Joab was fiercely loyal to his master. He killed, plotted, scorned curses, and risked his life for his king, and later, for his own reasons. In spite of his loyalty and remarkable courage, Joab's years as an assassin and warrior ended in personal and spiritual destruction.

Joab fought beside David in his early battles against King Saul's army. After Saul's death, the kingship was in question; those loyal to Saul fought David and his supporters until Saul's troops were defeated and their commander Abner ran for his

life. During the chase that followed, Abner killed Joab's brother Asahel.

Joab wanted revenge. When David made peace with Abner in order to reunite the nation, Joab falsely accused Abner of deceit. David stood by Abner, however, and Israel was united under his rule. Displaying the ruthlessness and tunnel vision that would eventually destroy him, Joab asked Abner to come to Hebron and then killed him in cold blood. Although David commanded Joab to publicly mourn his brother's killer, Joab remained loyal and acted—however rashly—for what he considered David's best interest.

When David was crowned king, the Jebusites held Jerusalem. As a way to reaffirm his loyalty, Joab was chosen to lead an attack to reclaim the city. At Jerusalem, the Jebusites placed blind and lame people at the gates. The Hebrews shrank back, fearing the people were cursed; only Joab was willing to defy the curse and attack. His bold victory at Jerusalem earned him command of all of David's forces.

On another occasion, Joab led handpicked troops into a hopeless battle. David's army was pinned between the Arameans and Ammonites; only Joab's reckless courage and skill saved them. After this, the Arameans feared Israel's military might and made peace.

Knowing the extent of Joab's loyalty, David turned to him in his most desperate and shameful hour. The story began while the Israelites were at war with the Ammonites and Arameans. In spring, when kings traditionally joined their troops, David stayed in Jerusalem. One afternoon, while standing on his roof terrace, he spied his neighbor—a beautiful woman—bathing. Thus began a now legendary story of adultery, murder, and remorse. David and the woman, Bathsheba, committed adultery. When Bathsheba became pregnant, they panicked, and David sent for Joab. He needed someone both loyal and unquestioning.

Joab went to the battlefront to order Bathsheba's husband, a soldier named Uriah, to speak with the king. David tried a ruse to pass off the child as Uriah's own; he encouraged Uriah to spend the night with Bathsheba before returning to the front. When Uriah's honor prevented him from taking comfort denied his comrades, David and Bathsheba faced national disgrace. David turned again to Joab, commanding him to place Uriah in the heart of the battle and withdraw. After enemy

Through the efforts of Joab, David claims victory over the Ammonites.

They fought shoulder to shoulder, building the strong bonds common to comrades of war. And, in spite of his poor judgment and rashness, Joab's loyalty to David had been sincere and without reserve.

One final act on Joab's part pushed David to his breaking point. As David grew old and frail, he could no longer rule. His second son, Adonijah, decided to usurp the throne. He prepared a sacrifice in his own honor and invited officials of Judah, all his brothers, and many important supporters, including Joab. When David heard this, he was furious and commanded the prophet Nathan to crown his son Solomon king. David

archers killed Uriah, David married the widowed Bathsheba to hide their adultery.

Increasingly, such violence became Joab's solution to problems. Although he mediated between David and his son Absalom during a period of estrangement, Joab turned against the prince the moment he saw a threat to his master. Absalom led a revolt and Joab's troops crushed the rebellion. In spite of David's command to treat his mutinous son with gentleness, Joab found and killed Absalom when his hair became entangled in tree branches. This vengeful murder was too much for David; he removed Joab as commander and replaced him with his nephew, Amasa. This may have put an axe to the root of loyalty in Joab's heart. From then on, he no longer looked out for David's best interests.

After years of killing on David's behalf, Joab was quite prepared to kill for himself. He waited for the opportune moment to eliminate his rival Amasa. They both were assigned to capture a rebel named Sheba. On the battlefield, Joab approached Amasa and, without warning, stabbed him to death. Even this second murder could not bring David to imprison or execute Joab. The two men were related—Joab was the son of David's sister—but their relationship went even deeper than blood. Joab had stood with David during his darkest hour.

never forgot the people who supported Adonijah; he remembered Joab's betrayal in particular. On his death bed, King David reminded Solomon of Joab's foolish and violent temperament. Recalling the murders of Abner and Amasa, David told Solomon that Joab should not die in peace. David's words were Joab's death sentence. Joab fled to the altar for sanctuary, but Solomon was unmoved; he commanded his servant to strike him down where he stood, bringing a violent end to Joab's destructive life.

For further study, see 2Sa 2:13-32; 3:22-31; 10–11; 14; 18:5-18; 19:1-13; 20:6-10; 23; 1Ki 1:1-10; 2:1-6,28-34.
2. 1Ch 4:14; descendant of Judah 1
3. Ezr 2:6; descendant of Pahath-moab; ancestor of resettlers in Judah

JOAH (JOH uh) *the Lord is brother*
1. 1Ch 6:21; descendant of Levi
2. 10 century B.C.; 1Ch 26:4; son of Obed-edom; head of temple gatekeeper family
3. 8 century B.C.; 2Ch 29:12; Levite; helped purify temple under Hezekiah
4. 8 century B.C.; 2Ki 18:18; official who spoke with Assyrians when Jerusalem was besieged
5. 7 century B.C.; 2Ch 34:8; official Josiah sent to help with temple repair

JOAHAZ (JOH uh haz) *the Lord has grasped;*
7 century B.C.; 2Ch 34:4; his son Joah helped
repair the temple

JOAKIM (JO uh keem) meaning unknown
1. 6 century B.C.; Sus 1:1; husband of Susanna 1
2. 4 century B.C.; Jdt 4:6; high priest from
Jerusalem who honored Judith

JOANAN (joh AY nuhn) meaning unknown; Lk
3:27; descendant of Zerubbabel; ancestor of Jesus

JOANNA (joh AN uh) *the Lord has been gracious;*
1 century A.D.; Lk 8:3; wife of Chuza; visited
Jesus's tomb

JOARIB (JOH ah rib) meaning unknown; 1Mac
2:1; ancestor of Judas Maccabeus

JOASH (JOH ash) *the Lord has given*
1. 19 century B.C.; 1Ch 7:8; son of Becher 1;
grandson of Benjamin
2. 1Ch 4:22; descendant of Judah 1
3. 12 century B.C.; Jdg 6:11; Abiezrite; father
of judge Gideon
4. 11 century B.C.; 1Ch 12:3; brother of
Ahiezer 2; joined David's army
5. 10 century B.C.; 1Ch 27:28; superintendent
of David's olive oil supply
6. 9 century B.C.; 1Ki 22:26; son of Ahab;
imprisoned prophet Micaiah
7. ruled 835–796 B.C.; 2Ki 11:2

The heir apparent to the throne of Judah, Joash
was kept in hiding for six years as a boy during the
reign of terror conducted by the wicked Queen
Athaliah, who had murdered all his other siblings.
He was raised in secret by his Aunt Jehosheba until
he was ready to be made king, replacing the murderous Athaliah, who had usurped the throne of
David.

Too young to rule in his own right, Joash relied
at first on the guidance of Jehosheba and her husband, the high priest Jehoiada. Jehoiada anointed
Joash king, but it was the people who crowned
him, thus setting precedent for kings ruling by
popular consent and mutual covenant.

Twenty-three years after assuming the throne at
age seven, Joash instigated some religious reform in
Israel (mostly temple repairs), but he tolerated
pagan worship. Soon after Jehoiada's death, Israel
under Joash alone become apostate and idolatrous.

*Joash, the heir apparent to the throne of Judah, replaces
his usurper Athaliah.*

When Jehoiada's son, the prophet Zechariah, confronted him about his wayward kingdom, Joash
had Zechariah killed. For that treacherous murder,
Joash himself was assassinated. In turn, Joash's
murder was later avenged when his son and successor, Amaziah, had the assassins executed.

For further study, see 2Ki 11–12; 14:1-6; 2Ch
23–24. Also called Jehoash 1.
8. 2Ki 13:9; see Jehoash 2

JOB (JOHB) meaning unknown; Job 1:1

The Book of Job records the story of a wealthy,
pious man whose good life turned to ashes because
God allowed Satan to test Job's faith. Jewish tradition has long honored Job for his faith and spiritual
endurance.

Job lived in the "land of Uz." Because the names
of Job's three friends mentioned in the story were
Edomite in origin, Uz may have been near Edom.
Some Hebrew traditions place Job in Hauran, a fertile area east of the Jordan River. In addition, because Job's lifespan is listed as 140 years, he may
have lived in the early patriarchal period.

Job's tale began in heaven, when God praised
him as an example of human faith. Satan, called
"the accuser" in the biblical record, dismissed Job's
faith, saying that he was righteous only because
God had blessed and protected him. Satan pro-

posed that if Job lost his wealth and loving family, Job would curse God to his face. God gave Satan the freedom to destroy anything but Job's life itself. Thus began this story of tested faith and adversity.

Satan swept down like a plague. Within one day, Job's herds had been stolen by nomadic raiders, his ten children died, and Job himself was struck with a repulsive disease that left him covered with infected sores. When his neighbors saw this deluge of calamities, they decided Job must have done something terrible to warrant such punishment and threw him out of the city.

Once a wealthy community leader sought out for his wisdom, Job now sat on an ash heap, scraping his sores with a bit of broken pottery. His wife looked at the destruction of their lives and counseled Job to "curse God and die." Satan had, indeed, destroyed nearly everything Job loved and valued.

Job was joined by three friends: Eliphaz, Bildad, and Zophar. For seven days, a common period of mourning for death or some great disaster, they sat silently with Job outside the city gates. Afterward, Job's first words were a wail of absolute despair. He cursed the day he was conceived and asked why he had been born. Job was confused; he had lived a good, righteous life, giving to the poor, caring for widows and fatherless children, and loving his own family. Why, then, had this happened to him? His question has been repeated throughout history to the present day: Why do bad things happen to innocent people?

Job's friends had quite a different perspective. Eliphaz spoke first, telling of a vision in which an angel asked whether any human could be righteous before God. He asked Job what he could have done to deserve such disastrous punishment, saying, "Do not despise the discipline of the Almighty." Eliphaz implied the orthodox understanding that adversity was the appropriate result of sin and that a good life was reward for righteousness. By that reasoning, of course, Job must have committed some grievous, hidden sin. Job held to his innocence. "Show me my wrong!" he said. After losing home and family, his only companions accused him. Job despaired; life was empty and futile. He cried out, "I will complain in the bitterness of my soul." Bildad spoke next, trying to reason with Job. He carefully laid out a logical justification for his friend's suffering and encouraged Job to ask God for forgiveness and help. Perhaps the most encouraging of Job's questionable comforters, Bildad assured Job that God would not reject a blameless person. If Job would repent, surely God would bring laughter and restoration. Job's response was a wish for death. "Would that I had died before any eye had seen me," he wept. For Job, not understanding why the God he had served and honored would allow disaster after disaster to fall upon him was more painful than even his physical suffering.

Job. Relief from lower panel of the sarcophagus of Junius Bassus, the Roman prefect. 359 A.D.

In this segment of the Book of Job, God's nature is examined alongside the question of human suffering and God's will. Job asked age-old questions, "Who is God?" and "How can humans ever understand him?" To Job, the loving God who created him could not also have created suffering. He asked these questions and found only silence in response.

The third friend, Zophar spoke in harsh confrontation. "What do you know of God?" he asked. Zophar had no doubt that Job's punishment was less than he actually deserved. In Zophar's eyes, the "deep things of God" were so high above human understanding as to be unreachable. He ridiculed Job's longing to understand God and his ways, calling his words babble and mockery. By then, Job had had his fill of his friends' counsel. He sarcastically approached them, saying, "No doubt you are the people, and wisdom will die with you." Their advice was like "proverbs of ashes"; Job would listen no more.

In a dialogue reminiscent of the Greek scholarly dramas written thousands of years later, Job debated his friends' judgment. Their convictions that sorrow and disaster do not happen to innocent people seemed untrue to Job. He challenged his friends to look at the world and to consider God. Job accused his friends, in turn, of speaking "falsely for God" because they could not understand that God was free and able to accomplish and allow anything—with or without human understanding. Job then repeated his determination to "contend with God" face to face; he would either be vindicated or die.

Each of Job's friends spoke a second time. They repeated their firm opinions that Job must repent for his secret sin and seek God's forgiveness. They urged him to turn to God, sure that he must have abandoned any real relationship or faith. As his friends continued their accusations, Job became increasingly desperate and despairing. He repeatedly

cried out to God about his life, using words like loathsome, repulsive, and hopeless. "Where is God?" he asked. He said, in effect, that the wicked often go unpunished, living long and happy lives, and that his friends were deceived and knew little of God's ways.

At this time, a bystander named Elihu entered the conversation. He first criticized Eliphaz, Bildad, and Zophar for their inability to defeat Job's reasoning, and then launched his own attack. Elihu, in fact, repeated many of his predecessors' arguments, urging Job to observe God's power displayed on the earth and admit that he could not understand divine wisdom or actions.

Job's final dialogue ended both his conflict and his suffering. Finally, "out of the whirlwind," God answered, "Who is this that darkens counsel by words without knowledge?" Then, both challenging and demonstrating his own absolute power, God asked where Job was when the earth was created, when the sun, moon, and stars were set on their paths and the seasons were established, bringing rain, snow, and harvest. He asked if Job had seen the exotic beasts like lions, ostriches, or mountain goats in their wild homes, or understood the strange sea monsters. God demanded to know who could do such things "under the whole heaven, who?"

In powerful, poetic verse, the Book of Job records God's description of the extent of his own knowledge and authority. These words challenged both Job's willingness to "contend with God" and his friends' poor advice. In claiming that God rewarded evil with suffering and good with prosperity, Eliphaz, Bildad, Zophar, and Elihu assumed an understanding of God's nature that humans do not have.

Job's encounter with the Almighty sheds light on his assumption that God was one who could be held accountable for his actions by humans. God's

> ➤ ◄
>
> *"For I know that my Redeemer lives, and that at the last he will stand upon the earth; and after my skin has thus been detroyed, then in my flesh I shall see God, whom I shall see on my side."*
>
> Job 19:25-27

oft-repeated question "Where were you?" asked, in effect, "Have you earned the right to question me?" Job said, "I lay my hand on my mouth . . . I have uttered what I did not understand, things too wonderful for me, which I did not know." Once, he admitted, he had only heard about God and thought he understood what he heard. Now, however, he had seen and experienced God firsthand and said, "I repent in dust and ashes." In the end, Job's friends were forgiven because of his prayers on their behalf, and Job's fortune and family were restored two-fold, as a blessing from the Lord for his faithfulness.

For further study, see the Book of Job; Ez 14:14; Jas 5:11; Sir 49:9.

JOBAB (JOH bab) *to call shrilly*
1. Gen 10:29; son of Joktan; ancestor of an Arabian tribe
2. Gen 36:33; pre-Israelite king of Edom
3. 15 century B.C.; Jos 11:1; Canaanite king of Madon who battled Joshua
4. 1Ch 8:9; descendant of Benjamin

JOCHEBED (JAHK uh bed) *the Lord is glory;* 16 century B.C.; Ex 6:20; wife of Amram; mother of Moses and Aaron

JODA (JOH duh) meaning unknown; Lk 3:26; descendant of Zerubbabel; ancestor of Jesus

JODAN (JOH dahn) meaning unknown; 5 century B.C.; 1Esd 9:19; married and divorced foreign wife after Exile

JOED (JOH ed) *the Lord is witness;* Ne 11:7; ancestor of Sallu 1

JOEL (JOH uhl) *the Lord is God*
1. 1Ch 7:3; descendant of Issachar 1
2. 1Ch 5:4; descendant of Reuben
3. 1Ch 5:12; Gadite chief who lived in Bashan
4. 1Ch 6:36; ancestor of Samuel
5. 11 century B.C.; 1Sa 8:2; son of Samuel; corrupt judge
6. 10 century B.C.; 1Ch 4:35; Benjaminite who joined David's army at Ziklag
7. 1Ch 11:38; see Igal 2
8. 10 century B.C.; 1Ch 15:7; Levite leader of Gershonites under David
9. 10 century B.C.; 1Ch 23:8; Gershonite; temple treasurer; possibly Joel 8

10. 10 century B.C.; 1Ch 27:20; Manassite officer in David's time
11. Joel 1:1

The Book of Joel begins with images of a locust plague destroying everything in its path. It describes Judah as a nation in desperate straits—their crops ruined and herds starving. Whether Joel experienced a plague or spoke symbolically about invading armies or a nation in ruin is unclear; however, he clearly saw the locusts as a judgment for sin. He called for repentance, and promised God's mercy. Joel prophesied that God would pour out his Spirit on all humans, men and women, old and young alike, with visions and prophecies. In the Acts of the Apostles, the apostle Peter cited this passage to explain that Pentecost fulfilled Joel's words. For further study, see the Book of Joel; Ac 2:14-21.
12. 8 century B.C.; 2Ch 29:12; Levite; purified temple in Hezekiah's day
13. 5 century B.C.; Ezr 10:43; descendant of Nebo 2; married and divorced foreigner after Exile
14. 5 century B.C.; Ne 11:9; chief officer of Benjaminites in Jerusalem after Exile

JOELAH (joh EE luh) *let him help;* 11 century B.C.; 1Ch 12:7; Benjaminite; joined David at Ziklag

The prophet Joel. Michelangelo (1475–1564), Sistene Chapel, Rome.

JOEZER (joh EE zuhr) *the Lord is help;* 11 century B.C.; 1Ch 12:6; warrior who joined David at Ziklag

JOGLI (JAHG lye) *exiled;* 15 century B.C.; Nu 34:22; father of Bukki the Danite who helped divide Canaan

JOHA (JOH uh) *the Lord is living*
1. 1Ch 8:16; descendant of Benjamin
2. 11 century B.C.; 1Ch 11:45; mighty man of David

JOHANAN (joh HAY nuhn) *the Lord is gracious*
1. 11 century B.C.; 1Ch 12:4; Saul's relative who joined David at Ziklag
2. 11 century B.C.; 1Ch 12:12; Gadite who joined David at Ziklag
3. 10 century B.C.; 1Ch 6:9; great-grandson of Zadok the priest of David
4. 8 century B.C.; 2Ch 28:12; father of Azariah 14
5. 7 century B.C.; 1Ch 3:15; son of King Josiah of Judah
6. 6 century B.C.; 2Ki 25:23; ally of Gedaliah the governor of Jerusalem
7. 5 century B.C.; Ezr 8:12; descendant of Azgad; returned to Judah
8. Ne 12:22; see Jehohanon 5
9. 1Ch 3:24; descendant of Zerubbabel
10. Ne 6:18; son of Tobiah 2; husband of Meshullam

JOHN (JAHN) *the Lord has been gracious*
1. 3 century B.C.; 1Mac 2:1; father of Mattathias
2. 3 century B.C.; 1Mac 8:17; father of Eupolemus; won concessions from Antiochus III
3. 3 century B.C.; 1Mac 2:2; oldest son of Mattathias; guerilla for Maccabeans
4. John Hyrcanus (JAHN her KAY nuhs); 2 century B.C.; 1Mac 13:53

John Hyrcanus led Israel after his father, Simon Maccabeus, died. A generation earlier, Jews led by Judas Maccabeus had rebelled against the Seleucid Empire and fought for their religious freedom. When Judas died, leadership passed to his brothers Jonathan and Simon. Simon won spiritual and political freedom for his people but was assassinated. At Simon's death, the position of chief priest passed to his son, John. This began the Hasmonean dynasty, a period in which descendants of Judas Mac-

cabeus ruled Israel as priest-kings for nearly 80 years. Although John made alliances with Rome, which opened the door to later Roman domination, the Hasmonean dynasty was visible evidence that the Maccabees had succeeded in lifting the "yoke of the heathen" from Israel's shoulders. For further study, see 1Mac 16:1-23.
5. 1 century A.D.; Jn 1:42; father of apostle Peter; also called Jonah 3
6. John the Baptist; 1 century A.D.; Mt 3:1

The life of John the Baptist was radical from its beginning. His parents, Elizabeth and Zechariah, were elderly and childless. When the angel Gabriel announced John's conception, his father doubted the angel's words and was struck dumb as punishment. After John was born, Zechariah's first words were an amazing prophecy about his son. Zechariah said God had chosen the child as a prophet of the Most High to prepare the way for the Lord, preaching salvation through forgiveness of sins. The news of this unusual birth spread across the entire hill country of Judea, where the family lived.

John was related to Jesus, as his mother was cousin or close kin to Mary, Jesus's mother. He was raised in an orthodox Jewish home; both parents came from priestly families where life centered around learning the Torah and religious and ethnic traditions of family, faith, and congregation. John may have been a Nazirite, a member of a religious order of devout Jews who took a vow to abstain from alcohol, from cutting their hair, and from touching the dead. Some scholars think he may also have lived with the Essenes, an ancient Jewish religious community committed to prayer, celibacy, study, and work. Such experiences may have helped shape John's sincere and rigorous faith.

In adulthood, John lived in the Judean hills, a hot, nearly waterless wasteland east of the Jordan River. He wore camel hair and leather, living a rustic life in this wilderness where God first called him to be a prophet. John was toughened physically and spiritually by desert life, and when he came down to the Jordan River, he was a man with a mission.

Today, John might be considered a revival preacher. For him, real faith must show itself in moral renewal. His bold invitation was, "Repent because the kingdom of God is at hand." He preached in the countryside about changed hearts and turning from sin, using baptism as a symbol of cleansing and forgiveness. The words "the kingdom of God is at hand" became a symbol of his ministry. Clearly, John saw something, or someone, on the horizon.

This odd-looking desert "wild man" attracted an audience of thousands. Some of his listeners became followers, learning from his preaching and asking to be baptized. They were impressed with his spirited preaching and the fact that he challenged the ritualism and legalism of the religious establishment of his day. Even Jesus came to the Jordan to ask for baptism by John.

Jesus traveled from Nazareth to request this baptism, but John refused, saying Jesus should baptize him. Jesus insisted, however, and as he came up from the water, he saw "the spirit of God descending like a dove.... And a voice from heaven said, 'This is my son, the beloved, with whom I am well pleased'" (Mt 3:16-17).

John's reputation grew, until people began to ask if he might be the messiah. John answered in true character. The messiah would come, "to baptize with the Holy Spirit and fire," he said. "But I am not worthy to carry his sandals" (Mt 3:11). Later, John instructed his disciples to follow Jesus, insisting that his own influence had to decrease in order that Jesus's might increase.

With preaching characterized by directness and confrontation, John fearlessly demanded faith and righteous moral choices. He spoke of people who valued religious ritual more than inner change as a "brood of vipers," and taught that faith must be followed by changed behavior. When he proposed radical acts, like telling a man with two coats to give one away, he drew everyone's attention, from the wealthiest Roman to the poorest beggar.

John's uncompromising nature eventually brought him trouble. When Herod Antipas, Rome's appointed ruler in Israel, married his brother's wife Herodias, John the Baptist condemned them publicly. Herodias was unaccustomed to embarrassment; she demanded that her husband imprison this Jewish preacher. When imprisoning John did not satisfy her desire for revenge, she arranged for his death. At a party for

John the Baptist fulfills his mission as the precursor to the messiah when he baptizes Jesus.

John, James, and Peter in the garden of Gethsemene with Jesus.

were part of Jesus's inner circle; he often spoke with them apart from the rest of the apostles, and only these three viewed the Transfiguration of Jesus and stayed with him in the garden of Gethsemene.

Many scholars think the apostle John was once a disciple of John the Baptist. The first chapter of John's Gospel tells that John the Baptist sent an unnamed disciple and Andrew (who became one of the 12) to Jesus.

John grew up in Bethsaida, learning the fishing trade from his father, Zebedee. According to Luke's Gospel, John and James were business partners with another pair of brothers, Simon (called Peter) and Andrew. One day Jesus saw the four men fishing and called out to them, "Follow me and I will make you fish for people." Luke records that they left everything—boats, equipment, and family—and followed him. James and John were impetuous, spirited men, as rugged as the Galilean hills. They were called Boanerges, or "sons of thunder."

John is remembered for his "thunder-like" actions and opinions. He once came upon someone casting out demons in Jesus's name and immediately tried to make the person stop. He neglected to ask Jesus's advice, and later he found that his Master would have taken the opposite approach.

The Gospels record one incident where John's inclination would have been literally thunderous. In Samaria, a region populated by half-Jews, Jesus was turned away by some villagers. This angered John and his brother, so they asked Jesus if he wanted them to call down fire to consume the village. Jesus was more disturbed by the brothers' lack of mercy than by the inhospitable villagers; he rebuked James and John sharply.

John is perhaps best known for wanting what he did not understand. He and James asked Jesus to give them seats of honor when he "came into his glory"; they were seeking a kind of honor that had no place in Jesus's kingdom. Jesus responded not with criticism, but with a challenge and a prophecy.

Herod's birthday, Herodias's daughter Salome danced erotically for the guests. Scripture records that Salome so enticed Herod that he offered her anything she wished. At her mother's direction, Salome demanded, and received, the head of John the Baptist on a platter.

Jesus called John the greatest prophet and grieved at his death. Although John's life was cut short, his ministry continued. Even 30 years later, when the apostle Paul came to Ephesus, he found a small group of John's disciples. Like their teacher, these 12 people were bold and ready to believe, holding on to the promise of the messiah.

For thousands of years, the Jewish people had waited for a messiah. Many Old Testament prophecies foretold a savior, but one in particular, found in Malachi 4:5, promised that a great prophet, like Elijah, would come before the messiah to prepare the people. Matthew stated that John the Baptist fulfilled this ancient prophecy by preparing Israel for the coming of Jesus.

For further study, see Mt 3:1-17; 11:2-19; 21:31-32; Mk 1:1-11; 6:14-29; Lk 1:5-25, 39-80; 7:18-35; Ac 1:6-9; 19:1-7.

7. John the Apostle; 1 century, A.D.; Mt 4:21

The New Testament often refers to Peter, James, and John—three Galilean fishermen who were among the first followers of Jesus. These three men

Jesus asked the brothers if they were able to "drink the cup that I drink" (Mk 10:38), referring to his impending death. Jesus then prophesied that the two would, indeed, "drink his cup," a foretelling of martyrdom for James and great loss for John. The ten other disciples were angry when they heard of the brothers' attempt to acquire recognition and honor. Jesus took that opportunity to teach his new, radical definition of honor and greatness. He said, "whoever wishes to become great among you must be your servant...for the Son of Man came not to be served but to serve, and to give his life as a ransom for many" (Mk 10:41-45).

John was also deeply sensitive. On one occasion, Jesus, James, and John went to the home of the Jewish leader Jairus, because the man's daughter had died. Though Jesus would later revive the girl, her tragic death obviously touched John, because he wept along with the mourners.

After the death and resurrection of Jesus, the followers of Jesus first were recognized as a movement within Judaism and then as a separate faith. John often traveled with Peter, preaching, healing, and teaching this new faith. The two men were arrested, imprisoned, beaten, and interrogated by the temple leaders. An angel once released them from prison while the doors remained locked and the guards stood outside.

John returned to Samaria, where he had once wanted to consume the village in fire because of their poor treatment of Jesus. On this visit, however, his purpose was quite different. Peter and John had been summoned by Philip, an evangelist, because some Samaritans had heard about and believed in Jesus. At that time, the followers of Jesus thought only Jews would believe; now their half-Jewish relatives, the Samaritans, not only believed, but asked for baptism. The apostles laid hands on the Samaritans and prayed for them to receive the Holy Spirit.

John remained in Jerusalem, as one of the leaders of the new

John records a vision, now known as the Book of Revelation, while exiled on the island of Patmos.

church. The New Testament credits him with authorship of three New Testament epistles and equates him with the John who was exiled to the island of Patmos where he recorded a vision now known as the Book of Revelation. The Bible does not record John's death, but some second-century records place him in Ephesus as a very old man.

For further study, see Mk 1:19-20; 3:17; 10:37; Lk 9:40-54; Jn 1:35-37; Ac 4:1-23; 8:14-25; 12:1-2; Gal 2:9; Rev 1–2.

8. John Mark; Ac 12:12; see Mark

9. 1 century A.D.; Ac 4:6; relative of Annas the priest; made ruling at Peter's trial

JOIADA (JOY uh duh) *the Lord knows*
1. 5 century B.C.; Ne 3:6; son of Paseah 3; repaired Jerusalem wall
2. 5 century B.C.; Ne 12:10; son of Eliashib 2; a form of Jehoiada 6

JOIAKIM (JOY uh kim) *the Lord exalts;* 6 century B.C.; Ne 12:10; priestly son of Jeshua; father of Eliashib 2 the priest

JOIARIB (JOY uh rib) *the Lord defends*
1. Ne 11:5; his descendants resettled in Jerusalem
2. 6 century B.C.; Ne 12:6; priest who returned to Judah after Exile
3. 5 century B.C.; Ne 11:10; priest; possibly Joiarib 2
4. 5 century B.C.; Ezr 8:16; learned man; retrieved Levites to serve at temple

JOKIM (JOH kim) *the Lord raises up;* 1Ch 4:22; descendant of Shelah 2

JOKSHAN (JAHK shan) meaning unknown; 20 century B.C.; Gen 25:2; son of Abraham by Keturah

JOKTAN (JAHK tan) *he will be made small;* Gen 10:25; grandson of Shem; source of 13 Arabian tribes

Jonah is spat onto shore near Ninevah by the great fish.

JONADAB (JOH nuh dab) *the Lord is noble*
1. 11 century B.C.; 2Sa 13:3; sly nephew of
David who planned seduction of Tamar
2. 9 century B.C.; 2Ki 10:15

Like his father Rechab, Jonadab was an ascetic
nomad who eschewed the corrupt city life and refused wine, farming, settled homes, and material
goods. Known as Jehonadab to those in the administration of his leader King Jehu, he actively
campaigned for religious reform. To prepare the
land for worship of God, Jonadab supported King
Jehu in ruthlessly suppressing the Baal worship that
previous rulers had promoted. With Jonadab
pledging zealous support, Jehu killed all who remained of the previous king's family and supporters. The pair ventured into Samaria, where under a
pretense of tolerance, they gathered together the
priests and prophets of the pagan god Baal and
then had them all executed. For Jonadab's brutal
but effective purging of idolatry, Jeremiah
promised that his followers (called Rechabites)
would never die out. For further study, see 2Ki 10;
Jer 35. Also called Jehonadab.

JONAH (JOH nuh) *dove*
1. 8 century B.C.; 2Ki 14:25

Jonah was a prophet when Israel was separated
into the two kingdoms of Israel and Judah. Although he counseled King Jeroboam II of Israel and
prophesied a successful campaign against the Syrians, his mission to bring God's word to one of Israel's
most violent enemies earned Jonah's place in history.

The Book of Jonah begins, "Now the word of
the Lord came to Jonah, son of Amittai, saying,
"Go at once to Nineveh . . . and cry out against it;
for their wickedness has come up before me" (Jnh
1:1-2). Jonah promptly ran in the opposite direction. Nineveh was a prominent Assyrian city, the
capital of the empire noted for its huge library, culture, and the physical beauty of its temples, public
gardens, and fortifying walls. The Assyrians were
also noted for their ferocity and cruelty in battle;
their troops would sweep through villages, killing
even infants with a viciousness that left neighboring nations trembling. Jonah had no interest in
preaching to the people of this city; he felt they deserved to remain in spiritual darkness.

Jonah went to Joppa, on the coast, and boarded a ship bound for Tarshish, probably a city on the western coast of the Mediterranean known for trade and metalwork. During the voyage, a storm nearly broke the ship apart. In the face of certain death, the sailors cried out, each to his own god. They pitched cargo into the sea and, in the process, found Jonah, sleeping in the hold. "Get up, call on your god!" they cried. "Perhaps your god will spare us a thought so we do not perish" (Jnh 1:6).

In ancient times, most tragedies were considered punishment for sin. With this perspective, the sailors cast lots to determine the guilty party, and the lot fell to Jonah. Jonah said they must throw him into the sea because his disobedience was the reason for the storm. Finally, when the storm increased so they could no longer control the ship, the men reluctantly threw him overboard. A great fish swallowed Jonah, and during the three days and nights spent in its belly, Jonah thanked the Lord for having saved him from drowning in the sea. The fish finally spat him onto the shore, only a day's walk from Nineveh.

Again, God instructed Jonah to go to Nineveh, taking the message that if the people did not change their ways, their city would fall in 40 days. To Jonah's astonishment and dismay, the Ninevites believed the message and repented. Even the king removed his robe, put on sackcloth, and covered himself with ashes as a symbol of repentance. The king commanded a citywide fast, saying "Who knows? God may relent and change his mind...so that we do not perish" (Jnh 2:9).

Jonah was furious when God did change his mind and spared the Ninevites. The Book of Jonah records Jonah's angry conviction that the Ninevites deserved any punishment they received, and instead God had given them forgiveness. Jonah said he would rather die than see his enemies receive mercy instead of punishment from God. In disgust, he walked east, outside the city gates, built a small shelter for himself, and waited.

Many scholars consider the building of a shelter as a sign that Jonah still hoped or expected God to destroy Nineveh. He found a spot that provided both safety and a view of the city and prepared to wait the appointed 40 days. While waiting, he learned a sobering lesson at God's hands. God made a broad-leafed plant grow to provide shade for Jonah's grim death-watch. Special note is made of Jonah's appreciation of the protection from the sun. When God sent a worm to kill the plant and remove the shade, Jonah's sorrow was noted as well. As the hot wind and sun beat down on Jonah's head, he once again said he would rather die than live. Then God spelled out his lesson in detail, saying, "You are concerned about the bush, for which you did not labor...should I not be concerned about Nineveh, that great city, in which there are more than a hundred and twenty thousand persons who do not know their right hand from their left, and also many animals?" (Jnh 4:9-11). The words "do not know their right hand from their left" refer to the people's spiritual darkness, yet God wanted them, and all people, to hear of him and repent. His words rebuke Jonah for having a narrow-minded, nationalistic view that kept him from caring about the people of Nineveh.

Nineveh's repentance seems to have been short-lived, as the prophets Zephaniah and Nahum later foretold its destruction as punishment for evil. The city was destroyed in 612 B.C., and its ruins were found by archaeologists in the late 19th century.

Jonah's story appears in the New Testament as a prophetic description of Jesus's death and resurrection. When people asked Jesus for a sign of his power, he said they would receive the "sign of Jonah." This referred to the three days Jesus was dead, paralleling Jonah's three days in the fish's belly, followed by his resurrection.

For further study, see the Book of Jonah; Zep 2:13-15; Na 1:1; 3:1; Mt 12:39-41; 16:4; Lk 11:29-32.
2. 5 century B.C.; 1Esd 9:23; Levite who married and divorced foreigner after Exile
3. 1 century A.D.; Mt 16:17; father of apostle Peter; also called John 5

JONAM (JOH nuhm) meaning unknown; Lk 3:30; ancestor of Jesus

JONATHAN (JAHN uh thuhn) *the Lord has given*
1. 1Ch 2:32; descendant of Judah 1
2. Jdg 18:30; descendant of Moses; household priest for Micah
3. 11 century B.C.; 1Ch 27:32; counselor and uncle to king David
4. 11 century B.C.; 1Sa 13:2
As King Saul's son and heir, Jonathan may have expected to reign himself one day, but instead he stepped aside for David, a friend who was closer than a brother. The relationship between David

and this humble, brave man is one of the Bible's great models of friendship and loyalty.

Jonathan is first mentioned in the Bible as the commander of 1000 soldiers. He led his soldiers against oppressing Philistine troops while his father attacked from the rear. The action brought an all-out Philistine offensive; soldiers on foot, horseback, and chariot flooded the Israelite troops, capturing the town of Michmash. Jonathan proved his military skill and personal courage again in the turning point of this conflict. The vastly overwhelmed Israelite troops faced Philistines more numerous than "the sand on the seashore" (1Sa 13:5). The people had fled, leaving only 600 Hebrew soldiers. Jonathan and his armor-bearer went to a cliff overlooking the Philistine camp, saying God could save Israel "by many or by few" (1Sa 14:6). The two men showed themselves to the Philistine troops and, when the enemies pursued, killed 20 soldiers.

Jonathan during his battle with the Philistines.

The story of two men killing 20 spread through the Philistine camp. The story grew with its telling until the Philistine troops panicked. The Israelites heard tremendous wailing from the camp and realized the Philistines were afraid. In the end, enough Israelite troops assembled to drive the Philistines into the hills.

Jonathan's friendship with David began when King Saul honored the young shepherd for killing the Philistine champion, Goliath. Jonathan made a symbolic gesture of friendship, giving David his tunic and weapons as a pledge. At first, David was greatly honored in the court, and his friendship with Jonathan grew. David was given command of some soldiers, and his stunning successes won admiration from the Israelites. When Saul heard them singing, "Saul has killed his thousands, and David his ten thousands" (1Sa 18:7), he was enraged and threatened David's life. Jonathan, however, remained a true friend, risking his father's anger and his own life to defend David.

David's life was often in danger from the jealous king. Once, Jonathan was able to convince his father that David meant him no harm, but only for a short time. When Saul's soldiers came to drag David from his bed and murder him, David fled to the city of Ramah. David met with Jonathan and asked what he had done to deserve such treatment. Jonathan first discounted David's claims, saying that he would have known if his father had ordered David's death. David convinced him that Saul knew the depth of their friendship and so hid his thoughts from Jonathan. During this conversation, Jonathan made a powerful, touching promise of faithfulness and friendship. He promised to warn David of any danger and, if needed, send him away to safety. Clearly, Jonathan feared that Saul might threaten his own life as well, because he said to David, "If [after this] I am still alive, show me the faithful love of the Lord; but if I die, never cut off your faithful love from my house" (1Sa 20:14-15).

Jonathan offered the following plan to test Saul's intentions: The next day, David would not come to a planned three-day feast but would hide in the fields instead. When David was missed, Jonathan would watch Saul's reaction. If Saul threatened David's life, Jonathan would come to the field and shoot an arrow far beyond David's hiding place as a signal to flee. During the feast, Saul demanded to know David's whereabouts. Jonathan lied, saying David had gone to Bethlehem, his family home, for

Jonathan and David with the head of Goliath.

a special sacrifice. Saul was furious; he berated Jonathan's loyalty to David, saying he had shamed his family and would never hold Israel's throne while David lived. Jonathan asked what his friend had done to deserve death. In uncontrolled rage, Saul threw a spear at his son. Jonathan escaped but knew then that David would be killed if Saul ever caught him.

Jonathan went to the fields with his bow and arrows the next day. He shot the arrows beyond David's hiding place, as planned. When Jonathan was alone, David crept out from the rocks where he had been hiding and bowed before his friend in thanks. The two embraced, kissed each other, and wept, knowing they might never be together again. "The Lord shall be between me and you, and between my descendants and your descendants, forever" (1Sa 20:42) they vowed.

David fled to the hills where he was joined by his brothers and many Israelites who were loyal to him. During the following months, all Israel was in chaos, as Saul made an attempt to destroy David and keep his Philistine enemies at bay. Although Jonathan knew that Saul was in the wrong, he stayed by his father's side.

Saul, Jonathan, and two of his brothers died in a battle with the Philistines, and David grieved for the whole family. The final piece of Jonathan's story occurred when David kept their final vow. After taking the throne, David found Jonathan's only surviving relative, a lame nephew named Mephibosheth, and provided for him out of his love for Jonathan.

For further study, see 1Sa 13–14; 18–20; 2Sa 1; 4:4; 9:1-13.

5. 11 century B.C.; 2Sa 15:27; son of David's high priest Abiathar

6. 11 century B.C.; 2Sa 23:32; mighty man of David

7. 10 century B.C.; 2Sa 21:21; son of Shimea; nephew of David

8. 10 century B.C.; 1Ch 27:25; son of Uzziah; overseer of town storehouses

9. 7 century B.C.; Jer 37:15; secretary of Zedekiah; imprisoned the prophet Jeremiah

10. 6 century B.C.; Ne 12:14; head of priestly family

11. 5 century B.C.; Ezr 8:6; father of Ebed 2

12. 5 century B.C.; Ne 12:35; father of priest Zechariah who dedicated Jerusalem wall

13. 5 century B.C.; Ezr 10:15; son of Asahel who opposed plan to divorce foreigners

14. 5 century B.C.; Ne 12:11; high priest

15. Jonathan the Maccabean; 2 century B.C.; 1Mac 2:5

In 160 B.C., Judea was controlled by the Seleucid Empire under Antiochus IV Epiphanes, who forbade the Jews to worship God and defiled the

Ruins of the fortress used by the Maccabees during their revolt against Antiochus IV Epiphanes. Beit Zur, Israel.

temple with sacrifices to Zeus. Judas Maccabeus led a rebellion that won religious but not political autonomy. However, when Antiochus appointed a Hellenistic (Greek) Jew as high priest, the fight began anew. When Judas died in battle, his brother Jonathan assumed leadership. He took advantage of the shaky Seleucid government to strengthen his army. Using alliances within the frequently changing Seleucid government to gain power, the Maccabeans reclaimed the position of chief priest. Later, a shift in power left Jonathan without support. He was tricked, taken prisoner, and executed. Leadership of the revolt then passed to Jonathan's brother Simon. For further study, see the Book of First Maccabees.

16. 2 century B.C.; 1Esd 8:32; leader returning from Exile

17. 2 century B.C.; 1Esd 9:14; judge who ruled on Jews divorcing foreign wives; possibly Jonathan 16

JORAH (JOHR uh) *rain;* 6 century B.C.; Ezr 2:18; ancestor of resettlers to Judah; also called Hariph 1

JORAI (JOHR eye) possibly *the Lord taught;* 1Ch 5:13; descendant of Gad

JORAM (JOHR uhm) *the Lord is exalted*
1. 1Ch 26:25; ancestor of David's treasurer Shelomith
2. 2Sa 8:10; see Hadoram 2
3. 2Ki 8:16; see Jehoram 2
4. 2Ki 8:21; see Jehoram 1

JORIM (JOHR im) *the Lord is exalted;* Lk 3:29; ancestor of Christ

JORKEAM (JOHR kee uhm) meaning unknown; 1Ch 2:44; descendant of Judah

JOSECH (JOH zek) meaning unknown; Lk 3:26; descendant of Jesus's ancestor Zerubbabel

Joseph's brothers sell him into slavery for 20 pieces of silver.

JOSEPH (JOH suhf) *may God add*
1. 18 century B.C.; Gen 30:24

When Joseph's father Jacob was young, his mother favored him, while his father favored his twin, Esau. This hurt both brothers and nearly destroyed their family. By practicing the same kind of favoritism toward his own 12 children, Jacob provoked conflict among the brothers and initiated a story that ultimately teaches forgiveness, loyalty, and God's farsightedness.

Jacob had a long, richly ornamented coat made for Joseph—a show of preference for his eleventh son that made the others angry and jealous. These feelings were aggravated when Joseph began having dreams that showed that he would one day lead the family. In the first dream, each of the brothers had a bundle of wheat, and Joseph's stood upright while his brothers' bundles bowed down. In the second dream, Joseph saw the sun, the moon, and 11 stars (recalling his father, mother, and eleven brothers) bow down to him. When Joseph reported his dreams to the family, the older brothers were outraged and even his father was disturbed.

Joseph's brothers soon had an opportunity to vent their anger when their father sent Joseph to meet them in the hills. They saw him from a distance, and decided to kill him, throw his body into a pit, and claim that wild animals had attacked the boy. Then "we shall see what will become of his dreams," they said (Gen 37:20).

Reuben, the eldest, was appalled at the idea. Thinking quickly, he suggested they throw Joseph into a pit and leave him for dead, after which Reuben planned to secretly rescue him. The brothers accepted this proposal. When Joseph arrived, they seized him, stripped the coat from his body, and threw him into a pit. Several of the brothers remained near the pit and sat down to eat. Traders bound for Egypt passed by, and their presence sparked a cruel idea: Why not sell their brother to make a profit and avoid the condemnation of fratricide? Since Reuben had left, Joseph had no advocate; they sold their 17-year-old brother into slavery for 20 pieces of silver.

Reuben made his way in secret to the pit and found Joseph missing. He came to his brothers in dismay, saying, "The boy is gone, and I, where can I turn?" (Gen 37:30). The brothers planned to dip Joseph's coat in goat's blood, pretend that a wild beast had killed him, and offer the coat as proof to their father. Whether Reuben feared his brothers or simply did not have the heart to tell the truth is unclear, but he agreed to this deception. When Jacob saw Joseph's bloody clothing, he could not be comforted.

Joseph was sold to Potiphar, captain of Pharaoh's guard. In time, Potiphar recognized his young servant's skill and trustworthiness and made Joseph steward over his estate. Where Potiphar saw skill, his wife saw a handsome face. She repeatedly attempted to seduce Joseph, once grabbing his garment as he pulled away from her. Hurt by his rejections, she accused him of attempted rape and used his garment as evidence. No slave could disprove such an accusation, and Joseph was imprisoned.

During this time, Pharaoh's personal cupbearer and baker were imprisoned also. Both men had peculiar dreams, and when they complained to Joseph that no interpretation was possible, he remarked that true interpretations came from God and offered to consult the God of Israel on their behalf. After listening to their dreams, Joseph told the cupbearer that Pharaoh would free him in three days and told the baker that Pharaoh would execute him in three days. In keeping with Joseph's interpretations, the baker was executed and the cupbearer returned to his duties at court, forgetting about Joseph altogether.

Some two years later, Pharaoh had a dream in which he stood by the Nile River and seven thin and seven fat cows came out of the water. The sickly, thin cows ate up the fat ones. This was followed by seven blighted ears of grain eating up seven healthy ears. The dream so disturbed him that he sent for magicians and wise men to ask for an interpretation. When no one could interpret Pharaoh's dream, the cupbearer's memory and conscience struck him simultaneously. He told Pharaoh about the incident in prison and Joseph's remarkable interpretation of the dreams, so Pharaoh sent for Joseph at once.

Joseph heard Pharaoh's dream and gave him an interpretation of warning, saying, "God has revealed to Pharaoh what he is about to do" (Gen 41:25). Joseph told Pharaoh that seven good years would be followed by seven years of terrible famine. He then outlined a plan by which the Egyptians

Potiphar's wife attempts to seduce the slave Joseph.

could be saved from starvation. The plan so pleased Pharaoh that he appointed Joseph as overseer of the kingdom with authority to organize grain storage for the next seven years.

During these years, Joseph married an Egyptian woman and fathered two sons. When the famine came, the neighboring nations starved, but Joseph's careful planning kept bread on Egyptian tables. The famine was so great that even in Canaan, Jacob and his sons ran out of food. Jacob sent Joseph's ten older brothers to Egypt to purchase grain, keeping Benjamin, the youngest, with him. When they were brought before Joseph, he instantly recognized them, although they did not know who he was.

Joseph first accused the brothers of spying and then had them imprisoned. The brothers pleaded their innocence, saying they were ten of 11 sons of the same man and wanted only food. Still not revealing himself, Joseph sold them grain but made them promise to return with their younger brother, keeping Simeon behind as hostage to ensure their return. Joseph then secretly hid their payment for the grain in their bags. On the journey home, the nine brothers discovered the money and feared that if they returned to Egypt they would be accused of thievery. When they told Jacob their father what had happened, he said he would let Benjamin return with them only if Reuben pledged the lives of his own two sons and Judah offered to take any blame upon himself. The brothers returned to Egypt, and to their great relief, Joseph welcomed them to his own home. At the sight of Benjamin, Joseph had to leave the room to hide his tears.

The brothers purchased grain again and prepared to leave. Joseph, however, wanted to keep Benjamin with him and so hid a silver cup in the boy's sack along with the money used to purchase the grain. When Joseph's servants found the cup in Benjamin's belongings, they had him arrested. Judah pleaded on his knees before Joseph for the life of young Benjamin. When Joseph heard that

> → ←
>
> *"God sent me before you to preserve for you a remnant on earth, and to keep alive for you many survivors."*
>
> Gen 45:7

their father might die of sorrow if Benjamin was lost, he sent his servants away and revealed his true identity. To the brothers' astonishment, Joseph expressed no desire for further revenge but wept so loudly that even the Egyptians heard him. He said, "So it was not you who sent me here, but God."

When Pharaoh heard that Joseph's brothers had come, he offered his own wagons to bring their families to Egypt. The 11 brothers went to Canaan, bringing gifts for their father from Joseph. They returned to Egypt, with Jacob and their extended family, in a caravan of 70 people. Jacob, now elderly and frail, was overjoyed at the promise of seeing the beloved son he had once mourned as dead.

From that time until his death, Joseph returned to Canaan once, to bury his father. Jacob's sons and their families were given land in Goshen. As Egyptians found sheepherders offensive, Joseph's family lived some distance from their Egyptian neighbors. This internal exile enabled them to keep their distinct religious and ethnic identity intact.

Joseph's ability to forgive his brothers has stood as an example in Judeo-Christian history. After all the hurt inflicted by his brothers, Joseph forgave them, saying, "Even though you intended to do harm to me, God intended it for good" (Gen 50:20). At his death, Joseph asked to be buried in Canaan, a request that was honored generations later when Moses took Joseph's remains back to Canaan during the Exodus.

For further study see, Gen 30:22; 35:16-26; 37; 39–50; Ex 1:1-8; 13:19; Jos 24:32.

2. 15 century B.C.; Nu 13:7; father of Igal the spy for Moses in Canaan

3. 10 century B.C.; 1Ch 25:2; son of Asaph the music minister

4. Lk 3:30; descendant of David

5. 6 century B.C.; Ne 12:14; head of priestly family in days of priest Joiakim

6. 6 century B.C.; Jdt 8:1; great-grandfather of Judith

7. 5 century B.C.; Ezr 10:42; one who married and divorced foreigner after Exile
8. Lk 3:24; descendant of Zerubbabel
9. 2 century B.C.; 2Mac 8:22; Maccabean fighter
10. 1 century A.D.; Mt 1:16

According to the Book of Matthew, Joseph was a descendant of David and a man of integrity, honor, and loyalty, but he was not the biological father of Jesus. When Joseph learned that his betrothed Mary was carrying someone else's child, he chose to end their engagement by quietly divorcing her. A "quiet divorce" (one involving just two other witnesses) would have saved Mary from the public disgrace of full court action against her. Joseph went through with the marriage, however, after an angel appeared to him in a dream, saying that the child was "of the Holy Spirit" (Mt 1:20).

Joseph protected Jesus, fleeing with his family to Egypt to escape the wrath and murderous intent of King Herod the Great. He also took Jesus to Jerusalem for the rite of purification or circumcision at the prescribed time. After returning with his family to Nazareth of Galilee, Joseph trained his son in the family business of carpentry.

According to Matthew 13:55, Joseph was the father of several children by Mary—four sons and several daughters. Although Mary and Jesus's brothers are mentioned throughout the Gospels, Joseph is conspicuously absent from all but the earliest years of Jesus's life.

For further study, see Mt 1:16–2:23; 12:46; 13:55-57; Mk 3:31; 6:3; Lk 1:26-38; 2:1-52; 4:22; Jn 2:12; 6:42; 7:3,27-28; 19:26-27; 1Co 9:5; Gal 1:19.
11. 1 century A.D.; Mt 13:55; brother of Jesus; also called Joses 1
12. Joseph of Arimathea; 1 century A.D.; Mt 27:57

Joseph of Arimathea, a wealthy and respected member of the Sanhedrin, did not take part in the resolution of the council to put Jesus to death. In fact, Joseph himself was looking for the kingdom of God and was a disciple of Jesus, something he kept secret because of his fear of the Jews. After the crucifixion of Jesus, Joseph secured permission from Pilate to remove the body of Jesus from the cross. He then provided fine linen for the burial, laid the body in his own unused rock tomb, and rolled a

Jesus as a young man at home with Mary and Joseph.

Joseph of Arimathea removes Jesus's body after the crucifixion. Rembrandt (1606–1669).

huge stone to the door of the tomb. For further study, see Mt 27:57-59; Mk 15:43-46; Lk 23:50-53; Jn 19:38.

13. 1 century A.D.; Ac 1:23; nominee to replace apostle Judas; also called Justus 1 and Barsabbas 1
14. 1 century A.D.; Ac 4:36; the given name of Barnabas

JOSES (JOH seez) *increaser*
1. Mk 6:3; see Joseph 11
2. 1 century A.D.; Mk 15:40; brother of James 4; son of Mary and Clopas

JOSHAH (JAHSH uh) *the Lord's gift;* 8 century B.C.; 1Ch 4:34; clan leader in genealogy of Simeon

JOSHAPHAT (JAHSH uh fat) *the Lord has judged*
1. 11 century B.C.; 1Ch 11:43; mighty man of David
2. 11 century B.C.; 1Ch 15:24; priest and trumpeter before ark upon its return

JOSHAVIAH (JAHSH uh VYE uh) meaning unknown; 11 century B.C.; 1Ch 11:46; son of Elnaam; mighty man of David

JOSHBEKASHAH (JAHSH buh KAY shuh) *he returns a hard fate;* 10 century B.C.; 1Ch 25:4; son of Heman; chief music minister under David

JOSHEB-BASSHEBETH 2Sa 23:8; see Jashobeam 1

JOSHIBIAH (JAHSH uh BYE uh) *the Lord causes to dwell;* 8 century B.C.; 1Ch 4:35; father of Jehu the Simeonite clan leader

JOSHUA (JAHSH oo uh) *the Lord is salvation*
1. 15 century B.C.; Ex 17:9
Under Moses's leadership, the entire population of Israel was freed from generations of slavery and oppression in Egypt. As they traveled through the wilderness to return to their ancient homeland, Moses took a group of refugees who had little understanding of their culture, faith, or national identity and reestablished them as a nation. During this grueling journey, Moses chose and trained leaders to assist him, and among the most gifted of these leaders was Joshua.

Joshua was originally named Hoshea. Soon after the Israelites' successful escape from Pharaoh, they were forced to fight for their lives against the Amalekites at Rephidim. Joshua led the Hebrew defense in a battle now famous in Israel's history because his troops were victorious only as long as Moses stood on the hillside with his staff raised. If Moses's arm dropped, the Amalekites gained advantage. Finally, Moses's brother, Aaron, and a man named Hur held up his hands until sunset, when the victory was complete. Evidently, Joshua's success in battle earned him his new name.

Only Joshua went with Moses to Mt. Sinai, where he spent 40 days and nights in God's presence. As Joshua guarded his tent, Moses received the Law and instructions for Israel's governing and religious life. When they returned to the camp and found that a golden calf had been created and worshiped as an idol, Joshua risked his life to stand with Moses as he confronted the Israelites' sin.

Joshua appeared at crucial points in the establishment of Israel as a spiritual and political nation. When Moses brought the people north from Mt. Sinai to the oasis of Kadesh-barnea, they stood at the doorway to Canaan, the land God had promised to give them as a home. Joshua was chosen to represent his tribe, Ephraim, on the team sent to survey the land. Twelve Hebrew men traveled some 40 days through Canaan to spy out the quality of the land and assess military strength. They discovered rich farm and grazing lands and beautiful countryside. However, they also found fortified cities and numerous armies, including the tall, powerful-looking Anakite tribesmen. The spies were frightened. At their return, they gave exaggerated reports that the country was populated by giants who could not possibly be defeated. Only Joshua and Caleb of Judah disagreed, as they were confident of Israel's military strength and God's support. Upon hearing reports about giants, the people wailed like mourners. When they began to talk about going back to Egypt, Joshua and Caleb tore their clothes in grief and begged the people to trust God's protection. The two were nearly stoned by the angry crowd.

Divine punishment for this lack of faith was quick to come and long in duration. Moses delivered the judgment: Even though the Israelites had been miraculously rescued from Egypt, they still did not believe. God's patience was ended; he would not permit any of the adults, except the families of Moses, Joshua, and Caleb, to enter Canaan. Ten of the spies died of plague, and the Israelites lived as homeless nomads for 40 years in the deserts near Kadesh-barnea.

Toward the end of this period, Moses officially recognized Joshua as Israel's new leader. The priest Eleazar blessed Joshua to confirm him as leader, judge, and preserver of the Law. The task of leading the Israelites into the Promised Land was a risky, bold endeavor. All of Joshua's military skill

Joshua battles the Amalekites during the Exodus to the Promised Land.

The Israelites cross the Jordan River with the ark of the covenant.

and faith in God were fully tested as his band of desert-dwelling nomads invaded fortified cities and challenged standing armies. The Book of Joshua records his battles, acts of courage, brilliant and foolish military strategies, and reliance on the power of God.

Canaan was a land of valleys and mountains that encouraged political divisions. Former nomadic tribes had settled in these regions, gradually forming separate kingdoms, each with its own chief or ruler. Military confrontations, invasions, and loose alliances were common, and the least powerful were open targets for military aggression on all sides. The Israelites were poised to claim Canaan as their land because God had promised it to their ancient ancestors. However, ownership had to be won through bloody battles and conquests.

First, the Israelites crossed the Jordan River to Gilgal, where the miracle of parting the Red Sea was repeated. In Gilgal, the young men were cir-

cumcised and all Israel celebrated Passover. After that, the battles of conquest began, and Israel's first victory, at Jericho, caught the attention of all Canaan. Jericho was a fortified city with double walls—the outer wall was six feet thick, and the inner one, 12. Joshua's men would have had to scale the formidable first wall, fight their way across the top, dodge projectiles in the space between, then repeat the feat at the second wall. Obviously, a direct assault would be costly and almost certain to fail. God directed Joshua to march his men, with seven priests and the ark of the covenant, around Jericho once each day for six days. On the seventh day, they were to march again, with priests blowing trumpets and a ram's horn. The people were to shout "with a great shout," and then Jericho's walls would fall. The wise, experienced military commander obeyed these seemingly pointless instructions, and for six days the people of Jericho saw an eerie spectacle—silent Israelite troops, marching to the sound of trumpets. On the seventh day the trumpets signaled a great shout, after which "the walls fell down flat, so the people charged straight ahead into the city and captured it" (Jos 6:20).

Some of Joshua's battles were unsuccessful. After helping the Israelites take Jericho, God prevented them from defeating the small city of Ai because of one man's transgression. A soldier named Achan had taken booty from Jericho despite God's specific directive not to do so. Achan's sin was discovered after the Israelites were repulsed at Ai, and he and his entire family were stoned to death and all their possessions were destroyed. Once this punishment had been meted out, the Israelites were able to take the city.

The Gibeonites were frightened by the tales of Jericho's defeat, so they sent two men, dressed in rags and eating moldy bread, to meet Joshua at Gilgal. The men claimed to be travelers and asked Joshua for a promise of peace. Joshua agreed, only to discover three days later he had been deceived; they were not distant travelers at all, but Gibeonites of a neighboring kingdom. However, Joshua had pledged peace in the name of God and was bound to it. The Gibeonites were, however, forced into slavery under Israel.

Joshua and his troops defeated city after city, even crushing a coalition of five northern kings. Joshua defeated 31 kings in his battles. In a custom common to the era and region, he exiled the conquered people and divided their land among the tribes of Israel. Although much of Canaan remained unconquered, Joshua allowed the tribes to separate and settle on their allotted land. He spent considerable time judging disputes and hearing complaints as the land was divided. Then Joshua sent representatives from each tribe to look at unconquered Canaanite territory with an eye to future conquest and division.

As Joshua saw his people settle in towns and villages, plant crops and raise their sheep, he saw his own mark on history. The Book of Joshua records this settlement, saying, "The Lord gave them rest on every side just as he had sworn to their ancestors.... Not one of the good promises that the Lord had made to the house of Israel had failed; all came to pass" (Jos 21:43-45).

Before his death, Joshua gathered his people for a final word. He reaffirmed that God would give them all the land between the River Jordan and the

> ⇥ ⇤
>
> *"...choose this day whom you will serve.... but as for me and my household, we will serve the Lord."*
>
> Jos 24:15

western coast, warned them about idol worship and foreign gods, and challenged them in the strongest terms that they had to choose between the God of Israel and the Egyptian idols their ancestors worshiped. Joshua's personal statement of faith has been repeated in words of commitment over the centuries. He said, "...choose this day whom you will serve... but as for me and my household, we will serve the Lord" (Jos 24:15).

For further study, see Ex 14; 17:8-16; 24:12-18; 32:1–33:11; Nu 13–14; 26:65; 27:12-23; Dt 1:19-40; 3:21-29; 31–34; the Book of Joshua.

2. 11 century B.C.; 1Sa 6:14; owner of field in Beth-shemesh
3. 7 century B.C.; 2Ki 23:8; governor of Jerusalem during reign of Josiah
4. Hag 1:1; see Jeshua 4
5. Lk 3:29; ancestor of Jesus

Joshua's men march around the walls of Jericho as seven priests blow trumpets.

JOSIAH (joh SIGH uh) *the Lord supports* or *fire of the Lord*

1. ruled 640–609 B.C.; 1Ki 13:2

After the reign of Solomon, son of the legendary King David, Israel split into separate nations, Israel and Judah. During this era of political and ethnic division, Josiah became Judah's sixteenth ruler. Although Josiah's grandfather had burned one of his own children as an offering to the pagan god Baal, and his father worshiped idols all his life, Josiah worshiped Israel's God. Though only a handful of Hebrew monarchs worshiped God in the generations before and after, Josiah was a man of faith like King David.

During the eighteenth year of Josiah's reign, renovation work was being done in the temple. At the king's order, the high priest Hilkiah reviewed the temple treasury in preparation for this significant expense. During the review, a Book of the Law was found (perhaps segments or an ancient copy of the Book of Deuteronomy).

The book was read to King Josiah, who listened intently to its descriptions of God's spiritual and moral standards. Josiah saw immediately how far the Hebrew people had strayed from God's ways and was horrified. He tore his clothes in a sign of horror or grief and told the high priest to pray for the nation, because their disobedience surely de-

served God's anger. Josiah did not know what to do. The priests consulted a respected prophet, Huldah, who confirmed Josiah's trepidation; she said God would destroy Judah, although not during his lifetime.

Josiah ordered the entire nation to the temple and required everyone, from the highest priest to the simplest laborer, to listen to God's commandments. To underscore their importance, Josiah read the words himself and made a public promise to keep God's decrees. This public reading of the Law began an era of radical reform. Josiah started in the temple, taking all vessels or items connected with the worship of Baal, Asherah, or other idols to be burned. He deposed Hebrew priests who made offerings to Baal, tore down buildings that housed temple prostitutes, and ground idols to dust. He defiled altars for the Assyrian worship of the sun, moon, and stars, and cut down sacred poles dedicated to Asherah and Baal, defiling those sites with human bones. Josiah attempted to stop the child sacrifice practiced by worshipers of the Ammonite god Milcom by defiling the entry to the valley of Hinnom, where the vile practice occurred.

In Bethel, Josiah found an altar built by Jeroboam, Israel's first king, in honor of an idol. From nearby tombs, he took human bones and burned them on the altar. This very act had been foretold by a Samaritan prophet many generations earlier. The prophecy was given to Jeroboam, cautioning that because of his idolatry, the priests he paid to serve at his Baal altars would someday be burned upon them.

The Hebrew people in Josiah's time knew so little of their spiritual and cultural heritage that even the celebration of Passover had been forgotten. When Josiah saw the instructions in the book of the Law, he realized that Passover had not been observed "since the days of the judges . . . or during all the days of the kings of Israel or of the kings of Judah" (2Ki 23:21-22). Josiah commanded a celebration of Passover in Jerusalem in the reconsecrated temple. This celebration revived not only the religious tradition of recalling God's rescue of the Hebrew people from slavery in Egypt, but also their ancient identity as a nation set apart by God.

Josiah's reign was marked by both spiritual and political upheaval. While he was bringing spiritual order at home, Judah's borders were constantly threatened by invaders. During this era, the Egyptians, Babylonians, and Assyrians kept smaller na-

King Josiah. Stained glass. Grace Episcopal Church, Manchester, New Hampshire.

tions like Israel and Judah in a constant state of fear; if one did not attack, the other might.

The Assyrians had long dominated the region. When the Babylonians and Medes united against Assyria, Pharaoh Neco of Egypt came to Assyria's aid, hoping to ensure his own position in the process. Josiah was a good king, but a poor military strategist. When Neco sent an envoy saying, in effect, "I have no quarrel with you; get out of my way," Josiah refused to back down. Judah's soldiers were confronted by Neco's vastly superior forces, and Josiah disguised himself in battle, hoping to kill the Egyptian monarch. In the ensuing battle (609 B.C.), Josiah was killed and Egypt's hold over Judah was strengthened.

The people of Judah grieved for their king. Whether they understood his religious reforms and commitment or not, they still loved him. The Book of Second Chronicles records that songs of grief for Josiah's death became part of Hebrew musical tradition and were written in an ancient book of laments. Even the prophet Jeremiah publicly grieved. Josiah was buried in his tomb in Jerusalem. His son, Jehoahaz, held Judah's throne for only three months before Pharaoh Neco of Egypt replaced him with his more compliant (and perhaps less principled) older brother, Jehoiakim.

For further study, see 1Ki 13:1-4; 2Ki 21:24; 22–23; 2Ch 34–36; Jer 1:1-3; Zep 1:1-6.
2. 6 century B.C.; Zec 6:10; son of Zephaniah

JOSIPHIAH (JAHS uh FYE uh) *the Lord adds;* 5 century B.C.; Ezr 8:10; father of Shelomith

JOTHAM (JAY thuhm) *the Lord is perfect*
1. 1Ch 2:47; descendant of Judah 1
2. 12 century B.C.; Jdg 9:5

In an attempt to solidify his power and establish the first monarchy over Israel, Abimelech, son of Gideon the judge, used mercenaries from Shechem to murder his 69 brothers. Only Jotham, the youngest brother, survived, and Abimelech set himself up as king. During his reign, Abimelech reintroduced idolatrous Baal worship to Israel. Jotham went into hiding but quickly emerged as a judge to deliver Israel and pronounce a curse on Abimelech. In Jotham's prophesy of doom, he used images of an olive tree, fig tree, worthless bramble (Abimelech), and forest fire (the destruction of Shechem). True to Jotham's double prophecy, the people of Shechem revolted against Abimelech.

Jotham survives a murder attempt by mercenaries sent by Abimelech.

The king's troops crushed the city, but Abimelech was killed during the fighting. For further study, see Jdg 8:31–9:57.
3. ruled 750–732 B.C.; 2Ki 15:5

King Jotham of Judah, like his brilliant father Uzziah, was known to follow the directives of the Lord, despite a lax policy toward the rampant paganism of his era. When his father was struck with leprosy, 25-year-old Jotham stepped up to rule with him as co-regent for ten years. The reigns of father and son, spanning 60 years altogether, were characterized by military strength and economic prosperity. But the Book of Second Kings hands down the same indictment on both of them: "Nevertheless, the high places were not removed; the people still sacrificed and made offerings" to pagan gods. Upon Jotham's death, his son Ahaz succeeded to the throne of Judah and promoted pagan worship and human sacrifice. For further study, see 2Ki 15:7,32-38; 2Ch 26:21–27:9.

JOZABAD (JAHZ uh bad) *the Lord has bestowed*
1. 11 century B.C.; 1Ch 12:4; Benjaminite defector to David at Ziklag
2. 11 century B.C.; 1Ch 12:20; Manassite military commander; joined David
3. 11 century B.C.; 1Ch 12:20; another military commander who joined David
4. 8 century B.C.; 2Ch 31:13; Levite in charge of temple offerings
5. 7 century B.C.; 2Ch 35:9; chief Levite under Josiah
6. 5 century B.C.; Ezr 8:33; Levite who weighed sacred gold and silver articles
7. 5 century B.C.; Ezr 10:22; priest who married and divorced foreigner after Exile
8. 5 century B.C.; Ezr 10:23; Levite who married and divorced foreigner after Exile
9. 5 century B.C.; Ne 8:7; Levite instructor of the Law
10. 5 century B.C.; Ne 11:16; chief Levite; settled in Jerusalem; possibly Jozabad 6, 8, or 9

JOZACAR (JAHZ uh cahr) *the Lord remembered;* 9 century B.C.; 2Ki 12:21; conspired to kill King Joash; also called Zabad 4

JOZADAK (JAHZ uh dak) *the Lord is righteous;* 6 century B.C.; Ezr 3:2; father of Jeshua 4; also called Jehozadak

JUBAL (JOO bahl) *sound;* Gen 4:21; son of Lamech; renowned father of flute and harp

JUCAL Jer 38:1; see Jehucal

JUDAH (JOO duh) *praised*
1. 18 century B.C.; Gen 29:35
Judah is among the best-known sons of Jacob because his offspring became Israel's tribe of Judah. When tricked into fathering children by his widowed daughter-in-law, Tamar, Judah also became an ancestor of Jesus.

Judah grew up in a divided, jealous household. His father, Jacob, had married his two cousins Rachel and Leah, but he only loved Rachel and favored her two sons over Leah's sons. Judah and his nine brothers so hated Joseph, the most favored son, that they considered killing him. Later, at

Judah solicits his daughter-in-law Tamar, who is posing as a prostitute.

Judah's suggestion, they sold the boy to traveling Midianite slave traders. Joseph ended up in Egypt and, years later, was able to save Jacob, Judah, and their entire extended family from starvation.

Judah married a Canaanite woman and fathered three sons—Er, Onan, and Shelah. Er married Tamar but died soon after, leaving her widowed and childless. In that culture, a brother-in-law was required to take a childless widow as his own wife and father her children, who would be recognized as his brother's children. In this way, the dead brother's name would continue. Onan was also childless. Since he did not want to father and raise children only to have them recognized as his brother's offspring, Onan "spilled his semen on the ground whenever he went in to his brother's wife" (Gen 38:9). This so displeased the Lord that Onan died also. Judah sent Tamar to her father's home to live as a widow until his youngest son, Shelah, became an adult. Tamar stayed until it became obvious that Judah would never keep his promise because he feared that Shelah, too, would die.

Tamar was desperate; not only would she be left without support when her father died, but her childlessness was considered shameful. Since Judah would not fulfill his obligations, Tamar took matters into her own hands. She dressed as a prostitute and waited by the side of the road for Judah. When he offered a goat in payment for her services, she demanded his staff, cord, and signet ring to hold until she received payment. Judah had his pleasure, but later, a servant sent to deliver the goat and collect the items left in pledge returned with this surprising news: Not only had the woman disappeared, but no prostitute even lived in the area. When Tamar became pregnant, Judah accused her of prostitution and was prepared to kill her. However, when she produced the staff, cord, and signet ring, Judah acknowledged his sin against her and accepted her twin sons as his own.

In later years, Judah was again the victim of a ruse designed to elicit justice. During a terrible region-wide famine, Jacob sent all his sons but Rachel's boy, Benjamin, to buy grain in Egypt. There, they were recognized by Joseph, the brother they had sold into slavery. However, Joseph hid his identity and accused his brothers of spying. He held one brother hostage and demanded that they bring Benjamin to him or forfeit the prisoner's life. To gain their father's permission to bring Benjamin back with them, Reuben had to offer his own sons as pledge for Benjamin's safety, and Judah had to take the blame (perhaps disinheritance or banishment) should Benjamin be harmed. When they arrived in Egypt, Joseph tried to keep Benjamin by hiding a silver cup in the boy's pack and accusing him of theft. Then, Judah pleaded with Joseph, saying that his father had already grieved for the death of one child and would die of a broken heart should he lose this second, beloved son. Judah's words were too much for Joseph to bear; he revealed his identity, forgave his brothers, and brought his family to Egypt where food would be available during the famine.

While the clan was in Egypt, Jacob grew frail and ill. As his father before him had done, Jacob blessed his sons before he died. In that day, a father's blessing was more than good wishes; it held spiritual power and, in Jacob's case, was prophetic as well. Jacob said his other sons would bow down to Judah. He called Judah a lion, indicating fearsome strength in battle. Finally, Jacob promised that Judah would rule, and the staff of leadership would not be taken from him or his descendants.

Throughout Israel's history, the tribe of Judah led and was more powerful than the others. After the Israelites escaped from slavery in Egypt and entered Canaan, the tribe of Judah received extensive land holdings, including the mountainous area surrounding Jerusalem. After the reign of Solomon, the nation split into separate kingdoms, northern Israel and southern Judah, and Judah's lands included the holy city Jerusalem.

Judah's descendants included David, a forefather of Jesus. The Book of Revelation records a vision in which a prophetic scroll is found, but only the "lion of the tribe of Judah, the Root of David . . . [is worthy to] open the scroll and its seven seals" (Rev 5:5). From early times, Christians have called Jesus the "lion of Judah," honoring him and his ancestor, Judah, the son of Jacob.

For further study, see Gen 37–38, 42:18-34; 46:12; 49:1,8-12; Nu 1:26-27; Jos 15:1-12; Mt 1:1-3.

2. Lk 3:30; ancestor of Jesus

3. 6 century B.C.; Ne 12:8; Levite; returned to Judah after Exile

4. 5 century B.C.; Ezr 10:23; Levite who married and divorced foreigner after Exile

5. 5 century B.C.; Ne 11:9; Benjaminite; resettled in Jerusalem

6. 5 century B.C.; Ne 12:34; helped dedicate Jerusalem wall

7. 5 century B.C.; Ne 12:36; priest and musician at Jerusalem wall dedication

JUDAHITES (JOO duh hights) 1Ch 12:16; people of Judah (the southern kingdom after the monarchy divided)

JUDAS (JOO duhs) *praised* or *hammer*
1. Judas Maccabeus; 2 century B.C.; 1Mac 2:4

From the time Assyria conquered Israel (722 B.C.) and Judah (587 B.C.) and exiled thousands of Jews, the area knew few periods of true peace. Rebellions, uprisings, and guerrilla warfare in the hills were all common during years of occupation by foreign troops. For centuries, Egypt, Assyria, and Babylon controlled their smaller neighbors. While these major powers fought, the less powerful nations had brief windows of peace and independence—at least until the next invasion. As Assyria's and Babylon's power waned, first the Persians and then the Greeks dominated the area. After Alexander the Great's death, the Seleucid Empire ruled all Israel, including Jerusalem. This was the time of Judas Maccabeus.

The Seleucid king, Antiochus IV Epiphanes, tried to wipe away the identity and heritage of any nations he conquered, so he set about crushing the Jews both spiritually and politically. Antiochus ordered that the temple be defiled and sacrifices to

Judas Maccabeus. Stained glass. Holy Cross Church, Minneapolis, Minnesota.

Zeus be made on the altar. All distinctive religious practices were outlawed and replaced with pagan worship. Soon it was forbidden to celebrate the Sabbath and traditional festivals, and parents who circumcised their sons were executed. In an effective but grisly show of power, Antiochus commanded that the body of the baby be hung around his dead mother's neck. In terror, many people abandoned their faith, but others stood firm, choosing to die as martyrs rather than abandon God's Law. Judas Maccabeus, his four brothers, and their father, Mattathias the priest, were among those who clung to their faith. When the king assigned soldiers to announce his regulations and require people to offer sacrifices to his god in 166 B.C., Mattathias and his sons refused, killed the soldiers, and fled to the hills, where people of similar conviction joined them.

Antiochus sent troops to hunt down the rebels. In the first battle, men, women, and children were massacred because they refused to fight on the Sabbath. Judas then took command, leading untried shepherds and tradesmen against professional troops. Judas's first two battles were surprising victories. In the first, he took the enemy commander's sword as a prize. In the second, Judas rallied his men with the words of the great warrior Joshua, saying that the Lord "can save by many or by few." Under his leadership, the Jews defeated vastly superior forces.

Word of the rebellion came to Antiochus. He assigned Lysias, an experienced commander, to deal with the Israelite problem, while he went to Persia to collect much-needed taxes. With half the Seleucid army, Lysias was to "wipe out and destroy the strength of Israel . . . [and] banish the memory of them from the place" (1Mac 3:35).

Lysias had 40,000 infantry and 40,000 cavalry troops. Judas and his people had only their faith in God. They prayed and fasted, "crying to heaven" for victory. Judas said, "Then all the Gentiles will know that there is one who redeems and saves Israel" (1Mac 4:11). Judas's troops defeated a Seleucid detachment at Emmaus, near Jerusalem. Then, Lysias came against Judas and 10,000 Israelites with 65,000 Syrian troops. The battle had only begun when Lysias realized that the Jews did not care whether they lived or died, but fought like wild men. The Jews' determination so intimidated the Seleucids that they withdrew from the battlefront.

During a two-year period when the Seleucids were occupied with battles elsewhere, Judas and his followers took Jerusalem. They were devastated by what they found; the temple had been ravaged, its gates burned, courts overgrown, and altar defiled. Judas chose priests who had been faithful to the Law to cleanse the sanctuary and remove unclean (sacrificial) stones. They replaced the defiled altar, rebuilt the sanctuary and temple interior, and made new vessels for worship.

This period of cleansing and renewal was a rededication of the nation as well as of the temple. In 164 B.C., a festival of rededication was held. The temple lamps were lit again, sacrifices and offerings were made, and the temple itself was decorated with "golden crowns and small shields" (1Mac 4:57). Judas and his brothers decided that each year their people would hold an eight-day celebration recalling the rededication of the temple. Today, Jews around the world celebrate Hanukkah, an eight-day "Feast of Dedication" or "Festival of Lights." According to the Hanukkah legend, the remaining cruse of undefiled oil, enough to burn for only one day, at God's intervention actually supplied light for all eight days of the temple rededication.

After reestablishing the temple, Judas tried to drive the last Seleucid forces from Israel. This brought swift action from the king, who sent Lysias and more than 120,000 soldiers to put down the rebellion. Faced with war elephants and heavy siege, the Jews seemed doomed. However, Lysias withdrew even though Jerusalem stood helpless, because political power struggles at home threatened the empire and his own position. The Seleucids left behind a Greek Jew who was amenable to their rule in the position of chief priest. Meddling with the priesthood was such an offense that the Maccabees decided that all Seleucid presence in Israel must end, so the military conflict continued. In 160 B.C., Judas Maccabeus was killed in battle at Elasa, and leadership of the rebellion passed to his brother Jonathan.

For further study, see the First Book of Maccabees.

2. 1 century B.C.; Ac 5:37; instigator of rebellion against Rome

3. 1 century A.D.; Mt 13:55

Judas was listed in the Gospels of Matthew and Mark as Jesus's brother, along with James, Joseph, and Simon. His name, a Greek form of Judah, was common to the era. Judas also wrote the Book of Jude, a pointedly Jewish book where he refers to himself only as a "servant of Jesus Christ and brother of James."

Judas was first mentioned in the Gospel account of one of Jesus's visits to his hometown of Nazareth. When the people heard Jesus teach in the synagogue, they were first struck by his wisdom and then responded with skepticism. They found it difficult to believe that the same Jesus whose brothers they knew as carpenters could have suddenly become an inspired teacher. Judas and his brothers may have shared this skepticism; the Gospels, at least, record that they did not believe until after Jesus's resurrection.

However belated, Judas's faith was sincere and highly moral—the kind of faith he urged his readers to emulate. Judas's unaddressed letter focuses on moral teaching from a markedly Jewish perspective, using Old Testament people and settings as the basis for his reasoning and illustrations. Judas's letter contains stern words about false teachers. He cautioned his readers not to assume that everyone who "talked faith" was truly a believer, but to evaluate words and deeds. He closed with a benediction now adopted by Christians throughout the world: "To him who is able to keep you from falling and to make you stand without blemish in the presence of his glory with rejoicing, to the only God our Savior, through Jesus Christ, our Lord" (Jude 1:24-25).

For further study, see Mk 6:3; the Letter of Jude. Also called Jude.

4. 1 century A.D.; Lk 6:16; son of James the disciple

5. Judas Iscariot (JOO duhs is KAYR ee uht) 1 century A.D.; Mt 10:4

Few names in history carry the stigma borne by the name Judas Iscariot. Judas was one of the 12 disciples, although the New Testament records little except that he was not Galilean and that Jesus entrusted him with the group's money. In his Gospel, John calls Judas a thief, and, along with Mark, records that Judas criticized Mary of Bethany for anointing Jesus's feet with costly ointment. The remaining references describe his treachery and death.

On Passover night before his death, Jesus washed all the disciples' feet—including Judas's—yet predicted one would betray him. John's Gospel clearly indicates Jesus knew the betrayer was Judas.

Judas betrays Jesus with a kiss in the garden of Gethsemene. Giotto (1266–1337).

Late that night, Judas contacted the chief priests and led the temple guards to the garden of Gethsemene. There, in an act that deeply saddened Jesus, he identified his Master by a kiss of greeting.

Judas received 30 pieces of silver for his information, but after Jesus's arrest he returned the money, saying, "I have sinned by betraying innocent blood" (Mt 27:4). Judas then hung himself. His body may have been left to rot, because Luke records that he fell and "his bowels gushed out" (Ac 1:18). The priests used Judas's tainted silver to buy a pauper's cemetery, appropriately called the "Field of Blood."

For further study, see Mt 26:14-25; 26:47–27:10; Mk 14:10-21,43-53; Lk 22:3-23,47-53; Jn 12:1-8; 18:2-12.

6. 1 century A.D.; Ac 9:11; hosted a blinded Saul in his Damascus home

7. 1 century A.D.; Ac 15:22; delivered letter outlining the acceptance of Gentiles into the early church

JUDE Jude 1:1; see Judas 3

JUDEANS (joo DEE uhnz) 2Ki 16:6; people of Judea (southern Palestine after kingdom of Judah ended)

JUDITH (JOO dith) *Jewess*
1. 20 century B.C.; Gen 26:34; daughter of Beeri; wife of Esau; see Oholibamah 1
2. 4 century B.C.; Jdt 8:1

Although the apocryphal Book of Judith may be an epic folktale, the message is one of courage and resourcefulness. According to the story, Judith was widowed during the reign of Nebuchadnezzar, in approximately 588 B.C. However, the story is set after the Babylonian Exile, in approximately 538 B.C. Some scholars think that this and other obvious errors were deliberately included so readers would not consider the story true.

Judith's city, Bethulia, was under siege. Although the invaders had been warned to avoid the power of Israel's God, the commander, Holofernes, said, "Who is God except Nebuchadnezzar?" He cap-

Judith and her maidservant with the head of Holofernes.

tured the water supply, and within 34 days, people were dying in the streets. Judith challenged the elders to rely on their faith in God, saying she would leave the city and the Lord would "deliver Israel by [her] hand" (Jdt 8:33). She prayed, dressed in her most stunning clothing, and left the city.

Judith was captured by the enemy. She asked to see Holofernes, claiming she would betray her people, and Holofernes was taken by her appearance and flattery. Judith assured the commander that Israel could not be defeated while God was with them. However, in their hunger, they had decided to eat consecrated food, and when they had done so, God's favor and protection ended. Judith promised to lead Holofernes through Israel to the throne in Jerusalem. Holofernes put his trust in Judith and held a celebratory banquet, hoping to seduce her. Judith took advantage of his attraction and encouraged Holofernes to "drink and be merry." When he was dead drunk, she cut off his head with his own sword.

The troops were terrified; without Holofernes's leadership, chaos reigned and they fled before the Israelites. Judith praised God and was honored by all Israel for the rest of her life.

For further study, see the Book of Judith.

JULIA (JOOL yuh) meaning unknown; 1 century A.D.; Ro 16:15; woman in Rome greeted by Paul

JULIUS (JOOL yuhs) meaning unknown; 1 century A.D.; Ac 27:1

The apostle Paul was taken before Agrippa, Israel's Roman ruler, accused of religious misconduct. Exercising his right as a Roman citizen, Paul asked for his case to be heard in Rome and was escorted there by a centurion, Julius. Luke records the centurion's kindness to Paul during the sea voyage, as when he allowed Paul to visit friends during a stop in Sidon. At one point, Paul advised that they stay the winter in Crete, but Julius ordered the ship to press on. During a heavy storm, an angel told Paul that the ship would wreck but the people would survive. As the ship drifted aimlessly, Paul advised Julius to cast off the lifeboat to ensure that the ship's crew would not abandon the passengers, and this time the centurion listened to him. Eventually the ship ran aground near the island of Malta. The Roman soldiers, fearing punishment if any of their prisoners escaped, planned to execute them all. Julius, "wishing to save Paul, kept them

The shipwreck at the island of Malta when Paul was in the custody of Julius.

from carrying out their plan" (Ac 27:43). As Paul had foretold, everyone on board made it safely to shore. For further study, see Ac 27:1-44.

JUNIA (JOO nee uh) meaning unknown;
1 century A.D.; Ro 16:7

Junia and coworker Andronicus were greeted in Paul's Letter to the Romans as fellow prisoners and "prominent among the apostles." Scholars find this short passage problematic because Junia is a woman's name; the status of women in the first century and scriptural standards for church leadership make it improbable that any woman would have held such a high position. The masculine name "Junias" appears in some later texts but may have been added by scribes who thought the feminine form was an earlier copyist's error. Whether a man or woman, this individual was commended by Paul as a leader in the early church.

JUSHAB-HESED (JOO shuhb HEE suhd) *loving-kindness is returned;* 6 century B.C.; 1Ch 3:20; son of Zerubbabel

JUSTUS (JUS tuhs) *just*
1. Ac 1:23; see Joseph 13
2. see Titius Justus
3. Col 4:11; see Jesus 3

KADMIEL (KAD mee uhl) *God is ancient*
1. 6 century B.C.; Ezr 2:40; family head of Levites that returned to Judah

2. 5 century B.C.; Ne 9:4; Levite; worship leader
3. 5 century B.C.; Ne 10:9; sealed covenant renewal; possibly Kadmiel 1 or 2

KADMONITES (KAD muh nights) Gen 15:19; obscure Phoenician tribe whose land was promised to Abraham

KAIWAN (KAY ih wahn) Am 5:26; star god identified with Saturn

KALLAI (KAL eye) meaning unknown; 6 century B.C.; Ne 12:20; head of priestly family under Joiakim

KAREAH (kuh REE uh) *bald head;* 7 century B.C.; 2Ki 25:23; father of Johanan 6 the ally of Gedaliah

KEDAR (KEE duhr) *powerful* or *dark* or *swarthy;* Gen 25:13; son of Ishmael

KEDEMAH (KED uh muh) *eastward;* Gen 25:15; son of Ishmael

KEILAH (kuh EYE luh) *enclosed;* 1Ch 4:19; descendant of Judah 1

KELAIAH (kuh LAY yuh) *the Lord is light;* 5 century B.C.; Ezr 10:23; married and divorced foreigner after Exile; also called Kelita 1

KELITA (kuh LYE tuh) *dwarf*
1. Ezr 10:23; see Kelaiah
2. 5 century B.C.; Ne 8:7; Levite; instructed people in the Law
3. 5 century B.C.; Ne 10:10; Levite; sealed covenant renewal; possibly Kelita 1 and 2

KEMUEL (KEM yoo uhl) *congregation of God*
1. 21 century B.C.; Gen 22:21; son of Nahor; nephew of Abraham; father of Aram
2. 15 century B.C.; Nu 34:24; Ephraimite whom Moses appointed to divide Canaan

3. 11 century B.C.; 1Ch 27:17; father of Hashabiah the officer over Levites in David's day

KENAN (KEE nuhn) *owner;* Gen 5:9; son of Enosh; descendant of Adam; see Cainan 1

KENAZ (KEE naz) *hunting*
1. 19 century B.C.; Gen 36:11; grandson of Esau
2. 15 century B.C.; Jdg 1:13; younger brother of spy Caleb; father of judge Othniel
3. 15 century B.C.; 1Ch 4:15; grandson of spy Caleb

KENITES (KEE nights) Gen 15:19; Canaanite metalworkers whose land in Palestine was given to Abraham

KENIZZITES (KEN uh zights) Gen 15:19; tribe in Palestine whose land was given to Abraham

KEREN-HAPPUCH (KAIR uhn HAP uhk) *horn of eye paint;* Job 42:14; youngest daughter born late to Job

KEROS (KEER ahs) *fortress* or *crooked;* Ezr 2:44; ancestor of temple servants who returned to Judah

KETURAH (keh TOOR uh) *incense;* 21 century B.C.; Gen 25:1; second wife of Abraham

KEZIAH (keh ZYE uh) *cassia;* Job 42:14; second daughter born late to Job

KISH (KISH) *power*
1. 12 century B.C.; 1Ch 8:30; Benjaminite; son of Jeiel; possibly uncle of Kish 2
2. 11 century B.C.; 1Sa 9:1; Benjaminite; father of King Saul
3. 1Ch 23:21; descendant of Levi
4. 8 century B.C.; 2Ch 29:12; Levite; helped purify temple
5. Est 2:5; Benjaminite; ancestor of Esther's cousin Mordecai

KISHI (KISH eye) *snarer;* 11 century B.C.; 1Ch 6:44; father of Ethan the music leader; also called Kushaiah

KITTIM (KIT im) meaning unknown; Gen 10:4; sons of Javan; a Japhethite tribe linked with Cyprus and Rome

KOHATH (KOH hath) *assembly;* 19 century B.C.; Gen 46:11; son of Levi; ancestor of Moses and Aaron

KOHATHITES (KOH hath ights) Nu 3:27; four family clans descended from Kohath the son of Levi the priest

KOLAIAH (koh LAY yuh) *voice of the Lord*
1. 7 century B.C.; Jer 29:21; father of Ahab the false prophet
2. Ne 11:7; ancestor of Sallu the resettler in Jerusalem

KORAH (KOHR uh) *bald*
1. 20 century B.C.; Gen 36:5; son of Esau and Oholibamah
2. 19 century B.C.; Gen 36:16; grandson of Esau; Edomite chief
3. 1Ch 2:43; descendant of Judah 1
4. 15 century B.C.; Ex 6:1
   This rebellious Levite was either a priest vying for position and authority over the established priesthood or a layperson insisting that "all the congregation are holy," not just Moses. When Korah and his followers rebelled against Moses and Aaron, and therefore against God, they were killed by an act of God. Korah suddenly died when he was buried and burned alive—by earthquake and fire—along with Dathan, Abiram, and 250 other leaders. Nonetheless, Korah's clan was spared. The "Sons of Korah" were noted musicians in the temple service (see Ps 42–49; 84–85; 87–88). The "way of Korah" later came to mean the path of greedy, complaining, power-hungry people. For further study, see Ex 6:21,24; Nu 16:1-49; 26:9-11; 1Ch 6:22,37; 9:19; Jude 1:11.

KORAHITES (KOR uh hights) Ex 6:24; sons of Korah the grandson of Levi; authors of 11 psalms

KORE (KOHR ee) *quail*
1. 11 century B.C.; 1Ch 9:19; son of Asaph; ancestor of temple gatekeepers
2. 8 century B.C.; 2Ch 31:14; Levite; distributed freewill offerings

KOZ (KAHZ) *thorn;* 1Ch 4:8; descendant of Judah 1

KUSHAIAH 1Ch 15:17; see Kishi

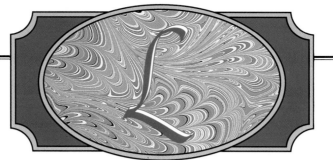

LAADAH (LAY uh duh) *festival;* 1Ch 4:21; descendant of Judah 1

LABAN (LAY buhn) *white;* 20 century B.C.; Gen 24:29

To escape the wrath of his brother Esau, whose birthright he had stolen, Jacob sought sanctuary with his mother's brother Laban. Laban was known for shrewd dealings in everything from marriage and dowry arrangements to labor and management negotiations, and he had two daughters to marry off, Leah and Rachel.

Jacob agreed to work seven years for Laban if he could then marry the younger daughter, Rachel. But on the wedding night, Laban substituted Leah for Rachel under the wedding veil; once Jacob and Leah had slept together, the marriage was consummated. When Jacob awoke next to the wrong woman, he realized too late that Laban had tricked him. When confronted by Jacob, Laban claimed he had carried out the deception only because it was necessary to marry off his older daughter before he could let the younger one wed; in truth, he feared he might not be able to find a husband for Leah. Jacob then agreed to take his beloved Rachel as his second wife and work seven more years for Laban.

Before he was done scheming, Laban had contracted for Jacob's services indefinitely. Jacob agreed to work in exchange for a share of the family sheep flocks, but Laban repeatedly gave Jacob less than he had earned. Still Jacob managed to accrue sizable wealth from his service with Laban. Eventually, much to Laban's dismay, Jacob was able to return home, taking Leah, Rachel, and their children with him.

For further study, see Gen 24; 27:41–28:5; 29:1-30; 30:25–32:5; 46:18.

LADAN (LAY duhn) meaning unknown
1. 1Ch 7:26; ancestor of Joshua the son of Nun
2. 1Ch 23:7; descendant of Gershon; also called Libni 1

LAEL (LAY uhl) *belonging to God;* 15 century B.C.; Nu 3:24; father of Eliasaph 2 the leader of the Gershonites

LAHAD (LAY had) *oppression;* 1Ch 4:2; descendant of Judah 1

LAHMI (LAH mye) *warrior;* 10 century B.C.; 1Ch 20:5; Philistine giant; brother of Goliath

LAISH (LAY ish) *lion;* 11 century B.C.; 1Sa 25:44; father of Michal's second husband Paltiel

LAMECH (LAY mek) *wild man*
1. Gen 4:18; descendant of Cain; first recorded polygamist
2. Gen 5:25; father of Noah

Jacob makes his agreement with Laban. Raphael (1483–1520).

LAODICEANS (LAY ah duh SEE uhns) Col 4:16; people from Laodicea (of Phrygia), city founded by Seleucid kings

LAPPIDOTH (LAP uh dahth) *torches* or *flames;* 13 century B.C.; Jdg 4:4; husband of the prophet Deborah

LASTHENES (LAS thuh neez) meaning unknown; 2 century B.C.; 1Mac 11:31; high official in charge of finances

LAZARUS (LAZ uh ruhs) *God has helped*
1. Lk 16:20

In the parable of the rich man and Lazarus (the only character in Jesus's parables to be given a name), Jesus described a man of means who dressed well and dined extravagantly every day. Meanwhile, at his gate, lay Lazarus the beggar—ill-fed, covered with sores, grasping for scraps from the rich man's table, with only dogs for company. Both men died. The beggar went to the nurture and safety of Abraham's bosom, while the rich man endured a tormented existence in Hades. The rich man begged that Lazarus be allowed to return to earth and give warning to the man's brothers so that they would not end up in Hades. Abraham responded by saying, "If they do not listen to Moses and the prophets, neither will they be convinced even if someone rises from the dead" (Lk 16:31). The story clearly offers caution against placing material gains ahead of the needs of others and also perhaps refers to the miracle Jesus performs in raising a man named Lazarus from the dead.
2. 1 century A.D.; Jn 11:1

Lazarus and his sisters, Mary and Martha, were Jesus's friends. He found comfort and welcome at their home in Bethany. Once, Lazarus became seriously ill and his sisters sent for Jesus. Oddly, Jesus responded by saying, "This illness...is for God's glory so that the Son of God may be glorified through it" (Jn 11:4). After waiting for two days, Jesus announced to his disciples that they should go with him to Bethany because Lazarus had died. Jesus said he had purposely delayed so the disciples might see a miracle even greater than healing. The disciples advised Jesus not to go, since he had nearly been stoned by Jews in that area, but Jesus insisted. His followers' fear is clear in Thomas's departing words, "Let us go, that we may die with him" (Jn 11:16).

Jesus restores Lazarus to life after four days in the tomb.

When Jesus arrived, Lazarus had been dead four days. Mary and Martha were grieving and wondered why Jesus had not come immediately. Jesus assured Martha that Lazarus would "rise again," and she took this as a reference to the final resurrection on the day of judgment. Jesus then said, "I am the resurrection and the life. Those who believe in me, even though they die, will live....Do you believe this?" (Jn 11:25-26). In one of the most direct and overt professions of faith in the Gospel, Martha proclaimed that Jesus was the Messiah and the Son of God.

Amidst cries that the decomposing body would smell, Jesus ordered that the stone be rolled away from Lazarus's tomb door. He prayed, then shouted, "Lazarus, come out," and Lazarus emerged, still wrapped in his burial cloths. When news of this miracle reached Jerusalem, the Jewish leaders feared everyone would follow Jesus, whom they considered a false messiah, so they began making plans to kill him.

For further study, see Jn 11:1–12:11.

LEAH (LEE uh) *wild cow;* 18 century B.C.; Gen 29:16

Leah became Jacob's first wife through deception. Jacob had arranged to marry Leah's sister Rachel, but on the day of the wedding, Rachel's father sent Leah in her place, disguised behind a veil. Jacob did not discover her true identity until after the marriage had been consummated and so had no recourse but to accept her as his first wife. He later took Rachel as his second wife and greatly favored her over Leah. He also favored the children born by Rachel over those born by Leah, which led to jealousy and betrayal within his family. Although Leah's marriage was cold, she was honored as a "mother of Israel," and the Levites, David, and Jesus came from her line. For further study, see Gen 27:41–28:5; 29:1–30:24; 49:31; Mt 1:2-3.

LEBANA (luh BAY nuh) *white;* Ne 7:48; ancestral head of family of temple servants; a form of Lebanah

LEBANAH Ezr 2:45; see Lebana

LECAH (LEE kuh) *walking;* 1Ch 4:21; descendant of Judah 1

LEGION (LEE juhn) *large number;* 1 century A.D.; Mk 5:9

A man living among the dead in a cemetery near Gadara was obviously tormented by demonic spirits or multiple personalities. Implying that he had a large number of evil spirits within him, he called himself "Legion; for we are many." He was referring to a Roman legion, which consisted of 5000 to 6000 infantry troops. When Jesus cast out this multitude of demons, they jumped into a herd of pigs, who then rushed into the sea and destroyed themselves. For further study, see Mt 8:28–9:1; Mk 5:1-20; Lk 8:26-39.

LEHABIM (lih HAY bim) Gen 10:13; a people descended from Egypt; possibly related to Libyans

LEMUEL (lem YOO uhl) *devoted to God;* Pr 31:1; king whose proverbial wisdom was taught to him by his mother

LETUSHIM (lih TOO shuhm) *oppressed;* Gen 25:3; son(s) of Dedan

LEUMMIM (LEE uh mim) *people;* Gen 25:3; son(s) of Dedan

LEVI (LEE vye) *joined*
1. 20 century B.C.; Gen 29:34

Levi was the third son of Jacob by his wife Leah, and the father of three sons—Gershon, Kohath, and Merari. He became a chief priest and founder of the priestly tribe bearing his name. His three sons then became the ancestral heads of the three main divisions of the priesthood—the Gershonites, the Kohathites, and the Merarites.

Levi and his sons did not bring very priestlike qualities to their positions. In a typically cruel and vengeful fashion, Levi and his brother Simeon avenged the rape of their sister Dinah by massacring an entire town rather than by punishing the one man who had committed the crime. Living up to this reputation for violence, the sons of Levi killed 3000 Hebrew rebels who defied Moses during the Exodus in the wilderness.

Jacob cursed this characteristic violence, knowing Levi and Simeon would pass along that trait to their sons. The tribe of Levi received no inheritance in the Promised Land—in part as punishment and in part to free them to fulfill their priestly duties. The Levites were then dependent on their brothers in other tribes, who gave their tithes and offerings to the temple service.

For further study, see Gen 29:34; 34:25-31; 35:23; 46:11; 49:5-7; Ex 1:2; 6:16; 32:25-29; Nu 3–4; 16:1; 18:20-24; 26:59; Jos 21; 1Ch 2:1; 6:1-47; Ezr 8:18.
2. Lk 3:24; ancestor of Christ
3. Lk 3:29; another ancestor of Christ
4. Mk 2:14; see Matthew

LEVITES (LEE vights) Ex 6:19; tribe of Levi; assisted priests in representing Israel before God

LIBNI (LIB nye) *white*
1. Ex 6:17; see Ladan 2
2. 1Ch 6:29; descendant of Merari and Levi

LIKHI (LIK high) *learned;* 1Ch 7:19; descendant of Manasseh

LINUS (LYE nuhs) meaning unknown; 1 century A.D.; 2Ti 4:21; attended to Paul in prison, presumably at Rome

LO-AMMI (LOH AM ee) *not my people;* 8 century B.C.; Hos 1:9; symbolic name for the son of the prophet Hosea

LOIS (LOH is) meaning unknown; 1 century A.D.; 2Ti 1:5; pious grandmother of Timothy

LO-RUHAMAH (LOH roo HAH muh) *not loved* or *not pitied;* 8 century B.C.; Hos 1:6; symbolic name for prophet Hosea's daughter

LOT (LAHT) *concealed* or *covering;* 22 century B.C.; Gen 11:27

Born at Ur of the Chaldees (in southern Iraq), Lot traveled with his father Haran and uncle Abraham, who was responding to God's call and promise of land and descendants. However, Lot separated himself from that godly influence and settled in the well-watered, well-populated Jordan area among "cities of the plain" (at the southern end of the Dead Sea). There he pursued the comforts and customs of the wicked city of Sodom. Against God's will, Lot not only moved his tent near Sodom but soon was "sitting in the gateway" as an elder of the sinful city.

Lot grew to be a wealthy herdsman, with many flocks, cattle, and tents. He and his family were kidnapped by marauding Canaanites, only to be rescued by Abraham. After returning to Sodom, Lot was visited by two angels, who warned him of God's plan to destroy the sinful city and told him he must flee or be destroyed also. For associating with such sinners, Lot paid dearly with the loss of his goods and his family; when Lot was told to flee the condemned Sodom without looking back, his wife looked back anyway and God turned her into a "pillar of salt."

Eventually, Lot and his descendants settled in the mountainous land of Moab. With his own two daughters, Lot conceived two sons—Moab and Ben-ammi, ancestors of the Moabites and Ammonites, respectively.

For further study, see Gen 11:27-31; 12:4-5; 13:1–14:16; 19:1-36; Dt 2:9-19; Lk 17:28-29; 2Pe 2:7.

Lot flees Sodom with his daughters while his wife looks back at the city.

LOTAN (LOH tan) *hidden;* 20 century B.C.; Gen 36:20; Horite chief; lived in Seir in Esau's day

LUCIUS (LOO shuhs) *light*
1. 1 century A.D.; Ac 13:1; Cyrenian Christian; a leader of the Antioch church
2. 1 century A.D.; Ro 16:21; leader of church at Rome; possibly Lucius 1

LUD (LUHD) possibly *bending;* Gen 10:22; son of Shem; ancestor of Semitic tribe, likely the Lydians

LUDIM (LOO deem) possibly *benders;* Gen 10:13; son(s) of Egypt (Mizraim); ancestor of a Hamite tribe from northern Africa

LUKE (LEWK) *light* or *bright;* 1 century A.D.; Col 4:14

Paul knew him best as a traveling companion, a "fellow worker," "fellow prisoner," and as "the beloved physican." Luke accompanied Paul as he traveled from Troas to Philippi and later from Philippi to Jerusalem. He also accompanied Paul during his final voyage to Rome.

Readers of the Bible know Luke best as the author of the Gospel According to Luke and the Acts of the Apostles. Luke's writings comprise a quarter of the New Testament. His two volumes show careful attention to geographic, nautical, and medical terminology, and give specific information about the political and historical backdrop of the time.

The only non-Jewish author of a New Testament book, Luke spoke for the poor and oppressed of society; the Gospel he presented included people normally rendered unacceptable by the religious or social elite of the time. Luke presents Jesus as the universal Savior, both in terms of history (tracing Jesus's genealogy back to Adam and Eve) and in terms of ethnic inclusivity. Luke's Gospel addresses the Gentiles, Romans, Samaritans, women, lepers, children, tax collectors, and prostitutes—any and all who fell outside the purview of ancient Judaism.

Some scholars believe Acts was written as a treatise for Paul as he defended the Christian faith to the authorities of the Roman Empire. Much depends on identifying the recipient of Acts, the "most excellent Theophilus." Luke's Gospel—an "orderly account" based on firsthand experience and eyewitness testimony—could have been used in the defense of Christianity and of Paul's apostleship.

For further study, see the Gospel According to Luke; the Acts of the Apostles; Col 4:10-17; 2Ti 4:11; Phm 1:24.

LYDIA (LID ee uh) meaning unknown; 1 century A.D.; Ac 16:14

Born in Thyatira of the Lydia region (western Turkey), Lydia later settled in Philippi in Macedonia (modern Greece). There she could market her expensive purple cloth among the social elite, military retirees, and ruling families. When she heard the apostle Paul speak in the business district at Philippi, she reaffirmed the decision she had made earlier to convert to Judaism and worship God alone; she become Europe's first convert to Christianity and a fine example of a successful Christian woman in the marketplace. She converted her whole household to Christianity and hosted the first European house church. For further study, see Ac 16:11-15,40.

LYSANIAS (lih SAY nee uhs) *ending sadness;* 1 century A.D.; Lk 3:1; ruler of Abilene (in Syria)

LYSIAS (LIS ee uhs) meaning unknown
1. Ac 21:31; see Claudius Lysias
2. 2 century B.C.; 1Mac 3:32

In 166 B.C., Antiochus IV Epiphanes ruled the Seleucid Empire, which included the vassal state of Judea. Antiochus tried to establish his power by outlawing all Jewish religious practices. In response, Judas Maccabeus led a rebellion, and Lysias, an experienced Seleucid commander, was sent to crush it. At first, the Israelites fought wildly, without regard for life or death, and Lysias withdrew. Later, he scattered Judas's troops and was preparing to take Jerusalem when word came of political unrest at home. He left immediately to support his king. Later, Lysias offered the Jews religious freedom without political control. The Jews rejected his proposal and continued their rebellion. In the end, Israel was able to oust Lysias and the Seleucid oppressors. For further study, see the Books of First and Second Maccabees.

LYSIMACHUS (LIS ee MAK uhs) meaning unknown
1. 2 century B.C.; 2Mac 4:29; Menelaus's brother; plundered temple
2. 2 century B.C.; AddEst 11:1; Alexandrian Jew; translator of the Book of Esther

MAACAH (MAY uh kuh) *oppression* or *stupid*
1. 21 century B.C.; Gen 22:24; son of Nahor and Reumah
2. 1Ch 2:48; concubine of Caleb
3. 1Ch 7:15; wife of Makir
4. 12 century B.C.; 1Ch 8:29; wife of Saul's ancestor Jeiel
5. 11 century B.C.; 1Ch 11:43; father of Hanan the mighty man of David
6. 11 century B.C.; 2Sa 3:3; mother of Absalom
7. 11 century B.C.; 1Ki 2:39; father of Achish the Philistine king; also called Maoch
8. 11 century B.C.; 1Ch 27:16; father of Shephatiah the officer of the Simeonite tribe
9. 10 century B.C.; 1Ki 15:2; wife of Rehoboam; mother of King Abijah; also called Micaiah 7

MAADAI (MAY uh dye) *the Lord is an ornament;* 5 century B.C.; Ezr 10:34; married and divorced foreigner after Exile

MAADIAH (MAY uh dye uh) *ornament;* 5 century B.C.; Ne 12:5; head of priestly clan; also called Moadiah

MAAI (MAY eye) meaning unknown; 5 century B.C.; Ne 12:36; musician at dedication of Jerusalem wall

MAASAI 1Ch 9:12; see Amashsai

MAASEIAH (MAY uh SEE yuh) *work of the Lord*
1. 11 century B.C.; 1Ch 15:18; played lyre upon ark's return
2. 9 century B.C.; 2Ch 23:1; commander who helped overthrow Queen Athaliah
3. 9 century B.C.; 2Ch 26:11; officer under King Uzziah
4. 8 century B.C.; 2Ch 28:7; son of King Ahab; killed in battle with King Pekah
5. 7 century B.C.; 2Ch 34:8; governor of Jerusalem; helped repair and purify temple

6. 7 century B.C.; Jer 21:1; father of priest Zephaniah
7. 7 century B.C.; Jer 29:21; father of false prophet Zedekiah
8. 7 century B.C.; Jer 35:4; doorkeeper who lived in the temple
9. 5 century B.C.; Ne 3:23; his son Azariah helped repair the Jerusalem wall
10. 5 century B.C.; Ezr 10:18; priest; married and divorced foreigner after Exile
11. 5 century B.C.; Ezr 10:21; another priest who married and divorced foreigner after Exile
12. 5 century B.C.; Ezr 10:22; a third priest who married and divorced foreigner after Exile
13. 5 century B.C.; Ezr 10:30; descendant of Pahath-moab; married and divorced foreigner
14. 5 century B.C.; Ne 8:4; aide to Ezra for reading of the Law
15. 5 century B.C.; Ne 8:7; Levite instructor in the Law
16. 5 century B.C.; Ne 10:25; leader who sealed covenant renewal
17. Ne 11:5; see Asaiah 4
18. 5 century B.C.; Ne 11:7; his descendant Sallu resettled in Jerusalem after the Exile
19. 5 century B.C.; Ne 12:41; priest and singer at Jerusalem wall dedication
20. 5 century B.C.; Ne 12:42; another priest and singer at Jerusalem wall dedication

MAASMAS (MAHS muhs) meaning unknown; 5 century B.C.; 1Esd 8:43; man sent by Ezra to bring priests to Jerusalem

MAATH (MAY ath) *small;* Lk 3:26; descendant of Zerubbabel; ancestor of Christ

MAAZ (MAY az) *wrath;* 1Ch 2:27; descendant of Jerahmeel

MAAZIAH (MAY uh ZYE uh) *God is a refuge*
1. 10 century B.C.; 1Ch 24:18; head of priestly clan

2. 5 century B.C.; Ne 10:8; priest; sealed covenant renewal

MACCABEUS 1Mac 2:4; see Judas 1

MACEDONIANS (mass ih DOH nee unz) Ac 16:9; people from province of Macedonia in northern Greece; active with Paul

MACHBANNAI (mak BAN eye) *clad with a cloak;* 11 century B.C.; 1Ch 12:13; warrior with David at Ziklag

MACHBENAH (mak BEE nuh) meaning unknown; 1Ch 2:49; descendant of Caleb

MACHI (MAY kye) *decrease;* 15 century B.C.; Nu 13:15; father of Geuel the Gadite spy of Canaan

MACHIR (MAY keer) *sold*
1. 19 century B.C.; Gen 50:23; son of Manasseh; great-grandson of Jacob
2. 10 century B.C.; 2Sa 9:4; man of Lo Debar; caretaker of Mephibosheth

MACHNADEBAI (mak NAD uh bye) *gift of the noble one;* 5 century B.C.; Ezr 10:40; son of Bani; married and divorced foreigner after Exile

MACRON 2Mac 10:12; see Ptolemy 2

MADAI (MAY dye) *middle;* Gen 10:2; son of Japheth; ancestor of the Medes

MADMANNAH (mad MAHN uh) *dunghill;* 1Ch 2:49; grandson of Caleb

MAGDIEL (MAG dee uhl) *God's choice gift;* Gen 36:43; Edomite chief; descendant of Esau

MAGOG (MAY gahg) meaning unknown; Gen 10:2

Magog was a son of Japheth whose name was later attached to a kingdom. Magog is the subject of prophecies by Ezekiel and by John in the Book of Revelation. The people of Magog were described as fierce warriors, skilled horsemen, and expert archers; possibly, they were the Scythians, who were renowned for their destructive warfare and barbarous ways. Gog, possibly the ruler of Magog, is linked with Meshech and Tubal—all from areas far north of Israel. The prophecies hold that Magog and allies from all parts of the earth will wage a war against Israel that will be so devastating it will take seven months just to bury the dead. John sees the war against Gog and Magog symbolically, as one between good and evil at the end of history. For further study, see 1Ch 1:5; Eze 38–39; Rev 20:7-10.

MAGOR-MISSABIB (MAY gohr MIS uh bib) *terror on every side;* 7 century B.C.; Jer 20:3; name given to Pashhur 3 by Jeremiah

MAGPIASH (MAG pee ash) *collector of stars* or *moth killer;* 5 century B.C.; Ne 10:20; sealed covenant renewal

MAHALALEEL (muh HAL uh LEE uhl) *praise of God;* Lk 3:37; ancestor of Christ; a form of Mahalalel

MAHALALEL (muh HAL uh lel) *praise of God*
1. Gen 5:12; see Mahalaleel
2. Ne 11:4; his descendant Athaiah resettled in Jerusalem

MAHALATH (MAY huh lath) meaning unknown
1. 20 century B.C.; Gen 28:9; daughter of Ishmael; wife of Esau
2. 10 century B.C.; 2Ch 11:18; granddaughter of David; wife of Rehoboam

MAHARAI (MAY huh rye) *swift* or *hasty;* 11 century B.C.; 2Sa 23:28; mighty man of David

MAHATH (MAY hath) *grasping*
1. 1Ch 6:35; descendant of prophet Heman
2. 8 century B.C.; 2Ch 29:12; temple Levite in Hezekiah's day

MAHAZIOTH (muh HAY zee ahth) *visions;* 10 century B.C.; 1Ch 25:4; son of Heman the seer; music minister

MAHER-SHALAL-HASH-BAZ (MAY huhr SHAL uhl HASH baz) *the spoil speeds and the prey hastens;* 8 century B.C.; Isa 8:1; Isaiah's son

MAHLAH (MAH luh) *weak* or *sickly*
1. 19 century B.C.; 1Ch 7:18; great-grandson of Manasseh

2. 15 century B.C.; Nu 26:33; daughter of Zelophehad; received father's inheritance

MAHLI (MAH lee) *weak* or *sickly*
1. Ex 6:19; descendant of Merari
2. 1Ch 6:47; descendant of Levi

MAHLON (MAH luhn) *sickly* or *mild;* 12 century B.C.; Ru 1:2; son of Elimelech and Naomi; first husband of Ruth

MAHOL (MAY hahl) *dance;* 1Ki 4:31; father or ancestor of four whom Solomon exceeded in wisdom

MAHSEIAH (mah SEE yuh) *the Lord is a refuge;* 7 century B.C.; Jer 32:12; ancestor of Seraiah 7 and Baruch

MALACHI (MAL uh ky) *my messenger;* 5 century B.C.; Mal 1:1

Malachi, the last of the minor prophets in the Old Testament, lived in Jerusalem between the Jews' return from the Babylonian Exile and the urban renewal efforts of Ezra and Nehemiah. The Jews had been released from captivity in Babylon when God heard their repentant cries, but they quickly strayed from the prescribed forms of worship after their return to Jerusalem. Malachi was sent as God's prophet to confront the spiritual and social sins of the people.

Malachi rebuked the priests for their dishonesty when they offered sickly sacrifices to God and kept the healthy animals for themselves. He bluntly told them they would never offer such poor sacrifices even to their governor. The Israelites violated the Law by divorcing their Jewish wives and marrying foreign women with beliefs contrary to theirs, while still offering regular sacrifices at the temple. Malachi not only called the Jews to task for violating the Law, but he also dealt harshly with them for stealing tithes and offerings that

Malachi. Stained glass. St. Mary's Basilica, Minneapolis, Minnesota.

were meant for God. He then rebuked them for openly doubting if there was any purpose in serving God.

Malachi did not hesitate to communicate harsh words of God's judgment for the people's persistent disobedience. However, Malachi's prophecy was also explicitly redemptive. He prophesied that in the midst of the punishment, God would preserve a faithful few. Malachi brought the message to the Jews that God was willing to return to his people if they would only return to him. His book ends with an important prophecy about Elijah that Matthew later applies to John the Baptist.

For further study, see the Book of Malachi.

MALCAM (MAL kam) *their king;* 1Ch 8:9; descendant of Benjamin

MALCHIAH (mal KYE uh) *the Lord is my king;* 7 century B.C.; Jer 21:1; son of King Zedekiah of Judah; owned cistern used to imprison Jeremiah

MALCHIEL (MAL kee uhl) *God is my king;* Gen 46:17; descendant of Gad

MALCHIJAH (mal KYE juh) *the Lord is my king*
1. 1Ch 6:40; descendant of Asaph the music minister
2. 10 century B.C.; 1Ch 24:9; head of division of priests under David
3. 7 century B.C.; Jer 21:1; father of Pashhur 3
4. 1Ch 9:12; ancestor of Adaiah the priest who resettled in Jerusalem
5. 5 century B.C.; Ezr 10:25; descendant of Parosh; married and divorced foreigner after Exile
6. 5 century B.C.; Ezr 10:25; another descendant of Parosh; married and divorced foreigner after Exile
7. 5 century B.C.; Ezr 10:31; descendant of Harim; married and divorced foreigner after Exile
8. 5 century B.C.; Ne 3:14; Recabite; helped repair wall of Jerusalem

9. 5 century B.C.; Ne 3:31; goldsmith; helped repair Jerusalem wall
10. 5 century B.C.; Ne 8:4; stood to Ezra's left when Law was read
11. 5 century B.C.; Ne 10:3; priest; sealed covenant renewal; possibly Malchijah 10
12. 5 century B.C.; Ne 12:42; priest; singer at Jerusalem wall dedication; possibly Malchijah 10 or 11

MALCHIRAM (mal KYE ruhm) *my king is exalted;* 6 century B.C.; 1Ch 3:18; son of Jehoiachin

MALCHISHUA (MAL kih SHOO uh) *my king saves;* 11 century B.C.; 1Sa 14:49; son of Saul; killed at Gilboa

MALCHUS (MAL kuhs) *ruler;* 1 century A.D.; Jn 18:10; priest's servant whose ear Peter cut off

MALLOTHI (MAL uh thigh) *the Lord has spoken;* 10 century B.C.; 1Ch 25:4; son of Heman; chief temple singer

MALLUCH (MAL uhk) *counselor*
1. 1Ch 6:44; Levite; ancestor of Ethan the music minister
2. 6 century B.C.; Ne 12:2; priest who returned to Judah
3. 5 century B.C.; Ezr 10:29; married and divorced foreigner after Exile
4. 5 century B.C.; Ezr 10:32; another who married and divorced foreigner after Exile
5. 5 century B.C.; Ne 10:4; priest; sealed covenant renewal; possibly Malluch 2
6. 5 century B.C.; Ne 10:27; leader; sealed covenant renewal

MAMRE (MAM ree) *strength* or *fatness;* 22 century B.C.; Gen 14:13; Amorite; ally of Abram who helped rescue Lot

MANAEN (MAN ee uhn) *comforter;* 1 century A.D.; Ac 13:1; prophet and teacher in Antioch church

MANAHATH (MAN uh hath) *resting place;* 20 century B.C.; Gen 36:23; son of Horite chief living in Seir

MANASSEH (muh NAS uh) *one who causes forgetfulness*
1. 19 century B.C.; Gen 41:51

Manasseh was born in Egypt to Joseph by Asenath, the daughter of an Egyptian priest. When Joseph's father Jacob was old and nearly blind, Manasseh and Ephraim (his younger brother) were presented by Joseph to receive their patriarch's blessing. Jacob reversed the order of blessing, indicating that the younger Ephraim and his descendants were more important than Manasseh and his descendants. The Ephraimites did indeed become the dominant tribe of Jacob, but Manasseh received a large share of the Promised Land, from the sea coast across the central hill country to the Jordan River. Jacob's blessing is still quoted in the benediction used by many Jewish parents: "God make you like Ephraim and like Manasseh" (Gen 48:20).

Manasseh and Ephraim receive the blessing of their grandfather Jacob.

For further study, see Gen 41:50-52; 48; Nu 1–2; 26; 32; Jos 13; 17; 21–22; 1Ch 5–7; 2Ch 30.

2. ruled 697–642 B.C.; 2Ki 20:21

Manasseh was only 12 when his father Hezekiah died and left him the throne of Judah. Unlike his father's godly reign, Manasseh's was replete with evil practices that ultimately led to the kingdom's collapse and its Babylonian captivity.

Manasseh practiced witchcraft and erected altars to false gods in the temple, but most detestable were the fiery sacrifices Manasseh made of his sons. Manasseh's leadership was so evil that the sins of Judah were worse than those of the heathen nations God had already destroyed before their eyes. God tried to get the attention of Manasseh and his people, but they paid him no regard. The abominable practices of Manasseh incited God's anger, and he allowed the king of Assyria to capture Manasseh, put a hook in his nose, bind him with bronze shackles, and take him to Babylon.

During his imprisonment, Manasseh humbled himself and prayed earnestly to God. God heard his prayer and restored him to his position as king of Jerusalem, where he served the remainder of his reign. Manasseh eliminated paganism in Judah, reformed their religious practices, and rebuilt the outer wall of the city. Manasseh's prayer (as found in the Apocrypha) portrays God not only as a God of justice but as a God of mercy and forgiveness who can pardon sins and restore a life and a nation.

For further study, see 2Ki 21:1-18; 2Ch 33:1-20; PrM 1:10

3. 5 century B.C.; Ezr 10:30; one who married and divorced foreigner after Exile

4. 5 century B.C.; Ezr 10:33; another who married and divorced foreigner after Exile

5. 5 century B.C.; Jdt 8:2; husband of Judith; wealthy farmer in Ephraim

MANNASEUS (man uh SEE uhs) meaning unknown; 5 century B.C.; 1Esd 9:31; priest who married and divorced foreigner after Exile

MANASSITES (muh NASS ights) Nu 7:54; descendants of Manasseh the son of Joseph; known for their valor

MANOAH (muh NOH uh) *rest;* 12 century B.C.; Jdg 13:2; father of Samson

MAOCH 1Sa 27:2; see Maacah 7

MAON (MAY ahn) *dwelling;* 1Ch 2:45; descendant of Judah 1

MAONITES (MAY ohn ights) Jdg 10:12; people of Maon (a city and desert) who oppressed Israel; possibly Meunim 1

MARA (MAHR uh) *bitter;* Ru 1:20; name Naomi used when widowed

MARESHAH (muh REE shuh) *hilltop*
1. 1Ch 2:42; firstborn son of Caleb; father of Hebron
2. 1Ch 4:21; descendant of Judah 1

MARK (MAHRK) *large hammer;* 1 century A.D.; Ac 12:12

Mark had a unique vantage point on the Gospel. The home of Mary, Mark's mother, was probably the secret meeting place not only for the Last Supper and other meetings Jesus had with his disciples, but for the early Christian gatherings recorded in the Acts of the Apostles.

The young Mark (also called John Mark) became a companion of two great missionaries—his cousin Barnabas and Paul. Mark traveled with them on their first journey from Antioch to Cyprus and Perga in Pamphylia. Without explanation, Mark decided to leave and return home. When planning a second journey with Paul, Barnabas wanted to invite Mark again. Paul steadfastly refused to take someone he considered a deserter. This resulted in a parting of the ways between Paul and Barnabas. Barnabas took Mark with him to his native Cyprus, while Paul chose another companion—Silas—to travel with him throughout Syria and Cilicia for the next three years.

Mark and Paul were evidently reconciled some ten years later, since Paul commended Mark to the church at Colossae, calling him his "fellow worker" and referring to him as "useful in my ministry." Peter referred to "my son Mark" in one of his letters. That fact has church historians speculating about the relationship between the two men. If Mark was a spiritual son to Peter, probably in Rome, then he would have had anecdotes and actual quotes from Peter's life and preaching. After Peter and Paul both suffered a martyr's death, Mark could then have borrowed from Peter's notes in penning his version of the life and ministry of Jesus. The Gospel According to Mark reveals that its author was a Jew working with the Gentiles in the first church at Jerusalem.

For further study, see the Gospel According to Mark; Ac 12:25; 15:37-39; Col 4:10; 2Ti 4:11; 1Pe 5:13. Also called John Mark.

MARSENA (mahr SEE nuh) meaning unknown; 5 century B.C.; Est 1:14; noble of Medo-Persia; advised Ahasuerus

MARTHA (MAHR thuh) *lady;* 1 century A.D.; Lk 10:38; sister of Mary 3 and Lazarus 2; follower of Jesus; see Lazarus 2, Mary 3

MARY (MAIR ee) *bitterness*
1. 1st century B.C.; Mt 1:18

Mary is first introduced in Scripture as a young virgin engaged to Joseph, a descendant of Abraham and David. According to Jewish custom, an engagement was linked to marriage in such a way that the fiancée was called wife. Any sexual relationship during this period was considered adultery. Ac-

cording to Jewish Law, if the wife were unfaithful, she would be stoned to death.

During her engagement, Mary was visited at her home in Nazareth by the angel Gabriel, who said to her, "Greetings, favored one! The Lord is with you" (Lk 1:28). Mary was evidently frightened at the angel's visit, since Gabriel told her not to be afraid. He then announced that she would become pregnant and have a child who would be called the Son of the Most High and he would inherit the throne of King David and reign forever. Mary answered, "How can this be, since I am a virgin?" (Lk 1:34). She did not doubt what Gabriel said but was confused about how it could happen. The angel explained that Mary would become pregnant by the power of the Holy Spirit, and she accepted this assignment for her life in spite of the shame and danger she would experience because of her pregnancy.

Mary received some other good news from Gabriel—her older relative Elizabeth had conceived a son six months earlier and was going to have a baby after a long life of childlessness. In

The angel Gabriel visits Mary and announces that she will bear a son.

Mary's joy, she traveled to the city of Judah in the hill country (about 80 miles from Nazareth) to visit Elizabeth and her husband Zechariah. When Mary arrived at their house and greeted them, the baby in Elizabeth's womb (John the Baptist) leaped for joy to hear the voice of the mother of Jesus. Elizabeth exuberantly expressed in a loud voice how blessed she was to be in the presence of Mary and the child she would bear. Following this demonstration of delight, Mary broke out in song—a song of praise and adoration to God for what he had done. Mary's song, known historically as the Magnificat, reflects some of the Old Testament psalms, as well as Hannah's song of praise in First Samuel after her son Samuel was born. The song demonstrates that Mary was well educated in the Old Testament and shows that she was a humble, God-fearing woman. She praises God for his mercy to the humble and poor and for his justice upon the rich and the proud.

Mary stayed with Elizabeth for three months, probably up to the birth and circumcision of John. For the remainder of her pregnancy, Mary returned to Nazareth, where her fiancé Joseph was ready to divorce her quietly rather than expose her to the public shame and punishment imposed on an adulteress in Jewish culture. But Joseph was visited in a dream by an angel who assured him that the child Mary carried was conceived by the Holy Spirit and would save his people from their sins. Joseph took Mary home as his wife and had no sexual relations with her before Jesus was born.

When Mary was in her last month of pregnancy, Caesar Augustus ordered a census to be taken of the entire Roman world. Mary and Joseph had to register in Bethlehem, the town of David, because Joseph belonged to the house of David. Because of the large influx of people to Bethlehem for the census, Mary and Joseph had no place to stay when she went into labor. The child was born humbly in a place where animals were kept and fed. Mary even graciously accepted guests to this manger-crib

> ➤ ➤
>
> *"Then Mary said,*
> *'Here am I, the servant of*
> *the Lord; let it be with me*
> *according to your word.'*
> *Then the angel departed*
> *from her."*
>
> Lk 1:38

when the unexpected shepherds arrived. She later entertained the kings from the East who came to worship Jesus and whose inquiries in Jerusalem had stirred up King Herod's jealousy and concern over Jesus's birth.

In obedience to Jewish Law, Mary and Joseph traveled to the temple in Jerusalem to have Jesus circumcised on the eighth day after his birth, to pay the redemption price for a firstborn child, and to offer two turtle doves or pigeons as an offering for Mary's purification ceremony (see Lev 12:2-4).

At the temple, Mary encountered two older people, Simeon and Anna, who wanted to hold her baby. To the amazement of Mary and Joseph, Simeon and Anna both gave thanks for Jesus and praised God for sending the Savior they had been waiting for.

When everything had been completed in Jerusalem to fulfill Jewish Law, Mary's life was again disrupted when an angel told Joseph to flee with his family to Egypt to escape Herod's attempt to kill Jesus. So Mary and her family were again traveling under adverse conditions, this time leaving in the middle of the night in secrecy. Mary, Joseph, and Jesus stayed in Egypt until Herod died and all danger was past. They returned to Nazareth and lived together as a family while Jesus grew to manhood.

Being devout Jews, Mary and Joseph made their yearly trek to Jerusalem for the Passover Feast. On their trip home from Jerusalem, when Jesus was 12 years old, Mary and Joseph experienced one of a parent's greatest fears—their child became separated from them and was nowhere to be found. Mary and Joseph traveled an entire day before realizing Jesus was not among the relatives and friends in their group. They returned to Jerusalem and agonized in their search for him for three days. They eventually found him in the temple, listening to the teachers and asking them insightful questions. Mary rebuked him for treating his parents uncaringly, but he gently rebuked them for not realizing

Mary, Joseph, and Jesus flee into Eygpt to escape Herod's attempt to kill Jesus.

he had to be in his Father's house. Mary did not realize that Jesus had to fulfill his duties and his purpose even at such a young age. Jesus obeyed his parents, though, and returned with them to Nazareth.

Mary was present at Jesus's first miracle when he changed the water to wine at a wedding in Cana. In fact, she prompted the miracle by telling Jesus that the supply of wine was exhausted and then telling the servants to obey Jesus's commands. Mary was also present when Jesus was crucified on the cross. She saw the son she bore suffer an indescribably cruel death, and she was unable to prevent it. She heard him cry out for something to drink, and she couldn't attend to his needs. But in all Jesus's agony, he still looked down at the foot of the cross, saw his mother, and told John, the beloved disciple, to care for her the rest of her life.

The only other time Mary is mentioned by name in Scripture is after Jesus's resurrection from the dead and ascension into heaven when she and Jesus's brothers met for prayer with the 11 remaining apostles, waiting for the promised gift of the Holy Spirit. In this aspect of Mary's life, she followed Jesus not as her son but as her Savior.

In ways that Mary could never have imagined, all generations since Christ have indeed called her blessed. Over the centuries, various teachings about the special nature of Mary have developed and been accepted by some and discarded by others. The Roman Catholic concept of the Immaculate Conception, for instance, states that Mary was born free from original sin. Other doctrines concerning Mary include the teaching that she perpetually remained a virgin and that on her death, her body was taken into heaven.

For further study, see Mt 1:16-25; 13:54-57; Lk 1–2; Jn 2:1-5; Jn 19:25-27; Ac 1:14; Gal 4:4.

2. 1 century A.D.; Ac 12:12

Although referred to only once in the Bible, Mary, the mother of Mark, owned the house that became the first Christian meeting place in Jerusalem. She evidently was a woman of some wealth, for she not only owned a house big enough to accommodate a large group of people, but she also had servants. Though the Bible does not say, tradition holds that Mary's home was also the place where the Last Supper was served and where the apostles and a group of women met and prayed following Jesus's ascension. Also, following Peter's extraordinary escape from prison, he went directly to Mary's house, where he found many people who had been praying for him. For further study, see Mk 14:13-16; Ac 1:12-14; 12:12-13.

3. 1 century A.D.; Lk 10:39

Mary lived with her brother Lazarus and her sister Martha. They were all close friends of Jesus and often opened up their home to him as he traveled through Bethany. Mary preferred sitting at Jesus's feet listening to what he said. Once, Martha complained that Mary was not helping her with chores, but Jesus gently rebuked her because Mary had chosen a better pursuit.

When Lazarus became very ill, the sisters sent for Jesus to come. He did come, but to the consternation of Mary, Lazarus died and was buried four days before Jesus arrived. Mary did not go out to greet Jesus but remained in the house with a group of mourners. When Martha came to get her to tell her that Jesus was asking for her, Mary quickly left the house and found him, falling at his feet and telling him how she regretted his late, untimely arrival. Jesus was deeply moved by her tears and asked to be taken to the tomb. There, Mary not only witnessed Jesus weeping over his good friend Lazarus but also heard him call in a loud voice for Lazarus to come forth. Mary's tears were replaced with joy when her brother returned to life through the power of Jesus.

Mary is mentioned again at another meal in her home in honor of Jesus, where she poured out on Jesus an entire pint of an expensive perfume (worth a year's wages) and then wiped his feet with her hair. When Judas Iscariot rebuked her for her wastefulness, Jesus admonished him to leave Mary alone.

For further study, see Lk 10:38-42; Jn 11:1–12:11.

4. Mary Magdalene; 1 century A.D.; Mt 27:56

As Jesus and his disciples traveled from town to town, a group of exceptional women followed and supported them wherever they went. Mary Magdalene was among these women. Indebted to Jesus, who had liberated her from demon possession, Mary followed him and gave money to his ministry.

Unswerving in her devotion, Mary was at the cross and observed Jesus endure this cruel method of Roman execution. Watching opposite the tomb where Jesus's body was taken, she witnessed his burial by Joseph of Arimathea. She saw the Romans roll an enormous stone in front of the tomb, closing off and sealing the burial place. After leaving the tomb, she maintained a vigil through the sabbath until the dawn of the next day and then returned to the tomb with anointing spices.

Atop the stone that had been rolled away from the entrance of the tomb sat a luminous angel—a truly frightening sight for the Roman guards and for Mary. John's Gospel says that Mary saw two other angels inside the tomb who asked her why she was crying. Mary then turned to see a man she thought was the gardener. She asked him to tell her where he might have carried Jesus's body. But when Jesus spoke her name, Mary recognized his voice and called him Rabboni, meaning *My Teacher*. After Jesus told her to go tell the disciples what she had heard, Mary immediately ran to tell them the news of his resurrection and the things Jesus had told her.

For further study, see Mt 27:56-61; 28:1; Mk 15:40-47; 16:1-9; Lk 8:2; 24:10; Jn 19:25; 20:1-18.

5. Mary, mother of James and Joses and probably the wife of Clopas, is referred to in the Scripture as "the other Mary." This Mary was present at Jesus's crucifixion, standing near his cross with Jesus's mother, sister, and Mary Magdalene. After Jesus's death, she was at his tomb and returned to it again two days later with Mary Magdalene to bring anointing spices. However, they found the tomb empty and met an angel who told them Jesus had risen. On her way to tell this news to the disciples, the two women met and talked with the risen Jesus. For further study, see Mt 27:56–28:10; Mk 16:1-7; Jn 19:25–20:1.

6. 11 century B.C.; Ro 16:6; Roman Christian praised for her hard work

MASH (MASH) meaning unknown; Gen 10:23; son of Aram; descendant of Shem; also called Meshech 2

MASSA (MAS uh) *burden;* 21 century B.C.; Gen 25:14; son of Ishmael; ancestor of a northern Arabian tribe

MATRED (MAY trid) *expulsion;* Gen 36:39; mother of Mehetabel the wife of King Hadad

MATRITES (MAY tri tehz) *rainy;* 1Sa 10:21; head of Benjaminite clan; King Saul was one

Mary Magdalene and others see an angel at the tomb of Jesus.

MATTAN (MAT uhn) *gift*
1. 9 century B.C.; 2Ki 11:18; priest of Baal slain when Queen Athaliah was overthrown
2. 7 century B.C.; Jer 38:1; his son Shephatiah threw Jeremiah into a cistern

MATTANIAH (MAT uh NIGH uh) *gift of the Lord*
1. 10 century B.C.; 1Ch 25:4; son of Heman the head of a division of temple singers
2. 2Ch 20:14; descendant of Asaph; ancestor of the prophet Jahaziel
3. Ne 12:35; descendant of Asaph; ancestor of the priest Zechariah
4. 1Ch 9:15; Levite whose descendants settled in Jerusalem; possibly Mattaniah 3
5. 8 century B.C.; 2Ch 29:13; Levite who helped purify temple
6. ruled 597–587 B.C.; 2Ki 24:17; last king of Judah; son of Josiah; also called Zedekiah 5
7. 6 century B.C.; Ne 12:8; Levite who returned to Judah after Exile
8. 6 century B.C.; Ne 13:13; grandfather of Hanan the assistant in temple storerooms; possibly Mattaniah 7
9. 6 century B.C.; Ne 12:25; temple gatekeeper in time of high priest Joiakim
10. 5 century B.C.; Ezr 10:26; married and divorced foreigner after Exile
11. 5 century B.C.; Ezr 10:27; married and divorced foreigner after Exile
12. 5 century B.C.; Ezr 10:30; married and divorced foreigner after Exile
13. 5 century B.C.; Ezr 10:37; married and divorced foreigner after Exile

MATTATHA (MAT uh thuh) *gift;* Lk 3:31; descendant of David

MATTATHIAH (mat uh THIGH uh) *gift of the Lord;* 5 century B.C.; 1Esd 9:43; aide to Ezra for teaching the Law

MATTATHIAS (MAT uh THI uhs) *gift of the Lord*
1. Lk 3:25; descendant of Zerubbabel
2. Lk 3:26; descendant of Zerubbabel
3. 2 century B.C.; 1Mac 2:1
Mattathias was a Jewish priest when the Seleucid king Antiochus IV Epiphanes outlawed Jewish religious practices. Soldiers commanded all Jews to sacrifice to Zeus, but Mattathias and his five sons killed them and fled to the hills, crying, "Let everyone who is zealous for the law…come out with me" (1Mac 2:27). In 166 B.C., a guerrilla war began. Mattathias and his sons led inexperienced Jews against trained Seleucid troops. The Jews would rather have died than give up their faith and so fought with a fierce abandon that forced the Seleucids to withdraw. Although Mattathias did not live to see the Seleucids' defeat, the example he set helped see his sons through to victory. For further study, see 1Mac 1–2.

MATTATTAH (MAT uh tuh) *gift;* 5 century B.C.; Ezr 10:33; married and divorced foreigner after Exile

MATTENAI (MAT uh nye) *gift of the Lord*
1. 6 century B.C.; Ne 12:19; priest under high priest Joakim
2. Ezr 10:33; married and divorced foreigner after Exile
3. Ezr 10:37; another who married and divorced foreigner after Exile

MATTHAN (MATH an) *gift;* 1 century B.C.; Mt 1:15; grandfather of Jesus's father, Joseph; also called Matthat 2

MATTHAT (MATH at) *gift*
1. Lk 3:29; ancestor of Jesus
2. Lk 3:24; see Matthan

MATTHEW Matthew (MATH yoo) *gift of the Lord;* 1 century A.D.; Mt 9:9
Unlike the rugged fishermen that Jesus had already called as disciples, Matthew (or Levi) worked as a Roman government employee—a detested tax collector, or publican. Jews who collected taxes for Rome were despised as traitors to their own people. Many also collected more taxes than Rome demanded, lining their own pockets at the expense of their countrymen. Due to their bad reputation and bad business practices, publicans were generally referred to as sinners.
Jesus first approached Matthew as he sat at his collection booth, simply saying "Follow me." Responding to this call, Matthew invited Jesus to his home for dinner. The guest list was diverse—many tax collectors, sinners, Jesus, and his disciples. This dinner affair was obviously visible to outsiders, for the Pharisees saw what was going on in Matthew's dining room and asked the disciples why Jesus was

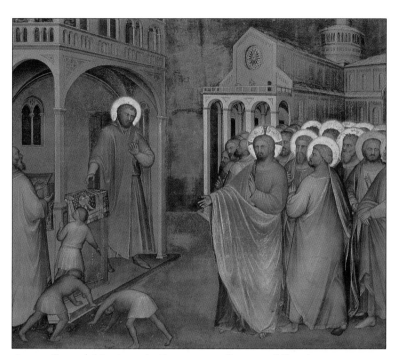

Jesus calls upon Matthew, the Roman tax collector, to follow him.

eating with tax collectors and sinners. Jesus defended not only Matthew but everyone he was sharing his meal with when he said, "For I have come to call not the righteous but sinners" (Mt 9:13).

In the Acts of the Apostles, after Jesus's ascension, Matthew met with the other disciples (11 in all since Judas Iscariot had died) to pray. Their meeting place was the Upper Room, probably in the home of Mary the mother of Mark. Here they joined with a group of faithful women followers of Jesus and other believers. At this meeting, Matthew cast his vote for the man who would replace Judas Iscariot as the twelfth disciple.

For further study, see the Gospel According to Matthew; Mk 2:13-17; 3:18; Lk 6:15; Ac 1:13. Also called Levi.

MATTHIAS (muh THI uhs) *gift of the Lord;* 1 century A.D.; Ac 1:23

After Jesus was last seen ascending into heaven, 120 of his followers gathered in the Upper Room (probably at the home of Mark's mother, Mary) to pray and await further instructions. It was decided that they needed to replace the betrayer Judas Iscariot, who had killed himself, so that the number of apostles would correspond to the number of tribes of Israel. The next apostle had to have been

in the company of the original 12, and he had to bear witness to the resurrection of Jesus. After praying and casting lots, Matthias was chosen to replace Judas. For further study, see Ac 1:13-28.

MATTITHIAH (MAT uh THIGH uh) *gift of the Lord*
1. 11 century B.C.; 1Ch 15:18; Levite harp player when ark returned to Jerusalem
2. 10 century B.C.; 1Ch 25:3; son of Jeduthun; head temple singer; possibly Mattithiah 1
3. 5 century B.C.; 1Ch 9:31; Levite; baked bread offerings for temple
4. 5 century B.C.; Ezr 10:43; descendant of Nebo; married and divorced foreigner after Exile
5. 5 century B.C.; Ne 8:4; aide to Ezra for reading the Law; possibly Mattithiah 3

MAZITIAS (muh ZEE tee uhs) meaning unknown; 5 century B.C.; 1Esd 9:35; descendant of Nooma

MEBUNNAI (meh BUN eye) *built;* 11 century B.C.; 2Sa 23:27; mighty man of David; also called Sibbecai

MEDAD (MEE dad) *beloved;* 15 century B.C.; Nu 11:26; Israelite elder; prophesied in the wilderness

MEDAN (MEE dan) *strife;* 21 century B.C.; Gen 25:2; son of Abraham by Keturah

MEDES (MEEDS) 2Ki 17:6

These ancient Indo-European people from Media in Asia Minor followed the religion of Zoroastrianism. The politics and history of Media were affected by the rise and fall of Persia, Babylonia, Syria, and Greece. For further study, see Ezr 6; Est 1; Da 6; 8; Ac 2:9.

MEHETABEL (muh HET uh bel) *God is doing good*
1. Gen 36:39; wife of Hadad the king of Edom
2. 6 century B.C.; Ne 6:10; grandfather of the traitor Shemaiah

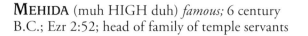

MEHIDA (muh HIGH duh) *famous;* 6 century B.C.; Ezr 2:52; head of family of temple servants

MEHIR (MEE huhr) *price* or *dexterity;* 1Ch 4:11; descendant of Judah 1

MEHUJAEL (meh HOO jee uhl) *God is smiting;* Gen 4:18; descendant of Cain

MEHUMAN (meh HOO muhn) *true;* 5 century B.C.; Est 1:10; eunuch who served King Ahasuerus

MELATIAH (MEL uh TYE uh) *the Lord has delivered;* 5 century B.C.; Ne 3:7; helped repair Jerusalem wall

MELCHI (MEL kye) *my king*
1. Lk 3:24; ancestor of Christ
2. Lk 3:28; another ancestor of Christ

MELCHIAS (mel KYE uhs) meaning unknown; 5 century B.C.; 1Esd 9:32; married and divorced foreigner after Exile

MELCHIEL (MEL kih ehl) meaning unknown; 5 century B.C.; Jdt 6:15; father of Charmis the city officer

MELCHIZEDEK *(*mel KIZ uh dek) *king of righteousness;* 22 century B.C.; Gen 14:18

His mysterious appearance and disappearance as a friend of Abraham and fellow worshiper of God has led to considerable speculation about Melchizedek's origins. Some speculate that this historical king-priest had no father or mother, nor any descendants, but existed eternally, such as the archangel Michael. In the New Testament, he is pictured as a supernatural figure whose untraceable origins and eternal life prefigure the divinity of Jesus Christ.

At the time Abraham met him, Melchizedek was king of Salem (short form of Jerusalem) and a priest of the Most High God. This was a most propitious meeting, at which this king-priest interceded on Abraham's behalf. Melchizedek offered bread and wine to the war-weary Abraham, a prayer of blessing for him, as well as praise to God for victory over Chedorlaomer and his allies, who

The king-priest Melchizedek offers bread and wine to the war-weary Abraham.

had previously kidnapped Abraham's nephew Lot. For this service, Abraham gave Melchizedek a tithe of all the bounty won in battle.

The Melchizedek mentioned in the Psalms may be the same one as in the Genesis account, or he may be the more symbolic idealized king-priest that would foreshadow Jesus's priestly ministry. According to the writer of Hebrews, the priesthood of Melchizedek was greater than Abraham (whom he blessed and received a tithe from) and greater than the Levitical or Aaronic priesthood (as Levi was subordinate to Abraham; hence also to Melchizedek). The greatness of Melchizedek would be exceeded only by Christ's perfect priesthood.

For further study, see Gen 14:17-24; Ps 110:4; Heb 5:5-10; 6:19–7:17.

MELEA (MEE lee uh) meaning unknown; Lk 3:31; descendant of David; ancestor of Christ

MELECH (MEE lek) *king;* 1Ch 8:35; descendant of Jonathan and Saul

MEMUCAN (meh MOO kuhn) *dignified* or *impoverished;* 5 century B.C.; noble of Medo-Persia who advised Ahasuerus

MENAHEM (MEN uh hem) *comforter;* ruled 752–742 B.C.; 2Ki 15:14; king of Israel who began paying tribute to Assyria

MENELAUS (MEN uh LAY uhs) *comforter;* 2 century B.C.; 2Mac 4:23

Before the Maccabean revolt, the Seleucids ruled Israel. The Seleucid king Antiochus IV Epiphanes accepted bribes to appoint Jason, a Greek Jew, as high priest. In 171 B.C., Jason sent tributes to King Antiochus via his servant, Menelaus, but Menelaus turned traitor—matching Jason's bribe and adding 300 talents of silver to purchase the priesthood for himself. Menelaus returned to Jerusalem, unqualified for priesthood in character and family line, but with the king's support. Fearing for his life, Jason fled the city. Later Menelaus bribed Antiochus's friends with temple treasures to kill Onias, a former high priest. He also helped Antiochus invade Jerusalem, massacre 80,000 people, and plunder the temple. After ten years, Menelaus's treachery caught up with him. He was executed by suffocation in a pit of ashes. For further study, see the Book of Second Maccabees.

MENESTHEUS (men ESTH ee uhs) meaning unknown; 2 century B.C.; 2Mac 4:21; father of General Apollonius

MENNA (MEN uh) meaning unknown; Lk 3:31; descendant of David; ancestor of Christ

MEONOTHAI (mee AHN uh thigh) *my dwelling;* 14 century B.C.; 1Ch 4:13; son of Othniel the judge

MEPHIBOSHETH (meh FIB oh sheth) *utterance of shame*
1. 11 century B.C.; 2Sa 4:4

Orphaned at the tender age of five when his grandfather King Saul and father Jonathan died fighting the Philistines, Mephibosheth grew up as a survivor. He was lame in both feet from a childhood accident, after which he was raised by a family nurse, by the family steward Ziba, and by Machir, a wealthy benefactor. Apparently, Mephibosheth could not care for himself and lived with anyone who could meet his special needs.

Having lost his family and all means of support, Mephibosheth was facing a dire situation, but David offered to adopt him in fulfillment of a pledge he had made to Jonathan. Out of covenant loyalty to Saul and Jonathan, David protected and provided for this orphan prince at great risk and expense to himself. Newly established kings such as David normally killed off anyone with a rival claim to the throne, which Mephibosheth clearly had.

Though heir to Saul's throne, Mephibosheth was not the threat to David that Ziba made him out to be or that David's followers thought him to be. Thanks to David's intercession, Mephibosheth survived one more murderous purge of Saul's household and went on to provide many descendants for Saul and Jonathan through his son Mica.

For further study, see 1Sa 20:14-17; 2Sa 4:4; 9:1-13; 16:1-4; 19:24-30; 21:7-9; 1Ch 8:34-38; 9:40. Also called Merib-baal.
2. 11 century B.C.; 2Sa 21:8; son of Saul and concubine Rizpah

MERAB (MEER ab) *increase;* 11 century B.C.; 1Sa 14:49; daughter of Saul promised to David

MERAIAH (muh RAY yuh) *rebellion;* 6 century B.C.; Ne 12:12; head of priestly clan under priest Joiakim

MERAIOTH (muh RAY ahth) *rebellious*
1. 12 century B.C.; 1Ch 6:6; descendant of Aaron; grandfather of Ahitub
2. 1Ch 9:11; descendant of David's high priest Zadok

MERARI (muhr AHR eye) *bitter*
1. 19 century B.C.; Gen 46:11; son of Levi; head of Merarite priestly clan
2. 5 century B.C; Jdt 8:1; father of Judith

MERARITES (meh RAY rights) Nu 4:29; descendants of Merari 1; a Levitical clan akin to Gershonites and Kohathites

MERED (MEER ed) *rebel;* 1Ch 4:17; descendant of Judah 1

MEREMOTH (MAIR uh mahth) *heights*
1. 6 century B.C.; Ne 12:3; priest who returned with Zerubbabel from Exile
2. 5 century B.C.; Ezr 8:33; priest who weighed silver and golden articles in temple
3. 5 century B.C.; Ezr 10:36; one who married and divorced foreigner after Exile
4. 5 century B.C.; Ne 10:5; priest; sealed covenant renewal; possibly Meremoth 1 or 2

MERES (MEER ez) *worthy;* 5 century B.C.; Est 1:14; noble of Medo-Persia; advised Ahasuerus

MERIB-BAAL 1Ch 8:34; see Mephibosheth 1

MERODACH (MAIR uh dahk) Jer 50:2
Babylonian god of war that was sometimes called Marduk; patron deity of Babylon's capital city; see Bel

MERODACH-BALADAN (MAIR uh dak BAL uh duhn) *Marduk* [a god] *has given a son;* ruled 721–710, 703 B.C.; 2Ki 20:12
Merodach-baladan was a clever and ambitious Babylonian ruler who managed to rise to some power through judicious military alliances and shrewd political moves. During his short reign, he constantly struggled against the powerful Assyrians. Eventually, the Assyrian king Sargon II took control of Babylon, but Merodach-baladan returned to power for a short time after Sargon's death. He receives mention in the Bible for sending envoys with gifts to Judah's King Hezekiah after Hezekiah had recovered from a deathly illness through God's intervention. Hezekiah greeted the envoys warmly and eagerly accepted their gifts, but the prophet Isaiah warned that Babylon would one day ransack Jerusalem and despoil the temple, which it did in 586 B.C. For further study, see 2Ki 20:12-19; Isa 39:1.

MESHA (MEE shuh) *freedom* or *retreat* or *salvation*
1. 1Ch 2:42; son of Caleb
2. 1Ch 8:9; descendant of Benjamin
3. 9 century B.C.; 2Ki 3:4
Mesha ruled Moab, a mountainous plateau region east of the Dead Sea, where he also raised sheep noted for the quality of their wool. Israel had dominated their Moabite neighbors for 40 years, demanding an exorbitant annual tribute of 100,000 lambs and the wool of 100,000 sheep. Mesha finally rose up against Israel's kings Ahaziah and Jehoram to throw off the yoke of oppression. The rebellion seemed to be failing until Mesha resorted to sacrificing his firstborn son to the gods of Moab; Israel then retreated in horror and forfeited the fruits of victory. For further study, see 2Sa 8:2; 2Ki 3.

MESHACH (MEE shak) meaning unknown; 7 century B.C.; Da 1:7; Daniel's friend; tested by fire; also called Mishael; see Shadrach

MESHECH (MEE shek) *draw* or *drag*
1. Gen 10:2; son(s) of Japheth; a nation in Asia Minor; symbol of evil
2. 1Ch 1:17; see Mash

MESHELEMIAH (muh SHEL uh MI uh) *the Lord repays;* 1Ch 9:21; chief temple gatekeeper; also called Shelemiah 1

MESHEZABEL (muh SHEZ uh bel) *God delivers*
1. 6 century B.C.; Ne 3:4; ancestor of repairer of Jerusalem wall
2. 5 century B.C.; Ne 11:24; Judahite; father of Pethahiah
3. 5 century B.C.; Ne 10:21; Jewish leader; sealed covenant renewal

MESHILLEMITH (muh SHIL uh mith) *repaid;* 1Ch 9:12; descendant of Immer; also called Meshillemoth 1

MESHILLEMOTH (muh SHIL uh mahth) *repaid*
1. Ne 11:13; see Meshillemith
2. 8 century B.C.; 2Ch 28:12; his son Berekiah opposed enslaving prisoners

MESHOBAB (muh SHOH bab) *restored;* 8 century B.C.; 1Ch 4:34; Simeonite leader in time of Hezekiah

MESHULLAM (muh SHOO luhm) *reconciliation* or *friendship*
1. 1Ch 8:17; descendant of Benjamin
2. 1Ch 5:13; head of Gadite family in Bashan
3. 1Ch 9:12; ancestor of priest Maasai
4. 8 century B.C.; 2Ki 22:3; grandfather of Josiah's secretary Shaphan
5. 7 century B.C.; 1Ch 9:11; descendant of high priest Zadok
6. 7 century B.C.; 2Ch 34:12; Levite supervisor of temple restoration
7. 6 century B.C.; 1Ch 3:19; son of Zerubbabel
8. 6 century B.C.; Ne 12:13; priest in days of Joiakim
9. 6 century B.C.; Ne 12:16; another priest in days of Joiakim
10. 6 century B.C.; Ne 12:25; Levite gatekeeper in time of Joiakim
11. 5 century B.C.; 1Ch 9:7; father of Sallu the settler in Jerusalem
12. 5 century B.C.; 1Ch 9:8; Benjaminite settler in Jerusalem
13. 5 century B.C.; Ezr 8:16; leader who returned to Judah with Ezra
14. 5 century B.C.; Ezr 10:15; opposed Ezra's decree to divorce foreigners
15. 5 century B.C.; Ezr 10:29; one who married and divorced foreigner after Exile
16. 5 century B.C.; Ne 3:4; priest who repaired Jerusalem wall
17. 5 century B.C.; Ne 3:6; one who repaired Jerusalem wall
18. 5 century B.C.; Ne 8:4; one at Ezra's left when Law was read
19. 5 century B.C.; Ne 10:7; priest who sealed covenant renewal
20. 5 century B.C.; Ne 10:20; leader who sealed covenant renewal
21. 5 century B.C.; Ne 12:33; leader who helped dedicate Jerusalem wall

MESHULLEMETH (muh SHOO luh meth) *reconciled* or *rewarded;* 7 century B.C.; 2Ki 21:19; wife of King Manasseh

METHUSELAH (muh THOO zuh luh) *man of the javelin* or *sent;* Gen 5:21; son of Enoch 2; longest-living human recorded in Bible

METHUSHAEL (muh THOO shee uhl) *man of God;* Gen 4:18; descendant of Cain; father of Lamech 1

MEUNIM (meh YOO nim) *dwelling* or *habitations*
1. 1Ch 4:41; family of exiles who lived in Arabia; also called Meunites
2. Ezr 2:50; ancestor of temple servant family who returned to Judah

MEUNITES 2Ch 20:1; possibly Maonites; see Meunim 1

ME-ZAHAB (MEH zay hab) *waters of gold;* Gen 36:39; grandfather of Mehetabel the wife of King Hadad

MIBHAR (MIB hahr) *choice;* 11 century B.C.; 1Ch 11:38; mighty man of David

MIBSAM (MIB suhm) *sweet odor*
1. 21 century B.C.; Gen 25:13; son of Ishmael; head of Ishmaelite tribe
2. 1Ch 4:25; descendant of Simeon

MIBZAR (MIB zahr) *fortress;* Gen 36:42; Edomite chief descended from Esau

MICA (MYE kuh) *who is like the Lord?*
1. 10 century B.C.; 2Sa 9:12; son of Mephibosheth; also called Micah 3
2. 1Ch 9:15; descendant of Asaph; also called Micaiah 3
3. 5 century B.C.; Ne 10:11; Levite who sealed covenant renewal

MICAH (MYE kuh) *who is like the Lord?*
1. 12 century B.C.; Jdg 17:1
    Micah, who lived in the hill country of Ephraim, stole 1100 pieces of silver from his mother. She cursed him for the act, and Micah felt compelled to return the money. She consecrated the money to the Lord but also used some of it to

have an idol made. Micah made a shrine for the idol in his home and installed one of his sons as priest. However, a Levite happened by, and Micah hired him as priest in place of his son. Later, when the men of Dan were on their way to conquer Laish, they stole Micah's cult objects and persuaded the Levite to join them. After their victory over Laish, the Danites rebuilt the city and set up Micah's idol for themselves. For further study, see Jdg 17–18.

2. 1Ch 5:5; descendant of Reuben

3. 1Ch 8:34; see Mica 1

4. 10 century B.C.; 1Ch 23:20; Levite listed among Kohathites

5. 8 century B.C.; Mic 1:1

Micah of Moresheth grew up in poor, hilly, war-torn Shephelah. He prophesied in Judah during the reigns of Jotham (750–732 B.C.), Ahaz (735–715 B.C.), and Hezekiah (729–686 B.C.). Micah called for both social reform and religious revival. The rich and politically connected were robbing the poor. For this injustice, Samaria suffered oppression and fell to Assyria, the region's greatest power, in 722 B.C. Micah also trumpeted mercy, social justice for the poor, and a humble walk with God as the essential requirements of faith. He taught that only religious revival could remove the social injustices of that day, and he also spoke of the Messiah from Bethlehem who would bring ultimate hope. For further study, see Jer 26:18; the Book of Micah.

6. 7 century B.C.; 2Ch 34:20; father of Abdon the official of Josiah; also called Micaiah 4

7. 5 century B.C.; Jdt 6:15; father of Uzziah the chief city officer in days of Judith

MICAIAH (mih KAY yuh) *who is like the Lord?*

1. 9 century B.C.; 1Ki 22:8

Micaiah risked his life and endured a spiteful prison sentence for prophesying death for King Ahab of Judah. His words contradicted those of other court prophets, who told Ahab he would be victorious in battle. Micaiah claimed that God had used a spirit to misinform these prophets in order to bring about Ahab's death. Micaiah's life was spared only when King Jehoshaphat, Ahab's ally from Israel, pled for him. Ahab chose not to heed the prophet's words and died in battle. For further study, see 1Ki 22:1-28; 2Ch 18:1-27.

2. 9 century B.C.; 2Ch 17:7; official of Jehoshaphat; taught the Law

3. Ne 12:35; see Mica 2

4. 2Ki 22:12; see Micah 6

5. 7 century B.C.; Jer 36:11; betrayed Jeremiah to King Jehoiakim

6. 5 century B.C.; Ne 12:41; priest and singer at Jerusalem wall dedication

7. 2Ch 13:2; see Maacah 9

MICHAEL (MYE kuhl) *who is like God?*

1. Da 10:13

Michael is an archangel with other angels under his authority. He is first mentioned by name as a prince who will support the prophet Daniel against the Persian king and protect the nation of Israel. Michael is later mentioned in a dispute with the devil over the body of Moses. The Bible does not mention what this dispute was, but it does say that Michael left the final judg-

Micah exhorts the Israelites to return to the Lord.

ment of Satan up to God. Michael is also mentioned in the Book of Revelation as the angel leading other angels in a heavenly battle against Satan and his fallen angels. Michael wins this battle, and Satan and his followers are expelled from heaven and cast to earth where they lead the whole world astray. For further study, see Da 10:21; 12:1; Jude 9; Rev 12:7-9.

2. 15 century B.C.; Nu 13:13; his son Sether was sent as a spy to Canaan

3. 1Ch 7:3; descendant of Issachar

4. 1Ch 5:13; descendant of Gad

5. 1Ch 5:14; descendant of Gad

6. 1Ch 6:40; ancestor of Asaph the music minister under David

7. 1Ch 8:16; descendant of Benjamin

8. 11 century B.C.; 1Ch 12:20; Manassite who joined David at Ziklag

9. 11 century B.C.; 1Ch 27:18; father of Omri the officer of Issachar tribe

10. 9 century B.C.; 2Ch 21:2; son of King Jehoshaphat

11. 5 century B.C.; Ezr 8:8; his son Zebediah headed a family who returned to Judah after the Exile

MICHAL (MY kuhl) *who is like God?;* 11 century B.C.; 1Sa 18:20

Michal's love for David caused her father Saul to use her as a pawn to destroy David. When Saul's plan failed, he gave Michal to David in marriage. Michal courageously protected her husband from her father, even sneaking David out a window and placing an idol with fake hair in bed with her when Saul sent soldiers to kill him. While David was in hiding, however, Saul gave Michal to Paltiel in marriage. When David became king after Saul's death, he sent for Michal, but their marriage was not the same. Her cynical arrogance manifested itself when she ridiculed David for dancing joyfully before the ark when it was returned to Jerusalem. His rebuke was the end of their once ideal relationship, and she bore no children as a result. For further study, see 1Sa 14:49; 18:20–19:17; 2Sa 6:12-23; 3:12-16.

MICHRI (MIK rye) *precious;* 1Ch 9:8; ancestor of Elah the Benjaminite resettler in Jerusalem

MIDIAN (MID ee uhn) *strife;* 21 century B.C.; Gen 25:24; son of Abraham and Keturah

The archangel Michael is depicted as a warrior dressed in battle attire.

MIDIANITES (MID ee uhn ights) Gen 37:28

Though related to Israel through Abraham's son Midian and by Moses's marriage to a Midianite, this tribe was singled out for destruction because they seduced the Israelites through sexual immorality into idolatrous religion. Gideon carried out that destruction. For further study, see Gen 25:1-2; Ex 2:15-22; Nu 25; Jdg 6–7.

MIJAMIN (MIJ uh min) *from the right side* or *fortunate*

1. 10 century B.C.; 1Ch 24:9; head of division of priests under David

2. 6 century B.C.; Ne 12:5; priest who returned to Judah after Exile; also called Miniamin 2

3. 5 century B.C.; Ezr 10:25; one who married and divorced foreigner after Exile

4. 5 century B.C.; Ne 10:7; priest who sealed covenant renewal; possibly Mijamin 2
5. 5 century B.C.; Ne 12:51; priest and trumpeter at Jerusalem wall dedication; possibly Mijamin 4

MIKLOTH (MIK lahth) *rods*
1. 12 century B.C.; 1Ch 8:32; son of Jeiel
2. 10 century B.C.; 1Ch 27:4; leader of army division under David

MIKNEIAH (mik NEE yuh) *the Lord possesses;* 11 century B.C.; 1Ch 15:18; harpist who played at ark's return

MILALAI (MIL uh lye) meaning unknown; 5 century B.C.; Ne 12:36; Levite musician; dedicated Jerusalem wall

MILCAH (MIL kuh) meaning unknown
1. 21 century B.C.; Gen 11:29; niece of Abraham; wife of Nahor; mother of Rebekah
2. 15 century B.C.; Nu 26:33; daughter of Zelophehad; received her father's inheritance

MILCOM (MIL kum) meaning unknown; 1Ki 11:5; deity of Ammonites; worship involved child sacrifice; also called Molech and Moloch

MINIAMIN (MIN eye uh mihn) *from the right side* or *fortunate*
1. 8 century B.C.; 2Ch 31:15; steward of temple offerings
2. Ne 12:17; see Mijamin 2

MIRIAM (MEER ee uhm) meaning unknown
1. 15 century B.C.; Ex 2:4

Miriam was born at a turbulent time in Jewish history—a time when the Israelites were being held as slaves in Egypt.

When Miriam was just a young girl of 12, Shiphrah and Puah, two Hebrew midwives, had been ordered by the king of Egypt to slaughter all Jewish baby boys as soon as they were born as a means of population control. Miriam's family suffered anguish when her mother Jochebed gave birth to Moses, for he was doomed to be thrown into the Nile along with the other male babies.

The family hid their baby boy as long as possible. Then Jochebed came up with a plan to save him. She built a basket out of papyrus, waterproofed it with tar, placed Moses in it, and hid it in the reeds. Miriam helped by keeping a vigil, faithfully watching the makeshift lifeboat from a discreet distance to see where it landed down river.

Pharaoh's daughter, going to the river to bathe, was the first to discover the little basket. Though she immediately recognized the baby as a Hebrew, which should have been his death sentence, she wanted to keep the child. Miriam quickly struck up a conversation with this curious daughter of Pharaoh and offered to fetch a Hebrew woman to nurse the baby. Pharaoh's daughter eagerly jumped at the chance to get someone else to help. That someone was Jochebed, who was then hired as a nursemaid for her own child.

Thanks to his sister's efforts, Moses was returned to his mother's arms. Miriam's ability to take charge and make quick decisions not only saved her little brother but was instrumental in eventually saving the nation of Israel, for it was Moses who went on to deliver the Israelites out of their bondage. Her brother become the adopted son of Pharaoh's daughter and then rose to greatness. As a member of Pharaoh's house, Moses learned "all the wisdom of the Egyptians and was powerful in words and deeds" (Ac 7:22). That education and reputation proved pivotal when Moses eventually led the Israelites out of Egypt.

During the Exodus of the Israelites from Egypt and their subsequent 40 years in the desert, Miriam shared leadership with her brothers Moses and Aaron. After the miracle of the Red Sea (when God parted the waters, allowing the Israelites to cross to safety on dry land), Miriam expressed her elation with song and dance. With tambourine in hand, she began to play and sing in praise and thanksgiving to God. The strength of her leadership then became evident—all the women followed her lead, singing and dancing in joyous and triumphant worship. As thousands of women celebrated openly, Miriam sang, "Sing to the Lord, for he has triumphed gloriously; horse and rider he has thrown into the sea" (Ex 15:21).

However, Miriam did not always sing praises to God for what he did, and she did not always support her brother Moses. She and Aaron both talked against Moses when he married a Cushite (Ethiopian) woman, but their irritation with Moses went beyond his choice of a wife. Miriam and Aaron rebelled against his leadership because they were jealous of his position of authority over Israel. They decided to express their resentment publicly:

"Has the Lord spoken only through Moses? Has he not spoken through us also?" (Nu 12:2).

No mention is made of how Moses reacted to his siblings' accusations, but God responded immediately and decisively. He called all three to the Tent of Meeting where he appeared to them in a cloud. He spoke directly to Miriam and Aaron, rebuking them for talking behind Moses's back and rebelling against his authority. God scolded them for speaking against his true and faithful servant and for resisting the leader he had placed over Israel. Before this divine confrontation was over, Miriam was left standing with leprosy that covered her entire body. In his anguish, Aaron begged Moses to help his sister. He begged Moses to forgive them of their sin. So Moses cried out to God to heal Miriam. God did heal her, but only after she was led away from the people and quarantined outside the camp for seven days. Miriam is not mentioned again until her death and burial at Kadesh in the Wilderness of Zin.

For further study, see Ex 15:20-21; Nu 12:1-15; 20:1; 26:59; Dt 24:9; 1Ch 6:3; Mic 6:4.

2. 1Ch 4:17; descendant of Judah 1

MIRMAH (MUHR muh) *fraud;* 1Ch 8:10; descendant of Benjamin

MISHAEL (MISH ee uhl) *who is what God is?*
1. 15 century B.C.; Ex 6:22; kinsman of Aaron; buried Aaron's sons
2. Da 1:6; also called Meshach; see Shadrach
3. 5 century B.C.; Ne 8:4; aide to Ezra for reading of the Law

MISHAM (MI sham) meaning unknown; 1Ch 8:12; descendant of Benjamin

MISHMA (MISH muh) *hearing*
1. 21 century B.C.; Gen 25:14; son of Ishmael
2. 1Ch 4:25; descendant of Simeon

MISHMANNAH (MISH man uh) *fatness;* 11 century B.C.; 1Ch 12:10; Gadite leader; joined David at Ziklag

MISPAR (MIS pahr) *number;* Ezr 2:2; ancestor of family that returned to Jerusalem; also called Mispereth

Pharaoh's daughter discovers the baby Moses as Miriam watches from a distance.

MISPERETH Ne 7:7; see Mispar

MITHREDATH (MITH ruh dath) *gift of Mithra*
1. 6 century B.C.; Ezr 1:8; treasurer of King Cyrus
2. 5 century B.C.; Ezr 4:7; official who opposed rebuilding Jerusalem

MIZZAH (MIZ uh) *terror;* 19 century B.C.; Gen 36:13; grandson of Esau by Basemath

MNASON (NAY suhn) meaning unknown; 1 century A.D.; Ac 21:16; Cypriot Christian who hosted Paul

MOAB (MOH ab) meaning unknown; 21 century B.C.; Gen 19:37; son of Lot by his oldest daughter

MOABITES (MOH uh bights) Gen 19:37
Amorites, Israelites, Assyrians, Arabians, and Romans each in turn occupied Moab, a land east of the Dead Sea. The Moabites, descendants of Lot, in turn oppressed Israel. Ruth, ancestor of Jesus, was a Moabite. For further study, see Nu 21–26; Dt 2; 34; Jdg 3; 11; Ru 1; 1Sa 14; 22; 2Ki 3; Isa 15–16; Jer 48; Eze 25.

MOADIAH Ne 12:5; see Maadiah

MOETH (MOH eth) meaning unknown; 5 century B.C.; 1Esd 8:63; Levite servant in the temple

MOLECH Lev 18:21; see Milcom

MOLID (MOH lid) *begetter;* 1Ch 2:29; descendant of Judah 1

MOLOCH Ac 7:43; see Milcom

MOMDIUS (mahm DEE us) meaning unknown; 5 century B.C.; 1Esd 9:34; priest who married and divorced foreigner after Exile

MOOSSIAS (moo SIGH uhs) meaning unknown; 5 century B.C.; 1Esd 9:31; priest who married and divorced foreigner after Exile

MORDECAI (MOHR duh kye) *consecrated to Marduk* [a pagan god]
1. 6 century B.C.; Ezr 2:2; one who returned to Judah with Zerubbabel
2. 5 century B.C.; Est 2:5
Mordecai is best known as the adoptive father of his orphaned cousin Esther. He raised Esther to have confidence, to respect her Jewish roots, and to remember all that he had done for her. Later, after she was selected to marry King Ahasuerus and become the Queen of Persia, she won the king's favor for her fellow Jews in exile and, with the help of Mordecai, reversed a death sentence against her people.

Mordecai came into conflict with the Persian prime minister Haman when he refused to bow down before Haman because he felt that such an act would be idolatrous. The vain Haman was outraged and plotted revenge against not just Mordecai but his people as well by ordering all Jews in Persia to be killed. Fortunately, Mordecai had gained the king's favor by earlier thwarting a plot against the king's life. Ironically, the king ordered Haman to oversee a procession in honor of his enemy Mordecai, which only served to fuel Haman's rage. In the end, Mordecai and Esther were able to expose to the king Haman's murder-

To Haman's dismay, the Persian king orders him to give Mordecai a procession of honor.

ous plot against the Jews. The king then ordered Haman to be hung on the gallows he had built for Mordecai. Further, Mordecai was given Haman's position as prime minister. The Feast of Purim, which is celebrated to this day by Jews grateful for their historic deliverance by Mordecai and Esther, came to be called Mordecai's Day by some Jews.

For further study, see Est 2–10.

MOSES (MO zuhs) *draw out;* 15 century B.C.; Ex 2:2

During a time when the Israelites were slaves in the land of Egypt, a new king began to fear the increase of the Israelites' numbers. In an attempt to control the Hebrew population, he ordered two Hebrew midwives to kill all newborn Hebrew boys. When they refused to obey, the king ordered his own people to drown the babies in the Nile River. It was in this tumultuous setting that Jochebed and Amram of the tribe of Levi gave birth to a son. Jochebed hid her son for three months, but when he grew more active, she put him in a basket made of papyrus and waterproofed with tar. Ironically, she stationed the little basket among the reeds of the Nile, the death site for Hebrew baby boys, while the baby's older sister Miriam kept watch. The baby boy was found by Pharaoh's daughter, returned to his mother for nursing, and later adopted by Pharaoh's daughter, who named him Moses because she drew him out of the water. Moses was an extraordinary child and he was raised and educated as a member of the royal household.

Forty years after his birth, Moses visited his own people as they toiled under the hands of their Egyptian slavemasters. Seeing an Egyptian beating one of the Hebrews, Moses put his Hebrew roots above his political position and murdered the Egyptian, hiding the body in the sand. But what he thought was a secret act of justified revenge turned out to be the demise of his high position in Egypt, for a Hebrew had witnessed the killing.

Fearing he would be executed for the murder, Moses fled to Midian. There he befriended seven sisters at a well by driving away a group of shepherds that were harassing them. He married one of the seven and began a life as a shepherd. One day, as he was leading his flock by Mt. Horeb, an angel of God appeared to him in the fire of a burning bush. As Moses came near the bush, God spoke directly to him, warning him not to come any closer and to take off his sandals, for he was standing on holy ground, the ground where God had chosen to appear in all his glory. Moses took off his sandals and hid his face, afraid to look at the almighty God.

The Israelites, in their despair, had cried out to God to be released from slavery. He heard their cries and decided to execute their deliverance through his servant Moses. But Moses was not sure he was the man to make it work. He questioned God time and time again, which prompted God to perform miracles so Moses would believe. Moses saw his staff become a snake and the snake become a staff again. He saw his own hand turn leprous, and he saw it restored. God told Moses how he would be able to turn water into blood before Pharaoh. Still, Moses hesitated, saying he was not a good enough speaker for the job, so God allowed Moses's older brother Aaron to go with him and speak for him.

In spite of Moses's lack of self-confidence, he was still a man who obeyed God. After securing a leave of absence from his shepherding job, Moses took his wife, sons, and Aaron to Egypt, carrying with him the staff that God would use against the Egyptians. Then began the series of requests to let the Israelites go, the recurrence of Pharaoh's flat denials, and the string of ten plagues meted out exclusively on the Egyptian people. Moses set the stage for an incredible display of God's power over the deadly forces of nature in order to convince Pharaoh and the other Egyptians of the foolishness of opposing the Hebrew God.

God allowed Moses and Aaron to be the initiators of the first nine plagues that had transformed the Nile into blood, covered the land with frogs, changed the dust to gnats, produced dense swarms

> → ←
>
> *"Never since has there been a prophet in Israel like Moses, whom the Lord knew face to face."*
>
> Dt 34:10

of flies, massacred the Egyptian livestock, festered boils on all people and animals, dispatched a devastating hailstorm, canopied the land with locusts, and dipped Egypt into total darkness. But for the last and most devastating plague, God was the initiator. God struck down all the Egyptians' firstborn sons, and there was loud wailing and utter anguish in every Egyptian household that night. The Israelites were spared the havoc of the plague by displaying blood on their doors. Moses and Aaron were summoned in the middle of the night by Pharaoh himself, whose own son had died. So great was his anguish at the death of his firstborn son that he told them to leave quickly with the Israelites.

Moses led a host of Israelites out of Egypt. Shortly after their departure, Pharaoh lusted for vengeance and pursued them with his army. He caught up with them when their backs were to the vast Red Sea. Apparently trapped and sure to be captured, the Israelites blamed Moses for leading them to destruction. Responding to God's directive, Moses raised his staff over the waters and parted them to create a path of escape. When the

Moses parts the Red Sea and creates a path of escape for the Israelites fleeing from Egypt.

Egyptian soldiers attempted to pursue, the waters rushed together and drowned them.

As Moses led a grumbling, complaining nation across the desert to Canaan, God provided water, manna, and quail for them. God also used Moses to give out his Law on Mt. Sinai, which was possibly the greatest appearance God made in the Old Testament. God knew Moses's high level of obedience to him, and with that confidence, he entrusted him with his Law—standards that would reveal the sinfulness of the human race. After warning the people they would die if they touched the mountain, Moses climbed Mt. Sinai in the middle of a thick cloud, with thunder and lightning on all sides, and smoke billowing up from it. The mountain was shaking violently and the sound of a trumpet was growing louder as Moses spoke. And then God himself spoke directly to his humble servant. He spoke his commandments, his principles for life, and his measurements for the sins of humanity. Moses spent 40 days and nights alone with God, whose presence caused Moses's face to shine so brightly that the people could not look directly at him and made the mountain itself shine for seven days afterward.

When Moses came down from the mountain, he had the Law, written with the finger of God, on tables of stone, and he had the instructions for the construction of the Tabernacle, the place where God would dwell with the people in the desert. But at the bottom of the mountain, Moses discovered a golden calf that the people had built and worshiped in their impatience for his return. Moses broke the two stones of God's Law and then fell prostrate and fasted for 40 days and nights, begging God not to completely destroy the people. God spared the Hebrew people and later gave Moses an identical set of stone tablets. Moses challenged the people to take a stand for God. The Levites, Moses's own tribe, rallied around him.

After many years of wandering, Moses effectively led the rebellious Israelites to the edge of the Promised Land, but on one occasion, the people complained that there was no water. God provided for them again by telling Moses to speak to a rock so that it would produce water. Instead of speaking to the rock, Moses struck it with his rod. His years of faithfulness and obedience were tainted by this single disobedient act, and he was not allowed to enter the Promised Land.

Angered by the Israelites' idolatry, Moses breaks the stone tables containing God's Law.

Moses died in the desert of Moab after spending another private time with God, who showed him a panoramic view of the Promised Land, the land he would never walk upon, from the top of Mt. Nebo. His epitaph at the end of Deuteronomy gives tribute to Moses, who performed miracles and showed God's mighty power more than any other in Israel.

For further study, see Ex 2–40; the Book of Numbers; the Book of Deuteronomy.

MOZA (MOH zuh) *departing* or *going forth*
1. 1Ch 2:46; son of Caleb
2. 1Ch 8:36; Benjaminite descendant of Jonathan and Saul

MUCHAEUS (MEW kay ee uhs) meaning unknown; 5 century B.C.; AddEst 1:16; advisor to King Ahasuerus

MUPPIM (MUP im) *obscurities;* 19 century B.C.; Gen 46:21; son of Benjamin

MUSHI (MOO shee) *drawn out;* Ex 6:19; son of Merari and head of Levite clan

NAAM (NAY uhm) *pleasant;* 15 century B.C.; 1Ch 4:15; son of Caleb the spy

NAAMAH (NAY uh muh) *pleasant*
1. Gen 4:22; daughter of Lamech by Zillah
2. 10 century B.C.; 1Ki 14:21; Ammonite wife of Solomon; mother of Rehoboam

NAAMAN (NAY uh muhn) *pleasantness*
1. 19 century B.C.; Gen 46:21; son of Bela; grandson of Benjamin
2. 9 century B.C.; 2Ki 5:1

As commander of the Syrian army, Naaman had a celebrated reputation for his military victories, and the Syrian king valued him greatly. However, Naaman had leprosy. Through the encouragement of his wife's Israelite servant girl, Naaman asked for the king's permission to travel to Israel for a cure. The king did not hesitate to let Naaman go and sent a letter to the Israelite king asking for Naaman's healing.

The Israelite king, thinking the request impossible, assumed the Syrians were trying to provoke a conflict. But Elisha the prophet heard about Naaman's problem and sent for him. When Naaman arrived at Elisha's house, a servant met him and instructed him to go wash seven times in the Jordan River. Naaman was angry and offended; he had expected the great prophet to personally perform some rite or ceremony over him. He went off in a rage, convinced that the waters in Damascus's rivers were just as good as the waters in Israel.

After Naaman's servants convinced him that healing did not always happen in a grandiose way, he went to the Jordan, dipped himself in it seven times, and was cured. In thankfulness, Naaman went to Elisha, told him of his faith in God, and offered him a gift, which Elisha refused. Elisha's servant Gehazi was not so gracious; he ran after Naaman to accept his gift and later lied to Elisha about what he had done. As punishment for his greed and deceit, Gehazi was afflicted with Naaman's leprosy.

For further study, see 2Ki 5.
3. 1Ch 8:7; descendant of Benjamin

NAAMATHITES (NAY am uh thights) Job 2:11; residents of Naameh in southwest Arabia; family name of Zophar

NAARAH (NAY uh ruh) *girl;* 1Ch 4:5; wife of Ashhur the leader of Tekoa (city southeast of Bethlehem)

Naaman dips himself in the Jordan River. Stained glass. Gloucester Cathedral, Gloucester, England.

NAARAI (NAY uh rye) *my youth;* 11 century B.C.; 1Ch 11:37; mighty man of David; also called Paarai

NAATHUS (NAE thus) meaning unknown; 5 century B.C.; 1Esd 9:31; priest who married and divorced foreigner after Exile

NABAL (NAY buhl) *foolish;* 11 century B.C.; 1Sa 25:3

This rancher and sheepherder was both wealthy and stingy. Despite having every reason and resource to be hospitable, Nabal had a reputation for being mean-spirited and inhospitable. Nabal's wartime prosperity was due, in part, to the diligent protective services of David's warriors. Yet when David's men asked for daily rations, Nabal balked and insulted the very men who were protecting him. His wife took it upon herself to plead with David not to punish them for her husband's ungratefulness and offered to provide food for David's men. While indulging in a feast, Nabal learned what his wife had done; shocked by the news, he had a heart attack and died some days later. His widow became David's wife.

NABATEANS (nab uh TEE unz) 1Mac 5:25

The Nabateans from Edom in southern Arabia were builders, traders, and excellent engineers. Their influence was felt throughout the Near East, especially in the century before and after Christ.

NABOTH (NAY buhth) possibly *a sprout* or *fruit;* 9 century B.C.; 1Ki 21:1

Naboth's vineyard was a family plot located at Jezreel, near Mt. Gilboa. Unfortunately, Naboth's family plot also adjoined King Ahab's winter palace, and the king wanted it for his garden. Rightly claiming a divine lease to keep the land within his family as a permanent inheritance in the Promised Land, Naboth refused to sell his land to King Ahab. Queen Jezebel schemed to acquire the land for her husband. She had Naboth falsely accused of blasphemy; he lost his life, and his land

Nadab and Abihu are consumed by heavenly fire for errantly performing new rituals.

was forfeited to the crown. The prophet Elijah challenged Ahab's actions in acquiring the land and predicted his ultimate demise. For further study, see 2Ki 9:25-26.

NACON (NAY kahn) *ready;* 11 century B.C.; 2Sa 6:6; owned threshing floor where Uzzah died; also called Chidon

NADAB (NAY dab) *generous* or *noble*
1. 15 century B.C.; Ex 6:23

Nadab and his brother Abihu died for errantly performing the newly established priestly rituals set during the Exodus from Egypt. The Bible indicates they offered "unholy fire," but the exact nature of their sin is unclear. Their punishment, however, is detailed as consumption by fire from heaven. The severity of their punishment served to instill fear of God and respect for new rituals at a time when God was inaugurating a new covenant with Israel. A similar rationale was implicit in the sudden deaths of Ananias and Sapphira for a small offense when the early church was being founded (Ac 5:1-11). For further study, see Ex 6:23-25; 24:1-11; 30:7-8; Lev 8–10; 16:12; Nu 16:46.
2. 1Ch 2:28; descendant of Judah 1
3. 12 century B.C.; 1Ch 8:30; son of Jeiel; possibly granduncle of Saul

4. ruled 909–908 B.C.; 1Ki 14:20

Nadab was the second king of Israel after the monarchy split into the northern and southern kingdoms of Israel and Judah. Nadab, like his father, did "evil in the sight of the Lord." Because the regime of his father, Jeroboam I, was so burdensome and oppressive, the whole Jeroboam family was the target of a conspiracy. Each and every son and grandson of that dynasty had to be wiped out, according to a prophetic word delivered by Ahijah of Shiloh. Baasha obliged, killing Nadab while the king was engaged in a siege of the Philistine city of Gibbethon. Baasha then became the third king of Israel. For further study, see 1Ki 15:25-31.

5. Tob 11:18; nephew of Tobit

NAGGAI (NAG eye) *meaning unknown;* Lk 3:25; ancestor of Jesus

NAHAM (NAY ham) *comfort;* 1Ch 4:19; descendant of Judah 1

NAHAMANI (NAY huh MAY nee) *compassionate;* 6 century B.C.; Ne 7:7; Jewish leader who returned to Judah

NAHARAI (NAY uh rye) *snorting;* 11 century B.C.; 2Sa 23:37; mighty man of David from Beeroth

NAHASH (NAY hash) *serpent*
1. 11 century B.C.; 1Sa 11:1; Ammonite king defeated by Saul
2. 11 century B.C.; 2Sa 10:2; Ammonite king who befriended David
3. 11 century B.C.; 2Sa 17:25; father of David's half-sisters Abigail and Zeruiah

NAHATH (NAY hath) *rest or descent*
1. 19 century B.C.; Gen 36:13; grandson of Esau; Edomite chief
2. 1Ch 6:26; ancestor of Samuel; also called Toah and Tohu
3. 8 century B.C.; 2Ch 31:13; Levite; served in temple under Hezekiah

NAHBI (NAH bye) *secret;* 15 century B.C.; Nu 13:14; Naphtali tribal leader sent to explore Canaan

NAHOR (NAY hohr) *snorting*
1. Gen 11:22; ancestor of Abraham
2. 22 century B.C.; Gen 11:26; brother of Abraham; husband of Milcah

NAHSHON (NAH shahn) *diviner;* 15 century B.C.; Ex 6:23; brother-in-law of Aaron; leader during Exodus

NAHUM (NAY hum) *comforter*
1. 7 century B.C.; Na 1:1

Like Jonah before him, the prophet Nahum was sent by God to the wicked and brutally murderous people of Nineveh to convince them to repent. Unlike Jonah, Nahum issued a harsh warning of God's inescapable justice rather than an offer of mercy and forgiveness. Jonah's message, while heeded at first, was eventually forgotten, and 100 years later, Nahum imposed on the "city of bloodshed" the same death sentence its people so freely meted out to others. Nahum's prophecy of Nineveh's fall was fulfilled in 612 B.C. For further study, see the Book of Nahum.

2. Lk 3:25; descendant of Zerubbabel

NAIDUS (nah EE dus) *meaning unknown;* 5 century B.C.; 1Esd 9:31; priest who married and divorced foreigner after Exile

NAOMI (nay OH mee) *pleasantness or my joy;* 12 century B.C.; Ruth 1:2

In the days when judges guided Israel, a famine forced many people to leave the country. Naomi, her husband Elimelech, and their two sons Mahlon and Chilion went to Moab, where food was more plentiful. While there, Elimelech died, leaving Naomi a widow and a single parent in a foreign country.

As many in her situation would do, Naomi cherished her sons as they grew. Her joy was great when they married fine Moabite women named Orpah and Ruth. But after ten years in Moab, both of her sons died, and Naomi was grieving again.

When Naomi heard that God had provided food again in Israel, she prepared to return to Bethlehem with her daughters-in-law. However, as she thought more about taking these two women out of their own land, she changed her plans and told them to go back to their own mothers. In her love for them, she gave them up. Orpah and Ruth both wept openly and confirmed their decision to go with Naomi, but Naomi insisted they return to their homes. In the end, Orpah finally said goodbye to Naomi, but Ruth clung to her and expressed her devotion and commitment to her dead husband's mother.

Naomi and Ruth arrived in Bethlehem, where Naomi changed her name to Mara, which means *bitter*, "for the Almighty has dealt bitterly with me." It was Naomi who convinced Ruth to work for a respectable relative named Boaz. He later bought from Naomi the land that had belonged to Elimelech and his two sons and took Ruth as his wife.

For further study, see the Book of Ruth.

NAPHISH (NAY fish) *numerous* or *breath;* 21 century B.C.; Gen 25:15; son of Ishmael; see Nephisim and Nephushesim

NAPHTALI (NAF tuh lye) *wrestle;* 20 century B.C.; Gen 30:8

Naphtali, the sixth son of Jacob, was so named because he was the outcome of an emotional wrestling match or tug-of-war between Rachel and Leah over the affection of their shared husband. An infertile and jealous Rachel offered Jacob her maidservant Bilhah, so that Rachel might be credited with bearing children through her. Naphtali, the product of that union, grew up in this blended family of four mothers and 13 children. As a member of this jealous household, he played a role in the saga of selling younger brother Joseph into slavery, seeking famine relief from Joseph in Egypt, and then moving the entire family to Egypt. Later, when the tribes of Jacob were allotted land in Canaan, Naphtali received extensive territory, stretching from the fertile Jezreel Valley and Sea of

Naomi entreats her daughters-in-law Ruth and Orpah to return to their own families.

Galilee to the northern border. For further study, see Gen 30:1-8; 46:24; 49:21; Nu 1–2; 26; Dt 33:23; Jos 19; Jdg 4; 1Ch 7:13.

NAPHTUHIM (NAF tuh him) Gen 10:13; sons of Egypt; people of the delta region of Lower Egypt

NARCISSUS (nahr SIS uhs) *daffodil;* 1 century A.D.; Ro 16:11; head of Christian household at Rome

NATHAN (NAY thuhn) *gift*
1. 1Ch 2:36; descendant of Judah 1
2. 11 century B.C.; 2Sa 23:36; from Zobah; father of mighty man of David
3. 11 century B.C.; 2Sa 7:2

Nathan, God's prophet and messenger to King David, reported good news as well as bad to the king. After supporting David's idea to build a temple to replace the portable tentlike tabernacle, Nathan disappointed the enthusiastic king when God revealed that his temple was to be built by David's successor, Solomon. Nathan had to tell the king that God had other plans for David's kingdom—an eternal kingdom established through his family line. It was Nathan's tact and diplomacy that helped David accept the fact that his son Solomon would build the temple.

Later, this prophet confronted King David over his adulterous affair with Bathsheba and the murder of her husband, Uriah. Nathan was cautious in approaching David about the subject. He told a story of a rich man who slaughtered a poor man's beloved pet lamb to serve a meal to a traveler. David condemned himself without realizing it when he told Nathan to make the man pay a four-fold retribution for the lamb and then put the man to death for his crime. Nathan then told David that he was the man in his story and that David would endure God's judgment for taking Bathsheba from her husband. As his punishment, David's own wives would commit adultery, not in secret as he had done but in broad daylight before his eyes. Nathan also informed him that his son by Bathsheba would die.

For further study, see 2Sa 7:2-17; 12:1-25; 1Ki 1:8-45; 4:4-5; 1Ch 17:1-15.
4. 10 century B.C.; 2Sa 5:14; son of David born in Jerusalem
5. 10 century B.C.; 1Ki 4:5; father of Azariah and Zabud; possibly Nathan 3 or 4

Nathan reproaches King David for his affair with Bathsheba and the murder of her husband, Uriah.

6. Tob 5:14; descendant of prophet Shemaiah
7. 5 century B.C.; Ezr 8:16; Jewish leader sent by Ezra to Iddo
8. 5 century B.C.; Ezr 10:39; married and divorced foreigner after Exile

NATHANAEL (nuh THAN ee uhl) *God has given*
1. 1 century A.D.; Jn 1:45; disciple of Jesus; see Bartholomew
2. Jdt 8:1; ancestor of Judith

NATHAN-MELECH (NAY thuhn MEL ek) *king's gift;* 7 century B.C.; 2Ki 23:11; official under King Josiah

NAZARENES (nazz uh REENS) Ac 24:5; people of Nazareth, an obscure town where Jesus grew up; also called Nazoreans

NAZIRITES (NAZZ uh rights) *separated ones;* Nu 6:4

Nazirites were Israelites who had entered into a special vow to God for all or part of their life for some specific purpose or service. They vowed abstinence from wine and grapes, refrained from using a razor on their hair, and eliminated all contact with dead bodies. Samson was dedicated as a Nazirite by his parents before birth; the prophet Samuel and John the Baptist may have been Nazirites also. For further study, see Nu 6; Jdg 13; 1Sa 1; Am 2:11-12.

NAZOREANS Mt 2:23; see Nazarenes

NEARIAH (NEE uh RYE uh) *child of the Lord*
1. 8 century B.C.; 1Ch 4:42; Simeonite leader; invaded Seir in days of Hezekiah
2. 1Ch 3:22; descendant of Zerubbabel

NEBAI (NEE bye) meaning unknown; 5 century B.C.; Ne 10:19; leader; sealed covenant renewal with God

NEBAIOTH (neh BAY uth) meaning unknown; 21 century B.C.; Gen 25:13; firstborn son of Ishmael

NEBAT (NEE bat) *view;* 10 century B.C.; 1Ki 11:26; father of King Jeroboam

NEBO (NEE boh) *height* or *the proclaimer*
1. Isa 46:1; Babylonian god of literature, wisdom, and the arts
2. Ezr 10:43; ancestor of one who married and divorced foreigner after Exile

NEBUCHADNEZZAR (NEB uh kuhd NEZ uhr) *may Nebo protect my boundary;* ruled 604–562 B.C.; 2Ki 24:1

Seven years after the fall of the Assyrian Empire to Babylon, a brutal prince named Nebuchadnezzar became king of Babylon. Even though Judah was a vassal of Babylon, Nebuchadnezzar attacked them and took their King Jehoiakim captive. The next king of Judah, Jehoiachin, surrendered to Nebuchadnezzar and became his prisoner. Neb-

uchadnezzar also brought many elite citizens of Jerusalem into captivity in Babylon. For those remaining in Jerusalem, he appointed Zedekiah as their king.

Nine years later, against the advice of the prophet Jeremiah, Zedekiah rebelled, causing Nebuchadnezzar to camp with his whole army outside the walls of Jerusalem for two years. Because of famine, the entire Jewish army broke through the city walls in the middle of the night. The Babylonians pursued them, capturing them and killing Zedekiah's own sons before his eyes. Zedekiah's eyes were put out, and he was bound and taken to Babylon. King Nebuchadnezzar then took every valuable article out of the Jews' sacred temple and burned down the temple, as well as the royal palace and every other building important to the Jews. He demolished the city walls and carried all the people except the very poor into captivity in Babylon where they stayed for 70 years.

During this time of Jewish captivity, Nebuchadnezzar proved to be a most influential, industrious, and vainglorious leader. Traces of this glory have been discovered by archaeologists: a most splendid palace, the sacred Procession Way adorned with 120 lions, and the Ishtar Gate trimmed with 575 dragons and bulls. Also attributed to him are the incredible temple to his god and the ziggurat, or temple-tower, of Babylon. The bricks in the city were inscribed with his name, indelibly identifying the city as his own. Nebuchadnezzar was also the originator of the Hanging Gardens, said to be one of the seven wonders of the ancient world. They were created on terraces overlooking the palace, allegedly to remind his wife of her native Media. His city was fortified with double walls and an artificial lake. The city's water supply system was intricately designed to draw water from the Tigris and Euphrates rivers. Under Nebuchadnezzar's rule, Babylon became the greatest center of trade, architecture, art, and astronomy of the time.

Nebuchadnezzar even governed the Jewish captives in a grand way. The chief of his court was ordered to bring in the most promising Jewish males for a three-year training program in preparation for future service to the king. The men had to be young, handsome, intelligent, alert, and physically perfect. Among those chosen men were Daniel, who was renamed Belteshazzar; Hananiah, who was renamed Shadrach; Mishael, who was renamed Meshach; and Azariah, who was renamed Abednego. As these men trained for Nebuchadnezzar's service, God gave them great knowledge and the ability to understand visions and dreams.

When Nebuchadnezzar began having disturbing dreams, he called upon all his magicians, enchanters, sorcerers, and astrologers to interpret them. When no one could decipher his dreams, he ordered the execution of all the wise men of Babylon. But Daniel went to the king and begged for more time. During the night, God revealed the meaning of the last dream to Daniel. Daniel explained that the dream meant that Nebuchadnezzar's great empire, and several lesser empires that would follow, would all fall one day, but that the kingdom established by God would last forever.

The king fell prostrate before Daniel and raised him to a place of honor and high position within the province of Babylon. Nebuchadnezzar also gave tribute to Daniel's God, who had revealed the meaning of the dream.

Yet King Nebuchadnezzar continued to elevate himself in Babylon. He built a gold statue nine stories high and decreed that everyone must bow down to the statue at the sound of certain music. Whoever did not fall down and worship Nebuchadnezzar would be thrown into a blazing furnace to die a terrible death. Shadrach, Meshach, and Abednego refused to bow down to a false god, so the king threw them into the blazing furnace, which he had heated seven times hotter than normal. To the king's amazement, the men were preserved from harm in that fiery furnace by a fourth man; not a single hair on their heads was singed. Nebuchadnezzar believed that the fourth man was an angel. The king was so impressed with the faith of these men and the power of their God that he made it illegal for anyone to say anything against their God, and he promoted them to a higher position in Babylon.

A subsequent dream and interpretation by Daniel foretold personal humiliation that Nebuchadnezzar would suffer. The prophecy was fulfilled 12 months later when the king was told by a voice from heaven that his royal authority had been stripped away and that he would live with wild animals, eating grass like cattle. Immediately, Scripture says, he began eating grass, the hair on his body grew like the feathers of an eagle, and his nails grew like the claws of a bird. In this horrifying condition, Nebuchadnezzar turned his eyes to heaven and praised God, honoring and glorifying him. Immediately, Nebuchadnezzar was restored to the throne of Babylon and became even greater than before. This time, however, he ruled in obedience to God. As Neb-

By order of King Nebuchadnezzar, Shadrach, Meshach, and Abednego are cast into the furnace.

uchadnezzar himself said of God, "He is able to bring low those who walk in pride" (Da 4:37).

For further study, see 2Ki 25; 2Chr 36; Jer 25–52; Eze 26–30; Da 1–4. Also called Nebuchadrezzar.

NEBUCHADREZZAR Jer 21:2; see Nebuchadnezzar

NEBUSHAZBAN (NEB uh SHAZ ban) *Nebo deliver me;* 7 century B.C.; Jer 39:13; chief Babylonian officer; freed Jeremiah

NEBUZARADAN (NEB uh zahr AY duhn) *Nabu* [a god] *has given offspring;* 6 century B.C.; 2Ki 25:8

King Nebuchadnezzar of Babylon raided and besieged Jerusalem during the second and third invasions of Judah in 597 and 586 B.C. Many high officials were executed, the temple was burned, furnishings were dismantled and taken as booty, the city walls were demolished, and the people were sent into exile. The high-ranking army commander and court official responsible for carrying all this out was Nebuzaradan. Yet he was kindly disposed toward Jeremiah the prophet, who had advised that Jerusalem submit to Babylon. Nebuzaradan entrusted him and other innocent civilians to Gedaliah, the Jewish noble whom he appointed as governor after the fall of Jerusalem. For further study, see 2Ki 25:8-20; Jer 39:9–40:6; 52:12-30.

NECO (NEE koh) meaning unknown; ruled 609–595 B.C.; 2Ki 23:29; Egyptian king who killed Josiah; see Pharaoh

NEDABIAH (NED uh BYE uh) *the Lord is willing;* 6 century B.C.; 1Ch 3:18; son of Jehoiachin

NEHEMIAH (NEE uh MYE uh) *the Lord comforts*
1. 6 century B.C.; Ezr 2:2; one who returned to Judah with Zerubbabel
2. 5 century B.C.; Ne 1:1

Nehemiah is renowned for putting together the many components of a long-term urban renewal strategy that rebuilt Jerusalem after its destruction and the people's 70-year captivity in Babylon. The opening chapter of Nehemiah's story takes place in Persia (modern Iran), where he worked as a cupbearer in the royal palace. A trusted official, he tasted the food for the Persian king Artaxerxes I. Nehemiah grieved and prayed when he heard the news of his beloved Jerusalem being devastated by war and pestilence. Appealing to his Persian master for help, he received a leave of absence, a letter of credit from the Persian king, and a government grant of timber from Asaph, the national forester. With these outside resources, he began to rebuild Jerusalem.

Nehemiah entered the community with sensitivity and confidence. For three days, he surveyed the community's needs without being intrusive by riding around town at night. Townspeople recognized his authority as coming from both God and the king, but he did not bask in his position. Instead he spoke of God's hand being behind his efforts. The people responded to his vision with anticipation and solidarity: "Let us start building!" (Neh 2:18). He organized the people of Judah and centered them on the task of rebuilding the walls of Jerusalem. The project came to serve as a focal point for the devastated community. As the work progressed, their sense of pride, of community, and of heritage began to return.

Neighboring authorities opposed Nehemiah's revitalization of Jerusalem. Tobiah the Ammonite, Geshem the Arab, and most notably, Sanballat the Horonite openly questioned his motives, tried to get the Jews to turn against their leader, and wrote a deceitful letter to the king to interfere with the effort. However, Nehemiah resisted their subterfuge by relying on God and human ingenuity. He set up prayer vigils appealing for divine help and appointed guards to watch over the work on the walls. In the end, he was able to restore the walls in the remarkable time of 52 days.

Once the building project was complete, Nehemiah recruited people to live in Jerusalem and reestablish the city from within. Even though Jerusalem was the holy city, this was not an easy task. The leaders of the people dwelt at Jerusalem, but most others preferred to live in the countryside. Everyone cast lots to see who would dwell in the city. Ninety percent could remain in their respective hometowns, but ten percent, a tithe of the people, would relocate to the abandoned city. Those who were drafted, and some who volunteered to relocate, were commended and blessed or ordained for this redemptive calling.

While the actual rebuilding of the walls took only 52 days, the redevelopment of the systems and values that hold a city together took generations. Nehemiah worked to address the decayed social conditions of his people. He initiated economic reform to the impoverished region and led a movement to return to their cultural traditions. With Nehemiah's support, the priest Ezra led his people in worship, in Bible study, and in the renewal of their covenant vows as families and as a community.

After an absence from his governorship, Nehemiah returned to his rebuilt city in 432 B.C. only to find that some of his reforms had not lasted. The city had relapsed and lost some of its original vision and commitment to serving the needy and honoring God. He spent his remaining years in office cleansing the people and the temple from foreign influences.

The Book of Nehemiah ends his story with the prayer, "Remember me, O my God, for good" (13:31). Today Nehemiah is remembered for implementing a plan of prayer, study, community values, and social justice that effectively restored the city of Jerusalem and the faith of Judaism.

The walls of Jerusalem were rebuilt in 52 days under the direction of Nehemiah.

For further study, see the Book of Nehemiah.
3. 5 century B.C.; Ne 3:16; son of Azbuk; helped repair Jerusalem wall

NEHUM (NEE hum) *comfort;* 6 century B.C.; Ne 7:7; resettled in Judah after Exile; also called Rehum 1

NEHUSHTA (neh HUSH tuh) *brazen* or *bronze;* 7 century B.C.; 2Ki 24:8; wife of Jehoiakim; mother of Jehoiachin

NEKODA (neh KOH duh) *sheep owner*
1. Ezr 2:48; head of family of temple servants
2. Ezr 2:60; ancestor of exiles who could not prove Israelite descent

NEMUEL (NEM yoo uhl) meaning unknown
1. Nu 26:12; see Jemuel
2. 15 century B.C.; Nu 26:9; Reubenite; brother of Dathan and Abiram

NEPHEG (NEE feg) *sprout*
1. Ex 6:21; son of Izhar; brother of Korah the rebel
2. 10 century B.C.; 2Sa 5:15; son of David born in Jerusalem

NEPHILIM (NEF ihl ihm) Gen 6:4
The Old Testament twice mentions this group of giants in a way that separates them from the people of God, but their origin and relationship to humanity is unclear. For further study, see Nu 13:33; compare to Anakim and Rephaim.

NEPHISIM (NEF ih sim) meaning unknown; Ezr 2:50; ancestor of temple servants; also called Nephushesim

NEPHUSHESIM Ne 7:52; see Nephisim

NER (NUHR) *light* or *lamp*
1. 12 century B.C.; 1Ch 8:33; grandfather of King Saul
2. 12 century B.C.; 1Sa 14:50; father of Abner; kinsman of Saul; possibly Ner 1

NEREUS (NEER ee uhs) *a sea god;* 1 century A.D.; Ro 16:15; Roman Christian greeted by Paul

NERGAL (NUHR gahl) 2Ki 17:30; war god of pestilence, disease, and death; worshiped in Medo-Persia

NERGAL-SHAREZER (NUHR gahl shahr EE zuhr) *Nergal* [a god] *protect the king;* 7 century B.C.; Jer 39:3; Babylonian official

NERI (NEER eye) *my lamp* or *lamp of the Lord;* Lk 3:27; ancestor of Jesus

NERIAH (nuh RYE uh) *the Lord is a lamp;* 7 century B.C.; Jer 32:12; father of Baruch 1 and Seraiah 7

NERO (NEER oh) meaning unknown; ruled A.D. 54–68; Ac 25:8
Accounts of his personal debauchery, extravagance, and persecution of Christians have made Nero out to be a monster. Some even thought him to be the Antichrist. However, the early church thrived under much of his reign, and the apostle Paul appealed to this Caesar for personal justice.

Nero tended not to bother with affairs of state, leaving those matters to others while he focused on his personal indulgences. Early in his reign, he specifically declared that he would not act as a judge. Consequently, Paul may not have had his case of misconduct tried before the Emperor even though he was sent to Rome for that reason.

Nero held that Christian activists were responsible for the famous fire that destroyed much of Rome in A.D. 64 and so mounted a campaign of brutal persecution against the church. Although the circumstances of Paul's death are not certain, he likely perished during this purge.

For further study, see Ac 25:8-12; 26:30-32; Ro 13:1-7; Php 4:22.

NETHANEL (nuh THAN uhl) *gift of God*
1. 15 century B.C.; Nu 1:8; one who led tribe of Issachar during Exodus
2. 11 century B.C.; 1Ch 2:14; son of Jesse; brother of David
3. 11 century B.C.; 1Ch 15:24; priest and trumpeter before the ark upon its return
4. 11 century B.C.; 1Ch 24:6; Levite; father of Shemaiah 4 the scribe
5. 10 century B.C.; 1Ch 26:4; son of Obed-edom; temple gatekeeper
6. 9 century B.C.; 2Ch 17:7; official sent by Jehoshaphat to teach the Law
7. 7 century B.C.; 2Ch 35:9; chief Levite; provided offerings for Passover
8. 6 century B.C.; Ne 12:21; head of priestly family in days of high priest Joiakim
9. 5 century B.C.; Ezr 10:22; priest who married and divorced a foreigner after Exile
10. 5 century B.C.; Ne 12:36; Levite musician at Jerusalem wall dedication

NETHANIAH (NETH uh NIGH uh) *gift of the Lord*
1. 10 century B.C.; 1Ch 25:2; son of Asaph; temple singer
2. 9 century B.C.; 2Ch 17:8; Levite; instructed people in the Law
3. 7 century B.C.; Jer 36:14; father of Jehudai the official of Jehoiakim
4. 6 century B.C.; 2Ki 25:23; father of Ishmael the murderer of Gedaliah
5. 5 century B.C.; 1Esd 9:34; one who married and divorced foreigner after Exile

NETOPHATHITES (neh TOH fuh thights) 1Ch 2:54; people from Netophah in Judah; two of David's mighty men were Netophathites

NEZIAH (neh ZYE uh) meaning unknown; Ezr 2:54; ancestor of temple servants that returned to Judah

NIBHAZ (NIB haz) meaning unknown; 2Ki 17:31; local deity worshiped by the Avvites (Assyrians)

NICANOR (nih KAY nohr) *conqueror*
1. 2 century B.C.; 1Mac 3:38; Syrian general sent by King Demetrius I to stop the Maccabean revolt in Judea
2. 1 century A.D.; Ac 6:5; disciple chosen to distribute food to Jerusalem Christians

NICODEMUS (NIK uh DEE muhs) *victor over the people;* 1 century A.D.; Jn 3:1

Nicodemus the Pharisee held a position on the Sanhedrin, the Jewish high council and ruling body. As a Pharisee, Nicodemus depended heavily upon his lineage and boasted with the other Pharisees that he was a descendant of the faithful Abraham. When Nicodemus came to talk to Jesus in the middle of the night, it was ironic that Jesus told him he had to be born again to see the kingdom of God. Evidently, Nicodemus took what Jesus said to

Nicodemus comes to Jesus to be taught.

mean another physical birth by entering again into his mother's womb, which was preposterous. Jesus admonished the learned Nicodemus for not knowing what the kingdom of God was all about.

Nicodemus kept an open mind and heart toward Jesus. Once, when the Pharisees sought to bring Jesus in for questioning, he even spoke up for Jesus, saying, "Our law does not judge people without first giving them a hearing to find out what they are doing, does it?" (Jn 7:51).

After Jesus's death, Nicodemus became more bold in following him. Accompanying Joseph of Arimathea, Nicodemus brought about 75 pounds of spices to anoint Jesus's body after Joseph received permission from Pilate to take the body for burial. Nicodemus assisted with burial preparations by helping Joseph wrap Jesus's body with the spices and strips of linen, in accordance with Jewish custom. Nicodemus and Joseph then took Jesus's body to a nearby garden, where they laid him in Joseph's own unused tomb.

For further study, see Jn 3:2-9; 7:50-52; 19:38-42,59.

NICOLAITANS (nik oh LAY ih tuns) Rev 2:6; heretical sect condemned by Christ for immorality

NICOLAUS (NIK uh luhs) *conqueror of the people;* 1 century A.D.; Ac 6:5

Nicolaus and six others from Greece were chosen to meet the daily food needs of the Greek widows who had been neglected (perhaps in favor of the Jewish widows), due to the growth of the early church in Jerusalem. These seven were also trusted with handling the cross-cultural issues involved in this ministry. Nicolaus was a "proselyte of Antioch," meaning he had previously converted from a pagan background to Judaism before becoming a Christian. He is not likely responsible for or related to the Nicolaitans, whose heretical doctrine was condemned at Ephesus and Pergamum (Rev 2:6,15). For further study, see Ac 6:1-6.

NIGER (NIGH juhr) *black;* 1 century A.D.; Ac 13:1; teacher at Antioch church who was also called Simeon

NIMROD (NIM rahd) *we will revolt* or *he that rules;* Gen 10:8

From Ham came Cush, who begat Nimrod, "first on earth to become a mighty warrior" and "a mighty hunter before the Lord." The beginnings of the Sumerian, Babylonian, Akkadian, and Assyrian empires are traceable to Nimrod, the father of empires and imperialism. Some scholars suggest that Nimrod may be Sargon the Great, king of Akkad, who flourished around 2300 B.C. Despite its eclipse by later cultural groups, the Sumerian-Akkadian culture begun by Sargon left a rich legacy of advanced urban civilization. For further study, see Gen 10:8-12; Mic 5:6.

NIMSHI (NIM shy) *the Lord reveals;* 10 century B.C.; 1Ki 19:16; grandfather of King Jehu

NIPHISH (NIGH fish) meaning unknown; 1Esd 5:21; ancestor of exiles who returned with Zerubbabel

NISROCH (NIS rahk) *eagle* or *hawk;* 2Ki 19:37; Assyrian god in whose temple King Sennacherib was killed

NOADIAH (NOH uh DYE uh) *the Lord assembles*
1. 5 century B.C.; Ezr 8:33; Levite; weighed sacred articles in temple
2. 5 century B.C.; Ne 6:14; prophet who opposed Nehemiah

NOAH (NOH uh) *rest* or *comfort*
1. Ge 5:29

The son of Lamech and the grandson of Methuselah, Noah appears in the tenth generation after Adam in the genealogies of Genesis. Singled out by God to preserve life on earth when all others proved undeserving, he became the center of one of the most familiar stories found in the Bible.

Noah and his family lived in a world so violent and so wicked that God decided he would not allow humans to exist any longer. However, in the midst of this decadence, there was one man—Noah—who had faith in God and lived a righteous and blameless life. God revealed to Noah his plan to destroy not only corrupt humanity but the physical earth in its entirety by a deluge of water not yet known to humankind.

So righteous was Noah that God made a covenant with him, a promise of safety for him and his family, and a place of preservation for two of every animal on the earth. In preparation for the floodwaters, God gave Noah a 120-year project, telling him to build an ark of cypress wood coated with pitch inside and out. God gave him precise instructions and dimensions; it was to be 450 feet long, 75 feet wide, and 45 feet tall. Noah did everything just as God commanded.

The task of gathering every kind of animal together in one place was improbable, but God helped by delivering the animals to him. Noah put the animals into the huge seafaring zoo, and when he and his wife, sons, and daughters-in-law all safely entered the ark, God closed the door. Noah was a little over 600 years old when God released the floodwaters and caused underground springs to burst open. Noah made the ark his home, managing his family and overseeing the feeding and cleaning of the animals, while the rains fell for 40 days and 40 nights on the entire earth. After 150 days, the waters had receded enough to reveal the mountain tops, and Noah and his menagerie landed on the mountains of Ararat. After 40 days, Noah opened the only window in the ark and released a raven, which kept flying back. Noah then set free a dove from the window, but it also returned. Seven days later, Noah again sent out the dove, and finally

Noah and his family build the ark in preparation for the flood.

Noah sees the olive leaf as a sign that he, his family, and the animals can soon leave the ark.

it returned with an olive leaf in its mouth. Noah then knew that vegetation had begun to grow, and soon they would be able to leave the ark. Seven more days passed, and Noah again released the dove. Noah was assured that the earth was again habitable when the dove did not return.

After the water dried up on the earth, Noah removed the covering from the ark and saw the dry land. Almost two months later, God told Noah and his family to leave the ark and liberate the animals. Noah, still obedient and faithful to God, stepped out of the ark and built an altar, giving praise to God for his deliverance. Noah took some clean animals and birds and sacrificed a burnt offering to God. God then promised to never again curse the earth or completely destroy it with water. As a sign of his pledge, God put a rainbow in the sky and promised to remember his covenant every time the

colorful arc appeared. Along with God's covenant and blessing, Noah and his sons also received God's command to be fruitful and multiply. God gave them authority and responsibility over all the animals and birds, and he gave them all living creatures as food to eat.

After abandoning life on the ark, Noah began a new life on the earth, an earth that would again provide a place to live for all people and animals. Like Adam and Eve, Noah and his family were the only people on the entire earth. They became the new origin of all the peoples of the world.

Noah soon established a career as a farmer, working the soil and growing grapes in his vineyard. His attempt to make wine from his crop, however, proved hazardous. Laying drunk and naked inside his tent, Noah was disgraced when he was seen in this state by his son, Ham. Ham told his brothers, who then walked backward into the tent to avoid seeing their naked father and covered him up. Upon waking up and discovering what had happened, Noah cursed his son Ham to a lifetime of servitude to his brothers. At the same time, Noah blessed Shem and Japheth with a servant and additional land.

For further study, see Ge 5:28-32; 6:8–9:29; Mt 24:38,39; Heb 11:7; 1Pe 3:20; 2Pe 2:5.
2. 15 century B.C.; Nu 26:33; daughter of Zelophehad; received her father's inheritance

NOBAH (NOH buh) *barking;* 15 century B.C.; Nu 32:42; Manassite who captured Kenath

NODAB (NOH dab) *nobility;* 1Ch 5:19; ancestor of Arabian tribe; possibly Kedemah

NOEBA (noh EE bah) meaning unknown; 1Esd 5:31; ancestor of returning exiles

NOGAH (NOH guh) *splendor;* 10 century B.C.; 1Ch 3:7; son of David born in Jerusalem

NOHAH (NOH hah) *rest;* 19 century B.C.; 1Ch 8:2; son of Benjamin

NOOMA (nuh OH mah) meaning unknown; 5 century B.C.; 1Esd 9:35; one who married and divorced foreigner after Exile

NUMENIUS (noo MEN ee uhs) meaning unknown; 2 century B.C.; 1Mac 12:16; son of Antiochus; envoy to Rome

NUN (NUN) *fish;* 15 century B.C.; Ex 33:11; father of Joshua

NYMPHA (NIM fuh) *sacred to the nymphs;* 1 century A.D.; Col 4:15; wealthy person who housed a Christian church

OBADIAH (OH buh DYE uh) *servant of the Lord*
1. 1Ch 7:3; descendant of Issachar
2. 11 century B.C.; 1Ch 12:9; Gadite commander; joined David at Ziklag
3. 11 century B.C.; 1Ch 27:19; father of Ishmaiah 2
4. 9 century B.C.; 2Ch 17:7; official of Jehoshaphat; taught the Law
5. 9 century B.C.; 1Ki 18:3

When Jezebel, the wicked wife of King Ahab and promoter of Baal worship in Israel, began killing priests of the Hebrew God, Obadiah tried to defend them from this persecution. He risked his life by hiding 100 priests in caves to keep Jezebel from killing them. Obadiah also risked his life by conveying a message from the prophet Elijah to King Ahab, since Elijah had a price on his head and all who harbored him were to be killed as well. Acting in his capacity as palace governor, Obadiah set up a contest between Elijah and the prophets of Baal to demonstrate that the God of Israel was far more powerful than that of Jezebel. For further study, see 1Ki 18.
6. 1Ch 8:38; descendant of Saul through Jonathan
7. 7 century B.C.; 2Ch 34:12; Levite; supervised temple restoration
8. 6 century B.C.; Ne 12:25; chief gatekeeper in days of Joiakim

The prophet Obadiah.

9. 6 century B.C.; Ob 1:1

Virtually nothing is known about the author of the prophetic Book of Obadiah. Scholars disagree on when the book was written, offering dates that range from the eighth to the fourth century B.C., but it was most likely written shortly after the Babylonian attacks on Jerusalem (605–586 B.C.). The shortest book of the Old Testament, Obadiah directs harsh criticism at Israel's neighbor Edom for its actions during the Babylonian invasion. A long history of enmity existed between Edom and Israel; on several occasions the Hebrews ruled over the Edomites, taking advantage of Edom's rich trade routes and extensive copper resources. However, the fact that the Edomites gloated over the demise of their brother Jews in the hour of Jerusalem's greatest need and humiliation galled Obadiah, and he predicted that under God's judgment they would one day be conquered and all their allies would become enemies. Obadiah points out that the conflict between these two groups extends back to the bitter conflict over inheritance between Esau, founder of the Edomites, and his brother Jacob, founder of the Israelites. For further study, see the Book of Obadiah.

10. 1Ch 3:21; descendant of Zerubbabel
11. 1Ch 9:16; see Abda 2
12. 5 century B.C.; Ezr 8:9; head of family that returned to Judah
13. 5 century B.C.; Ne 10:5; priest; sealed covenant renewal

OBAL (OH buhl) *to be bare;* Gen 10:28; son of Joktan; source of Arabian tribe; also called Ebal 2

OBED (OH bed) *worshiper* or *servant*
1. 11 century B.C.; Ru 4:17; son of Ruth and Boaz; grandfather of David
2. 1Ch 2:37; descendant of Judah 1
3. 11 century B.C.; 1Ch 11:47; mighty man of David
4. 10 century B.C.; 1Ch 26:7; grandson of Obed-edom; temple gatekeeper
5. 9 century B.C.; 2Ch 23:1; his son Azariah helped overthrow Queen Athaliah

OBED-EDOM (OH bed EE duhm) *servant of Edom*
1. 11 century B.C.; 2Sa 6:10

Proximity to the sacred ark of the covenant brought with it tremendous privilege and liability.

The ark contained the tablets brought down by Moses from Mt. Sinai and symbolized God's presence and his pact with the Israelites. For some time the ark had been in the hands of Philistine enemies, but King David had won it back and was returning it to Jerusalem. While transporting it, Uzzah had died for touching the ark without proper reverence. Fearful of further ritual violations and their repercussions, David halted his efforts to transport the ark and left it in the care of a foreigner, Obed-edom, who had offered his house to store the ark. For taking this risk, God blessed his entire household. Obed-edom the Gittite was either one of David's bodyguards from Gath or a Levite from Gath Rimmon in Dan. For further study, see 2Sa 6:1-15; 1Ch 13:1-14; 15:18-25; 16:5,38; 26:4-8,15.
2. 11 century B.C.; 1Ch 15:18; son of Jeduthun; chief gatekeeper under David
3. 9 century B.C.; 2Ch 25:24; temple treasurer under King Amaziah of Judah

OBIL (OH bil) *camel driver;* 10 century B.C.; 1Ch 27:30; Ishmaelite overseer of King David's camels

OCHRAN (AHK ruhn) *trouble;* 15 century B.C.; Nu 1:13; father of Pagiel the tribal leader during the Exodus

ODED (OH ded) *restorer* or *counter*
1. 10 century B.C.; 2Ch 15:1; father of prophet Azariah
2. 8 century B.C.; 2Ch 28:9; prophet; opposed enslaving captives of Pekah

ODOMERA (OH duh MAIR uh) meaning unknown; 2 century B.C.; 1Mac 9:66; nomad defeated by Jonathan

OG (AHG) meaning unknown; 15 century B.C.; Nu 21:33; Amorite king; defeated by Israelites and Moses

OHAD (OH had) *strength;* 19 century B.C.; Gen 46:10; son of Simeon

OHEL (OH hel) *tent;* 6 century B.C.; 1Ch 3:20; son of Zerubbabel

OHOLAH (oh HOH luh) *tent;* Eze 23:4; sister of Oholibah; harlot symbolic of Samaria

OHOLIAB (oh HOHL lee ab) *father's tent;* 15 century B.C.; Ex 31:6; craftsman on tabernacle with Bezalel

OHOLIBAH (oh HOH lee bah) possibly *my tent is in her;* Eze 23:4; sister of Oholah; harlot symbolic of Jerusalem

OHOLIBAMAH (oh HOH lih BAH muh) *tent of the high place*
1. Gen 36:14; see Judith 1
2. Gen 36:41; Edomite chief; descendant of Esau

OLAMUS (OH lih muhs) meaning unknown; 5 century B.C.; 1Esd 9:30; son of Mani who returned from Exile

OLYMPAS (oh LIM puhs) meaning unknown; 1 century A.D.; Ro 16:15; Roman Christian greeted by Paul

OMAR (OH mahr) *speaker;* 19 century B.C.; Gen 36:11; son of Eliphaz; grandson of Esau

OMRI (AHM ree) possibly *to thrive* or *to live long*
1. 1Ch 7:8; descendant of Benjamin
2. 10 century B.C.; 1Ch 27:18; officer over tribe of Issachar in David's day
3. ruled 885–874 B.C.; 1Ki 16:16

Zimri had made himself king of Israel after assassinating Elah, but his reign, headquartered in Tirzah, was short-lived: only seven days. With his army backing him up, Omri deposed the usurper. Zimri committed suicide while Omri's army was besieging the city of Tirzah.

To consolidate his power and gain control of strategic trade routes, Omri made the city of Samaria the new capital of the northern kingdom of Israel. Ahab, Omri's son and successor, completed construction on this capital city, built to rival Jerusalem in the lasting beauty of its buildings. In due time, the whole area surrounding the prominent city became known as Samaria and its residents as Samaritans.

To hold on to power and heal years of internal strife in Samaria, Omri conquered Moab, made numerous concessions to Syria, and cemented ties with Phoenicia by marrying off Ahab to Jezebel,

daughter of the Phoenician king. However, this political marriage opened the door to the pagan worship of Baal so hotly contested by the Hebrew prophets Elijah and Elisha.

Many historical observers cite Omri as one of Israel's most effective leaders for bringing order and security to a divided nation. His influence was so great that for centuries after his death, neighboring nations referred to Israel as the house of Omri. In contrast, the few biblical verses that describe his reign label him as one of Israel's most wicked kings, primarily because he openly allowed idol worship. "He did more evil than all who were before him" (1Ki 16:25).

For further study, see 1Ki 16:15-29; 20:34; 2Ki 8:26; 2Ch 22:2; Mic 6:16.
4. 1Ch 9:4; his descendant Uthai resettled in Jerusalem

ON (AHN) *strength;* 15 century B.C.; Nu 16:1; Reubenite leader; joined Korah in rebellion against Moses

ONAM (OH nam) *vigorous*
1. 20 century B.C.; Gen 36:23; son of Shobal the Horite chief
2. 1Ch 2:26; descendant of Judah 1

ONAN (OH nan) *vigorous;* 19 century B.C.; Gen 38:4; son of Judah; killed for disobedience

ONESIMUS (oh NES ih muhs) *profitable* or *useful;* 1 century A.D.; Col 4:9

Rancher and landowner Philemon started, or at least hosted, a house church in the Lycus valley near Ephesus, a major urban hub and the strategic city for reaching "all Asia" with the Gospel. Philemon also had a household of slaves, one of whom was Onesimus. For unknown reasons, Onesimus stole money from his master and ran off, turning up some years later in Rome, where he met the apostle Paul.

Onesimus likely wanted to get lost in a Western city where he could start life over as a freedman, perhaps under a new guise or with false identity papers. Paul was living under house arrest at the time (A.D. 60–62), which meant he could still entertain visitors. Paul and his associates met Onesimus, evangelized him, and discipled him; soon Onesimus had a new identity in Christ. However, a runaway slave, if caught, had to be returned to his former master for restitution. By Roman law, the master could execute his runaway slave or sell him off into slavery again.

Following the law, Paul sent Onesimus back to the Lycus valley with a letter of endorsement. Onesimus hand-carried this letter 1,000 miles back to Asia, where the unsuspecting, and perhaps unforgiving, Philemon would be waiting. In that brief letter, Paul greeted the house church, prayed for its leaders, praised Philemon for his good works and loving character, and made an appeal for Onesimus. Paul referred to Onesimus as "my child" and said his conversion had created a use for the once useless slave, playing on the meaning of his name. He suggested Philemon take Onesimus back "no longer as a slave, but more than a slave, a beloved brother." Paul also said he would assume responsibility for any debt Onesimus owed and then pointed out that Philemon owed Paul his life for having converted him to Christianity.

Philemon now faced a dilemma: If word got out that all a slave had to do to become free was to steal money, run away, and adopt Christianity, there would soon be no more slaves to work the profitable farms in the valley. Yet as a Christian, Philemon felt bound by the arguments of Paul, his trusted friend and the one to whom he owed his life. Paul died a few years later in a Roman prison and never found out what Philemon decided or what happened to Onesimus.

The next written record of Onesimus is by Ignatius of Antioch, whose little-known letter of A.D. 110 survives among the later writings of the early church leaders. When arrested on false charges and marched off to Rome for trial and imminent execution, Ignatius spent the next nine consecutive nights writing letters to encourage the churches he had to leave behind. From Smyrna, he wrote a letter to the church at Ephesus, addressing its bishop (chief pastor) by name—Onesimus. Catholic and Protestant scholars concur that this is the same Onesimus that Paul helped to free, indicating a remarkable restoration of this runaway slave.

For further study, see the Letter of Paul to Philemon.

ONESIPHORUS (on uh SIF uh ruhs) *profit-bringer;* 1 century A.D.; 2Ti 1:16; aide to Paul during imprisonment

ONIAS (oh NIGH uhs) meaning unknown
1. 4 century B.C.; 1Mac 12:7; Onias I the high priest in Jerusalem
2. 2 century B.C.; 1Mac 12:7

Onias III, high priest in Judea during the reign of the Seleucid king Seleucus IV, came from a respected family with a priestly lineage documented all the way back to Solomon's time. He lived in an era of political confusion when the Seleucid and Ptolemaic empires vied for control of the Middle East. Onias supported Egypt, but his cousins betrayed their country to the Seleucids, even revealing secret locations of temple treasures. King Seleucus's minister, Heliodorus, searched for the treasure and was struck down in the temple by a vision. Only Onias's prayers saved him. Onias lost his position to his brother, Jason, who offered a bribe to the king. Later, Jason was replaced—also through bribery—by his servant

Ashurbanipal, who is thought to be the same as Osnappar, conquers an Elamite city. Stone bas-relief, palace of Nineveh, Iraq.

Menelaus. Menelaus stole sacred temple treasures and had Onias killed for protesting the sacrilege. For further study, see 1Mac 12; 2Mac 3,4; 4Mac 4:1-16.

OPHIR (OH fuhr) *rich* or *fat;* Gen 10:29; son of Joktan; descendant of Shem

OPHRAH (AHF ruh) *fawn;* 14 century B.C.; 1Ch 4:14; grandson of Othniel

OREB (OHR eb) *raven;* 12 century B.C.; Jdg 7:25; Midianite leader killed by Gideon's forces

OREN (OHR en) *fir tree;* 1Ch 2:25; descendant of Jerahmeel and Judah

ORNAN 1Ch 21:15; see Araunah

ORPAH (OHR puh) possibly *neck;* 12 century B.C.; Ru 1:4; Moabite wife of Kilion; daughter-in-law of Naomi

OSNAPPAR (os NAP uhr) meaning unknown; ruled 668–627 B.C.; Ezr 4:10

Osnappar sent a letter to King Artaxerxes of Persia urging him to stop the Jews from rebuilding the walls of Jerusalem, but the rebuilding project progressed unhindered. Osnappar is usually identified with Ashurbanipal, who is known from extra-biblical sources as the son who succeeded Esar-haddon to the throne of Assyria in 668 B.C. Hence, the otherwise unknown Osnappar could be one of last great kings of Assyria. Ashurbanipal captured Thebes in Egypt (663 B.C.) and frequently raided such groups as the Syrians, Phoenicians, and Arabs. On one such raid in 641 B.C., Ashurbanipal sacked Elam and deported its natives to Samaria, an act the Bible attributes to Osnappar.

OTHNI (AHTH nih) meaning unknown; 10 century B.C.; 1Ch 26:7; son of Shemaiah; temple gatekeeper

OTHNIEL (AHTH nee uhl) possibly *God is might* or *lion of God;* 14 century B.C.; Jos 15:17

Othniel was the first to conquer and occupy the city of Kiriath-sepher, or Debir, which then was awarded to him as his share in the Promised Land. For his military success, he also won Caleb's daughter Achsah as his wife. With Achsah, Othniel became an ancestor of an officer in King David's cab-

The judge Othniel. Stained glass. Lincoln Cathedral, Lincoln, England.

inet. While family ties to Caleb proved fortuitous for the courageous Othniel, he is best known as the first of four judges or deliverers of Israel, whom the "Spirit of the Lord came upon" in a special way to deliver God's people. Othniel served as peacemaker for 40 years after overthrowing the oppressive Cushan-rishathaim, king of Mesopotamia. For further study, see Jos 15:16-17; Jdg 1:13; 3:7-11.

OTHNIAH (oth NIGH ah) meaning unknown; 5 century B.C.; 1Esd 9:28; one who married and divorced foreigner after Exile

OX (AHKS) meaning unknown; 6 century B.C.; Jdt 8:1; grandfather of Judith 2

OZEM (OH zuhm) meaning unknown
1. 1Ch 2:25; son of Jerahmeel; descendant of Judah 1
2. 11 century B.C.; 1Ch 2:15; son of Jesse; older brother of David

OZIEL (AHZ ih el) meaning unknown; Jdt 8:1; ancestor of Judith 2

OZNI Nu 26:16; see Ezbon 1

PAARAI 2Sa 23:35; see Naarai

PADON (PAY dahn) *redemption;* Ezr 2:44; ancestor of temple servants who returned to Judah

PAGIEL (PAY gee uhl) possibly *alloted by God* or *fortune of God;* 15 century B.C.; Nu 1:13; leader of the tribe of Asher during Exodus

PAHATH-MOAB (PAY hath MOH ab) *ruler of Moab*
1. Ezr 2:6; ancestor of family that returned to Judah
2. 5 century B.C.; Ne 10:14; leader who sealed covenant renewal

PALAL (PAY lal) *judge;* 5 century B.C.; Ne 3:25; rebuilder of Jerusalem wall

PALLU (PAL oo) *famous* or *conspicuous;* Gen 46:9; son of Reuben; grandson of Jacob

PALTI (PAL tih) *the Lord delivers* or *my deliverance*
1. 15 century B.C.; Nu 13:9; Benjaminite leader who explored Canaan
2. 11 century B.C.; 1Sa 25:44; Benjaminite to whom Saul gave David's wife Michal; also called Paltiel 2

PALTIEL (PAL tee uhl) *God delivers* or *God is my deliverance*
1. 15 century B.C.; Nu 34:26; leader from tribe of Issachar; helped divide Canaan
2. 2Sa 3:15; see Palti 2

PARMASHTA (pahr MASH tuh) *stronger;* 5 century B.C.; Est 9:9; one of Haman's ten sons slain by Jews

PARMENAS (PAHR muh nuhs) *steadfast;* 1 century A.D.; Ac 6:5; disciple charged with distributing food to the poor in the Jerusalem church

PARNACH (PAHR nak) meaning unknown; 15 century B.C.; Nu 34:25; father of Elizaphan 2

PAROSH (PAIR ahsh) *flea*
1. Ezr 2:3; head of family that returned to Jerusalem
2. 5 century B.C.; Ne 10:14; leader who sealed covenant renewal

PARSHANDATHA (pahr shan DAY thuh) possibly *made for battle;* 5 century B.C.; Est 9:7; one of Haman's ten sons killed by Jews

PARTHIANS (PAHR thi uhns) Ac 2:9; residents of Parthia, southeast of the Caspian Sea in Persia (modern Iran)

PARUAH (puh ROO uh) *blooming;* 10 century B.C.; 1Ki 4:17; father of Jehoshaphat the governor under Solomon

PASACH (PAY sak) meaning unknown; 1Ch 7:33; descendant of Asher

PASEAH (puh SEE uh) *limping*
1. 1Ch 4:12; descendant of Judah 1
2. Ezr 2:49; head of temple servant clan that returned to Judah
3. 5 century B.C.; Ne 3:6; father of Joiada 1 the rebuilder of the Jerusalem wall

PASHHUR (PASH hur) *destruction all around*
1. Ezr 2:38; head of priestly family that returned to Judah
2. 6 century B.C.; Jer 38:1; father of Gedaliah 3
3. 6 century B.C.; Jer 20:1
The son of Immer the priest, Pashhur was the chief officer in the temple, second in authority only to the high priest. It was his responsibility to keep order in the temple, and he did so severely. In response to Jeremiah's harsh criticisms and predictions of God's wrath bringing doom on Israel, Pashhur had the great prophet beaten and put in

stocks for a day. After Jeremiah's release, he continued to foretell the destruction of Jerusalem, and he specifically named Pashhur as one who would suffer in exile. For further study, see Jer 20:1-6.
4. 7 century B.C.; Jer 21:1; official of Zedekiah; helped throw Jeremiah in cistern; possibly Pashhur 2 or 3
5. 1Ch 9:12; ancestor of Adaiah the priest who resettled in Jerusalem
6. 5 century B.C.; Ne 10:3; priest; sealed covenant renewal

PATHRUSIM (puh THROO sim) *southerners;* Gen 10:14; son(s) of Egypt; people of Pathros in Upper Egypt

PATROBAS (PAT ruh buhs) *paternal;* 1 century A.D.; Ro 16:14; Roman Christian greeted by Paul

PATROCLUS (PAT ruh klus) meaning unknown; 3 century B.C.; 2Mac 8:9; father of Nicanor

PAUL (PAWL) *little;* 1 century A.D.; Ac 7:58
As Stephen, the first Christian martyr, was being stoned for his faith, Paul (also called Saul) watched in approval. That day sparked a great persecution against the church, scattering Christians in Jerusalem throughout Judea and Samaria in fear. At the head of this persecution was Paul, a Jew educated in Greek culture and born a Roman citizen. He made it his mission to destroy the church, going from house to house and dragging Christian men and women to prison. Ironically, he would later become the apostle who did more to spread the Christian religion than anyone up to that point; he became a leader in establishing a worldwide church within 40 years of Jesus's death, and by

example he showed Christians how to face persecution with courage and faith.

After Stephen's death, Paul threatened Christians with arrest and death for quite some time. He sought and received authority from the high priest to travel to Damascus and arrest Christians there. On his way to Damascus, however, he was surrounded by a bright light, which blinded him and knocked him to the ground. He heard a voice saying, "Saul, Saul, why do you persecute me? I am Jesus, whom you are persecuting" (Ac 9:4-5). Jesus then told him to go into the city where he would be told what to do. The sightless Paul was led by his companions into Damascus, where a disciple named Ananias restored his sight by causing huge scales to fall from his eyes. After spending several

The Conversion of St. Paul. Michelangelo (1475–1564).

days with Jesus's disciples there, Paul embraced the faith of the Christians he had been victimizing, and he began preaching about Jesus, astonishing his listeners with his sudden transformation from persecutor to preacher.

After many days of powerful preaching in Damascus, the tables were turned and the Jews sought to kill him. Paul escaped by being lowered over the city walls in a basket and fleeing to Jerusalem, where he stayed with Peter for 15 days. Paul had a suspicious reception from the other disciples until Barnabas interceded for him, relating the details of his conversion. Paul passionately spoke and debated with the Grecian Jews in Jerusalem until they also tried to kill him. After he was taken to Caesarea and put on a ship to Tarsus for his safety, the church had a period of peace and grew stronger and larger.

Paul traveled extensively, preaching and establishing churches. His activities are recorded in the Acts of the Apostles, and his letters to the churches he established tell how his desire to preach was not thwarted by the physical, emotional, or spiritual resistance he received on his journeys. He wrote to the Corinthian church of the afflictions, hardships, and calamities he had endured. He mentioned beatings, imprisonments, riots, labors, sleepless nights, and hunger as some of the circumstances he and his companions had suffered through for their faith.

Paul's ambitious mission began at the church of Antioch where Paul and Barnabas were first commissioned. From Antioch, Paul set off on his first missionary journey, just as enthusiastic for the cause of Christ as he had previously been zealous for the destruction of those who believed in Christ. Paul and Barnabas traveled to Seleucia and on to Salamis on the island of Cyprus, and to Paphos, the seat of the Roman proconsul Sergius Paulus. One of the proconsul's servants was a magician named Elymas Bar-Jesus, who tried to prevent Paul from preaching the Christian message to his master. But Paul ruthlessly exposed him as a charlatan, and the proconsul accepted Paul's message about Jesus. From there, Paul went to Perga, Pisidia, Iconium, and Lystra, where he healed a cripple, causing the crowd to declare Paul and Barnabas gods. They went on to Derbe and then arrived back at Antioch. The churches they visited were those of the ancient Roman province of Galatia.

Fourteen years after Paul had fled for his life from Jerusalem, he returned with Barnabas and Titus to a conference of Jewish leaders. It was decided at this Jerusalem Council that Peter, James, and John would preach to the Jews, and Paul and Barnabas would go to the Gentiles.

When it came time for Paul to travel again, he and Barnabas disagreed over whether John Mark should go with them. Paul and Barnabas parted ways, Barnabas traveling with John Mark, and Paul accompanied by Silas. Paul next went west to Troas by the sea where he crossed to Neapolis, then to Philippi, Apollonia, Thessalonica, Berea, Athens, Corinth, Ephesus, Caesarea, Jerusalem, and back to Antioch.

On Paul's third missionary journey, he revisited the places of the first and second journeys, strengthening the churches he had established. He went from Ephesus to Tyre and Caesarea, and finally to Jerusalem, where he was received warmly by the Christians. However, a large group of Jews were belligerent toward him, not only because they thought he had brought a Gentile into the temple, but because they believed he was teaching Jews to turn away from Moses and the sacred rite of circumcision. In an effort to convince the people that these reports were not true and that he was living in obedience to the Law, Paul purified himself and went to the temple to make an offering.

When a group of Jews recognized him in the temple, they stirred up a huge crowd and eventually the whole city turned against him. After an

> ⟩ ⟨
>
> *"But the Lord said to him, '...he is an instrument whom I have chosen to bring my name before Gentiles and kings and before the people of Israel.'"*
>
> Ac 9:15

angry mob dragged him from the temple and attempted to kill him, news reached the commander of the Roman troops that there was a riot in the city. When the troops arrived, the crowd stopped beating Paul. He was subsequently arrested and chained by the Romans, who had to carry him away from the mob. Because of Paul's Roman citizenship, the commander of the army granted him permission to speak to the irate crowd, who listened to his story until he told how God had sent him to preach to the Gentiles. At that point, the mob shouted for his death as they threw their clothes and dirt at him. The commander ordered him whipped and questioned, but Paul's proof of Roman citizenship terminated any further actions by the troops, since it was illegal to flog a Roman citizen who had not been found guilty.

Paul's preaching in Ephesus prompted some sorcerers to burn their books of magic and accept Christianity.

Paul was turned over to the highest Jewish tribunal of that day, the Sanhedrin, made up of Pharisees and Saduccees. When Paul spoke before this ruling body, the chief priest Ananias ordered those standing nearby to strike him on the mouth. Typical of his forward personality, Paul replied, "God will strike you, you white-washed wall!" (Ac 23:3). The dispute over Paul became so violent that the Roman troops had to rescue him and bring him to the barracks.

While the Jews were forming a conspiracy to kill him, the Romans secretly removed Paul from Jerusalem, taking him to Caesarea, where Governor Felix imprisoned him for two years. When Festus took over as governor, Felix decided to leave Paul in prison as a favor to the Jews. The conspirators tried to convince Festus to take Paul to Jerusalem, but Festus insisted that Paul be tried in Caesarea. Since King Agrippa had stopped by to pay his respects to the governor, Festus involved the king in the dispute over Paul. After hearing Paul's story, the king announced he could find nothing in Paul that deserved death or imprisonment.

Paul was handed over to a centurion named Julius who protected him and traveled with him and several others by ship to Italy, where they arrived safely, in spite of a shipwreck from a huge storm at sea and a three-month delay at the island of Malta. In Rome, Paul was allowed to live by himself except for a soldier who guarded him. He stayed there two years and boldly preached about the kingdom of God to everyone who came to see him, as well as to people in other provinces through letters he sent by emissaries.

During Paul's imprisonments, he wrote to the Philippians, Ephesians, Colossians, and Philemon. History records a letter from Clement of Rome to the Corinthians, written about A.D. 96, which is an epitaph to Paul, commending his exemplary life and his "notable pattern of patient endurance." The Bible does not record Paul's death, but in his last message to Timothy just prior to the traditional date of his death, Paul indicates that his end is near. The fourth-century church historian Eusebius records that Paul was taken to Rome and beheaded in Nero's persecution in A.D. 67.

For further study, see the Acts of the Apostles, Romans, 1 Corinthians, 2 Corinthians, Galatians, Ephesians, Philippians, Colossians, 1 Thessalonians, 2 Thessalonians, 1 Timothy, 2 Timothy, Titus, and Philemon.

PEDAHEL (PED uh hel) *God has redeemed;* 15 century B.C.; Nu 34:28; Naphtali tribal leader; inherited land

PEDAHZUR (ped DAH zuhr) *the rock has redeemed;* 15 century B.C.; Nu 1:10; father of Gamaliel the leader of the Manassites

PEDAIAH (puh DAY yuh) *the Lord has redeemed*
1. 11 century B.C.; 1Ch 27:20; father of Joel the officer over the Manassites in David's day
2. 7 century B.C.; 2Ki 23:36; father of Zebidah the mother of Jehoiakim
3. 6 century B.C.; 1Ch 3:18; third son of Jehoiachin; adoptive father of Zerubbabel; see Shealtiel
4. Ne 11:7; his descendant Sallu resettled in Jerusalem
5. 5 century B.C.; Ne 3:25; rebuilder of the Jerusalem wall
6. 5 century B.C.; Ne 8:4; one who stood on Ezra's left at the reading of the Law
7. 5 century B.C.; Ne 13:13; manager of food storerooms in Jerusalem; possibly Pedaiah 5 or 6

PEKAH (PEE kuh) *he opens* or *he sees;* ruled 740–732 B.C.; 2Ki 15:25

King Pekah of Israel came to power by assassinating King Pekahiah but was assassinated himself in office by Hoshea. His reign continued the idolatrous ways of King Jeroboam and brought war and suffering to his people. Pekah and King Rezin of Syria unsuccessfully tried to coerce Judah's kings, Jotham and later Ahaz, to join them in a revolt against their Assyrian oppressors. Pekah and Rezin went into battle alone, dividing and conquering many cities in their fight for independence from Assyria. In the end, the Assyrian king Tiglath-pileser III proved too much for them; Pekah was left with a defeated and depleted nation. For further study, see 2Ki 15:25–16:5; 2Ch 28:5-15.

PEKAHIAH (PEH kuh HIGH uh) *the Lord opens* [the eyes]; ruled 742–740 B.C.; 2Ki 15:22; son and successor of King Menahem of Israel

PELAIAH (puh LAY yuh) *the Lord is marvelous*
1. 5 century B.C.; Ne 8:7; Levite interpreter of the Law
2. 5 century B.C.; Ne 10:10; Levite; sealed covenant renewal; possibly Pelaiah 1
3. descendant of Zerubbabel

PELALIAH (PEL uh LYE uh) *the Lord judges;* Ne 11:12; ancestor of priest who resettled in Jerusalem

PELATIAH (PEL uh TYE uh) *the Lord delivers*
1. 8 century B.C.; 1Ch 4:42; led Simeonites who destroyed Amalekites in Seir
2. 7 century B.C.; Eze 11:1; leader in Jerusalem whose death was prophesied by Ezekiel
3. 1Ch 3:21; descendant of Zerubbabel
4. 5 century B.C.; Ne 10:22; Jewish leader; sealed covenant renewal with God

PELEG (PEE leg) *division* or *channel;* Gen 10:25; descendant of Shem; ancestor of Abraham

PELET (PEE let) *deliverance*
1. 1Ch 2:47; Judahite; descendant of Caleb
2. 11 century B.C.; 1Ch 12:3; Benjaminite who joined David

PELETH (PEE leth) *swiftness*
1. 15 century B.C.; Nu 16:1; father of On the Reubenite leader who rebelled against Moses
2. 1Ch 2:33; descendant of Judah 1

PELETHITES (PEE leth ights) 2Sa 8:18; select company of David's bodyguards

PENINNAH (peh NIN uh) possibly *coral;* 12 century B.C.; 1Sa 1:2; fertile wife of Elkanah

PENUEL (peh NOO uhl) *face of God*
1. 1Ch 4:4; descendant of Judah 1
2. 1Ch 8:25; descendant of Benjamin

PERESH (PEER esh) meaning unknown; 1Ch 7:16; descendant of Manasseh

PEREZ (PEER ez) *bursting forth;* 19 century B.C.; Gen 38:29; twin born to Judah and Tamar

PERIDA (puh RYE duh) *divided;* Ne 7:57; servant of Solomon; descendants returned to Judah; a form of Peruda

PERIZZITES (PAIR uh zights) Gen 13:7

The Perizzites of Canaan were encountered by Abraham and conquered by Joshua, but they seduced Israel into idolatry. Later, they became subservient to Solomon. For further study, see Gen 15:20; 34:30; Ex 3:8, 17; Jos 3:10; 11:3-12; 12:8; 17:15; 24:11; Jdg 1:4-5; 3:5-6.

PERSEUS (PUHR see uhs) meaning unknown; 2 century B.C.; 1Mac 8:5; last king of Macedonia

Jesus washes Peter's feet in a symbolic act of humility.

PERSIANS (PUHR zyuhns) Ezr 4:9

Persia (modern Iran) appears in the biblical record at the height of its power in the ancient world. Succeeding the Babylonian kingdom in the mid-sixth century B.C., the Persian Empire was the major political force in the Middle East until it fell before Alexander the Great in 331 B.C. Many Persian kings—including Cyrus, Darius, and Artaxerxes—played a role in the history of the Israelites, returning them to their homeland to end the Babylon Exile and giving them religious autonomy. For further study, see the Book of Ezra; the Book of Nehemiah; Est 1; Da 6; 10; the First Book of Esdras.

PERSIS (PUHR sis) *persian woman;* 1 century A.D.; Ro 16:12; Christian woman in Rome greeted by Paul

PERUDA Ezr 2:55; see Perida

PETER (PEE tuhr) *rock;* 1 century A.D.; Mt 4:18

Peter, also called Simon, was a fisherman who became one of Jesus's first disciples. At times he exhibited unwavering faith, yet at other times his faith was greatly shaken in the face of adversity. He made bold confessions of commitment to Jesus, but at one point denied ever knowing Jesus.

Peter first lived in Bethsaida but later resided in Capernaum, where his brother Andrew personally introduced him to Jesus. Andrew eagerly told Peter that he had found the Messiah. Upon meeting Peter, Jesus called him by name (Simon) and then changed his name to Peter. Little did Peter know that one day he would confess that Jesus was the Son of the living God, and Jesus would call him the foundation of the church and the recipient of the keys to the kingdom of heaven.

Following these first events with Jesus, Peter was evidently with him constantly, observing his ministry firsthand. Though Peter saw his own mother-in-law healed by Jesus, it was as one of the inner circle of disciples closest to Jesus (along with James and John) that he really experienced the heart of Jesus's ministry. These three were the only ones invited to go with Jesus to the house of Jairus to see Jesus raise his daughter from the dead amidst the crying and wailing of the mourning family. These three men were the only ones taken up on a high mountain with Jesus to witness his transfiguration, where his face shone like the sun and his clothes became dazzling white. They witnessed the appearance of Moses and Elijah and heard them talk to Jesus. It was the zealous Peter who offered to build three houses on the mountain—one for Jesus, one for Moses, and one for Elijah.

These same three disciples were also with Jesus at the place of his greatest sorrow—Gethsemane. Peter, along with James and John, fell asleep while Jesus prayed and grieved over his impending death. This prompted Jesus to admonish Peter and the others for forsaking their Master at his hour of greatest need.

> → ←
>
> *"And Jesus answered him '... And I tell you, you are Peter* [Petros]*, and on this rock* [petra] *I will build my church, and the gates of Hades will not prevail against it.'"*
>
> Mt 16:17-18

Besides his weak moment in the garden of Gethsemane, Peter also had his times of untimely bluntness. After Jesus explained his own impending death, Peter reprimanded him by saying, "This must never happen to you!" Just as strong as Peter's reprimand was Jesus's rebuke of Peter: "Get behind me, Satan! You are a stumbling block to me." Another display of Peter's boldness was his fearless attempt to walk on water to meet Jesus. When his faith turned to apprehension over the storm, Peter began to sink and cried out for help. Jesus caught him before he sank and chided him for doubting. When Jesus washed the disciples' feet in an act of humility and servanthood, Peter again exhibited a zeal that overpowered his wisdom when he humbly refused to let Jesus wash his feet. Jesus answered, "Unless I wash you, you have no share with me." Peter immediately offered not just his feet, but his hands and his head as well.

Even though Peter steadfastly declared that he would lay down his life for Jesus, he ended up denying his association with Jesus completely. On the night of Jesus's arrest, Peter displayed his skill and bravery with his sword by cutting off the right ear of the high priest's servant. But then he followed this heroic act with a show of cowardice in the courtyard of Caiaphas when he denied three times that he was one of Jesus's disciples. Following his third denial, a rooster crowed, fulfilling Jesus's prediction at the Last Supper that Peter would deny him three times before the cock crowed.

Peter's failures, however, did not overshadow his faith or his passion. After receiving news that Jesus had risen from death, Peter ran to the tomb to see for himself. When Peter entered the place where Jesus had been buried and saw the linen burial wrappings, he immediately believed that Jesus had indeed risen from the dead.

Peter was among the other disciples when Jesus later appeared to show them his wounded hands and side and to perform many miracles. His next encounter with Jesus was at the Sea of Galilee as Peter and his friends returned from a fruitless day of fishing. Jesus addressed a great crowd of people gathered on the shore. When he finished speaking, Jesus told Peter to put his net into the deep water on the right side of the boat. Though he was skeptical, Peter did what Jesus instructed and found himself hauling in more fish than he and his co-workers could handle. One of the other disciples cried out, "It is the Lord!" Peter needed no further instruction. Leaving the others to bring in the huge haul of fish by themselves, Peter rewrapped himself in his outer garment, impetuously jumped overboard, and swam ashore to be the first to personally greet his Master.

Once on shore, the disciples were invited to a breakfast of fish and bread cooked on an open fire. Following this private early morning meal, Jesus asked Peter three times if he loved him, and three times Peter answered, "You know that I love you."

A rooster crows in the courtyard of Caiaphas as Peter denies he is one of Jesus's disciples.

Jesus gave Peter a commission to "feed my sheep," thus beginning Peter's position as the founder of the universal church.

After receiving the Holy Spirit on Pentecost, the disciples began preaching in a variety of foreign tongues, which drew the attention of large crowds. Some were amazed by the disciples' display, but others questioned it, attributing it to drunkenness. Spurred by these accusations, Peter stood up and addressed the crowd in a loud voice, explaining what led to the events of Pentecost and telling them to repent. His sermon was responsible for the conversion of about 3000 people that day.

After Pentecost, Peter healed a lame beggar who was being carried to the temple gate where he was taken every day to beg. Many people in the temple crowded around Peter and John, amazed by the miracle they had performed. Peter preached to these people in Jesus's name until the Sadducees became so disturbed that they seized Peter and John and put them in jail. The Jewish rulers on the high council, though baffled at their courage and knowledge, commanded Peter and John not to speak or teach in the name of Jesus. The disciples refused, and the council finally released them out of sheer frustration. Peter and John's prayer after their release was not lacking in majesty or grandeur. They raised their voices together in prayer to God for his mighty deeds and in supplication for the ability to speak God's word more boldly. After they prayed, their meeting place was shaken, they were filled with the Holy Spirit, and they spoke the word of God fearlessly.

More and more people believed their message, and the healing ministry of Peter (as well as the other disciples) flourished. However, persecution also flourished, as Jewish leaders were filled with jealousy. Arrest, trial, jail, escape, and a refusal to quit preaching prompted Peter to declare, "We must obey God rather than any human authority." The rulers wanted to kill Peter and the other defiant apostles, but Gamaliel, a teacher of the Law, intervened on their behalf. He reasoned that if their activities were of human origin, they would eventually fail. Peter continued preaching even though the church

was persecuted and scattered and some followers of Jesus were martyred.

While praying in the town of Joppa, Peter experienced a vision that would eventually take the church in a new direction. He saw a huge linen sheet descend from the sky, holding within it a variety of animals considered to be unclean and uneatable under Jewish Law. A voice instructed Peter to kill and eat the animals, telling him "What God has cleansed, you must not call common." Peter was also told in the vision that he should accompany a group of men who had come to see him. The men brought him to the house of a Gentile soldier who wished to hear Peter preach. Peter realized then that the vision was an instruction to him to open the church to non-Jews. Although this policy would cause great controversy among Jewish believers, Peter, among others, fought and won the battle to accept Gentiles into the church.

Peter was later arrested and imprisoned by King Herod, but he escaped with the assistance of fervent prayer and an angel sent by God. Herod's anger over the jailbreak precipitated the execution of the prison guards. After reporting to the believers who were praying for him at the house of Mary, Peter left and went to another place. His activities thereafter are not recorded in Scripture, but Paul mentions that some years later, he went to Jerusalem for a two-week visit with Peter for Paul's own edification. Eleven years later, Paul confronted Peter at the first all-church council at Antioch over

Peter impulsively jumps into the Sea of Galilee to swim ashore to greet Jesus.

the issue of whether Gentiles had to first become Jews (be circumcised) in order to become Christians.

Although the details of Peter's activities late in life are uncertain, he is credited with the authorship of two biblical epistles. The First Letter of Peter encourages Christians to persevere in their faith in the face of suffering and persecution, while the Second Letter primarily expresses concern and warnings regarding the dangers of false teachers and division within the church. While no sources document Peter's death, church tradition holds that he suffered martyrdom at the hands of the Roman Emperor Nero sometime in the middle of the first century A.D.

For further study, see Mt 16–17, 26; Mk 8–9, 14; Lk 9, 22; Jn 13:31-38; 18:15-27; 21:15-23; Ac 1–5; 9–12; 15; First Letter of Peter; Second Letter of Peter. Also called Cephas, Simon.

PETHAHIAH (PETH uh HIGH uh) *the Lord opens up*
1. 10 century B.C.; 1Ch 24:16; head of priestly division appointed by David
2. 5 century B.C.; Ezr 10:23; Levite who married and divorced foreigner after Exile
3. 5 century B.C.; Ne 9:5; Levite; led public confession and renewal; possibly Pethahiah 2
4. 5 century B.C.; Ne 11:24; Judahite; agent of King Artaxerxes

PETHUEL (puh THOO uhl) meaning unknown; Joel 1:1; father of Joel the prophet

PEULLETHAI (pee UHL uh thigh) possibly *reward* or *work of the Lord;* 10 century B.C.; 1Ch 26:5; son of Obed-edom; gatekeeper under David

PHALTIEL (FAL tih el) meaning unknown; 5 century B.C.; 2Esd 5:16; leader who came to Ezra after Ezra's vision

PHANUEL (fuh NOO uhl) *face of God;* 1 century B.C.; Lk 2:36; Asherite; father of Anna the prophet

PHARADATHA (fair uh DATH uh) meaning unknown; AddEst 9:8; son of Haman

PHARAKIM (FAIR uh kim) meaning unknown; 1Esd 9:8; ancestor of returning temple servants

PHARAOH (FAYR oh) *great house;* Gen 12:15
The Egyptian pharaoh was considered a god among men and a man among the gods, performing a priestly and monarchical role. The pharaoh's renowned temples, statues, and pyramid tombs attest to the religious link between his ancestors (all dead kings) and their gods, who worked together for the welfare of Egyptians. The link between various pharaohs was not necessarily by bloodline but by religious tradition.

The unnamed pharaohs of Abraham's day, of Joseph's day, and of Moses's lifetime cannot be identified with certainty, as the dates involved are conjectural. Some have suggested that the pharaoh from Joseph's time dates from the Hyksos period of Egyptian history (about 1700–1550 B.C.). The Hyksos took over the political machinery from the pharaohs proper, likely after a coup, without interfering with Egyptian culture, and ruled in a manner much more benevolent to outsiders than the common image of the oppressive pharaohs of Moses's day. During the Hyksos dynasty, many Semites ruled as viziers. Joseph could have fit that tradition. The Hyksos were Semitic-Asiatics who served in various capacities: administrators, chancellors, vassals, and even legitimate kings.

Five pharaohs or Egyptian kings are named in Scripture: Shishak (950–929 B.C., see 1Ki 11:40; 14:25-26; 2Ch 12:2-9); So (about 725 B.C., see 2Ki 17:4); Tirhakah (690 B.C., see 2Ki 19:9; Isa 37:9); Neco (610–595 B.C., see 2Ki 23:28-35; 2Ch 35: 20-22; 36:4; Jer 46:2); and Hophra (589–570 B.C., see Jer 44:30).

For further study, see Gen 12; 39–50; Ex 1–14; Isa 19; 30; Eze 29–32; Ac 7.

PHARES (FAIR eez) meaning unknown; 5 century B.C.; 1Esd 5:5; descendant of David

PHARISEES (FAYR uh sees) *separated ones;* Mt 3:7
The Pharisees were scribes and lawyers known for their fanatical devotion to the Law, especially the traditions about tithing and ritual purity. Such legalisms made it difficult for them to accept the teachings of Jesus. Nicodemus and Paul were two notable Pharisees who did convert to Christ; Gamaliel was one who remained open-minded about the Christian movement but was not documented as a convert. Pharisees fought with Jesus, who pictured their hypocrisy in his parables, and

with Sadducees, a more liberal party. Other comparable political parties in Jewish society at the time were the Herodians, who were loyal to Rome; the Zealots, who were revolutionaries against Rome; and the Essenes, who were detached purists and celibates. For further study, see Mt 23; Mk 2; 7:1-23; Lk 7:36-50; 11:37-54; 18:9-14; Jn 3:1; 7:45-52; Ac 23:6-10; Php 3:5.

PHASIRON (fuh SIGH ruhn) meaning unknown; 1Mac 9:66; his descendants were killed by Jonathan Maccabeus

PHICOL (FYE kahl) possibly *strong* or *mouth of all;* 21 century B.C.; Gen 21:22; Philistine commander in days of Abraham

PHILEMON (fy LEE muhn) *friendship;* 1 century A.D.; Phm 1:1

Philemon was a house church leader in the Lycus valley near Ephesus, where he owned profitable land and slaves. One of his slaves, Onesimus, stole money from him and fled to Rome, where he met the apostle Paul and was converted to Christianity. A runaway slave, if caught, had to be returned to his former master, and could be returned to slavery or killed as the master chose. Those who sheltered runaway slaves could also be held financially liable. Assuming Philemon would be unforgiving toward his runaway slave, perhaps even to Paul, the apostle wrote a compassionate letter on behalf of Onesimus, asking Philemon to accept him as a brother not as a slave. Paul's request serves as the biblical basis for abolishing slavery and other forms of institutionalized racism. For further study, see the Letter to Philemon.

PHILETUS (fye LEE tuhs) *beloved;* 1 century A.D.; 2Ti 2:17; heretical teacher at Ephesus

PHILIP (FIL ip) *lover of horses*
1. ruled 359–336 B.C.; 1Mac 1:1; king of Macedonia; father of Alexander the Great
2. ruled 220–179 B.C.; 1Mac 8:5; king of Macedonia; father of Perseus
3. 2 century B.C.; 1Mac 6:14; friend of Antiochus IV Epiphanes; foe of Lysias
4. 2 century B.C.; 2Mac 5:22; brutal Phrygian governor of Jerusalem
5. 1 century A.D.; Mt 14:3; Herod Philip I; father of Salome; see Herod 4

Philip and the Ethiopian eunuch. Stained glass. St. Peter's Church, Albany, New York.

6. ruled 4 B.C.–A.D. 34; Lk 3:1; Herod Philip II; husband of Salome; see Herod 5
7. 1 century A.D.; Mt 10:3

Philip was first introduced to Jesus the day after Andrew and Peter had become disciples. All three were fishermen from the same hometown, Bethsaida. Philip, in turn, told his friend Nathanael to "come and see" the Messiah for himself and become a disciple. Although Philip followed Jesus faithfully, he seemed to fall short of understanding the powerful implications of Jesus's work. Just before Jesus performed the miracle of the loaves and fishes, he asked Philip how they could feed the crowd of 5000. Philip responded by thinking of money—a material solution—rather than by turning to the power of God, as Jesus did. Amid the confusion of the Last Supper, when Jesus spoke of denial and his death, Philip asked for a sign to bolster his faith: "Lord, show us the Father, and we

will be satisfied." Again, Philip's words showed a lack of understanding of the true nature of Jesus. For further study, see Mk 3:18; Lk 6:14; Jn 1:43-48; 6:5-7; 12:21-22; 14:8-21; Ac 1:13.
8. 1 century A.D.; Ac 6:5

Philip did much to carry out Peter's mandate to open the church to Gentiles and to other people traditionally shut out from Jewish society. As one of the leaders of the early church in Jerusalem, he helped meet the material needs of the Greek-speaking widows in the community, extending the church's social services to non-Jews. As an evangelist working with the apostle Peter, Philip brought the Gospel to the mixed-race Samaritans. On the road from Samaria, he encountered a royal eunuch from Ethiopia and led him to conversion; the eunuch returned to his homeland and spread the Gospel there. In his later years, Philip raised and trained four gifted daughters to prophesy and preach. Thus Philip pushed the frontiers of evangelism—moving beyond his deacon's role and his parish—to embrace a wide variety of people who were typically ignored by earlier evangelists. For further study, see Ac 6:1-7; 8:1-13,26-40; 21:8-9.

PHILIPPIANS (fih LIP pih anz) Php 4:15; inhabitants of Philippi, a Roman colony in eastern Macedonia (modern Greece)

PHILISTINES (fih LIH steenz) Gen 10:14

Originally Aegean Sea people, the Philistines migrated to Canaan and renamed it Palestine. Operating from the five major strongholds of Gaza, Ashkelon, Ashdod, Ekron, and Gath, they became Israel's perennial enemies. For further study, see Gen 26; Jdg 10; 13–16; 1Sa 4–7; 13–14; 17–18; 23–31; 2Sa 3; 5; 8; 21; 23; Jer 47; Eze 16; 25.

PHILOLOGUS (fil LAHL uh guhs) *lover of learning;* 1 century A.D.; Ro 16:15; Roman Christian greeted by Paul

PHILOMETOR (fil uh MEE tor) meaning unknown; 2 century B.C.; 2Mac 4:21; Egyptian ruler; also called Ptolemy and Philopator

PHILOPATOR 3Mac 1:1; see Philometor

PHINEAS (FIN ee uhs) *the Nubian* or *the negro;* 1Esd 8:2; priest-grandson of Aaron

PHINEHAS (FIN ee uhs) *the Nubian* or *the negro*
1. 15 century B.C.; Ex 6:25

As the son of Eleazar and grandson of Aaron the priest, Phinehas inherited his role as Israel's third high priest when Aaron died. Phinehas served in this position faithfully for 19 years. While his duties centered around such mundane tasks as transporting special vessels and trumpets to the sanctuary, he was repeatedly involved in violent acts of retribution on those who violated God's Law. He led a fierce attack against the Benjaminites for the rape and murder of a foreign woman traveling across their camp. He averted a campaign of retribution against several tribes accused of idolatry, when he inspected their temple and determined it was within the confines of the Law. Phinehas's most notable act brought an end to a devastating plague sent by God on the Israelites for engaging in ritual sex with Midianite women; after that practice had been openly denounced, Phinehas ran a spear through the Hebrew Zimri and the Midianite priestess Cozbi, who were continuing to perform these pagan rites. His zealous act prompted God to lift the plague and entrust Phinehas's descendants with the care of the priesthood. Phinehas headed a long line of priests, unbroken until the Romans sacked Jerusalem in A.D. 70. For further study, see Nu 25:1-18; 31:6; Jos 22:9-34; 24:33; Jdg 20:28; 1Ch 6:4,50; 9:20; Ezr 7:5; 8:2; Ps 106:30.
2. 12 century B.C.; 1Sa 1:3; wicked son of Eli; guilty of graft, idolatry, and immorality; see Hophni
3. 5 century B.C.; Ezr 8:33; father of priest Eleazar who weighed temple articles

PHINOE (FIN oh ee) meaning unknown; 1Esd 5:31; ancestor of Jews who returned with Ezra

PHLEGON (FLEG ahn) *burning;* 1 century A.D.; Ro 16:14; Roman Christian greeted by Paul

PHOEBE (FEE bee) *radiant* or *bright;* 1 century A.D.; Ro 16:1-2

At the end of Paul's letter to the church at Rome, he commended Phoebe to them and asked them to welcome her in the Lord when she came to their church. It is commonly believed that she delivered Paul's letter to the church. Phoebe was a deaconess in her own church in Cenchrea, a village on Corinth's east harbor. It is uncertain whether the position of deaconess was a definite office or merely a general term for community service. Phoebe was known for assisting Paul during his visits to Corinth and Cenchrea, and for helping many other people. Paul mentioned in his letter what a great help she had been to him and others. He urged the Roman church to treat his "sister" well and give her any help that she might need.

PHOENICIANS (foh NEE shih uhns) Ob 1:20

Living in the narrow coastal plains of Syria, Phoenicians were seafaring, shipbuilding, and tree-felling allies of David and Solomon, but they led Israel astray by worshiping Baal and Astarte. For further study, see 1Ki 5; 9; 11; 18; Isa 23; Eze 26–28; Ac 11:19; 15:3; 21:2-3.

PHYGELUS (fye JEL uhs) *fugitive;* 1 century A.D.; 2Ti 1:15; one who deserted Paul in Asia

PILATE (PY luht) *javelin carrier;* governed A.D. 26–36; Mt 27:2

Pontius Pilate served as the fifth Roman governor of Judea. His 10-year governorship was marred by controversy and, in many respects, incompetence. Though an expert at compromise, he earned no respect or allegiance, and he was readily manipulated and outmaneuvered by others.

Although Judea was occupied by Rome, the Jews still maintained some autonomy in following their religious laws and customs. The Sanhedrin (the Jewish governing council led by the high priest Caiaphas) was still in place, although its actions were subordinate to the secular law of Rome. Tension frequently erupted when Roman interests came into conflict with Jewish religious practices, and Pilate typically mishandled these situations.

Pontius Pilate washes his hands, symbolically cleansing himself of responsibility in Jesus's death.

In Pilate's day, Jerusalem was the only city in the Roman Empire without a statue of Emperor Tiberius in the city square. So Pilate ordered images of the emperor erected throughout the city, even facing the temple. He did so without any consideration for the Jewish belief in one God. An angry crowd 7000 strong gathered the next day to protest outside his residence in Caesarea. They protested for a week, until Pilate prepared to use force on the crowd. The Jews, however, were willing to die rather than defile their city and temple with graven images, and Pilate never gave the order for his soldiers to disperse the people. This incident foreshadowed things to come at the trial of Jesus, when the crowd would again sway Pilate.

Pilate erred another time when he used funds from the temple to finance his aqueduct project. This violation of the temple treasury caused an uproar and near riot among the Jewish people. This time Pilate did use his troops to suppress the crowd; thousands were trampled to death in the chaos. He received a severe reprimand from Rome but remained in office.

Luke reports another incident of mismanagement when he holds Pilate responsible for the killing of some Galileans while they were offering sacrifices (Lk 13:1). Pilate made one final error in judgment in A.D. 36, ordering an attack on a group of Samaritans. This time, Pilate was ordered back to Rome and then exiled from Italy. Although the record is unclear, it seems that shortly thereafter he committed suicide, as was customary among Roman nobles convicted of a crime.

All four Gospels record Jesus's trial and conviction, but John gives more insight into the particular role of Pilate. While the Sanhedrin had ruled that Jesus was guilty of blasphemy, they had no law to put anyone to death, so they decided to bring him before Pilate with the capital charge of treason for claiming to be the King of the Jews. A large group of Jews had ushered Jesus to Pilate's palace early on the Friday morning before Passover. Pilate asked Jesus if he was the King of the Jews, and Jesus answered that he was indeed a king, but his kingdom was not of this world. Pilate saw no crime against Rome and ordered that the case be taken to the Judean ruler Herod Antipas.

Herod refused to get involved and merely made a fool of Jesus. Dressed in a purple robe and a crown of thorns, Jesus was beaten, whipped, mocked by the soldiers, and returned to Pilate.

Three times Pilate tried to exonerate Jesus, wanting no part in his death. But the angry crowd relentlessly shouted, "Crucify him! Crucify him!"

To appease the Jews, the government customarily released a prisoner of their choice every year at Passover. Pilate suggested releasing Jesus as this token prisoner, but the the crowd asked instead for Barabbas, a known murderer and insurrectionist. A disbelieving Pilate went before the huge crowd with a wash basin and publicly washed his hands, claiming, "I am innocent of this man's blood; see to it yourselves" (Mt 27:24). He then released Barabbas and handed Jesus over for crucifixion.

For further study, see Mt 27; Mk 15; Lk 23; Jn 18–19.

PILDASH (PIL dash) possibly *steely* or *flame of fire;* 21 century B.C.; Gen 22:22; son of Nahor; nephew of Abraham

PILHA (PIL hah) *millstone;* 5 century B.C.; Ne 10:24; leader who sealed covenant renewal

PILTAI (PIL tye) *the Lord is my deliverer;* 6 century B.C.; Ne 12:17; head of priestly family under priest Joiakim

PINON (PYE nahn) meaning unknown; Gen 36:41; Edomite chief descended from Esau

PIRAM (PYE ruhm) possibly *wild ass* or *zebra;* 15 century B.C.; Jos 10:3; Amorite king; attacked Gibeon; defeated by Joshua

PISPA (PIS puh) possibly *dispersion;* 1Ch 7:38; descendant of Asher

PITHON (PYE thahn) *harmless* or *gift of mouth;* 10 century B.C.; 1Ch 8:35; great-grandson of Saul's son Jonathan

POCHERETH-HAZZEBAIM (PAHK uh reth HAZ uh BAY uhm) *gazelle hunter;* Ezr 2:57; ancestor of returnees to Judah

PONTIUS see Pilate

PORATHA (pohr AY thuh) meaning unknown; 5 century B.C.; Est 9:8; one of Haman's ten sons slain by Jews

The Egyptian Potiphar takes Joseph as a household slave.

PORCIUS Ac 24:27; see Festus

POSIDONIUS (PAHS ih DOH nee uhs) meaning unknown; 2 century B.C.; 2Mac 14:19; Nicanor's envoy to Judas Maccabeus

POTIPHAR (PAHT ih fuhr) *whom Re* [the sun god] *has given;* 20 century B.C.; Gen 37:36

Captain Potiphar was either prison-keeper or chief butler and cook in the Egyptian royal court. In either position, this officer of Pharaoh catered to extremely rich Egyptians. He lived in an ornate house that required several servants to attend to all the cooking, gardening, hospitality, and entertainment. Potiphar engaged in the international slave trade to manage his household affairs, and he purchased Joseph from his jealous brothers for this purpose. Potiphar quickly promoted Joseph to manage his household. When Joseph was wrongly accused of rape by Potiphar's flirtatious wife, Potiphar had him imprisoned. For further study, see Gen 37:36; Gen 39:1-23.

POTIPHERA (pah TIF uhr uh) *given by Re* [the sun god]; 20 century B.C.; Gen 41:45; father-in-law of Joseph 1

PRISCA Ro 16:3; see Priscilla

PRISCILLA (prih SIL uh) meaning unknown; 1 century A. D.; Ac 18:2

When Priscilla chose to wed Aquila, a Jewish former slave, she undoubtedly shocked her wealthy Roman family. Tentmakers by trade, Priscilla and her husband Aquila took Paul on as a business partner. When Emperor Claudius forced all Jews to leave Rome, Priscilla and Aquila took their business and Gospel ministry to Corinth and Ephesus. As a result, they started three churches—at Rome, Corinth, and Ephesus. Because Priscilla's name more often appears before Aquila's, some scholars feel she was the leader of their joint efforts. For further study, see Ac 18:1-3,18-28; Ro 16:3; 1Co 16:19; 2Ti 4:19. Also called Prisca.

PROCHORUS (PRAH kohr uhs) *leader in a chorus;* 1 century A.D.; Ac 6:5; deacon who oversaw food program

PRODIGAL SON (PRAHD i guhl suhn) *extravagant* or *lavish* or *wasteful;* Lk 15:11

The Prodigal Son was not so named in the Bible, but he was the foolish son in one of Jesus's parables who asked for an early inheritance and subsequently squandered it on wild living in another country. When a famine hit, he got a job feeding pigs in the field. His hunger was so great that he even craved their food. The Prodigal Son realized that even his father's hired men had food to spare. He longed for home and determined to return and work as a servant. The repentant son expressed how unworthy he was to be his father's son, but he was met with his father's unconditional love and forgiveness and restored to his place in the family in spite of his brother's objections. The parable is meant to convey the attitude of forgiveness that God expresses to those who repent of their sins. For further study, see Lk 15:11-32.

PTOLEMY (TAHL uh mee) meaning unknown
1. ruled 323–30 B.C.; AddEst 11:1

Ptolemy was a general title of the dozen Greek kings who ruled Egypt from the death of Alexander the Great until Rome conquered Egypt. Though no Ptolemaic king is named in the Bible, certain prophecies in the Book of Daniel appear to foreshadow this period of history. Several references in the Apocrypha and other extra-biblical sources document these reigns.

Alexander the Great, the "warrior king" of Daniel 11:3, had his empire divided "not to his posterity" but between his two major generals. Descendants of Ptolemy I Soter ruled Egypt for 300 years. The other major general, Seleucus I Nicator, established a similar dynasty of Greek rulers over Syria.

Ptolemy I Soter (323–283 B.C.) warred against the Seleucid dynasty to gain control of Phoenicia and Palestine. He resettled Jewish prisoners in Alexandria—the military capital and intellectual center of the region.

His son, Ptolemy II Philadelphus (283–246 B.C.), also battled the Seleucids. His Alexandrian Library—one of the seven wonders of the ancient world—helped spread Greek culture throughout the Middle East, and he also built the great Pharos lighthouse. He commissioned 70 Jewish students of the Bible to translate the Old Testament from Hebrew into Greek.

Ptolemy III Euergetes battled the Seleucids for as long as he reigned (246–222 B.C.). During this time, synagogues were first established in Egypt for Jews living far from Jerusalem.

The Prodigal Son returns home and receives his father's forgiveness.

During the reign of Ptolemy IV Philopater (222–205 B.C.), Egypt defeated Syria and its Seleucid ruler, Antiochus III.

Ptolemy V Epiphanes (205–180 B.C.) brought peace through the intermarriage of these two dynasties. This particular Ptolemy wrote the famous Rosetta Stone that later allowed archaeologists to decipher the Egyptian hieroglyphic alphabet.

For further study see Da 11; the Four Books of Maccabees.

2. 2 century B.C.; 1Mac 16:11; son of Abubus; assassinated Simon in an attempt to become governor; also called Macron.

3. 2 century B.C.; AddEst 11:1; son of Dositheus the priest; brought the Book of Esther to Egypt

PUAH (POO uh) possibly *splendid one*

1. 20 century B.C.; 1Ch 7:1; son of Issachar; went to Egypt with grandfather Jacob; also called Puvah

2. 15 century B.C.; Ex 1:15

When the Israelites were held captive in Egypt under Pharaoh's harsh rule, Puah and her colleague, Shiphrah, worked as Hebrew midwives. As Pharaoh became fearful that the Israelites might become too

numerous and revolt, Puah and Shiphrah were told to kill all the male babies born to the Hebrews. However, the midwives refused to do as Pharaoh told them. When asked why they let the baby boys live, they explained that the Hebrew women were too energetic and robust, giving birth before they arrived. For further study, see Ex 1.

3. 12 century B.C.; Jdg 10:1; father of Tola the judge

PUBLIUS (PUB lee uhs) *common* or *popular;* 1 century A.D.; Ac 28:7; chief official on Malta; Paul healed his father

PUDENS (POO denz) *modest;* 1 century A.D.; 2Ti 4:21; Christian who sent greetings to Timothy

PUL 2Ki 5:19; see Tiglath-pileser III

PURAH (PYOOR uh) *branch* or *fruit;* 12 century B.C.; Jdg 7:10; servant of Gideon who spied on Midianite camp

PUT (PUT) meaning unknown; Gen 10:6; son of Ham; could be founder of Libyans

PUTIEL (POO tee uhl) *he whom God gives;* 15 century B.C.; Ex 6:25; father-in-law of Eleazar the son of Aaron

PUVAH Gen 46:13; see Puah 1

PYRRHUS (PEER uhs) *fiery red;* 1 century A.D.; Ac 20:4; father of Paul's companion Sopater

QUARTUS (KWOHR tus) *fourth;* 1 century A.D.; Ro 16:23; Christian in Corinth; greeted Romans through Paul

QUEEN OF HEAVEN (KWEEN uv HEH vuhn) Jer 7:18; the Babylonian goddess of love and war; also called Ishtar

QUINTUS MEMMIUS (KWIN tuhs MEM ee uhs) meaning unknown; 2 century B.C.; 2Mac 11:34; conveyed Lysius's concessions to Jews

QUIRINIUS (kwih RIN ee uhs) meaning unknown; 1 century A.D.; Lk 2:2; Roman governor of Syria at time of Jesus's birth

The Hebrew midwives Puah and Shiphrah appear before Pharaoh.

RAAMAH (RAY uh muh) possibly *trembling* or *greatness;* Gen 10:7; ancestor of Cushite or Arabian tribe

RAAMIAH (RAY uh MI uh) possibly *the Lord has thundered;* 6 century B.C.; Ne 7:7; Israelite chief; also called Reelaiah

RABSHAKEH (rab SHAH kuh) possibly *chief cupbearer;* 7 century B.C.; 2Ki 18:17; officer of Sennacherib of Assyria

RACHEL (RAY chuhl) *ewe;* 20 century B.C.; Gen 29:6

Jacob was sent to find his uncle Laban at the urging of his mother Rebekah, who wanted him to find a wife and escape his brother Esau's anger. On his trip to Mesopotamia, Jacob fell in love with a woman named Rachel, who turned out to be Laban's daughter. He met her at a well where he stopped to ask directions and ended up helping her water her father's sheep.

After Jacob worked for his uncle for a month, Laban offered to pay him for his labors. However, Jacob told Laban that he would work seven more years for him if, in return, he could marry Rachel. When the seven years had passed, Laban deceived Jacob by sending his veiled daughter Leah to Jacob's bed instead. He justified his decision by saying it was the custom to give the older daughter in marriage first.

Laban agreed, however, to give Rachel to Jacob in a week if he would serve him another seven years, and Jacob agreed. Rachel was Jacob's favorite wife, and he loved her more than Leah. However, God allowed Leah to have many children, while Rachel was barren. In Rachel's desperation, she told Jacob, "Give me chil-dren, or I shall die!" But Jacob became angry with her, exclaiming that he wasn't the one who had kept her from having children.

The rivalry and jealousy between the two sisters became so great that Rachel and Leah both used their maids as surrogate mothers to try to outdo each other. Leah had six sons and a daughter before the distraught Rachel had her first child, Joseph. Rachel died giving birth to her second son Benjamin and was buried on the way to Bethlehem.

For further study, see Gen 29–30; 35:16-29; Jer 31:15; Mt 2:18.

RADDAI (RAD eye) *trampling;* 11 century B.C.; 1Ch 2:14; son of Jesse; older brother of David

The sisters Rachel and Leah.

RAGUEL (RAG yoo uhl) *friend of God* or *God is a friend;* Tob 3:7; kinsman of Tobit; father of Sarah 2

RAHAB (RAY hab) *broad*
1. 15 century B.C.; Jos 2:1

When Joshua began his leadership of Israel, he started his plan to enter the Promised Land by sending spies out to survey the opposition. Two spies slipped into the city of Jericho and entered the home of Rahab, a prostitute, whose house was on the city wall. When soldiers came looking for the spies, she hid the Israelites and told the soldiers that the two had left at nightfall. Like the other inhabitants of Jericho, Rahab had heard of the victories the Israelites had already won with the help of their God and of the miracle he had performed by parting the Red Sea to save them. Convinced that the Israelite God was "indeed God in heaven above and on earth below," she asked the spies to reward her for her assistance by sparing her and her family

Rahab hides the spies of Joshua.

when the Israelites came to take Jericho. The spies promised her safety if she tied a scarlet cord in her window and had all her relatives in her house at the time of the attack. When the way was clear, she let the spies down by a rope through her window and warned them to hide in the hills for three days. When the Israelites destroyed Jericho, they rescued Rahab and her family before setting fire to the city. She became the wife of Salmon and the mother of Boaz in the lineage of Jesus. She was mentioned among the great heroes of the faith in Hebrews 11. For further study, see Jos 2:2-21; 6:17-25; Mt 1:5; Heb 11:31.
2. Isa 30:7; mythical sea monster; symbolic of Egypt

RAHAM (RAY ham) *mercy* or *love;* 1Ch 2:44; Judahite descendant of Caleb

RAKEM (RAY kuhm) meaning unknown; 1Ch 7:16; descendant of Manasseh

RAM (RAM) *exalted*
1. Job 32:2; head of family of Job's advisor Elihu
2. Ru 4:19; ancestor of David and Jesus; also called Arni
3. 1Ch 2:25; firstborn son of Jerahmeel

RAMIAH (ruh MYE uh) *the Lord is high;* 5 century B.C.; Ezr 10:25; one who married and divorced foreigner after Exile

RAPHA (RAY fuh) *he has healed;* 19 century B.C.; 1Ch 8:2; last son of Benjamin

RAPHAEL (RA fi el) *God heals* or *God is fearsome;* Tob 3:17

The angel Raphael visited the city of Nineveh to assist two Hebrews living there in exile. Tobit had been blinded in the course of performing a religious ceremony, and Sarah had been possessed by a demon that prompted her to kill each of her seven husbands on their wedding night before the marriage was consummated. Raphael assumed the name and bodily presence of Tobit's relative Azariah, and then instructed Tobit's son Tobias on how to cure both Tobit and Sarah. After Raphael's intervention, Tobias married Sarah, and Tobit recovered a large sum of money that had been lost. For further study, see the Book of Tobit.

Rebekah offers water and lodging to Abraham's servant.

RAPHAH (RAY fuh) meaning unknown; 1Ch 8:37; descendant of Jonathan the son of Saul; also called Rephaiah 2

RAPHAIN (RAY fuh in) meaning unknown; Jdt 8:1; ancestor of Judith

RAPHU (RAY foo) *once healed;* 15 century B.C.; Nu 13:9; father of Palti the Israelite spy in the land of Canaan

RAZIS (RAH zis) meaning unknown; 2 century B.C.; 2Mac 14:37; devout Jew; died violently fighting Nicanor

REAIAH (ree AYE yuh) *seen by the Lord*
1. 1Ch 4:2; descendant of Judah 1
2. 1Ch 5:5; descendant of Reuben
3. Ezr 2:47; ancestor of family of temple servants

REBA (REE buh) *fourth;* 15 century B.C.; Nu 31:8; Midianite king killed by Israelites under Moses

REBECCA Ro 9:10; see Rebekah

REBEKAH (ruh BEK uh) meaning unknown; 21 century B.C.; Gen 22:23

Rebekah was the daughter of Bethuel and the grandniece of Abraham, but she also became Abraham's daughter-in-law when she married his son Isaac. The aging Abraham had made his chief servant promise that he would find his son Isaac a wife, not among the Canaanites but among his own relatives in his own country. His servant was not to take Isaac with him to find a wife but was to rely upon an angel to show him who the willing woman would be. The servant, even as he was praying, found Rebekah, a courteous, kind woman who offered him water and gave him lodging with her family. She, as well as her family, agreed that she should travel to Canaan to marry Isaac.

When they arrived in Canaan, Isaac saw Rebekah coming, riding on a camel. She got down from her camel and went to him. They were married, but Rebekah remained barren for 20 years. Finally, after Isaac pleaded with the Lord, Rebekah bore twin sons, Jacob and Esau. The twins were in conflict even in the womb; Jacob was born clutching at Esau's heel. The favoritism of Isaac for Esau and Rebekah for Jacob increased the brothers' strife. Rebekah, who overheard Isaac promising Esau his inheritance, was determined to obtain it for Jacob. She helped Jacob deceive the elderly Isaac into granting him Esau's birthright.

When Rebekah died, she was buried in a tomb in a cave at Machpelah, the same place where Abraham, Sarah, Isaac, and Leah were buried.

For further study, see Gen 24–27; 49:31; Ro 9:10. Also called Rebecca.

RECHAB (REE kab) *horseman*
1. 11 century B.C.; 2Sa 4:2
After King Saul's death and David's ascent to the throne, Saul's son Ishbaal was David's only remaining rival. Two of Ishbaal's captains, Rechab and Baanah, thought that killing their leader would gain them favor with David and perhaps a rich reward. As Ishbaal lay napping in bed, they crept up on him, stabbed him in the stomach, beheaded him, and then went to great lengths to bring his head to David. However, Rechab and Baanah poorly misjudged David's character. For their act of cruelty and treason, a furious David had them both executed and disgraced in death. For further study, see 2Sa 1:1-16; 4:1-12.
2. 2Ki 10:15; ancestor of Jonadab the ally of Jehu against Ahab
3. 5 century B.C.; Ne 3:14; his son Malkijah helped repair the Jerusalem wall

RECHABITES (REE kab ights) Jer 35:5
To avoid tainting themselves with corrupt city life, these simple tent-dwellers withdrew to the desert and refused wine-making, seed-planting, home-building, and material goods. Jeremiah promised this godly tribe, founded by Jonadab, the son of Rechab, that they would never die out; professed followers of this group still live in Yemen and Iraq.

REELAIAH Ezr 2:2; see Raamiah

REELIAH (ree uh LYE uh) meaning unknown; 6 century B.C.; 1Esd 5:8; one who returned with Zerubbabel from Exile

REGEM (REE guhm) *friend;* 1Ch 2:47; Judahite; descendant of Caleb

REGEM-MELECH (REE guhm MEH lek) *friend of the king;* 6 century B.C.; Zec 7:2; delegate from Bethel who asked Jerusalem priests about fasting

REHABIAH (REE huh BYE uh) *the Lord has made wide;* 15 century B.C.; 1Ch 23:17; son of Eliezer; grandson of Moses

REHOB (REE hahb) *broad* or *open*
1. 11 century B.C.; 2Sa 8:3; father of Hadadezer the king of Zobah
2. 5 century B.C.; Ne 10:11; Levite; sealed covenant renewal

REHOBOAM (REE huh BOH uhm) *the people is extended;* ruled 930–913 B.C.; 1Ki 11:43
Rehoboam was the son of Solomon, born to Naamah, an Ammonite princess. He ascended to the throne at age 41 and saw his kingdom split in two under his reign.

Though born and raised in Jerusalem, Rehoboam held his coronation in Shechem, which would become his capital after the division of the monarchy. When northern leaders came to him seeking respite from the heavy taxes they had endured under Solomon, Rehoboam told them, "Now, whereas my father laid on you a heavy yoke, I will add to your yoke. My father disciplined you with whips, but I will discipline you with scorpions" (1Ki 12:14). His intolerable response prompted ten tribes of Israel to break away under the leadership of Jeroboam, leaving only the tribes of Judah and Benjamin loyal to the new king. Rehoboam attempted to raise an army to subdue the ten northern tribes of Israel, but he abandoned this idea when the prophet Shemaiah told him the division of the Hebrews was part of God's punishment for their sins during the reign of Solomon.

Rehoboam's 17-year reign over Judah was spiritually lax; he allowed pagan worship and other foreign practices to supersede the Hebrew Law. Like his father, Rehoboam took many foreign wives; his favorite, Maacah, gave birth to Abijah, whom he named as his successor. Eventually, his people were reduced to a vassal state under Egypt's King Shishak.

For further study, see 1Ki 11:43–12:27; 14:21–15:6; 2Ch 9:31–12:16.

REHUM (REE hum) *merciful*
1. Ezr 2:2; see Nehum
2. 6 century B.C.; Ne 12:3; chief priest who returned to Judah
3. 5 century B.C.; Ezr 4:8; Persian officer; wrote letter opposing rebuilding of Jerusalem
4. 5 century B.C.; Ne 3:17; rebuilder of Jerusalem wall
5. 5 century B.C.; Ne 10:25; leader who sealed covenant renewal

REI (REE eye) *friendly;* 10 century B.C.; 1Ki 1:8; loyal friend of David during Adonijah's coup attempt

REKEM (REE kuhm) *friendship* or *flowered*
1. 15 century B.C.; Nu 31:8; king of Midian killed during battle with Israelites
2. 1Ch 2:43; descendant of Caleb

REMALIAH (REM uh LYE uh) *the Lord adorns;* 8 century B.C.; 2Ki 15:25; father of Pekah the king of Israel

REPHAEL (REF ay el) *God heals;* 10 century B.C.; 1Ch 26:7; tabernacle gatekeeper; son of Shemaiah 5

REPHAH (REE fuh) *healing* or *support;* 1Ch 7:25; grandson of Ephraim

REPHAIAH (ref FAY yuh) *the Lord heals*
1. 1Ch 7:2; descendant of Issachar
2. 1Ch 9:43; see Raphah
3. 8 century B.C.; 1Ch 4:42; Simeonite leader; fought Amalekites
4. 1Ch 3:21; descendant of David
5. 5 century B.C.; Ne 3:9; repairer of Jerusalem wall

REPHAIM (REF ah yuhm) Gen 14:5
The Rephiam were feared much like the giant Anakim and Nephilim. The last known member of this group was King Og of Bashan. Rephaim later became a term applied by Israel to people who were dead and gone. For further study, see Gen 15:20; Dt 2:11; 3:13; Jos 12:4; 13:12. Also called Zamzummim.

REPHAN (REE fan) meaning unknown; Ac 7:43; idol worshiped by Israelites; associated with Saturn; possibly Kaiwan

RESAIAH (ruh SAYEE uh) meaning unknown; 6 century B.C.; 1Esd 5:8; returnee from Exile

RESHEPH (REE shef) *flame;* 1Ch 7:25; descendant of Ephraim

REU (REE oo) *friendship;* Gen 11:18; descendant of Shem; ancestor of Abraham

REUBEN (ROO ben) *behold a son;* 20 century B.C.; Gen 29:32
The firstborn of Jacob's 12 sons, Reuben lived in a household rife with jealousy and bitterness. Being the oldest, he played a large role in the plot to sell his younger brother Joseph into slavery by making

Reuben and his brothers carry out their plot against Joseph. Stained glass. St. Mary Redcliffe, Bristol, England.

a veiled effort to save Joseph's life when his other brothers plotted against him. Years later, Reuben offered his own two sons as hostages when Joseph exacted justice on his brothers. Thus Reuben gained a reputation for honor and power.

Reuben lost favor with his father, however, by sleeping with Bilhah, one of his father's concubines. This rash act was a move to presumptuously claim his rights as firstborn, since the eldest son usually inherited his father's concubines.

Reuben fathered four sons and resettled them with the rest of Jacob's clan in the eastern delta region of Egypt called Goshen. By Moses's blessing, Reuben's tribe would grow quite large. The Reubenites were pastoral people who grazed their considerable livestock on land east of the Jordan when they returned to Canaan after the Exodus from Egypt.

For further study, see Gen 29:32; 30:14; 35:22-23; 37:1-36; 42:22-37; 46:8-9; 48:5; 49:3-4; Ex 6:14; Nu 1:20-21; 32:1-33; Dt 21:15-17; 33:6; 1Ch 5:1.

REUBENITES (ROO ben ights) Nu 2:10

Descendants of Jacob's oldest son Reuben, the Reubenites settled into a peaceful and pastoral existence east of the Jordan River. They were taken into exile for a time by the Assyrian ruler Tiglath-pileser III. For further study, see Ex 6:14; Nu 1–2; 13:4; 16:1; 26:7; 32; Jdg 5:15-16; Jos 13; 22.

REUEL (ROO uhl) *friend of God*
1. 20 century B.C.; Gen 36:4; son of Esau by Basemath
2. 16 century B.C.; Ex 2:18; Midianite priest; father-in-law of Moses; possibly Jethro
3. 1Ch 9:8; Benjaminite; ancestor of resettler in Jerusalem

REUMAH (ROO muh) meaning unknown; 21 century B.C.; Gen 22:24; concubine of Nahor the brother of Abraham

REZIN (REE zin) meaning unknown
1. ruled 740–732 B.C.; 2Ki 15:37

King Rezin of Syria joined with King Pekah of Israel to attack King Ahaz of Judah, who had refused to assist Rezin and Pekah in revolting against their Assyrian masters. Ahaz had been warned by the prophet Isaiah to protect Jerusalem by putting his trust in God rather than in any military al-

liances. Instead, Ahaz panicked and bribed Tiglath-pileser III of Assyria to rescue him.

The Assyrian king then marched on Damascus and besieged the city for two years. In this Syro-Ephraimite War, Tiglath-pileser managed to kill Rezin, destroy his army, annex Syria and most of Israel, and deport Syrian citizens, thus effectively eliminating Syria as an independent nation.

For further study, see 2Ki 15:37–16:9; Isa 7:4.
2. Ezr 2:48; ancestor of temple servants after the Exile

REZON (REE zuhn) *prince;* 10 century B.C.; 1Ki 11:23; king of Damascus; Solomon's enemy; possibly Hezion

RHESA (REE suh) meaning unknown; 6 century B.C.; Lk 3:27; son of Zerubbabel

RHODA (ROH duh) *rose;* 1 century A.D.; Ac 12:13; servant girl at the home of Mary the mother of Mark

RHODOCUS (ROH duh kus) meaning unknown; 2 century B.C.; 2Mac 13:21; Maccabean soldier; turned traitor at Beth-zur

RIBAI (RYE bye) *pleader;* 11 century B.C.; 2Sa 23:29; Benjaminite; father of Ithai the mighty man of David

RIMMON (RIM ahn) *pomegranate*
1. 2Ki 5:18; Syrian deity of thunder, lightning, and rain
2. 11 century B.C.; 2Sa 4:2; his sons Rechab and Baanah murdered Saul's son Ish-bosheth

RINNAH (RIN uh) *praise to God* or *song;* 1Ch 4:20; son of Shimon; descendant of Judah 1

RIPHATH (RYE fath) Gen 10:3; son of Gomer; people of the Upper Euphrates area; also called Diphath

RIZIA (rih ZYE uh) meaning unknown; 1Ch 7:39; descendant of Asher

RIZPAH (RIZ pah) *hot stone;* 11 century B.C.; 2Sa 3:7

Rizpah, concubine to King Saul, is first mentioned in the Bible after Saul's death, when one of

Saul's generals is accused of having seduced her. She appears again later, near the end of David's reign, during a three-year famine sent by God as punishment for Saul's massacre of the Gibeonites. In an effort to atone for Saul's deed, David agreed to hand over to the Gibeonites seven of Saul's sons, two of which were his sons by Rizpah. The Gibeonites killed all seven and left them out in the open. In her sorrow, Rizpah spread sackcloth for herself on a rock to keep watch over her dead sons until the harvest was finished and the rains came. When David heard about this devoted mother, he buried her sons in a family tomb in Ephraim. For further study, see 2Sa 3:8-11; 21:1-14.

RODANIM (ROH duh nim) Gen 10:4; son of Japheth; ancestor of islanders in Aegean area

Rizpah tirelessly watches over her dead sons.

ROHGAH (ROH guh) *clamor;* 1Ch 7:34; descendant of Asher

ROMAMTI-EZER (roh MAM tih EE zuhr) *highest help;* 10 century B.C.; 1Ch 25:4; chief of temple singers

ROMANS (ROH muhnz) Jn 11:48

During New Testament times, the Romans controlled most of the known world around the Mediterranean, including Judea. As their vast empire spread, the Romans merged elements of various religions into their own pantheon of gods, including Greek mythology and several eastern cults. Like Babylon in the Old Testament, the Roman Empire became a New Testament symbol of paganism, idolatry, and oppression. Roman presence in Judea influenced the political climate of the region during Jesus's ministry; in fact, some Jews believed that Jesus's role as Messiah was to free Judea from Roman tyranny. Roman law was crucial to the process and outcome of the trials of Jesus and the apostle Paul. Rome also played a major role in the development of the early church. At first, Christianity was tolerated and even protected. In the second half of the first century, however, Rome adopted a policy of brutal persecution against the church. Christianity eventually became the dominant religion of the Roman Empire in its waning years under Emperor Constantine. For further study, see Ac 22–28; Ro 1; 1Mac 8; 12; 14.

ROSH (ROHSH) *head;* 19 century B.C.; Gen 46:21; son/grandson of Benjamin

RUFUS (ROO fuhs) *red*
1. 1 century A.D.; Mk 15:21; brother of Alexander; son of Simon of Cyrene
2. 1 century A.D.; Ro 16:13; Christian at Rome greeted by Paul; possibly Rufus 1

RUTH (ROOTH) *companion* or *friend* or *satiated;* 12 century B.C.; Ru 1:4

A famine in Bethlehem forced Naomi, her husband Elimelech, and their two sons Mahlon and Chilion to go to Moab, where Elimelech died. Naomi's sons married Moabite women, Ruth and Orpah. After a while, both sons died, leaving Ruth and Orpah widows. When they heard there was food in Israel, Ruth, Orpah, and Naomi prepared to go there. However, as Naomi thought about taking these women out of their land, she reconsidered and told them to go back to their mothers. Ruth and Orpah both wept openly, confirming their loyalty to Naomi, but Naomi insisted they return since she could not produce more sons to replace their deceased husbands. Orpah finally said good-bye, but Ruth refused to leave Naomi.

Once in Bethlehem, Naomi convinced Ruth to work in the wheat fields. Boaz, the owner of the field, noticed Ruth and was drawn to her. He told his foreman to instruct the workers to secretly help her and protect her from attacks.

Under Israelite Law, a dead man's nearest relative had the right to marry or "redeem" his widow. If he refused, that right would pass on to the nearest kin. Since Boaz was Mahlon's relative, he waited at the city gate for a closer relative to claim redemption rights to Ruth. One was willing to buy Mahlon's land but not to marry Ruth. The relative agreed that Boaz could marry Ruth and took off one sandal and handed it to Boaz to seal their arrangement. Ruth and Boaz were married and had a son named Obed, who had a son named Jesse, who became the father of David, Israel's most illustrious and loved king.

For further study, see the Book of Ruth.

The widow Ruth works in the wheat fields of Boaz.

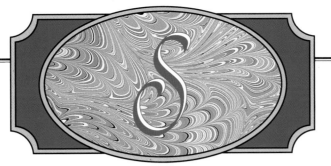

SABEANS (suh BEE uhnz) Job 1:15

The Sabeans settled southwestern Arabia (modern Yemen) and established themselves as traders from Africa all the way to India. During Solomon's reign, their queen visited Israel to test his wisdom and view his riches. For further study, see 1Ki 10; 2Ch 9; Job 1:15; 6:19; Ps 72:10,15; Isa 45:14; 60:6; Eze 27:22-23; 38:13; Joel 3:8.

SABTA (SAB tuh) meaning unknown; 1Ch 1:9; son(s) of Cush; a Hamite or Arabian tribe; a form of Sabtah

SABTAH Gen 10:7; see Sabta

SABTECA (SAB tuh kuh) meaning unknown; 1Ch 1:9; son(s) of Cush; a Hamite or Arabian tribe; a form of Sabtecah

SABTECAH Gen 10:7; see Sabteca

SACHAR (SAY kahr) *reward*
1. 11 century B.C.; 1Ch 11:35; father of Ahiam the mighty man of David; also called Sharar
2. 10 century B.C.; 1Ch 26:4; son of Obed-edom; gatekeeper under David

SACHIA (suh KYE uh) meaning unknown; 1Ch 1:9; descendant of Benjamin

SALA Lk 3:32; see Salmon

SALAMIEL (suh LAM ee el) possibly *God is friend;* Jdt 8:1; ancestor of Judith

SALATHIEL (suh LAY thee el) meaning unknown; Mt 1:12; ancestor of Jesus

SALLAI (SAL eye) meaning unknown
1. 5 century B.C.; Ne 11:8; Benjaminite resettler in Jerusalem
2. 5 century B.C.; Ne 12:20; priest who returned to Judah from Exile

SALLU (SAL oo) meaning unknown
1. 6 century B.C.; Ne 12:7; priest who returned to Judah from Exile
2. 6 century B.C.; 1Ch 9:7; Benjaminite; helped rebuild Jerusalem wall

SALMA (SAL muh) possibly *strength* or *clothed*
1. 1Ch 2:51; descendant of Caleb; founder of Bethlehem
2. 1Ch 2:11; see Salmon

SALMON (SAL muhn) meaning unknown; 1Ch 2:11; ancestor of Jesus through Boaz; also called Sala and Salma 2

SALOME (suh LO mee) *peaceable*
1. 1 century A.D.; Mk 15:40

Wife of Zebedee and mother of the apostles James and John, Salome is best known for her zealous attempt to gain high positions for her sons in heaven. After Jesus had predicted his death, burial, and resurrection, Salome asked him if one of her sons could sit at his right hand and the other at his left in his kingdom. Jesus explained that those positions would be granted by his Father. When the other ten disciples became angry with James and John for seeking such positions in heaven, Jesus taught them that "whoever wishes to be great among you must be your servant" (Mt 20:26). Salome observed Jesus's crucifixion and was also among the women who came with spices to the tomb to anoint Jesus's body. For further study, see Mk 16:1; Mt 20:20-28; 27:56.
2. 1 century A.D.; Mk 6:22

Salome and her parents, Herodias and Philip, were related to Herod the Great. Herodias left Philip and married Herod Antipas, her uncle. Since this marriage was forbidden by law, John the Baptist openly criticized Herod and Herodias, for which he was arrested. Herodias wanted him dead for his comments against her, but Herod refused to execute him. Salome danced before Herod at his birthday party, pleasing him and his guests so

Salome displays the head of John the Baptist, killed by King Herod at her request.

SAMARITANS (suh MAR ih tuhns) Mt 10:5

Samaria was both the capital city and the region of the one-time northern kingdom of Israel. Rival Jews cultivated a hatred of Samaritans, whom they regarded as "mixed race" Hebrews, tainted by foreign blood through intermarriage with Assyrian colonists and by their false worship. Samaritans distinguished themselves from Jews by revering only a modified version of the Torah (the first five books of Moses), while excluding the rest of the Old Testament entirely. Despite all these differences in their worship of God, both groups observed the Sabbath and circumcision and anticipated the messiah and a Judgment Day. Some scholars date the religious break between the two groups of Israelites to Eli building a rival sanctuary at Shiloh in 1100 B.C. Others point to the Assyrian Empire capturing the city of Samaria in 722 B.C. and deporting thousands of its residents. Others date the rift to a conflict between Governor Sanballat of Samaria and Governor Nehemiah of Jerusalem in 450 B.C. But the definitive split occurred when Samaritans built a sanctuary for themselves on Mt. Gerazim within a century of their return from the Babylonian Exile. Eventually, the Samaritans were excommunicated by the Jews around A.D. 300. The positive New Testament images of the Samaritan woman at the well, the immortalized Good Samaritan in Jesus's parable, and the Samaritans evangelized by Philip and the early church round out the biblical picture of these people. For further study, see 1Ki 16; 20–22; 2Ki 6; 10; 13–18; Isa 10; Eze 16; Hos 7–13; Am 3–8; Mic 1; Lk 10; 17:16; Jn 4:1-40; Ac 8:1-25.

much that he agreed to grant her whatever she wished. After conferring with her mother, Salome asked for John the Baptist's head on a platter. Regretfully, the king fulfilled his promise by having John beheaded and presenting the head to Salome, who in turn gave it to her mother. Salome's name is not in the Bible except by implication as the daughter of Herodias. For further study, see Mk 6:14-29.

SALTHAS (SAL thuhs) meaning unknown; 5 century B.C.; 1Esd 9:22; priest who married and divorced foreigner after Exile

SALU (SAY loo) meaning unknown; 15 century B.C.; Nu 25:14; father of Zimri the Simeonite killed by Phinehas

SAMATUS (say MAY tuhs) meaning unknown; 5 century B.C.; 1Esd 9:34; Levite who married and divorced foreigner after Exile

SAMGAR-NEBO (SAM gahr NEE boh) *having to do with* [the god] *Nebo;* 7 century B.C.; Jer 39:3; Babylonian prince

SAMLAH (SAM luh) *garment;* Gen 36:36; pre-Israelite king of Edom

SAMSON (SAM suhn) *sun's man* or *distinguished;* 11 century B.C.; Jdg 13:24

Manoah wanted to be a father, but he and his wife could not conceive until the Lord solved their infertility problem. An angel announced they would soon have a son: "It is he who shall begin to deliver Israel from the hand of the Philistines" (Jdg 13:5). Israel and Philistia were neighbors, but the Philistines were the dominant power of the region and their presence was a corrupting influence on the culture of Israel.

The angel told Manoah that his son, Samson, would be bound to a Nazirite's vow. The Nazirite's vow was one of abstinence and consecration. According to the Law of Moses (Nu 6:1-21), Nazirites would abstain from consuming alcohol or any drink made from grapes to symbolize their disdain of worldly culture. Nazirites also abstained from cutting their hair, touching dead bodies, and eating anything considered unclean. The Nazirites were a consecrated class of women and men who would choose to take the vow to set themselves apart for special use by God. The vow was taken in order to concentrate mental, physical, and spiritual energies for a particular task. Nazirite vows could be limited to the formative years or to special periods of consecration. In Samson's case, being a Nazirite was a permanent calling and one that he did not choose for himself.

Samson broke every rule set down for him as a Nazirite. His first breach was in marrying a non-Jewish Philistine woman and drinking wine at his wedding. Later, Samson touched the decaying carcass and ate honey from the in-nards of a lion he had killed. Samson must have known he was breaking two aspects of the Nazirite's vow, for he purposely kept these incidents from his parents.

Despite his rebellion, Samson proved an effective if unwitting tool of God. His indulgent actions and vengeful temper led to conflict between Israel and Philistia. Enraged over owing a suit of clothes to each of 30 Philistines who had cheated him in a wager, Samson paid his debt by killing 30 innocent Philistines, stripping them, and delivering their garments. After having his Philistine wife taken away, he again sought vengeance, this time by lighting the tails of foxes on fire and sending them through the Philistines' fields to burn the crops. After additional killings, he was finally hunted down and turned over to Philistine soldiers, but he promptly killed 1000 of them armed only with the jawbone of an ass.

When the impulsive Samson took the Philistine Delilah as his lover, he shared with her the secret of his superhuman strength—his unshaven hair. When the Philistine lords found out and shaved his head one night, yet another Nazirite vow was broken and his strength left him. Blinded and enslaved

Sampson's uncut hair, the source of his strength, is shaved by Delilah and the Philistines.

by the Philistines, he appealed to the power of God for vengeance. Because of his faith, his strength was restored, and Samson tore down a Philistine temple, killing himself and thousands of his enemies.

Samson presents an enigma to believers—almost as much as he did to the pagan Philistines. Remarkable for his moral weakness as well as his physical strength, he is both an unlikely and all-too-familiar hero. His limited virtues and obvious vices belie the fact that he was a hero of faith to Jews and Christians alike.

For further study, see Nu 6; Jdg 13–16; Heb 11:32-34.

SAMUEL (SAM yoo uhl) *name of God* or *God hears;* 11 century B.C.; 1Sa 1:20

Elkanah and Hannah were a devout couple from Ramathaim-zophim in the hill country of Ephraim. Hannah had long been childless, and on an annual pilgrimage to the shrine at Shiloh, she promised the Lord that if she was given a son, he would be consecrated to God's service.

In time, she gave birth to a child she called Samuel, because God had heard her. Hannah kept her promise and brought the toddler to Shiloh, formally dedicated him, and left him there to be reared by Eli the priest. As he grew, Samuel learned to help with the religious services, wearing a linen ephod, or priestly apron. Every year Hannah and Elkanah came to Shiloh to worship, and each time Hannah brought Samuel a robe she had made for him. The boy thrived in this environment, cared for by Eli and admired by the people who came to Shiloh.

One night, while Samuel was still a boy, God revealed himself to the lad. At first, Samuel thought he heard the voice of the aging high priest, and he went to him. Eli sent Samuel back to bed. The third time this happened, Eli told Samuel that it was the Lord calling and instructed Samuel in the way he should answer. When God spoke again, he told Samuel about the downfall of the house of Eli because of the corruption of Eli's two sons, the priests Hophni and Phinehas. The next morning Eli insisted that Samuel tell him what he had heard. When Samuel told him everything, it became clear that God had made Samuel a prophet, and news of this spread everywhere.

When Israel was defeated by the Philistines at the battle of Aphek, Eli's two sons were killed, and the sacred ark of God's covenant was captured. Old

Eli was devastated when he heard the news, and he fell over backward, broke his neck, and died.

The ark of the covenant was a troublesome presence to the Philistines: The pagan deity Dagon fell down in front of it twice and was broken, and the people of Ashdod were struck with tumors. Feeling the judgment of Israel's God on them, the Philistines sent the ark back to the Hebrews. It was taken to Kiriath-jearim and remained there for some 20 years.

Samuel called the people to gather at Mizpah, near Jerusalem. He challenged them to turn away from pagan gods, to repent, and to serve the God of Israel only. While the Israelites fasted, prayed, and offered burnt sacrifices to the Lord, the Philistine army approached to attack them. Samuel cried out to God for help, and the Philistines were thrown into confusion and retreated. Samuel marked this victory by setting up a stone to the Lord and naming the place Ebenezer, which means *stone of help.* After this, Samuel's role as a prophet and a religious judge was established throughout the land. He settled in Ramah, close to Jerusalem,

The priest Eli raised Samuel as his own son.

built an altar to the Lord, and administered justice to Israel there.

When Samuel was old, he appointed his sons, Joel and Abijah, as judges in Beersheba. They did not follow Samuel's ways; instead they were like Eli's sons, taking bribes and perverting justice. Their wickedness caused deep discontent among the elders of Israel, and they went to Samuel demanding a monarch to rule them. Up to that point, the 12 Hebrew tribes had not had an earthly king; however, they were loosely bound by their common history, culture, and religious beliefs. God was their ruler and his commandments were their law.

Samuel felt displeased and rejected by the demand for a ruler, and he prayed about the matter. At God's bidding, the judge lectured the people about the evils of kingship, and what they could expect from the one who would reign over them. Undeterred by Samuel's words, the people insisted on having a king to govern them and lead them in battle. Samuel finally had to agree to their demand and told the leaders to return home. Sometime later, a young Benjaminite named Saul was out looking for a missing herd of donkeys that belonged to his father, Kish. God had revealed to Samuel that Saul was the one selected to become the first king of Israel. When Saul sought the seer's advice about the missing animals, Samuel detained him. Early the next morning, Samuel poured oil on Saul's head and anointed him ruler over Israel. At the end of the meeting, Samuel foretold signs that would confirm Saul's calling, and these came to pass as predicted.

Samuel then called a meeting of all Israel at Mizpah. Once again he upbraided the people over their decision to have a king. He proceeded with the drawing of lots and finally Saul was confirmed as Israel's choice. Saul was brought out, and Samuel presented the tall new ruler to the populace. They hailed him as king, and Samuel informed Israel of the rights and responsibilities of the kingship and recorded them in a book, which he placed in the sanctuary. After this, Saul returned to his father's house in Gibeah.

Saul's first opportunity to prove his kingly abilities was a success: With a military victory against the Ammonites secured, Samuel called the Israelites together, and Saul's kingship was publicly confirmed at Gilgal amid sacrificing to the Lord and great rejoicing. In his farewell address to Israel, Samuel, now elderly, reminded the people that even though they now had a king, only the Lord could preserve them, as he had done in the past, and they should serve him. To underline the significance of his words, he called on the Lord to send thunder and rain, and when it came the people were terrified.

Sometime later, the Philistines again appeared to threaten the Israelites. Saul, unable to wait for Samuel to come and make ritual sacrifices to the Lord before battle, presumed to do them himself. When Samuel arrived, he rebuked Saul for his actions and warned him that because of his disobedience his kingdom would not continue. He told Saul that the next king would be "a man after God's own heart" (1Sa 13:14).

After pushing back the Philistines, Saul went after the Amalekites with specific instructions from Samuel to annihilate the entire tribe in the Lord's name. Once again, Saul took matters into his own hands. He overpowered the enemy but spared King Agag and allowed his men to take the enemy's best livestock. Samuel confronted Saul's behavior and ominously told the king that the kingdom had been torn from him that day. After this, Samuel treated Saul as a reprobate and made no more official visits to see him. Samuel's next task was to visit Bethlehem and secretly anoint young David, the

> ➔ ←
>
> *"As Samuel grew up, the Lord was with him and let none of his words fall to the ground. And all Israel from Dan to Beersheba knew that Samuel was a trustworthy prophet of the Lord."*
>
> 1Sa 3:19-20

son of Jesse, as Israel's next king. The elders were both awed and fearful when the prophet and judge arrived in their town. He was clearly well known and was a powerful, inspiring figure in spite of his advanced years.

Later, when Saul became jealous of David and tried to kill him, David escaped to Ramah to the safety of Samuel. Saul sent messengers after him and finally went after David himself, but he became caught up in the religious fervor surrounding Samuel and the prophets there, and David's life was spared.

The aged prophet died while Saul was still king. Samuel was buried at Ramah and was mourned by all of Israel. After Samuel's death, Saul, seeking help, attempted to consult the spirit of Samuel through an old witch of Endor. When Samuel's spirit appeared, the frightened king was rebuked by the words of Samuel and sternly warned about the defeat of Israel and his impending death. The king fainted when he heard the news, and the next day the prediction came true.

Samuel is a key figure in Israel's history. This austere, uncompromising man of God was diligent in a variety of roles, not only as seer, religious judge, and prophet, but also in organizing and conducting religious services and festivals for the people of Israel. In the Old Testament, he is recognized as a man of prayer and intercession, and the New Testament acknowledges Samuel as a hero of faith.

For further study, see 1Sa 1–16; 19; 28; Ps 99:6; Heb 11:32.

Samuel anoints David, the son of Jesse, as Israel's king.

SANBALLAT (san BAL uht) *may Sin* [the moon god] *give him life;* 5 century B.C.; Ne 2:10

Sanballat was the long-time governor of Samaria during the time the Jews were exiled in Babylon. He may have been considered the governor of Judah as well, until Nehemiah assumed that position. With Tobiah the Ammonite and Geshem the Arab, Sanballat vehemently opposed Nehemiah's efforts to rebuild the walls of Jerusalem, using ridicule and mockery, rumors and lies. Despite Sanballat's efforts, Nehemiah was successful in restoring the city. For further study, see Neh 2; 4; 6.

SAPH (SAF) meaning unknown; 10 century B.C.; 2Sa 21:18; descendant of Philistine giants; also called Sippai

SAPPHIRA (suh FYE ruh) *beautiful* or *sapphire;* 1 century A.D.; Ac 5:1; wife of Ananias 4; see Ananias 4

SARAH (SAYR uh) *princess*
1. 22 century B.C.; Gen 11:29

Sarah (first known as Sarai) was a beautiful woman. She was Abraham's half-sister on his father Terah's side, and she became Abraham's wife before the family left Ur of the Chaldees on the journey to Haran. On their way, famine forced Sarah and her family to stop in Egypt. To avoid falling victim to the custom that one could kill a foreigner to take his wife, Abraham (then called Abram) passed her off as his sister. Pharaoh brought Sarah into his household and gave her alleged brother lavish gifts. When Pharaoh's household became afflicted with plagues, he learned the truth about Sarah and Abraham. Upset by the deception, he returned Abraham's wife to him and told the Hebrew family to leave. Sarah also posed as Abraham's sister at the court of King Abimelech of Gerar. God intervened in that situation, and Sarah returned to Abraham instead of joining Abimelech's household.

Sarah was childless—a situation made harder by the Lord's promise that Abraham's offspring would be a great nation. Sarah offered Abraham her Egyptian slave, Hagar, as his concubine. When Hagar became pregnant, Sarah was so jealous that she mistreated Hagar, who ran away for a time. When she returned, Ishmael was born.

Sarah was 90 when the Lord told Abraham that she would bear a son. Sarah laughed when she heard this news, but in due time the child was born

An angel visits Sarah and reminds her that God has promised her a son.

and named Isaac. Even after Isaac's birth, conflict erupted between Sarah and Hagar, and Sarah demanded that Abraham send Hagar and Ishmael away from the household. Sarah died at the age of 127 and was buried beside Abraham in the family tomb at Hebron.

For further study, see Gen 12–23; Isa 51:2.
2. Tob 3:7

In the apocryphal story of Tobit, Sarah was married and widowed seven times because a demon, Asmodeus, killed each of her husbands in their bridal chamber. Her sorrow became so great that she considered hanging herself. Only thinking of her father's grief kept her from suicide. As Sarah prayed for release, Tobit, a pious Jew in a distant city, also prayed for release—from his blindness. God sent the angel Raphael to heal them both. Sarah married Tobit's son, Tobias. Raphael told Tobias to burn the organs of a fish to eliminate the demon and be saved from his predecessors' fate. When Tobias brought Sarah to his home, Raphael said to smear the gall of the fish on Tobit's eyes. As Tobias obeyed, his father's blindness was healed. Raphael revealed himself as an angel and blessed Tobias and Sarah. For further study, see the Book of Tobit.

SARAI Gen 11:29; see Sarah 1

SARAPH (SAIR uhf) *burning;* 1Ch 4:22; Judahite ruler in Moab and Lehem

SARASADAI (SAIR uh SAY dah ee) *Shaddai [God] is a rock;* Jdt 8:1; ancestor of Judith

SARBACHA (sar BAK uh) meaning unknown; AddEst 9:8; son of Haman

SAREA (SAR ee uh) meaning unknown; 5 century B.C.; 2Esd 14:24; one of five scribes who recorded Ezra's words

SARGON II (SAHR gahn) *he [the god] has established the kingship;* ruled 722–705 B.C.; Isa 20:1

King Sargon II of Assyria sacked Samaria in 722 B.C. and deported, according to his annals, 27,290 residents to Mesopotamia. He then repopulated the region with people from the East. Sargon proved to be a formidable war chief against whom no political alliance prevailed. He was related to three Assyrian kings: his father, Tiglath-pileser III; his brother and predecessor, Shalmaneser V; and his son, Sennacherib. When Sargon II was assassinated in 705 B.C., Sennacherib succeeded him as king of Assyria. For further study, see 2Ki 17:3-6; 18:9-12; Isa 20:1-6.

SAROTHIE (suh ROH thee) meaning unknown; 10 century B.C.; 1Esd 5:34; Solomon's servant; ancestor of returnees from Exile

SARSATHAEUS (sar SAY tha ee us) meaning unknown; AddEst 1:14; advisor to King Artaxerxes

SARSECHIM (sar SEE kim) *master of wardrobes* or *chief of the eunuchs;* 6 century B.C.; Jer 39:13; Babylonian commander at Jerusalem

SATAN (SAY tuhn) *adversary;* 1Ch 21:1

His name means *adversary,* and as that would imply, Satan is portrayed in the Bible as the chief antagonist of God and humanity. In the New Testament he is called Abaddon and Apollyon, both meaning *destroyer.* He is also called Beelzebul, Belia, the Enemy, the accuser of our comrades, the devil, the deceiver of the whole world, the great dragon, the evil one, a murderer, the father of lies, the ruler of the power of the air, the ruler of this world, the ancient serpent, and the tempter. His many different names and descriptive references do not confuse his character, but serve to identify him as the source of all aspects of evil. Beginning with the temptation of Adam and Eve, the Bible consistently depicts Satan as the great deceiver who not only tried to foil God's plan for all humankind, but who still prowls around like a roaring lion, "looking for someone to devour" (1Pe 5:8).

According to some interpretations, the prophet Ezekiel presents Satan as a created being with limitations and describes him in his original state as the model of perfection—blameless, full of wisdom, and perfect in beauty. However, as a result of these exceptional qualities, he grew extremely proud and used his wisdom for evil rather than good, desiring

Posing as a serpent, Satan entices Adam and Eve to eat fruit from the forbidden tree.

to be like God and to rule over him. Because of his rebellious ambition and self-deification, Satan was cast from heaven and hurled to the earth, where he was given the temporary position of "ruler of the power of the air" (Eph 2:2). The Book of Revelation depicts this event as a war in heaven where Michael and his angels fought against the "dragon" and his angels. The dragon was defeated and thrown down with his angels to the earth because there was no longer any place for them in heaven. Thus began the conflict between God and Satan, good and evil, divine will and self will, holiness and sin, life and death.

Even though Satan is neither eternal nor all powerful, he still has the ability to seduce and deceive the human race. After his fall from heaven, he began his pursuit of people without delay, tricking and misleading Eve into believing that God didn't really say what she heard him say. Adam and Eve gave in to Satan's allure, allowing him to succeed in establishing control over humankind. Scripture, however, does not leave the human race without hope in the face of this powerful evil. The Bible states that through the death and resurrection of God in the flesh (Jesus Christ), the power of Satan was broken so that "through death he [Jesus] might destroy the one who has the power of death, that is, the devil" (Heb 2:14).

The conflict between Satan and God is one of the ongoing themes throughout the entire Bible. The struggle is mentioned as early as the third chapter of Genesis where God told the serpent— identified in the Book of Revelation as Satan—that there would be enmity between him and the woman's offspring (Jesus). The winner was chosen when God said to the serpent, "he will strike your head, and you will strike his heel."

Likewise, the conflict between Satan and humanity repeatedly appears as a theme in Scripture.

> *"He was a murderer from the beginning and does not stand in the truth, because there is no truth in him. When he lies, he speaks according to his own nature, for he is a liar and the father of lies."*
>
> Jn 8:44

The story of Job begins when the "heavenly beings came to present themselves before the Lord, and Satan also came among them" (Job 1:6). A lively discussion followed in which God questioned Satan about the righteousness and faithfulness of Job. Satan subsequently challenged God with the cynical prospect that, if afflicted with tragedy his wealthy servant Job would curse God. With God's permission, and limited to what God would allow, Satan inflicted suffering upon Job by destroying all his possessions and everyone he loved. Through all of his losses, however, Job did not turn his back on God. When Satan again appeared before God, he sarcastically attributed Job's allegiance to the fact that he had never suffered physical pain himself. Again with God's permission, Satan covered Job with horrible sores from the soles of his feet to the top of his head. Still Job did not curse God and sin. This biblical account allows the reader to actually witness a discourse in heaven between the two archenemies—between good and evil—and to see the outcome of victory on the side of good.

Aside from the fact that Satan wants every human being to succumb to his temptations, his ultimate goal is to destroy God's plan and usurp his position. His most concentrated effort to do so was his temptation of Jesus in the desert. After Jesus's baptism, where God announced that this was his Son in whom he was well pleased, Jesus retreated to the desert and fasted for 40 days and 40 nights. While Jesus was very hungry and weak, Satan attempted to convince him of the futility of his ministry and prove to Jesus the benefits of worshiping him. Satan first worked on his physical weaknesses by telling him to turn the stones into bread, but Jesus answered by saying that spiritual needs were more significant than physical needs. Then Satan took him to the highest point of the temple, challenging him to use his supernatural powers and hurl himself to the ground so God would use his angels to rescue him. But Jesus rebuked Satan for tempting him. Satan then offered to give him all the kingdoms of the world if Jesus would only bow down and worship him. His offer not only confirms that Satan does have temporary authority over the world (thus his power to give it away), but it establishes his paramount desire—to be superior to God. Jesus instantly rebuked him and declared that God was the only one to be worshiped. In each one of his triumphs over Satan's temptations, Jesus used quotes from the Old Testament to oppose and resist Satan's schemes.

In his unsuccessful attempt to make Jesus sin and shift his allegiance, Satan was attempting to destroy God's plan to send the Messiah as the savior of the world. The principal role of the Messiah was to destroy the works of Satan; when Jesus was

crucified on a Roman cross, he also destroyed Satan's power over humanity, offering potential deliverance from Satan's control to every person. According to Scripture, in the futile display of Satan's power in the desert and at Jesus's victory on the cross, Satan was defeated by the only one who has authority over him.

However, Scripture also says that even though the war with Satan was won at the cross, the conflict between good and evil continues. The Bible tells of an ongoing warfare and prophesies of a final battle that will seal the inevitable doom of Satan and his followers. In the Gospel According to Matthew, Jesus alluded to an eternal fire prepared for the devil and his angels. The Book of Revelation describes the final judgment that will be meted out upon the devil and his followers. Satan's future includes confinement in a sealed bottomless pit for 1000 years, a time period that some scholars interpret literally and some metaphorically. During this time, the earth will be in peace, free from the deceptive and enticing customs of Satan. At the end of the 1000 years, Satan will be loosed from the pit for a period of time during which he will resume his ambition to destroy and delude the world. In the end, he and his angels will be defeated eternally and thrown into the lake of fire and brimstone where "they will be tormented day and night forever and ever" (Rev 20:10).

For further study, see Gen 3:15; 1Ch 21:1; Job 1; 2; Zec 3:1,2; Mt 4:1-11; 12:24-26; 25:41; Jn 8:44; 16:11; 2Co 4:4; Eph 6:10-18; 1Th 3:5; Heb 2:14-15; 1Pe 5:8-11; 1Jn 5:19-20; Jude 9; Rev 9:11; 12:4-17; 20:1-10.

Satan challenges the fasting Jesus to show his power by turning stones into bread.

SAUL (SAHL) *asked*

1. ruled 1050–1010 B.C.; 1Sa 9:2

Saul came from a wealthy, influential family. He worked for his father, Kish, who was from the tribe of Benjamin, growing wheat and herding donkeys. Saul was at least a head taller than most men and extremely good looking. Despite this, he looked upon himself modestly and surely never envisioned that he would one day become the first king of his people.

The Bible begins the story of Saul as he was searching for his father's lost donkeys. He turned to the prophet Samuel for assistance and was given instead a most surprising dewere threatening from several sides. Previously, the Israelites had a simple political structure, a loose alliance of the 12 tribes that had no true central authority. They did rely occasionally on the leadership of judges; however, the judges were not real rulers but deliverers who were raised to prominence by God to guide the nation during times of military or spiritual need. This system had often left the Israelites vulnerable to the armies of more organized nations, and the people called for a strong king to rule them after the fashion of other nations. Such a request showed that Israel lacked faith in God and his protection; nonetheless, God instructed Samuel, the last of the judges, to name Saul as monarch.

The people delighted in Saul's first military victory—a surprise attack at night against the Ammonites. Two years later, Saul challenged the formidable Philistines with a force of 3000 men (1000 were under the command of Saul's oldest son Jonathan). The Philistine army—equipped with charioteers, horsemen, and foot soldiers, all armed with superior weapons—caused the fearful Israelite troops to hide in caves or flee across the Jordan River. But when Jonathan and his armor bearer single-handedly killed 20 Philistine soldiers in a surprise at-

David plays the lyre before King Saul.

cree. Pouring oil over the young man's head, Samuel revealed, "The Lord has anointed you ruler over his people Israel" (1 Sa 10:1) and told Saul that the Spirit of the Lord would possess him and make him a new man. Saul was reluctant to assume this new role of king; in fact, when his selection was announced to the people of Israel, he was hiding among the pack animals in the hope that he would be passed over. The job was daunting; he was taking control of a country with no government agencies, no economic system, no military security, and no religious harmony at a time when oppressors

tack, the entire Philistine force panicked and was defeated by the remaining 600 Israelites. Saul went on to further military victories against the Amorites, the Zobahites, the Arameans, the Ammonites, and the Amalekites, and his popularity grew tremendously.

Despite his military campaigns, Saul's relations with Samuel were failing. As king, Saul made the military decisions, but Samuel, as priest, was responsible for overseeing the religious aspects of army life to ensure that Israel remained in God's favor. During one battle with the Philistines, after impatiently waiting seven days for Samuel to come and administer a burnt offering, Saul took religious affairs into his own hands by performing the sacrifice himself. Samuel warned Saul that for this sin, God would one day replace him with a new, more worthy king.

A penitent Saul ordered a fast for his troops during the battle of Michmash, vowing to kill any soldier who broke it. His son Jonathan, unaware of the decree, ate wild honey and encouraged his hungry soldiers to do the same. Saul was prepared to order the death of his son but relented when the people objected because of Jonathan's great success in battle.

Saul again clashed with Samuel during the conquest of the Amalekites. Samuel had advised that holy retribution be wrought on these people and that they and their livestock be slaughtered. Saul took Agag, their king, captive and allowed the troops to take sheep and cattle as plunder to offer as sacrifices to God. Samuel responded harshly, saying "Surely, to obey is better than sacrifice" (1Sa 15:22), and he once again told Saul that God would bring another to take his place. Saul begged for clemency but was refused. As Samuel turned to leave, Saul grabbed the priest's robe. It tore, prompting Samuel to compare the incident to God ripping the kingdom of Israel from Saul. This was the last time that the two saw each other alive.

In time, Samuel secretly anointed a new king— David. In the years that followed, Saul became distraught and emotionally unstable as he waited with dread for his kingdom to be taken from him. His advisors sought a musician to soothe his torment. Ironically, the gifted young lyrist they chose was none other than the king-to-be, David. Saul showed great love for the lad, taking him in as his armor bearer. While acting in this capacity, David had his famed encounter with the giant Goliath, and his renown among the people began to grow. As David's popularity flourished, Saul became increas-

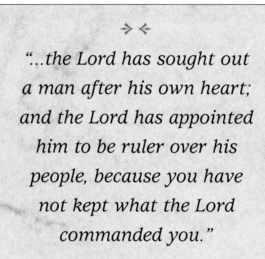

"...the Lord has sought out a man after his own heart; and the Lord has appointed him to be ruler over his people, because you have not kept what the Lord commanded you."

1Sa 13:13-14

ingly jealous and vengeful, and he eventually recognized David as the one who would replace him.

Saul's jealousy consumed him, and he sought to kill David, first by sending him to the front lines against the Philistine army under the pretense of awarding his daughter Merab in marriage if David were victorious. When David returned triumphant, the disappointed and surprised king changed his mind and awarded David his second daughter, Michal. Saul was foiled again, however, when David and Michal actually fell in love.

As Saul's hatred of David grew and became more obvious, his kingship began to lose support, even within his own family. His son Jonathan, who had become close friends with David, refused to aid his father in his schemes. Likewise, Michal actively helped David escape from Saul's increasingly blatant attempts to murder him.

David ultimately had to flee, and Saul relentlessly pursued him throughout Israel. Despite the resources available to him as king, Saul was unable to capture David or his supporters, and the more he tried, the more foolish he looked. His errors twice gave David the opportunity to slay him, but David allowed Saul to live both times out of respect for Saul's divinely appointed office.

While Saul concentrated his efforts on finding David, Israel faced a threat from the gathering Philistine army. Saul wanted divine guidance for the impending battle, but his prophet Samuel had died. In a desperate and misguided attempt to reach God, Saul went to a sorcerer from Endor, hoping to summon the spirit of Samuel. The prophet did appear and predicted imminent death for Saul and his family. In battle the next day, the Philistines slaughtered Saul's army and three of his sons—Jonathan, Abinadab, and Malchishua. Wounded by an arrow, Saul himself begged his armor bearer to finish the job and kill him. When his servant refused, Saul fell on his own sword. The Philistines cut off Saul's head, stripped off his armor, and hung his body and those of his sons on a wall as carrion. Later, some Israelites retrieved the bodies and gave them a proper burial and respectful funeral.

Saul's great successes were clearly overshadowed by personal struggles with other people and by inner conflicts and rebellion against God. His promising life and favored position as the first sovereign of Israel were eclipsed by his rebellion, his sins, and his all-consuming jealousy. He proved himself a fool in attempting to destroy God's choice for Israel's next king, and he was humiliated in death. The hope of Israel—the king for whom they had implored God—ended his life a disgrace to himself and to his entire nation.

For further study, see 1Sa 9–29; 31.

2. Ac 7:58; see Paul

SCEVA (SEE vuh) 1 century A.D.; Ac 19:14

When Paul began to heal the sick and diseased residents of Ephesus, many in the helping profession took notice and became jealous. Some began imitating him, including seven Jewish exorcists in the Sceva clan. They invoked "the Jesus whom Paul proclaims" to exorcise a demon from a possessed man. The spirit said it recognized the authority of Jesus and Paul but did not know the seven mystics and so set upon them and drove them away "naked and wounded." When word of this encounter with the sons of Sceva spread throughout Ephesus, Jews and Greeks alike were awestruck by the apparent power of Jesus's name. Some practicing sorcerers even denounced their witchcraft, burned their books of magic, and became Christians. For further study, see Ac 19:11-20.

SCYTHIANS (SITH ee uhns) Col 3:11; a barbarous people and nomadic raiders of the Black Sea region

SEBA (SEE buh) meaning unknown; Gen 10:7; son(s) of Cush; a Hamite or Arabian tribe

SECUNDUS (se KUN duhs) *second;* 1 century A.D.; Ac 20:4; Paul's traveling companion from Thessalonica

SEGUB (SEE gub) *the deity is lifted up*
1. 19 century B.C.; 1Ch 2:21; son of Hezron; descendant of Judah 1
2. 9 century B.C.; 1Ki 16:34; son of Heil; died while helping his father rebuild Jericho

SEIR (SEER) *hairy* or *rugged;* Gen 36:20; ancestor of the Horites, who settled in the mountainous Seir region

SELED (SEE led) *lifted up;* 1Ch 2:30; descendant of Jerahmeel and Judah

SELEMIA (seh LEE mih ah) meaning unknown; 5 century B.C.; 1Esd 14:24; one of five scribes who recorded for Ezra

SELEUCUS IV PHILOPATOR (suh LOO kuhs FIL o pay tor) meaning unknown; ruled 187–175 B.C.; 2Mac 3:3; son of Antiochus the Great

SEMACHIAH (SEM uh KYE uh) *the Lord has sustained;* 10 century B.C.; 1Ch 26:7; Levite gatekeeper under David

SEMEIN (SEM ee in) meaning unknown; Lk 3:26; ancestor of Christ

A wounded Saul falls upon his own sword in a battle with the Philistines.

SENAAH Ezr 2:35; see Hassenaah

SENNACHERIB (suh NAK uhr ib) *Sin* [the moon god] *has increased the brothers;* ruled 705–681 B.C.; 2Ki 18:13

    Sennacherib advanced to the throne of Assyria by usurping the claim of his older brother when their father, Sargon II, died. He is known for the extensive military campaigns that he ably and mercilessly executed across the Middle East and for the elaborate construction work that he ordered in his capital city of Nineveh. Early in his rule, several of the vassal states in his empire rose in rebellion, including Judah. The Assyrian army swept across the empire and quelled the rebellion easily. Marching on Judah, they took village after village, amassing some 200,000 prisoners in their advance to Jerusalem. King Hezekiah of Judah attempted to appease Sennacherib by sending him tribute, but the Assyrian army was soon encamped outside Jerusalem. Hezekiah turned to God for help, and "That very night the angel of the Lord set out and struck down one hundred eighty-five thousand" (2Ki 19:35) of the soldiers in the siege force, effectively destroying Sennacherib's once formidable military power. The Assyrian king returned to Nineveh in defeat, and several years later was murdered by two of his own sons. For further study, see 2Ki 18:13–19:37; 2Ch 32; Isa 36–37.

SEORIM (see OHR im) meaning unknown; 10 century B.C.; 1Ch 24:8; head of division of priests under David

SEPHARVITES (SEH fuhr vights) 2Ki 17:31; inhabitants of Sepharvaim; practiced child sacrifice

SERAH (SEER uh) *abundance;* 20 century B.C.; Gen 46:17; daughter of Asher; granddaughter of Jacob and Zilpah

SERAIAH (suh RAY yuh) *the Lord is prince* or *the Lord has prevailed*
1. 14 century B.C.; 1Ch 4:13; son of Kenaz; brother of judge Othniel
2. 1Ch 4:35; descendant of Simeon
3. 11 century B.C.; 2Sa 8:17; secretary of David; also called Shavsha, Sheva 2, and Shisha
4. 7 century B.C.; 2Ki 25:18; high priest when Jerusalem was conquered by Nebuchadnezzar

5. 7 century B.C.; Jer 36:26; tried to arrest Baruch and Jeremiah
6. 7 century B.C.; Jer 51:59; son of Neriah; brother of Baruch; received Jeremiah's prophecy scroll
7. 6 century B.C.; 2Ki 25:23; army officer allied with Gedaliah at Mizpah
8. Ezr 2:2; see Azariah 20
9. 6 century B.C.; Ne 12:1; head of priestly family that returned to Judah
10. 5 century B.C.; Ne 10:2; priest who sealed covenant renewal; possibly Seraiah 9
11. 5 century B.C.; Ne 11:11; see Azariah 27

SERED (SEER ed) *deliverance* or *fear;* 19 century B.C.; Gen 46:14; eldest son of Zebulun

SERGIUS PAULUS (SUHR jee uhs PAWL us) meaning unknown; 1 century A.D.; Ac 13:7; convert of Paul's ministry

SERON (SEER ohn) meaning unknown; 2 century B.C.; 1Mac 3:13; Seleucid general sent to crush Maccabean revolt

SERUG (SEER ug) *branch;* Gen 11:20; descendant of Shem; ancestor of Abraham

SESTHEL (SES thel) meaning unknown; 1Esd 9:31; ancestor of some who married and divorced foreigners after Exile

SETH (SETH) *appoint;* Gen 4:25
    Adam and Eve had suffered the loss of their first two sons—Abel was murdered and Cain was banished for the crime. To compensate them in their grief and loss, God "appointed" Seth as a replacement offspring. Over 100 years later, this third son of Adam and Eve gave birth to Enosh. The Genesis account notes that after the birth of Seth and his son Enosh, "people began to invoke the name of the Lord," that is, they began pursuing the spiritual aspect of being made "in the likeness of God." Seth fathered many other sons in his 912-year lifetime, thus establishing the human race. Noah, the ancestor of all humanity after the Flood, was a descendant of Seth through Enosh. For further study, see Gen 4:25–5:8; 1Ch 1:1.

SETHUR (SEE thur) *hidden;* 15 century B.C.; Nu 13:13; Asherite leader sent to explore Canaan

SHAAPH (SHAY af) *balm*
1. 1Ch 2:49; son of Caleb by Maacah
2. 1Ch 2:47; Judahite in clan of Caleb

SHAASHGAZ (shay ASH gaz) *lover of beauty* or *servant of the beautiful;* 5 century B.C.; Est 2:14; eunuch of King Ahasuerus in charge of concubines

SHABBETHAI (SHAB uh thye) *sabbath-born*
1. 5 century B.C.; Ezr 10:15; Levite involved in dispute about divorce of foreign wives
2. 5 century B.C.; Ne 8:7; Levite interpreter of the Law; possibly Shabbethai 1
3. 5 century B.C.; Ne 11:16; chief Levite in Jerusalem after wall was rebuilt; possibly Shabbethai 1

SHADRACH (SHAD rak) *command of Aku* [a moon god] or *I am very fearful;* 6 century B.C.; Da 1:6

While living in Babylon during the Exile, several promising young Jewish boys were taken into the court of the Babylonian king Nebuchadnezzar for training and service. Among them were Hananiah (who was given the Babylonian name Shadrach), Daniel the prophet (renamed Belteshazzar), Mishael (renamed Meshach), and Azariah (renamed Abednego). These four young men quickly rose to prominence in the court, winning the respect and admiration of the king. Although tempted with all the indulgences of court life, the young men remained true to their Jewish heritage.

Shadrach, Meshach, and Abednego earned the king's wrath when, true to their God's Law, they refused to bow down to a gold idol set up by Nebuchadnezzar. The enraged king ordered them to be cast into a fiery furnace for refusing to participate in his idolatry. When Nebuchadnezzar came to see them burn, however, he was amazed to find them walking about freely in the flames along with a fourth figure having the "appearance of a god." For their faith and devotion, the three young men had been protected from the flames by an angel. Recognizing the power of the God of Israel, Nebuchadnezzar released the three youths, elevated their position in the court, and issued a decree banning any criticisms of their religion.

For further study, see Da 1:1–3:30.

SHAGEE 1Ch 11:34; see Shammah 3

SHAHARAIM (SHAY huh RAY im) *double dawn* or *double warning;* 1Ch 8:8; Benjaminite living in Moab

SHALLUM (SHAL uhm) *reward*
1. 1Ch 7:13; see Shillem
2. 19 century B.C.; 1Ch 4:25; son of Shaul 1; grandson of Simeon

Shadrach, Meshach, and Abednego miraculously survive in the fiery furnace.

3. 1Ch 2:40; descendant of Jerahmeel and Judah
4. 8 century B.C.; 2Ch 28:12; father of Jehizkiah the Ephraimite leader
5. 8 century B.C.; 2Ki 15:10; son of Jabesh; king of Israel; killed Zechariah
6. 7 century B.C.; 1Ch 6:12; father of the high priest Hilkiah
7. 7 century B.C.; 2Ki 22:14; keeper of King Josiah's wardrobe; husband of Huldah
8. 7 century B.C.; Jer 32:7; uncle of Jeremiah; father of Hanamel; possibly Shallum 7
9. 7 century B.C.; Jer 35:4; father of Maaseiah the temple doorkeeper
10. 1Ch 3:15; also called Jehoahaz 3
11. Bar 1:7; ancestor of Jehoiakim the high priest
12. Ezr 2:42; ancestral head of gatekeepers that returned to Judah
13. 5 century B.C.; 1Ch 9:17; gatekeeper at temple after Exile
14. 5 century B.C.; Ezr 10:24; gatekeeper who married and divorced foreigner after Exile; possibly Shallum 13
15. 5 century B.C.; Ezr 10:42; descendant of Binnui; married and divorced foreigner
16. 5 century B.C.; Ne 3:12; son of Hallohesh; helped repair Jerusalem wall with his daughters
17. 5 century B.C.; Ne 3:15; another who helped repair Jerusalem wall

SHALMAI (SHAL mye) *the Lord is recompenser;* Ne 7:48; ancestor of temple servants who returned to Judah; also called Shamlai

SHALMAN (SHAL muhn) meaning unknown; Hos 10:14; one who sacked Beth-arbel

SHALMANESER V (SHAL muh NEE zuhr) *Salman* [a god] *is leader;* ruled 727–722 B.C.; 2Ki 17:3

Shalmaneser V was the name that Ululai, the governor of Babylon, assumed when he seized the throne following the death of Tiglath-pileser III, king of Assyria. He is best known for conducting a three-year siege of Israel, which then fell into the hands of his successor, Sargon II, in 722 B.C. The siege was precipitated by King Hoshea of Israel, who, in his seventh year as a vassal king, refused to pay the annual tribute to Assyria. Hoshea was hoping to throw off Assyrian domination but instead instigated the fall of the northern kingdom. For further study, see 2Ki 17:3-6; 18:9-10.

SHAMA (SHAY muh) *he has heard;* 11 century B.C.; 1Ch 11:44; son of Hotham; mighty man of David

SHAMGAR (SHAM gahr) *foreigner* or *stranger;* Jdg 3:31; minor judge; killed many Philistines

SHAMHUTH (SHAM huth) meaning unknown; 10 century B.C.; 1Ch 27:8; commander of division of David's army

SHAMIR (SHAY muhr) *sharp point* or *thorn;* 11 century B.C.; 1Ch 24:24; Levite whose family served in tabernacle

SHAMLAI Ezr 2:46; see Shalmai

SHAMMA (SHAM uh) *fame* or *desolation;* 1Ch 7:37; son of Zophah; leader of Asher tribe

SHAMMAH (SHAM uh) *fame* or *desolation* or *waste*
1. 19 century B.C.; Gen 36:13; Edomite; son of Reuel; grandson of Esau
2. 11 century B.C.; 1Sa 16:9; third son of Jesse; older brother of David; also called Shimea 3, Shimeah 2, and Shimeil 10
3. 11 century B.C.; 2Sa 23:11; one of three elite mighty men of David; also called Shagee
4. 11 century B.C.; 2Sa 23:25; another mighty man of David; also called Shammoth

SHAMMAI (SHAM eye) *famous* or *waste*
1. 1Ch 2:28; Judahite; descendant of Jerahmeel
2. 1Ch 2:44; descendant of clan of Caleb and Judah
3. 1Ch 4:17; descendant of Judah 1

SHAMMOTH 1Ch 11:27; see Shammah 4

SHAMMUA (SHAM moo uh) *renowned* or *heard*
1. 15 century B.C; Nu 13:4; Reubenite leader sent to explore Canaan
2. 10 century B.C.; 2Sa 5:14; son of David and Bathsheba; Solomon's brother; also called Shimea 4
3. Ne 11:17; ancestor of resettlers in Jerusalem; also called Shemaiah 16
4. 6 century B.C.; Ne 12:18; head of priestly family under Joiakim

SHAMSHERAI (SHAM shuh rye) *hero;* 1Ch 8:26; descendant of Benjamin

SHAPHAM (SHAY fuhm) *bare* or *vigorous* or *youthful;* 8 century B.C.; 1Ch 5:12; chief Gadite living in Bashan

SHAPHAN (SHAY fuhn) *rock badger* or *rabbit*
1. 7 century B.C.; 2Ki 22:12; father of Ahikam; grandfather of Gedaliah the governor
2. 7 century B.C.; 2Ki 22:3; aide who brought Josiah the Law; possibly Shaphan 1
3. 7 century B.C.; Jer 29:3; father of Elasah the courier to exiles; possibly Shaphan 1 or 2
4. 7 century B.C.; Eze 8:11; father of Jaazaniah the idolator in the temple in Ezekiel's vision

SHAPHAT (SHAY fat) *he has judged*
1. 15 century B.C.; Nu 13:5; Simeonite sent by Moses to explore Caanan
2. 10 century B.C.; 1Ch 27:29; official in charge of David's herds
3. 10 century B.C.; 1Esd 5:34; Solomon's servant; ancestor of returnees from Exile
4. 9 century B.C.; 1Ki 19:16; father of prophet Elisha
5. 1Ch 3:22; descendant of Zerubbabel
6. 8 century B.C.; 1Ch 5:12; Gadite chief living in Bashan

SHARAI (SHAIR eye) meaning unknown; 5 century B.C.; Ezr 10:40; one who married and divorced foreigner after Exile

SHARAR 2Sa 23:33; see Sachar 1

SHAREZER (shuh REE zuhr) *he has protected the king*
1. 7 century B.C.; 2Ki 19:37; son and murderer of King Sennacherib
2. 6 century B.C.; Zec 7:2; delegate from Bethel who traveled to Jerusalem to ask priests about fasting

SHASHAI (SHAY shy) meaning unknown; 5 century B.C.; Ezr 10:40; descendant of Binnui who married and divorced foreigner after Exile

SHASHAK (SHAY shak) *assaulter;* 1Ch 8:14; son of Elpaal; descendant of Benjamin

SHAUL (SHAWL) *asked*
1. 19 century B.C.; Gen 46:10; son of Simeon by a Canaanite woman
2. Gen 36:37; pre-Israelite king of Edom
3. 1Ch 6:24; Kohathite; descendant of Levi

SHAVSHA 1Ch 18:16; see Seraiah 3

SHEAL (SHEE uhl) *request;* 5 century B.C.; Ezr 10:29; one who married and divorced foreigner after Exile

SHEALTIEL (shee AL tee uhl) *I have asked of God;* 6 century B.C.; Ezr 3:2; first son of Jehoiachin; father of Zerubbabel; see Pedaiah 3

SHEARIAH (SHEE uh RYE uh) *the Lord considers* or *God's gate;* 1Ch 8:38; son of Azel; descendant of King Saul

SHEAR-JASHUB (SHEER JAH shub) *a remnant shall return;* 8 century B.C.; Isa 7:3; Isaiah's son; a symbol of the prophecy that some Hebrews would one day return after Exile

SHEBA (SHEE buh) *oath*
1. Gen 10:7; son of Ramaah; founder of Hamite or Arabian tribe
2. Gen 10:28; son of Joktan; descendant of Shem
3. Gen 25:3; son of Jokshan; grandson of Abraham
4. 10 century B.C.; 2Sa 20:1; Benjaminite who began rebellion against David
5. 8 century B.C.; 1Ch 5:13; head of Gadite family in days of Jotham

SHEBANIAH (sheb uh NIGH uh) meaning unknown
1. 11 century B.C.; 1Ch 15:24; priest and trumpeter at ark's return
2. 5 century B.C.; Ne 9:4; Levite; participant in covenant renewal
3. 5 century B.C.; Ne 10:4; priest; sealed covenant renewal
4. 5 century B.C.; Ne 10:10; Levite; sealed covenant renewal, possibly Shebaniah 2
5. 5 century B.C.; Ne 10:12; another Levite who sealed covenant renewal; possibly Shebaniah 2

SHEBER (SHEE buhr) *lion;* 1Ch 2:48; son of Caleb by Maacah

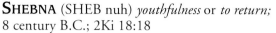

SHEBNA (SHEB nuh) *youthfulness* or *to return;*
8 century B.C.; 2Ki 18:18

Shebna served as a senior official under King Hezekiah and exerted considerable influence over the king's household and perhaps over Judah's standing army. He also served as an ambassador to negotiate with the Assyrians, who felt threatened by Hezekiah's pro-Egyptian policies. These same policies were opposed by the prophet Isaiah, who warned Judah to be solely dependent on God for protection. Shebna had the dubious distinction of being the only individual singled out by name for condemnation in all of Isaiah's oracles. Isaiah condemned Shebna for his overwhelming pride, noting especially his self-aggrandizing tomb (the kind reserved only for kings). Isaiah predicted he would be thrust out of office (he was replaced by Eliakim) and die in exile. For further study, see 2Ki 18:18–19:2; Isa 22:15-25; 36:3–37:2,22-29. Also called Shebnah.

SHEBNAH 2Ki 18:18; see Shebna

SHEBUEL (SHEH boo uhl) meaning unknown
1. 11 century B.C.; 1Ch 23:16; Levite; officer in charge of treasurers under David
2. 1Ch 25:4; see Shubael 2

SHECANIAH (SHEK uh NIGH uh) *dweller with the Lord*
1. 10 century B.C.; 1Ch 24:11; head of division of priests under David
2. 8 century B.C.; 2Ch 31:15; priest; distributed contributions among other priests
3. 6 century B.C.; Ne 12:3; priest who returned to Judah
4. Ezr 8:3; his descendant Hattush returned to Judah with Ezra
5. 1Ch 3:21; descendant of Zerubbabel; possibly Shecaniah 4
6. 5 century B.C.; Ne 3:29; father of Shemaiah 22
7. 5 century B.C.; Ezr 8:5; head of family that returned to Judah after Exile
8. 5 century B.C.; Ezr 10:2; favored Ezra's divorce reform
9. 5 century B.C.; Ne 6:18; father-in-law of Nehemiah's enemy Tobiah

SHECHEM (SHEK uhm) *shoulder*
1. 20 century B.C.; Gen 34:2; son of Hamor; seduced and proposed to Dinah

2. Nu 26:31; descendant of Manasseh
3. 1Ch 7:19; descendant of Manasseh

SHEDEUR (SHED ee uhr) *shedder of light;* 15 century B.C.; Nu 1:5; father of Elizur; Reubenite leader

SHEERAH (SHEE uh ruh) meaning unknown; 19 century B.C.; 1Ch 7:24

Sheerah, the daughter or granddaughter of Ephraim, oversaw the building of three major cities: Lower and Upper Beth Horon and Uzzen-sheerah. The two Beth Horons were located along the mountain pass between the territories of Benjamin and Ephraim, some ten miles northwest of Jerusalem. Due to their strategic location on the route into Palestine, these two cities saw much bloodshed, including battles against the Amorites, Philistines, and Syrians. The upper city housed the fortified military barracks, while the lower city held the farmer's market. For further study, see Jos 10:6-15; 1Ki 9:17; 1Ch 7:24; 2Ch 8:5.

SHEHARIAH (SHEH huh RYE uh) meaning unknown; 1Ch 8:26; descendant of Benjamin

SHELAH (SHEE luh) *prayer*
1. Gen 10:24; descendant of Shem; father of Eber; ancestor of Abraham
2. 19 century B.C.; Gen 38:5; son of Judah and Shua

SHELEMIAH (SHEL uh MYE uh) *the Lord is recompense*
1. 1Ch 26:14; see Meshelemiah
2. 7 century B.C.; Jer 36:14; his grandson Jehudi took Jeremiah's scroll
3. 7 century B.C.; Jer 37:3; his son Jehucal threw Jeremiah into cistern
4. 7 century B.C.; Jer 37:13; his son Irijah arrested Jeremiah
5. 7 century B.C.; Jer 36:26; official who tried to arrest Baruch and Jeremiah
6. 5 century B.C.; Ne 3:30; his son Hananiah helped rebuild Jerusalem wall
7. 5 century B.C.; Ezr 10:39; descendant of Binnui; married and divorced foreigner after Exile
8. 5 century B.C.; Ezr 10:41; another descendant of Binnui who married and divorced foreigner
9. 5 century B.C.; Ne 13:13; priest appointed as temple treasurer by Nehemiah

SHELEPH (SHEE lef) *drawn out;* Gen 10:26; son of Joktan; ancestor of southern Arabian tribe

SHELESH (SHEE lesh) possibly *third;* 1Ch 7:35; descendant of Asher

SHELOMI (shuh LOH mye) *my peace;* 15 century B.C.; Nu 34:27; his son Ahihud helped divide the land in Canaan

SHELOMITH (shuh LOH mith) *peaceful*
1. 15 century B.C.; Lev 24:11; her son was accused of blasphemy and stoned to death during the Exodus
2. 1Ch 23:18; Levite descendant of Izhar; also called Shelomoth 2
3. 10 century B.C.; 2Ch 11:20; child of King Rehoboam and Maacah
4. 6 century B.C.; 1Ch 3:19; daughter of Zerubbabel
5. 5 century B.C.; Ezr 8:10; head of family that returned to Judah

SHELOMOTH (shuh LOH mahth) *peaceful*
1. 11 century B.C.; 1Ch 23:9; Gershonite; head of family of Levites in David's time
2. 1Ch 24:22; see Shelomith 2
3. 10 century B.C.; 1Ch 26:25; descendant of Eliezer the son of Moses; temple treasurer

SHELUMIEL (shuh LOO mee uhl) *God is peace;* 15 century B.C.; Nu 1:6; leader of Simeonites during Exodus

SHEM (SHEM) *renown* or *name;*
Gen 5:32

Noah's oldest son Shem was one of eight human survivors of the Flood to touch down on Mt. Ararat and settle in that mountainous kingdom. He and his wife were childless before the Flood, but afterward (at 110 years of age), Shem fathered five sons—Elam, Asshur, Arpachshad, Lud, and Aram. Shem and his sons are credited by scholars with fathering the five Semitic nations of Persia, Assyria, Chaldea, Lydia, and Syria. That makes Shem the father of the ancient Near East peoples generally and the Israelites specifically (through Arpachshad's descendant Eber). For further study, see Gen 5:32–11:11; 1Ch 1:4,17.

SHEMA (SHEE muh) possibly *fame* or *rumor*
1. 1Ch 2:43; descendant of Caleb
2. 1Ch 5:8; descendant of Reuben
3. 1Ch 8:13; head of Benjaminite family who helped defeat Philistines
4. 5 century B.C.; Ne 8:4; aide to Ezra in reading of the Law

SHEMAAH (shuh MAY uh) possibly *fame;* 11 century B.C.; 1Ch 12:3; Benjaminite whose sons joined David

SHEMAIAH (shuh MAY yuh) *the Lord hears*
1. 1Ch 4:37; ancestor of Simeonites active in Hezekiah's reign
2. 1Ch 5:4; descendant of Reuben
3. 11 century B.C.; 1Ch 15:8; Levite who assisted David in bringing ark to Jerusalem
4. 10 century B.C.; 1Ch 24:6; Levite scribe active in temple service
5. 10 century B.C.; 1Ch 26:4; son of Obed-edom; head of family of gatekeepers
6. 10 century B.C.; 1Ki 12:22

As a prophet, Shemaiah advised King Rehoboam during his reign over Judah. When the ten northern tribes broke off from Rehoboam to form the northern kingdom, Shemaiah kept the king from waging war to bring them back by revealing that this course of events was God's will. Five years later, when Egypt's King Shishak was raiding sev-

Noah's sons Shem, Ham, and Japheth.

eral of Judah's cities, Shemaiah again prophesied that this was the Lord's punishment for Rehoboam's abandonment of God. When Rehoboam took Shemaiah's word to heart and repented, God spared Judah. For further study, see 1Ki 12:20-24; 2Ch 11:2-4; 12:1-15.

7. 9 century B.C.; 2Ch 17:8; Levite; taught the Law in Judah

8. 8 century B.C.; 2Ch 29:14; Levite; purified temple in Hezekiah's day

9. 8 century B.C.; 2Ch 31:15; assistant to Kore the Levite in charge of offerings

10. 7 century B.C.; 2Ch 35:9; chief Levite in Passover celebration under Josiah

11. 7 century B.C.; Jer 26:20; father of prophet Uriah

12. 7 century B.C.; Jer 36:12; his son Delaiah supported preservation of Jeremiah's scroll

13. 7 century B.C.; Jer 29:24; opponent of Jeremiah

14. Ne 12:36; Levite descended from Asaph

15. 6 century B.C.; Ne 10:8; priest who returned to Judah after Exile

16. 1Ch 9:16; see Shammua 3

17. 5 century B.C.; 1Ch 9:14; Levite who resettled in Jerusalem

18. 5 century B.C.; Ezr 8:13; one who returned to Judah after Exile

19. 5 century B.C.; Ezr 8:16; one sent to Iddo to bring Levites to Jerusalem

20. 5 century B.C.; Ezr 10:21; priest who married and divorced foreigner after Exile

21. 5 century B.C.; Ezr 10:31; one who married and divorced foreigner after Exile

22. 5 century B.C.; Ne 3:29; son of Shecaniah; helped rebuild Jerusalem wall

23. 5 century B.C.; Ne 6:10; false prophet hired to trick Nehemiah to commit sacrilege

24. 5 century B.C.; Ne 10:8; priest; sealed covenant renewal

25. 5 century B.C.; Ne 12:34; Jewish leader; participant in Jerusalem wall dedication

26. 5 century B.C.; Ne 12:35; Levite musician at Jerusalem wall dedication

27. 5 century B.C.; Ne 12:42; priest in choir at Jerusalem wall dedication

28. 1Ch 3:22; descendant of Zerubbabel

SHEMARIAH (SHEM uh RYE uh) *the Lord keeps*
1. 11 century B.C.; 1Ch 12:5; Benjaminite warrior; defected to David at Ziklag

2. 10 century B.C.; 2Ch 11:19; son of King Rehoboam and Mahalath

3. 5 century B.C.; Ezr 10:32; married and divorced foreigner after Exile

4. 5 century B.C.; Ezr 10:41; another who married and divorced foreigner after Exile

SHEMEBER (shem EE buhr) meaning unknown; 22 century B.C.; Gen 14:2; king of Zeboiim; ally of Sodom

SHEMED (SHEE med) *destruction;* Gen 14:2; built towns of Ono and Lod; descendant of Benjamin

SHEMELIAH (shem eh LYE ah) meaning unknown; Tob 5:14; friend of Tobit

SHEMER (SHEE muhr) *watch*
1. 1Ch 6:46; Merarite Levite; ancestor of David's music minister

2. 9 century B.C.; 1Ki 16:24; owner of hill on which Samaria was built

SHEMIDA (shuh MYE duh) meaning unknown; Nu 26:32; ancestral head of Manassite clan

SHEMIRAMOTH (shuh MEER uh mahth) meaning unknown
1. 11 century B.C.; 1Ch 15:18; lyrist before the ark of the covenant

2. 9 century B.C.; 2Ch 17:8; Levite; taught the Law throughout Judah

SHEMUEL (SHEM yoo uhl) *heard by God;* 15 century B.C.; Nu 34:20; Simeonite who allotted land in Canaan

SHENAZZAR (shuh NAZ uhr) *protected by Sin* [a god]; 6 century B.C.; 1Ch 3:18; son of Jehoiachin

SHEPHATIAH (SHEF uh TYE uh) *the Lord is judge*
1. 11 century B.C.; 1Ch 12:5; Benjaminite; joined David at Ziklag

2. 10 century B.C.; 2Sa 3:4; son of David and Abital

3. 10 century B.C.; 1Ch 27:16; Simeonite officer in David's day

4. 10 century B.C.; Ezr 2:57; Solomon's servant whose descendants returned to Judah

5. 9 century B.C.; 2Ch 21:2; son of Jehoshaphat; brother of Jehoram
6. Ezr 2:4; ancestor of family who returned to Judah after Exile
7. Ne 11:4; ancestor of Judahite who resettled in Jerusalem
8. 7 century B.C.; Jer 38:1; official who threw Jeremiah into cistern
9. 5 century B.C.; 1Ch 9:8; his son Meshullam resettled in Jerusalem

SHEPHI 1Ch 1:40; see Shepho

SHEPHO (SHEE foh) *bareness;* 20 century B.C.; Gen 36:23; son of Shobal the Horite chief in Esau's day; also called Shephi

SHEPHUPHAM Nu 26:39; see Shephuphan

SHEPHUPHAN (sheh FOO fan) meaning unknown; 19 century B.C.; 1Ch 8:5; ancestor of Shuppim; also called Shephupham

SHEREBIAH (SHAIR uh BYE uh) *the Lord's burning heat*
1. 6 century B.C.; Ne 12:8; Levite; returned to Judah after Exile
2. 5 century B.C.; Ezr 8:18; head of Levites recruited from Iddo for temple service
3. 5 century B.C.; Ne 10:12; Levite; sealed covenant renewal; possibly Sherebiah 1 or 2
4. 5 century B.C.; Ne 12:24; chief Levite under priest Eliashib; possibly Sherebiah 2

SHERESH (SHEER esh) *root;* 1Ch 7:16; descendant of Manasseh

SHESHAI (SHEE shy) *princely* or *free;* 15 century B.C.; Nu 13:22; giant descended from Anak

SHESHAN (SHEE shan) *princely* or *free;* 1Ch 2:31; Judahite with no sons; gave daughter to Egyptian slave

SHESHBAZZAR (shesh BAZ uhr) *may Sin* [a god] *protect the father;* 6 century B.C.; Ezr 1:8

   After the decree of King Cyrus of Persia, Sheshbazzar, the prince of Judah, was among the first group of exiles permitted to go back to Jerusalem to rebuild the temple. Sheshbazzar was made governor and put in charge of the 5400 sacred temple vessels that had been stolen by the Babylonians and were returned to Jerusalem with the Jews. Sheshbazzar was also responsible for laying the foundations of the temple. After the return to Jerusalem, Zerubbabel emerged as the leader of the repatriated exiles. Since both Sheshbazzar and Zerubbabel were from royalty, had Babylonian names, and played significant roles in the return, some scholars suggest that Sheshbazzar and Zerubbabel were the same person. However, the biblical evidence supports the idea that they were separate individuals. For further study, see Ezr 1; 5:14-16. See Zerubbabel.

SHETHAR (SHEE thahr) *star* or *commander;* 5 century B.C.; Est 1:14; noble of Medo-Persia; advisor to King Ahasuerus

SHETHAR-BOZENAI (SHEE thahr BAHZ uh nye) *star of splendor;* 6 century B.C.; Ezr 5:3; opposed temple rebuilding

SHETHITES (SHETH ights) *sons of tumult;* Nu 24:17; descriptive name for Moabites in Balaam's oracle

SHEVA (SHEE vuh) meaning unknown
1. 1Ch 2:49; son of Caleb by Maacah; descendant of Judah 1
2. 2Sa 20:25; see Seraiah 3

SHILHI (SHIL high) *armed;* 10 century B.C.; 1Ki 22:42; grandfather of King Jehoshaphat

SHILLEM (SHIL uhm) *compensation;* 19 century B.C.; Gen 46:24; son of Naphtali; also called Shallum 1

SHILONITES (SHY luh nights) 1Ki 11:29; people from Shiloh; some resettled in Jerusalem after Exile

SHILSHAH (SHIL shuh) *third;* 1Ch 7:37; descendant of Asher

SHIMEA (SHIM ee uh) *fame* or *God has heard*
1. 1Ch 6:30; descendant of Merari
2. 11 century B.C.; 1Ch 6:39; Levite; kinsman of Asaph the music minister
3. 1Ch 2:13; see Shammah 2
4. 10 century B.C.; 1Ch 3:5; son of David

SHIMEAH (SHIM ee uh) *fame* or *God has heard*
1. 11 century B.C.; 1Ch 8:32; relative of King Saul who resided in Jerusalem; also called Shimeam
2. 2Sa 13:3; see Shammah 2

SHIMEAM 1Ch 9:38; see Shimeah 1

SHIMEATH (SHIM ee ath) *fame* or *hearing;* 9 century B.C.; 2Ki 12:21; Ammonite mother of King Joash's murderer

SHIMEI (SHIM ee eye) *the Lord hear me*
1. Ex 6:17; ancestral head of Levite clan
2. 1Ch 4:26; in genealogy of Simeon
3. 1Ch 5:4; descendant of Reuben
4. 1Ch 6:29; descendant of Merari
5. 1Ch 6:42; in genealogy of David's musician, Heman; possibly Shimei 1
6. 1Ch 8:21; in geneaology of Benjamin
7. 1Ch 23:9; Levite descendant of Gershon; possibly Shimei 5
8. Est 2:5; descendant of Kish; ancestor of Mordecai
9. 10 century B.C.; 2Sa 16:5
   As King David fled to safety during his son Absalom's coup attempt, Shimei the Benjaminite publicly cursed the king and accused him of wrongfully taking the throne from his predecessor Saul. David restrained his soldiers, who were eager to kill Shimei for the affront. When David returned after Absalom's defeat, Shimei begged for and received forgiveness for his words. On his deathbed, however, David cautioned his successor, Solomon, to rid himself of Shimei. Solomon had Shimei confined to the city limits of Jerusalem and then had him executed when Shimei violated that order. For further study, see 2Sa 16:5-13; 19:16-23; 1Ki 2:8-9, 36-46.
10. 2Sa 21:21; see Shammah 2
11. 10 century B.C.; 1Ki 1:8; officer of David; loyal during Adonijah's attempted coup
12. 10 century B.C.; 1Ch 25:3; son of Jeduthun; head of division of music ministers
13. 10 century B.C.; 1Ch 27:27; overseer of King David's vineyards
14. 10 century B.C.; 1Ki 4:18; district governor under Solomon; possibly Shimei 11
15. 8 century B.C.; 2Ch 29:14; Levite descendant of Heman; helped purify temple

16. 8 century B.C.; 2Ch 31:12; helped with temple treasury; possibly Shimei 15
17. 6 century B.C.; 1Ch 3:19; grandson of Jehoiachin
18. 5 century B.C.; Ezr 10:23; Levite who married and divorced foreigner after Exile
19. 5 century B.C.; Ezr 10:33; another who married and divorced foreigner after Exile
20. 5 century B.C.; Ezr 10:38; a third who married and divorced foreigner after Exile

SHIMEON (SHIM ee uhn) *hearing;* 5 century B.C.; Ezr 10:31; married and divorced foreigner after Exile

SHIMON (SHY muhn) meaning unknown; 1Ch 4:20; descendant of Judah 1

SHIMRATH (SHIM rath) *watcher;* 1Ch 8:21; descendant of Benjamin

SHIMRI (SHIM ree) *vigilant*
1. 1Ch 4:37; descendant of Simeon
2. 11 century B.C.; 1Ch 11:45; father of Jediael the mighty man of David
3. 10 century B.C.; 1Ch 26:10; son of Hosah and Merarite; tabernacle gatekeeper
4. 8 century B.C.; 2Ch 29:13; Levite; helped purify temple in Hezekiah's day

SHIMRITH (SHIM rith) *vigilant;* 9 century B.C.; 2Ch 24:26; mother of King Joash's murderer; also called Shomer 2

SHIMRON (SHIM rahn) *a guard* or *a watch-place;* 19 century B.C.; Gen 46:13; son of Issachar

SHIMSHAI (SHIM shy) *bright* or *sun-child;* 5 century B.C.; Ezr 4:8; opponent of rebuilding Jerusalem wall

SHINAB (SHY nab) *tooth of the father;* 22 century B.C.; Gen 14:2; King of Admah; defeated by Chedorlaomer

SHIPHI (SHY fye) *overflow;* 8 century B.C.; 1Ch 4:37; father of Ziza 2

SHIPHRAH (SHIF ruh) *beauty;* 15 century B.C.; Ex 1:15; Hebrew midwife who refused to kill male babies; see Puah

SHIPHTAN (SHIF tan) *judge;* 15 century B.C.; Nu 34:24; his son Kemuel divided land of Canaan

SHISHA 1Ki 4:3; see Seraiah 3

SHISHAK (SHEE shak) meaning unknown; ruled 945–925 B.C.; 1Ki 11:40; Egyptian king; fought Israelites; see Pharaoh

SHITRAI (SHY trye) meaning unknown; 10 century B.C.; 1Ch 27:29; shepherd of flocks in Sharon

SHIZA (SHY zuh) *splendor;* 11 century B.C.; 1Ch 11:42; father of Adina the mighty man of David

SHOBAB (SHOH bab) meaning unknown
1. 1Ch 2:18; son of Caleb; descendant of Judah 1
2. 10 century B.C.; 2Sa 5:14; son born to David in Jerusalem

SHOBACH (SHOH bak) *enlarging;* 10 century B.C.; 2Sa 10:16; Syrian general; died in war; also called Shophach

SHOBAI (SHOH bye) *captive;* Ezr 2:42; ancestral head of family of gatekeepers

SHOBAL (SHOH buhl) meaning unknown
1. 20 century B.C.; Gen 36:20; Horite chief living in Seir
2. 1Ch 2:50; grandson of Caleb; founder of Kiriath-jearim
3. 1Ch 4:1; ancestral source of the Zorathites; possibly Shobal 2

SHOBEK (SHOH bek) possibly *conqueror;* 5 century B.C.; Ne 10:24; Jewish leader; sealed covenant renewal

SHOBI (SHOH bih) *captive;* 10 century B.C.; 2Sa 17:27; son of King Nahash; brought food to David

SHOHAM (SHOH ham) *precious stone;* 11 century B.C.; 1Ch 24:27; head of Levite family who served under David

SHOMER (SHOH muhr) *keeper* or *watcher*
1. 1Ch 7:32; descendant of Asher
2. 2Ki 12:21; see Shimrith

SHOPHACH 1Ch 19:16; see Shobach

SHUA (SHOO uh) *help*
1. Gen 38:2; see Bath-shua 1
2. 1Ch 7:32; daughter of Heber the leader of tribe of Asher

SHUAH (SHOO uh) *depression* or *prosperity;* 21 century B.C.; Gen 25:2; son of Abraham by Keturah; led a desert tribe

SHUAL (SHOO uhl) *fox* or *jackal;* 1Ch 7:36; in genealogy of Asher

SHUBAEL (SHOO bay uhl) meaning unknown
1. 1Ch 24:20; Levite descendant of Amram
2. 10 century B.C.; 1Ch 25:20; son of Heman; chief of singers under David; also called Shebuel 2

SHUHAH (SHOO huh) *depression* or *prosperity;* 1Ch 4:11; brother of Chelub

SHUHAM Nu 26:42; see Hushim 1

SHUHITES (SHOO hights) Job 2:11; descendants of Shuah the son of Abraham; maybe from Suhu in northern Syria

SHUNAMMITES (SHOO nam mights) 1Ki 1:3; natives of Shunem

SHUNI (SHOO nih) *resting;* 19 century B.C.; Gen 46:16; son of Gad; ancestral head of clan

SHUPPIM (SHUP im) *serpents*
1. 19 century B.C.; 1Ch 7:12; descendant of Benjamin; tribal leader
2. 10 century B.C.; 1Ch 26:16; gatekeeper in city of David

SHUTHELAH (SHOO thuh luh) meaning unknown
1. 19 century B.C.; Nu 26:35; son of Ephraim; ancestral source of Ephraimites
2. 1Ch 7:21; descendant of Ephraim the son of Joseph

SIA Ne 7:47; see Siaha

SIAHA (SIGH uh huh) *assembly;* Ezr 2:44; ancestor of family of temple servants; also called Sia

SIBBECAI 2Sa 21:18; see Mebunnai

SIDONIANS (sih DAWN ih uhns) Dt 3:9; inhabitants of Sidon, a major city in ancient Phoenicia criticized in the Old Testament as a place of idolatry and materialism

SIHON (SIGH hahn) *sweeping away;* 15 century B.C.; Nu 21:21; Amorite king; slain in battle with Israelites

SILAS (SI luhs) *of the woods;* 1 century A.D; Ac 15:22

Silas traveled on Paul's second missionary journey through Syria, Asia Minor, Macedonia, and Thessalonica. Silas had been a Jerusalem synagogue attendant who preserved the scrolls and Scriptures, and his Roman citizenship, writing ability, and ties to the Jerusalem church proved useful for the church at large. The Jerusalem Council of apostles and elders appointed Silas and three others to write and deliver their landmark decision to all outlying churches regarding ethical guidelines for Gentile converts. Silas was imprisoned with Paul at Philippi when an earthquake destroyed the jail and freed all the prisoners. For further study, see Ac 15:22-41; 16:16–18:5; 2Co 1:19; 1Th 1:1; 2Th 1:1; 1Pe 5:12. Also called Silvanus.

SILVANUS 2Cor 1:19; see Silas

SIMEON (SIM ee uhn) *hearing* or *he hears*
1. 20 century B.C.; Gen 29:33; son of Jacob and Leah
2. Lk 3:30; descendant of David; ancestor of Jesus
3. 1Mac 2:1; ancestor of Mattathi the father of Judas Maccabeus
4. 1 century B.C.; Lk 2:25

Having been promised by the Holy Spirit that he would not die without seeing the Messiah, Simeon encountered Jesus at the temple in Jerusalem. Mary and Joseph had brought the infant there to consecrate their firstborn son with an offering, as Jewish custom demanded. Simeon saw Jesus as the fulfillment of the Holy Spirit's promise to him and identified him as the salvation of Hebrew and Gentile alike. Simeon also foresaw that Jesus's parents would be hurt by the controversy surrounding their son. The aged prophet Anna also came forward that day and confirmed Simeon's words. For further study, see Ex 13:2; Lev 12:1-8; Lk 2:25-38.

SIMEONITES (SIM ee uhn ights) Nu 2:12; descendants of Simeon the son of Jacob; settled in southern Canaan

SIMON (SIGH muhn) *he hears* or *hearing*
1. 3 century B.C.; Sir 50:1; high priest called The Just
2. 2 century B.C.; 1Mac 2:3

Simon was the second son of the Maccabean priest Mattathias. When Israel fell to the Seleucid Empire, Simon's father refused the Seleucids' demands to abandon Judaism and worship their god. Mattathias led his sons and like-minded Jews into the hills and fought against the Seleucid forces. After his brothers were killed, Simon lead the rebellion for 12 more years. When the Seleucid ruler King Demetrius II was threatened by a usurper, Simon cleverly supported the king. Demetrius emerged victorious, and he gratefully granted Israel's freedom and appointed Simon chief priest.

Simeon with Jesus at the temple of Jerusalem. Stained glass. Sacred Heart Church, Concord, New Hampshire.

Simon and Judas, two of the Maccabeans who led the revolt against the Seleucid Empire.

Several years later, Simon was murdered by a traitorous son-in-law. For further study, see 1Mac 1–16. Also called Thassi.

3. 1 century A.D.; Jn 6:71; father of Judas Iscariot
4. Mt 4:18; see Peter
5. 1 century A.D.; Mt 10:4

Simon, one of Jesus's 12 apostles, was called the Zealot or the Cananaean (meaning *zealous one*), indicating that he may have been a member of the Zealot party. These fanatical nationalists of Judea opposed the Roman occupation and advocated violence to regain their autonomy. Such Zealots gave Galilee the reputation as the seedbed of revolutionaries in the eyes of Rome. Some scholars note that the description of Simon may mean he was a supporter of zealous adherence to Jewish Law rather than of revolution. As one of the apostles, Simon participated in the events leading to the death of Jesus and witnessed his resurrection from the dead and his ascension into heaven. For further study, see Mk 3:18; Lk 6:15; Ac 1:13.

6. 1 century A.D.; Mt 13:55; brother of Jesus
7. 1 century A.D.; Lk 7:40

As a Pharisee, Simon was charged with interpreting and enforcing Jewish Law, and he considered it inappropriate to consort with any who did not also follow this Law. While entertaining Jesus in his home, Simon became outraged and even doubted Jesus's piousness when Jesus welcomed a sinful woman who approached him. The woman bathed Jesus's feet with her tears, wiped them dry with her hair, and anointed them with oil in an effort to gain his blessing. After offering the woman forgiveness for her sins, Jesus explained to Simon that even though the woman was a sinner, she had expressed a greater love for him than had the self-righteous Pharisee. For further study, see Lk 7:36-50.

8. 1 century A.D.; Mt 26:6; leper in Bethany in whose house Jesus's feet were perfumed
9. 1 century A.D.; Mk 15:21; Cyrenian who carried cross for Jesus
10. 1 century A.D.; Ac 8:9

Simon the Sorcerer was heralded throughout Samaria for his apparent magical abilities and supernatural powers. When Philip brought the Gospel to the land, however, Simon and a great many others converted and became baptized. Simon stayed close by Philip and saw him perform miracles. Later Peter and John arrived and brought the Holy Spirit upon many of the converts by laying their hands on them. Simon revealed a lack of understanding of God's power when he offered them money to share this ability with him. Peter condemned him severely for his attempt and said that his "heart is not right before God" (Ac 8:21). Simon listened to Paul's warning and repented of his desire to wield God's power for his own use. For further study, see Ac 8:9-25.

11. 1 century A.D.; Ac 9:43; tanner in Joppa with whom Peter stayed

SINITES (SIGH nights) Gen 10:17; a tribe of Canaanites who settled in northern Phoenicia (modern Lebanon)

SIPPAI 1Ch 20:4; see Saph

SIRACH (SIGH rak) meaning unknown; Sir 50:27; grandfather of Jesus Ben Sira the author of the Book of Sirach

SISERA (SIS uhr uh) meaning unknown
1. 13 century B.C.; Jdg 4:2; Canaanite commander of King Jabin's army; defeated by Deborah; killed by Jael
2. Ezr 2:53; ancestor of temple servant family that returned to Judah

Sisinnes (sih SIN neez) meaning unknown; 6 century B.C.; 1Esd 6:3; Syrian governor; protested temple restoration

Sismai (SIS mye) meaning unknown; 1Ch 2:40; in genealogy of Judah

Sithri (SITH rye) *the Lord is protection;* Ex 6:22; Kohathite Levite; in family of Moses and Aaron

So (SOH) meaning unknown; 8 century B.C.; 2Ki 17:4; king of Egypt to whom Hoshea appealed

Soco (SO coh) *thorny;* 1Ch 4:18; descendant of Judah 1; son of Heber

Sodi (SOH dih) *my secret;* 15 century B.C.; Nu 13:10; father of Gaddiel the spy in Canaan

Solomon (SAHL uh muhn) *peaceable;* ruled 970–930 B.C.; 2Sa 12:24

By all accounts, King Solomon was the wisest man of his era, a master of proverbial lore, and an insightful problem-solver. Despite his famed sagac-

ity, he was often discouraged and led astray by others; he made a number of compromises, and eventually his heart grew cold to God. Such contradictions make it difficult for those seeking to study the reputed wisdom of Solomon.

Solomon succeeded to the throne of Israel in an unprecedented manner: Unlike Saul or David, he did not have the triumphant military war record or the charismatic personality to be anointed king. Instead he had the political pull of Bathsheba, his mother and David's favorite wife. Although others were in line ahead of him for the throne, Solomon won the kingship through the influence that his mother and Nathan the prophet wielded over David. To solidify his hold on power, Solomon had his half-brother and potential usurper Adonijah killed, while he himself entered into many political marriages. Later, Solomon's faith would be eroded by the influence of the religions of his many foreign wives—among whom were Hittites, Moabites, Edomites, Sidonians, and Ammonites.

Early in his reign, Solomon received a vision of God while performing a sacrifice. When God asked the young king what gift he wanted, Solomon asked for wisdom to "discern between good and

Solomon orders the death of a child to determine which of two women is the mother.

evil" (1Ki 3:9) so that he might be a better ruler of God's people. The request so pleased God that he also bestowed a blessing of wealth and prosperity on the king. The famous decision in which Solomon resolved a dispute over an infant served to demonstrate that God had granted Solomon's request. Two women claimed custody of the same small child, and the king determined which was the true mother by ordering the child cut in half and divided between the women. When one of them insisted on giving the child up in order to let it live, Solomon ruled that she must be the child's parent.

Solomon established a strong centralized monarchy and an even tax system for his people. He divided the nation into 12 regions, each of which was responsible for provisioning the court for one month of the year. He established strong trading alliances with other nations that quickly made him fabulously wealthy. He also undertook extensive building projects, dedicating seven years to building the temple his father had dreamed of and almost twice that long to erecting his own sumptuous palace. Foreign slaves were used in the building projects, but he also conscripted Israelite laborers on a large scale. Between the heavy taxes and the enforced building projects, Solomon's accomplishments placed a crushing economic burden on his subjects.

Solomon's other main interest was women. He reportedly had an astounding 700 wives and 300 concubines. Many of the marriages were calculated to foster internal political alliances or international relations or to increase Solomon's world-famous wealth, and the great king's downfall is attributed to these pursuits. Although he clearly accomplished much in a material sense, he let go of the ways of God in pursuing these ends and brought the nation and himself to strife. To accomodate the demands of many of his foreign wives, Solomon freely allowed pagan worship in a variety of forms and so

> ⇥ ⇤
>
> *"God said to (Solomon)*
> *'...Indeed I give you a wise*
> *and discerning mind;*
> *no one like you has been*
> *before you and no one*
> *like you shall arise*
> *after you.'"*
>
> 1Ki 3:11-12

lost God's favor. In punishment, Solomon's peaceful reign was disrupted toward the end of his life by threats of violence from outside the nation. More importantly, the heavy burdens he placed on his people prompted the kingdom to be torn in two shortly after his death; ten of Israel's tribes broke away to form the northern kingdom, while only two, Judah and Benjamin, remained loyal to the house of David.

Solomon was a prolific writer and is credited with having authored some 3000 proverbs, 1000 songs, and several books of the Bible. Some of his writings indicate that Solomon was keenly aware that the material accomplishments of his reign meant nothing next to the spiritual decay of his life. Despite all his women, wealth, and fame, his words sometimes convey a deep cynicism and lack of joy. In the Book of Ecclesiastes, Solomon warns of focusing one's efforts on self instead of on God. "I saw all the deeds that are done under the sun; and see, all is vanity and a chasing after the wind" (Ecc 1:14). From his failures and pain, and with the wisdom of hindsight, he concludes, "Remember your creator in the days of your youth.... Fear God, and keep his commandments; for that is the whole duty of everyone. For God will bring every deed into judgment, including every secret thing, whether good or evil" (Ecc 12:1,13–14).

For further study, see 1Ki 1–14; 1Ch 28–29; 2Ch 1–9. For books of Scripture credited to Solomon, see Proverbs 1–21, Ecclesiastes, and the Song of Solomon. In Jewish tradition, he is also credited with writing the apocryphal book the Wisdom of Solomon. ·

SOPATER (SOH pat uhr) *of sound parentage;* 1 century A.D.; Ac 20:4; Paul's escort; also called Sosipater 2

SOPHERETH Ne 7:57; see Hassophereth

SOSIPATER (soh SIP uh tuhr) *defending one's father*
1. 2 century B.C.; 2Mac 12:19; commander in Maccabean army
2. Ro 16:21; see Sopater

SOSTHENES (SAHS thuh neez) meaning unknown
1. 1 century A.D.; Ac 18:17
Sosthenes likely acted as prosecuter when the apostle Paul was brought to court in Corinth accused of violating religious customs. When Paul was acquitted of the false charges, the crowd that levied the accusations turned on Sosthenes and beat him. Yet, as a result of granting Paul his freedom of speech, Sosthenes was won over by Paul's Gospel. Along with Crispus, another synagogue ruler at Corinth, Sosthenes became a convert. This may be the same Sosthenes mentioned later as a copyist in Paul's First Letter to the Corinthians. For further study, see Ac 18:1-17; 1Co 1:1.
2. 1Co 1:1; companion of Paul; possibly Sosthenes 1

SOSTRATUS (suh STRAH tuhs) meaning unknown; 2 century B.C.; 2Mac 4:28; Syrian commander; tax collector

SOTAI (SOH tye) meaning unknown; 10 century B.C.; Ezr 2:55; descendant of Solomon's servants

STACHYS (STAY kis) *ear* [of grain]; 1 century A.D.; Ro 16:9; Roman Christian greeted by Paul

STEPHANAS (STEF uh nuhs) *crown;* 1 century A.D.; 1Co 1:16
Stephanas and his household were the first Christian converts in Achaia and some of the founding members of the Corinthian church. His family members were among the few people personally baptized by the apostle Paul when he was in Corinth. In his letter to the Corinthian church while in Ephesus, Paul commended Stephanas's family for their devotion to the service of other Christians. He encouraged the Corinthians to serve this family since they were promoting the church and working as co-laborers with him. Finally, Paul urged the Corinthians to give recognition to Stephanas, Fortunatus, and Achaicus, who had come to Ephesus and encouraged him there. For further study, see 1Co 16:15-17.

Stephen is stoned to death for blasphemy. Stained glass. St. Stephen's Church, Edina, Minnesota.

STEPHEN (STEE vuhn) *crown* or *crown-bearer;* 1 century A.D.; Ac 6:5
Acclaimed "a man full of faith and the Holy Spirit" (Ac 6:5), Stephen was chosen as one of the first seven deacons of the early Christian church. As a Greek-speaking Christian, he was entangled in the controversy over whether or not to open the Gospel to non-Jews. For his arguments using Scripture to promote the spread of the Gospel, Stephen was convicted of blasphemy by the the Jewish high council and stoned to death, becoming the first Christian martyr. Elements of his trial and death are parallel to those of Jesus; in court he and Jesus were accused of similar crimes, and at his death Stephen commended his spirit to God and asked that his executioners be forgiven as Jesus had done on the cross. While Stephen's arguments eventually did open up the church to outsiders, his conviction and death sparked a short-term persecution of the church throughout Jerusalem. For further study, see Ac 6–7.

SUA (SOO ah) meaning unknown; 1Esd 5:29; ancestor of temple servants returning from Exile

SUAH (SOO uh) possibly *sweeping* or *riches* or *distinction;* 1Ch 7:36; in genealogy of Asher

SUBAI (SOO bye) meaning unknown; 1Esd 5:30; ancestor of temple servants that returned to Jerusalem after Exile

SUBAS (SOO bas) meaning unknown; 10 century B.C.; 1Esd 5:34; servant of Solomon whose ancestors returned from Exile

SUCCOTH-BENOTH (SUHK koth BEE noth) *booths* or *tabernacles of daughters;* 2Ki 17:30; deity worshiped by Babylonians

SUKKIIM (SUHK kim) meaning unknown; 2Ch 12:3; a tribe (perhaps African) who invaded Judah with King Shishak

SUSANNA (soo ZAN uh) *lily*
1. 6 century B.C.; Sus 1:2

The apocryphal book of Susanna depicts Susanna, daughter of Hilkiah, as a beautiful, God-fearing Jewess educated in the Law by her parents. Her husband, Joakim, was a leader in the Jewish community during the Babylonian Exile, and their spacious home, with its attached walled garden, was a gathering place for elders and judges.

Two of the elders desired Susanna because of her beauty and plotted to seduce her. Knowing that she often walked in the garden, they hid there, waiting until she came alone to bathe. They asked her to have intercourse with them and threatened to accuse her of adultery if she refused.

Susanna did refuse and cried out for help. When people came in response to her cries, the two elders claimed they had seen her commit adultery with a young man. Susanna was taken before the judges where the accusations were heard.

Although no proper trial was conducted, the elders' testimony was taken at face value, and Susanna was sentenced to be stoned. Only the prophet Daniel, then a young man, spoke out in protest. He criticized the judges for condemning a righteous woman without a trial. Daniel then demanded to question the two accusing elders separately. He asked each man to say where he and his colleague were standing when they saw the alleged adultery take place. The first said, "under a mastic tree," but the second said, "under an evergreen

oak." The elders' lie and Susanna's innocence were then obvious to the assembly. The two elders were executed in her place and Susanna was honored by her family and community as a righteous woman.

For further study, see the Book of Susanna.
2. 1 century A.D.; Lk 8:3; follower of Christ during his ministry

SUSI (SOO sih) *my horse;* 15 century B.C.; Nu 13:11; father of Gaddi the spy in Canaan

SYNTYCHE (SIN tih kee) *fortunate;* 1 century A.D.; Php 4:2; Philippian woman in conflict with Euodia

SYRIANS see Arameans

Susanna is accosted by two elders as she prepares to bathe.

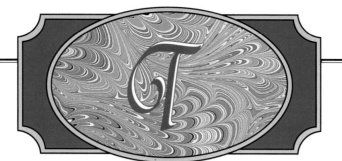

TABBAOTH (TAB ay ahth) possibly *rings;* Ezr 2:43; head of family of temple servants that returned to Judah

TABEEL (TAY bee uhl) *God is good*
1. 8 century B.C.; Isa 7:6; father of pretender or puppet king after Ahaz was deposed
2. 5 century B.C.; Ezr 4:7; Samaritan who opposed rebuilding Jerusalem wall

TABITHA (TAB i thuh) *gazelle;* 1 century A.D.; Ac 9:36

While Peter was in Lydda healing a paralytic named Aeneas, a woman named Tabitha (Dorcas in

Peter brings Tabitha back to life. Stained glass. Quigley Seminary North, Chicago, Illinois.

Greek) became ill and died in nearby Joppa. She was respected for doing good and helping the poor. The disciples sent two men to get Peter who, upon his arrival, was taken to an upstairs room where the body lay attended by mourners. Peter asked them to leave the room, and then, down on his knees praying, he told Tabitha to get up. She opened her eyes and sat up. Peter helped her to her feet and presented her to the people. News of the miracle spread quickly and prompted a great many people to accept Peter's teachings of the Gospel. For further study, see Ac 9:36-40.

TABRIMMON (tab RIM ahn) *Rimmon [a god] is good;* 10 century B.C.; 1Ki 15:18; Syrian king; father of Ben-hadad I

TAHAN (TAY han) meaning unknown
1. Nu 26:35; ancestral head of Ephraimite clan
2. 1Ch 7:25; descendant of Ephraim

TAHASH (TAY hash) possibly *dolphin;* 21 century B.C.; Gen 22:24; son of Nahor by Reumah; nephew of Abraham

TAHATH (TAY hath) *compensation*
1. 1Ch 6:24; Kohathite listed in Levite genealogy
2. 1Ch 7:20; descendant of Ephraim
3. 1Ch 7:20; another descendant of Ephraim

TAHPENES (TAH puh neez) possibly *wife of the king;* 10 century B.C.; 1Ki 11:19; Egyptian queen

TAHREA (TAH ree uh) *flight;* 1Ch 9:41; son of Micah; great-grandson of Jonathan; also called Tarea

TALMAI (TAL mye) possibly *makes furrows* or *my furrows* or *bold*
1. 15 century B.C.; Nu 13:22; son of Anak; driven out from Hebron
2. 11 century B.C.; 2Sa 3:3; king of Geshur; grandfather of Absalom; father-in-law of David

TALMON (TAL mahn) possibly *violent* or *brightness*
1. Ezr 2:42; ancestor of gatekeepers that returned to Judah
2. 5 century B.C.; 1Ch 9:17; Levite gatekeeper; resettled in Jerusalem

TAMAR (TAY mahr) *palm tree*
1. 19 century B.C.; Gen 38:6
When Judah's wicked son Er died, leaving his widow Tamar childless, Judah gave his son Onan to her so she would be able to have a child. According to custom, a brother-in-law was obligated to provide his brother's childless widow with a child, but that child would be considered the heir and descendant of the deceased man. Unwilling to fulfill this duty, Onan would spill his semen on the ground when he lay with Tamar. God was angered by his actions and put him to death. Judah sent Tamar to live with her father until the time that his youngest son, Shelah, would be old enough to give her a son. Fearing that Shelah would die as his brothers had, Judah never sent him to fulfill this familial obligation.

In time, Judah's wife died. After his period of mourning had passed, Tamar learned that he would be traveling to Timnah. She covered her face with a veil and posed as a prostitute at a point on Judah's route. Not recognizing her as his daughter-in-law, he solicited her, offering a young goat in payment. Tamar agreed to sleep with him but requested he leave his signet, cord, and staff as collateral. When Judah later sent a friend with his payment, Tamar was nowhere to be found. Some months later, Judah learned that Tamar had become pregnant; he ordered her burned to death for her impropriety. As she was being led to the fire, Tamar produced Judah's signet, cord, and staff. Recognizing them, Judah conceded that "she is more in the right than I" (Gen 38:26) and so rescinded her death sentence. Tamar gave birth to twin boys, Perez and Zerah. Perez was in the direct line of the ancestry of David, and thus the line of Jesus. Tamar is one of only four women mentioned by Matthew in Jesus's genealogy.

For further study, see Gen 38; Ru 4:12; 1Ch 2:4; Mt 1:3.
2. 10 century B.C.; 2Sa 13:1; sister of Absalom; raped by half-brother Amnon
3. 10 century B.C.; 2Sa 14:27; daughter of Absalom

TAMMUZ (TAM uhz) Eze 8:14; Babylonian fertility god; husband/brother of Ishtar

TANHUMETH (tan HOO meth) *comfort;* 7 century B.C.; 2Ki 25:23; his son Seraiah 7 joined Gedaliah

TAPHATH (TAY fath) possibly *a drop;* 10 century B.C.; 1Ki 4:11; daughter of Solomon; wife of Ben-abinadab

TAPPUAH (TAP poo uh) *apple;* 1Ch 2:43; descendant of Caleb and Judah

TAREA 1Ch 8:35; see Tahrea

TARSHISH (TAHR shish) meaning unknown
1. Gen 10:4; son(s) of Javan; people who lived in the western Mediterranean
2. 1Ch 7:10; descendant of Benjamin
3. 5 century B.C.; Est 1:14; noble of Medo-Persia; advisor to King Ahasuerus

TARTAK (TAHR tak) meaning unknown; 2Ki 17:31; deity worshiped by Avvites in Samaria after 8 century B.C.

TATTENAI (TAT uh nigh) meaning unknown; 6 century B.C.; Ezr 5:3; Persian governor under Darius; helped rebuild temple

TEBAH (TEE buh) possibly *slaughter;* 21 century B.C.; Gen 22:24; son of Nahor and Reumah; nephew of Abraham

TEBALIAH (TAB uh LYE uh) *the Lord has purified;* 10 century B.C.; 1Ch 26:11; tabernacle gatekeeper

TEHINNAH (tuh HIN uh) *supplication;* 1Ch 4:12; founder of city of Ir-nahash

TEKOITES (TUH koh ights) Ne 3:5
The Tekoites lived in the city of Tekoa in Judah, just south of Jerusalem. King David and Jonathan the Maccabean both sought refuge there at different times. The prophet Amos was a Tekoite. For further study, see 2Sa 14; 23:26; 1Ch 2:24; 4:5; 11:28; Jer 6:1; Am 1:1; 1Mac 9:33.

Thomas touches the wounds of the risen Jesus.

TELAH (TEE luh) possibly *breach;* 1Ch 7:25; descendant of Ephraim

TELEM (TEE lem) *a lamb* or *oppression;* 5 century B.C.; Ezr 10:24; gatekeeper who married and divorced foreigner after Exile

TEMA (TEE muh) meaning unknown; 21 century B.C.; Gen 25:15; son of Ishmael; source of inhabitants of Tema in northern Arabia

TEMAH (TEE muh) meaning unknown; Ezr 2:53; ancestor of temple servants that returned to Judah after Exile

TEMAN (TEE muhn) meaning unknown
1. 19 century B.C.; Gen 36:11; grandson of Esau; Edomite chief
2. Gen 36:42; Edomite chief; descendant of Esau

TEMANITES (TEE muhn ights) Gen 36:34; Edomites from Teman, home of Job's friend Eliphaz

TEMENI (TEM uh nigh) meaning unknown; 1Ch 4:6; descendant of Judah 1

TERAH (TEER uh) possibly *wandering* or *wild goat;* 23 century B.C.; Gen 11:24; father of Abraham, Nahor, and Haran

TERESH (TEER esh) possibly *desire* or *greedy;* 5 century B.C.; Est 2:21; guard who plotted Ahasuerus's death; also called Tharra

TERTIUS (TUHR shee uhs) *third;* 1 century A.D.; Ro 16:22; one to whom Paul dedicated letter to Romans

TERTULLUS (tuhr TUL uhs) *third;* 1 century A.D.; Ac 24:1; prosecuted Paul before Felix

THADDAEUS (THAD ee uhs) possibly *large-hearted* or *courageous;* 1 century A.D.; Mt 10:3; apostle of Christ; possibly Judas 4

THARABA (THAHR ah bah) meaning unknown; 5 century B.C.; AddEst 1:10; eunuch who served King Artaxerxes

THARRA AddEst 1:10; see Teresh

THASSI 1Mac 2:3; see Simon 2

THEODOTUS (thee UH doh tus) meaning unknown; 2 century B.C.; 2Mac 14:19; Nicanor's envoy to Judas Maccabeus

THEOPHILUS (thee AHF uh luhs) *loved by God;* 1 century A.D.; Lk 1:3; addressee of Luke's two books

THESSALONIANS (thes suh LOH nee uhns) 1Th 1:1; inhabitants of the Greek city of Thessalonica

THEUDAS (THYOO duhs) meaning unknown; 1 century A.D.; Ac 5:36

Theudas was a Judean messianic figure who led 400 followers in a rebellion against Roman authority, only to be ruthlessly wiped out. His example was used in an argument by the renowned Rabbi Gamaliel to urge other Jewish leaders to show tolerance toward the apostles and their preaching. Gamaliel pointed out that such movements would fail without the intervention of Jewish leaders if they had solely human origins, but that they would persevere in spite of their efforts if supported by God. His reasoning prompted the Jewish high council to allow the apostles to continue their preaching about Jesus. Some confusion surrounds the story of Theudas and his followers. Extra-biblical sources mention a rebel leader with that name who acted some years after Gamaliel's speech. The region at that time was a hotbed of insurrection against Rome, however, and it is not unlikely that more than one rebel leader was named Theudas.

THOMAS (TAHM uhs) *the twin;* 1 century A.D.; Mt 10:3

Thomas the apostle was known for his loyalty, courage, and practicality, but he is best remembered as "Doubting Thomas." He was absent the first time the resurrected Jesus entered a locked room and visited ten of the remaining eleven apostles. When he heard their description of the event, Thomas told the others that he would believe Jesus had risen only if he could see and touch the wounds in his hands and side. When Jesus appeared to them again one week later, the doubting apostle saw and felt the wounds of the crucifixion and professed his belief. Jesus responded by saying, "Have you believed because you have seen me? Blessed are those who have not seen and yet have come to believe" (Jn 20:29). Some extra-biblical sources hold that Thomas traveled to India, founded a church in present-day Kerala, and was martyred. For further study, see Mk 3:18; Lk 6:15; Jn 11:16; 14:5; 20:24-29; 21:2.

TIBERIUS (ti BEER ee uhs) *son of the Tiber;* ruled A.D. 14–37; Lk 3:1

Tiberius Claudius Nero Caesar became Claudius Caesar Augustus at age 55 and ruled the Roman Empire until his death at age 78. He was in his fifteenth year as emperor (A.D. 28) when John the Baptist began preaching. Jesus discussed the emperor when some Pharisees attempted to trick him by asking whether or not it was right for Jews to pay taxes to Rome. Saying no would have cast Jesus as an insurrectionist, but saying yes would have been in conflict with some interpretations of Jewish Law. Jesus responded by displaying a coin that

Emperor Tiberius. Marble head from first-century Phrygia in Asia Minor.

had Tiberius's image stamped on it, saying, "Give to the emperor the things that are the emperor's, and to God the things that are God's" (Mk 12:17). Tiberius was also the unnamed Caesar in Rome during the trial and execution of Jesus. Extra-biblical sources indicate Tiberius was an austere, cautious, and sometimes morose man. Fearful of treachery, he conducted numerous trials for treason. For further study, see Mt 22:15-22; Mk 12:13-17; Lk 20:20-26; 23:2; Jn 19:12,15.

TIBNI (TIB nigh) possibly *man of straw;* ruled 885–880 B.C.; 1Ki 16:21; challenged Omri for the throne of Israel

TIDAL (TYE duhl) meaning unknown; 21 century B.C.; Gen 14:1; king of Goiim; took Sodom and Gomorrah

TIGLATH-PILESER III (TIG lath pih LEE zuhr) *my trust is in the heir of* [the temple] *E-sharra;* ruled 745–727 B.C.; 2Ki 15:19

Tiglath-pileser III enlarged and revived the Assyrian Empire, which took control of Babylon for the first time in five centuries and dominated the ancient Near East. He outwitted, outflanked, and totally subjugated his enemies, deporting many captive Jews in his expansionist policies. When King Pekah of Israel and King Rezin of Syria decided to revolt against Assyrian dominance, they tried persuading King Ahaz of Judah to join them.

When Ahaz refused, they attacked him, and Ahaz appealed to Tiglath-pileser III for help. Extra-biblical records indicate that the Assyrian king then marched through Galilee and Israel and took control of Damascus in 732 B.C. Many Israelites were captured and deported—154,000 in one year. Pekah and Rezin paid for their revolt with their lives. Tiglath-pileser III was also known in the biblical record as Pul, perhaps his personal name, as opposed to his Babylonian throne name. His son and sucessor was Shalmaneser V. For further study, see 2Ki 15:19-20,29; 16:7-10; 1Ch 5:26; 2Ch 28:20. Also called Tilgath-pilneser.

TILGATH-PILNESER 1Ch 5:6; see Tiglath-pileser III

TIKVAH (TIK vuh) *hope*
1. 7 century B.C.; 2Ki 22:14; father-in-law of the prophet Huldah; also called Tokhath
2. 5 century B.C.; Ezr 10:15; his son Jahzeiah opposed divorce of foreign wives after Exile

TILON (TYE lahn) *scorn;* 1Ch 4:20; descendant of Judah

TIMAEUS (tim MAY uhs) *to be unclean* or *highly prized;* 1 century A.D.; Mk 10:46; father of blind beggar Bartimaeus

TIMNA (TIM nuh) *restraining*
1. 20 century B.C.; Gen 36:12; concubine of Esau's son Eliphaz
2. 20 century B.C.; Gen 36:22; sister of Lotan the Horite chief in Seir
3. Gen 36:40; Edomite chief; descendant of Esau

TIMNITES (TIM nights) Jdg 15:6; inhabitants of Timnah, from where Samson took a wife

TIMON (TIM mahn) *deemed worthy;* 1 century A.D.; Ac 6:5; deacon chosen by Jerusalem church to work with poor

TIMOTHY (TIM uh thee) *man who honors God*
1. 2 century B.C.; 1Mac 5:6; Ammonite leader who fought Judas Maccabeus

A triumphant King Tiglath-Pileser III. Relief from the royal palace in Nimrud, 730 B.C.

Timothy. Stained glass. St James's, Bouroughbridge, England.

2. 1 century A.D.; Ac 16:1

Timothy's life was marked by assets and liabilities, virtues and weaknesses, yet he became one of Paul's chief associates and the bishop of Ephesus. Born to a pagan Greek father and a pious Jewish mother, Timothy was raised as a Jew and converted to Christianity when Paul visited his hometown of Lystra. Paul became Timothy's father in the faith and his mentor for missionary work. Paul selected Timothy as his associate because of his bicultural background and the respect accorded him by the people at Lystra and Iconium. In joining Paul's second missionary journey, Timothy had to submit to painful adult circumcision and imprisonment in Roman jails.

Young Timothy was placed in charge of certain projects at Ephesus. Apparently due to his age, however, he suffered some lack of respect. Timothy also suffered bouts of ill health and moments of anxiety. Hence, his mission to Corinth was cut short and considered a failure by some. Paul warned the Corinthians to go easy on Timothy and

named the more forceful Titus as his apostolic delegate there.

Despite his reputation for being timid, sickly, and even lustful, Timothy proved to be most sensitive, affectionate, and loyal. Paul and the church elders laid hands on Timothy to impart a special endowment for ministry that would help him persevere in hard times, hoping that he would be able to compensate through divine grace for whatever was lacking in his faith and character.

For further study, see Ac 16:1-5,16-40; 17:14; 18:5; 19:22; 20:4-5; Ro 16:21; 1Co 4:14-17; 16:10-11; 2Co 1:18-20; Php 2:19-24; the First Letter of Paul to Timothy; the Second Letter of Paul to Timothy.

TIRAS (TYE ruhs) *longing;* Gen 10:2; son of Japheth; a people possibly of Thrace on the Balkan peninsula

TIRHAKAH (tuhr HAY kuh) meaning unknown; 8 century B.C.; 2Ki 19:9; king of Egypt and Ethiopia; see Pharaoh

TIRHANAH (tuhr HAY nuh) possibly *favor* or *kindness;* 1Ch 2:48; Judahite; son of Caleb by Maacah

TIRIA (TEER ee uh) meaning unknown; 1Ch 4:16; descendant of Judah 1

TIRZAH (TUHR zuh) possibly *pleasing* or *willing;* 15 century B.C.; Nu 26:33; daughter of Zelophehad who petitioned to receive inheritance from her father

TISHBITES (TISH bights) 1Ki 17:1; residents of Tishbe (in Gilead); Elijah the prophet was one

TITIUS JUSTUS (TISH ee us JUS tuhs) meaning unknown; 1 century A.D.; Ac 18:7; Corinthian convert; hosted Paul

TITUS (TI tus) meaning unknown; 1 century A.D.; 2Co 2:13

Titus, a Greek-speaking Gentile, did not undergo circumcision as part of his conversion under the apostle Paul. Thus, his conversion became a key example for Paul to use in his arguments to the first church council at Jerusalem concerning the acceptance of Gentiles into the church. Based partly on the example of Titus, the council decided that rituals such as circumcision were not needed to supplement God's grace and that acceptance of Christ was the only thing necessary to belong to the church.

Titus accompanied Paul on his missionary journeys and was given a variety of difficult tasks. He used his strength of character to solidify many local churches: at Corinth in southeastern Greece; on the Mediterranean island of Crete; at Nicopolis in northwestern Greece; and in Dalmatia on the Balkan Peninsula. In these lands, Titus had to overcome strong opposition and battle to maintain church doctrine. Often he had to reject a divisive member from the fellowship of the church, as at Corinth. Among the Cretans, who were viewed as "liars, evil beasts and lazy gluttons," Titus proved himself to be a dependable, diligent, and effective motivator. In his 20-year ministry, Titus was recognized for having the strength, tact, and diligence to spread and preserve church teaching in the face of difficult intellectual opposition.

For further study, see 2Co 2:13; 7:6-16; 8:6,16-24; 12:18; Gal 2:1-3; 2Ti 4:10; the Letter of Paul to Titus.

TITUS MANIUS (TY tuhs MAN y uhs) meaning unknown; 2 century B.C.; 2Mac 11:34; Roman emissary to Maccabeans

TOAH (TOH uh) meaning unknown; 1Ch 6:34; Levite ancestor of Samuel; also called Nahath and Tohu

TOB-ADONIJAH (tub ad on NIGH juh) *the Lord, my Lord, is good;* 9 century B.C.; 2Ch 17:8; taught the Law in Judah

TOBIAH (toh BYE uh) *the Lord is good*
1. Ezr 2:60; ancestor of returnees to Judah with Zerubbabel
2. Ne 2:10; opposed rebuilding of Jerusalem wall

TOBIAS (too BYE uhs) *the Lord is [my] good*
1. Tob 1:9
Tobias is featured in the apocryphal Book of Tobit. In this pious and romantic Jewish folktale, Tobias helps heal both his new wife Sarah and his father Tobit.

According to the story, Tobit, a righteous Israelite taken captive in Nineveh, suffers from blindness and is near death. He bids Tobias to follow a guide and reclaim a fortune of silver that Tobit had given to a friend in Media some 20 years before for safe keeping. The guide Tobias chooses is a man calling himself Azariah, who is actually the angel Raphael in disguise. Raphael intends to cure Tobit of his blindness.

En route to Media, Azariah and Tobias camp along the Tigris River. When a fish bites his feet, Tobias catches it and Azariah tells him to preserve its heart, liver, and gall for future use as medicine. Before Tobias reaches his destination, he meets Sarah, a distant relative who has been possessed by a demon. The demon (Asmodeus) has mysteriously caused the death of her husband on their wedding night each of the seven times she has married. Following Azariah's instructions, Tobias takes her as his wife and burns the fish's liver and heart on their wedding night, driving out the demon.

Tobias then proceeds on his own to find the hidden treasure, return to Nineveh, and apply the gall of the fish he caught earlier to Tobit's eyes. Tobit is healed and lives another 50 years, while Tobias cares for him. Eventually, Tobias returns to Media and lives there with Sarah and her family.

For further study, see the Book of Tobit.
2. 2 century B.C.; 2Mac 3:11; father of Hyrcanus; steward of temple fund

TOBIEL (TO bee ehl) *God is [my] good;* 8 century B.C.; Tob 1:1; father of Tobit

TOBIJAH (tob BYE juh) *the Lord is good*
1. 9 century B.C.; 2Ch 17:8; Levite sent to teach the Law in Judah
2. 6 century B.C.; Zec 6:10; brought gold and silver from Exile for high priest's crown

TOBIT (TOH bit) *my goodness;* Tob 1:1
Tobit narrates in the first person the apocryphal book that bears his name. In the unfolding of this romantic and moralizing Jewish folktale, set in the eighth century B.C. but written around 200 B.C., Tobit is the hero. He reaps the rewards of faithfully obeying his God while in exile, even by observing Jewish dietary and burial laws in defiance of Assyrian law.

As the story opens, Tobit experiences the calamity and guilt associated with blindness. The innocent result of sparrow droppings getting into his eyes, this blindness severely tests Tobit's faith in

Tobias and his guide, the angel Raphael, on the road to Media.

God, who is supposed to reward the righteous and punish only the guilty. Tobit despairs of life itself over his affliction and apparent abandonment by God, but he never relinquishes his faith.

Tobit sends his son Tobias on a journey to reclaim some valuables. Assisted by the angel Raphael in human form, Tobias not only finds the treasure, wins a wife, and cures her of possession by a demon, but he also learns how to cure Tobit of his blindness. Returning home triumphantly, Tobias follows the angel's instructions to apply the gall of a fish to his father's eyes and restores his sight. Tobit is healed and lives another 50 years under the attentive care of Tobias.

For further study, see the Book of Tobit.

TOGARMAH (toh GAHR muh) *bony* or *strong;* Gen 10:3; Japhethite tribe allied with ancient Tyre and Magog

TOHU 1Sa 1:1; see Toah

TOI (TOH eye) *wandering* or *error;* 11 century B.C.; 2Sa 8:9; king of Hamath; congratulated David; also called Tou

TOKHATH 2Ch 34:22; see Tikvah 1

TOLA (TOH luh) *worm*
1. 19 century B.C.; Gen 46:13; son of Issachar; went to Egypt with Jacob
2. 12 century B.C.; Jdg 10:1; minor judge; led Israel for 23 years

TOU 1Ch 18:9; see Toi

TROPHIMUS (TRAHF ih muhs) *nourishing;* 1 century A.D.; Ac 20:4
Trophimus the Ephesian was a well-meaning disciple who accompanied Paul on part of his third missionary journey. While in Jerusalem, however, he inadvertently contributed to Paul's arrest. Paul was incorrectly accused of profaning the temple by bringing Trophimus, a Gentile, into a part of the temple that non-Jews were not allowed to see. For this, Paul was brought to court in Jerusalem and was eventually imprisoned in Rome. Evidently, Trophimus stayed with Paul as he was taken to Rome for trial, but he became ill and stayed behind at Miletus in southwest Asia Minor. Trophimus may have been killed later during the infamous persecution of the church by the Roman emperor Nero. For further study, see Ac 21:1-29; 2Ti 4:20.

TRYPHAENA (tri FEE nuh) *dainty;* 1 century A.D.; Ro 16:12; Christian woman at Rome whom Paul greeted

TRYPHO (TRAY foh) *magnificent* or *luxurious;* 2 century B.C.; 1Mac 11:39
Though not a member of the Seleucid dynasty that had ruled Syria since the days of Alexander the Great, the ambitious military commander Trypho deposed two kings and assumed the throne for himself in 143 B.C. Jonathan, the Jewish priest and leader of the Maccabean revolt against the Syrians, first supported Trypho but was later murdered by him. Jonathan's brother and successor, Simon, sided against Trypho with Antiochus VII Sidetes, the brother of one of the kings Trypho had usurped. Antiochus's army pursued Trypho from Antioch to Dor on the Palestinian coast and then besieged the city. General Trypho escaped by ship to Orthosia, where he apparently committed suicide. For Simon's support, the Jews were granted religious autonomy by Antiochus when he regained the throne. For further study, see 1Mac 11:39-40, 54-56; 12:39–13:34; 15:10-39.

TRYPHOSA (tri FOH suh) *delicate;* 1 century A.D.; Rom 16:12; Christian woman praised for her hard work

TUBAL (TOO bahl) meaning unknown; Gen 10:2; son(s) of Japheth; a people living near Cappadocia (modern Turkey)

TUBAL-CAIN (TOO bahl CAYN) meaning unknown; Gen 4:22; son of Lamech; master metalworker

TYCHICUS (TIK ih kuhs) *fortuitous* or *chance;* 1 century A.D.; Ac 20:4; Paul's friend and special envoy

TYRANNUS (tuh RAN uhs) *tyrant;* 1 century A.D.; Ac 19:9; Ephesian who rented Paul his school for ministry

TYRIANS (TYE ree uhns) 1Ch 22:4; Phoenicians, akin to Sidonians, from the coastal city of Tyre

UEL (OO uhl) *will of God;* 5 century B.C.; Ezr 10:34; married and divorced foreigner after Exile

ULAM (OO lam) *first*
1. 1Ch 7:16; descendant of Manasseh
2. 1Ch 8:39; Benjaminite; descendant of Jonathan and Saul

ULLA (UL uh) *yoke* or *elevation;* 1Ch 7:39; descendant of Asher

UNNI (UHN eye) *afflicted;* 1Ch 15:18; 11 century B.C.; Levite who played lyre before ark of the covenant

UNNO (UHN oh) *afflicted;* 6 century B.C.; Ne 12:9; Levite who returned to Judah after Exile

UR (UHR) *flame;* 11 century B.C.; 1Ch 11:35; father of Eliphal the mighty man of David

URBANUS (uhr BAY nuhs) *pleasant* or *urbane;* 1 century A.D.; Ro 16:9; Roman Christian greeted by Paul

URI (YOO rye) *fiery* or *enlightened*
1. 15 century B.C.; Ex 31:2; father of Bezalel the craftsman in charge of building the tabernacle
2. 11 century B.C.; 1Ki 4:19; father of Geber the district governor under Solomon
3. 5 century B.C.; Ezr 10:24; Levite gatekeeper; married and divorced foreigner after Exile

URIAH (yoo RYE uh) *the Lord is light* or *a flame*
1. 10 century B.C.; 2Sa 11:3

Uriah the Hittite was a soldier in King David's army. While the army under Joab was besieging the Ammonite capital of Rabbah, David committed adultery with Uriah's wife, Bathsheba. When Bathsheba became pregnant, David sent a message for Uriah to return home, hoping that he would have relations with Bathsheba and think that he was the father of the child. The plan failed when Uriah refused to indulge himself in any activities that his comrades in the field could not enjoy. David sent Uriah back to the encampment with a sealed letter for Joab, instructing Joab to put Uriah at the forefront of the battle in an unprotected position to ensure that he would die. After Uriah was killed, David married Bathsheba. The prophet Nathan foretold that God would punish David for this crime. For further study, see 2Sa 11; 1Ki 15:5.
2. 8 century B.C.; 2Ki 16:10; chief priest under King Ahaz; built an Assyrian altar

The siege of Rabbah, where Uriah is killed.

3. 8 century B.C.; Isa 8:2; priest under Ahaz; witness to Isaiah's prophecy; possibly Uriah 2
4. 7 century B.C.; Jer 26:20; prophet from Kiriath-jearim; killed by Jehoiakim
5. 5 century B.C.; Ezr 8:33; father of Meremoth 1
6. 5 century B.C.; Ne 8:4; aide to Ezra in reading of the Law

URIEL (YOOR ee el) *God is light* or *flame of God*
1. 11 century B.C.; 1Ch 6:24; Levite of the Kohathite clan and ancestor of Samuel
2. 2Ch 13:2; see Absalom 2
3. 2Esd 4:1
Along with Michael, Gabriel, and Raphael, Uriel is an angel featured in the pseudepigraphal Book of Enoch. This extra-biblical Jewish writing says that Uriel issued warnings to Noah about the wicked state of human affairs and the coming flood. Speaking with Enoch, Uriel discussed fallen angels, false worship, the fate of the wicked, astronomy, and even the lunar calendar. In the Apocrypha (another set of extra-biblical writings from the time between the Testaments), Uriel is the angel who rebuked Esdras for questioning the ways of God. In later literature, Uriel is the angel of Paradise who interceded for Adam and Abel. He is also, reportedly, the angel who wrestled with Jacob at Peniel. For further study, see 2Esd 5:20; 10:28; Gen 3–6; 32.

UTHAI (OO thigh) *helpful*
1. 5 century B.C.; 1Ch 9:4; Judahite; resettled in Jerusalem after Exile
2. 5 century B.C.; Ezr 8:14; head of family that returned to Judah after Exile

UZ (UHZ) meaning unknown
1. Gen 10:23; son(s) of Aram; likely settled Wadi Sirhan in northern Canaan, home of Job
2. 21 century B.C.; Gen 22:21; son of Nahor and Milcah; Abraham's nephew
3. 21 century B.C.; Gen 36:28; son of Dishan the Horite chief who lived in Seir

UZAI (UH zye) *hoped for;* 5 century B.C.; Ne 3:25; his son Palal helped rebuild Jerusalem wall

UZAL (OO zuhl) *wanderer;* Gen 10:27; son(s) of Joktan; a people that settled a city near Medina (Arabia)

UZZA (UHZ uh) *strength*
1. 1Ch 8:7; descendant of Benjamin
2. Ezr 2:49; ancestor of temple servants that returned to Judah after Exile

UZZAH (UHZ uh) *strength*
1. 1Ch 6:29; Levite descendant of Merari
2. 11 century B.C.; 2Sa 6:3; son of Abinadab; killed by God for touching the ark of the covenant

UZZI (UHZ eye) *my strength*
1. 1Ch 7:2; descendant of Issachar
2. 1Ch 7:7; descendant of Benjamin
3. 1Ch 6:6; priest in Eleazar's line
4. 1Ch 9:8; ancestor of Benjaminite resettler in Jerusalem
5. 6 century B.C.; Ne 12:19; head of priestly family in days of high priest Joiakim
6. 5 century B.C.; Ne 11:22; descendant of Asaph; officer of Levites in Jerusalem
7. 5 century B.C.; Ne 12:42; Levite; helped dedicate wall of Jerusalem

UZZIA (uh ZYE uh) *the Lord is my strength;* 11 century B.C.; 1Ch 11:44; mighty man of David

UZZIAH (uh ZYE uh) *the Lord is my strength*
1. 11 century B.C.; 1Ch 27:25; father of Jonathan the overseer for King David
2. 1Ch 6:24; Levite descendant of Kohath
3. ruled 792–740 B.C.; 2Ki 14:21
Frequently referred to by the name Azariah, Uzziah was a successful expansionist king of Judah, noted for the longest total reign (52 years). He acted as coruler with his father Amaziah for the first 25 years of his reign and as coruler with his son Jotham for the last ten years of his life. Uzziah was instructed by a teacher named Zechariah "in the fear of God," and he followed these teachings early in his reign.
As king, Uzziah rebuilt Judah's army and succeeded as a warrior, defeating the Philistines and the Arab states and annexing their territory. He also built cities and fortifications and promoted agriculture. Because "he loved the soil" (2Ch 26:10), he built towers and cisterns to protect and irrigate the wilderness for farmers and vinedressers.
As his success grew, however, so did his pride. Uzziah saw fit to tolerate pagan worship, and he presumptuously assumed certain duties reserved only for Hebrew priests. He was severely chastised

by priests for his attempt to make an incense offering in the temple and was subsequently afflicted with leprosy. It was at this time that he went into seclusion and shared his authority with his son.

For further study, see 2Ki 15:1-7; 2Ch 26:1–27:2; Isa 1:1; 6:1; Hos 1:1; Am 1:1; Zec 14:5. Also called Azariah.

4. 5 century B.C.; Ne 11:4; father of Athaiah the Judahite resettler in Jerusalem
5. 5 century B.C.; Ezr 10:21; priest who married and divorced foreign wife
6. 5 century B.C.; Jdt 6:15

In the apocryphal tale of Judith, Uzziah was an elder in the city of Bethulia in Ephraim when it was besieged by the Assyrian general Holofernes. Although Holofernes had been cautioned to avoid Israel and its powerful God, he put his faith in his enormous army and ignored the warning. After suffering 34 days of the siege, Uzziah and the other elders of the city prepared to surrender. Judith, a beautiful young widow, chided them for lacking faith in the protection of God. Judith dressed elegantly and went out to meet Holofernes, pretending to betray her people. Holofernes took her to his tent, planning to question and seduce her. Judith encouraged Holofernes until he became drunk, and then she beheaded him with his own sword.

Priests expel King Uzziah from the temple as he attempts to make an offering of incense.

Judith returned with Holofernes's head, and Uzziah led a procession in her honor. When the Assyrian soldiers discovered their commander's body, they were terrified, and Uzziah sent troops to drive them away. For further study, see Jdt 6–8.

UZZIEL (uh ZIH uhl) *God is my strength*
1. 1Ch 7:7; descendant of Benjamin
2. Ex 6:18; a Levite son of Kohath; ancestor of the Uzzielites
3. 1Ch 25:4; see Azarel 2
4. 8 century B.C.; 1Ch 4:42; Simeonite leader; invaded Seir to defeat Amalekites
5. 8 century B.C.; 2Ch 29:14; Levite; helped purify temple in days of Hezekiah
6. 5 century B.C.; Ne 3:8; goldsmith who helped rebuild Jerusalem

UZZIELITES (uh ZYE ehl ights) Nu 3:27; descendants of tribal family of Uzziel 2

VAIZATHA (VI zuh thuh) meaning unknown; 5 century B.C.; Est 9:9; son of Haman slain by Jews

VANIAH (vuh NIGH uh) meaning unknown; 5 century B.C.; Ezr 10:34; son of Bani; married and divorced a foreigner after Exile

VASHTI (VASH ti) *beautiful woman;* 5 century B.C.; Est 1:9

In the midst of a raucous celebration held for the military leaders, nobles, and supporters of King Ahasuerus of Persia (also called King Xerxes I), the king summoned his wife Vashti to present herself so the guests could admire her beauty. The queen boldly refused to subject herself to this ogling, causing embarrassment for Ahasuerus and alarm to his guests. It was feared that her action would prompt a wave of similar defiance by women throughout the kingdom. The king listened to his distraught advisors and decreed that Vashti be banned from his presence, which told all other women "that every man should be master in his own house" (Est 1:20). God used this abuse and banishment of Vashti to bring Esther, a Hebrew living in exile in Persia, to the throne. As the new queen, Esther was able to free the Jews from Persian persecution. For further study, see Est 1–2.

VOPHSI (VAHF sigh) *rich;* 15 century B.C.; Nu 13:14; father of Nahbi

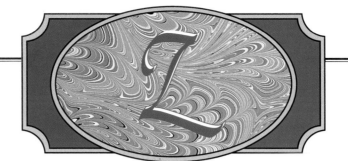

ZAAVAN (ZAY uh van) possibly *unquiet* or *to tremble;* 20 century B.C.; Gen 36:27; son of Ezer the Horite chief

ZABAD (ZAY bad) *gift* or *endowment*
1. 1Ch 7:21; descendant of Ephraim
2. 1Ch 2:36; Judahite in genealogy of Jerahmeel
3. 11 century B.C.; 1Ch 11:41; mighty man of David; possibly Zabad 2
4. 9 century B.C.; 2Ch 24:26; assassin of King Joash; also called Jozacan
5. 5 century B.C.; Ezr 10:27; one who married and divorced foreigner after Exile
6. 5 century B.C.; Ezr 10:33; another who married and divorced foreigner after Exile

7. 5 century B.C.; Ezr 10:43; another who married and divorced foreigner after Exile

ZABBAI (ZAB eye) meaning unknown
1. 5 century B.C.; Ne 3:20; his son Baruch helped rebuild Jerusalem wall
2. 5 century B.C.; Ezr 10:28; one who married and divorced foreigner after Exile

ZABDI (ZAB dye) possibly [the Lord] *has given*
1. 1Ch 8:19; descendant of Benjamin
2. 10 century B.C.; 1Ch 27:27; overseer of David's wine cellars
3. 10 century B.C.; Ne 11:17; descendant of Asaph; also called Zaccur 4 and Zichri 7

Zacchaeus climbs a tree to get a glimpse of Jesus.

4. Jos 7:1; ancestral head of Judahite family; also called Zimri 2

ZABDIEL (ZAB dee uhl) *God is my gift*
1. 11 century B.C.; 1Ch 27:2; father of Jashobeam the mighty man of David
2. 5 century B.C.; Ne 11:14; chief officer of priests who resettled in Jerusalem
3. 2 century B.C.; 1Mac 11:17; Arabian leader; decapitated King Alexander Balas

ZABUD (ZAY buhd) *bestowed;* 10 century B.C.; 1Ki 4:5; priest; personal advisor to King Solomon

ZABUTHEUS (zah BOO thee us) meaning unknown; 5 century B.C.; AddEst 9:9; one of Haman's ten sons killed by Jews

ZACCAI (ZAK eye) possibly *the Lord has remembered* or *pure* or *innocent;* Ezr 2:9; head of family that returned to Judah

ZACCHAEUS (ZAK ee uhs) *pure*
1. 2 century B.C.; 2Mac 10:19; Maccabean who besieged two Idumean cities
2. 1 century A.D.; Lk 19:2

Zacchaeus, chief Jewish tax collector for the Romans at Jericho, wanted to see Jesus when he came to the city. Being short in stature, he had to climb a tree to get a glimpse of Jesus through the crowd. As Jesus passed by, he looked up and bid Zacchaeus to host him at his house. The crowd, who viewed Zacchaeus as a traitor assisting in the Roman oppression of his people for his own monetary benefit, was outraged. After this encounter with Jesus, however, Zacchaeus became a new man, vowing to repay the poor and all those he had defrauded. Jesus told the crowd that salvation had come to a son of Abraham and his household that day, and he reminded the self-righteous crowd that his mission was to seek and redeem the lost. For further study, see Lk 19:1-10.

ZACCUR (ZAK uhr) *remembered*
1. 15 century B.C.; Nu 13:4; father of Shammua the Reubenite leader sent to explore Canaan
2. 1Ch 4:26; descendant of Simeon
3. 1Ch 24:27; Levite descendant of Merari
4. 1Ch 25:2; see Zabdi 3
5. 5 century B.C.; Ezr 8:14; one who returned to Judah after Exile

Zadok and Nathan at the coronation of Solomon. Stained glass. Beverley Cathedral, Beverley, England.

6. 5 century B.C.; Ne 3:2; rebuilder of Jerusalem wall
7. 5 century B.C.; Ne 10:12; Levite; sealed covenant renewal with God
8. 5 century B.C.; Ne 13:13; father of Hanan the assistant temple treasurer

ZADOK (ZAY dahk) *righteous*
1. 10 century B.C.; 2Sa 8:17

Zadok, the son of Ahitub, was a loyal high priest in King David's court. When David fled Jerusalem during his son Absalom's insurrection, Zadok and a priest named Abiathar began to follow him out of Jerusalem, carrying with them the ark of the covenant. David told them to turn back with the ark and return with their two sons to Jerusalem, in hopes that he would also return there someday as king. From Jerusalem, the two priests kept David informed of Absalom's actions by sending their sons to him as couriers. After the death of Absalom,

Zadok and Abiathar encouraged the people of Judah to ask for David's reinstatement as king.

Later Zadok was involved in the events that surrounded the succession of David's son Solomon to the throne. When David was old and ready to step down, his son Adonijah took over the throne without David knowing it. At the urging of his wife Bathsheba, David summoned Zadok, the prophet Nathan, and a military leader named Benaiah to prepare to anoint Solomon king of Israel. These three men mounted Solomon on David's mule and rode to Gihon where Zadok anointed him king. They blew the trumpet and the people said, "Long live King Solomon!" (1Ki 1:39). All of David's loyal supporters followed Solomon into Jerusalem, where they pronounced him king. In fear, Adonijah gave up the throne and begged Solomon for mercy.

Zadok was mentioned in First Chronicles as "a young warrior." Ezekiel, a descendant of Zadok, identifies all the priests as "sons of Zadok."

For further study, see 2Sa 15:24-36; 19:11-14; 1Ki 1; 1Ch 12:26-28; 27:17.
2. 9 century B.C.; 2Ki 15:33; grandfather of King Jotham of Judah
3. 1Ch 6:12; Aaronite descendant of Zadok 1
4. 5 century B.C.; Ne 3:4; rebuilder of Jerusalem wall
5. 5 century B.C.; Ne 3:29; priest; helped with reconstruction of Jerusalem
6. 5 century B.C.; Ne 10:21; leader who sealed covenant renewal; possibly Zadok 4
7. 5 century B.C.; Ne 13:13; scribe responsible for temple treasuries
8. Mt 1:14; descendant of Zerubbabel; ancestor of Christ

ZAHAM (ZAY ham) *hateful;* 10 century B.C.; 2Ch 11:19; son of Rehoboam I by David's granddaughter Mahalath

ZALAPH (ZAY laf) *caper plant;* 5 century B.C.; Ne 3:30; his son Hanun helped rebuild Jerusalem wall

ZALMON 2Sa 23:28; see Ilai

ZALMUNNA (zal MUN uh) *deprived of shade* or *shelter;* 12 century B.C.; Jdg 8:5; Midianite king defeated by Gideon

ZAMBRIS (ZAM bris) meaning unknown; 1Esd 9:34; ancestor of returning Levites

ZAMOTH (ZAY moth) meaning unknown; 1Esd 9:28; ancestor of returning Levites

ZAMZUMMIM Dt 2:20; see Rephaim

ZANOAH (zuh NOH uh) *swamp;* 1Ch 4:18; son of Jekuthiel; grandson of Mered; descendant of Judah 1

ZAPHENATH-PANEAH (ZAF uh nath puh NEE uh) possibly *the god speaks and he* [Joseph] *lives;* 19 century B.C.; Gen 41:45; name given to Joseph 1 by Pharaoh

ZARIUS (ZAR ee us) meaning unknown; 1Esd 1:38; brother of King Jehoiakim

ZATHOLTHA (zah THOHL thah) meaning unknown; 5 century B.C.; AddEst 1:10; eunuch servant of King Artaxerxes

ZATTU (ZAT oo) *lovely*
1. Ezr 2:8; ancestor of family whose members returned to Judah
2. 5 century B.C.; Ne 10:14; Jewish leader; sealed covenant renewal

ZAZA (ZAY zuh) meaning unknown; 1Ch 2:33; Judahite descendant of Jerahmeel

ZEBADIAH (ZEB uh DYE uh) *the Lord has bestowed*
1. 1Ch 8:15; descendant of Benjamin
2. 1Ch 8:17; another descendant of Benjamin
3. 11 century B.C.; 1Ch 12:7; Benjaminite warrior; son of Jeroham from Gedor
4. 10 century B.C.; 1Ch 26:2; son of Meshelemiah; tabernacle gatekeeper
5. 10 century B.C.; 1Ch 27:7; son of Asahel; brother of Joel; leader in David's army
6. 9 century B.C.; 2Ch 17:8; Levite whom King Jehoshaphat sent to teach the Law
7. 9 century B.C.; 2Ch 19:11; a judge from Judah under King Jehoshaphat
8. 5 century B.C.; Ezr 8:8; descendant of Shephatiah who resettled his family in Judah
9. 5 century B.C.; Ezr 10:20; priest who married and divorced foreigner after Exile

ZEBAH (ZEE buh) *sacrifice* or *victim of sacrifice;* Jdg 8:5; Midianite king; killed along with Zalmunna by Gideon

ZEBEDEE (ZEB uh dee) *my gift* or *gift of the Lord;* 1 century A.D.; Mt 4:21

When the fishermen James and John were called to follow Jesus as disciples, "they left their father Zebedee in the boat with the hired men, and followed him." Zebedee may also have enjoyed another tie to Jesus. Some researchers speculate that his wife was a woman named Salome who gave financial support to Jesus's ministry. Zebedee and his wife made an even greater contribution to the cause of Christianity 15 years later when their son James was martyred. For further study, see Mt 4:18-22; 20:20-23; Mk 1:16-20; Lk 5:1-10.

ZEBIDAH (zuh BYE duh) *given;* 7 century B.C.; 2Ki 23:36; mother of King Jehoiakim

ZEBINA (zuh BYE nuh) *purchased;* 5 century B.C.; Ezr 10:43; married and divorced foreigner after Exile

ZEBUL (ZEE buhl) possibly *exalted* or *lord;* 12 century B.C.; Jdg 9:28; governor of Shechem under Abimelech

ZEBULUN (ZEB yoo luhn) *endowed* or *honor;* 20 century B.C.; Gen 30:20

Zebulun was so named because Jacob's first wife, Leah, was not first in her husband's heart, and she hoped that with the birth of her sixth son, Zebulun, Jacob might finally "honor" her. Zebulun grew up in Jacob's competitive family of four mothers and 13 children, each vying for a position of honor. He participated in the family calamities that led to selling his younger brother Joseph into slavery, seeking famine relief from Joseph in Egypt, and moving his family, including three sons, to Egypt. Later, when the tribes of Jacob were allotted land in Canaan, Zebulun's descendants were marked to become a maritime people bordering the land of Sidon, although they settled in western Galilee some miles from the Mediterranean Sea. For further study, see Gen 30:1-8; 46:14; 49:13; Nu 1–2; 26; Dt 33:18; Jos 19; Jdg 4–5; 12; Mt 4:13-16.

ZEBULUNITES (ZEB yoo luhn ights) Nu 2:7; tribe of Jacob's son Zebulun

Jesus calls James and John, sons of Zebedee, to follow him.

ZECHARIAH (ZEK uh RYE uh) *the Lord remembers*

1. 1Ch 5:7; listed in genealogy of Reuben

2. 12 century B.C.; 1Ch 9:37; son of Jeiel; relative of Saul; also called Zecher

3. 11 century B.C.; 1Ch 15:18; Levite; played lyre as ark returned to Jerusalem

4. 11 century B.C.; 1Ch 15:24; priest and trumpeter during the procession of the ark

5. 11 century B.C.; 1Ch 24:25; head of Levites; descended from Isshiah; possibly Zechariah 3

6. 10 century B.C.; 1Ch 26:2; son of Meshelemiah; chief of temple gatekeepers

7. 10 century B.C.; 1Ch 26:11; fourth son of Hosah; temple gatekeeper

8. 10 century B.C.; 1Ch 27:21; Manassite tribal officer over Gilead

9. 9 century B.C.; 2Ch 17:7; official sent by King Jehoshaphat to teach the Law

10. 9 century B.C.; 2Ch 20:14; Levite descendant of Asaph; father of Jahaziel 4

11. 9 century B.C.; 2Ch 21:2; son of Jehoshaphat; killed when his brother became king

12. 9 century B.C.; 2Ch 24:20; son of priest Jehoiada; killed by idolatrous King Joash

13. 8 century B.C.; 2Ch 26:5; one who influenced King Uzziah into seeking God

14. 8 century B.C.; 2Ki 18:2; grandfather of King Hezekiah

15. ruled 753 B.C.; 2Ki 14:29; son and successor of King Jeroboam II of Israel

16. 8 century B.C.; Isa 8:2; son of Jeberekiah; assisted prophet Isaiah

17. 8 century B.C.; 2Ch 29:13; Levite descendant of Asaph; purified temple

18. 7 century B.C.; 2Ch 34:12; Kohathite Levite; supervised temple reconstruction

19. 7 century B.C.; 2Ch 35:8; temple administrator; contributed to Passover feast

20. Ne 11:12; ancestor of priest who resettled in Jerusalem

21. Ne 11:4; ancestor of one who resettled in Jerusalem

22. Ne 11:5; ancestor of one who resettled in Jerusalem

23. 6 century B.C.; Ezr 5:1

The prophet Zechariah. Michelangelo (1475–1564), Sistene Chapel, Rome.

Zechariah the prophet, the son of Berechiah and the grandson of Iddo, was born in Babylon during the Exile but returned with others to Jerusalem in 538 B.C. He was a contemporary of Haggai the prophet, Zerubbabel the governor, and Darius I the Persian king. Like the prophets Jeremiah and Ezekiel, Zechariah was also a priest from the tribe of Levi. The first eight chapters of the Book of Zechariah contain visions delivered between 520 and 518 B.C. that encourage those in Jerusalem to work at rebuilding the temple. The remaining six chapters are oracles of judgment and salvation that describe a time in the future when Israel will be redeemed by God. This section contains a great many statements that have been interpreted as describing Jesus and his ministry. Jesus and several New Testament writers used passages from

Zechariah to show that Jesus was the promised Messiah. For further study, see Ezr 5:1; 6:14; the Book of Zechariah.

24. Mt 23:35; prophet; son of Berechiah; possibly Zechariah 12 or 23

25. 6 century B.C.; Ne 12:16; head of priestly family in days of the priest Joiakim

26. 5 century B.C.; Ezr 8:3; leader who returned to Judah with Ezra

27. 5 century B.C.; Ezr 8:11; another who returned to Judah with Ezra

28. 5 century B.C.; Ezr 8:16; leader; Ezra's delegate to retrieve Levites from Casiphia; possibly Zechariah 26 or 27

29. 5 century B.C.; Ezr 10:26; one who married and divorced foreigner after Exile

30. 5 century B.C.; Ne 8:4; one who stood on Ezra's left at the reading of the Law

31. 5 century B.C.; 1Ch 9:21; temple gatekeeper; returned after Exile; possibly Zechariah 6

32. 5 century B.C.; Ne 12:35; Levite descendant of Asaph; musician at Jerusalem wall dedication

33. 5 century B.C.; Ne 12:41; priest and trumpeter who played at Jerusalem wall dedication

34. 1 century A.D.; Lk 1:5

Zechariah was considered a devout and worthy priest, but his faith faltered in his old age when God finally announced that he would answer Zechariah's long-standing prayers for a son. The angel Gabriel told the priest that his elderly, barren wife Elizabeth would bear a son, whom they should name John. Zechariah asked for proof that they

Unable to speak, Zechariah writes that his child's name should be John, as the angel instructed him.

finally would be granted a child so late in life, and he was struck dumb for doubting the word of God's messenger. When Elizabeth finally delivered the baby boy, Zechariah followed the angel's instructions and signaled that the child's name should be John. His speech returned to him on naming the child, and he immediately began to praise God. He offered a prophecy concerning Jesus and John, saying that God was about to fulfill his promise of a savior for Israel and that his son, John the Baptist, "will be called the prophet of the Most High; for you will go before the Lord to prepare his ways" (Lk 1:76). For further study, see Lk 1:5-25,59-80.

ZECHER 1Ch 8:31; see Zechariah 2

ZEDEKIAH (ZED uh KI uh) *the Lord is my righteousness*
1. 9 century B.C.; 1Ki 22:11; son of Chenaanah; false prophet to King Ahab
2. Bar 1:1; ancestor of Baruch the scribe of Jeremiah
3. 7 century B.C.; Jer 29:21; false prophet among Babylonian exiles
4. 7 century B.C.; Jer 36:12; official under King Jehoiakim
5. ruled 597–586 B.C.; 2Ki 24:17
  At the age of 21, Zedekiah (formerly Mattaniah) became king of Judah, marking a period of unforgettable disaster for the Jewish nation. He was appointed as a vassal king by Nebuchadnezzar, king of Babylon, after Judah's King Jehoiachin was exiled to Babylon with his mother, wives, and national leaders. Nebuchadnezzar also deported Judah's 7000-member army and 1000 of the nation's finest craftsmen and artisans, leaving only the poor and inexperienced to run the country. The prophet Jeremiah described the remnant as "rotten figs that are so bad they cannot be eaten" (Jer 29:17). Zedekiah's 11-year reign was characterized by the same idolatrous practices and disregard for God's commands as those of the kings preceding him, and the prophet Jeremiah predicted that Babylon would destroy Jerusalem as God's punishment for these practices.
  Zedekiah continually ignored and mocked the warnings of the prophets, and he foolishly joined Egypt in a rebellion against the superior Babylonian forces. Jerusalem was besieged for two years, and conditions became so poor that some reportedly resorted to cannibalism. Zedekiah desperately asked Jeremiah for a miracle from God, but he refused to accept the prophet's directive from God—to surrender peacefully to Nebuchadnezzar. Babylonian soldiers eventually broke through the walls of the city and began slaughtering the people and burning the temple and the palaces. The fleeing Zedekiah and his army were captured about 15 miles away and taken to Babylon. After Zedekiah was forced to witness the execution of his own young sons, the Babylonians gouged out his eyes, bound him in bronze shackles, and put him in prison until the day of his death.
  For further study, see 2Ki 24–25; 1Ch 3:15-16; 2Ch 36; Jer 21; 34; 37:1–39:7; 52:11; La 4:10.
6. 5 century B.C.; Ne 10:1; priest; sealed covenant renewal with God

ZEEB (ZEE eb) *wolf;* 12 century B.C.; Jdg 7:25; Midianite leader; captured and killed by Ephraimites

ZELEK (ZEE luhk) *fissure;* 11 century B.C.; 2Sa 23:37; Ammonite; mighty man of David

ZELOPHEHAD (zeh LOH fuh had) *shadow of fear;* 15 century B.C.; Nu 26:33
  Zelophehad of the tribe of Manasseh died in the wilderness after the Exodus from Egypt. He had no sons to inherit his name or his share of the Promised Land, but he did have five enterprising daughters: Mahlah, Noah, Hoglah, Milcah, and Tirzah. In an unprecedented case, these five women appealed to Moses and the other leaders for their right to claim their father's inheritance. Moses consulted with God and determined that the daughters' claim was valid. He passed their father's share of the Promised Land to them and established the precedent of female inheritance. A restriction was later added saying that women who inherit property must marry within their own tribe so that their holdings stay within that tribe. For further study, see Nu 27: 1-11; 36:1-13.

ZEMARITES (ZEM uh rights) Gen 10:18; a tribe of northern Canaan who likely settled a city now called Sumra

ZEMIRAH (zuh MYE ruh) *song;* 1Ch 7:8; descendant of Benjamin's son Becher

ZENAS (ZEE nuhs) *gift of Zeus;* 1 century A.D.; Tit 3:13; expert in Roman and Jewish law; Paul's lawyer

ZEPHANIAH (ZEF uh NIGH uh) *the Lord has hidden* or *the Lord has treasured*
1. 1Ch 6:36; Kohathite; ancestor of Heman the music minister
2. 7 century B.C.; Zep 1:1
   A contemporary of the prophet Jeremiah, Zephaniah prophesied during the early reign of the religious reformer King Josiah. His criticisms centered on the rampant pagan practices of the people and on the corruption of civil and religious leaders. His words may have lent support to Josiah's efforts to reestablish the Mosaic Law beginning in 621 B.C. In the Book of Zephaniah, he predicts Jerusalem's inevitable fall, which comes at the hands of the Babylonians in 586 B.C., and he speaks of God's judgment also falling on the foreign nations of Moab, Ammon, Philistia, and Assyria. Only a penitent remnant of Zion and her pagan neighbors would escape judgment and enjoy God's future kingdom. For further study, see 2Ki 23:4-20; the Book of Zephaniah.
3. 7 century B.C.; 2Ki 25:18; chief priest in Jerusalem under King Zedekiah
4. 6 century B.C.; Zec 6:10; father of Josiah and Hen; returned to Judah

ZEPHI (ZEE fye) meaning unknown; 19 century B.C.; 1Ch 1:36; grandson of Esau; Edomite chief; also called Zepho

ZEPHO Gen 36:11; see Zephi

ZEPHON (ZEE fahn) possibly *watching;* 19 century B.C.; Nu 26:15; son of Gad; traveled with Jacob to Egypt

ZERAH (ZEER uh) possibly *shining* or *dawning*
1. 19 century B.C.; Gen 36:13; grandson of Esau; an Edomite chief
2. 19 century B.C.; Gen 38:30; son of Judah and Tamar; twin brother of Perez
3. Nu 26:13; descendant of Simeon; possibly Zohar 2
4. Gen 36:33; father of Bela the pre-Israelite king of Edom
5. 1Ch 6:21; Gershonite; ancestor of Asaph the music minister
6. 10 century B.C.; 2Ch 14:9; Cushite king; led a powerful army against Asa

ZERAHIAH (ZAIR uh HIGH uh) *the Lord has shined forth*
1. 1Ch 6:6; Levite; descendant of Eleazar
2. 5 century B.C.; Ezr 8:4; his son Eliehoenai returned to Judah with Ezra

ZERAHITES (ZEE rah hights)
1. Nu 26:13; descendants of Zerah the Simeonite

The prophet Zephaniah.

Zerubbabel and the high priest Jeshua. Stained glass. Oude Kerk, Delft, Netherlands.

2. Nu 26:20; descendants of Zerah the Judahite; Achan was one

ZERAIAH (zeh RYE ah) meaning unknown; 5 century B.C.; 1Esd 8:34; leader among those who returned from Exile

ZERDAIAH (zer DAYE ah) meaning unknown; 5 century B.C.; 1Esd 9:28; Levite who returned from Exile

ZERESH (ZEER esh) *gold;* 5 century B.C.; Est 5:10; wife of Haman; suggested he build gallows for Mordecai

ZERETH (ZEER eth) *splendor;* 1Ch 4:7; listed in genealogy of Judah

ZERI 1Ch 25:3; see Izri

ZEROR (ZEER ohr) *tied;* 1Sa 9:1; Benjaminite; ancestor of Saul

ZERUAH (zuh ROO uh) *leprous;* 10 century B.C.; 1Ki 11:26; mother of Jeroboam

ZERUBBABEL (zuh RUB uh buhl) *seed of Babylon;* 6 century B.C.; 1Ch 3:19

Zerubbabel, a member of the royal house of King Jehoiachin of Judah, was among the Jews taken captive by Babylon for 70 years, during which time Jerusalem was destroyed and the temple was burned. In 538 B.C., King Cyrus of Persia conquered Babylon and subsequently signed an edict permitting the Israelites to return home to restore their city and rebuild the temple. Some 42,360 Jews packed their belongings and returned to Jerusalem. The first (and most prominent) person mentioned from this group was Zerubbabel. Along with Jeshua the high priest, Zerubbabel built an altar and sacrificed burnt offerings to God. Charged with rebuilding the temple, they subcontracted masons and carpenters to do the work; they also traded food and oil with Sidon and Tyre (in Lebanon) for fine cedar logs for building. The temple plans followed Solomon's plans for the first temple, though on a smaller scale.

After the foundation was built and celebrations took place, the work was interrupted by Samaritans who claimed the right to help rebuild the temple. After Zerubbabel denied them access to the temple, they wrote a slanderous letter to Darius, the new king of Persia, who then ordered work on the temple suspended.

Zerubbabel and Jeshua received permission from King Darius to resume construction 18 years later. The work was finished five years later in 515 B.C. This place of worship stood until A.D. 70, when it was destroyed by Rome under Emperor Titus.

A few scholars suggest that Zerubbabel may have been the same person as Sheshbazzar, another key figure in the restoration of the temple.

For further study, see Ezr 2–5; Neh 7:7; 12:1, 47; Mt 1:12-13. See Sheshbazzar.

ZERUIAH (zuh ROO yuh) meaning unknown; 11 century B.C.; 1Sa 26:6; David's sister; mother of Joab, Abishai, and Asahel

ZETHAM (ZEE thuhm) *olive tree;* 10 century B.C.; 1Ch 23:8; son of Ladan; a Gershonite; temple treasurer

ZETHAN (ZEE thuhn) *olive tree;* 1Ch 7:10; listed in genealogy of Benjamin

ZETHAR (ZEE thahr) possibly *conqueror;* 5 century B.C.; Est 1:10; eunuch servant of King Ahasuerus

ZEUS (ZOOS) *bright sky of day;* Ac 14:12

The Romans equated the Greek god Zeus with their supreme god, Jupiter. In the second century B.C., Syrian occupiers profaned the temple in Jerusalem by dedicating it to Zeus. Some 200 years later, residents of Lystra believed the apostle Barnabas to be Zeus after he and Paul performed a miraculous healing. For further study, see Ac 14:12-13; 2Mac 6:2.

ZIA (ZYE uh) possibly *the trembler;* 1Ch 5:13; listed in genealogy of Gad

ZIBA (ZIH buh) possibly *plant* or *branch;* 11 century B.C.; 2Sa 9:2

Ziba was a servant in the house of King Saul charged with caring for Saul's lame grandson Mephibosheth. By the time David assumed the throne from Saul, Mephibosheth was the only surviving member of Saul's line. In an effort to gain Saul's inheritance, Ziba alleged that Mephibosheth was disloyal to the new king. At first, David accepted Ziba's word and positioned him as steward of Saul's estate. Later, when Mephibosheth pleaded innocent to the accusations, David divided the estate between Ziba and Mephibosheth. For further study, see 2Sa 9:1-13; 16:1-4; 19:24-30.

The Greek god Zeus. Statue from the temple of Zeus.

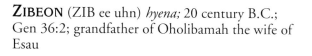

ZIBEON (ZIB ee uhn) *hyena;* 20 century B.C.; Gen 36:2; grandfather of Oholibamah the wife of Esau

ZIBIA (ZIB ee uh) *gazelle;* 1Ch 8:9; listed in genealogy of Benjamin

ZIBIAH (ZIB ee uh) *gazelle;* 9 century B.C.; 2Ki 12:1; mother of King Joash

ZICHRI (ZIK rye) *remembered* or *my remembrance*
1. Ex 6:21; Levite in family of Moses and Aaron
2. 1Ch 8:19; listed in genealogy of Benjamin
3. 1Ch 8:23; another listed in Benjamin's genealogy
4. 1Ch 8:27; a third listed in Benjamin's genealogy
5. 11 century B.C.; 1Ch 26:25; father of Shelomith the Levite official in David's day
6. 11 century B.C.; 1Ch 27:16; father of Eliezer the Reubenite officer
7. 1Ch 9:15; see Zabdi 3
8. 10 century B.C.; 2Ch 17:16; father of Amasiah the army commander under Jehoshaphat
9. 9 century B.C.; 2Ch 23:1; father of Elishaphat the army commander under Jehoiada
10. 8 century B.C.; 2Ch 28:7; Ephraimite warrior who killed King Ahaz's son Maaseiah
11. 6 century B.C.; Ne 12:17; head of priestly family in line of priest Joiakim
12. 5 century B.C.; Ne 11:9; father of Joel the chief Benjaminite officer

ZIHA (ZYE huh) *dried*
1. Ezr 2:43; ancestor of temple servants that returned to Judah
2. 5 century B.C.; Ne 11:21; overseer of temple servants under Nehemiah

ZILLAH (ZIL uh) *shadow* or *protection;* Gen 4:19; wife of Lamech; mother of Tubal-cain

ZILLETHAI (ZIL uh thigh) *shadow* or *protection*
1. 1Ch 8:20; listed in genealogy of Benjamin
2. 11 century B.C.; 1Ch 12:20; military leader; joined David at Ziklag

ZILPAH (ZIL puh) *dropping* or *sprinkling;* 20 century B.C.; Gen 29:24; maidservant of Leah; mother of Gad and Asher

ZIMMAH (ZIM uh) [the Lord has] *planned*
1. 1Ch 6:20; Levite descendant of Gershon
2. 8 century B.C.; 2Ch 29:12; his son Joah helped purify temple

ZIMRAN (ZIM ran) possibly *the singer;* 21 century B.C.; Gen 25:2; son of Abraham and Keturah

ZIMRI (ZIM rye) possibly *my song*
1. 15 century B.C.; Nu 25:6; Simeonite leader; slain by Phinehas for adultery
2. 1Ch 2:6; see Zabdi 4
3. 1Ch 8:36; Benjaminite descendant of Jonathan and Saul
4. ruled 7 days in 885 B.C.; 1Ki 16:9; officer of Elah; killed king and seized throne of Israel

ZINA (ZYE nuh) meaning unknown; 1Ch 23:10; Levite listed in genealogy of Gershonites; also called Zizah

ZIPH (ZIF) *refining place*
1. 1Ch 2:42; grandson of Caleb; descendant of Judah 1
2. 1Ch 4:16; listed in genealogy of Judah

ZIPHAH (ZIF uh) *lent;* 1Ch 4:16; Judahite; son of Jehallelel

ZIPHITES (ZIF ights) 1Sa 23:19; inhabitants of Ziph, a city near Hebron (in southeastern Judah), where David hid from Saul

ZIPPOR (ZIP ohr) *bird;* 15 century B.C.; Nu 22:2; father of Balak the Moabite king who opposed Israelites

ZIPPORAH (zi POR uh) *sparrow* or *swallow;* 15 century B.C.; Ex 2:21

Zipporah was one of seven daughters of Jethro, a priest in Midian. Moses had a chance meeting with these seven sisters at a well where they were trying to water their father's flock. When Moses drove away some shepherds who threatened the women, Jethro invited Moses to stay with him and gave his daughter Zipporah to him in marriage. Their children were Gershom and Eliezer. When Moses returned to Egypt, Zipporah and their sons accompanied him. On the way, God rebuked Moses over a circumcision matter, prompting Zipporah to circumcise one of their sons herself. She touched her son's foreskin to Moses's feet and said, "Truly you are a bridegroom of blood to me!" (Ex 4:25). Zipporah and her sons returned to Jethro and rejoined Moses after the Exodus. For further study, see Ex 2:15-22; 4:24-26; 18:1-8.

ZIZA (ZYE zuh) meaning unknown
1. 10 century B.C.; 2Ch 11:20; son of Rehoboam and Maacah
2. 8 century B.C.; 1Ch 4:37; Simeonite leader in days of Hezekiah

ZIZAH 1Ch 23:11; see Zina

ZOBEBAH (zoh BEE buh) meaning unknown; 1Ch 4:8; son of Koz the Judahite tribal leader

Moses meets his future wife Zipporah and her six sisters at the well in Midian.

ZOHAR (ZOH hahr) possibly *yellow-red* or *white* or *shining*
1. 21 century B.C.; Gen 23:8; his son Ephron sold Abraham a burial site
2. 19 century B.C.; Gen 46:10; son of Simeon who went to Egypt with Jacob; possibly Zerah 3

ZOHETH (ZOH heth) *strong* or *proud;* 1Ch 4:20; in genealogy of Judah

ZOPHAH (ZOH fuh) *bellied jug;* 1Ch 7:35; in genealogy of Asher

ZOPHAI 1Ch 6:26; see Zuph

ZOPHAR (ZOH fuhr) possibly *young bird;* Job 2:11; most condemning of Job's three comforters; see Eliphaz

ZORATHITES (ZOH rath ights) 1Ch 2:53; people of Shobal 3 or the Danite city of Zorah; Manoah was one

ZOSARA (zuh SAR ah) meaning unknown; 5 century B.C.; AddEst 5:10; wife of Haman

ZUAR (ZOO uhr) *little one;* 15 century B.C.; Nu 1:8; his son Nethanel led Issacharites during Exodus

ZUPH (ZUF) possibly *honeycomb;* 1Sa 1:1; Ephraimite ancestor of Elkanah and Samuel; also called Zophai

ZUR (ZUHR) *rock*
1. 15 century B.C.; Nu 25:15; Midianite king; his daughter was killed by Phinehas
2. 12 century B.C.; 1Ch 8:30; Benjaminite listed in genealogy of Saul

ZURIEL (ZUHR ee uhl) *God is a rock;* 15 century B.C.; Nu 3:35; leader of Merarite clan at time of Exodus

ZURISHADDAI (ZUHR ih SHAD dye) *the Almighty is a rock;* 15 century B.C.; Nu 1:6; father of Shelumiel

ZUZIM (ZOO zihm) *powerful ones;* Gen 14:5; a pre-Israelite tribe of Ham (east of Jordan River)

Index

A

Aaron, 6–7, 76, 94, 189, 212–213, 215
  descendants of, 83, 176
  grandson Phinehas, 247
Abaddon, 7, 268
Abednego, 7, 63–64, 223–224, 275
Abel, 7–8, 17, 56, 274
  mother Eve, 92
  and Uriel, 300
Abiathar, 8, 17, 22, 303–304
Abigail, 8–9, 26, 68
Abihu, 6, 9, 76, 219
Abijah, son of Rehoboam, 9, 256
Abijah, son of Samuel, 9, 265
Abimelech, king of Gerar (c. Abraham), 10, 14, 267
Abimelech, king of Gerar (c. Isaac), 10
Abimelech, son of Gideon, 10, 181
Abinadab, son of Saul, 10, 272
Abiram, rebel, 10, 189
Abishag, 10–11, 17, 69
Abishai, 11
Abner, 11–12, 26, 131, 158
Abraham (Abram), 12–14, 58, 73, 107
  burial place, 256
  descendant(s) of, 113, 133, 228
  grandniece Rebekah, 255
  wife Sarah (Sarai), 267
  and Lot, 193
  and Melchizedek, 206–207
  son Isaac, 128
  son Ishmael, 131–132
Absalom, 8, 11, 14–15, 17, 26, 69, 126, 159, 282, 303
  and Ahithophel, 23
  murder of Amnon, 27
Achaicus, 15, 288
Achan, 15, 178
Achsah, 16, 57, 235
Adam, 16–17
  and Eve, 91–92
  son Abel, 7
  son Cain, 56–57
  and Uriel, 300
Adonijah, 8, 11, 17–18, 48, 50, 69, 159, 286, 304
Adoni-zedek, 18
Adrammelech, 18, 86

Adullam band, 68
Aegean islanders, 140
Aeneas, 18, 290
Agag, 18, 265, 272
Agagites, 18, 109
Agrippa. See Herod Agrippa II.
Agrippina, 60
Ahab, 18–20, 33, 147, 210, 233
  and Ben-hadad II, 51
  daughter Athaliah, 146
  and Naboth, 219
  and Obadiah, 231
  and worship of Baal, 38, 42, 78–80, 157
Ahasuerus (Xerxes I), 20, 35, 87, 88–89, 214, 301
Ahaz, 21, 117, 129, 181, 210, 240, 258, 294
Ahaziah, son of Ahab, 20, 145
Ahaziah, son of Jehoram, 39, 208
Ahijah, prophet, 22, 151–152, 220
Ahimelech, 8, 22
Ahinoam, wife of David, 22, 27, 68
Ahisamach, 23, 54
Ahithophel, 23, 47, 126
Ahitub, 23, 303
Ai, 15, 18, 178
Ain es-Sultan, 82
Akkadia, 229
Alcimus, 23, 71
Alexander of Ephesus, 25, 126
Alexander Balas, 24–25, 32, 71, 72
Alexander the Great, 24, 241, 251
Alexandrian Library, 251
Amalek, 6, 25,
Amalekites, 6–7, 25, 75, 265, 272
Amasa, 11, 26, 159
Amaziah, 26, 28, 144, 160, 300
Amelekites, 176
Amel-Marduk, 144
Amittai, 26, 168
Ammon, 69, 93, 309
Ammonites, 11, 27, 59, 75, 193, 265, 271, 286
Amnon, 14–15, 17, 27
Amorites, 27, 58, 271, 278
Amos, 27–28, 130, 152, 291
Amram, 6, 28, 215
Anakim, 28, 104

Anakites, 28, 177
Ananias, 29–30, 219, 239
Andrew, 30, 166, 241
Andronicus, 30, 188
Anna, prophet, 30, 201, 284
Annas, 30–31, 56
Antioch, 45, 238, 244
Antiochus III (the Great), 31, 252
Antiochus IV Epiphanes, 31–32, 66, 71, 105, 171–172, 184, 204, 207
Antiochus V Eupator, 32, 71
Antiochus VI Epiphanes Dionysus, 32
Antiochus VII Sidetes, 32, 298
Apollos, 33
Apollyon, 7, 33, 268
Aquila, 33, 250
Arabs, 33
Aram, son of Shem, 33, 279
Arameans, 33, 144, 271. See also Syrians.
Aram (Syria). See Syria.
Ararat, 229
Aretas, 34
Aristarchus, 34, 71
Aristobulus, 115
Armenia, 46
Arpachshad, 35, 279
Artaxerxes I Longimanus, 35, 225, 235, 241
Artemis, 35–36, 72
Asa, 36, 43, 146
Asahel, 12, 36–37, 158
Asaph, 37
Asenath, 37, 198
Ashbel, 37
Ashdod, 247, 264
Asher, 37, 96
Asherah, 19, 37–38, 78, 117, 157, 180
Ashkelon, 247
Ashurbanipal, 235
Asia Minor, 24
Asmodeus, 38, 267, 296
Asshur, 38, 279
Assyria(ns), 20, 21, 38–39, 86, 117, 125, 129, 168, 181, 229, 235, 274, 279, 309
Astarte, 19, 39, 248
Astyages, 39, 62
Athaliah, 39, 144, 160